INSTEAD OF VIOLENCE

Edited and with notes and introductions [

A R T H U R *myron and* L I L A   W E I N B E R G

Other books by the editors

Arthur Weinberg:
ATTORNEY FOR THE DAMNED

Arthur and Lila Weinberg:
THE MUCKRÁKERS
VERDICTS OUT OF COURT

nstead of Violence

Nritings by the great advocates of
eace and nonviolence throughout history

3EACON PRESS   BOSTON

International Standard Book Number: 0-8070-1569-5

Third printing, November 1971

All the care possible has been taken to obtain permission from the copyright owners to reprint articles and selections protected by copyright; any errors or omissions are unintentional and will be rectified in any future printings upon notification to the editors, who wish to express their gratitude for permission to reprint material from the following sources:

Acts for Peace, and the author, for "Sanity and Survival" by Jerome D. Frank, published in *Fresh Thoughts on War,* Series No. 2.

George Allen & Unwin Ltd. for *Above the Battle,* by Romain Rolland, translated by C. K. Ogden; and for *Perpetual Peace,* by Immanuel Kant.

The Atlantic Monthly for "The War Against War," by Havelock Ellis.

Roger N. Baldwin for "Faith of a Heretic," published in *The Nation.*

Ernest Benn Ltd. for *James Nayler: The Rebel Saint,* by Emilio Fogelklou; and for "Patriotism" from *Facts and Comments,* by Herbert Spencer.

Vinoba Bhave for "The True Nature of *Ahimsa* and Our Duty," published in "The Task of Peace-making: Report of the World Pacifist Meeting Sanhinijetan and Sevagram"; Visva-Bharati Publishing Dept., Calcutta, 1951.

John A. Brittain for *Newer Ideals of Peace,* by Jane Addams, published by the Macmillan Company, New York.

Cambridge University Press, New York, for letter to Oliver Cromwell by George Fox, from the *Journal of George Fox,* vol. 1, edited from the MSS by Norman Penny.

The Christian Century for "The United States vs. Arle Brooks," copyright 1941 Christian Century Foundation; for the answers of Harry Emerson Fosdick and Ernest Fremont Tittle to "If America Is Drawn into the War Can You, as a Christian, Participate in It or Support It?"—both copyright, 1941, Christian Century Foundation; and for "Pilgrimage to Nonviolence," by Martin Luther King, Jr., © 1960 by Christian Century Foundation.

The Condé Nast Publications, Inc., for "Disturber of the Peace," an interview with Robert Pickus, published in *Mademoiselle,* © 1961 by Street and Smith Publications, Inc.

Abraham Cronbach for his address delivered at Fellowship Farm, Pa.

Daedalus, the American Academy of Arts and Sciences, and the author, for "The Case for Unilateral Disarmament" from *Arms Control,* by Erich Fromm; reprinted also by permission of George Braziller, Inc., publisher of the hard-cover edition, *Arms Control, Disarmament, and National Security.*

Dodd, Mead & Co. for "The End of War," from *No More War!,* by Linus Pauling, © 1958, 1962, by Linus Pauling.

Danilo Dolci for his address at the Anti-Nuclear Arms Convention in New Delhi.

The Educational Foundation for Nuclear Science, Inc., and the author, for "Are We on the Road to War?" by Leo Szilard, published in *Bulletin of Atomic Scientists.*

Sigmund Freud Copyrights Ltd., and International Series of Open Letters—No. 2, for Dr. Freud's letter to Albert Einstein, "Why War?", published by the International Institute of Intellectual Cooperation, Paris, 1933.

Harper & Row for *Pointing the Way,* by Martin Buber, edited and translated by Maurice Friedman, copyright 1957 by Martin Buber; and for *The Mysterious Stranger,* by Mark Twain.

Harper & Row, and the author, for "Pacifism in Personal Relations," by John Haynes Holmes, from *Pacifism in the Modern World* edited by Devere Allen.

Gerald Heard for "The Significance of the New Pacifism," a pamphlet.

Holt, Rinehart and Winston for *A Pilgrimage of Ideas*, by Sherwood Eddy, copyright 1934, 1962, by Sherwood Eddy; and for *Love—The Law of Life*, by Toyohiko Kagawa, translated by J. Fullerton Gressitt.

Holt, Rinehart and Winston, and the Estate of George Lansbury, for "My Pilgrimage for Peace," copyright 1938 by George Lansbury.

Holt, Rinehart and Winston, and A. & C. Black Ltd., for *Peace or Atomic War?* by Albert Schweitzer; © 1958 by Albert Schweitzer.

Aldous Huxley for "Pacifism and Philosophy," a pamphlet.

Stephen King-Hall for "Common Sense in Defence," published by K-H Services, Ltd., London.

Liberation magazine for "The Way to Disarmament," by Rajendra Prasad; and for "A Lawyer's Case for Civil Disobedience," by Harris Wofford.

Dwight Macdonald for "Neither Victims Nor Executioners," by Albert Camus, translated by Dwight Macdonald; for "Reflections on War," by Simone Weil; and for "Letter to Judge" by Arthur Wiser, with the author's permission also; all three published in *Politics* magazine.

Macmillan & Co. Ltd., London, for "War: Then and Now," from *Peace and War* by Guglielmo Ferrero, translated by Bertha Pritchard.

The Magnes family for "The Old America and the New" from *War-time Addresses, 1917-1921*, by Judah Magnes, published by Thomas Seltzer, New York.

Maurice F. McCrackin for his statement before the Cincinnati Presbytery's Judicial Commission.

The Mennonite Publishing House for *The Complete Writings of Menno Simons*, translated from the Dutch by Leonard Verduin, edited by John Christian Wenger.

The Meredith Press for *The Biology of War* by G. F. Nicolai.

A. J. Muste for "Something To Die For," from *How to Deal With a Dictator*, published by Fellowship Publications.

Otto Nathan, trustee, Estate of Albert Einstein, for *Einstein on Peace*, edited by Otto Nathan and Heinz Norden, published by Simon and Schuster; © 1960, by Estate of Albert Einstein.

The Navajivan Trust, Ahmedabad, for "My Faith in Nonviolence" and "The Future" from *Non-Violent Resistance*, by Mahatma Gandhi; published by Shocken Books, New York.

New Directions, and the author, for "Murder the Murderer," from *Remember to Remember*, by Henry Miller; copyright 1947 by New Directions.

Harold Ober Associates for "I Think I'll Sit This One Out," by Milton Mayer, published in the *Saturday Evening Post;* copyright 1939 by The Curtis Publishing Company.

Mrs. Kirby Page for *Now Is the Time to Prevent a Third World War*, by Kirby Page.

Peace News, and the author, for "Disobedience Against Polaris," by Herbert Read.

Pendle Hill, and the author, for "Pacifist Program in Time of War, Threatened War, or Fascism" by Richard B. Gregg, Pendle Hill pamphlet No. 5.

Judge Justine Wise Polier for the address by Stephen S. Wise at the Free Synagogue, New York.

The Progressive magazine for "I Will Keep My Soul," by James Farmer; for "The Case Against Civil Defense," by Sidney Lens; and for "Peace and War and the Intellectuals," by Harold Taylor.

Paul R. Reynolds & Son for "The Moral Equivalent of War," by William James, from *Memoirs and Studies*.

Bertrand Russell for "On Civil Disobedience."

Siegfried Sassoon for *Memoirs of an Infantry Officer*, published by Faber and Faber Ltd., London.

The *Saturday Review*, and the author, for "A Strange Kind of Love," by Lillian Smith.

Roderick Seidenberg for "I Refuse to Serve," published in *The American Mercury*.

Dr. A. C. Sen for *Asoka's Edicts*, by A. C. Sen, published for the Institute of Indology by the Indian Publicity Society, Calcutta.

Simon and Schuster, Inc., for "A Modest Proposal," from *The Rule of Folly*, by James R. Newman, © 1962 by James R. Newman.

Suhrkamp Verlag, Frankfurt/M., for "An Einen Staatsminister," from *Krieg und Frieden*, by Hermann Hesse, copyright 1946 by Fretz & Wasmuth Verlag AG, Zurich.

Norman Thomas for "War's Heretics: A Plea for the Conscientious Objector," published in *The Survey*.

The Universal House of Justice for "The Pitiful Causes of War, and the Duty of Everyone to Strive for Peace," from *Paris Talks*, 10th ed., by Abdul Baha, published by the National Spiritual Assembly of the Baha'is of the British Isles.

Visva-Bharati Publishing Department, Calcutta, for an address by Vinoba Bhave.

War Resisters International for an address by Lord Ponsonby, published in the *War Resister*, No. 43.

The War Resisters League for "Conscience in Action," from *The Way to Freedom*, by Evan W. Thomas.

The Westminster Press, Philadelphia, and Lutterworth Press, London, for *The Divine Imperative*, by Emil Brunner, translated by Olive Wyon, copyright 1947 by W. L. Jenkins.

Norbert Wiener for "A Scientist Rebels," published in the *Atlantic Monthly*.

For our mothers:

Blanche Hyman Shaffer [1895-1958]
Anna Avedon Weinberg [1894-1947]

Acknowledgments

In making the selections for this book, the editors have tried to present a full spectrum of representative thinking on the questions of peace, non-violence, civil disobedience, and passive resistance. In some instances, certain pieces were not available because of copyright difficulties where either the estate or the author himself refused permission. To those who did give us their permission, we are most grateful.

The editors alone, of course, are responsible for the selection, and for the opinions and interpretation in the introductions. But many people have helped us prepare the book; to them our heartfelt thanks. To our friends Zalman and Mitzi Alper, at whose home, around a dinner table, this book was first conceived; to our friends and editors Richard L. Grossman and Jill Kneerim, who enthusiastically accepted the idea, encouraged and helped us; to Professor Merle F. Curti, University of Wisconsin, who spent time with the editors and read the manuscript, as did Professor Paul A. Schilpp of Northwestern University, Sidney Lens, and Fran Coughlin. We owe thanks also to our cousin, Dr. Stanley L. Chyet, of Hebrew Union College, whose invaluable counsel was always available, and to the college itself, which was most cooperative; also to our friend Claire Rooz, who translated the Hermann Hesse piece from the German.

Others who have helped us include Lord Bertrand Russell, Henry Miller, Dr. Abraham Cronbach of Hebrew Union College, A. J. Muste, Norman Thomas, Dr. Evan Thomas, Roger Baldwin, Dr. John Haynes Holmes, Arthur Wiser, Dr. Carl Hermann Voss, Dr. Homer Jack, Dr. Maurice Friedman at Sarah Lawrence College, Marjorie V. Edwards, curator, Swarthmore College Peace Collection, Norman Bentwick, Deborah Ann Berman, executive director, Friends of Danilo Dolci, Inc., Dr. Jonathan Magnes, Hebrew University, Jerusalem, Gisela Stein, Brooklyn College, Dr. J. K. Senior, Fred W. Thompson and Ahlyce Kaplan.

We are grateful as well to the staff of Newberry Library in Chicago, which was most cooperative, to the Chicago Public Library, to both Harper and Swift libraries at the University of Chicago, to the New York Public Library, and to the Swarthmore College Peace Collection.

Last, but not least, we owe thanks to our daughters—Hedy Merrill, Anita Michelle, and Wendy Clare—who bore with us, patiently, lovingly and proudly, as we worked on the book.

ARTHUR *and* LILA WEINBERG

Chicago, Illinois
September, 1963

CONTENTS

INTRODUCTION *xxi*

1 AFTER THE ATOMIC BOMB [1946 to the present]

Introduction 3

1963/ Pope John XXIII *asks the world to halt the arms race* 7 ✓
". . . not by the force of arms, but by the light of reason . . ."

1962/ Lillian Smith *writes of a strange kind of love* 13
". . . no limit on compassion . . ."

1962/ Rajendra Prasad *calls for unilateral disarmament* 15
". . . break the vicious circle of mutual fear and distrust . . ."

•1962/ Danilo Dolci *asks humanity to cure itself of violence* 22 .
". . . the greatest impediment to war is . . . the point of maturity which men who do not want war have reached . . ."

1962/ Leo Szilard *suggests the election of government officials solely on the issue of war and peace* 26
"The problem which the bomb poses to the world cannot be solved except by abolishing war, and nothing less will do."

1962/ Harold Taylor *says the time has come for intellectuals to come to terms with the issues of war and peace* 36
"We must turn to the invention of new alternatives . . ."

1962/ Sidney Lens *condemns civil defense for giving a treacherous sense of security* 42
". . . it makes us more willing to 'go the brink' . . ."

1961 / James Farmer *reports on a Freedom Ride* 45
". . . to reach the common humanity of our fellow men . . ."

1961 / Herbert Read *calls for a revolt of the instincts of man against the threat of mass destruction* 49
"We must release the imagination of the people . . ."

1961 / Bertrand Russell *sets out the case for nonviolent civil disobedience in combating the nuclear peril* 51
". . . it is only a small part of what the world needs . . ."

1961 / James R. Newman *suggests:* "Let our children go" 57
"Suppose they gave a war and no one came?"

1961 / Albert Luthuli *explains why Africans have chosen nonviolence to turn enmity into amity* 60
"Nothing which we have suffered . . . has turned us from our chosen path."

1961 / Robert Pickus *shows that pacifism is working in most areas of life except war* 62
"It isn't even a moral question of whether war is right or wrong, but does it work? And I say no."

1961 / Harris Wofford *presents the lawyer's case for civil disobedience* 64
". . . every command of the law should be seen as a question."

1960 / Martin Luther King, Jr., *traces his pilgrimage to nonviolence* 69
"The choice is either nonviolence or nonexistence."

1960 / Peace organizations *give their rules for public witness demonstrations* 75
". . . and show peaceful intent."

1960 / Jerome D. Frank *declares that war-making man is modifiable* 77
"If mice can be trained, why cannot man?"

1960 / Erich Fromm *defines his one main concern* 83
"If we should all perish in the nuclear holocaust . . . it would be because the consensus of stupidity has prevented man from seeing reality . . ."

1960 / Maurice F. McCrackin *refuses to pay taxes if the money is used to prepare for war* 86
"There are other voices that I must obey."

1960 / Stephen King-Hall *presents a plan for the nonviolent resistance of enemy occupation* 90
". . . a positive assault on the minds of the occupying forces."

1960/ Abraham Cronbach *says that the only national defense is international amity* 92

"Pacifism holds that the ideal and the practical do not fall apart."

1958/ Linus Pauling *urges research for peace* 95 ✓

"The time has now come for man's intellect to win out . . ."

1958/ Albert Schweitzer *calls for a new trust among all peoples* 100

"The spirit is a mighty force for transforming things."

1955/ Fifty-two Nobel Laureates *plead for nations to renounce force* 101

"A nation that engages in a total war thus signals its own destruction and imperils the whole world."

1954/ A. J. Muste *discusses the workability of nonviolence* 103

"Our firm conviction as pacifists is that it is not possible to achieve democracy by undemocratic means."

1953/ Martin Buber *believes that genuine dialogue between people can overcome conflict* 108

"Let us release speech from its ban! Let us dare, despite all, to trust!"

1949/ Vinoba Bhave *is not afraid of world wars, but rather of small wars and quarrels* 112

". . . the all-merciful God sends world war to free man's mind from limitations . . ."

1947/ Norbert Wiener *points out that to provide scientific information is not necessarily an innocent act* 116

". . . to disseminate information about a weapon in the present state of our civilization is to make it practically certain that the weapon will be used."

1947/ Emil Brunner *perceives that war has begun to outlive its purpose* 118

"To claim that war is the *ultima ratio* of politics is simply a superstition."

✓ 1946/ Kirby Page *reminds nations that the only defense against atomic war is the prevention of all war* 120

"Preparedness to wage war with these new weapons will perpetuate anarchy . . ."

1946/ Albert Camus *visualizes an endless struggle between violence and friendly persuasion* 122

"All I ask is that, in the midst of a murderous world, we agree to reflect on murder and make a choice."

1946/ Albert Einstein *believes a permanent peace cannot be prepared by threats* 124

"Everything that is done in international affairs must be done from the viewpoint of whether it will advance or hinder the establishment of world government."

2 IN THE FACE OF FASCISM [1933-1945]

Introduction 131

1945/ Arthur Wiser *explains why he walked out of Civilian Public Service camp No. 94* 134

"I am obligated to live in the manner which I believe right and to refuse to participate in any program or activity which I believe wrong."

1943/ Evan Thomas *explains that peace can be demanded only on the basis of conscience* 138

"A sizable minority of individuals who are honest . . . can end the sordid evil of war."

1941/ Henry Miller *says: "Murder the murderer."* 143

"I am prepared to do anything which may be demanded of me in the service of humanity—except to kill."

1941/ Harry Emerson Fosdick *explains why he cannot participate in the war even if the United States is drawn into it* 146

"I will not prostitute the ministry of Jesus Christ to the sanction and support of war."

1941/ Ernest Fremont Tittle *states the case for Christian pacifism* 151
"The only way out of the world's misery is, I believe, the doing of good."

1941/ Arle Brooks *defends his refusal to register for the draft* 157
"Conscription is a denial of the democracy for which I have worked."

1939/ Richard B. Gregg *assures pacifists that the sacrifice of oneself is an affirmation of a greater unity* 158

"If we give our suffering . . . we are simply paying a debt."

1939/ Milton S. Mayer *announces he is "going to sit this one out"* 162

"I am trying to keep my eye on the ball in spite of my hatred of a man called Hitler."

1937/ George Lansbury *calls on all European nations to abolish war* 164

"If Jesus Christ came through that door with Julius Caesar and Napoleon beside him, to whom would you kneel?"

1937/ Lord Ponsonby *insists that teaching hate is a crime*   169
". . . violence sows the seed of hatred . . ."

1935/ Gerald Heard *diagnoses war as a symptom of a diseased civilization*   173
"The causes of war can only be eliminated by creating neutralizing causes."

1935/ Aldous Huxley *shows that peace is a by-product of a certain way of life*   176
". . . if enough people set out to experience the spiritual reality in which men are united, then there will be peace . . ."

1934/ Sherwood Eddy *explains how he made his decision for peace*   180
"I think I have found a better weapon than a machine gun."

1934/ Ernst Toller *offers a program for teaching the love of peace*   183
". . . peace is not a state but a risk."

1933/ Guglielmo Ferrero *finds war nothing but a form of collective suicide*   184
"The heart and not the head will decide our future."

1933/ Simone Weil *asks if a revolution can be accomplished without war*   186
". . . the worst betrayal will always be to subordinate ourselves to the Apparatus . . ."

3 THE WAR TO END WARS [1914-1932]

Introduction   193

1932/ Stephen Wise *warns his congregation against supporting the deepest and most terrible sin of men*   197
"The war came, and to my everlasting regret, I took sides."

1932/ Roderick Seidenberg *describes the prison life of conscientious objectors*   199
"We had offended military pride. We must be broken."

1932/ Sigmund Freud *examines the nature of man's aggressive instincts*   202
"All that produces ties of sentiment between man and man must serve us as war's antidote."

1930 / Mahatma Gandhi *describes his means of battle*   211
1940
"Nonviolence is a weapon of the strong."

1929/ Toyohiko Kagawa *says violence is its own destruction*   214
"Men who fear to make the sacrifice of love will have to fight."

1929/ John Haynes Holmes *sees pacifism taking hold in personal relationships*   215
"The armed man is disappearing from contemporary life. The armored home is as antiquated as a medieval castle."

1927/ Rosika Schwimmer *petitions for naturalization*   222
"If it is a question of fighting, as much as I desire American citizenship, I would not seek the citizenship."

1920/ Judah Magnes *supports the right of all men to speak freely*   229
"Only when speech and writing are left in the background and actual overt acts of physical violence and bloodshed are committed has a people's government the right to intervene."

1919/ Scott Nearing *shows war to be a social curse*   231
"To my mind the great curse of war is that it is built on fear and hate."

1918/ Eugene V. Debs *offers his defense to the court*   233
"Gentlemen of the jury, I am accused of having obstructed the war. I admit it. Gentlemen, I abhor war. I would oppose the war if I stood alone."

1918/ G. F. Nicolai *shows that morality and humanity are inseparable*   236
"If humanity wins, the death-knell of war will have sounded."

1918/ Roger Baldwin *refuses to obey the draft*   237
"I am fully aware that my position is extreme . . ."

1917/ Siegfried Sassoon *speaks for the soldiers*   240
"I am making this statement as an act of willful defiance of military authority . . ."

1917/ John Reed *asks, "Whose war?"*   241
"With lies and sophistries they will whip our blood until we are savage . . ."

1917/ Max Eastman *challenges conscription*   244
"For what specific purposes are you shipping our bodies, and the bodies of our sons, to Europe?"

1917/ Randolph Bourne *takes the American intellectuals to task for their lack of thinking*   246
"The American intellectuals, in their preoccupation with reality, seem to have forgotten that the real enemy is war rather than imperial Germany."

1917/ Norman Thomas *makes a plea for the conscientious objector*
253

". . . only the free spirit can finally determine for a man the highest service he can render."

1917/ Norman Angell *answers the question, "If a German attacked your wife . . ."* 257

"If we undertake to defend our lives and our womenfolk by force, shall we be dragged by an unbreakable chain to war and militarism?"

1917/ Hermann Hesse *challenges a minister of state to end the dilemma of war* 262

"I wish that one of these days, in a moment of peace, you would read a profile of Christ, a poem by Goethe, a saying by Lao-Tse."

1917/ Meyer London *speaks in Congress against declaring war on Germany* 265

"I shall not permit anyone to vote that my arm should be stretched to kill a fellow human being."

1916/ Alfred H. Fried *predicts that pacifism will survive its failure to prevent the First World War* 270

"Pacifism does not need to unlearn."

1916/ Floyd Dell *explains his special brand of nonresistance* 273

"A little murder now and then, of a passionate and unreasoned sort, will do society little harm. It is to the reasoned belief in murder, and in other forms of force, that I object."

1916/ Mark Twain *foresees war a million years ahead* 276

"The loud little handful—as usual—will shout for the war."

1915/ Emma Goldman *calls "preparedness" the road to universal slaughter* 277

"The human mind seems to be conscious of but one thing, murderous speculation."

1914/ Romain Rolland *calls for an end to the homicidal fury in Europe* 282

"Love of my country does not demand that I shall hate and slay those noble and faithful souls who also love theirs."

1914/ Karl Liebknecht *votes "no" in the Reichstag* 285

"This war, desired by none of the people concerned, has not broken out in behalf of the welfare of the German people or any other."

4 ORGANIZING FOR PEACE [1815-1914]

Introduction   291

1911 / Abdu'l Bahá *deplores man's descent to slaying*   295
"It is for their tombs these men are fighting."

1911 / Havelock Ellis *predicts that peace will offer great scope for daring and adventure*   297
"Those persons who are burning to display heroism may rest assured that the course of social evolution will offer them every opportunity."

1910 / William James *proposes a moral equivalent of war*   300
"The only thing needed henceforth is to influence the *civic* temper as past history has inflamed the military temper."

1908 / Charles E. Jefferson *urges Christians to batter down institutions that make war*   304
"Don't be afraid of being too radical. There are enough conservatives to render your radicalism harmless."

1907 / Jane Addams *observes the passing of the war virtues*   305
". . . peace would no longer be an absence of war, but the unfolding of world-wide processes making for the nurture of human life."

1906 / Bertha von Suttner *explains how she came to write* Lay Down Your Arms   308
"The idea dawned on me and soon became a deep-set conviction, that war was an institution handed down to us by the barbarians."

1903 / Clarence Darrow *decries violence and force as punishment*   311
"No amount of treatment can reclaim an evil heart if the treatment is administered without love."

1902 / Frédéric Passy *salutes the future of arbitration*   316
"The future . . . shall belong to neither war, nor division, nor hatred."

1898 / Jean de Bloch *describes the burdens of "armed peace"*   320
". . . slow destruction in consequence of expenditure . . . for war, or swift destruction in the event of war . . ."

1898 / Leo Tolstoy *pleads for each man to follow his own reason and conscience*   324
"We must not obey men more than God, and no matter what they may do, we cannot and will not obey them."

c. 1893/ Herbert Spencer *deplores the cry of "Our country, right or wrong!"* 329

"When men hire themselves out to shoot other men . . . asking nothing about the justice of their cause, I don't care if they are shot themselves."

1861/ Alfred Love *urges a friend not to serve as a chaplain in the Civil War* 332

"Acknowledging war a horrible evil, and yet accepting it on account of the cause . . . is not calculated to lessen its enormity . . ."

c. 1855/ Elihu Burritt *proposes a working man's strike against war* 340

"The yoke will gall and bend alike victors and vanquished . . ."

1852/ William Lloyd Garrison *denies that nonresistance is a state of "passivity"* 345

"It is a state of activity, ever fighting the good fight of faith, ever foremost to assail unjust power . . . in a world-wide spirit."

1849/ Victor Hugo *calls on all nations to hasten the day of international unity* 347

"A day will come when a cannon will be exhibited in public museums, just as an instrument of torture is now, and people will be astonished how such a thing could have been."

1849/ Henry David Thoreau *calls men to the duty of civil disobedience* 353

". . . must the civilian ever for a moment . . . resign his conscience to the legislator?"

1847/ Theodore Parker *protests against the Mexican War* 355

"Let us remonstrate; let us petition; let us command."

1846/ Thomas Cooper *says the regeneration of the world depends on moral resistance* 361

"The consciousness of right, even for an hour, is worth a million years passed in mere animal enjoyment."

1845/ Charles Sumner *declares the victories of peace to be higher than the triumphs of war* 365

"Let the grandeur of man be discerned . . . in the establishment of perpetual peace."

1842/ William Jay *insists that man is not compelled to do evil* 369

". . . our lusts, although natural to us, are not unconquerable."

1841/ William E. Channing *asks, "Has the duty of obeying government no bounds?"* 371

"A declaration of war cannot sanction wrong, or turn murder into a virtuous deed."

1839/ Adin Ballou *charts a course for nonresistants* 375
"The real power which restrains the world is moral power . . ."

1838/ Ralph Waldo Emerson *declares that the cause of peace is not the cause of cowardice* 377
"If peace is to be maintained, it must be by brave men . . . [who will] carry their life in their own hands . . . and will not seek another man's life."

1833/ Thomas Carlyle *describes the soldiers of Dumdrudge* 383
"Their governors had fallen out . . . and had the cunning to make these poor blockheads shoot."

1832/ Thomas Grimke *calls the law of violence the law of murder* 384
". . . nor shall the sword be employed to deliver, much less to avenge us."

1828/ Joshua P. Blanchard *envisions a patriotism based on pacific principles* 386
"Let the love of country be shown not by guarding it with a fence of terror . . ."

1827/ William Ladd *urges men to give public testimony for peace* 388
"Seek those *men,* as well as things, that make for peace . . ."

1825/ Thomas Hancock *condemns "necessity" as an excuse for war* 392
"Fear pictures imaginary dangers."

1823/ Jonathan Dymond *suggests that civil disobedience is the final duty of Christians* 399
"Let them then be willing to avow their opinions and to defend them."

1817/ Noah Worcester *shows that war is the effect of a popular delusion* 401
". . . rulers of nations are as likely to be misled by their passions and interests as other men."

5 THE RISE OF PROTESTANT PACIFISM
[1400-1814]

Introduction 407

1795/ Immanuel Kant *outlines the basis of perpetual peace* 410
"Reason . . . makes the state of peace . . . an immediate duty."

c. 1782/ Job Scott *shows war to be incompatible with Christianity* 414
"What trait of the mind of Christ did I follow when I defied death?"

✓ 1778/ Anthony Benezet *warns that the consequences of war are timeless* 420

". . . the means are infinitely disproportionate to the end."

1693/ William Penn *demonstrates that peace is not merely the end of war* 424

"Peace is maintained by justice, which is a fruit of government, as government is from society, and society from consent."

1676/ Robert Barclay *cites the Christian roots of nonviolence* 426

". . . The Prince of Peace . . . hath expressly prohibited his children all violence . . ."

1660/ James Nayler *exalts peace on his deathbed* 429

"There is a spirit which I feel, that delights to do no evil, nor to revenge any wrong . . ."

1654/ George Fox *swears to Oliver Cromwell that he will do no violence* 430

"I doe deny the carrying or drawing of any carnall sword against any . . ."

1625/ Hugo Grotius *points out that in the conflict of arms, laws are silent* 431

"I saw . . . license in making war of which even barbarous nations would have been ashamed."

1514/ Erasmus *questions whether man was shaped to war* 435

". . . nature, or rather God, hath shaped this creature, not to war, but to friendship . . ."

c. 1536-1559/ Menno Simons *condemns the use of carnal weapons* 438

"Our weapons are . . . patience, silence, and hope, and the word of God."

6 BEFORE GUNS [Sixth century B.C.-1400 A.D.]

Introduction 443

c. 316-c. 397/ Saint Martin *withdraws from Julian's army* 448

". . . allow me now to become a soldier to God."

c. 295/ Maximilian *refuses to be conscripted into the Roman army* 449

"I am a Christian and cannot fight . . ."

250/ Origen *says Christians need not fight for their kings* 450

". . . putting on the whole armor of God."

c. 160-c. 230/ Tertullian *asks if it is lawful to make an occupation of the sword*   451

". . . neither does military service hold out escape from punishment of sins . . ."

66 A.D./ Agrippa *urges the Jews not to undertake war against the Romans*   453

". . . to what end do you so much boast of your liberty?"

✓ B.C.-A.D./ The Bible   461

"Nation shall not lift up sword against nation, neither shall they learn war any more."

c. 233 B.C./ Asoka *proclaims no living beings are to be killed*   463

"The Beloved of the gods wishes all beings noninjury, restraint [and] impartiality . . ."

411 B.C./ Aristophanes' *Lysistrata strikes for peace*   466

"To make the men make peace, there's but one way."

c. 430 B.C./ Motse *shows that the gentlemen of the world are confused about the difference between righteousness and unrightousness*   470

". . . when such a great wrong as attacking a state is committed, people do not know they should condemn it."

520 B.C./ Buddha *pities a man who abuses him*   471

"The virtuous man cannot be hurt . . ."

c. 550 B.C./ Lao-Tse *says that he who rejoices at the destruction of human life is not fit to be trusted with power*   473

"He who goes forward to use weapons of war honors . . . instruments of evil omen."

INTRODUCTION

"We have arrived at that point, my friends, when war does not present the possibility of victory or defeat. War would present to us only the alternative in degrees of destruction. There could be no truly successful outcome."

"General and complete disarmament is the avenue leading to the deliverance of mankind from the calamities of war. . . . Long live peace throughout the world!"

These are not the words of avowed pacifists or peace marchers. The first statement was made at Trinity College by a former President of the United States and commanding general of the Supreme Allied Forces during World War II, Dwight D. Eisenhower. The second comes from a report made by the Premier of Soviet Russia, Nikita S. Khrushchev.

In peacetime, nations generally agree that war is insane, impractical, barbarian and futile. But throughout history, war and violence have been the traditional means for settling disputes.

Parallel to war and violence throughout history runs the constant argument put forward by individuals and groups to convince the world that there is another way to settle differences. These men and women hope that bloodshed and force will disappear. They are the peace-seekers, the gadflies attacking the institution of war. The opinion and arguments of these people make up this book. Their ideas and programs go under many names: nonresistance, passive resistance, pacifism, civil disobedience, nonviolent resistance, Gandhian *satyagraha*. But they share one common outlook: that human affairs on the personal, national and even international levels can be settled by nonviolent means—by arbitration, mediation, conciliation. Their general theme says: Instead of violence, let's use peaceful means to find a solution. Let's sit down and talk things over.

If we must have conflict, let it be in the arena of ideas rather than on the battlefield.

The diversity of their viewpoints within this one framework is apparent in this volume. But the underlying theme is always the same: the futility of physical violence.

"I am an enemy of war," says one adherent. "But I believe that for some causes there is such a thing as a just war, and in such causes I will support my leaders." And so there have been holy wars and crusades.

"I am a pacifist," another will say. "But I know specific evils greater than the evil of war." Thus American pacifists supported the North in its war against the South to abolish slavery, and across the world advocates of peace fought in the war against Hitler and fascism.

"I oppose capitalist warfare," says a third, "but I will support class warfare and revolution."

The absolutist brooks no deviation from his pacifist tenets. "I refuse to use physical force," he says, "either in support of my government or in my personal life."

Another will say: "I am against war and will do all in my power to prevent it; but once my country joins, I will support the war effort."

"I work for the peace movement," says a newcomer to the scene, "because I oppose the use of nuclear weapons."

Clearly, pacifism is no unified philosophy. Its name derives from the Latin word "peacemaker," but each pacifist has his own terms, different from the others'. Many of them, whom we here call "pacifists" for convenience, would object to the appellation; in fact only the loosest general definition encompasses them all. Their ideas are based in most instances on Judeo-Christian or Hindu ethics. The secular pacifists have founded their philosophies on humanitarianism, or on political ideas like socialism and anarchism. But whether religious or secular, in the general philosophy of pacifism and in the methods of nonviolence lies a respect for the individual and a belief in mutual aid and cooperation.

The absolute pacifist categorically follows the commandment "Thou shalt not kill" and, further, denies the right of any man to commit violence against any other individual, no matter what the circumstances. He denies the right of magistrates to pass death sentences and of executioners to carry them out. But even men who think of themselves as absolute pacifists have disagreed on particular points. Leo Tolstoy took an absolute stand, but he differed with the American absolutist Adin Ballou who conceded that force might be used in handling drunkards and the insane.

An eternal question that has divided pacifist opinion (and generally separates the strict absolutists from the others) is whether a man has the right to use force when his family or he himself is attacked. John Haynes Holmes, an American clergyman known for his absolute pacifism, held that "to resort to force from motives of self-defense is as perilous as to resort to force from motives of liberation." * But as always there were differences of opinion, and the British pacifist Norman Angell answered him: "If I have a moral objection to tearing off a man's face with a piece of hot metal because his government has disagreed with mine as to whether Austrian or Russian influence shall dominate the Balkans, must I also stand aside when some drunken savage attacks a child?"

Pacifism, of course, has never belonged only to the absolutists. Men who call themselves pacifists base their lives on a philosophy of love and understanding and on the absolute dignity of man. Pacifism is their philosophy; nonviolence, civil disobedience and passive resistance are their methods. These methods have been borrowed by many people whose goal is not necessarily international peace. Aldous Huxley said in 1936, "The best way of dealing with typhoid is not to cure it, but to prevent its breaking out. Pacifism is to war what clean water and clean milk are to typhoid; it makes the outbreak of war impossible. But though mainly preventive, pacifism is also . . . a technique of conflict—a way of fighting without the use of violence." †

Modern history is full of examples of movements using the methods of pacifism to other ends. Outstanding among them is Mahatma Gandhi's long campaign for Indian freedom. The nonviolent tradition so closely associated with Gandhi's name is as much a means toward an end as it is an end in itself. Gandhi, after all, took part in the Boer War, the so-called Zulu rebellion, and in World War I. "I would rather have India resort to arms in order to defend her honor," he said, "than that she would, in a cowardly manner, become or remain a helpless witness to her own dishonor." But he made clear his preference: "I believe that nonviolence is infinitely superior to violence, forgiveness is more manly than punishment." ‡

The nonviolent methods of the American integration struggle, too, are means to an end rather than the end itself, although many of its leaders are absolute pacifists in their philosophy. "The method of nonviolent resistance is effective in that it has a way of disarming the opponent," Martin Luther King, Jr., has said. "It exposes his moral defenses, it weakens his morale and at the same time it works on his conscience. Nonviolent resistance also provides a creative force through which men can channelize their discontent. It does not require that they abandon their discontent. . . . Nonviolence saves it from degenerating into morbid bitterness and hatred." §

* John Haynes Holmes, *New Wars for Old*, Dodd, Mead and Co., New York, 1916.
† Aldous Huxley, *What Are You Going to Do About It?*, Chatto & Windus, London, 1936.
‡ From *Young India*, August 11, 1920.
§ Address quoted in *Time*, August 3, 1962.

In the middle of the nineteenth century, the Hungarians used passive resistance against the Austrian emperor's attempt to subordinate them. He was forced to capitulate and grant Hungary her own constitution. In the early twentieth century, Gandhi led the Indian population of South Africa in a successful nonviolent campaign to win the abolition of registration and the head-tax, and to gain positive rights for their minority.

By using nonviolent resistance against the Nazis during World War II, the Danish people were able to save most of their Jewish population. Teachers in Norway led a nonviolent strike, refusing to submit to Nazi pressures. And Adolf Hitler in his New Year's 1944 proclamation to the German people tried to explain the Nazi reverses in Italy and North Africa by the "sabotage and paralyzation" created by passive resistance on the part of his enemies.

Pacifism—and its methods—is today considered a rebel movement by its advocates. It has grown from scattered statements by individuals against war and injustice in the past into an organized radical social-action movement. There are pacifists at work in the United States among Freedom Riders seeking racial equality, among opponents of capital punishment, among nonviolent marchers protesting nuclear tests.

In this book we have tried to present the ideas of pacifism and nonviolence through the writings of those who have advocated these principles. The representation encompasses a variety of individuals from all political, economic, social, and religious walks of life. It will be seen that there has been no more consistency in the pacifist movement than in any other human endeavor that has survived for as many centuries. Only one thing links the movement's protagonists from the sixth century B.C. to the present day: their denial of violence as a just instrument for settling disputes.

1

AFTER THE ATOMIC BOMB

[1946 to the present]

The atomic bombs dropped on Hiroshima and Nagasaki brought a new variation on an ancient theme: *nuclear* pacifism.

"Hiroshima made me a pacifist," says former U.S. congresswoman Helen Gahagan Douglas. "Reason has made it clear that war is no longer usable as an instrument of foreign policy, and that war in the future would be senseless. But man has so long used force to gain his ends that it is hard for him to believe that arms no longer are serviceable. And so the arms race, which has cost untold billions of dollars since the end of World War II and has brought no security for the world, goes on. Man's mental block: his continued faith in arms. Man does not dare let go his weapons as long as he holds to the myth that they will make him safe. They will not. Only reason will. I am not advocating the laying down of arms in a military world; but I may come to that." *

Some men who were already pacifists were shocked into new tactics by Hiroshima. Dr. Paul A. Schilpp, professor of philosophy at Northwestern University, says, "Up until the bomb dropped on Hiroshima, I was a pacifist. With the dropping of the bomb I became convinced, and have been ever since, that pacifism is not going to stop World War III any more than it stopped World War II or World War I. Though I have not changed my pacifism as a long-range position and underlying principle, instead of preaching pacifism I am preaching world government." *

Nuclear weapons have given the peace movement a great sense of urgency. Since total destruction is possible, disarmament and peace have become essential to the continuance of life as we know it. Pacifists cite the famous remark of Dr. Albert Einstein that he did not know what

* In conversation with the editors.

the weapons of a third world war would be, but in a fourth world war they would be "sticks and stones."

Today the peace movement probably has more adherents than ever before, and any person who wishes to join an organization working for peace or disarmament has a variety of choice that would have dazzled his ancestors. The International Peace/Disarmament Directory, which its publishers claim is "fairly comprehensive," lists more than 1,400 groups and subgroups and more than 350 periodicals working for the cause. A more conservative list published in the Sane World newsletter, encompassing only groups outside of the United States, shows three international coordinating organizations, eight international groups, and almost 100 groups in forty-three countries. Many of these newer peace groups have grown out of the efforts of the earlier peace societies.

These groups encompass a whole spectrum: there are protagonists of unilateral or of multilateral disarmament; absolute pacifists and nuclear pacifists; advocates of nonviolence and civil disobedience; religious pacifists and believers in Gandhian satyagraha.

In the United States, the principal nuclear peace group is the Committee for a Sane Nuclear Policy, generally called just SANE. Its executive director, Homer Jack, points out that though many of the group's members and leaders are pacifist, SANE is not. "We are pragmatic, not absolutist," he explains. "We believe that modern war does not work and that other methods are needed to allow change, yet keep the peace in the modern world. Herein we differ from some organizations which oppose war primarily on religious or ethical grounds." *

Another American group that has grown up in recent years is the Women's Strike for Peace, which started with the slogan "End the arms race—not the human race." They have been active in demonstrations and meetings, and their representatives have visited Washington, Moscow and Geneva in the crusade against war.

There are two major organizations that work at coordinating peace groups across the world. One is the International Confederation for Disarmament and Peace; the other, the World Council of Peace. The International Confederation for Disarmament and Peace was established —with its final form still to be discussed—at a congress in Oxford, England, in January 1963. The World Council of Peace, founded in London in 1950, is often considered to be the leading Communist voice for peace and disarmament because it is generally in line with Soviet policy.

* From an address, "What SANE Is and Is Not," delivered in New York City, November 15, 1962.

(At its most recent congress, held in Moscow in July 1962, the council managed to get representation, in the form of guests and observers, from nonaligned peace organizations. It issued a test-ban appeal to the nuclear powers.)

There are smaller-scale peace organizations in practically all civilized countries. These groups benefit from having a voice in a larger organization. Among the ones affiliated with the World Council of Peace are the Australian Peace Council, the Ceylon Peace Council, the Polish Peace Committee, the Soviet Peace Committee, the Mongolian Peace Committee and the Deutscher Friedensrat in East Germany.

Peace organizations represented at the Oxford meeting for the establishment of the International Confederation for Disarmament and Peace included Ostermarsch der Atomwaffengegner (West Germany), Irish Campaign for Nuclear Disarmament, Kampagnen Mod Atomvaabon (Denmark), Yugoslav League for Peace, Independence and Equality of Peoples, Aktionsgruppen Mot Svensk Atoombomb (Sweden) and the Campaign for Nuclear Disarmament (New Zealand).

Also throughout the world are chapters of such peace organizations as the International Fellowship of Reconciliation, United Nations Association, War Resisters International, World Association of World Federalists, and the Women's International League for Peace and Freedom.

In the years since World War II there have been, of course, many international conferences more limited in their representation than those at Oxford or London. There was the meeting of East-West scientists at Pugwash, the meetings of American and Russian intellectuals at Dartmouth, the Crimea, and Andover, and the Accra Assembly in Ghana with representatives from nonaligned organizations.

Public demonstration is one of the chief weapons of the peace movement. The demonstrations are peaceful, and demonstrators adhere to strict rules of conduct. They owe a great deal, in method and idea, to Mahatma Gandhi.

In England, "ban the bomb" demonstrations have attracted large numbers of supporters and a great deal of attention. Bertrand Russell, who has been a key figure in more than one such demonstration, has explained why this kind of action is so important. Civil disobedience to protest nuclear arms, he says, "can do a great deal, because it can make people aware that if they go on as they are going there will almost certainly be a nuclear war and that will be very, very horrible. You see, a great many people think, 'Oh, there'll never be a war. They'll never use those weapons.' Well, we make people aware that that's irrational, that if things go on as they are there will be a war." *

To focus the world's attention on the folly of the nuclear-arms race, demonstrators have sat vigils and fasted, used sitdowns and marches, refused to participate in air-raid drills and trespassed on military projects; they have petitioned their elected officials; they have campaigned for the election of candidates who have a peace orientation; they have refused to pay taxes that will go to build up armaments.

In England there have been five Easter Aldermaston marches with tens of thousands participating; in the United States there have been annual Easter marches against the bomb.

In 1960-61 a band of Western peace marchers, including thirteen from the United States, walked into Moscow to complete a ten-month trek which started in San Francisco. On their way they had distributed a leaflet printed in six languages, including Russian, urging unilateral disarmament and an end to conscription. "When one country disarms first, it opens the way for others to do the same. Some nation must find the courage to act first," it said. "In the nuclear age war is outdated. . . . In this new situation we believe that nonviolence—such as Gandhi used for the freedom of India, and the Norwegian teachers used in resisting Hitler—can best defend and enlarge freedom and justice."

One of the sponsors of the march was the Committee for Nonviolent Action, which also had organized protests against nuclear tests on land in 1957, against nuclear tests at sea through the voyage of the *Golden Rule* in 1958 and the voyages of *Everyman I* and *II* in 1962, against land-based missiles in 1959, and against sea-launched missiles, including the launching of the Polaris submarine.

Nonviolent demonstrations are not the property of the peace movement alone. The methods preached and used by Gandhi in his long campaign to free India of British rule have been adopted by causes and movements in many countries. The most sustained and outstanding of these is the Negro's campaign for equal rights in every realm of American life. Nonviolence has been the rule all through the sit-ins, the wade-ins, the freedom rides. The warfare is "soft and gentle" and yet "grim and frightening," as masses of men and women, and even children, offer themselves up without battle to enforce new legislation and wider opportunity.

For *satyagraha* to be effective, discipline is all-important. Gandhi himself on three different occasions between 1919 and 1922 called off his

* Quoted in *Newsweek*, August 20, 1962.

nonviolent crusade because of inadequate discipline among his followers, and each time he fasted as a personal penance for the violence of his people.

Peaceful demonstration and the widespread fear of nuclear war show that man's enduring wish for peace is more vital today than it was in World War II, stronger than it was when the First World War was declared, more powerful than ever in recorded history. With so many peace organizations at work, with presidents and premiers of nations talking peace, with the destructiveness of nuclear weapons unquestionable, will the peace ideal be won? Will man survive?

Pope John XXIII
asks the world to halt the arms race

POPE JOHN [Angelo Giuseppe Roncalli, 1881-1963], *became head of the Roman Catholic Church in 1958. He was elected as an interim pope, but he far exceeded these expectations and turned out to be one of the greatest popes the Church ever had. In an effort to "restore the simple and pure lines that the face of the Church of Jesus had at its birth," he called an Ecumenical Council for the first time in more than ninety years. "Pacem in Terris," issued April 10, 1963, is the last of eight encyclicals he wrote during his five-year reign, and it will undoubtedly remain his most enduring monument.*

Where the civil authority uses as its only or its chief means either threats and fear of punishment or promises of rewards, it cannot effectively move men to promote the common good of all. Even if it did so move them, this would be altogether opposed to their dignity as men, endowed with reason and free will. As authority is chiefly concerned with moral force, it follows that civil authority must appeal primarily to the conscience of individual citizens, that is, to each one's duty to collaborate readily for the common good of all. Since by nature all men are equal in human dignity, it follows that no one may be coerced to perform interior acts. That is in the power of God alone, who sees and judges the hidden designs of men's hearts.

Those therefore who have authority in the state may oblige men in conscience only if their authority is intrinsically related with the authority of God and shares in it.

By this principle the dignity of the citizens is protected. When, in fact, men obey their rulers, it is not all as men that they obey them, but through their obedience it is God, the provident Creator of all things, whom they reverence, since he has decreed that men's dealings with one another should be regulated by an order which he himself has established. Moreover, in showing this due reverence to God, men not only do not debase themselves but rather perfect and ennoble themselves. For to serve God is to rule.

Since the right to command is required by the moral order and has its source in God, it follows that, if civil authorities legislate for or allow anything that is contrary to that order and therefore contrary to the will of God, neither the laws made nor the authorizations granted can be binding on the consciences of the citizens, since God has more right to be obeyed than men. . . .

It is with deep sorrow that we note the enormous stocks of armaments that have been and still are being made in more economically developed countries, with a vast outlay of intellectual and economic resources. And so it happens that, while the people of these countries are loaded with heavy burdens, other countries as a result are deprived of the collaboration they need in order to make economic progress.

The production of arms is allegedly justified on the grounds that in present-day conditions peace cannot be preserved without an equal balance of armaments. And so, if one country increases its armaments, others feel the need to do the same; and if one country is equipped with nuclear weapons, other countries must produce their own, equally destructive.

Consequently, people live in constant fear lest the storm that every moment threatens should break upon them with dreadful violence. And with good reason, for the arms of war are ready at hand. Even though it is difficult to believe that anyone would deliberately take the responsibility for the appaling destruction and sorrow that war would bring in its train, it cannot be denied that the conflagration may be set off by some uncontrollable and unexpected chance. And one must bear in mind that, even though the monstrous power of modern weapons acts as a deterrent, it is to be feared that the mere continuance of nuclear tests, undertaken with war in mind, will have fatal consequences for life on the earth.

Justice, then, right reason and humanity urgently demand that the arms race should cease. That the stockpiles which exist in various countries should be reduced equally and simultaneously by the parties concerned. That nuclear weapons should be banned. And that a general agreement should eventually be reached about progressive disarmament and an effective method of control. In the words of Pius XII, our predecessor of happy memory: "The calamity of a world war, with the economic and social ruin and the moral excesses and dissolution that accompany it, must not be permitted to envelop the human race for a third time."

All must realize that there is no hope of putting an end to the building up of armaments, nor of reducing the present stocks, nor, still less, of abolishing them altogether, unless the process is complete and thorough and unless it proceeds from inner convictions: unless, that is, everyone sincerely cooperates to banish the fear and anxious expectation of war with which men are oppressed. If this is to come about, the fundamental principle on which our present peace depends must be replaced by another, which declares that the true and solid peace of nations consists not in equality of arms, but in mutual trust alone. We believe that this can be brought to pass, and we consider that it is something which reason requires, that it is eminently desirable in itself and that it will prove to be the source of many benefits.

In the first place, it is an objective demanded by reason. There can be, or at least there should be, no doubt that relations between states, as between individuals, should be regulated not by the force of arms, but by the light of reason, by the rule, that is, of truth, of justice and of active and sincere cooperation.

Second, we say that it is an objective earnestly to be desired in itself. Is there anyone who does not ardently yearn to see war banished, to see peace preserved and daily more firmly established?

And finally, it is an objective which will be a fruitful source of many benefits, for its advantages will be felt everywhere by individuals, by families, by nations, by the whole human family. The warning of Pius XII still rings in our ears: "Nothing is lost by peace. Everything may be lost by war."

Since this is so, we, the vicar on earth of Jesus Christ, Savior of the world and author of peace, and as interpreter of the very profound longing of the entire human family, following the impulse of our heart, seized by anxiety for the good of all, we feel it our duty to beseech men, especially those who have the responsibility of public affairs, to spare no labor in order to insure that the world events follow a reasonable and human course.

In the highest and most authoritative assemblies, let men give serious thought to the problem of a peaceful adjustment of relations between political communities on a world level: an adjustment founded on mutual trust, on sincerity in negotiations, on faithful fulfillment of obligations assumed. Let them study the problem until they find that point of agreement from which it will be possible to commence to go forward toward accords that will be sincere, lasting and fruitful.

We, for our part, will not cease to pray God to bless these labors so that they may lead to fruitful results.

Recent progress of science and technology has profoundly affected human beings and influenced men to work together and live as one family. There has been a great increase in the circulation of ideas, of persons and of goods from one country to another, so that relations have become closer between individuals, families and intermediate associations belonging to different political communities, and between the public authorities of those communities. At the same time the interdependence of national economies has grown deeper, one becoming progressively more closely related to the other, so that they become, as it were, integral parts of the one world economy. Likewise the social progress, order, security and peace of each country are necessarily connected with the social progress, order, security and peace of all other countries.

At the present day no political community is able to pursue its own interests and develop itself in isolation, because the degree of its prosperity and development is a reflection and a component part of the degree of prosperity and development of all the other political communities.

The unity of the human family has always existed, because its members were human beings all equal by virtue of their natural dignity. Hence there will always exist the objective need to promote, in sufficient measure, the universal common good, that is, the common good of the entire human family.

In times past, one would be justified in feeling that the public authorities of the different political communities might be in a position to provide for the universal common good, either through normal diplomatic channels or through top-level meetings, by making use of juridical instruments such as conventions and treaties, for example: juridical instruments suggested by the natural law and regulated by the law of nations and international law.

As a result of the far-reaching changes which have taken place in the relations between the human family, the universal common good gives rise to problems which are complex, very grave, and extremely urgent, especially as regards security and world peace.

On the other hand, the public authorities of the individual political communities—placed as they are on a footing of equality one with the other—no matter how much they multiply their meetings or sharpen their wits in efforts to draw up new juridical instruments, are no longer capable of facing the task of finding an adequate solution to the problems mentioned above. And this is not due to a lack of good will or of a spirit of enterprise, but because of a structural defect which hinders them.

It can be said, therefore, that at this historical moment the present system of organization and the way its principle of authority operates on a world basis no longer correspond to the objective requirements of the universal common good.

There exists an intrinsic connection between the common good on the one hand and the structure and function of public authority on the other. The moral order, which needs public authority in order to promote the common good in human society, requires also that the authority be effective in attaining that end. This demands that the organs through which the authority is formed, becomes operative and pursues its ends, must be composed and act in such a manner as to be capable of bringing to realization the new meaning which the common good is taking on in the historical evolution of the human family.

Today the universal common good poses problems of world-wide dimensions, which cannot be adequately tackled or solved except by the efforts of public authorities endowed with a wideness of powers, structure, and means of the same proportions: that is, of public authorities which are in a position to operate in an effective manner on a world-wide basis. The moral order itself, therefore, demands that such a form of public authority be established.

A public authority, having world-wide power and endowed with the proper means for the efficacious pursuit of its objective, which is the universal common good in concrete form, must be set up by common accord and not imposed by force. The reason is that such an authority must be in a position to operate effectively, yet, at the same time, its action must be inspired by sincere and real impartiality: in other words, it must be an action aimed at satisfying the objective requirements of the universal common good. The difficulty is that there would be reason to fear that a supernatural or world-wide public authority, imposed by force by the more powerful political communities, might be or might become an instrument of one-sided interests and even should this not happen, it would be difficult for it to avoid all suspicion of partiality in its actions, and this would take from the efficaciousness of its activity.

Even though there may be pronounced differences between political communities as regards the degree of their economic development and their military power, they are all very sensitive as regards their juridical equality and their moral dignity. For that reason, they are right in not easily yielding in obedience to an authority imposed by force, or to an authority in whose creation they had no part, or to which they themselves did not decide to submit by conscious and free choice.

Like the common good of individual political communities, so too the universal common good cannot be determined except by having regard to the human person. Therefore, the public authority of the world community, too, must have as its fundamental objective the recognition, respect, safeguarding and promotion of the rights of the human person. This can be done by direct action when required, or by creating on a world scale an environment in which the public authorities of the individual political communities can more easily carry out their specific functions.

Just as within each political community the relations between individuals are governed by the principle of subsidiarity, so too the relations between the public authority of each political community and the public authority of the world community must be regulated by the light of the same principle. This means that the public authority of the world community must tackle and solve problems of an economic, social, political and cultural character which are posed by the universal common good. For, because of the vastness, complexity and urgency of those problems, the public authorities of the individual states are not in a position to tackle them with any hope of a positive solution.

The public authority of the world community is not intended to limit the sphere of action of the public authority of the individual political community, much less to take its place. On the contrary, its purpose is to create, on a world basis, an environment in which the public authorities of each political community, its citizens and intermediate associations, can carry out their tasks, fulfill their duties and exercise their rights with greater security.

As is known, the United Nations Organization (U.N.O.) was established on June 26, 1945, and to it there were subsequently added intergovernmental agencies with extensive international tasks in the economic, social, cultural, educational and health fields. The United Nations Organization had as its essential purpose the maintenance and consolidation of peace between peoples, fostering between them friendly relations, based on the principles of equality, mutual respect and varied forms of cooperation in every sector of human society.

An act of the highest importance performed by the United Nations Organization was the Universal Declaration of Human Rights, approved in the General Assembly of December 10, 1948. In the preamble of that declaration, the recognition and respect of those rights and respective liberties is proclaimed as an ideal to be pursued by all peoples and all countries.

Some objections and reservations were raised regarding certain points in the declaration. There is no doubt, however, that the document represents an important step on the path toward the juridical-political organization of the world community. For in it, in most solemn form, the dignity of a person is acknowledged to all human beings. And as a consequence there is proclaimed as a fundamental right, the right of free movement in the search for truth and in the attainment of moral good and justice, and also the right to a dignified life, while other rights connected with those mentioned are likewise proclaimed.

It is our earnest wish that the United Nations Organization—in its structure and in its means—may become ever more equal to the magnitude and nobility of its tasks, and that the day may come when every human being will find therein an effective safeguard for the rights which derive directly from his dignity as a person, and which are therefore universal, inviolable and inalienable rights. This is all the more to be hoped for since all human beings, as they take an ever more active part in the public life of their own political communities, are showing an increasing interest in the affairs of all peoples, and are becoming more consciously aware that they are living members of a world community.

Lillian Smith
writes of a strange kind of love

LILLIAN SMITH [1897-   ] *is an American writer who won acclaim for* Strange Fruit, *a novel about the tragedy of segregation. In* Killers of the Dream *she explored the psychological basis of prejudice. In 1950 she was awarded a special citation for distinguished contribution to American letters by the National Book Award Committee. "A Strange Kind of Love" was published in the* Saturday Review *in October 1962.*

The nonviolent protesters are demanding their rights, yes; but at the same time they are offering us not "black supremacy," not a black KKK, not black mobs, but gifts of good will, conciliation, forgiveness. They don't want to take our rights away (as do the Black Muslims); they only want theirs. But the big story, which many are missing, is that now has come *their* time to heal broken relationships, to "give presents" of mutual forgiveness, and a mutual bearing of spiritual burdens.

This arouses in some, not warmth, not gratitude, not awe, but anxiety. They find this strange love offered us, this passion for our common welfare and common future extremely disturbing. One man said this: "Let the Black Muslims come! I prefer them to these damned nonviolent niggers. I know what to do with a Black Muslim." But what does one do when offered forgiveness and love? This means we've "gotta straighten things out," as one white put it. And how hard this now seems to people who had convinced themselves that a little token desegregation would do it—then business could go on as usual, art could go on as usual, philosophy, religion could go on as usual, politics. . . .

And now—now we know better.

A man must accept limits to his rebellion, as Camus so wisely said, whether it is rebellion against the past or the future. If the word "moderation" has any meaning left in it after its misuse for the past decade, it lies in this necessity to accept limits. The nonviolent group has done so: its members exclude physical violence and verbal arrogance; they exclude resentment; they try never to refuse a chance for conciliating talks. But they put no limit on each individual's capacity for forgiveness, no limit on compassion, no limit on willingness to help bear the white man's psychic burdens.

This is, in effect, a tremendous spiritual challenge to white southerners—one many of us are unable to rise to at present. These acts, these words—how are we to answer? Where have *we* put the limits to our rebellion against change? Are limits set only against mobs, terrorists, arsonists, demagogues? Only against the closing of our schools? Have we set limits to our arrogance, our hubris, our complacency, our refusal to see what the future demands of us? Can we meet compassion with compassion, justice with justice, reconciliation with reconciliation? There can be no limits to love, it must be (and is) durable and long-lasting; there can be no limits to honor and justice and mercy.

Only a profound humility can say, "We have done wrong and are even now doing wrong." It requires character to be humble, character to accept this "strange love" offered by Negroes to help us bear the burdens of our common future and our common fears.

This strange love is the essence of the Christian religion; its roots go deep into the Jewish religion; it is what valid religion is about. That superb writer, Charles Williams, now dead but well remembered in England, a friend of T. S. Eliot and C. S. Lewis, speaks in his essays and novels more clearly than any contemporary writer of the love that says, "Let me bear your fear for you; you can then do what you need to do; let me ease you of your anxiety; I cannot do your work, this you must do, but I can bear your fear." And though the leaders of the nonviolent movement have not used these words, they, in their ritualistic acts and their conciliating talk, are saying to the white South: "You have no need to fear revenge or malice from us; all we ask is that you let us help bear the fears you have for the future; all we want is to help meet that future with courage—and with grace."

But many whites turn away saying, "They make mistakes, too; they are not always forgiving, some of their leaders do foolish things." Of course they do. Some of their leaders have not as yet made their own Orphic journey; others commit tactical errors; a few are not spiritually concerned enough for this òrdeal; some of the college kids are thinking more about their rights than they are of what they will do with these rights; some of the young northern whites in the movement feel more anger toward white southerners than compassion, though all are courageous.

This is true. And, because they have undertaken a rigorous vocation, they must demand all that is possible of themselves or get out of the movement. But all groups, all movements, even saints come short of perfection. What this group is saying to the South and the nation is worth listening to; worth reaching out for; let us stifle our angry shouts and try to hear the "small voice" that is speaking to us. It is possible this philosophy, these conciliating, nonviolent acts may save us (even though some say we don't "deserve" saving) from the "eye for an eye, the tooth for a tooth" rage of those black supremacists who have succumbed to a ravening hunger for revenge. *If we listen in time.*

Rajendra Prasad

calls for unilateral disarmament

RAJENDRA PRASAD [1884-1963], *the first president of the Indian Republic, was an associate of Mahatma Gandhi. A lawyer by profession, he joined with Gandhi in the Champaran agrarian movement and was imprisoned for his participation in this act of civil disobedience. "The Way to Disarmament" was an address given by Prasad at the opening session of the Anti-Nuclear Arms Convention in New Delhi in 1962. The meeting was sponsored by the Gandhi Peace Foundation.*

From time immemorial man has been known to quarrel with man, employing such weapons as were available to him at the time. The emphasis has gradually shifted from personal bravery to the efficiency and destructiveness of the weapons. The result has been gradual progress from the ax to the atom bomb. At the same time man has not only lost much of his heroism and chivalry but his conscience has become more and more deadened to the finer feeling of humanity. War is fast becoming a push-button affair. The question therefore naturally arises: how is humanity to be saved from the destruction which is inevitable if the misuse of scientific and technological advance goes unchecked or unregulated? It would seem that the wheel has come full circle and the *reductio ad absurdum* of the logic of violence or brute force is almost complete. If man has sense he must see that he has not only to cry halt to the mad rush toward the final disaster but that he must reverse his direction. This was what Mahatma Gandhi meant when he said that ultimate nonviolence was the only safe defense not only for the individual but also for nations. To him this was not a theoretical proposition but a highly practical plan. He applied it in the struggle for freedom by India, and, however limited the scope and application of the principle, the objective was achieved.

However, we who have met here have no illusions that the spiritual principle for which Mahatma Ghandi stood will today be acceptable to the world at large. Our objective is a limited one—namely, the cessation of nuclear tests, banning of nuclear weapons and total disarmament. This would, of course, include the banning of the manufacture and use of nuclear weapons and the destruction of the existing nuclear stockpiles.

If it were only a question affecting two combatants, who could fight it out between themselves and destroy each other, one could sit back complacently and say: "If they are so minded let them do their worst to each other and be damned." But unfortunately the very future of humanity is at stake. Slaughter of the innocent and the guilty alike on a mass scale is bad enough. It becomes infinitely worse if not only the living but also many generations of those yet to be born are doomed to be afflicted with congenital physical and mental defects. The nonaligned and neutral people are as much involved as those who are knowingly or unknowingly engaged in the criminal conspiracy of creating weapons and conditions that would spell their own annihilation no less than that of others.

There is no known defense against a nuclear attack once it is launched. The only thing that the target country can do is to perfect a system of instant retaliation that would be able to function even when the rest of the country has been reduced to an atomic wreckage. It can, however, be poor consolation to the victim of a nuclear attack to know that after he has been wiped out of existence a similar fate would overtake the adversary.

It has been said that the only way to prevent a nuclear war is to develop an adequate nuclear deterrent. But the strategy of deterrence can be rendered ineffective by several causes. It may be rendered ineffective by the failure or malfunctioning of a radar warning system, by a misinterpretation of the signal given by it or even by a meteor striking the earth. Any of these things could create the illusion that a thermonuclear war was on and touch off an unintended thermonuclear war. On several recent occasions such a disaster was only narrowly averted. It is said that the moon, at least once, and the flights of geese, repeatedly, were mistaken for Russian missiles. Again, an unintended nuclear war may be precipitated by a sudden nervous breakdown of an important military officer or official. Nor must it be forgotten that a non-nuclear war can easily develop into a nuclear war. Finally, it does not require much imagination to see that if the race for nuclear supremacy continues, nuclear weapons will be more and more widely distributed. When many nations possess such weapons, the chances of a nuclear war breaking out are immensely increased. An irresponsible head of a small chauvinistic state may be tempted to employ nuclear weapons against a neighbor and thereby precipitate a global thermonuclear war.

Even if deterrence succeeds, the mounting scale of expenditure on armaments resulting from the nuclear-arms race will be such as to impoverish the nations concerned and deprive mankind of much of the fruits of scientific advance. . . .

A race for nuclear weapons, if it remains unchecked, can have only three possible results:

It may lead to a thermonuclear war between East and West which will result in the annihilation of whole populations on either side, destroy civilization and turn the world into a radioactive wasteland.

Or, as Bertrand Russell points out, assaults on heavenly bodies by the competing powers may take the place of exploding nuclear weapons in the attempt by each to demonstrate its superior counterforce capacity to the other side. "It may well happen," says Russell, "that means will be found to cause them [celestial bodies] to disintegrate. The moon may split and crumble and melt. Poisonous fragments may fall on Moscow and Washington or more innocent regions. Hate and destructiveness having become cosmic will spread madness beyond its present terrestrial confines."

The insane race for supremacy in thermonuclear weapons may lead to the financial bankruptcy of the countries concerned and turn the whole world into a vast slum inhabited by fear-ridden neurotics.

How is it, one may ask, that with all these disastrous consequences staring them in the face, the powers still engage in the nuclear-arms race? Why cannot they agree to stop the ruinous competition and dump their armaments into the sea? The reason is that both sides are in the grip of mutual fear, suspicion and distrust, and these do not make for sanity. The only cure for fear, Mahatma Gandhi taught us, is faith, for suspicion sincerity, and for distrust, trust.

We have seen disarmament conferences dragging on their weary course endlessly, only to bog down in a morass of equivocation and double talk. Diplomats hold forth on disarmament but are not prepared to abjure war. In the absence of fundamental sincerity, talks at these conferences become a maneuvering for a position of advantage by each participant at the expense of his adversary. It is obviously to the advantage of a power that has attained superiority in nuclear weapons to try to freeze nuclear armaments at their present level. But a rival power that is trying to overtake and outstrip it in the race for armaments would naturally object to this. Similarly, a power that has a lead in regard to the conventional weapons and forces might agree to the abolition of nuclear weapons, but a power that is inferior in conventional armaments will wish to make up its deficiency by arming itself with nuclear weapons. In the same way, a power that has already conducted a sufficient number of nuclear tests and holds the balance of advantage in the research on nuclear weapons can very well offer with a show of virtue to call for a moratorium on further tests to put its rival in the wrong box if it tries to overtake it in the nuclear race, and use it as an excuse for a further series of tests when it is ready for them. A proposition for simultaneous disarmament evokes the fear in the free world that if free nations disarmed, Communism would, by engineering revolutions with the help of its fifth columns in the non-Communist countries, destroy the free way of life and force the Soviet system upon them.

The straightest and simplest way to break through this vicious circle would be for all powers to abjure the use of force altogether, and this abjuration would have to be reflected in their domestic policies. There may be an agreement to enforce collective sanctions, economic and other, not involving the use of force, against any power that violates the agreed code.

If any one country, taking courage in both hands, unilaterally disarmed, it would break this vicious circle of mutual fear and distrust and pave the way for universal disarmament. Such a nation would go down in history as the benefactor of mankind and the world would not allow it to fall a victim to aggression. We have of late seen one African country after another achieve independence, not by the use of military force but under pressure of world opinion. Since India has had the unique privilege of engaging in a successful nonviolent struggle for independence, under the leadership of Mahatma Gandhi, it will be urged that she should set the example, if her appeal for unilateral disarmament is to carry any weight. I consider this to be a perfectly legitimate challenge. My appeal is addressed to India no less than to the other countries of the world.

It may, however, be that some other country is better qualified than India to take the lead in this respect and will succeed more quickly than we. Mahatma Gandhi was once asked if he, after fifty years of striving, had not been able on his own admission to demonstrate the full power of nonviolence of his conception, what chance was there for others to succeed even in a thousand years? He replied:

It may take some a thousand years, and it may take others only one year. Do not think that, if in spite of my fifty years' practice of it I am still imperfect, it must take you many more years. No, there is no rule of three here. You may succeed quicker than I.

He even envisioned some Western nation, by dint of its training in discipline and organization, and its martial valor, attaining the goal of nonviolence before India, though he never ceased to hope that India would not allow itself to be beaten in the race.

It is, however, arguable that this consummation cannot be achieved at a stroke. It will take time. True, one cannot jump off a running train. Even a man going at more than ordinary speed cannot all of a sudden stop at the last step. The pace can always be adjusted to the circumstances, provided the will is there and a clear recognition of what needs to be done.

So far as the Gandhi Peace Foundation is concerned, the line of unadulterated nonviolence, or *ahimsa,* is the only line that it can take. It cannot seek palliatives by compromising on this point or by speaking in an uncertain voice for the sake of expediency. World peace is its goal but the means for its attainment also have to be peaceful, i.e., truthful and nonviolent. It cannot associate itself with the use of armed force, even for the attainment of peace. . . .

We must have faith that the free way of life cannot be destroyed so long as it is enshrined in the hearts of individuals who are prepared to die for it without anger or ill will in their hearts. A plan for nonviolent defense, however, can have for its object only the preservation of a way of life that is based on honest industry, and the right to enjoy in full the fruit of such industry, coupled with equality and individual freedom, not a way of life based on exploitation, inequality, class distinction, class pride and class rule.

Far from insuring the triumph of one way of life, nuclear weapons only promise the extinction of all life. On the other hand, instances can be multiplied to show that military defeat, occupation and annexation of a country did not result in the disappearance of the nation or its way of life—Poland, Ireland, Czechoslovakia are there, to mention only a few. During the last World War, resistance movements sprang up in several countries under German occupation. The victims of Nazi aggression realized that capitulation by the forces of their respective governments did not necessarily mean the end of popular resistance to occupation. It was further noted that these movements were most successful where they were carried on, largely if not wholly, by moral, i.e., nonviolent means. An outstanding instance of this is provided by the resistance movement in Norway. Violent resistance, where it was tried, proved efficacious only to the extent to which it was the reflection of moral resistance, or the measure of the will to resist in terms of readiness to suffer, and of the intensity of sympathy and active or passive support for the thousands of non-terrorists.

The employment of nuclear weapons is only a part of the technique of terror. The idea behind it is that if the tyrant can demonstrate his undoubted capacity to exterminate the adversary, the latter is bound to submit. But if the adversary learns the art of dying without submission or a sense of defeat, if he develops the awareness that there is in us something which the armaments cannot destroy and which survives even the destruction of our physical body, the power of armaments, nuclear or other, will be sterilized. For it is not the physical destruction of the adversary that the tyrant desires as a rule, but only to bend him to his will.

> At the back of the policy of terrorism is the asssumption that terrorism if applied in a sufficient measure will produce the desired result, namely, bend the adversary to the tyrant's will. But supposing a people make up their mind that they will never do the tyrant's will, nor retaliate with the tyrant's own methods, the tyrant will not find it worth his while to go on with his terrorism. If sufficient food is given to the tyrant a time will come when he will have had more than surfeit.

This was what happened in our own case. The British could have tried to put us down in 1930 by methods which they adopted in 1857 to suppress the Indian Revolt. But we did not give them the chance, because we were, by and large, nonviolent; and even though our nonviolence was not of the purest type, it worked. Lord Irwin had to declare that his government could not impose "the peace of the grave" on India, even though they had the capacity.

Asked whether the atom bomb had not rendered obsolete the weapon of nonviolence, Mahatma Gandhi answered that on the contrary, nonviolence was the only thing that was now left in the field.

> It is the only thing that the atom bomb cannot destroy. I did not move a muscle when I first heard that the atom bomb had wiped out Hiroshima. On the contrary, I said to myself, "Unless now the world adopts nonviolence, it will spell certain suicide for mankind."

A little before his death he was asked by a journalist how he would use nonviolence against the atom bomb. He said:

> *I would meet it by prayerful action. . . . I would come out in the open and let the pilot see that I had not a trace of evil against him. The pilot would not see my face at such a height, I know. But the longing in our heart that he will not come to harm will reach up to him and his eyes would be opened.*

To provide the antidote to the atom bomb, however, requires nonviolence of the highest type. It may be asked whether this would not make too heavy a demand on human nature. Answering this question, Mahatma Gandhi said:

> *The critics gratuitously assume the impossibility of human nature, as it is constituted, responding to the strain involved in nonviolent preparation. But that is begging the question. I say, "You have never tried the method on any scale. In so far as it has been tried, it has shown promising results."*

. . . After all, the change in our outlook and way of life demanded by Gandhiji, by adopting nonviolence or *ahimsa,* is not more drastic than that resulting from our going in the opposite direction. It only requires foresight, faith and determination to leave the trodden path and chalk out a new one which would be for the benefit not only of the present generation but also countless generations to come. If we feel ourselves unable to undertake and achieve this at one step, let us at least make a move in the right direction by banning all nuclear tests as a preliminary step toward the removal of the threat to human survival that confronts us today, and thus give humanity breathing time to think out and adopt further steps to rid the world of fear, distrust and suspicion, which lie at the root of violence.

Danilo Dolci

asks humanity to cure itself of violence

DANILO DOLCI [1924-   ], *an Italian reformer and idealist, was born in Trieste, studied architecture and town planning in Rome and Milan, and in 1952 went to western Sicily to study classical architecture. By then he had already been imprisoned—during World War II—for refusing military service. The misery he saw in Sicily decided him to move there and devote his life to fighting poverty. In 1956 he led a "strike in reverse" where several hundred unemployed Sicilians, to protest a lack of work, repaired a long-neglected road on a voluntary basis with no promise of pay. Dolci and twenty-four others were arrested, tried and convicted, but the court, while sentencing them to terms of imprisonment, expressed appreciation of "the high moral value of Dolci's action." Dolci delivered the speech below in June 1962 to the Anti-Nuclear Arms Convention in New Delhi.*

The main difficulty in eliminating armaments, not to be too naive, is found in the measure of our inability to substitute some other equally strong or stronger and more efficient means of defense than that of being armed. That is to say, in brief:

1. I do not believe there can be truly effective action for peace except to the degree that there are people who believe, from personal experience, in the necessity of struggling, of cooperating, and of living according to the principles and practice of nonviolence.

2. It is urgent and indispensable that the people should understand, that every man should understand the danger and take part in protests, in the most active possible way, against the lunatic possibilities which threaten the existence of all of us. However, even more important than such protests is that people should know and prepare not only checks and obstacles but also ways and means for the construction of lasting peace. One should remember the advice of Gandhi ("there is always a risk that once the consciousness of disaster and the feelings of disgust have been dissipated, the world will return to violence with renewed zeal")—and the fact that more and more easily will bombs be able to be made privately.

3. Action stemming from the people themselves is therefore essential—(and this is truly and deeply revolutionary: in so far as it does not have revolutionary force it is a concession to things past and out of date, to reaction and to death). The people must take part in some local action, however small, so long as it has precise aims and is well planned. In this

way they may learn how great are the possibilities of common action: and in this there is much which bears directly on the possibilities for peace. It is of fundamental importance that every individual, group and nation, working together at every level, should state and understand their problems; what it is they want and what the effective solutions are. One should therefore encourage the making of organic, open and nonviolent plans, by the people themselves wherever possible, which will thus cause the growth of research into ideas for local action, which in turn will become regional plans and slowly develop into bigger, more enveloping ones. Aldo Capitini, the organizer of the Italian March for Peace, would say: "We must promote a nonviolent federalism from below."

4. There can never be true peace, organic peace I should say, while hunger, poverty, ignorance, exploitation, unemployment, colonialism and institutional restrictions on life itself are still to be found in the world. We should not allow ourselves to be lulled by superficial moments of calm or by the mildness of certain peoples: mild to the point of undernourishment and traditionally humiliated, without hope. Armed violence is not the only kind of violence: one should remember that privileged conservatives try in every possible way to "maintain order," above all by ensuring that they are strong in arms and in armies, but appealing to the principles of law and civil rights in doing so.

5. In so far as a person, group or nation is underdeveloped and has not yet reached the best of which it is capable and finds it hard to fulfill its creative possibilities, so conflicts are bound to occur; only when such potentialities as exist in each person, group or nation are realized do they arrive at the necessary level of serenity to understand the way and possibilities of peace. It is therefore fundamental to discover, study, keep in mind and value the particular experience and contribution that each person, group and nation can make, so that a new world culture, morality, political system and a new life can take for nourishment that which is authentic and is offered by the various cultures. To this end the development of the sociology of planning at the group, at the national, and at the international level is important.

6. How can people be sure that they themselves determine the issues of war and peace when, as yet, they do not feel, and indeed are not, masters of their own small today or of their immediate tomorrow? Vast numbers still believe themselves impotent in the face of fundamental problems, not having the necessary experience to understand that development and improvement are possible if men are determined to have them. All actions through which men can experience the possibilities of their own creative development, according to their own true individual, group and collective interests, as a result assuming choice and responsibility, are therefore the essential seminaries for training the leaders necesssary for a

world which aims at a sane way of human development. To condition human life by external means is dangerous if, at the same time, there is no strong leavening action at the social level.

7. It is not enough to rely on the good will of those at the top—politicians, religious and cultural leaders. *By themselves they do not know and they cannot succeed.* He who has the greatest burden of responsibility, even when working and striving in the best possible way so that everyone may possess essential values, is in danger of thinking that he knows what in fact he does not know, and of seeing as uniform things which are not at all uniform. He is also in danger of constantly repeating his own point of view and propositions without listening to others, always thinking the other side wrong, imagining that others, plotting all manner of subterfuges and mean acts, do not mean well and cannot be sincere, and discounts the fact that for his own part he is bound to advance with violence (and to increase it) to save truth, justice and peace itself: this then is the key to peaceful action? to peace? And yet in just this, so primitive morally, consists the greatest part of political action at the summit of the major powers.

8. Thus a great educational effort is required, by means of which humanity may recognize itself, may be cured and renew itself. A longstanding illness, to be cured, needs deep, fundamental treatment. The greatest impediment to war, and the only real one, is, in the final analysis, determined by the point of maturity which the men who do not want war have reached. And this maturity, this self-education, is not produced, evidently, by making or by listening to speeches, but in fact by making plans, by seeking answers, by living together, working together in the field and by becoming aware together. Very often working in depth, not only for immediate results, happens also to be the safest and surest way. To disarm means to accelerate and improve development; but this is also reversible.

9. Certainly there are only too many irrational elements and situations of power, tension and explosive force. For this very reason one needs such a strong and organic life of nonviolence—implacably strong when necessary—to prevent violence from exploding at all levels. To search for a solution to these problems, having said NO to war and violence as instruments for resolving them, means, in fact, to search for and discover the techniques of nonviolence. In order not to risk wasting one's effort in some vague attempt at propaganda, one must have one's feet firmly on the ground in the struggle, while one's vision may reach far ahead. One must form centers for open development from the grass roots which will deepen, widen and multiply as time goes on—like new cells tending to link together in new tissue.

10. To resign oneself to doing or letting others do what one is not

profoundly convinced of, and not to seek coherence at the highest level of one's carefully examined conscience, is to fail to lead a true life. We are easily satisfied with a certain point of development of our own as individuals, as groups or as nations; but in communication we grow. Our relationships cannot be compared with a rock or with a wave; they are far more articulate and far more complex. The misunderstandings which may occur in one day, if well faced, may give opportunities for growing richer in the days which follow. If on the one hand it seems to me an abstract moralism to say, "It's enough that we are pure: the problem will solve itself," on the other hand to suppose that one can resolve the problem by some improvised external formula savors of the ancient world, superstitious, magical, childlike: it denotes an insensitivity to the proportions of the problem, of the disease. I have been amazed to hear people say at certain congresses: "But we've come here to try and resolve the problems of the atomic threat, not to solve educational, social and economic problems."

Effective agreements, effective coordination, can exist only among effective personalities: of individuals, groups, regions, nations.

11. Must we really wait until everyone has understood before we can eliminate war and atomic weapons? If it is true, as indeed it is, that there are things which are imperative, and are indispensable conditions, such as, in the first place, the nonmassacre of people, then these things must be accepted by those who have the responsibility of power. Since humanity stands above the nation, it is ever more necessary to actuate every form of coordinating international authority. It is necessary to continually improve the function and the authority of both international and supranational organisms.

12. Every atom must be sane, organic. In each atom love, truth, the best possible development—that is peace—should be reconquered: nothing can be definitely acquired or discounted. In this field as in others, pretenses, tricks and selfish acts cannot be expected to produce sincerity, loyalty and cooperation; just as lentils do not grow from potatoes. Tuberculosis and leprosy do no good in themselves even when life is so strong as to resist, in spite of illness and blunders, making use of whatever remains on the positive side, destroying and absorbing the germs of death, of chaos and of nothingness, or neutralizing them as with the pearl.

Leo Szilard

suggests the election of government officials solely on the issue of war and peace

LEO SZILARD [1898-   ] *was born in Budapest and came to the United States in 1937. The first patent in America in the field of atomic energy was issued to Dr. Szilard and Enrico Fermi. Albert Einstein based his historic letter telling President Roosevelt of the potentialities of the atom bomb on the work of these two scientists. Dr. Szilard was against dropping the bomb on Japanese cities during World War II; he was active in fighting a Congressional bill which, if passed, would have given the development of atomic energy in the United States to an agency not under the civilian control of the President. In 1959 Szilard was given the Atoms for Peace Award. The selection below is part of a lecture which he has delivered at American universities and colleges. Because of this address, the Council for a Livable World was formed.*

The problem which the bomb poses to the world cannot be solved except by abolishing war, and nothing less will do. But first of all, we must back away from the war to which we have come dangerously close. . . .

America cannot be made secure by keeping ahead in an atomic arms race, and an agreement providing for arms control is a necessary first step toward abolishing war.

An agreement on arms control does not seem to be, however, "around the corner." It might very well be, therefore, that *in the immediate future* America would have to take certain unilateral steps. Some of the steps would be taken in order to reduce the present danger of war; other steps would be taken so that if a war breaks out, which neither America nor Russia wants, it may be possible to bring hostilities to an end before there is an all-out atomic catastrophe.

Such unilateral steps are not adequate substitutes for negotiated agreements, and they can carry us only part of the way, but still there are some unilateral steps which should be taken at the present time and I propose to discuss at this point what these steps may be.

The issue of bomb tests and the issue of bomb shelters are peripheral issues; they are more the symptoms of the trouble we are in than the cause of the trouble, and I propose to turn now to issues which I believe to be more relevant.

1. Nothing is gained by America's winning meaningless battles in the cold war, and a change of attitude in this regard is urgently needed.

Take the International Atomic Energy Agency in Vienna, for instance. This organization has at present no function whatsoever, and if it is maintained in existence at all, it should be maintained as an exercise in cooperation among nations.

The first director of this agency was an American, and his term expired recently. Since, next to America, the Soviet Union is the most important atomic power, America could have proposed that the next director of the agency be a Russian. Instead, America proposed a Swede, who was not acceptable to the Russians, and since America had the votes she was able to win one more victory in a meaningless battle of the cold war.

All this "victory" accomplished was to reduce the chances of finding some useful function for this agency, because the Russians resent being pushed around in this agency and there is no way for us to force them to play ball.

I believe that it would be important for the government to reach a major policy decision, and for the President to issue an executive order against fighting meaningless battles in the cold war.

We have a cultural exchange program with the Russians but their State Department and our State Department are playing a game of "If you hit our scientists, we shall hit your scientists." Accordingly, our State Department imposes senseless travel restrictions on our Russian colleagues who visit this country. These travel restrictions are not aimed at the safeguarding of any secrets, but are merely a way of hitting back at travel restrictions which the Soviet government occasionally imposes on American scientists who travel about in Russia.

I believe that representations ought to be made, at as high a level of the administration as is necessary, for the Secretary of State to find some other assignment in the State Department for those who have, up till now, handled the East-West Cultural Exchange Program.

2. I believe that America could and should make unilaterally two crucially important policy decisions and that she should proclaim these decisions.

First of all, America should resolve and proclaim that she would not resort to any strategic bombing of cities or bases of Russia (either by means of atomic bombs or conventional explosives), except if American cities or bases are attacked with bombs, or if there is an unprovoked attack with bombs against one of America's allies.

Further, America should make a second policy decision and should proclaim this decision. In order to understand the meaning and relevance of this second decision, it is necessary to consider the following:

Soon after the war, when Russia did not as yet have any atomic bombs, she proposed that the bomb be outlawed. This could take the form of a unilateral pledge, given by each atomic power, that it would not resort to the use of atomic bombs, either for the purpose of attacking cities or bases, or as a tactical weapon to be used against troops in combat. Recently, Sulzberger of *The New York Times* discussed with Khrushchev the possibility of such unilateral pledges, renouncing the use of the bomb. Khrushchev said, on this occasion, that if there were a war, even if at first only conventional weapons were used, subsequently the side which is about to lose the war would find it impossible to abide by its pledge and would resort to the use of the bomb.

This brings out what I believe to be the crux of the issue, that today it might still be possible to resist force with force, but the objective of the use of force must no longer be victory. The objective must only be to make a conquest difficult and expensive.

If such force is used, then an all-out war, which neither side wants, can be avoided only if both sides recognize that the use of force must not be aimed at victory, or anything approaching victory.

Keeping this point of view in mind, *America* could and *should* adopt *the policy that, in case of war, if she were to use atomic bombs against troops in combat, she would do so only on her own side of the prewar boundary.*

In case of war America would then be bound by a pledge to this effect as long as Russia imposed a similar restraint on her conduct of the war.

Manifestly, this type of use of atomic bombs would be a defensive operation and moreover, it would be a very effective defensive operation, either on the part of Russia or on the part of America, as long as the restraints remain in effect on both sides.

Such a pledge would be no less clear than the simple pledge renouncing the use of the bomb, but it would be much easier to keep and therefore it would be a more believable pledge. And if neither side aimed at anything approaching victory, then it would substantially reduce the danger of an all-out war.

When I discussed this issue in Germany three years ago, people there said that if the ground forces of the allies were pushed back to the Rhine, and America used atomic bombs against troops in combat between the Rhine and the Oder-Neisse line, many West German cities might be destroyed by American bombs. I do not know to what extent West German cities could be spared by a judicious tactical use of atomic bombs by American forces, but I do know that if America were to use bombs beyond the prewar boundary, West German cities would be destroyed by Russian bombs.

Recently, the United Nations Assembly vetoed with a more than two-thirds majority, fifty-five against twenty, to outlaw the use of atomic bombs in war. The use of atomic bombs in warfare was declared by the

Assembly to be a crime and a violation of the United Nations Charter. Since the machinery of the United Nations was set up for the purpose of maintaining peace among the smaller nations, assuming the cooperation of the great powers to this end, attempts to regard a two-thirds vote of the Assembly as legally binding must necessarily fail. Still, the United States must not fly in the face of world opinion and simply disregard the vote of the General Assembly, when a two-thirds vote of the Assembly expresses the legitimate concern of the great majority of the nations that the use of atomic bombs in warfare might lead to a world catastrophe. Rather, out of respect for world opinion and in its own interest, the United States ought to go as far toward complying with it as valid considerations for its own security permit. The restrictions on the use of atomic bombs in case of war which I am advocating, are advocated with this end in view.

Western Europe is not inferior to Russia either in manpower or in resources and it would be possible for Western Europe to build up within five years conventional forces to the point where it could renounce the use of atomic bombs against troops in combat in case of war. But even this would be to no avail unless the nations involved give up any thought of fighting limited wars for "limited objectives" and resort to force only to make a conquest difficult and, with luck, to prevent it.

As long as there is no agreement providing for arms control, and Russia remains in possession of large stockpiles of bombs, America has no choice but to maintain a strategic atomic striking force. However, it should maintain such a force only as protection against America's or her allies' being attacked with bombs. The number of bombs retained for this purpose need not be very large, and more important than the number of bombs retained is the invulnerability of the bases from which they would be launched. If these bases are invulnerable, so that no single massive attack against them could substantially damage America's ability to retaliate, then America needs to retain only enough bombs to be able to destroy in retaliation a substantial number of Russia's cities, after giving due notice to permit their orderly evacuation.

It must be made clear, however, that if America adopts the policy here advocated, she thereby renounces the threat of strategic bombing as a general *deterrent* bcause she could then make this threat only in case Russia should drop bombs, and drop them on *our* side of the prewar boundary.

I, personally, do not believe that America would lose much by giving up the threat of strategic bombing, because the deterrent effect of such a threat is negligible unless the threat is believable.

If America were to threaten to drop bombs on a large number of Russian cities in case of war, knowing full well that Russia would retaliate by dropping bombs on a large number of American cities, such a threat would be tantamount to a threat of murder and suicide. The threat of murder and suicide would not be a believable threat, in the context of the so-called Berlin crisis, nor would it be a believable threat in the context of any other similar conflict in which America's rights and interests may be at stake, but not America's existence as a nation.

Those responsible for the planning of strategy in the Department of Defense would concede this much.

According to persistent press reports there is, however, an increasingly influential school of thought in the Department of Defense which holds that, in case of war with Russia, America may engage in strategic bombing, aimed at the destruction of Russian rocket bases and strategic air bases. America would not bomb any of Russia's cities if she can help it, as long as Russia did not bomb any of America's cities.

This school of thought holds that, at present, Russia does not have many long-range rocket bases and strategic air bases, that the location of many of these bases is known, and that most of them are vulnerable and could be destroyed by attacking them with bombs. By building enough long-range solid-fuel rockets (Minutemen) and submarines capable of launching intermediate range solid-fuel rockets (Polaris) America may be able to keep ahead in this game for the next five years.

Those who advocate such a policy believe that if America should succeed in knocking out, say, 90 per cent of Russia's strategic atomic striking forces, then the Russians would probably speak to us as follows: "We have enough rockets left to destroy a large number of American cities, but we know that if we did this America may retaliate by destroying all of our cities. Therefore, we are going to hold our fire and we propose to negotiate peace. We concede that the power balance has now shifted in America's favor and we are now willing to yield on a number of issues on which we took an inflexible stand prior to the outbreak of hostilities." If this were to happen America would have won a victory even though it may be a victory in a limited sense of the term only.

Naturally if there is a war and America resorts to the bombing of bases in Russia, one could not expect the Russians to sit idly by and watch America picking up step by step one base after another. It follows that America would have to start the strategic bombing of Russian bases with a sudden, massive attack and to try to destroy all vulnerable Russian bases of known location, in the first attack.

There are, of course, people in the Department of Defense who have serious doubts that America would actually carry out such a first strike against bases, in case of war, yet they believe that—at the present juncture—it is a good thing to threaten to bomb Russian bases in case of war because this is a more believable threat than the threat of "murder and suicide."

I do not know just how believable this threat is, but I do know that at best we are purchasing an increased restraint on Russia's part for a year or two, and that we are purchasing it at a very high price. For whether we adopt such a strategy or merely give Russia the impression that we have adopted such a strategy, we are provoking an all-out atomic arms race and may within a very few years reach the point of no return, in this regard.

Therefore, I believe that it is imperative to oppose: (a) the adoption of plans which call for a first strike against Russian rocket and strategic air bases in case of war, and (b) the adoption of the policy of "deterring" Russia, with the threat that America would resort to such a first strike in case of war. I believe that the rejection of both these policies is an attainable political objective because there is considerable doubt within the administration of the wisdom of these policies.

3. *America could and should resolve that atomic bombs and the means suitable for their delivery, which are supplied by her and which are stationed in Europe, shall remain in the hands of American military units which are under American command, rather than be placed under the control of NATO.* As long as America is committed to defend Western Europe, there is no valid argument for turning over bombs to the control of other Western European nations.

Germany is going to put increasingly strong pressure on the United States government to turn over such equipment to NATO control, and I would be in favor of balancing any such pressure by bringing domestic political counterpressure to bear on the government.

America should stand firm in opposing the production of atomic and hydrogen bombs by Germany as well as the production of means suitable for their delivery.

It is conceivable, of course, that all attempts to achieve arms control may fail and that in the end it will not be within the power of the United States to prevent Germany from producing its own bombs and rockets. At about the same time the United States may however also free herself from her commitments to defend Germany against external military intervention. But we are not concerned at this point with developments that may conceivably occur in the unpredictable future.

4. Not every issue can be solved by Congress' passing a law, and there are borderline issues where political action alone can bring no solution because the specific knowledge is lacking of how to go about the solution. The issue of general disarmament seems to be such a borderline issue.

I believe that, at the present time, little could be gained by bringing pressure on the administration to enter into formal negotiations with Russia on the issue of general disarmament, because—as they say, "You can lead a horse to the water, but you can't make him drink."

I believe that no substantial progress can be made toward disarmament until Americans and Russians first reach a meeting of the minds on the issue of how the peace may be secured in a disarmed world.

American reluctance to seriously contemplate general disarmament is largely due to uncertainty about this point. If it became clear that a satisfactory solution of this issue is possible, many Americans may come to regard general disarmament as a highly desirable goal.

On the issue of how to secure the peace in a disarmed world, progress could probably be made reasonably fast, through nongovernmental discussions among Americans and Russians. *I believe that such discussions ought to be arranged through private initiative, but with the blessing of the administration.*

The Russians know very well that America is *not* ready seriously to contemplate general disarmament and this, to my mind, explains why, in spite of being strongly motivated for disarmament, the Russian government displays in its negotiations on this issue much the same attitude as does the American government. As far as negotiations on disarmament are concerned, hitherto both governments have been mainly guided by the public-relations aspect rather than by the substantive aspect of the issue.

The Soviet Union's attitude might change overnight, however, if it became apparent that America was becoming seriously interested in disarmament.

The Russians are very much aware of the economic benefits they would derive from disarmament, and I believe that the Soviet Union would be willing to pay a commensurate price for obtaining it. It stands to reason that this should be so, for the Soviet Union spends on defense an even larger fraction of her industrial output than America does.

America is at present committed to protect certain territories which are located in the geographical proximity of Russia. In the case of general disarmament, America would not be able to live up to any such commitments. Disarmament would therefore be politically acceptable to America only if it is possible for her to liquidate her present commitments—without too much loss of prestige and without seriously endangering the interests of the other nations involved.

Khrushchev seems to be very much aware of this. Therefore, if it came to serious negotiations on the issue of disarmament, and if it became manifestly necessary to reach a political settlement in order to permit America to liquidate her military commitments, then the Soviet Union might go a long way toward seeking an accommodation.

5. General disarmament may, if we are lucky, eliminate war, but it would not end the rivalry between America and Russia.

It is a foregone conclusion that American efforts toward creating an orderly and livable world will be frustrated in southeast Asia and Africa because of our failure to devise forms of democracy which would be viable in these regions of the world. The task of devising forms of democracy which would be suitable to the needs of such areas is not a task that the government can handle. Various forms of democracy may have to be devised which are tailor-made to fit the various areas. *A major private group could tackle and ought to tackle this problem.* If it is not solved, more and more underdeveloped nations may become dictatorships; some of them may have a rapid succession of dictator after dictator and, in the end, the people may have to choose between chaos and Communism.

It is a foregone conclusion that America's efforts to raise the standard of living of underdeveloped nations may be frustrated in those areas where the birth rate is high, infant mortality is high, and there is little arable land left. Improvement in the standard of living will initially lead to a fall in infant mortality, and if the birth rate remains high, the population will shoot up so rapidly that economic improvements will not be able to catch up.

Our failure to develop biological methods of birth control, suitable for the needs of such areas, is responsible for this state of affairs. The development of such methods is not a task which the government can undertake. The government could not create research institutes which would attract scientists who are ingenious and resourceful enough to come up with an adequate solution. *A major private group could and should tackle this problem.*

If it should turn out that it is possible to formulate a set of political objectives on which reasonable people could generally agree, and if these objectives could count on the all-out support of a sizable and dedicated minority, then I should be impelled to go further, and I would plan to go further along the following lines:

I would ask about fifteen distinguished scientists to serve as fellows of a council which might be called Council for Abolishing War or perhaps Council for a Livable World. The fellows (who are all scientists) would elect the board of directors, but membership on the board would not be restricted to scientists.

This council would, first of all, assemble a panel of political advisors, and then in close consultation with these advisors, it would formulate two sets of objectives. To the first set belong those objectives which cannot be attained at the present time through political action because it would take further inquiry, and perhaps even real research to know, in concrete terms, what needs to be done. To the second set belong those objectives which can be pursued through political action because it is clear what needs to be done.

The fellows of the council would set up a research organization aimed at the pursuit of the first set of objectives, and they would elect the trustees of that organization. The fellows of the council would also set up a political organization aimed at the pursuit of the second set of objectives, and they would elect the board of directors of that organization. Because one of the major functions of the second organization would be to lobby, we may refer to it for our purposes as the lobby.

The council would hold hearings, perhaps one every four months, and would subsequently proclaim in detail the immediate political objectives it proposes to advocate. It would communicate these objectives, perhaps in the form of a series of pamphlets, to all those who are believed to be seriously interested. Those who regularly receive the communications of the council would be regarded as members of the movement, if they are willing *actively* to support *at least one* of the several specific objectives proclaimed by the council.

It seems to me that there is no need to enlist those who are interested as members of an organization. What one needs to create is not a membership organization, but a movement.

The articulate members of the movement would be expected to discuss the relevant issues with editors of their newspaper and various columnists and other opinion makers in their own community. They would be expected to write to, and in other ways to keep in touch with, their congressman and the two senators of their own states.

One of the functions of the lobby would be to help the members of the movement clarify their own minds on the political objectives they wish actively to support.

The members of the movement would be regarded as pledged to vote in the primaries as well as in the elections. As far as Federal elections are concerned, they would be pledged to cast their vote, *disregarding domestic issues,* solely on the issue of war and peace.

The members of the movement would be regarded as pledged annually to spend 2 per cent of the income on campaign contributions. The members would be asked to make out a check payable to the recipient of the campaign contribution but to mail that check to the Washington office of the lobby for transmission. In this manner the lobby would be in a position to keep track of the flow of campaign contributions.

Those in high-income brackets may be left free to contribute 3 per cent after taxes rather than 2 per cent before taxes.

All members of the movement would be free to wear an emblem

that would identify them as members of the movement, if they wish to do so.

Those who cannot spend 2 per cent of their income on campaign contributions may regard themselves as supporters of the movement if they spend either 1 per cent of their income or $100 per year, according to their preference. Such supporters of the movement may receive the advice and guidance of the lobby on the same terms as the members of the movement.

So that each member of the movement may know where his contribution should go, in order to be most effective in furthering the political objectives which he has chosen to pursue, the lobby would keep in touch with each member. The lobby would keep the members informed about the particular contests for seats in Congress which are of interest to the movement; but it may advise one member to take an interest in one of these contests and another member to take an interest in another of these contests.

For covering the operating expenses of the lobby and the research organization (which would be maintained independently from and operated parallel to the lobby), one would look to the members of the movement. Each year a certain group of the members would be asked by the lobby to contribute 2 per cent of their income to it, rather than to spend it for political contributions. One year this group might be composed of those whose names start with the letter *C*. Another year it might be composed of those whose names start with the letter *R*, etc.

The movement must not wield the power that it may possess crudely. People in Washington want to be convinced, they do not want to be bribed or blackmailed. He who gives consistently financial support to certain key members of Congress may evoke their lasting friendship and may count on their willingness to listen to him as long as he talks sense. He who talks to members of Congress, but does not talk sense, will not accomplish anything of lasting value, even if he temporarily sweeps some members of Congress off their feet by making huge political contributions to them.

There are many intelligent men in Congress who have insight into what goes on; the movement could help these men to have the courage of their convictions. There are others in Congress who are not capable of such insight; the only thing to do with them is not to return them to Congress, and to replace them with better men. This may make it necessary to persuade better men to run in the primaries and to stand for election. To find such better men must be one of the main tasks of the movement, and the lobby must be prepared to help members of the movement to perform this task.

Harold Taylor

says the time has come for intellectuals to come to terms with the issues of war and peace

HAROLD TAYLOR [1914-   ] *was president of Sarah Lawrence College for fourteen years. Upon retirement he traveled for six months in Asia and Russia on a special Ford Foundation grant, studying the educational and political problems of the Eastern countries. Since 1960 he has been teaching, lecturing on college campuses and writing on philosophy, education and the problems of world peace and disarmament. In 1960 he was instrumental in organizing a committee on peace research with a group of six eminent scientists, to cooperate in the development of research projects related to the prevention of war. In 1961 the committee was organized into a more permanent form as the Peace Research Institute; Dr. Taylor is vice-president. "Peace and War and the Intellectuals" appeared in* The Progressive *in July 1962.*

The intellectual as an institutional member of world culture is a recent man. In fact, it is only in recent years that we have had organized intellectual communities emancipated from the control of the church, the state and the elite. For four hundred years the universities of the Western world have been responsible for collecting and transmitting the history, culture and knowledge of the world and for acting as a stabilizing, integrating and creative force in the advancement of knowledge and civilization.

The new circumstances of the present age have changed all that.

The universities and the intellectual community have been captured by the organized establishment, by governments, and by military-industrial institutions of the Soviet Union and the Western countries. The vast body of the world's research, ranging through the social sciences and the natural sciences to technology and engineering, is now organized, directly or indirectly, by governments to deal with questions and projects whose character is determined by their relevance to political, economic and, ultimately, military control.

In the United States, in the Soviet Union, in England, in Communist China, in India, there are men in the field of science who have it in their power to work for the solution of the problem of human survival. They could, if they wished, drop all work on weapons systems and military strategy; they could assert that the morality of science demands that the scientist turn all his efforts to saving the human race and creating a richer life for everyone. Why don't they?

They are committed to political and social values which they have learned to accept through the lives they have led and the social system which has nurtured them. They are not dealing with each other as individual men, but as symbols and creatures of systems in which the two key words are not "life" and "death" but "Communism" and "anti-Communism."

What a curious pair of concepts with which to shape human destiny. What a narrow and parochial framework within which to organize human lives and human action. How deadly the effect of their dialectic, how tragic the consequences of their mutual disregard of the human. How deliberate their disregard of the reality of the problems of real men of real flesh and blood.

The international community of scientists and scholars has no need for such abstractions. It is the moral duty of scholars to stay outside narrow ideologies and to join together as internationalists who share a common interest in the invention of new knowledge and in the enhancement of human lives. In the field of science and in the arts, it is up to each man to decide what problems he will struggle to solve.

Yet in our country this choice is being forced by a combination of social, political and economic pressures which have now placed our major scientific resources in the hands of the military and government bureaucracy. The universities, the major counterforce to naked power and material values, have themselves been seduced by a mixture of money and invitations to patriotic duty, until research budgets for studies of weapons systems, military security, cold war politics and industrial development occupy major research facilities in the country's institutions. In a dispute last year between the military and one of our larger universities, for example, a university research project was revealed to consist of studies of "relative merits of beachheads and airdrop centers, use of big bombers for close infantry battle support, techniques in psychological warfare, obsolescence factors in weapons industries, civil defense requirements, and military factors in economic growth."

One views any dispute between the military and the universities with a gleam of hope that at last the universities may be coming to their senses and refusing to demean their true aims by becoming the instruments of war. This dispute, however, was not about the role of the university in peace and war, but about what was referred to by the university as "ethical differences," which turned out to be, in the words of a university spokesman, the "university's responsibility not to touch on decisions, but to do good research" without regard for the conclusions brought about by scientific inquiry. In other words, the issue was not the conversion of the intellect to war-making but simply whether or not the scientist might do his assigned tasks without being badgered by the military hierarchy. The only result of the dispute was that the military developed a new organization to deal with the university; most of the same scientists continue to dance to the same martial tunes under a different bandmaster.

Scientists and engineers, sophisticated in the play of automated war games, use computers to simulate almost all military situations. Professor John George Kemeny of Dartmouth, the distinguished mathematician who was a consultant at Los Alamos, has made the brilliant suggestion that when international tension makes war seem imminent, all the relevant data on weapons systems and destructive power be fed into computers, both the attacking and defending sides showing what they can do, and a simulated war be fought, with international referees, the victor to be decided by the computers. This would release each side from the necessity of actually building the weapons systems or of killing millions of people with them, and still provide the militarists and the politicians with games they can play.

A more immediate plan might be to divert the huge scientific resources of the United States away from an almost total concern with war strategy and its derivatives to disarmament and peace strategy and rearrange the present incredible imbalance of emphasis represented by a $52,000,000,000 military budget as against a $6,000,000 disarmament appropriation. Such a dramatic shift in emphasis would create a fundamental change in our contemporary national attitude. Yet, as James Baldwin says, "Societies are never able to examine, to overhaul themselves; this effort must be made by that yeast which every society cunningly and unfailingly secretes. This ferment, this disturbance, is the responsibility and the necessity of writers."

This ferment *is* the responsibility and the necessity, not only of writers, but of the universities, the scientists, and the scholars. The universities and the intellectual community exist to challenge accepted truth and accepted values, to create new conceptions, to stand against the organized establishment, as that part of the social organism which works as the brain and the conscience of the entire enterprise. Unless they are prepared to embrace this mission, they condemn themselves to a history of service to the establishment, whatever the establishment may be.

The time has come for the members of the American intellectual community to confront themselves bluntly with the issue of war and peace and to come to terms with it. In a safer time it was possible to argue that the role of the intellectual could be fulfilled by advancing knowledge on any front, that political decision-making was the responsibility of the electorate, of which the intellectual was simply another member.

If this were ever true, it is no longer so in the 1960s. During World War II the intellectual resources of the entire country were mobilized on a national scale for war action—for making the bomb, for the Office of Strategic Services, for the Office of War Information, for research and development, for military educational projects. The universities became an integral part of the military system.

The difference between then and now is that the degree of seriousness in the situation is currently greater, the possibility of world destruction is closer. But the question of what the intellectual is to do about it is, in the present time, a matter for his personal decision and only indirectly of government policy. In the case of the scientists and scholars, a choice exists between working on military research, either inside or outside government, or pursuing research which has no military meaning, while the power of the scientist inside government and the Defense Department grows vastly greater than that of the scientist outside. For the rest of the intellectual community, the choice is not so apparent, but it is equally real. It depends upon one's assessment of the present situation and the extent to which one feels morally involved.

There are two new conditions which now exist which never existed before:

The United States government cannot protect its citizens from annihilation in a nuclear war.

Decisions of policy and strategy in relation to peace and war have become so complex and so intermingled with economic, political, scientific, military and moral factors that they are being made by intellectuals, principally scientists, in and out of uniform. . . .

Until we apply to peace strategy the same concentration of brain power now being applied to military problems, we will not find the solutions we seek. Nor will the world believe that we are as serious about peace as we are about war. No one, including the Russians, doubts our military capacity. . . . But where is the evidence of our capacity and our will to bring about disarmament?

What evidence there is comes from studies like those of the economic arrangements which would be necessary in a disarmed America and a disarmed world, studies which have been carried out, first under the initiative of scholars outside government—men like Kenneth Boulding, Émile Benoit, Walter Millis and Seymour Melman—and more recently by some of these men and others for the Disarmament Agency. But we do not yet have a full-scale research plan of economic redevelopment for a peacetime economy in the United States. Until we do, who can believe that we fully intend to rearrange our society to accommodate a serious disarmament policy?

Certainly the reallocation of military contracts can disrupt entire communities, entire cities, entire areas of American society. This, more than anything else, gives the American citizen a stake in an increased military budget at a time when our problems are not in the last analysis military, but are social, political, economic and moral.

Other evidence of our will for peace comes from the renewal of American efforts to negotiate seriously with the Russians on disarmament, this time with a detailed plan which can serve as a basis for solving the practical problems of parity of arms and stability within the military environment. But at the same time we have clung to our decision to renew testing in the atmosphere when, without serious hazard, we could have made a sharp break with the past and set out on a new course of unilateral initiatives.

When we look for encouragement and new grounds for the belief that peace is possible, we find it in the work, in this country and abroad, by scientists and scholars who, on their own initiative, have tackled the practical problems of achieving peace and whose sense of social responsibility has led to the formation of groups for international exchange of ideas like the Soviet-American collaboration of scientists through the Council on Science and World Affairs. The recent announcement of American-Soviet cooperation in research in outer space holds out new hope that within the international scientific community we will find a place to invent alternatives to cold war competition.

The American intellectual community need not wait for the formation of international or national research groups by governments. We can look to our universities and colleges as centers of research and action for peace. Within the university curriculum itself we can establish seminars, study groups, research projects and research institutes, like the University of Michigan Center for Research on Conflict Resolution, or the Canadian Peace Research Institute to be established at McGill University. The coordinating agency for doing so already exists in the Peace Research Institute in Washington.

The study of the issues involving peace and war takes the scholar and the student into areas of research in which the combined efforts of natural scientists, social scientists, philosophers and humanists are necessary to the resolution of the issues, and a new and significant realignment of the traditional disciplines becomes not only possible but necessary. . . .

Were we to establish across the country in our colleges and universities centers for the study and discovery of strategies toward peace, we would have a flow of new ideas to match the flow of events and find imaginative solutions to the problems of social change before the conflict such change generates can erupt into violence. These new institutes could easily be arranged within existing university structures. What is needed is a radical redirection of the kind of research now being carried on and a concern for its relevance to the major issues now affecting the international order. Almost the whole of our research in the past has been after the fact, or in explanation of the status quo. We must turn to the invention of new alternatives for the solution of problems which, if left to governments and chance, will run their course into mass violence.

We must consider such projects as a World University, on the base of the United Nations, a university whose student body and faculty is world-wide, whose curriculum consists of the world's problems, beginning with the problems of peace and war, whose graduates would be those deeply educated in a world view, free of the parochialism of the nation-state, yet conscious of the meaning of national differences. These would be scholars and young men and women who would form an international agency, educated to meet the issues of a new world, ready to take up the task of planning the future in advance of its disasters. We already have precedents for such research and education in the World Health Organization, the International Agency for the Peaceful Use of Atomic Energy, and the projects of the United Nations Secretariat.

We also have the prototype of these international students among our own American youth who have already taken the lead in many of our colleges in tackling issues which range from the race problem, aid to underdeveloped countries, and the Peace Corps, to student research projects and conferences in disarmament and peace strategy. In many instances these students are ahead of the university faculty members, both where the degree of their involvement and the degree of their sophistication in seeking out alternatives to cold war policy are concerned.

Those who speak disparagingly of the college men and women who have been active in the peace movement, and who say that the students act without knowledge on matters which they do not understand, should be required to face the responsible and informed reports which the students have prepared, and to answer student arguments against present deterrence policy. They should also be prepared to answer the students' question as to why the academic community has not given leadership to the public, as well as to students, in meeting the issues which are currently being raised within American society and the world order. The intellectual has a responsibility to meet the blind and aggressive attitudes of those committed to the American right by strong and vigorous statements against the growing national habit of treating the use of reason in international affairs as if it were a sign of softness. It is the duty of the intellectual to engage himself in the issues, to open up the area of public debate, to add his voice to the support of intelligent solutions to national problems.

To unite the cultures, the immediate task is to bring the full resources of the human mind to bear on the major issues of peace and war. Until we are prepared to do this, we leave the world's future to the ultras, to the military, to the blind forces of history, to the ideologies, to governments, and to chance. We may still choose to act, and it is high time we did.

Sidney Lens

*condemns civil defense for giving a treacherous
sense of security*

SIDNEY LENS [1912-   ] *is a lifelong union official and writer. He
has written and lectured on foreign affairs, labor and other political subjects. Lens is one of four editors of* Liberation *magazine, a Gandhian
monthly, but he considers himself only partly Gandhian in philosophy.
He is a nuclear pacifist. The essay here was first printed as part of "The
Case Against Civil Defense" in the February 1962 issue of* The Progressive.

A civil defense program, whether its rationale is based on the moderate and superficially reasonable "insurance" argument or the harsher insist-ence on "making the deterrent credible," sharpens the dilemma facing America. As a nation we want to cling to the power and security our strength has given us. We are challenged now by a hostile ideology in the Soviet world and by a pyramiding revolution in what was once the colonial world. How do we defend our power in a situation that seems to be disintegrating all around us?

The traditional answer, military might, proved adequate in the past to secure America's position in the world.

It was almost inevitable, then, that although Hiroshima opened a new era in warfare and canceled out the axioms of thousands of years, we still cling to the concept of yesterday—that power rests on military might. In the heightened tensions that came in the post-World War II world we have responded in a characteristically emotional manner—as Dr. Jerome Frank, noted psychiatrist at Johns Hopkins University, recently pointed out in the *Bulletin of the Atomic Scientists*—by re-gressing "to solutions which worked in the past." We are groping in the past for parallels with the present. We cannot yet grasp the vital fact that while armaments may have secured power yesterday, they are not equal to the task today or in the future.

"In the past," anthropologist Margaret Mead says, "no matter what kingdoms fell or what civilizations crumbled, the march of mankind could continue. But this is no longer true."

War, in the past, was the ultimate act in defending national policy. Through wars it was possible to extend empires or hold onto those already fashioned. It was possible, through armed force, to protect trade or sustain or suppress revolutions. But in the nuclear age war can serve none of these purposes, for, as Air Force General Curtis LeMay points out, "No one can win a modern war. Even the victor loses."

Subconsciously, at least, every thoughtful American knows that victor and vanquished in the next war will both be destroyed. When Albert Einstein was asked what weapons would be used in World War III, he said he didn't know, but he was certain that in World War IV they would be "sticks and stones." In our very bone and marrow, most of us are convinced this is true. But since, as a nation, we regress to former solutions, the arms race continues, and the ordinary citizen faces a painful dilemma: how to plan survival when there seems little prospect for survival.

We try to "solve" these problems in a number of unrealistic ways. The first, and, as Dr. Frank points out, "the most primitive way," is simply to disregard the existence of the danger. Writers and scientists who spoke yesterday of total destruction in modern war gradually accustom themselves to believe it "thinkable," even "tolerable." Much of the daily press and magazines like *Time* and *Life* reduce the danger through "fraud by computer" to a mere 3 per cent dead as a result of nuclear attack, and Colonel Mawrence concludes that with proper measures only 900,000 (one-half of one per cent) of our people would perish. This denial of reality only adds to the development of a more belligerent foreign policy, makes negotiations that much more difficult, and brings nuclear war that much closer. We learn to speak of "overkill"—we have enough weapons to kill the Russians many times over.

Another internal emotional defense is fatalism. The man on the street says, "There have always been wars and always will be." If the "big one" drops, he tells the pollsters, "we're going to die anyway." He absolves himself from responsibility in any public decisions. But this fatalism is unrealistic. It is true that wars have been almost ever-present in history, but it is not true that man cannot change his patterns of thinking and living. In the course of time—it took centuries—we have been able to eliminate human sacrifice, slavery and other forms of brutality.

Dr. Jack N. Peterman, of the Chicago Psychological Club, tells us that when two wolves fight each other, the one which is near defeat bares his jugular vein as an invitation to the victor for the coup de grâce. The winner, however, backs off at this point and refuses to kill his opponent. "We have not yet learned, like the wolf," says Dr. Peterman, "to stop short of extinction." But there is no reason why societies that can send artificial satellites around the earth cannot discover for themselves the values that motivate even wolves. There is no reason why mankind cannot learn the same primitive lesson in sanity.

Another manifestation of man's present frustration is his quest for elusive panaceas, such as civil defense. In their concern about the present and future of human existence, many thoughtful Americans cling to this tiny hope and blind themselves from an objective examination of the totality of the problem.

Yet there are rational solutions if we will only face up honestly to the totally new dimensions of war that arrived with the nuclear age. There is risk, of course, in every alternative. There is risk in the arms race and its theory of deterrence—risk of accidental war, risk, as President Kennedy has pointed out, of ceaseless escalation. There is risk also in disarmament. Mere disarmament in itself will certainly not resolve the world's political frictions. There may even be some cheating and "brush fire" wars.

Yet, which risk is preferable: the one which virtually assures annihilation, or the one which offers time to work out world difficulties? The arms race only makes more difficult the task of negotiating every problem, whether it be Formosa, Vietnam, the Congo, Berlin, or Cuba—for each source of tension intensifies the arms race itself. But disarmament would at the very least gradually evolve a climate of hope, to replace our own suffocating atmosphere of near-certain doom.

Certainly there would be conflict—man cannot exist without conflict. Certainly there would be dispute, argument, harassment. Yet in a disarmed world the *risk* to life itself would not be nearly so great. The climate of reduced tension would make it possible for man to concentrate on the peaceful pursuits of conquering hunger, poverty and ignorance. The tense climate today makes the achievement of these goals difficult, for the world's energies are channeled into the primary emphasis on a "defense" that cannot defend.

Of course the pursuit of disarmament will be difficult. I am not suggesting that we have only to say yes to disarmament and no to civil defense to achieve the first and destroy the need for the second. What I am suggesting is that we are so wedded to the patterns of the past that we have not truly tried—hard enough—to achieve complete, universal disarmament by negotiated agreement. We are quick to give our treasure, our energies and our brains, and, if need be, our lives, to the development of new monsters of war and new gadgets of defense, but we are slow and stingy in exploring new frontiers of peacemaking. . . .

James Farmer
reports on a Freedom Ride

JAMES LEONARD FARMER [1920-   ] *is national director of the Congress of Racial Equality. His father was a scholar; his grandfather, a slave. Before becoming national director of CORE, Farmer was program director of the National Association for the Advancement of Colored People, and also an international representative of the State, County and Municipal Employees Union in New York. "I Will Keep My Soul" appeared in* The Progressive *magazine in November 1961.*

On May 4 of this year I left Washington, D.C., with twelve other persons on a risky journey into the South. Seven of us were Negro and six were white. Riding in two regularly scheduled buses, one Greyhound, the other Trailways, traveling beneath overcast skies, our little band—the original Freedom Riders—was filled with expectations of storms almost certain to come before the journey was ended.

Now, six months later, as all the world knows, the fire-gutted shell of one bus lies in an Alabama junk yard, and some of the people who almost died with it are still suffering prolonged illnesses. A dozen Freedom Riders nearly gave up their lives under the fierce hammering of fists, clubs and iron pipes in the hands of hysterical mobs. Many of the victims will carry permanent scars. One of them lies in a Detroit hospital critically ill from a cerebral hemorrhage, a direct result of the beating he took. Others have lost their jobs or have been expelled from school because of their participation in the rides. More than 350 men and women have been jailed in a half dozen states for doing what the Supreme Court of the United States had already said they had a right to do. The Interstate Commerce Commission has now issued an historic ruling in behalf of interstate bus integration which may indeed mean that the suffering of the past six months has not been in vain.

Why did we ride? What is the meaning of it all? Has the whole thing been a stunt, a gimmick engineered by irresponsible publicity seekers? Has America's prestige been damaged in the eyes of the world by the events that grew out of the Freedom Rides? These are questions frequently asked, and I think the answer should not be required to wait upon the verdict of history.

In 1946 the Supreme Court ruled in the Irene Morgan decision that segregation of interstate passengers in seating on buses was an unconstitutional burden upon commerce. A Freedom Ride later that year, called the "Journey of Reconciliation," cosponsored by the Congress of Racial Equality and the Fellowship of Reconciliation, demonstrated that segregated seating was still enforced on buses in the upper Southern states, and that anyone who challenged this segregation was subject to arrest and threatened violence. Through the years since that time reports have come into the office of the Congress of Racial Equality (CORE) of continuing segregation in seating on buses, especially in the deep South.

In 1960 the Supreme Court issued a ruling, in the Boynton case, banning segregation in the terminal facilities used by interstate passengers. Yet in the months that followed, reports continued to pour into our office indicating that the South was defying the Supreme Court's edict, just as some of the southern states have defied the court's school desegregation rulings. It was to close this gap between the interpretation and the implementation of the law that the Freedom Riders rode.

Who were the Freedom Riders? By what right did we seek to "meddle in the South's business"? Ever since the election of Rutherford B. Hayes to the Presidency in 1876, and the bargain with the South which it entailed, the southern states have maintained that what they do with the Negro is their own business, and "outsiders" have no right to interfere. The Freedom Riders rejected this essentially states' right doctrine of race relations. None of us, in the North or in the South, can afford the moral luxury of unconcern about injustice. Further, the states' rights doctrine is just as outmoded on the domestic scene as nineteenth-century isolationism is on the international. Today, how can we think of outsiders keeping hands off injustice in Alabama, when outsiders all over the world can be threatened with destruction by events in a faraway place like Laos? How would the dead of Korea view Mississippi's claim that only Mississippians have a right to concern themselves with injustice in that state?

So we came from all over the country, from both races and of all ages, to test compliance with the law, to exercise the right of all Americans to use all transportation facilities with the dignity of equality, to shake Americans out of their apathy on this issue and expose the real character of segregation to the pitiless scrutiny of a nation's conscience.

Outsiders? As Americans, from whatever state, all of us are Mississippians and Minnesotans, Carolinians and Californians, Alabamans and Arizonans. No American can afford to ignore the burning bus and the bloody heads of the mob's victims. Who can fail to be stirred by the new convicts for conscience, black and white, who walked with pride into southern jails, especially in Mississippi, surrendering their own personal freedom in the struggle for a greater freedom for everyone?

Jail at best is neither a romantic nor a pleasant place, and Mississippi jails are no exception. The first twenty-seven Freedom Riders to arrive in Jackson saw the inside of two different jails and two different prisons —the Jackson City Jail, the Hinds County Jail, the Hinds County Prison Farm, and the State Penitentiary at Parchman. Jails are not a new experience for many of the riders, but the Freedom Riders were definitely a new experience for Mississippi jails. For the first time, penal authorities in the citadel of segregation had a glimpse of the new Negro and the emancipated white. I do not think these jailers will ever be quite the same again after their experience. Nor will the other prisoners, black and white, be the same again, after having seen in the flesh men and women who do not believe segregation to be in the very nature of things, and who are willing to defy it.

Prison authorities frequently said, and really seemed to believe, that other Negro prisoners like things the way they are and have no sympathy with us, and that it was for our own protection that we were isolated from them. However, whenever the guards were not present, the Negro trusties went out of their way to show their sympathy by word and deed. "Keep up the good work," one said. "I admire you guys and what you are doing," said another. "I wish I could do the same thing, but I have to do what these people tell me to do." They smuggled newspapers in to us, delivered notes and messages between our cell block and that of the girl Freedom Riders, and passed on rumors which they had heard in the jail or in the community.

One night at the county jail, a voice called up from the cell block beneath us, where other Negro prisoners were housed. "Upstairs!" the anonymous prisoner shouted. We replied, "Downstairs!" "Upstairs!" replied the voice. "Sing your freedom song." And the Freedom Riders sang. We sang old folk songs and gospel songs to which new words had been written, telling of the Freedom Ride and its purpose. We sang new words to old labor songs, too. One stanza rang out: "They say in Hinds County no neutrals have they met. You're either for the Freedom Ride or you 'tom' for Ross Barnett." Then the downstairs prisoners, whom the jailers had said were our enemies, sang for us. The girl Freedom Riders, in another wing of the jail, joined in the Freedom Ride songs, and for the first time in history, the Hinds County jail rocked with singing of songs of freedom and brotherhood.

One evening at the county jail, after a rumor of our imminent transfer to the state penitentiary had reached us, the jailer came quietly to our Freedom Riders cell block. He called me, and we stood there with the bars between us, chatting. He did most of the talking. He told me about his family, his wife, and four or five children—the good records they had made in schools, including Ole Miss. He told me of his son's prowess in sports and of the children's marriages and his grandchildren. He told me, too, of his dislike of violence, and of his children's upbringing in that regard. The jailer stood there talking for more than an hour, in the first conversation we had had with him. This, I am sure, was his way of saying goodbye, and of telling us that he respects the Freedom Riders, and that whatever unpleasantness we might meet at the state penitentiary would be something of which he did not approve.

Mississippians, born into segregation, are human too. The Freedom Riders' aim is not only to stop the practice of segregation, but somehow to reach the common humanity of our fellow men and bring it to the surface where they can act on it themselves. This is a basic motive behind the Freedom Rides, and nonviolence is the key to its realization.

It is not only that southerners and other Americans have been shaken in their unjust racial practices, or out of their lethargy. Now, as a result of the Freedom Rides, the world at large, and especially the developing nations of Africa and Asia, have been offered the opportunity of viewing a new, more constructive approach to America's racial dilemma. If the world looks now it will see that many dedicated and conscientious Americans of both races, rather than sweeping the dirt of discrimination under the rug, are striving, at any cost, to remove the dirt from their house. If Africans witnessed our national shame in the necessity for the Freedom Rides, they saw our nation's hope and promise in the fact that there were so many Americans willing to risk their freedom and even their lives to erase that shame.

The world and America saw also the Freedom Rider's challenge to the traditions and fears which have immobilized so many Negroes in Dixie. In terminals in the South, and on the buses, many Negro passengers took the Freedom Riders' cue and dared to sit and ride "first class." This was another purpose of the rides themselves: to break down the voluntary submission of Negroes to racial injustice, a submission created by generations of suppression with the rope and with fire and with economic reprisal. As I entered the white waiting room in one terminal in the South, a Negro woman passenger from the same bus caught my eye and anxiously beckoned me to follow her into the dingy but safe colored section. Moments later, when she saw me served at the lunch counter in the white section, she joined me for a cup of coffee.

There is a new spirit among Negroes in Jackson. People are learning that in a nonviolent war like ours, as in any other war, there must be suffering. Jobs will be lost, mortgages will be foreclosed, loans will be denied, persons will be hurt, and some may die. This new spirit was expressed well by one Freedom Rider in the Mississippi state penitentiary at Parchman. The guards threatened repeatedly, as a reprisal for our insistence upon dignity, to take away our mattresses. "Come and get my mattress," he shouted. "I will keep my soul."

Herbert Read

calls for a revolt of the instincts of man against the threat of mass destruction

SIR HERBERT READ [1893-   ] *is a poet, writer, critic, and interpreter of modern art and literature. He explains in the introduction to his book* Anarchy and Order *that "revolutionary realism for an anarchist in an age of atom bombs is specific; the bomb is now the symbol, not of anarchy, but of proletarian power." In 1961 Read participated in the mass sit-down protest in London against Polaris submarines. Here he explains his reasons.*

The case for civil disobedience is the case of individual conscience against the authority of government. So long as the government is absolute and tyrannical, there are few reasonable people who would not admit the right of the individual to revolt when his conscience is outraged by a power that has no respect for humanity.

The problem becomes more difficult when the government is a democratic one and claims to represent the will of the people. But even a democratic government represents only a majority of the people, and sometimes by a very small margin.

The case for civil disobedience in a democratic state is not so obvious as it is in a tyrannical state, but modern democracy is a very impure institution. Its authority rests on an election in which many diverse and inconsistent policies are presented to the public, and any one vote may be determined by one of a hundred issues. There has never been a vote on the unequivocal issue of peace or war, and certainly never a vote on whether our country should commit itself to the manufacture and use of atomic weapons.

But even if there had been such a vote and a majority was in favor of such a policy, I should still be prepared to disobey the authority of a government that proposed to use such weapons against our fellow men.

I believe there are convincing strategical and political arguments for nuclear disarmament, but I will not use them on this occasion. They are known to most of you and have been expounded with more political acumen than I can claim to possess. My intention to commit an act of civil disobedience in opposition to official policy that contemplates atomic warfare is neither strategical nor political: it is instinctive.

War itself is instinctive. Its immediate causes are economic, but governments would not be able to delude their people into aggressive and murderous acts but for certain frustrations common to us all—emotional tensions caused in us by social conventions that are basically an aspect of the struggle for survival. Frustration automatically arouses aggressive impulses—this is one of the most established of all psychological laws.

To survive without war the society of nations must so arrange its economy and morals that frustration is not entailed with mutual danger to its constituent members, but that is a long-term policy for statesmen, and meanwhile the stockpile of atomic weapons increases. Frustration too increases. Stupid and bewildered men rise to power and the whole fate of humanity is attached to a very delicate trigger.

To have reached this state of imminent peril is in itself an unparalleled disaster, for which the statesmen and scientists of the world have forfeited all moral authority. Not one of us has any longer any faith in political action. The more conferences and committees we arrange and attend, the farther away we seem to get from any immediate and practical intention to disarm.

This stalemate must be broken, but it will never be broken by rational argument. There are too many right reasons for wrong actions on both sides. It can be broken only by instinctive action. An act of disobedience is or should be collectively instinctive—a revolt of the instincts of man against the threat of mass destruction.

Instincts are dangerous things to play with, but that is why, in the present desperate situation, we must play with instincts. The apathetic indifference of the majority of people to the very real threat of universal destruction is partly due to a lack of imagination, but the imagination does not function in the present situation because it is paralyzed by fear in its subconscious sources.

We must release the imagination of the people so that they become fully conscious of the fate that is threatening them, and we can best reach their imagination by our actions, by our fearlessness, by our willingness to sacrifice our comfort, our liberty, and even our lives to the end that mankind shall be delivered from pain and suffering and universal death.

Bertrand Russell

sets out the case for nonviolent civil disobedience in combating the nuclear peril

LORD BERTRAND RUSSELL [1872-   ] *is a mathematician and philosopher, and winner of the Nobel Prize for Literature in 1950. During World War I he favored conscientious objection to military service. He was above draft age himself, but he served a prison term for his stand against conscription. He is now considered the spiritual leader of the mass-action civil-disobedience movement in England. He does not consider himself technically a pacifist because he feels that in some circumstances force is justifiable. Russell delivered the address "On Civil Disobedience" at Birmingham, England, in 1961.*

My main purpose this afternoon is to set out the case for nonviolent civil disobedience as one of the methods to be employed in combating the nuclear peril. Many people believe that this method is not likely to achieve its purpose, and some have moral objections to it on principle. Most of them will admit that nonviolent civil disobedience is justified when the law demands the individual concerned to do something which he considers wicked. This is the case of conscientious objectors. But our case is a somewhat different one. We advocate and practice nonviolent civil disobedience as a method of causing people to know the perils to which the world is exposed and in persuading them to join us in opposing the insanity which affects, at present, many of the most powerful governments in the world. I will concede that civil disobedience as a method of propaganda is difficult to justify except in extreme cases, but I cannot imagine any issue more extreme or more overwhelmingly important than that of the prevention of nuclear war. Consider one simple fact: if the present policies of many great powers are not radically changed, it is in the highest degree improbable that any of you here present will be alive ten years hence. And that is not because your peril is exceptional. It is a universal peril.

"But," objectors will say, "why cannot you be content with the ordinary methods of political propaganda?" The main reason why we cannot be content with these methods alone is that, so long as only constitutional methods were employed, it was very difficult—and often impossible—to cause the most important facts to be known. All the great newspapers are against us. Television and radio gave us only grudging and brief opportunities for stating our case. Politicians who opposed us were reported in full, while those who supported us were dubbed "hysterical" or were said to be actuated by personal hostility to this or that politician. It is very largely the difficulty of making our case known that drove some of us to the adoption of illegal methods. Our illegal actions, because they had sensational news value, were reported, and here and there, a newspaper would allow us to say why we did what we did.

It was a most noteworthy fact that not only was our demonstration of February 18 very widely reported in every part of the world but, as an immediate consequence, all sorts of newspapers—both here and abroad—demanded and printed statements of our case which, until then, they would have rejected. I think also that the spectacle, even in photographs, of so very many serious people, not looking like freaks as newspapers had said we did, caused a widespread belief that our movement could not be dismissed as an outbreak of hysterical emotionalism.

Both popular and official ignorance of the main facts concerned has begun to grow less, and we hope that, in time, some members of the government, and perhaps one or two great newspapers, may acquire some knowledge as to the terrible problems about which they lightheartedly dogmatize.

Some of our critics who oppose nonviolent civil disobedience on principle say that we rely upon bullying and not upon persuasion. Alas, we are very far removed from being strong enough to bully anybody; and, if we ever were strong enough, present methods would have become unnecessary. I will take as typical of the arguments of our opponents a letter in *The Guardian* of March 29 from the Bishop of Willesden. You may think it rash to oppose a bishop on a moral issue, but—greatly daring—I will attempt the task. The bishop says that our demonstrations are intended to force our views upon the community, rather than merely to assert them. He has not, himself, experienced, as we have, the difficulty of asserting anything loudly enough to be heard when all the major organs of publicity are combined in an attempt to prevent our case from being known. Nonviolent civil disobedience, according to the bishop, is a use of force by a minority to compel the majority to submit. This seems to me one of the most farfetched and absurd arguments that I have ever heard. How can a minority of unarmed people, pledged to nonviolence, impose their will against all the forces of the Establishment backed by public apathy? The bishop goes on to say that such methods can lead to anarchy or dictatorship. There have, it is true, been many instances of minorities acquiring dictatorship. The Communists in Russia and the Nazis in Germany are outstanding examples. But their methods were not nonviolent. Our methods, which are nonviolent, can only succeed by persuasion.

There are two arguments which are often employed against nonviolent civil disobedience. One is that it alienates people who might otherwise be supporters, and the other is that it causes dissension within the antinuclear movement. I will say a few words about each of these. I have no wish whatever to see nonviolent civil disobedience adopted by *all* opponents of nuclear weapons. I think it is well that organizations both practicing and abstaining from nonviolent civil disobedience should exist to suit different temperaments. I do not believe that the existence of an organization practicing nonviolent civil disobedience prevents anybody from joining an organization which does not. Some may *say* that they are deterred by distaste for fanatical extremists, but I think these are all people who would in any case find something to deter them. I think, on the contrary, that our movement has a vigor and magnetism which attracts large numbers who might otherwise remain indifferent.

As for dissensions, they, I agree, are regrettable, but they are totally unnecessary. There is no reason why societies practicing different techniques should not exist side by side without finding fault with each other. I think this has come to be recognized. I have, for my part, a very great admiration for what the C.N.D. has done and I hope its work will continue to prosper. But I think the work of those who believe in nonviolent civil disobedience is at least equally valuable, especially while to the newspapers it has the attraction of novelty.

Many people say that, while civil disobedience may be justified where there is not democracy, it cannot possibly be right where everybody has a share of political power. This sort of argument is one which is willfully blind to very obvious facts. In practically every so-called democratic country there are movements similar to ours. There are vigorous movements in the United States. In Canada they are not far from acquiring power. Naturally the movement in Japan is very powerful and very convinced. Moreover, take the problem of people under twenty-one. If the governments have their way, these people will all be slaughtered without having any legal means of giving weight to their wish to survive. Consider, again, the way in which opinion is manufactured in a nominally democratic country. Great newspapers belong to rich and powerful people. Television and radio have strong reasons for not offending the government. Most experts would lose their position and their income if they spoke the truth.

For these reasons the forces that control opinion are heavily weighted upon the side of the rich and powerful. Those who are neither rich nor powerful can find no ways of counterbalancing this overweight except such as the Establishment can decry with the support of all who profit by the status quo. There is in every great modern state a vast mechanism intended to prevent the truth from being known, not only to the public, but also to the governments. Every government is advised by experts and inevitably prefers the experts who flatter its prejudices. The ignorance of important public men on the subject of nuclear warfare is utterly astounding to those who have made an impartial study of the subject. And from public men this ignorance trickles down to become the voice of the people. It is against this massive artificial ignorance that our protests are directed. I will give a few instances of this astonishing ignorance:

The *Daily Mail* in a report on civil defense stated that fallout decays rapidly once it is down on the ground and that, therefore, people who had taken refuge in shelters would not have to stay there very long. As a matter of fact, to take only two of the most dangerous ingredients of fallout—Strontium 90 has a half life of twenty-eight years and Carbon 14 has a half life of 5,600 years. These facts make it seem as if people would have to stay in the shelters as long as from the building of the pyramids to the present day.

To take a more important example, the Prime Minister recently stated without any qualification that "there will be no war by accident." I have not come across one nongovernment expert who has studied this subject who does not say the opposite. C. P. Snow, who has an exceptional right to speak with authority, said in a recent article: "Within at the most ten years, some of these bombs are going off. I am saying this as responsibly as I can. *That* is a certainty." John B. Witchell, an engineer, who resigned his position as a member of Canada's Atomic Research Board in protest against the government's nuclear-armament policies, stated in a recent speech: "The demand for instantaneous retaliation leads to a hair-trigger situation which renders nuclear war a statistical certainty." He went on to say that those whom he calls "the official liars" will say that mistakes will be impossible. He replied to them: "Let me say emphatically, positively, there can be no safeguard which can be considered adequate."

I could give many other quotations expressing the same view, and none expressing the opposite view except from government employees. Mr. Macmillan should know these facts, but evidently does not.

I will give another example of the Prime Minister's cheerful ignorance: Speaking in Ottawa quite recently he alluded to the signs of neutralism in Britain and told the Canadians not to be worried by them. He said, "If ever the call comes to them, the young will go straight from the ranks of the neutralists into the ranks of Her Majesty's Forces, as they have so often done in the past." They will have to be rather quick about it, as his own government has told us that they will only have four minutes' notice. At the end of the four minutes they will be dead, whether in Her Majesty's Forces or still among the neutralists. The ancient rhetorical language associated with war is so ingrained that Mr. Macmillan is quite unable to realize its complete remoteness from modern military facts.

It is not only that the organs of publicity are slow to publish facts which militate against official policy. It is also that such facts are unpleasant and, therefore, most people soon forget them. What proportion of the inhabitants of Britain know the official report by the U.S. defense minister of probable casualties in a nuclear war with present armament? His official guess was 160,000,000 in the U.S., 200,000,000 in the U.S.S.R. and everybody in Britain and Western Europe. He did not regard this as a reason for changing American policy. When one combines this estimate with the near certainty of a nuclear war if present policies continue, it is obviously not unjust to say that the government of Britain is favoring a course which, if persisted in, will lead to the death of every one of us. It may seem odd that a majority of the British public supports the policy leading to this dreadful disaster. I do not think that British voters would continue to do so if the facts were brought to their notice so emphatically that they could no longer forget them. This is part of our purpose and part of what makes spectacular action necessary.

Most people in Britain are not aware of the attitude taken by armament experts in America to the British alliance and to the British desire to be a nuclear Power. The most learned and detailed account of American policy in these matters is Herman Kahn's big book *On Thermonuclear War*.

He is remarkably cold-blooded and makes careful arithmetical estimates of probable casualties. He believes that both America and Russia could more or less survive a nuclear war and achieve economic recovery in no very long time. Apparently—though on this he is vague—they are both to set to work at once on preparations for another nuclear war, and this sort of thing is to go on until not enough people are left alive for it to be possible to make a bomb. All this has shocked liberal-minded Americans who have criticized Mr. Kahn with great severity, not realizing, apparently, that he is only expounding official American policy.

There is, however, another aspect of his discussions which is of special interest to Britain. He holds that Britain as an ally adds nothing to the strength of America. He argues at length that, if Russia were to attack Britain without attacking the United States, the United States would not intervene in spite of obligations under NATO. He shows no objection to British neutrality, and explicitly regrets the lack of success for the suggestion that Britain should form a nonnuclear club of which it should be a member. Britons who are orthodox in armament policy do not seem to be aware of this American opinion. It hurts their national pride since it considers British military power negligible and the protection of Britain during war totally impossible. British opponents of British neutralism all argue vehemently that the West would be weakened if Britain became neutral. But, apparently, this is not the opinion of orthodox American armament experts.

It is not only unpleasant facts that the public ignores: it is also some facts which ought to be found pleasant. Khrushchev has repeatedly offered complete disarmament by agreement combined with any degree of inspection that the West may desire. The West shrugs its shoulders and says, "Of course, he is not sincere." This, however, is not the argument that really weighs with Western governments. Khrushchev proclaims his hope that Communists will conquer the world by peaceful propaganda. Western governments fear that they cannot produce equally effective counterpropaganda. As Dulles said, in an unguarded moment, "We are losing this cold war, but we might win a hot one." He did not explain what he meant by "winning," but I suppose he meant that, at the end, there might be six Americans and four Russians.

Doubts as to sincerity have at least as much justification if entertained by the Russians toward us as they have if entertained by us toward the Russians. The British Commonwealth has lately voted unanimously for universal and complete disarmament. Since in this matter there is complete agreement with Khrushchev, while America is adverse, it might have been thought that the vote of the British Commonwealth, including Britain, would lead to a *rapprochement* with the Soviet government. Instead of this, however, Kennedy and Macmillan have recently been tightening up the alliance and proposing agreements which would make British disarmament totally impossible. We cannot therefore take the British vote in the Commonwealth as indicating the sincere wishes of the British government.

I think that while we are engaged in campaigning for British unilateralism it is important to bear in mind the more distant objectives which give international meaning to our efforts. Let us consider for a moment what international aims must form part of any attempt to put an end to nuclear war. The first thing to realize is that, if there are not to be nuclear wars, there must not be wars, because any way is sure to become nuclear no matter what treaties to the contrary may have been concluded. And if there is not to be war, there must be machinery for settling disputes by negotiation. This will require an international authority which shall arbitrate disputes and be sufficiently powerful to compel obedience to its awards. None of this can possibly come about while relations between East and West are as strained as they are now, and while weapons of mass extermination keep the whole world in a state of nuclear terror. Before anything that seriously diminishes the risk of nuclear war can be achieved, there will have to be a treaty between America and Russia and China, and an agreement to ban—not only nuclear weapons—but also chemical and biological weapons. All this may seem beyond the power of Britain to help or hinder. I do not think that it is. Negotiations between the East and West ever since 1945 have been abortive because only the two contesting blocks were represented in the negotiations, and each of them, from motives of prestige, felt unable to make the slightest concession to the other. If there is ever to be a detente between Russia and America, it will have to be brought about by the friendly mediation of neutrals. Britain, if neutral, could play an important part in this beneficent work, whereas Britain can do nothing in this direction while remaining a member of NATO.

These as yet somewhat distant vistas should, I think, be in our minds while we are engaged in what might seem an exclusively national campaign. We have to remember that weapons of mass extermination, once invented, remain a potential threat even if none are actually in being. For this reason, we have to remember, further, that, unless war is completely eliminated, the human race is doomed. To put an end to war, which has dominated human life for 6,000 years, is no easy task. It is a heroic task, a task worthy of all the energies and all the thought of every sane man throughout the world. I think this larger vista may help in difficult times to prevent discouragement and disillusion. I think that our campaign is the best thing that Britons not in government posts can do, though it is only a small part of what the world needs.

James R. Newman

suggests: "Let our children go."

J A M E S R. N E W M A N [1907-   ] *is an American writer who edited the four-volume* World of Mathematics *and* Science and Sensibility.

He has served as counsel to the U. S. Senate Committee on Atomic Energy and in a number of other government positions. The selection here was a letter to the Washington Post *in 1961 called "A Modest Proposal."*

I address myself to the Eminences and the Serenities. I make them a Modest Proposal. Let our children go.

A nuclear war, which day by day seems more likely, may very well end human life. But suppose, more cheerfully, that only the people of the Northern Hemisphere are exterminated; that in the Southern Hemisphere it will still be possible, somehow, for some persons to survive. Why should we not transport our young children to these regions as a refuge? The merits and advantages of the Proposal are obvious and many, as well as of the highest importance.

For *first,* as I cannot conceive any sane person capable of human feeling would challenge, the war to come, if war comes, is not the children's concern. Our quarrels, our bitterness, our hatred, our fears do not possess them. Our heroes and our devils are not theirs. They have barely begun their lives, they are not ready to end them for Causes. They are too innocent and foolish to realize that death is preferable to life under alien creeds. I recall a story which Carl Sandburg told of a little girl, perhaps his granddaughter, who, after hearing his description of a battle of the Civil War, observed, "Suppose they gave a war and no one came." There is no reason to suppose that children, unless forced, would come to our war.

Second, the conduct of the war would be so much less Burdensome if the children were removed. It would be unnecessary to yield to niceties, to observe amenities, to nurse the sick, to shield the weak, to spare the infirm. With the children gone, without the distractions and temptations of their cries and complaints, we could give ourselves over completely to the serious business at hand. There would be many fewer mouths to feed, less need for water and air and bandages and whole blood. Children are notoriously subject to epidemic diseases; thus a prolific source of infection would be eliminated.

The savings in money alone would be immense, and would not only pay to transport the children and maintain them until they could fend for themselves, but would leave a handsome margin for use in vigorous prosecution of the war. I have made a rough calculation for U.S. children which bears on the point. Say we take many of the children from the ages of two to twelve—the younger are too frail, the older are more stable and could be useful to us at home—then we shall have about 25,000,000 to transport and keep. For this purpose, allow $1,000 a head. The total is $25,000,000,000, a sum well under half our annual military appropriation.

Surely this is not too much to spend, considering the advantages to be gained.

Third, we rid ourselves once for all of the Incubus of a shelter program. What a relief no longer to have to pretend! What a comfort simply to face the facts! No sensible person, even among scientists, believes in the efficacy of shelters. Down one goes to the well-stocked, cozy hole. Then what? There is the gentle patter of fallout on the roof; one is shielded from the blast; the light of a thousand suns (or is it now a million suns?) does not penetrate. The lares and penates are there. The family is snug. Father is pedaling the air pump. Mother is preparing a tuna-fish casserole. The radio is on. Splendid. But when does one come up and what is there to come up to? Anarchy? Cannibalism? The living dead? Bloated corpses? Troublesome questions. And even more troublesome is the effect of fire and heat, a subject which none of the experts and no one in the Establishment has seen fit to discuss. I lay this omission, of course, to delicate feelings. It would, I believe, undermine morale to be reminded of the fire storms over Tokyo, Hamburg, Dresden, where a mere few thousands of tons of high explosives produced atmospheric convulsions.

Now with weapons, each of which may yield the equivalent of ten, or fifty, or a hundred million tons of high explosives, the fire storm produced by a single bomb will, I am reliably informed by an article in the *Scientific American,* vaporize the structures and burn off the vegetation of an area of at least 15,000 square miles. Even in a deep shelter the occupants will be quickly barbecued. What a dreadful thing to contemplate. It is enough to make cowards of us all. The necrophiles, the bitter ones, the incandescent patriots, those among the aged and ailing who take comfort in the thought that their demise will coincide with that of mankind: these endorse the view that shelters will give shelter. But secretly they laugh at our innocence. We must encourage them. If we are to die for the Cause, let us not cheapen and betray the sacrifice: Away with the shelters, and all will become clear.

Fourth, there is the grave moral issue of suicide. The law forbids it to the individual. On a national scale, however, it is apparently acceptable. Do we not, after all, make the law? Thus we may write its exceptions. Still, the question nags us, can we require the suicide of those who have no voice in the making of the laws, viz., children? It is a fine point, and none would venture to say how our leaders would feel compelled to decide it. My Proposal disencumbers them of this obligation.

Fifth, there must be many who, like myself, have a Weakness for children. In format and freshness they are much preferable to the larger editions, their parents. Children are unwrinkled, unwarped. They are healthy. They smell nice. They are not cynical. They suppose life to be an end in itself. Properly nourished, watered and cared for, they grow up. When grown they can breed. The dead do not breed. Quite recently the eminent geneticist Herman Muller described a scheme for setting up large-scale sperm banks. Sperm could be stored indefinitely; it could be classified according to the characteristics of the males who produced it. Human evolution would thus, in a sense, come under man's own control. Yet the scheme presupposes the continuance of women. It is my impression that sperm by itself will yield no fruit. Here again the Proposal is vindicated; for there will be female as well as male children: instead of storing germ plasm we will be storing the young themselves and thus assure the future.

For the moment I have said enough. I am anxious that Wise men consider my Proposal. Is it Feasible? (Less feasible, say, than a journey to the planets?) Is it Visionary? (More visionary than the preservation of Freedom by a nuclear war?) Is it too Costly? Is there yet time to execute it—in part at least if not in whole? Could it be made a matter of International Cooperation? Is a country without children worth living in? Perhaps not. In that case some better course must be found. Let the Wise men define it.

Albert Luthuli

explains why Africans have chosen nonviolence to turn enmity into amity

ALBERT JOHN LUTHULI [1899-   ], an ex-Zulu tribal chief, was the first native African to receive a Nobel Peace Prize. The 1960 prize was awarded him in recognition of the peaceful methods he was using in his fight against apartheid, the South African racial-segregation policy. Since 1952, Luthuli has been president general of the banned African National Congress. The South African government gave Luthuli the choice of resigning from the National Congress or giving up his elective chieftainship of the Abase-Makolweni Tribe of the Zulus. He answered that a chief is first of all leader of his people, and only secondarily a government official. The government dismissed him. Since 1952, he has been subjected to three arrest bans which limit his movement to a small area. What follows here is part of his acceptance speech for the Nobel prize.

The golden age of Africa's independence is also the dark age of South Africa's decline and retrogression.

Education is being reduced to an instrument of subtle indoctrination. Slanted and biased reporting in the organs of public information, a creeping censorship, book banning and blacklisting, all these spread their shadows over the land.

But beneath the surface there is a spirit of defiance.

The people of South Africa have never been a docile lot, least of all the African people. We have a long tradition of struggle for our national rights, reaching back to the very beginning of white settlement and conquest 300 years ago.

We, in our situation, have chosen the path of nonviolence of our own volition. Along this path we have organized many heroic campaigns.

The bitterness of the struggle mounts as liberty comes step by step closer to the freedom fighters' grasp. All too often, the protests and demonstrations of our people have been beaten back by force, but they have never been silenced.

Through all this cruel treatment in the name of law and order, our people, with few exceptions, have remained nonviolent.

Nothing which we have suffered at the hands of the government has turned us from our chosen path of disciplined resistance. It is for this, I believe, that this award is given.

The true patriots of South Africa, for whom I speak, will be satisfied with nothing less than the fullest democratic rights.

In government we will not be satisfied with anything less than direct individual adult suffrage and the right to stand for and be elected to all organs of government.

In economic matters we will be satisfied with nothing less than equality of opportunity in every sphere, and the enjoyment by all of those heritages which form the resources of the country which up to now have been appropriated on a racial "whites only" basis.

In culture we will be satisfied with nothing less than the opening of all doors of learning in nonsegregatory institutions on the sole criterion of ability.

In the social sphere we will be satisfied with nothing less than the abolition of all racial bars.

We do not demand these things for people of African descent alone. We demand them for all South Africans, white and black.

Let me invite Africa to cast her eyes beyond the past and, to some extent, the present with her woes and tribulations, trials and failures, and some successes, and see herself an emerging continent, bursting to freedom through the shell of centuries of serfdom.

This is Africa's age—the dawn of her fulfillment, yes, the moment when she must grapple with destiny to reach the summits of sublimity, saying ours was a fight for noble values and worthy ends, and not for lands and the enslavement of man.

Still licking the scars of past wrongs perpetrated on her, could she not be magnanimous and practice no revenge? Her hands of friendship scornfully rejected, her pleas for justice and fair play spurned, should she not nonetheless seek to turn enmity into amity?

Though robbed of her lands, her independence and opportunities . . . should she not see her destiny as being that of making a distinctive contribution to human progress and human relationship with a peculiar new African flavor enriched by the diversity of cultures she enjoys, thus building on the summits of present human achievement an edifice that would be one of the finest tributes to the genius of man?

In a strife-torn world, tottering on the brink of complete destruction by man-made nuclear weapons, a free and independent Africa is in the making, in answer to the injunction and challenge of history:

"Arise and shine, for thy light is come."

Acting in concert with other nations, she is man's last hope for a mediator between the East and West, and is qualified to demand of the great powers to "turn the swords into ploughshares" because two-thirds of mankind is hungry and illiterate.

Africa's qualification for this noble task is incontestable, for her own fight has never been and is not now a fight for conquest of land, for accumulation of wealth or domination of peoples, but for the recognition and preservation of the rights of man and the establishment of a truly free world.

Robert Pickus

shows that pacifism is working in most areas of life except war

ROBERT PICKUS [1923-   ] *is national coordinator of Turn to Peace, the coordinating center for thirty-eight organizations concerned with achieving a disarmed world under law. He has worked on race relations problems and in the labor and cooperative movements. He was a Fulbright Fellow in England, and during World War II he served in the Office of Strategic Services.* At one time Pickus was peace secretary *of the American Friends Service Committee in Chicago; later he worked on their national staff.* He is an associate editor of Liberation. *This is an interview published in* Mademoiselle *in 1961.*

But are men good enough to get rid of violence, to get rid of war?

Those are two different questions. We've got rid of slavery, but we still have exploitation, and in one form or another we're likely to have it always. But the move from a world that accepts slavery to a world that rejects it and is working on problems of exploitation is an important move. Isn't it possible that we could get rid of war, while people went on being nasty to their wives, occasionally kicking stray dogs? Wouldn't that still be an important advance? I'm not talking about saintliness or the best of all possible worlds when I talk of getting rid of war. I'm talking about the minimal understandings necessary if the human story is to go on. We've got to recognize that organization for war is no longer right and no longer rational, that we must turn our energies to developing alternate methods for the defense of our values. The startling thing is that in almost every other area of life we've already rejected violence. In penology we don't think punishment is the real answer any more. We don't throw the mentally ill into chains. The kind of pacifism I mean is already working in most other areas of life. It's only here in the question of war that there's been a failure of thought. Beat a child? No. But jump into a plane and destroy a city of a million human beings . . . yes sir!

Aren't there any causes worth the sacrifice of human life through warfare?

It isn't the sacrifice of human life that's at stake—most pacifists are willing to put their own lives quite literally on the line in order to further their beliefs—it's your phrase "through warfare." The point is, can causes we care for be furthered by war? To me it's clear that they can't. You only collaborate in spreading the very attitudes and actions you wanted to stop. It isn't even a moral question of whether war is right or wrong, but does it work? And I say no.

Assuming war can't serve our values, still they are under attack. . . .

That's the problem we must think about. It's tragic that so few intelligent people have been willing to start at that point—ruling out organized violence as a solution and then saying, "All right, what do we do instead?" All our intellectual efforts have been set in the context of one basic assumption: that organization for war is still right and rational for people holding democratic values—by which I don't mean voting, but a view of what a human being is and why there's dignity and value simply in the fact of being human. If this is the ground you stand on, then you have to rule out mass-organized violence and start searching for an alternative. The trouble with many pacifists is that they haven't faced the consequences of renouncing the violent solution.

Do you think war has ever achieved what people wanted it to?

I can't make an absolute statement about violence in the preatomic past, but I will about now. Herman Kahn's book, *On Thermonuclear War,* has done the peace movement a great service by carrying the premises involved in the use of violence to their logical conclusion. He's demonstrated that a commitment to violence today is not limited, not discriminate, not proportionate; that if you go along that road you must be willing to accept the final results. I think many people assume that somehow it'll never happen—even though so much of the whole life of our society is organized around war; still say, *"But* it's unthinkable. The whole point in preparing for war is to prevent war." But Kahn says, in effect, "Nonsense, you can't prepare for war intelligently unless you face the fact that it may come. And if it comes, this is what it will cost, and we must do something about the cost."

Harris Wofford

presents the lawyer's case for civil disobedience

HARRIS L. WOFFORD [1926-   ] *was adviser to President John F. Kennedy on civil rights and racial matters during the 1960 presidential campaign; before that, he had been consultant to the Federal Commission on Civil Rights. While he was Associate Professor of Law at the University of Notre Dame, Wofford wrote "A Lawyer's Case for Civil Disobedience." It first appeared in* Liberation *magazine in 1961.*

I could make a case for civil disobedience based on St. Augustine's description of the "melancholy and lamentable judgments"—the injustices—inherent in the law in this sinful City of Man, and, with pacifism as a check on the commission of new injustices, call for peaceful resistance to unjust laws. It is a good American case, defended and demonstrated by Thoreau and by a whole generation of abolitionists. "Unjust laws exist," said Thoreau. "Shall we be content to obey them, or shall we endeavor to amend them, and obey them until we have succeeded, or shall we transgress them at once?" Thoreau asked, as I think we each must ask. His answer was: "If this injustice is part of the necessary friction of the machine of government, let it go, let it go: perchance it will wear smooth . . . but if it is of such a nature that it requires you to be an agent of injustice to another, then, I say, break the law. Let your life be a counter friction to stop the machine." So he advised the abolitionists not "to wait till they constitute a majority of one." It is enough, he said, "if they have God on their side, without waiting for that other one." And he went to prison for refusing to pay taxes to a government that was upholding slavery by imprisoning and returning runaway slaves. He said that "under a government which imprisons any unjustly the true place for a just man is also prison." But people did not understand and a distant aunt paid his taxes for him and he was put out of prison after only a one-night stand. Still, I think, his apocryphal answer to Emerson made an imprint on the American mind. When Emerson asked him why he was in jail, Thoreau replied, "Why are you outside?"

But I do not think I am a pacifist and I know I am not an anarchist and I did pass the bar. So I want to make a lawyer's case for civil disobedience. We have been reading Justice Holmes in my class, and as always he has renewed my passion for this jealous mistress, the law, whose loyal lover I claim to be even as I stand here advocating civil disobedience. By the way, there is a Thoreau text for this, too. "They are the lovers of law and order who observe the law when the government breaks it."

Now, I realize that this involves a paradox—a central paradox of natural-law jurisprudence—that for many people spells anarchy. One man's natural law is all too often another's poison. For Socrates there was a higher law whispering to him from outside the cave of this world that told him it was the nature of man and the first principle of the teaching profession to ask questions—to question everything—and that therefore he should not obey the edict of Athens abridging his freedom of speech. But the Athenians who served him the hemlock were also obeying the highest law they knew, the need to preserve their society from subversion. I think you will agree with me that at least this one act of civil disobedience proved to be effective. For out of the cheerful prison-going and death of Socrates we learn academic freedom, and I would say that Socrates also teaches us the first principle of any republic, the principle established for this republic by the First Amendment.

I suppose that almost everyone here would agree that civil dis obedience would be justified toward any man-made law prohibiting the public worship of God. St. Thomas said that human laws contrary to divine law ought nowise to be obeyed. The Church has gone to the catacombs before, in its exercise of the freedom of religion. And the lives of many martyrs and saints should be enough to convince us of the educational potentialities of such civil disobedience. The question is, where else in the field of law and on what other occasion is civil disobedience also necessary and proper?

I would cite the second part of the First Amendment, freedom of speech, and the principle of equal protection of the laws in the Fourteenth Amendment, as two other areas where any laws in conflict with these commands of the natural law, according to my view of man's nature, ought to be civilly disobeyed.

But as soon as I say this, I have opened a Pandora's box from which many furies may fly, including the present disobedience of the Supreme Court's school decisions by many white citizens in the South. If you doubt that the white resistance to desegregation is based, in part at least, on a firmly held and often conscientiously held, though to me wrongheaded view of natural law, then listen to this colloquy from the *Congressional Record*. Senator Eastland asked: "Is not the segregated way of life a better life? Is not that the law of nature?" And Senator Thurmond replied: "Well, that is the way God made the races. I presume it is."

And yet, despite the risks involved in letting loose differing ideas of natural law to contend with each other, I believe that there is a great hope for the law, particularly for the law of a republic, at the bottom of this Pandora's box. That hope is embodied in a view of law that transcends the old idea which says that law is nothing but the command of the sovereign. In a republic, or with men who like Mark Twain's Connecticut Yankee have the idea of a republic in their heads, every command of the law should be seen as a question.

A Socratic philosopher of the law, Scott Buchanan, has stated this thesis to show how "Law teaches those who make and obey it"—and I would add, disobey it. "Laws," he says, "are questions asked by God, history, nature, or society to be answered by men individually and collectively. This formulation penetrates the heart of human freedom. It says that no law, not even divine law, cancels out human freedom; the answer can be Yes or No or something else. It also tacitly warns of consequences of the answer. But primarily it forces the human being to think about ends, or purposes."

In this view, there is implicit in each law the alternatives of obedience, or of civil disobedience with full acceptance of the consequences. Once we no longer see law as a mechanical thing, once we free ourselves from the idea that as good citizens we have no choice but to obey any law passed by the legislature, no matter how bad, then of each law we must ask ourselves, is this a law that I should obey? Is it a just law? Is it so unjust that it needs to be resisted from the very inception, and cannot await the slow process of parliamentary reform?

So we are back with Thoreau, but with a difference. He thought in terms of disobedience serving as a counterfriction to stop the whole machine of the law. I am presenting civil disobedience as a natural and necessary part of the great due process of our law, that process of persuasion through which we govern ourselves. Civil disobedience, as I see it, is a kind of persuasion, the persuasion of last resort, within the boundaries of the law, sometimes the only kind available.

Of course any kind of disobedience of law may have the effect of persuasion, just as force can at times be a powerful persuader. The disobedience of the prohibition laws was violent, secret, rather cynical and largely uncivil, yet it finally led to the repeal of the Eighteenth Amendment. But this kind of disobedience was truly beyond the legal pale. By teaching disrespect for this one law, it was indeed subversive of the law. To have been *civil* disobedience, the resistance to prohibition would have had to be open, in the sight and knowledge of the authorities, and those thus disobeying the law should have not only been prepared to accept the consequences, but should have deliberately invited them. If those who considered the Eighteenth Amendment a violation of their natural right to drink had courted the jails in protest, if they had, as Gandhi urged his countrymen, entered the prisons "as a bridegroom enters the bride's chamber," I think the Twenty-first Amendment would probably have come sooner. Certainly it would have come better. I do not think we would have had the organized crime that came in the wake of the less respectful forms of persuasion that were used.

Civil disobedience is within the legal pale—within the Canons of Ethics of our profession—because it involves the highest possible respect for the law. If we secretly violated the law or tried to evade it or violently sought to overthrow it, that would be disloyalty to the idea of law itself. But when we openly disobey a law that we hold to be unjust and ask for the penalty, we are saying that we so little respect the law that we belong in jail until it is changed. Thus Socrates refused to listen to his friends' plea for his escape from the verdict of Athens but chose instead to peacefully drink the hemlock, giving the respect he considered due to the state and to the laws in which he had lived and had his being.

Is this anarchy? I hope not, for I agree with Justice Brandeis that our government is "the potent, the omnipresent teacher" that "teaches the whole people." And I do not agree with Thoreau that "the law will never make men free." It is through law that we, like Socrates, find our freedom. But the law will play its full role as teacher only when we look upon it as a question. For it is the voice of our body politic with which we must remain in dialogue.

If the proposition to which we are dedicated is self-government, then we must respond to the law, resist it, change it, and fulfill it, even as it challenges, changes, and educates us. Civil disobedience is one way in which we can exercise the choice that the law gives us. It is the choice that makes us free.

Now, I have not even come to Gandhi, and all I will say about him is that he, too, was a lawyer—trained in London's Inner Temple—and I think he always saw civil disobedience as a constitutional form of persuasion, as a way to reach and move the minds and hearts of people and thus mold the law.

Nor have I tried to consider the many uses and abuses of this theory. I recall a Kentucky mayor who called on his people to adopt Gandhi's method of fighting injustice, as the only remaining form of resistance to court-imposed integration. The mayor added that of course the white people wouldn't want Gandhi to come to their town however useful his idea of civil disobedience might be for their purposes.

This doesn't disturb me. For the beauty of civil disobedience is that, in part at least, it answers a problem of law that has bothered people from St. Thomas to the present. Aquinas held that laws contrary to human good were not binding in conscience except in order to avoid "scandal or disturbance." Since violent disobedience, in the violent centuries that followed, did indeed often cause scandal and disobedience contrary to the common good, St. Thomas' exception has generally proved to be the rule, at least the rule for lawyers. But *civil* disobedience by its nature avoids the kind of scandal or disturbance that St. Thomas rightly feared.

In fact, what is wrong with the theory of civil disobedience in this country is not that our jails would fill. For jail-going is not the natural disposition of most men. A little jail-going against some of our laws might be good yeast to leaven the lump of our modern leviathan. Civil disobedience could be an antidote to the centralization and standardization of our life, to the sense of fatality of the multitude as well as to the tyranny of the majority. We certainly need some kind of Socratic gadfly to stir society from its dogmatic slumbers.

No, the problem, I fear, is rather that by nature we seem more inclined to disobey not unjust laws but just ones. We all engage in civil disobedience in the form of jaywalking or speeding, to name only two popular varieties. But we hesitate to resist an unjust law. We do not take personal responsibility for injustice. Instead of taking Socrates straight, we seem to prefer the comic version. I am referring to Aristophanes' portrayal in *The Clouds,* where the student of Socrates says: "But I wish to succeed, just enough for my need, and to slip through the clutches of the law." But there again, we are free to choose which Socrates—which inner light or higher law—to follow, and it is the choice that makes us free.

Martin Luther King, Jr.
traces his pilgrimage to nonviolence

MARTIN LUTHER KING, JR. [1929-   ] *is the spiritual leader of the American Negroes' nonviolent campaign against segregation. He directed the bus boycott in Montgomery, Alabama, in 1955; he maintained the morale of his demonstrators despite bombings, arrests and beatings; and he won. He was at the head of sit-in demonstrations throughout the South. All over the United States in the strongholds of racial prejudice, Martin Luther King has been a key figure in the constant nonviolent pressure for equal rights. His methods are Gandhian, and he strictly maintains them. The article here appeared in 1960.*

Ten years ago I was just entering my senior year in theological seminary. Like most theological students I was engaged in the exciting job of studying various theological theories. Having been raised in a rather strict fundamentalistic tradition, I was occasionally shocked as my intellectual journey carried me through new and sometimes complex doctrinal lands. But despite the shock the pilgrimage was always stimulating, and it gave me a new appreciation for objective appraisal and critical analysis. My early theological training did the same for me as the reading of Hume did for Kant: it knocked me out of my dogmatic slumber.

At this stage of my development I was a thoroughgoing liberal. Liberalism provided me with an intellectual satisfaction that I could never find in fundamentalism. I became so enamored of the insights of liberalism that I almost fell into the trap of accepting uncritically everything that came under its name. I was absolutely convinced of the natural goodness of man and the natural power of human reason.

The basic change in my thinking came when I began to question some of the theories that had been associated with so-called liberal theology. Of course there is one phase of liberalism that I hope to cherish always: its devotion to the search for truth, its insistence on an open and analytical mind, its refusal to abandon the best light of reason. Liberalism's contribution to the philological-historical criticism of Biblical literature has been of immeasurable value and should be defended with religious and scientific passion.

It was mainly the liberal doctrine of man that I began to question. The more I observed the tragedies of history and man's shameful inclination to choose the low road, the more I came to see the depths and strength of sin. My reading of the works of Reinhold Niebuhr made me aware of the complexity of human motives and the reality of sin on every level of man's existence. Moreover, I came to recognize the complexity of man's social involvement and the glaring reality of collective evil. I came to feel that liberalism had been all too sentimental concerning human nature and that it leaned toward a false idealism.

I also came to see that liberalism's superficial optimism concerning human nature caused it to overlook the fact that reason is darkened by sin. The more I thought about human nature the more I saw how our tragic inclination for sin causes us to use our minds to rationalize our actions. Liberalism failed to see that reason by itself is little more than an instrument to justify man's defensive ways of thinking. Reason, devoid of the purifying power of faith, can never free itself from distortions and rationalizations.

In spite of the fact that I had to reject some aspects of liberalism, I never came to an all-out acceptance of neo-orthodoxy. While I saw neo-orthodoxy as a helpful corrective for a liberalism that had become all too sentimental, I never felt that it provided an adequate answer to the basic questions. If liberalism was too optimistic concerning human nature, neo-orthodoxy was too pessimistic. Not only on the question of man but also on other vital issues neo-orthodoxy went too far in its revolt. In its attempt to preserve the transcendence of God, which had been neglected by liberalism's overstress of his immanence, neo-orthodoxy went to the extreme of stressing a God who was hidden, unknown and "wholly other." In its revolt against liberalism's overemphasis on the power of reason, neo-orthodoxy fell into a mood of antirationalism and semifundamentalism, stressing a narrow, uncritical Biblicism. This approach, I felt, was inadequate both for the church and for personal life.

So although liberalism left me unsatisfied on the question of the nature of man, I found no refuge in neo-orthodoxy. I am now convinced that the truth about man is found neither in liberalism nor in neo-orthodoxy. Each represents a partial truth. A large segment of Protestant liberalism defined man only in terms of his essential nature, his capacity for good. Neo-orthodoxy tended to define man only in terms of his existential nature, his capacity for evil. An adequate understanding of man is found neither in the thesis of liberalism nor in the antithesis of neo-orthodoxy, but in a synthesis which reconciles the truths of both.

During the past decade I also gained a new appreciation for the philosophy of existentialism. My first contact with this philosophy came through my reading of Kierkegaard and Nietzsche. Later I turned to a study of Jaspers, Heidegger and Sartre. All of these thinkers stimulated my thinking; while finding things to question in each, I nevertheless learned a great deal from study of them. When I finally turned to a serious study of the works of Paul Tillich I became convinced that existentialism, in spite of the fact that it had become all too fashionable, had grasped certain basic truths about man and his condition that could not be permanently overlooked.

Its understanding of the "finite freedom" of man is one of existentialism's most lasting contributions, and its perception of the anxiety and conflict produced in man's personal and social life as a result of the perilous and ambiguous structure of existence is especially meaningful for our time. The common point in all existentialism, whether it is atheistic or theistic, is that man's existential situation is a state of estrangement from his essential nature. In their revolt against Hegel's essentialism, all existentialists contend that the world is fragmented. History is a series of unreconciled conflicts and man's existence is filled with anxiety and threatened with meaninglessness. While the ultimate Christian answer is not found in any of these existential assertions, there is much here that the theologian can use to describe the true state of man's existence.

Although most of my formal study during this decade has been in systematic theology and philosophy, I have become more and more interested in social ethics. Of course my concern for social problems was already substantial before the beginning of this decade. From my early teens in Atlanta I was deeply concerned about the problem of racial injustice. I grew up abhorring segregation, considering it both rationally inexplicable and morally unjustifiable. I could never accept the fact of having to go to the back of a bus or sit in the segregated section of a train. The first time that I was seated behind a curtain in a dining car I felt as if the curtain had been dropped on my selfhood. I had also learned that the inseparable twin of racial injustice is economic injustice. I saw how the systems of segregation ended up in the exploitation of the Negro as well as the poor whites. Through these early experiences I grew up deeply conscious of the varieties of injustice in our society.

Not until I entered theological seminary, however, did I begin a serious intellectual quest for a method to eliminate social evil. I was immediately influenced by the social gospel. In the early 50s I read Rauschenbusch's *Christianity and the Social Crisis,* a book which left an indelible imprint on my thinking. Of course there were points at which I differed with Rauschenbusch. I felt that he had fallen victim to the nineteenth-century "cult of inevitable progress," which led him to an unwarranted optimism concerning human nature. Moreover, he came perilously close to identifying the kingdom of God with a particular social and economic system—a temptation which the church should never give in to. But in spite of these shortcomings Rauschenbusch gave to American Protestantism a sense of social responsibility that it should never lose. The gospel at its best deals with the whole man, not only his soul but his body, not only his spiritual well-being, but his material well-being. Any religion that professes to be concerned about the souls of men and is not concerned about the slums that damn them, the economic conditions that strangle them and the social conditions that cripple them is a spiritually moribund religion awaiting burial.

After reading Rauschenbusch I turned to a serious study of the social and ethical theories of the great philosophers. During this period I had almost despaired of the power of love in solving social problems. The "turn the other cheek" philosophy and the "love your enemies" philosophy are only valid, I felt, when individuals are in conflict with other individuals; when racial groups and nations are in conflict a more realistic approach is necessary. Then I came upon the life and teachings of Mahatma Gandhi. As I read his works I became deeply fascinated by his campaigns of nonviolent resistance. The whole Gandhian concept of satyagraha (satya is truth which equals love, and graha is force; satyagraha thus means truth-force or love-force) was profoundly significant to me. As I delved deeper into the philosophy of Gandhi my skepticism concerning the power of love gradually diminished, and I came to see for the first time that the Christian doctrine of love operating through the Gandhian method of nonviolence was one of the most potent weapons available to oppressed people in their struggle for freedom. At this time, however, I had a merely intellectual understanding and appreciation of the position, with no firm determination to organize it in a socially effective situation.

When I went to Montgomery, Alabama, as a pastor in 1954, I had not the slightest idea that I would later become involved in a crisis in which nonviolent resistance would be applicable. After I had lived in the community about a year, the bus boycott began. The Negro people of Montgomery, exhausted by the humiliating experiences that they had constantly faced on the buses, expressed in a massive act of noncooperation their determination to be free. They came to see that it was ultimately more honorable to walk the streets in dignity than to ride the buses in humiliation. At the beginning of the protest the people called on me to serve as their spokesman. In accepting this responsibility my mind, consciously or unconsciously, was driven back to the Sermon on the Mount and the Gandhian method of nonviolent resistance. This principle became the guiding light of our movement. Christ furnished the spirit and motivation while Gandhi furnished the method.

The experience in Montgomery did more to clarify my thinking on the question of nonviolence than all of the books that I had read. As the days unfolded I became more and more convinced of the power of nonviolence. Living through the actual experience of the protest, nonviolence became more than a method to which I gave intellectual assent; it became a commitment to a way of life. Many issues I had not cleared up intellectually concerning nonviolence were now solved in the sphere of practical action.

A few months ago I had the privilege of traveling to India. The trip had a great impact on me personally and left me even more convinced of the power of nonviolence. It was a marvelous thing to see the amazing results of a nonviolent struggle. India won her independence, but without violence on the part of Indians. The aftermath of hatred and bitterness that usually follows a violent campaign is found nowhere in India. Today a mutual friendship based on complete equality exists between the Indian and British people within the Commonwealth.

I do not want to give the impression that nonviolence will work miracles overnight. Men are not easily moved from their mental ruts or purged of their prejudiced and irrational feelings. When the underprivileged demand freedom, the privileged first react with bitterness and resistance. Even when the demands are couched in nonviolent terms, the initial response is the same. I am sure that many of our white brothers in Montgomery and across the South are still bitter toward Negro leaders, even though these leaders have sought to follow a way of love and nonviolence. So the nonviolent approach does not immediately change the heart of the oppressor. It first does something to the hearts and souls of those committed to it. It gives them new self-respect; it calls up resources of strength and courage that they did not know they had. Finally, it reaches the opponent and so stirs his conscience that reconciliation becomes a reality.

During recent months I have come to see more and more the need for the method of nonviolence in international relations. While I was convinced during my student days of the power of nonviolence in group conflicts within nations, I was not yet convinced of its efficacy in conflicts between nations. I felt that while war could never be a positive or absolute good, it could serve as a negative good in the sense of preventing the spread and growth of an evil force. War, I felt, horrible as it is, might be preferable to surrender to a totalitarian system. But more and more I have come to the conclusion that the potential destructiveness of modern weapons of war totally rules out the possibility of war ever serving again as a negative good. If we assume that mankind has a right to survive then we must find an alternative to war and destruction. In a day when sputniks dash through outer space and guided ballistic missiles are carving highways of death through the stratosphere, nobody can win a war. The choice today is no longer between violence and nonviolence. It is either nonviolence or nonexistence.

I am no doctrinaire pacifist. I have tried to embrace a realistic pacifism. Moreover, I see the pacifist position not as sinless but as the lesser evil in the circumstances. Therefore I do not claim to be free from the moral dilemmas that the Christian nonpacifist confronts. But I am convinced that the Church cannot remain silent while mankind faces the threat of being plunged into the abyss of nuclear annihilation. If the Church is true to its mission it must call for an end to the arms race.

In recent months I have also become more and more convinced of the reality of a personal God. True, I have always believed in the personality of God. But in past years the idea of a personal God was little more than a metaphysical category which I found theologically and philosophically satisfying. Now it is a living reality that has been validated in the experiences of everyday life. Perhaps the suffering, frustration and agonizing moments which I have had to undergo occasionally as a result of my involvement in a difficult struggle have drawn me closer to God. Whatever the cause, God has been profoundly real to me in recent months. In the midst of outer dangers I have felt an inner calm and known resources of strength that only God could give. In many instances I have felt the power of God transforming the fatigue of despair into the buoyancy of hope. I am convinced that the universe is under the control of a loving purpose and that in the struggle for righteousness man has cosmic companionship. Behind the harsh appearances of the world there is a benign power. To say God is personal is not to make him an object among other objects or attribute to him the finiteness and limitations of human personality; it is to take what is finest and noblest in our consciousness and affirm its perfect existence in him. It is certainly true that human personality is limited, but personality as such involves no necessary limitations. It simply means self-consciousness and self-direction. So in the truest sense of the word, God is a living God. In him there is feeling and will, responsive to the deepest yearnings of the human heart: this God both evokes and answers prayers.

The past decade has been a most exciting one. In spite of the tensions and uncertainties of our age something profoundly meaningful has begun. Old systems of exploitation and oppression are passing away and new systems of justice and equality are being born. In a real sense ours is a great time in which to be alive. Therefore I am not yet discouraged about the future. Granted that the easygoing optimism of yesterday is impossible. Granted that we face a world crisis which often leaves us standing amid the surging murmur of life's restless sea. But every crisis has both its dangers and its opportunities. Each can spell either salvation or doom. In a dark, confused world the spirit of God may yet reign supreme.

Peace organizations
give their rules for public witness demonstrations

THIS DISCIPLINE *for public witness demonstrations, based on a nonviolent philosophy and technique, was an outgrowth of the civil defense demonstrations in New York City in 1958. It was published in 1960 and has been endorsed by twelve peace organizations which now work together on various projects.*

DISCIPLINE FOR PUBLIC WITNESS DEMONSTRATIONS

Introduction

Achievement of these objectives is greatly enhanced if all demonstrators conduct themselves in a friendly and orderly manner. A disorderly demonstration is more likely to arouse opposition than support. Violence on the part of the demonstrators will almost certainly retard, rather than advance, the work of the peace movement. Demonstrations can be an opportunity to communicate our friendliness and concern for others in and outside of the demonstration and to begin to express specifically the concept of altruistic love. The following discipline is designed to facilitate this expression.

All persons are asked to accept the following discipline during the time they are participating in this demonstration. If you feel you cannot cooperate with all of the aspects of the discipline, *please leave the demonstration at an appropriate time.* The sponsors have no desire to limit spontaneity or dictate to the consciences of others. The discipline exists only to minimize the likelihood of rioting and violence and to increase the power of the demonstrations.

1. We will not use physical violence regardless of what may be done to us by others.

2. Our attitude toward persons who may oppose us will be one of understanding, and of respect for the right of others to hold and express whatever views they wish.

3. We will not be violent in our attitude, make hostile remarks, shout or call names. If singing or chanting is indicated, it will be in a manner consistent with the nonviolent spirit of the demonstration.

4. We will adhere to the planned program of action for each demonstration, unless a change of plan is communicated to us by the demonstration's sponsors or their representatives. We will not initiate any unannounced action, unless it has been explicitly approved by the sponsors.

5. We recognize that conducting an orderly demonstration depends upon mutual cooperation and respect between participants and those who have organized and are responsible for the demonstration. (If requests are made for action which you feel are unwise, you will have an opportunity to discuss your complaint fully with the responsible persons after the demonstration, if it is not possible at the time. If a request is made which you cannot accept, please quietly disassociate yourself from the demonstration.)

6. If questioned by passers-by, representatives of the press or other mass media, participants are encouraged to express their own opinion about themselves, their reasons for joining the demonstration, etc., making clear that these are their personal convictions. However, where possible, all questions concerning the policies of the demonstration should be referred to the sponsors or their representatives. The questioner should be given a copy of the demonstration's official leaflet.

7. In our contact with the police and other officials, we will:
   A. Maintain an attitude of understanding for the responsibilities with which they are charged.
   B. Be courteous at all times.
   C. Be completely open in announcing what we plan to do.
   D. Accept all requests which are reasonable.

8. We will be as truthful as possible in all statements.

9. *In case of violence.* Demonstration plans will always be announced to the police and in general their cooperation should be expected. However, in a large crowd there is always the possibility of violence from arbitrary policy interference, passers-by or participants. In such situations, the demonstrators must carefully follow the directions of the sponsors and their representatives.

The demonstrators might be requested to disperse as quickly and as quietly as possible in order to avoid incidents. It is usually better to take up grievances with the authorities after the demonstration than to try to settle them on the spot.

Sitting down might, in some cases, reduce the number of possible injuries in an emergency situation. Since sitting will probably be interpreted as civil disobedience and noncompliance, such action should be undertaken only upon the specific requests of the demonstration's sponsors or their representatives,* or if it is agreed upon in advance as the method of action of the particular demonstration.

Those who witness molestation or brutality on the part of the police may render a service by making a note of the numbers on the badges of those involved.

The following organizations have endorsed this discipline for public witness demonstrations for peace in New York City:

American Friends Service Committee
Committee for Nonviolent Action
Greenwich Village Peace Center—Peace Action Committee
National Committee for A SANE Nuclear Policy
New York Committee for a General Strike for Peace
New York Fellowship of Reconciliation
Student Peace Union
Tompkins Square Peace Center
War Resisters League
Women's Direct Action
Women's Strike for Peace
Women's International League for Peace and Freedom

* Demonstrators who have sat down and are offering nonviolent resistance to the police are urged to act in a way that does not imply disrespect for the police but is designed to prevent injuries and show peaceful intent.

Jerome D. Frank
declares that war-making man is modifiable

DR. JEROME D. FRANK [1909-   ] *is a professor of psychiatry at Johns Hopkins University School of Medicine and the psychiatrist-in-charge, psychiatric outpatient department, Johns Hopkins Hospital. He is concerned with the question of survival in the nuclear age and has written numerous articles on the psychological aspects of disarmament. In 1960, while he was in California, Dr. Frank presented two television broadcasts on alternatives to violence in international conflict.*

The essence of the nonviolent approach to the resolution of conflict is to meet violence with calm courage and willingness to accept suffering, without ceasing to resist, but also without hating the attacker. Violent behavior tends to elicit fear, hatred, and counterviolence from the person attacked, and this in turn, intensifies the attacker's zeal. The basic psychological insight of nonviolence is that if the victim remains unfrightened, calm and friendly, this inhibits the aggressor. By demonstrating to his adversary that he is willing to suffer for his beliefs, and that he is concerned for his attacker's welfare as well as his own, the practitioner of nonviolence tries to weaken the will of his persecutor and to win him over, not to beat him down.

It is often argued that nonviolence can never work because it flies in the face of human nature. Man is a fighter by instinct, it is said, and any line of thinking which denies this is doomed to futility. This may well be true. Human beings seem to enjoy killing for sport, and history is a sequence of bouts of mass killing called war. But if it is true, then mankind will probably become extinct, like many species before him, since in a nuclear world he cannot wage many wars without extinguishing himself.

Fortunately, there is considerable evidence to suggest that the habit of resort to war as a means of settling international disputes could be changed. Man is a very modifiable creature, and his behavior depends a lot on his past training. Dr. Scott, an animal psychologist, has shown that mice can be trained to fight, or not to fight. And if mice can be trained, why cannot man? Many personal disputes that formerly were settled by duels or armed conflict are now peacefully settled through recourse to law. Furthermore, there are in the world societies that are perfectly peaceful, and others that are very warlike, and some societies are peaceful at one period of their existence and warlike at another. In short, there is no reason to think that the habit of resorting to war as a means of settling international disputes is unmodifiable.

There is no denying that war has met certain important human needs such as the thirst for glory, self-sacrifice, heroism and group solidarity. The prospects of eliminating it would be brightened if we could develop other ways of meeting these needs. Years ago the great American psychologist William James called for a "Moral Equivalent of War," to satisfy the legitimate human drives for which this was the main outlet. With remarkable foresight he suggested something like the CCC under Roosevelt, in which young people could work together dedicated to a common cause. Modern means of communication and technology make it possible now to apply this idea on a worldwide scale. At a recent conference with Russian scientists, I discovered to my astonishment that the Russians seemed to welcome the proposal to send teams of Russian and American youth to help in the development of the backward countries of the world. Such an endeavor would have exciting potentialities.

A second new opportunity for finding a moral equivalent for war lies in the coming conquest of space. This endless frontier offers unlimited chances for heroism, self-sacrifice and group solidarity. In the end it may be one of the greatest hopes for the maintenance of peace on earth.

The strongest ground for hope is the existence of many successful examples of both individual and group nonviolence. If it works sometimes, it should be possible to make it work more often.

At the community and national levels there are the striking examples of Gandhi in India and Martin Luther King in Alabama. In both these situations nonviolent techniques proved extremely effective means for achieving the aims of an oppressed group. Now, it's perfectly obvious that the measures these two men used would not work in every situation. For one thing, both were working within the framework of a religious orientation which is not shared by many segments of humanity. Gandhi was, and King still is, a man of very rare character and courage. Both men used this method in a society in which they could command widespread publicity. They also advocated measures which had considerable support in the ruling group of the society, and they could appeal to the laws and ideals of the ruling group. Because of these special features and others, people are apt to dismiss the nonviolent approach as impossible for America in the present international scene. Let us consider some of the major objections briefly. Let us point out, first, that Gandhi's methods might work against the English, who have a long tradition of respect for the individual, but would never work against a Communist dictatorship. To this it may be said that the same British who yielded to Gandhi's program in India do not hesitate to use extreme brutality in Kenya where they have been opposed by the violence of the Mau Mau. There is nothing special about the English that makes them reluctant to use violence in all situations. Nonviolent methods might be hard to use against a dictatorship and would probably entail considerable suffering and loss of life. But the success of nonviolent resistance depends on its power to undermine the will of the oppressor, and there is no reason to think that a tyrant's henchmen, who, after all, are more like other human beings than they are different from them, would be permanently immune to this type of pressure.

A second objection is that nonviolence has only been tried within countries, and would not work at an international level. Undoubtedly this method would require considerable modification before it could be used to resolve conflicts between countries. Any large nation, however, which adopted a program of working toward the nonviolent settlement of disputes could command even more publicity than Gandhi and King, which would enable it to mobilize similar feelings in its own allies and in neutral countries, and even in enemy countries, because there are many groups in every land who have come to see the impossibility of continuing to resort to force as a means of settling international disputes.

The most telling objection to nonviolence is that, though it might be suitable for Hindus, who have a long tradition of this sort of thing, it would never be acceptable to Americans, who are thoroughly accustomed to fighting violently for what they believe, if necessary. To this it may be pointed out, first, that persons who as individuals might use violence to defend themselves or their families against attack—and in some situations probably should do so—that these very same persons can commit themselves to nonviolent methods when these are in the service of a well worked-out program and have strong group support. Only about 100 of Gandhi's followers were fully committed to his philosophy. The vast majority of the people who waged the successful nonviolent campaign against British rule were ordinary mortals, like you and me, many of whom had used violence in other situations. And King's followers were members of an American minority which has long been accused of being exceptionally prone to violence.

But the most important point is that Gandhi and King have shown that nonviolent resistance could work in settings in which no one would have predicted they would have been successful before they tried it. They have achieved a breakthrough in the conduct of human affairs which should be taken very seriously. The task now is to develop and modify it so it could be successfully applied at the international level.

Since the doctrine of nonviolence is easily misunderstood, a few points about it should be emphasized. It does not seek to eliminate conflict from the world, but views conflict as a stimulus to creative solutions in which both sides gain. For example, King named the movement to end segregation in buses in Montgomery, Alabama, the Montgomery Improvement Association. He saw the struggle as one to benefit all the citizens of Montgomery, white and colored, by eliminating an evil that harmed them all. Nonviolence has nothing to do with passive submission or surrender, but represents rather a determination to fight actively for what one believes, with all possible means short of violence. It is not a method for cowards, since it requires more courage and steadiness of purpose than the use of violence.

Nonviolence is not an easy or immediate solution. Obviously, it requires a long period of education, preparation and training as to how to act in the eventuality that one's opponent decides to use force. A nonviolent approach to the settlement of international problems does not by any means guarantee victory, and many lives might well be lost in such an effort. If one takes this approach seriously, one has to be willing to risk one's life in the cause of peace as much as in the cause of war. Resorting to violence doesn't guarantee victory either, and does guarantee the loss of many more lives, and in all probability, the destruction of all parties involved. Finally, it should be obvious that nonviolence does not imply underestimation of the evils of Communism or willingness to surrender to it. Many aspects of the Communist way of life are repugnant to us, and Communism is an expansionist movement which seeks continually to extend its sphere of domination and does not shrink from ruthless measures to achieve its goals. The examples of Hungary and Tibet are still fresh in our minds.

I am confident, however, that people in the Communist countries share the hunger for liberty that is common to all mankind; and that as the standard of living improves in these countries, they will put increasing pressure on their leaders to grant them greater freedom. As a matter of fact, this seems to be occurring already. Visitors to Russia in recent years agree that, although personal liberty is still markedly restricted compared to this country, it is steadily gaining ground. Any relaxation of the tensions of the arms race would probably accelerate this process, since the fear of America impedes the movement of Russia toward liberty, as our fear of Russia erodes liberty in this country.

To make the discussion of nonviolence more concrete, let me consider in conclusion what the consequences of a unilateral, limited but definite disarmament move might be, assuming that it were made not out of fear, but out of conviction that the American way of life can be defended and promulgated in a nuclear world only by nonviolent means. Because of Russia's distrust of us, their first reaction would probably be that this was a ruse, a trick, in order to gain some hidden advantage. They would therefore become doubly alert and tense, and for a while the danger of disaster would probably be increased. This would mean that the initial disarmament move would have to be very clear and simple, and would have to be persisted in long enough to convince the Russians of its genuineness. There would also have to be opportunity for inspection by them and probably by an international group. When the Russians finally became convinced that we meant it, there are four possibilities as to what they might do. First, they might launch a destructive nuclear attack on us. The danger of this is extremely small. For the chief incentive for such an attack is the fear that we might someday get strong enough to make a pre-emptive attack on them, and this incentive would be removed. Second, they might send over an army of occupation. I think this, too, is unlikely, because occupation of a country as large as ours would be a great strain on their resources, especially if they knew they would be met by a population fully determined to resist them by nonviolent means and well trained to do so. If they did occupy us, however, then we would have to rely on nonviolent resistance, and this would probably be costly in lives, and might not succeed. Still, it would be much less costly, and have a much better chance of succeeding, than nuclear war. For as long as human beings exist, the spark of liberty will stay alive. One sure way of extinguishing it forever is through the destruction of the human race by a nuclear holocaust.

Third, in the event of a unilateral disarmament step by us, Russia might well step up its pressure, backed by superior military power, on neutral countries and peripheral areas, in an effort to undermine our influence. This is indeed a danger, but it must be remembered that there are many kinds of influence. Our disarmament move would, of course, have to be accompanied by measures which would increase economic and medical aid, self-help programs, and other kinds of influence in uncommitted areas sufficiently to offset the influence our opponents had gained through military predominance. In other words, we would have to convince these countries that they had a genuine community of interest with us. Then they would be motivated to resist Communist domination for their own sakes, not for ours. Probably we would fail in some areas. On the other hand, our most powerful form of influence would be the example of disarmament, since this would, in all probability, meet with a great positive response in the peoples of the entire world, including those in Russia.

Modern atomic, bacteriological and chemical weapons are no respecters of ideology. They look just as terrible to all peoples, and all humanity longs to be relieved of the threat they represent. So there would be real reason to hope that the fourth possibility might come to pass—that a genuine disarmament move on our part, based on a renunciation of force as a means of settling international conflicts, would lead to reciprocal moves by other nations, and so gradually usher in the era of peaceful competition which both Russia and America claim to desire.

As this little flight of fancy makes clear, commitment to the nonviolent means of settling international disputes is not an easy or simple solution, and is certainly not an immediate one. It would require considerable advance education, preparation and training. It might entail great suffering and could not be certain of success. The main ground for advocating it is that ultimately it offers the only hope for the continuance of the human adventure. Renunciation of force has become a necessity for human survival. The only question is whether it will come before or after a catastrophe. Fortunately, there is yet time to work for the peaceful, prosperous and free world which all mankind seeks, and in which human beings can for the first time realize their potentialities.

Erich Fromm

defines his one main concern

ERICH FROMM [1900-   ] *is a psychoanalyst, social philosopher, and writer. He was born in Frankfort, Germany; his training in analysis was at Munich and later at the Psychoanalytical Institute in Berlin. He came to the United States in the early thirties and became a citizen. He has taught at several universities in this country, including Columbia and Yale. The article here, "The Case for Unilateral Disarmament," was published in* Daedalus *in 1960.*

One cannot discuss the question of what might happen as a result of unilateral disarmament—or, for that matter, of any mutual disarmament —without examining some psychological arguments. The most popular one is that "the Russians cannot be trusted." If "trust" is meant in a moral sense, it is unfortunately true that political leaders can rarely be trusted. The reason lies in the split between private and public morals: the state, having become an idol, justifies any immorality if committed in its interest, while the very same political leaders would not commit the same acts if they were acting in behalf of their own private interest. However, there is another meaning to "trust in people," a meaning which is much more relevant to the problem of politics: the trust that they are sane and rational beings, and that they will act accordingly. If I deal with an opponent in whose sanity I trust, I can appreciate his motivations and to some extent predict them, because there are certain rules and aims, like that of survival or that of commensurateness between aims and means, which are common to all sane people. Hitler could not be trusted because he was lacking in sanity, and this very lack destroyed both him and his regime. It seems quite clear that the Russian leaders of today are sane and rational people; therefore, it is important not only to know what they are capable of, but also to predict what they might be motivated to do.

This question of the leaders' and the people's sanity leads to another consideration which affects us as much as it does the Russians. In the current discussion on armament control, many arguments are based on the question of what is *possible* rather than on what is *probable*. The difference between these two modes of thinking is precisely the difference between *paranoid* and *sane* thinking. The paranoiac's unshakable conviction in the validity of his delusion rests upon the fact that it is logically possible, and, so, unassailable. It is logically possible that his wife, his children and colleagues hate him and are conspiring to kill him. The patient cannot be convinced that his delusion is *impossible:* he can only be told that it is exceedingly *unlikely.* While the latter position requires an examination and evaluation of the facts and also a certain amount of faith in life, the paranoid position can satisfy itself with the possibility alone. I submit that our political thinking suffers from such paranoid trends. We should be concerned, not with the possibilities, but rather with the probabilities. This is the only sane and realistic way of conducting the affairs of national as well as individual life.

Again on the psychological plane, there are certain misunderstandings of the radical disarmament position which occur in many of the discussions. First of all, the position of unilateral disarmament has been understood as one of submission and resignation. On the contrary, the pacifist as well as the humanist pragmatists believe that unilateral disarmament is possible only as an expression of a deep spiritual and moral change within ourselves: it is an act of courage and resistance—not one of cowardice or surrender. Forms of resistance differ in accordance with the respective viewpoints. On the other hand, Gandhists and men like King-Hall advocate nonviolent resistance, which undoubtedly requires the maxium of courage and faith; they refer to the examples of Indian resistance against Britain or Norwegian resistance against the Nazis. This point of view is succinctly expressed in *Speak Truth to Power:*

> *Thus, we dissociate ourselves from the basically selfish attitude that has been miscalled pacifism, but that might be more accurately described as a kind of irresponsible antimilitarism. We dissociate ourselves also from utopianism. Though the choice of nonviolence involves a radical change in men, it does not require perfection. . . . We have tried to make it clear that readiness to accept suffering—rather than inflict it on others—is the essence of the nonviolent life, and that we must be prepared if called upon to pay the ultimate price. Obviously, if men are willing to spend billions of treasure and countless lives in war, they cannot dismiss the case for nonviolence by saying that in a nonviolent struggle people might get killed! It is equally clear that where commitment and the readiness to sacrifice are lacking, nonviolent resistance cannot be effective. On the contrary, it demands greater discipline, more arduous training, and more courage than its violent counterpart.*

Some think of armed resistance, of men and women defending their lives and their freedom with rifles, pistols, or knives. It is not unrealistic to think that both forms of resistance, nonviolent or violent, might deter an aggressor from attacking. At least, it is more realistic than to think that the use of thermonuclear weapons could lead to a "victory for democracy."

The proponents of "security by armament" sometimes accuse us of having an unrealistic, flatly optimistic picture of the nature of man. They remind us that this "perverse human being has a dark, illogical, irrational side." They even go so far as to say that "the paradox of nuclear deterrence is a variant of the fundamental Christian paradox. In order to *live,* we must express our willingness to kill and to die." Apart from this crude falsification of Christian teaching, we are by no means oblivious of the potential evil within man, and of the tragic aspect of life. Indeed, there are situations in which man must be willing to die in order to live. In the sacrifices necessary for violent or nonviolent resistance, I can see an expression of the acceptance of tragedy and sacrifice. But there is no tragedy or sacrifice in irresponsibility and carelessness: there is no meaning or dignity in the idea of the destruction of mankind and of civilization. Man has in himself a potential for evil; his whole existence is beset by dichotomies rooted in the very conditions of his existence. But these truly tragic aspects must not be confused with the results of stupidity and lack of imagination, with the willingness to stake the future of mankind on a gamble.

Finally, to take up one last criticism, directed against the position of unilateral disarmament: that it is "soft" on Communism. Our position is precisely based on the negation of the Soviet principle of the omnipotence of the state. Just because the spokesmen for unilateral disarmament are drastically opposed to the supremacy of the state, they do not want to grant the state the ever-increasing power which is unavoidable in the arms race, and they deny the right of the state to make decisions which can lead to the destruction of a great part of humanity and can doom future generations. If the basic conflict between the Soviet system and the democratic world is the question of the defense of the individual against the encroachment of an omnipotent state, then, indeed, the position for unilateral disarmament is the one which is most radically opposed to the Soviet principle.

After having discussed the case for unilateral disarmament (in the broad sense), I want to return to the practical proposition of unilateral steps toward disarmament. I do not deny that there are risks involved in this limited form of unilateral action, but considering the fact that the present method of negotiations has produced no results and that the chances that they will in the future are rather slim, considering furthermore the grave risk involved in the continuation of the arms race, I believe that it is practically and morally justified to take this risk. At present we are caught in a position with little chance for survival, unless we want to take refuge in hopes. *If* we have enough shelters, *if* the

"United States' active offenses and active defenses can gain control of the military situation after only a few exchanges," we might have only five, or twenty-five, or seventy-five million killed. However, if these conditions do not materialize, "an enemy could, by repeated strikes, reach almost any level of death and destruction he wishes." (And, I assume, the same threat exists for the Soviet Union.) In such a situation, "when nations are poised at the last moment when an agreement appears possible to end the risk of horrifying war, unleashed by fanatics, lunatics, or men of ambition," it is imperative to shake off the inertia of our accustomed thinking, to seek for new approaches to the problem, and above all, to see new alternatives to the present choices that confront us.

Maurice F. McCrackin

refuses to pay taxes if the money is used to prepare for war

MAURICE F. MCCRACKIN [1905-   ] *was a Presbyterian pastor in Cincinnati, Ohio. In 1948 he stopped paying his Federal income tax because a portion of the tax would be used for military affairs and war preparations. He stopped filing his returns in 1957 because they aided the revenue department in collecting the taxes. When he was subpoenaed to appear in court with his financial records, he refused. He was carried into the courtroom and sentenced to six months in jail. On his release, the Cincinnati Presbytery censured him and in 1960 suspended him from the ministry. This is his statement to the presbytery during the trial.*

I do not think of the defense in this trial as a defense of me as a person, but rather the defense of a principle and that, the right of a Christian, yes, a Presbyterian Christian to follow what he believes to be God's will as it has been shown to him in Jesus Christ. . . .

In June 1945 I was offered the position of co-pastor of the West Cincinnati St. Barnabas Church. Since the church was in a racially inclusive neighborhood and because of my deep interest in church union and cooperation, I gladly accepted the opportunity to share in this venture undertaken by the Episcopal and Presbyterian denominations, and began work in August of the same summer. Two months later we opened a settlement house at what was the St. Barnabas Episcopal Church building. Before the federation of the two congregations Negroes were not welcome at either church, and so children and teenagers came by the hundreds to enjoy the activities at the new settlement house. Soon we organized a Community Council and tried to come to grips with community problems. Ties in church and settlement house were growing strong and meaningful. Camp Joy opened to children of all races and creeds, and with integrated camping and a racially mixed staff, children and teenage young people grew in self-awareness and in respect and love for one another.

All the while our community work was expanding, cold war tensions were increasing. Nuclear bombs were fast being stockpiled and reports were heard of new and deadlier weapons about to be made. Fresh in my mind were the bombed cities of Hiroshima and Nagasaki. In the crowded, deprived areas of these two cities were people working as we were now working in Cincinnati to build a happier, healthier community. There were nurses, teachers, domestic workers, laborers and secretaries. There were babies, children, young people and adults living together, playing and working together and praying together. The bomb fell and they, their institutions, their community organizations, all were destroyed.

It came to me that if churches, settlement houses, schools, if anything is to survive in Cincinnati or anywhere else, something must be done about the armaments race, a race which has always resulted in war. I preached against violence, against hatred, against wars, cold or hot. I preached about the dangers which the entire world faced and which had been made so vividly clear by renowned scientists. I was preaching, but what was I doing? We must build peace in our local communities; this we were doing but what about the international community? When I thought of Hiroshima and Nagasaki and of other cities in so-called enemy countries, which we were preparing to incinerate with even more deadly and devastating weapons, I said to myself, "I can no more give consent to the committing of this terrible atrocity against cities in Japan, Russia or any other country than I would give my consent to such acts of barbaric cruelty being committed against my friends and neighbors surrounding the church and neighborhood house." Long before, I had decided that I would never again register for the draft nor would I consent to being conscripted by the government in any capacity. Nevertheless each year around March 15 without protest I sent my tax payments to the government. By giving my money I was helping the government do what I so vigorously declared was wrong. I would never give my money to support a house of prostitution or the liquor industry, a gambling house or for the purchase and distribution of pornographic literature. Yet year after year I had unquestionably been giving my money to an evil infinitely greater than all of these put together, since it is from war's aftermath that nearly all social ills stem.

Income tax paid by the individual is essential to the continuance of the war machine. Over 50 per cent of the military budget is paid for by individuals through their income tax payments and 75 to 80 per cent of every dollar he pays via income tax goes for war purposes.

Again I examined what the principle of personal commitment to Jesus meant to me. Through the years I have tried to achieve a personal relationship with Jesus. This is the burden of the Christian gospel, that Jesus can be known personally and that he can bring a saving power into a man's life. For us as Christians to know Jesus personally has reality only as we try earnestly to grow more like him "unto the measure of the stature of his fullness." If we follow Jesus afar off, if we praise his life and teachings but conclude that neither applies to our daily living, what are we doing but denying and rejecting him? Jesus speaks with authority and with love to every individual, "Follow me. Take up your cross. Love one another as I have loved you." What would Jesus *want* me to do in relation to war? What *must* I do if I am his disciple? This was the conclusion I reached: If I can honestly say that Jesus would support conscription, throw a hand grenade, or with a flame thrower drive men out of caves, to become living torches—if I believe he would release the bomb over Hiroshima or Nagasaki, then I not only have the right to do these things as a Christian, I am even obligated to do them. But if, as a committed follower, I believe that Jesus would do none of these things, I have no choice but to refuse at whatever personal cost, to support war. This means that I will not serve in the armed forces nor will I voluntarily give my money to help make war possible.

Having had this awakening, I could no longer in good conscience continue full payment of my Federal taxes. At the same time I did not want to withdraw my support from the civilian services which the government offers. For that reason I continued to pay the small percentage now allocated for civilian use. The amount which I had formerly given for war I now hoped to give to such causes as the American Friends Service Committee's program and to other works of mercy and reconciliation which help to remove the roots of war.

As time went on I realized, however, that this was not accomplishing its purpose because year after year the government ordered my bank to release money from my account to pay the tax I had held back. I then closed my checking account and by some method better known to the Internal Revenue Service than to me, it was discovered that I had money in a savings and loan company. Orders were given to this firm, under threat of prosecution, to surrender from my account the amount the government said I owed. I then realized suddenly how far government is now invading individual rights and privileges: money is given in trust to a firm to be kept in safety and the government coerces this firm's trustees into a violation of that trust. But even more evil than this invasion of rights is the violence done to the individual conscience in forcing him to give financial support to a thing he feels so deeply is wrong. I agree wholeheartedly with the affirmation of Presbytery made in February of 1958, that, "A Christian citizen is obligated to God to obey the law but when in conscience he finds the requirements of law to be in direct conflict with his obedience to God, he must obey God rather than man."

Disobedience to a civil law is an act against government, but obedience to a civil law that is evil is an act against God.

At this point it came to me with complete clarity that by so much as filing tax returns I was giving to the Revenue Department assistance in the violation of my own conscience, because the very information I had been giving on my tax forms was being used in finally making the collection. So from this point on, or until there is a radical change for the better in government spending I shall file no returns. . . .

The nations seem unable to agree on any negotiated disarmament, and certainly there is little hope that in the foreseeable future any will do so unilaterally. At no time in human history, therefore, has there been such an acute necessity for individuals to disarm unilaterally, to behave as moral and responsible human beings and to do what they know to be right, beginning now. Some have said that this is the age of the common man. However, if we are to survive, it must become the age of the uncommon man. Unilateral, personal disarmament means that we will accept only work which contributes to the peace, welfare and uplift of mankind. One by one people are responsible for the most horrible crimes. These are not bad people, they are good people, many socially concerned, pillars of church and society. Yet, with little or no inward protest they respond to the state's demands to do all kinds of ghastly jobs—to perfect the H bomb or the more terrible cobalt bomb, to work in laboratories to perfect still more deadly nerve gas or to help spawn insects which will be more deadly germ carriers. The state persuades these and others that they are not really responsible for what they are doing, that they are only small cogs in a big machine and if they have guilt it is so slight they shouldn't worry over it.

Leo Tolstoy described this evil process of rationalization in his book *The Kingdom of God Is Within You.* He asks, "Is it possible that millions of men can go on calmly committing deeds which are so manifestly criminal, such as are the murders and tortures they commit, simply from fear of punishment? Surely these things would not exist were not the falsehood and brutality of their actions hidden from all classes of men by the system of political organization. When such deeds are committed, there are so many instigators, participants and abettors that no single individual feels himself morally responsible. The rulers of the state always endeavor to involve the greatest number of citizens in the participation of the crimes which it is to their interest to have committed. Some demand it, some confirm it, some order it and some execute it."

This evil chain of violence and death must be broken and it will be broken when enough individuals say to the state, "You may order me to do something I believe wrong, but I will not execute your command. You may order me to kill, but I will not kill nor will I give my money to buy weapons that others may do so." There are other voices that I must obey. I must obey the voice of humanity which cries for peace and relief from the intolerable burden of armaments and conscription. I must obey the voice of conscience, made sensitive by the inner light of truth. I must obey the voice heard across the centuries, "Love your enemies, pray for those who despitefully use you and persecute you." In obedience to these voices lies the only path to brotherhood and peace. And these are the voices I must obey.

Stephen King-Hall

presents a plan for the nonviolent resistance of enemy occupation

STEPHEN KING-HALL [1893-   ] *is a retired commander of the Royal Navy. During his military career, he served in the Great Fleet and on submarines during World War I. He was a member of Parliament and worked in various war-related jobs during World War II. In his introduction to the pamphlet* Common Sense in Defense, *published in 1960, Commander Sir Stephen King-Hall points out that he spent twenty years of his life "studying and preparing for the business of war, and I cannot honestly repent for these past activities." He adds, however, that he wishes he sometimes had the "moral courage" to take up the position of the pacifists, since he believes "it to be the view which Jesus Christ would have taken."*

One must always remember that our *object* is to defend and maintain our way of life and, as the assumption is that it is the enemy's intention to convert or force us to adopt his way of life, which for our present purpose we can assume would be Communism, our first task should be to make sure that our people know all about the merits of our way of life (and its defects) and why and in what respects it is preferable to Communism. The principle that attack is the best means of defense is as true in the sphere of psychological war as it is in the violence of military operations. We should not therefore regard our psychological civil defense as a kind of passive resistance; we should think rather in terms of a positive assault on the minds of the occupying forces. As it is impossible in modern conditions for an army of occupation to be isolated from the population, it is perfectly possible for the people to have influence with the occupiers if they know how to set about it and if they can communicate with them. I should therefore regard it as a perfectly sensible civil-defense activity on the part of anyone who seriously believes that the Russians might wish to occupy this country that they should advocate an extensive educational campaign of lessons in Russian as a spare-time occupation.

There is definite evidence that Russian troops who had been in close contact with the Hungarian people for many months before the revolt were unreliable and had to be replaced by formations from the Asiatic areas of the Soviet Union.

However, this is a very large and (unfortunately) unexplored subject so I will conclude these reflections upon it by saying:

(a) The usually accepted notion that collaboration with the enemy is wrong may need further examination if by collaboration is meant having contact and relations with him designed to change his mind.

(b) In the nuclear age there is small consolation in being "liberated" through a nuclear attack by an ally.

(c) It seems to me perfectly logical to argue that, given a nation adequately prepared and trained to deal psychologically with an invader in an ideological struggle (which is what modern wars are), the potential occupier might well decide that it was positively dangerous to allow any substantial number of his people to take up residence as occupying troops in the midst of such a nation. It is at least worthy of note that today (1960) it is the rulers of the Soviet Union and the other Communist states who refuse to give their peoples more than a very limited freedom to visit the West or read Western newspapers. Why?

(d) The whole question of the use of phychological resistance and attack by a people carefully trained on a national scale to be not a nation-in-arms but a nation-in-nonviolent-techniques requires detailed and expert examination. But this is not the place to begin that task.

Moreover I must insist that I have only included this subject for the benefit of those people who seem to take it for granted that as a matter of course we should be occupied by the Russians if we abandoned nuclear weapons. I think such an occupation is in the highest degree improbable but if I am wrong I submit that there is also a modern answer to this defense problem.

Abraham Cronbach

says that the only national defense is international amity

DR. ABRAHAM CRONBACH [1882-   ] *is an absolute pacifist, which means that he does not believe in the use of force either in personal or international relations. Professor emeritus of social studies at the Hebrew Union College—Jewish Institute of Religion, Dr. Cronbach withdrew from the ministry in 1919 because he felt his "views on public questions are such as to render the average pulpit position no longer tenable." In 1924, he tried to found a Jewish peace organization similar to that of the Quakers. But it was not until 1942 that a Jewish Peace Fellowship was formed. In 1946 when Nazi and Nazi-dominated officials were being brought to trial, Dr. Cronbach urged that "the Jews might beseech clemency for their tormentors and the slayers of their people." In 1960 he delivered the address here in Pennsylvania.*

I have been asked to speak upon the subject of pacifism. I am myself a pacifist. You, or most of you are not pacifists. You will be taking issue with some of that which I will be saying. But, differ as you may, I have no grudge against you. I respect your opinion. I respect your opinion because I respect your personality. Your personality is sacred. Your personality is God-given.

What is pacifism? Pacifism is the persuasion that the idealistic is the practical and that the nonidealistic is the impractical. Often we hear people say about a proposal: "That is a splendid idea, a fine vision, a noble theory, but will it work? Will it pan out in practice?"

Such is not the attitude of pacifism. Pacifism holds that the ideal and the practical do not fall apart. For the pacifist, the ideal and the practical coincide.

There are two points on which the pacifist and the nonpacifist agree. Pacifist and nonpacifist are in accord that "War is hell."

Another point of accord between pacifist and nonpacifist relates to love of country. We should stand by our country. We should protect and defend our country. We should be loyal to our country.

Wherein then do the two differ? They differ in this: While both agree that our country should be defended, the pacifist denies that war is national defense. The pacifist calls war not national defense but national jeopardy.

Those who speak of war as national defense do so on the assumption that their side is going to win. No one supposes that the defeated side is defended. The defeated side has to suffer not only the expenditures and the agonies of war but, in addition, the penalties and the reparations imposed by the victor. Each side enters the war expecting to win. If it did not expect to win, no country would enter a war. But how do you know that your side is going to win? Your side might be the loser. Then what comes of your national defense?

We fought the First World War "to make the world safe for democracy." We won that war. We prevailed. But what happened to democracy? Democracy suffered a tragic setback. When we entered the Second World War, we were told that, once we had overthrown Hitler, then we would be safe. We did overthrow Hitler. But, in the very moment of our triumph, the persons who told us that victory would bring us security, those identical persons were the ones who warned us that now our peril was greater than it had ever been before. England was a victor in that war. Yet the war-wrought sufferings of England were such that Englishmen began to question whether the plight of England could have been worse had England been not victorious but defeated. We Jews were among the winners in that war. We Jews were identified with the victorious allies. Yet we Jews, with our six million slain and our unnumbered homeless—see how we Jews were defended! How aptly did that American war correspondent express himself when, from the fighting front in Italy, he cabled to his newspaper in the United States: "Wars are won by those that do not wage them, and that nation prospers which keeps its youth alive."

And now we have entered the era of nuclear war. Albert Einstein (who surely knew something about nuclear energy) said that, if a third world war is fought with atomic weapons, the fourth world war will be fought with clubs. In other words, we shall be back to savagery, back to the jungle, back to cave dwelling, civilization annihilated.

War does not defend. Nor does armament defend. We often hear that, if only we were sufficiently armed, then we would be safe. Then no country would dare attack us. Then we would be in a position to maintain the peace of the world. All of which was precisely and exactly the doctrine of Hitler and of Mussolini. They likewise "spoke from strength." They likewise piled up armament "to maintain the peace of the world"; with what results, history has already recorded.

For years we have been spending on armament more and more billions annually. Yet, year by year, we have been told that now our peril is greater than it has ever been before. The very people who have been insisting upon our need to spend more and more for armament are the selfsame people who, after we do procure the armament, tell us that now our danger is worse than ever. And they are right. As our armament increases, our peril increases. The more we arm, the more our enemy arms.

To defend our country, one step must be that of getting our enemies to disarm. But the only way we can get our enemies to disarm is for ourselves to disarm.

We accuse our enemies of imperialism. In every war each side accuses the other of imperialism. What makes a country imperialistic? One cause of imperialism is the fear of invasion. A country seizes adjacent territory in order to keep that territory from becoming a launching place of invasion against itself. The way to stop imperialism is to remove the fear of invasion. To remove the fear of invasion, we must disarm and lead other countries to disarm.

Another cause of imperialism is the need for raw materials, markets, and other economic advantages. To scotch imperialism, we must enable every country in the world to obtain the raw materials, the markets, and the other economic advantages which it seeks, and to obtain them without imperialism, to obtain them by the peaceful ways of commerce. What country will submit to the costs and the miseries of imperialism if, by easier means, it can procure what it needs? Aptly did a noted journalist once write: "If goods do not cross boundary lines, soldiers will." International trade is an important device for national defense.

One can imagine America speaking to our present enemy, Russia: "Russia, we have been devoting most of our thought and most of our treasure to the project of hurting you. Now we have changed. Henceforth we devote our thought and our treasure to doing you good. We want you to be good to us. How can we expect you to be good to us if we are not good to you? Russia, you desire for your people a rising standard of living. You wish for your people ever better things in the way of food, clothing, housing, medical care, education, recreation and the rest. We wish to help your people obtain those things. We can do this by trading with you. If we trade with you, we benefit ourselves as well as you. Also we can place you or your allies among the nations receiving our foreign aid.

"Only this word of warning, Russia. In order to help you, America must be free. We must be untrammeled in pursuing what we call the American way of life. If any nation molests us or fetters us, our power to do you good will be impaired. Were you or any other nation to interfere with us, our willingness to help you would continue, but our power to help would be diminished. Russia, you cannot injure us without injuring yourself."

It would also enhance our safety were we to discontinue saying about Russia the hateful things which we have been saying. A few years ago we said those hateful things about Germany and about Japan. There was a time when we said them about Spain. There was a time when we said them about the southern Confederacy. Before that, we said them about Mexico and, farther back, we said them about England. And, after every war, it developed that, just as untrue as were the evil things our enemy said about us, equally untrue were the evil things we said about the enemy.

War does not defend. Armament does not defend. The only national defense is international amity.

Linus Pauling
urges research for peace

LINUS PAULING [1901-   ] *is a prominent scientist who was awarded the 1954 Nobel Prize in Chemistry for his research into the nature of the chemical bond. In the late fifties, Dr. Pauling initiated a petition campaign to obtain signatures of scientists who urged "an international agreement to stop further testing of nuclear weapons." More than 11,000 scientists in forty-nine countries signed. He was subpoenaed by the United States Senate Internal Security Committee and was asked to disclose the names of persons who aided him in this campaign. He de-*

clined to do so, explaining that he felt the names would be used for reprisals against them. The committee eventually dropped the request. The selection here is taken from No More War! *which came out in 1958.*

I believe that there will never again be a great world war, if only the people of the United States and of the rest of the world can be informed in time about the present world situation. I believe that there will never be a war in which the terrible nuclear weapons—atom bombs, hydrogen bombs, superbombs—are used. I believe that the development of these terrible weapons forces us to move into a new period in the history of the world, a period of peace and reason, when world problems are not solved by war or by force, but are solved by the application of man's power of reason, in a way that does justice to all nations and that benefits all people.

I believe that this is what the future holds for the world, but I am sure that it is not going to be easy for the world to achieve this future. We have to work to prevent the catastrophe of a cataclysmic nuclear war, and to find the ways in which world problems can be solved by peaceful and rational methods.

In the past, disputes between groups of human beings have often been settled by war. At first the wars were fought with stones and clubs as weapons, then with spears and swords, and then with bows and arrows. During the last few hundred years they have been fought with guns, and recently with great bombs dropped from airplanes—blockbusters containing one ton or even ten tons of TNT.

There may in the past have been times when war was a cruel but effective application of the democratic process, when force was on the side of justice. Wars fought with simple weapons were often won by the side with the greater number of warriors.

Now war is different. A great mass of people without nuclear weapons, without airplanes, without ballistic missiles cannot fight successfully against a small group controlling these modern means of waging war.

The American people were successful in their revolt against Great Britain because modern weapons had not yet been developed when the American Revolution broke out.

It is hard for anybody to understand how great a change has taken place in the nature of the world during the past century or two, and especially during the last fifty years. The world has been changed through the discoveries made by scientists. Everything has been changed by these discoveries—the food we eat, the clothes we wear, the methods of controlling disease, the methods of transportation and communication, the conduct of international affairs, the ways of waging war—all are different now from what they were a few decades ago.

Never again will there be the world of William Shakespeare, the world of Benjamin Franklin, the world of Queen Victoria, the world of Woodrow Wilson.

The scientific discoveries that have changed the world are manifold. I think that the greatest of all scientific discoveries, the greatest discovery that has been made since the discovery of the controlled use of fire by prehistoric man, was the discovery of the ways in which the immense stores of energy that are locked up in the nuclei of atoms can be released.

Many scientists contributed to this discovery. Among them we may mention some of the great ones—Pierre and Marie Curie, Albert Einstein, Ernest Rutherford, Niels Bohr, Ernest Lawrence, Frédéric and Irène Joliot-Curie, Otto Hahn, Enrico Fermi.

This discovery, by providing power in essentially unlimited quantities for the future world, should lead through its peaceful applications to a great increase in the standards of living of people all over the world.

It is this discovery also that has changed the nature of war in an astounding way.

The Second World War, like earlier wars, was fought with molecular explosives. Trinitrotoluene, TNT, is the one that was most used. TNT can be manufactured by the reaction of nitric and sulfuric acids with the hydrocarbon toluene, which can be obtained from petroleum. It is not very expensive—somewhere around twenty-five cents a pound. One pound of TNT can do a lot of damage; about the same as one stick of dynamite. It can demolish a small house and kill several people. A one-ton blockbuster, a bomb containing 2,000 pounds of TNT, can demolish a large building and may kill a hundred people or more.

During the Second World War many shells and bombs containing TNT and other explosives were fired at or dropped on cities and other targets in the warring countries. The total amount of explosives used in the whole of the Second World War came to about three million tons of TNT.

At the beginning of the Second World War the discoveries in the field of nuclear physics had just reached such a point as to cause a number of scientists to recognize that it might be possible to manufacture immensely powerful bombs involving nuclear reactions, and also to make nuclear power plants.

The world had indeed entered into a new stage of development in 1945, when the atom bombs were dropped on Hiroshima and Nagasaki and the United States began to build up its stockpile of thousands of these terribly destructive weapons, each one capable of destroying a medium-sized city and killing a hundred thousand people.

Albert Einstein was justified in his great apprehension, his fear that the possession of weapons of destruction a thousand times more powerful than the greatest that were ever used before would lead to catastrophe for the world.

And now we have the H-bomb!

Now the United States, the U.S.S.R. and Great Britain have stockpiles of hydrogen bombs and superbombs that are one thousand times more powerful still than the atomic bombs that were dropped on Hiroshima and Nagasaki!

In 1945 the world changed from the period of TNT blockbusters, with war as in the Second World War, when one large bomb could kill ten people or a hundred people, into its second period, the period of the great atomic bombs, each capable of killing one hundred thousand people. In 1952 the world moved into the *third* period, when the bombs became not just one thousand or ten thousand times more powerful than the blockbusters, but *one million* or *ten million* times as powerful—*one thousand times more powerful than the Hiroshima and Nagasaki bombs.*

If a war were to break out today, it is probable that one bomb would explode over New York, and kill ten million people. One bomb would explode over London, and kill ten million people. One bomb would explode over Moscow, and kill six million people. One bomb would explode over Leningrad, and kill three million people. One bomb would explode over Chicago, and kill four million people. One bomb would explode over Los Angeles, and kill three million people. And these cities themselves would be smashed flat, over an area ten miles or twenty miles in diameter. The cities and the regions around them would be rendered uninhabitable for years by the deposited radioactivity. The initial attacks in such a war would kill eighty-three million Americans and seriously injure another twenty-five million.

The bomb that could destroy the greatest city in the world and kill ten million people is not something imaginary. Bombs of this sort—hydrogen bombs and superbombs—have been made and have been exploded. Bombs have been tested that have an explosive power as great as fifteen megatons—an explosive power equivalent to fifteen million tons of TNT, fifteen million one-ton blockbusters.

Each one of these bombs is one thousand times more powerful than the Hiroshima bomb or the Nagasaki bomb. Each one of them has an explosive energy five times as great as that of all of the bombs used in the Second World War.

Albert Einstein was apprehensive, fearful, in 1946, when the world had passed into the period of atomic bombs, little nuclear bombs such that each bomb equals one hundred thousand people killed. How much more reason do we have now for fear about the future of the world, now that we have moved into the period of great nuclear weapons, with each bomb equal to as many as ten million people killed!

We are truly forced into abandoning war as the method of solution of world problems, the method of resolution of disputes among nations. President Eisenhower and other great national leaders have stated that the stockpiles of these terrible nuclear weapons are deterrents—that they will serve as deterrents against aggression, deterrents against war. There is little doubt that the nuclear weapons have been effective in preventing the outbreak of great wars during recent years.

But disputes between nations still need to be settled. In the past, world problems have often been settled by war, sometimes in such a way as to correspond to justice and sometimes to injustice. If the nuclear stockpiles continue to serve effectively as deterrents and to prevent war from breaking out, there still remains the task of solving the great world problems.

It is evident that these problems now need to be settled by the processes of negotiation, arbitration, the formulation and application of a sound system of international law. *We need to begin now to make international agreements.*

I am not alone in this belief. I think that the great majority of the scientists in the world and the great majority of the people in the world believe that there must be no more war, that the great stockpiles of terribly destructive nuclear weapons must not be used, that the time has come for morality and justice to take their proper place of prime importance in the conduct of world affairs, that world problems should be settled by international agreements and the application of international law.

On January 13, 1958, I presented to the United Nations a petition to which 9,235 scientists, of many countries in the world, had subscribed. In this petition we urged that immediate action be taken to effect an international agreement to stop the testing of all nuclear weapons. We pointed out that if testing continues and the possession of the nuclear weapons spreads to additional governments there will be greatly increased danger of outbreak of a cataclysmic nuclear war through the reckless action of some irresponsible national leader. We mentioned also the damage that is being done to the health of human beings all over the world and to the pool of human germ plasm that determines the nature of future generations by the bomb tests, which spread radioactive elements over every part of the world. We mentioned that an international agreement to stop the testing of nuclear bombs now could serve as the first step toward averting the possibility of a nuclear war that would be a catastrophe for all humanity. Our proposal is that we begin now the new era of peace and international law, by making an international agreement to stop the bomb tests.

It is proposed that the great world problems be solved in the way that other problems are now solved—by working hard to find their solution—by carrying on *research for peace.* It is proposed that there be set up a great research organization, the World Peace Research Organization, within the structure of the United Nations. This organization should include many scientists, representing all fields of science, and many other specialists, in all fields of knowledge. They would attack world problems by imaginative and original methods, and would work steadily in this attack, year after year.

The time has now come for man's intellect to win out over the brutality, the insanity of war.

Albert Schweitzer
calls for a new trust among all peoples

ALBERT SCHWEITZER [1875-   ], *Alsatian medical missionary, philosopher and musician, was awarded the Nobel Peace Prize in 1953. At the age of twenty-one he decided that he would consider himself justified in living for science and art until he was thirty, and that after that he would devote himself "to the direct service of humanity." He started to study medicine when he was thirty. Six years later he moved to Africa and opened a hospital at Lambarene, where he has lived ever since. The selection here is from an appeal broadcast from Norway in 1958.*

We live in a time when the good faith of peoples is doubted more than ever before. Expressions throwing doubt on the trustworthiness of each other are bandied back and forth. They are based on what happened in the First World War when the nations experienced dishonesty, injustice and inhumanity from one another. How can a new trust come about? And yet, it must.

We cannot continue in this paralyzing mistrust. If we want to work our way out of the desperate situation in which we find ourselves, another spirit must enter into the people. It can only come if the awareness of its necessity suffices to give us strength to believe in its coming. We must presuppose the awareness of this need in all the peoples who have suffered along with us. We must approach them in the spirit that we are human beings, all of us, and that we feel ourselves fitted to feel with each other; to think and to will together in the same way.

The awareness that we are all human beings together has become lost in war and through politics. We have reached the point of regarding each other only as members of a people either allied with us or against us and our approach—prejudice, sympathy or antipathy—are all conditioned by that. Now we must rediscover the fact that we—all together—are human beings, and that we must strive to concede to each other what moral capacity we have. Only in this way can we begin to believe that in other peoples as well as in ourselves there will arise the need for a new spirit which can be the beginning of a feeling of mutual trustworthiness toward each other. The spirit is a mighty force for transforming things. We have seen it at work as the spirit of evil which virtually threw us back from striving toward a culture of the spirit into barbarism. Now let us set our hopes on the spirit's bringing peoples and nations back to an awareness of culture.

At this stage we have the choice of two risks: the one lies in continuing the mad atomic-arms race with its danger of an unavoidable atomic war in the near future; the other in the renunciation of nuclear weapons, and in the hope that the United States and the Soviet Union, and the peoples associated with them, will manage to live in peace. The first holds no hope of a prosperous future; the second does. We must risk the second.

Fifty-two Nobel Laureates
plead for nations to renounce force

On July 15, 1955, a group of Nobel laureates, following a meeting at Mainau, Germany, issued an appeal to all countries.

We, the undersigned, are scientists of different countries, different creeds, different political persuasions. Outwardly, we are bound together only by the Nobel Prize, which we have been favored to receive. With pleasure we have devoted our lives to the service of science. It is, we believe, a path to a happier life for people. We see with horror that this very science is giving mankind the means to destroy itself. By total military use of weapons feasible today, the earth can be contaminated with radioactivity to such an extent that whole peoples can be annihilated. Neutrals may die thus as well as belligerents.

If war broke out among the great powers, who could guarantee that it would not develop into a deadly conflict? A nation that engages in a total war thus signals its own destruction and imperils the whole world. We do not deny that perhaps today peace is being preserved precisely by the fear of these weapons. Nevertheless, we think it is a delusion if governments believe that they can avoid war for a long time through the fear of these weapons. Fear and tension have often engendered wars. Similarly it seems to us a delusion to believe that small conflicts could in the future always be decided by traditional weapons. In extreme danger no nation will deny itself the use of any weapon that scientific technology can produce.

All nations must come to the decision to renounce force as a final resort of policy. If they are not prepared to do this they will cease to exist.

Lord Edgar Douglas Adrian, *Cambridge*
Kurt Alder, *Köln*
Max Born, *Bad Pyrmont*
Walther Bothe, *Heidelberg*
Percy William Bridgman, *Cambridge*
Adolf Butenandt, *Tübingen*
Arthur H. Compton, *St. Louis*
Henrik Damn, *Copenhagen*
Clinton Joseph Davisson, *Charlottesville*
P. A. M. Dirac, *Oxford*
Edward A. Doisy, *St. Louis*
Gerhard Domagk, *Wuppertal*
Joseph Erlanger, *St. Louis*
Hans K. von Euler-Chelpin, *Stockholm*
James Franck, *Chicago*
Otto Hahn, *Göttingen*
Werner Heisenberg, *Göttingen*
P. S. Hench, Rochester, *Minnesota*
Gustav Hertz, *Leipzig*
George von Hevesy, *Stockholm*
C. Heymans, *Gent*
Frédéric Joliot-Curie, *Paris*

Irène Joliot-Curie, *Paris*
E. C. Kendall, *Princeton*
Sir Hans Krebs, *Oxford*
Richard Kuhn, *Heidelberg*
Max von Laue, *Berlin*
Fritz Lipman, *Boston*
A. E. Moniz, *Lisbon*
Paul Hermann Müller, *Basel*
H. J. Muller, *Bloomington*
William Murphy, *Boston*
Wolfgang Pauli, *Zurich*
Linus Pauling, *Pasadena*
C. F. Powell, *Bristol*
Sir Chandrasekhara Venkata Raman,
    Bangalore
Th. Reichstein, *Basel*
Lord Bertrand Russell, *Richmond*
L. Ruzicka, *Zurich*
F. F. Sillanpää, *Helsinki*
Frederick Soddy, *Brighton*
W. M. Stanley, *Berkeley*

A. J. Muste

discusses the workability of nonviolence

ABRAHAM JOHN MUSTE [1885-   ] *came to the United States from Holland when he was still a child. In 1909 he was ordained a minister of the Dutch Reformed Church, but resigned from the pulpit in 1918 when he could not reconcile his pacifist convictions with the war. He was active in the American labor movement and was one of the first to use the "sit-down" tactic in a strike in the United States. Muste has devoted his life to active leadership in labor, civil liberties and peace, and has often been arrested for the part he has taken. Muste is Chairman of the Committee for Non-violent Action, member of the executive committee of the War Resisters League, one of the four editors of Liberation, and secretary emeritus of the Fellowship of Reconciliation. The selection here was originally part of a pamphlet published in 1954.*

There are two ultimate questions we must now consider. If we may use a military figure to state a pacifist case, we can say that one is the question of what we fight *for;* the other of what we fight *with* and rely on for a sense of security.

Paradoxically, life is worth living for those who have something for which they will gladly give up life. Individuals and nations need something beyond themselves to which they give unconditional homage and devotion. A nation cannot exist if it has no purpose save to exist, to survive at any cost and on any terms. It needs a spiritual goal. In the words of the Psalmist, "Except the Lord build the city, they labor in vain that build it."

It is equally true that in the final analysis the weapons with which a nation must fight are spiritual. Its defense and security are spiritually based, or they do not really exist. Even military men recognize that without morale, a spiritual factor, the biggest and best equipped army in the world is a shell. In answer to the question, "What constitutes the bulwark of our own liberty and independence?" Lincoln replied: "It is not our frowning battlements, our bristling sea coasts, our army and our navy. These are not our reliance against tyranny. *All of these may be turned against us without making us weaker for the struggle. . . . Our defense is in the spirit which prized liberty as the heritage of all men, in all lands everywhere."*

A people thus devoted to a spiritual goal and thus skilled in wielding spiritual weapons would have immense driving and staying power.

It would have a faith that other peoples, especially the long downtrodden masses, could embrace in place of the Communist faith that has so vast an attraction for them now. . . .

The Western world in its concept of democracy, the United States in "the American dream," and Christians in their gospel and ethic of love, of evil, overcome not by evil but by good, have knowledge of such a spiritual goal. The difficulty is that we do not pursue this goal. On the one hand are a lot of ordinary folks who have never truly been taught that there are other, better means for dealing with Communism than the shooting-mad-dogs technique. There are the hard-boiled who have no scruples. Then there are the many varieties of sophisticated intellectual and spiritual leaders. These people, however they phrase it in words, think that it is pointless, at least in this modern age, to call upon governments and nations to behave ethically, not to mention in a Christian way, to repent of the sins of atomic and biological war and to trust in God. With the chanting of the magic word "utopianism," these people dismiss the challenge and the hope of building brotherhood on earth as in heaven. Alas, not a few peace workers are among them, placing their reliance on some device by which an unrepentant and essentially unbelieving nation will on the basis of self-interest work out an agreement with an unrepentant and avowedly unbelieving Communist regime that will bring peace!

On the other hand, if in any typical Protestant church of a Sunday morning I were to say pretty much what I have here been writing about centering our national policy around the needy children of the world, Christian hearts would be touched and Christian heads would be nodded gravely in assent. And then, as the Roper polls show, these good Christian folk would agree nearly to the man that it was also right and wise for the United States to keep adding to the H-bomb stockpile as the best way to keep the godless, Christ-denying Communists from coming over here and closing Christ's churches!

Two pastors of the French Reformed Church were put into a concentration camp during World War II for refusal to conform to anti-Semitic laws enacted by the Pétain regime. The Communists in the camp were impressed by two men who seemed to them to behave like early Christians, for they accepted a second imprisonment in the camp rather than sign a piece of paper promising obedience to collaborationist laws, though few got a second chance to get out of a concentration camp in those days. "Why should anybody hesitate to sign a piece of paper, even if it tells a lie?" was the Communist reaction.

So impressed were they, in fact, that they began to spend several hours every day with the pastors in studying the New Testament. When the pastors were on the point of being released again, one of the Communists said to them in parting: "We recognize that your faith is superior to ours. This way of life which Jesus taught and lived everybody ought to live. And everybody will," he added, "after the revolution."

The problem of morale and faith facing the West is here vividly laid bare. It is that the Christian nations, Christian churches, Christian people are in thorough agreement with that Communist. Again the "enemy" is ourselves. We and that Communist are agreed that the Christian faith and way are superior; agreed that someday it has to prevail; and agreed that this will come to pass after we—Communists and Christians—have made it possible for our ways of life to survive and prevail by our respective impure and violent means. The Communists believe it will come to pass "after the revolution" when they are in control. American Christians believe it will come after they by the threat or use of their atomic arsenal have got things under control. But they all unite in the grand chorus: "But it isn't practical *now!*"

At an earlier stage we found that it is not possible to be absorbed at one and the same time in the power struggle and in the task of spreading general well-being across the world and building a stable world economy. We are faced with a choice of goals.

A choice of means must likewise be made, however we may shrink from it. Our firm conviction as pacifists is that it is not possible to achieve democracy by undemocratic means, to overcome Communism by resorting increasingly to Communist methods, to save the values of Christian civilization by throwing them overboard as modern war requires us to do. On the positive side it is our conviction that love translated into concrete action for human brotherhood is the way to overcome evil and that the spiritual power which flows through men when they give themselves to God in faith and obedience is real and the most potent force in the universe.

In this context we always come up against the question, "Will it work?" Will it work with the Russians, the Communists, the totalitarians? In the abstract and in general people are usually willing to grant the pacifist case, but the concrete enemy of the moment is always a *special* case. Nor would pacifists deny that totalitarianism in its modern forms and equipped with modern weapons of thought control, regimentation and terrorism presents a tremendous challenge to pacifists. It does also to the advocates of any other method for meeting aggression and tyranny, a point which nonpacifists sometimes overlook. Their record, as we pointed out at length in the beginning of this essay, is not one of success!

But what is the pacifist's answer to the question of workability? We are now dealing with the problem of practicality on another level than a short way back when we were dealing with the political-economic approach versus the military. There it was a question of "calculated risk," and we argued that on that basis the chances were that if the United States continued in the power struggle and armaments race, it would lose the battle against Communism. If, on the contrary, it embarked on a policy of devoting its skills and resources to developing a sound global economy, it would probably win. Now we are dealing with moral or spiritual values. In Christian terms we are proposing that men apply Christ's method of uncalculating love, of feeding the enemy and so on, rather than depending upon the sword for defense or liberation.

Stating the matter in other terms, we are here thinking of the morally responsible human being. All who believe in some kind of moral order, whether or not they are Christians or consider themselves religious at all, face a crucial problem in connection with war. The question is not whether one is going to die in war; at the appointed time all men, and nations also, die. This is in the order of nature. The question for the morally responsible being is what happens to *himself* if he becomes a murderer, drops atomic bombs on little enemy children instead of trying to bring them food and healing. The question is what *moral* price he is prepared to pay for his country's victory in war.

When on this level the Christian is asked whether the way of uncalculating love—of not "offending one of these little ones" behind the Iron Curtain—"works" in some immediate political sense, his first answer is bound to be that he doesn't think this is any of his business. God whom he knows in Christ commands love. He does not promise success to today's Christian any more than he did to Jesus. Indeed, there is sure to be a cross in the picture somewhere. One of the signs that we are off the track is that everything goes smoothly and all men speak well of us. When the Christian asks God for victory, success, a blank check, he has ceased to believe in God.

The morally responsible person will give essentially the same answer. He has to be true, in the final pinch, to the highest that he knows. He has to be able to live with himself. If his moral standard amounts to obeying whatever orders some government gives him (remember the Nuremberg doctrine of the guilt of *individual* Nazis) or if his standard is what he can get away with, then he is no longer a moral being. This is why, in fact, any human being not bereft of sanity altogether "draws a line somewhere," at some point says, "I can do no other."

The modern pacifist draws the line at participation in atomic and bacteriological war. When he is asked whether this pacifism is "politically effective," his reply is: "If human beings do not draw this line, then where will they draw the line? What are they waiting for?" In the great drama, *Jakobowski and the Colonel,* Jakobowski, the refugee, says to the Nazi colonel who has just been engaged in torturing certain victims: "There is one advantage that the hunted has over the hunter—namely, that he is not the hunter." The advantage is an ultimate one: not to join the hunters. If a man loses it, there is nothing to compensate for the loss.

Totalitarian regimes do indeed present a grave problem, and our argument in no sense proceeds on the basis of minimizing the evil of such regimes. But the familiar argument that Gandhi could get by with nonviolence in dealing with the British but that nonviolence is no good in dealing with this or that other regime in practice means that *any* methods have to be used with the latter. This clearly means surrender of the moral life. It is capitulation to the amoral or antimoral philosophy of Bolshevism: any means is justified because *my* end is good. Indeed, it is to fall lower than this in the moral scale because it amounts to saying: "The mere survival of my country at any cost and by any means in a naked struggle for power is justified." It is to enthrone the doctrine of military necessity as the moral imperative and to deny, utterly and finally, that "he who seeketh his life shall lose it."

There is a curious quirk in the thinking of people today. They will witness several world wars, as my generation has, and yet continue preparations for atomic and biological war, having from experience of the loss of life involved in past wars a frightening notion of what human as well as material cost future war will entail. Then somebody proposes that nonviolence would be a better way and they say, "But somebody might get killed!"

This familiar argument shows what an almost unbreakable hold the war pattern has on the thinking of people. Somehow the slaughter of untold millions in war seems rational or inevitable to them and "somebody might get killed" is conclusive ground for giving no further thought to a method the efficacy of which Gandhi demonstrated in at least one great political struggle. In almost any other realm, people would have open minds to some further experimenting with the new method. In this realm the U.S. government will have a $50,000,000 military budget and not appropriate a nickel for research in nonviolence, and many persons, including intellectual and spiritual leaders, either accept this outright or then go along after making a feeble protest which is dignified as "critical support of the war policy." What a rut for thinking to be in at what is probably the most critical moment in human history. What *faith* in material things and military means is here revealed!

If men are not willing to practice the way of nonviolence with the same kind of commitment and recklessness of cost or consequences as they practice the way of war and as Communists work for Communism, clearly nonviolence will not work.

Martin Buber

believes that genuine dialogue between people can overcome conflict

MARTIN BUBER [1878-   ], *a Jewish theologian and philosopher, is a cultural Zionist rather than a political one. He was born in Vienna, raised in Galicia, and studied in Vienna, Berlin and Zurich. After Hitler's rise to power in Germany, Buber moved to Jerusalem and joined the faculty of the Hebrew University. He is known as an interpreter of modern Jewish thought to the non-Jewish world. "You cannot truly love God," he writes, "if you do not love your fellow man, and you cannot truly love your fellow man if you do not love God." The address that follows was given September 27, 1953, when Dr. Buber was awarded the Peace Prize of the German Book Trade at Frankfurt am Main, in Paulskirche.*

Hearkening to the human voice, where it speaks forth unfalsified, and replying to it, this above all is needed today. The busy noise of the hour must no longer drown out the *vox humana,* the essence of the human which has become a voice. This voice must not only be listened to, it must be answered and led out of the lonely monologue into the awakening dialogue of the peoples. Peoples must engage in talk with one another through their truly human men if the great peace is to appear and the devastated life of the earth renew itself.

The great peace is something essentially different from the absence of war.

In an early mural in the town hall of Sienna the civic virtues are assembled. Worthy, and conscious of their worth, the women sit there, except one in their midst who towers above the rest. This woman is marked not by dignity but rather by composed majesty. Three letters announce her name: Pax. She represents the great peace I have in mind. This peace does not signify that what men call war no longer exists now that it holds sway—that means too little to enable one to understand this serenity. Something new exists, now really exists, greater and mightier than war, greater and mightier even than war. Human passions flow into war as the waters into the sea, and war disposes of them as it likes. But these passions must enter into the great peace as ore into the fire that melts and transforms it. Peoples will then build with one another with more powerful zeal than they have ever destroyed one another.

The Siennese painter had glimpsed this majestic peace in his dream alone. He did not acquire the vision from historical reality, for it has never appeared there. What in history has been called peace has never, in fact, been aught other than an anxious or an illusory blissful pause between wars. But the womanly genius of the painter's dream is no mistress of interruptions but the queen of new and greater deeds.

May we, then, cherish the hope that the countenance which has remained unknown to all previous history will shine forth on our late generation, apparently sunk irretrievably in disaster? Are we not accustomed to describe the world situation in which we have lived since the end of the Second World War no longer even as peace but as the "cold" phase of a world war declared in permanence? In a situation which no longer even seeks to preserve the appearance of peace, is it not illusory enthusiasm to speak of a great peace which has never existed being within reach?

It is the depth of our crisis that allows us to hope in this way. Ours is not a historically familiar malady in the life of peoples which can eventuate in a comfortable recovery. Primal forces are now being summoned to take an active part in an unrepeatable decision between extinction and rebirth. War has not produced this crisis; it is, rather, the crisis of man which has brought forth the total war and the unreal peace which followed.

War has always had an adversary who hardly ever comes forward as such but does his work in the stillness. This adversary is speech, fulfilled speech, the speech of genuine conversation in which men understand one another and come to a mutual understanding. Already in primitive warfare fighting begins where speech has ceased; that is, where men are no longer able to discuss with one another the subjects under dispute or submit them to mediation, but flee from speech with one another and in the speechlessness of slaughter seek what they suppose to be a decision, a judgment of God. War soon conquers speech and enslaves it in the service of its battle cries. But where speech, be it ever so shy, moves from camp to camp, war is already called in question. Its cannon easily drown out the word; but when the word has become entirely soundless, and on this side and on that soundlessly bears into the hearts of men the intelligence that no human conflict can really be resolved through killing, not even through mass killing, then the human word has already begun to silence the cannonade.

But it is just the relation of man to speech and to conversation that the crisis characteristic of our age has in particular tended to shatter. The man in crisis will no longer entrust his cause to conversation because its presupposition—trust—is lacking. This is the reason why the cold war which today goes by the name of peace has been able to overcome mankind. In every earlier period of peace the living word has passed between man and man, time after time drawing the poison from the antagonism

of interests and convictions so that these antagonisms have not degenerated into the absurdity of "no-farther," into the madness of "must-wage-
war." This living word of human dialogue that from time to time makes
its flights until the madness smothers it, now seems to have become life-
less in the midst of the nonwar. The debates between statesmen which
the radio conveys to us no longer have anything in common with a human conversation: the diplomats do not address one another but the face-
less public. Even the congresses and conferences which convene in the
name of mutual understanding lack the substance which alone can elevate the deliberations to genuine talk: candor and directness in address
and answer. What is concentrated there is only the universal condition
in which men are no longer willing or no longer able to speak directly to
their fellows. They are not able to speak directly because they no longer
trust one another, and everybody knows that the other no longer trusts
him. If anyone in the hubbub of contradictory talk happens to pause and
take stock, he discovers that in his relations to others hardly anything
persists that deserves to be called trust.

And yet this must be said again and again, it is just the depth of the
crisis that empowers us to hope. Let us dare to grasp the situation with
that great realism that surveys all the definable realities of public life, of
which, indeed, public life appears to be composed, but is also aware
of what is most real of all, albeit moving secretly in the depths—the latent
healing and salvation in the face of impending ruin. The power of turning that radically changes the situation, never reveals itself outside of crisis. This power begins to function when one, gripped by despair, instead
of allowing himself to be submerged, calls forth his primal powers and
accomplishes with them the turning of his very existence. It happens in
this way both in the life of the person and in that of the race. In its depths
the crisis demands naked decision: no mere fluctuation between getting
worse and getting better, but a decision between the decomposition and
the renewal of the tissue.

The crisis of man which has become apparent in our day announces
itself most clearly as a crisis of trust, if we may employ, thus intensified,
a concept of economics. You ask, trust in whom? But the question already contains a limitation not admissible here. It is simply trust that is
increasingly lost to men of our time. And the crisis of speech is bound
up with this loss of trust in the closest possible fashion, for I can only
speak to someone in the true sense of the term if I expect him to accept
my word as genuine. Therefore, the fact that it is so difficult for present-
day man to pray (note well: not to hold it to be true that there is a God,
but to address him) and the fact that it is so difficult for him to carry on
a genuine talk with his fellow men are elements of a single set of facts.
This lack of trust in Being, this incapacity for unreserved intercourse

with the other, points to an innermost sickness of the sense of existence. One symptom of this sickness, and the most acute of all, is the one from which I have begun: that a genuine word cannot arise between the camps.

Can such an illness be healed? I believe it can be. And it is out of this, my belief, that I speak to you. I have no proof for this belief. No belief can be proved; otherwise it would not be what it is, a great venture. Instead of offering proof, I appeal to that potential belief of each of my hearers which enables him to believe.

If there be a cure, where can the healing action start: Where must that existential turning begin which the healing powers, the powers of salvation in the ground of the crisis, await?

That peoples can no longer carry on authentic dialogue with one another is not only the most acute symptom of the pathology of our time, it is also that which most urgently makes a demand of us. I believe, despite all, that the peoples in this hour can enter into dialogue, into a genuine dialogue with one another. In a genuine dialogue each of the partners, even when he stands in opposition to the other, heeds, affirms and confirms his opponent as an existing other. Only so can conflict certainly not only be eliminated from the world, but be humanly arbitrated and led toward its overcoming.

To the task of initiating this conversation those are inevitably called who carry on today within each people the battle against the antihuman. Those who build the great unknown front across mankind shall make it known by speaking unreservedly with one another, not overlooking what divides them but determined to bear this division in common.

In opposition to them stands the element that profits from the divisions between the peoples, the contrahuman in men, the subhuman, the enemy of man's will to become a true humanity.

The name Satan means in Hebrew "the hinderer." That is the correct designation for the antihuman in individuals and in the human race. Let us not allow this Satanic element in men to hinder us from realizing man! Let us release speech from its ban! Let us dare, despite all, to trust!

Vinoba Bhave

is not afraid of world wars, but rather of small wars and quarrels

VINOBA BHAVE [c. 1894-   ] *is considered by many people to be the new Gandhi. He is an Indian mystic who was Gandhi's first choice to be arrested and imprisoned during India's civil disobedience campaign in 1942. Bhave initiated the* Bhoodan *(land-gift) movement. "While God keeps strength in me," he has said, "I shall tour the country and beg for land for the landless." In 1949 at the World Pacifist meeting in the Sevagram session, Bhave spoke on "The True Nature of* Ahimsa *and Our Duty."*

The power that drew you here has ceased to exist today in physical form, but it is my daily experience that in its spiritual form it is present here even more than before. Had Bapu been alive, he would have offered you the nectar of his spiritual thoughts. It is not given to us to offer you that. But you can see the little work we are doing here. The defects that you may discover—and there are many—are all ours; and if you see any good therein, take it that it springs from the immortal nectar of his thoughts.

Ahimsa is not merely nonparticipation in destructive activities; it principally manifests itself in constructive activities—services which lead to the upward growth of man. People say that the Goddess of Ahimsa has no weapons; I say that that is wrong. The Goddess of Ahimsa has very powerful weapons at her command. They are the weapons of love and are, therefore, creative and not destructive. Yet they do destroy; they destroy hatred, inequity, hunger and disease. It is true, however, that the weapons of *ahimsa* look small in size and slow in action.

People say that these small tools of ours will not work in this machine age. But we gave them a trial and found by experience that they do work even in this machine age. We plied the spinning wheel and the hand mill and we found that in spite of the machine age, the wheel gave us the yarn and the hand mill the flour. Then we went further with the experiment and you can see some of the results.

Our main shortcoming is that we have not yet been able to identify ourselves fully with the poor around us. As far as I can see, this is not possible so long as we do not give up our dependence on money and do not rely completely on body labor. We do perform a certain amount of body labor, but it is not enough. We should pledge ourselves to earn our bread through body labor alone, and free ourselves from dependence on money. Without this, *ahimsa* can never manifest itself as a great power. I believe to the very letter what Jesus Christ said (and would paraphrase it thus): "It is easier for a camel to pass through the eye of a needle than for the rich (one attached to money) to enter heaven (i.e., realize *ahimsa*)," however much he may profess it by mouth. My mind is working on these lines in these days. I am trying to think out how we may put this principle into immediate practice. I am trying to persuade my friends to leave money alone and get going with production. It is yet to be seen how far I shall succeed in this.

Now let me briefly place before you what I think about world peace. The whole world today is thinking of a third world war and if we continue to think about it constantly, it may well come about. But I am not afraid of world wars. I am rather afraid of small wars and quarrels. To me a world war appears to come very close to nonviolence. I always say to friends who believe in violence, "If by reason of your faith [in violence], you cannot take the vow of nonviolence, do not bother about it. But at least take this vow, that if you fight at all, you will fight world wars, and that you will on no account fight small wars or busy yourselves with petty quarrels." I have even said that world wars are from God. When we do not understand what is right straightaway, the all-merciful God sends world war to free man's mind from limitations and make him think in terms of humanity as a whole. This is a big step forward toward *ahimsa*. But this is not true of small wars. They are the sworn enemies of *ahimsa* and all the time push *ahimsa* further and further away. We therefore ought to be on our guard against these. Those who believe in violence are not unaware of this. Their effort, therefore, is to prevent world wars as far as possible and to go on with small wars.

Once we realize that *ahimsa* has mainly to fear from local and small wars, our task becomes easy and we get the right direction. That sets us to the service of the people around us and we endeavor to see that there is no discord within our field of service. Then we turn our eyes inward, and realize the need for the purification of our minds. This leads us to the right solution of our problems. But if our minds always dwell on the bogey of world wars we do not get down to the root of the matter, but become involved in superficial thinking and external organizations only.

This leads me to my views about organization. . . . "If along with service, we purify our lives, we may become receptacles of God's light. After all, it is he who will achieve it. We can only be tools in his hands. But in order to be such tools, we must be altogether humble, and reduce ourselves to zero. But mere organization cannot produce the light of nonviolence. It can be produced only through the purification of life." Very often we think of *ahimsa*, but do so in terms of *himsa*. None the less, use of wrong words leads us astray. For instance, we speak of an army of peace. We think that we should maintain a standing army of peace so that it could be detailed immediately to offer resistance and self-immolation whenever there is a breach of peace in any part of the world. But here is a point that needs thought. The farther you send an army of violence the better for it; for its duty is to hate. Therefore, the less it knows its opponents or the more false its notions about them are, the more intense will be its hatred. But in nonviolence we have to conquer through love. Therefore, an army of peace can serve better only in a familiar field. What sort of an army would that be? It will be a band of social workers engaged in producing food by daily manual labor and in serving the afflicted, completely identifying itself with all fellow beings in a spirit of humility. What should be the weapons of this army? As described by St. Tulsidas in the *Ramayana,* and as Gandhiji has laid down in the rules of his *Ashram,* they are the vows of truth, nonviolence, self-control and the like. Call these observances weapons if you will, but it is an entirely different concept.

The light of *ahimsa* cannot be spread by the external and formal mechanism of organizations. History shows that Jesus came alone and the light that he brought pervaded the world—not through church institutions or "Christian" governments, but in spite of them. The light inspires us even today. The same is true of the Buddha. He was a prince but his message could not be spread by the authority of the state. It spread because he threw his kingdom away like a wisp of straw.

After all, what is it that will spread nonviolence? It is not the body that can do it, for the body is an embodiment of violence. *Ahimsa* is assimilated to the extent one rises above one's body. Nonviolence is the natural state of the soul. What *ahimsa,* therefore, needs is the quest of the spirit, the purification of the mind, service of living creatures, love universal and fearlessness. This has become with me such an unshakable conviction that I keep on telling myself in the words of St. Francis: "Do not get entangled in organizations."

I do not wish to dilate upon these ideas at length. You are all men of experience and have made your own experiments. In all humility I have briefly placed my ideas before you and you will please take whatever you find worthy of consideration.

You have come here with great faith in the hope of gaining something from this country. I believe that your hopes will not be belied. "I look upon the world with the eye of friendship, so that the world may also look on me with the same eye." This is the message of the Vedas given to India in very ancient times. In historical times, the Lord Buddha by his life revealed the same truth in this country. Although we have not yet been able to put it into practice satisfactorily, still history bears witness that even in its days of power and glory, India hardly ever invaded another country. It comes easily to an ordinary Indian villager to think of all men as brothers, while the idea of nationalism does not come easily to him. And it is in the villages that real India lives. Even in the worst days of the British government's oppression in this country, our great national poet was busily engaged in founding a world university at Santiniketan, The Abode of Peace, and singing songs of universal love, and our political leader taught us lessons in *ahimsa* and strictly forbade the use of violence even for the winning of freedom. We made many mistakes, but we lived and worked for thirty years within the limitations set by him. It is but natural, therefore, if you expect something from this country.

The question is: In which direction are we going after the passing away of Gandhiji? Also, in which direction is our government going? I cannot speak of the future. But as I see things today, I feel consolation that Gandhiji's best colleague, Pandit Jawaharlal Nehru, leads our country at present. Whatever may be the shortcomings of his government in internal affairs, its whole weight so far as international affairs are concerned, is thrown on the side of world peace and the freedom of all nations.

None the less, our people do feel some darkness after Gandhiji's death. Some feel that we have perhaps begun to forget Bapu. The fact is, that they to whom this remark might apply never cared for Bapu's principles even during his lifetime; but those who had enshrined him in their hearts have not forgotten him. Even so there *is* darkness, and I think that the reason is that we remember Bapu too much. Whenever there is an occasion for some deliberation our first thought is always: What did Bapu say or do in such a situation? This manner of thinking sometimes throws us into darkness instead of leading us toward light. But this will not go on for long. Gradually we shall begin to think for ourselves about *ahimsa* and have courage to make new experiments on our own account. Even if that does not come about, there is no great cause for anxiety because by God's grace we too shall not live forever. He will take us away and will send others in our place, who will think with fresh minds. They will become God's instruments and will carry on the work so dear to his heart, until *ahimsa* pervades the world. Therefore, please do cherish hopes about India. It is this hope of yours which makes us weaklings strong; and how can hope, which gives strength even to the weak, fail to make the hopeful all the more strong?

Norbert Wiener

*points out that to provide scientific information is
not necessarily an innocent act*

NORBERT WIENER [1894-   ], one of the United States' out-
standing mathematicians, has been at the Massachusetts Institute of
Technology since 1919. During the Second World War, Professor
Wiener did research for the United States government in the field of
guided missiles. A scientist of an aircraft corporation queried Professor
Wiener for the technical account of a certain line of research that he had
conducted in the war. He refused the request with the letter that follows.
It later appeared—in January 1947—in The Atlantic Monthly.

SIR:

I have received from you a note in which you state that you are
engaged in a project concerning controlled missiles, and in which you
request a copy of a paper which I wrote for the National Defense Research Committee during the war.

As the paper is the property of a government organization, you are
of course at complete liberty to turn to that government organization
for such information as I could give you. If it is out of print as you say,
and they desire to make it available for you, there are doubtless proper
avenues of approach to them.

When, however, you turn to me for information concerning controlled missiles, there are several considerations which determine my reply. In the past, the comity of scholars has made it a custom to furnish
scientific information to any person seriously seeking it. However, we
must face these facts: The policy of the government itself during and after the war, say in the bombing of Hiroshima and Nagasaki, has made it
clear that to provide scientific information is not a necessarily innocent
act, and may entail the gravest consequences. One therefore cannot escape reconsidering the established custom of the scientist to give information to every person who may inquire of him. The interchange of ideas
which is one of the great traditions of science must of course receive certain limitations when the scientist becomes an arbiter of life and death.

For the sake, however, of the scientist and the public, these limitations should be as intelligent as possible. The measures taken during the
war by our military agencies, in restricting the free intercourse among
scientists on related projects or even on the same project, have gone so
far that it is clear that if continued in time of peace this policy will lead

to the total irresponsibility of the scientist, and ultimately to the death of science. Both of these are disastrous for our civilization, and entail grave and immediate peril for the public.

I realize, of course, that I am acting as the censor of my own ideas, and it may sound arbitrary, but I will not accept a censorship in which I do not participate. The experience of the scientists who have worked on the atomic bomb has indicated that in any investigation of this kind the scientist ends by putting unlimited powers in the hands of the people whom he is least inclined to trust with their use. It is perfectly clear also that to disseminate information about a weapon in the present state of our civilization is to make it practically certain that that weapon will be used. In that respect the controlled missile represents the still imperfect supplement to the atom bomb and to bacterial warfare.

The practical use of guided missiles can only be to kill foreign civilians indiscriminately, and it furnishes no protection whatsoever to civilians in this country. I cannot conceive a situation in which such weapons can produce any effect other than extending the kamikaze way of fighting to whole nations. Their possession can do nothing but endanger us by encouraging the tragic insolence of the military mind.

If therefore I do not desire to participate in the bombing or poisoning of defenseless peoples—and I most certainly do not—I must take a serious responsibility as to those to whom I disclose my scientific ideas. Since it is obvious that with sufficient effort you can obtain my material, even though it is out of print, I can only protest *pro forma* in refusing to give you any information concerning my past work. However, I rejoice at the fact that my material is not readily available, inasmuch as it gives me the opportunity to raise this serious moral issue. I do not expect to publish any future work of mine which may do damage in the hands of irresponsible militarists.

I am taking the liberty of calling this letter to the attention of other people in scientific work. I believe it is only proper that they should know of it in order to make their own independent decisions, if similar situations should confront them.

Emil Brunner

perceives that war has begun to outlive its purpose

EMIL BRUNNER [1889-   ] *is a Swiss Protestant theologian of Fundamentalist principles whose theology has been compared with that of Karl Barth. He is a professor of theology at the University of Zurich in Switzerland. The selection here is from his book* The Divine Imperative, *published in 1947.*

When the necessity for war is argued from the point of view of history, the supporters of this view entirely overlook the fact that we have reached a point in history at which all analogies drawn from the past break down. The nations have been brought into such close contact with one another, the world has become, to such a large extent, an economic and cultural unity, the idea of an organic connection between the nations has become such a reality that our traditional political conceptions have become useless. The relation of the nations to one another is already so close—not primarily through ethical developments but through purely natural developments—that it is now far more like that relation which used to exist between the tribes of one people, than like that which till recently existed between the nations, and still forms the basis of our political thought. Objective interest in the abolition of war is today greater than all national interests, however justifiable, exactly, as for instance, some time ago the interest in the creation of the unified national state was greater than even the most justifiable interest of the individual tribes. The process of combining in order to form a greater unity is always costly—even the process of forming the present national states cost a great deal; and yet we know that it was inevitable. The hour has now come when a further step toward combination must be taken; for already the one prime necessity of avoiding war—and indeed all that the "next war" would mean—demands it. . . .

To attempt to outline any scheme of the way in which this universal unity is to be attained, however, would be to indulge in purely fanciful speculation. One fact alone can be indicated as moving in the right direction; that is, the development of international law, which is a big step toward this unity. To a great extent—and indeed to a hitherto unparalleled extent—the law of the jungle among the nations has already been overcome, both as the result of purely natural developments and under the influence of Christian thought. In a few decades, to an extent which was wholly unexpected, the administration of international justice has become a fact; the altered temper of the nations has gained an expression, in their estimate of war, which, although it does not yet mean very much in the political sphere, is all the more significant as a sign of the direction in which thought is moving. The nations are beginning to perceive—obviously before their theologians!—that war has begun to outlive its purpose, that war is a way of putting an end to international tension which the world can no longer afford, that the unqualified sovereignty of individual nations no longer corresponds to the actual conditions, that the only alternative to race suicide is the nonmilitary way of settling difficulties between nations. Where war has reached this stage of development it has lost every particle of ethical justification.

To claim that war is the *ultima ratio* of politics is simply a superstition. This is the case only so long as one nation must fear that another will not renounce this *ultima ratio*. Conflict between groups of human beings will last so long as these groups exist; conflict between nations would exist even if war never came into consideration as a method at all, because everyone was convinced of its suicidal character; conflict would still exist, even if the idea that it was possible to protect one's nation by force of arms were seen to be an illusion. We have no idea what the substitute for war would be. We cannot play the part of Providence, but ethical reflection is called to meet the new facts with new ways of thought. Therefore, if a nation were to disarm, and render itself "defenseless"—in the old sense of the world—in order to prepare the way for the new form of "security," such action would not be a sign of political folly but of political wisdom, since it would demonstrate the possibility of a new way of political action. Again, when conscientious and politically sane citizens refuse to render a service to the state which used to be considered a very real service, but has now, in their opinion, become politically useless, they show political wisdom; this is shown by the fact that they regard this refusal as the command of God to them, not in the legalistic sense of fanatics, but in the concrete sense of political responsibility—that is, in a quite different sense from those who refuse this service simply on the ground of the command: "Thou shalt not kill," or on the basis of the Sermon on the Mount. They will bear witness to this new point of view by taking without complaint the punishment imposed upon them by the state, knowing well that the state does not yet see what they see, and thus that it regards what they are doing as service to the state as "a refusal to serve."

When a new order is struggling to come into being and to shake off the shackles of the old order, the idea of order itself begins to waver, and this leads to hesitation about the ethical obligation of obedience to the state. An ethical right to revolution which can be expressed in general terms does not exist; but the necessity does arise of making a choice between the new order which is coming into being and the old order which is falling into decay. Even the Christian cannot evade this necessity, for no one can. Where the old order no longer performs its service of providing for order a new order is necessary, whose "tragedy" consists in the fact that it must first of all do away with the old "order," that it may establish real order in place of a sham order. In itself it is impossible to justify revolution from the ethical point of view even when it takes place for the sake of a better order, for it elevates anarchy to the level of a principle, and in so doing it destroys the basis of all morality. But just as the duty of obedience to the state is always qualified by obedience to God's command, so also it is qualified by the possibility that God intends to destroy the old order because it has degenerated into a sham. But only unavoidable necessity will avail to protect this dangerous action from the reproach of rebellion against God.

Kirby Page

reminds nations that the only defense against atomic war is the prevention of all war

KIRBY PAGE [1890-1957] *has been described by* The New York Times *as "an itinerant social evangelist for peace." In 1915 he was ordained a minister of the Disciples of Christ. But throughout his life he spent more time preaching the gospel of peace than he did as a minister of the church. He was assistant secretary for the Y.M.C.A. in Houston, and in 1916-17 was a Y.M.C.A. worker in France and England. From 1926-34, he edited* The World Tomorrow, *and then became a contributing editor to* The Christian Century. *He was also vice-chairman of the Fellowship of Reconciliation. "War in the Atomic Age," written in 1946, is part of a chapter from* Now Is the Time to Prevent a Third World War.

A nation's preparedness to wage atomic war will have disastrous effects upon its relations with other peoples, through increased suspicion, deeper fear, more bitter enmity, and counterpreparedness to wage atomic war. So long as nations and alliances are frantically preparing to annihilate enemies with atomic energy, mutual aid in the solution of common problems on an adequate scale will be impossible. Effective forms of international government can never be operated so long as nations are preparing to wage war. The international mind and the international heart can never function adequately so long as the race of atomic armaments continues. Preparedness to wage war with these new weapons will perpetuate anarchy among the nations and will surely lead to a suicidal third world war if it is continued. It will be sheer madness to engage in a race of atomic armaments.

A nation's preparedness to wage atomic war will also have devastating consequences upon its own scale of values and code of morals. It will be morally paralyzing for America to prepare for the mass promiscuous killing of millions of human beings in Soviet Russia or in some other land. If we indoctrinate the youth of our land with the idea that they must be ready to kill Russian wives and babies in order to protect their own families, we will thereby destroy the very foundations of high morality. All exalted concepts of morality are based on reverence for human life and recognition of human solidarity. A low estimate of the worth of human life is essential to the training of our young men in the science of human slaughter.

The spiritual effects of preparedness to massacre millions of human beings are even more appalling. Every basic doctrine of Christianity is nullified to the degree that we accept the ideas and practices of atomic war: the fatherhood of God, the brotherhood of man, the inestimable value of human life, the kinship of all peoples, the duty and privilege of sympathy and compassion and affection, the responsibility of the strong to bear the burdens of the weak, the overcoming of evil with goodness, the redemptive power of self-giving forgiving love, the supremacy of spiritual forces over material might. We can take Jesus seriously and strive earnestly to follow him, or we can prepare to wage atomic war, but it is utterly impossible to do both at the same time.

The only defense against the ravages of atomic war is the prevention of that war through mutual aid in the solution of common problems under a reign of international law functioning through appropriate agencies of world government undergirded by mutual understanding and mutual confidence.

Albert Camus

visualizes an endless struggle between violence and friendly persuasion

ALBERT CAMUS [1913-1960], *essayist, playwright, novelist, won the Nobel Prize for Literature in 1957. He was born in eastern Algeria of illiterate parents, and went to France when he was 23. When France was taken by the Germans in 1940, Camus played an important role in the French resistance movement, first in Lyons, then in Paris. He was editorial writer for* Combat, *a daily newspaper of the French Resistance, where this article first appeared in 1946.*

Yes, we must raise our voices. Up to this point, I have refrained from appealing to emotion. We are being torn apart by a logic of history which we have elaborated in every detail—a net which threatens to strangle us. It is not emotion which can cut through the web of a logic which has gone to irrational lengths, but only reason which can meet logic on its own ground. But I should not want to leave the impression . . . that any program for the future can get along without our powers of love and indignation. I am well aware that it takes a powerful prime mover to get men into motion and that it is hard to throw one's self into a struggle whose objectives are so modest and where hope has only a rational basis —and hardly even that. But the problem is not how to carry men away; it is essential, on the contrary, that they not be carried away but rather that they be made to understand clearly what they are doing.

To save what can be saved so as to open up some kind of future— that is the prime mover, the passion and the sacrifice that is required. It demands only that we reflect and then decide, clearly, whether humanity's lot must be made still more miserable in order to achieve far-off and shadowy ends, whether we should accept a world bristling with arms where brother kills brother; or whether, on the contrary, we should avoid bloodshed and misery as much as possible so that we give a chance for survival to later generations better equipped than we are.

For my part, I am fairly sure that I have made the choice. And, having chosen, I think that I must speak out, that I must state that I will never again be one of those, whoever they be, who compromise with murder, and that I must take the consequences of such a decision. The thing is done, and that is as far as I can go at present. . . . However, I want to make clear the spirit in which this article is written.

We are asked to love or to hate such and such a country and such and such a people. But some of us feel too strongly our common humanity to make such a choice. Those who really love the Russian people, in gratitude for what they have never ceased to be—that world leaven which Tolstoy and Gorky speak of—do not wish for them success in power politics, but rather want to spare them, after the ordeals of the past, a new and even more terrible bloodletting. So, too, with the American people, and with the peoples of unhappy Europe. This is the kind of elementary truth we are likely to forget amidst the furious passions of our time.

Yes, it is fear and silence and the spiritual isolation they cause that must be fought today. And it is sociability (*"le dialogue"*) and the universal intercommunication of men that must be defended. Slavery, injustice and lies destroy this intercourse and forbid this sociability; and so we must reject them. But these evils are today the very stuff of history, so that many consider them necessary evils. It is true that we cannot "escape history," since we are in it up to our necks. But one may propose to fight within history to preserve from history that part of man which is not its proper province. That is all I have to say here. The "point" of this article may be summed up as follows:

Modern nations are driven by powerful forces along the roads of power and domination. I will not say that these forces should be furthered or that they should be obstructed. They hardly need our help and, for the moment, they laugh at attempts to hinder them. They will, then, continue. But I will ask only this simple question: What if these forces wind up in a dead end, what if that logic of history on which so many now rely turns out to be a will o' the wisp? What if, despite two or three world wars, despite the sacrifice of several generations and a whole system of values, our grandchildren—supposing they survive—find themselves no closer to a world society? It may well be that the survivors of such an experience will be too weak to understand their own sufferings. Since these forces are working themselves out and since it is inevitable that they continue to do so, there is no reason why some of us should not take on the job of keeping alive, through the apocalyptic historical vista that stretches before us, a modest thoughtfulness which, without pretending to solve everything, will constantly be prepared to give some human meaning to everyday life. The essential thing is that people should carefully weigh the price they must pay. . . .

All I ask is that, in the midst of a murderous world, we agree to reflect on murder and to make a choice. After that, we can distinguish those who accept the consequences of being murderers themselves or the accomplices of murderers, and those who refuse to do so with all their force and being. Since this terrible dividing line does actually exist, it will be a gain if it be clearly marked. Over the expanse of five continents throughout the coming years an endless struggle is going to be pursued between violence and friendly persuasion, a struggle in which, granted, the former has a thousand times the chances of success than that of the latter. But I have always held that, if he who bases his hopes on human nature is a fool, he who gives up in the face of circumstances is a coward. And henceforth, the only honorable course will be to stake everything on a formidable gamble: that words are more powerful than munitions.

Albert Einstein

believes a permanent peace cannot be prepared by threats

ALBERT EINSTEIN [1879-1955] *won a 1921 Nobel Prize for his work in theoretical physics. He had been born in Germany, but when Hitler took power Einstein left the country to become a United States citizen. In 1939 he wrote President Franklin D. Roosevelt that it would be possible to produce a nuclear bomb, but he himself never worked directly on the research project which developed the bomb. He had become a pacifist during World War I, and the horrors of the explosions over Hiroshima and Nagasaki only deepened his convictions. For a time he was honorary chairman of the War Resisters International, and after the Second World War he played a prominent role in the world-government movement. On May 29, 1946, Dr. Einstein delivered the radio address that follows to a Chicago rally of the Students for Federal World Government.*

I have been deeply impressed with a talk I had with three students from the University of Chicago. It made me realize that there is indeed a sense of responsibility and initiative at work among the younger generation in this country. These students fully realize that the destiny of their generation will be decided in the next few years. And they are resolved to exert as much influence as they can on the course of events.

Just what is the situation? The development of technology and military weapons has resulted in what amounts to a shrinking of our planet. Economic intercourse between countries has made the nations of the world more dependent upon one another than ever before. The offensive weapons now available leave no spot on earth secure from sudden, total annihilation. Our only hope for survival lies in the creation of a world government capable of resolving conflicts among nations by judicial verdict. Such decisions must be based upon a precisely worded constitution which is approved by all governments. The world government alone may have offensive arms at its disposal. No person or nation can be regarded as pacifist unless they agree that all military power should be concentrated in the hands of a supranational authority, and unless they renounce force as a means of safeguarding their interests against other nations.

Political developments, in this first year since the end of the Second World War, have clearly brought us no closer to the attainment of these goals. The present Charter of the United Nations does not provide either for the legal institutions or the military forces which would be necessary to bring real international security into being. Nor does it take into account the actual balance of power in the world today. Real power is today concentrated in a few hands. It is no exaggeration to say that the solution of the crucial problem depends solely upon the achievement of a far-sighted agreement between this country and Russia. If such an agreement were brought about, these two powers alone would be able to prevail upon all other nations to renounce their sovereignty to the degree necessary for the attainment of universal military security.

Many people say that, in the present circumstances, fundamental agreement between the United States and the Soviet Union is impossible. Such an assertion might be justified had America made a really serious effort in that direction since the end of the war. It seems to me that America has done just the opposite: It was not wise to admit Fascist Argentina into the United Nations over Russia's protest. Further, there was no need to keep on producing more and more atomic bombs and to spend twelve billion dollars in a single year on armaments, when there was no military threat in sight. Nor was there any sense in denying Trieste to Yugoslavia, a former ally who was in real need of this port that has, in fact, little economic significance to Italy, a former enemy country. There is no point in further enumerating all the details which indicate that nothing was done by the United Nations to mollify Russia's distrust. In fact, we have done much toward fostering this distrust which the events of the last several decades make only too understandable.

Enduring peace will come about, not by countries continuing to threaten one another, but only through an honest effort to create mutual trust. One should assume that the desire to bring about decent conditions for mankind on this planet as well as the fear of unspeakable annihilation would render those in positions of responsibility wiser and more dispassionate. But you cannot wait for this to happen, my young friends. You must attempt to galvanize the younger generation into insisting on a far-sighted policy of peace. If you do that, you will not only achieve effective protection for yourselves; you will deserve the gratitude of your country and of posterity to a larger degree than any generation before you.

[*In addition to this broadcast to the Chicago student rally, Einstein was interviewed by Paul Arthur Schilpp, Professor of Philosophy at Northwestern University, and by a student officer of the National Organization of Student Federalists.*]

Q (by Professor Schilpp): Professor Einstein, what, precisely, is the real difference between world government and the United Nations Organization? . . .

A: By world government I understand an institution whose decisions and rules are binding upon the individual member states. . . . In its present form the United Nations does not possess the powers of a world government, because its decisions and judgments have no binding power over the individual member states.

Q (by student leader): . . . My fellow students and I would very much like to know what you think we, the future leaders of the world, can do to achieve a federation of the world such as the original thirteen states achieved in this country 160 years ago.

A: First of all, the younger generation must ascertain what minimal conditions must be met to stop future military threats among the various nations or a combination of nations. The next task would be to spread this knowledge throughout the country. The third task would require the kind of organizational activity that would influence the members of Congress and the individual state assemblies in a way which reflects the will of the people on the subject of peace.

Q (by Professor Schilpp): Do you believe that mutual envy and hatred among nations can be overcome by a world government?

A: No, of course not. But a world government would be able to prevent such natural emotional reactions from leading to acts of violence among nations.

Q (by student leader): Does any other industrial country in the world possess the natural resources and scientific ability to produce atomic weapons?

A: Other countries, undoubtedly, command enough such resources and ability to constitute an unending and intolerable threat to each other.

Q (by Professor Schilpp): From this last answer, Professor Einstein, I take it that you, who know as much as any living person about the threat of atomic bombs to the future of humanity, consider the establishment of real world government an inescapable necessity to be realized at the earliest possible moment.

A: There can no longer be any doubt about its being an absolute necessity. For this reason everything that is done in international affairs must be done from the viewpoint of whether it will advance or hinder the establishment of world government.

2

IN THE FACE OF FASCISM

[1933-1945]

The late twenties and early thirties had been an era of optimism among pacifists. Their theme was generally universal disarmament and support for the League of Nations. A few governments were proud to be called pacifistic.

Undergraduates at Oxford in England pledged that they would not fight for king or country under any circumstances. In America, the Rabbinical Assembly declared, "The world has risked so much for war. Let it risk as much for peace." A questionnaire sent to Protestant ministers in the United States revealed that 67 per cent of those who answered felt the church should neither support nor sanction any future war.

Pope Pius XI concluded his allocation to the Sacred College of Cardinals: "If peace is truly desired we invoke peace, we bless peace, we pray for peace. If by chance there should be some who, owing to the phenomenon of suicide and homicidal manner, truly prefer war to peace, then we have another prayer which it will become our duty to utter, and we would say to the Blessed Lord, 'Disperse the people who want war.' "

These were the peace voices of the early 1930s.

The peace movement was gaining momentum; its ranks were swelling with workers, intellectuals, students. Its adherents came from all the social, economic, and political strata of society. There were religious men and Communists, the uncompromising War Resisters International and the respectable Carnegie Endowment for International Peace.

The Intercollegiate Disarmament Council in the United States polled college campuses and reported that 39 per cent of the students who voted opposed involvement in any war; an additional 33 per cent said they would take part only if the country were attacked; and only 28 per cent said they would participate in any war that had the approval of the President and was declared by Congress. An editor of a college paper summed it up by saying, "It will take more than flag-waving and bugle-calls to empty the colleges for another war."

The active peace movement now had a strong international feeling. Groups were talking across national borders. When the War Resisters International held its triennial conference, twenty-one different countries were represented. Notable for their absence were Bolshevik Russia, Fascist Italy, and Nazi Germany.

The diversity in political, social and economic opinion of the various peace advocates brought a schism into the movement. It began to divide on the issue of the Spanish Civil War. Many who had called themselves pacifists but who were opposed only to imperialist or capitalist wars came out in defense of the Loyalist cause in Spain. They looked on the war there as the beginning of a second world war, and they felt that the defeat of Franco was imperative to the future peace of the world. In January 1937 Norman Thomas contended in *The Nation* that "the pacifism which makes mere abstention from war the supreme command will not deliver mankind from new cycles of war and new dark ages of oppression. It is unrealistic and mad to say that it does not matter who wins in Spain if only the guns are stilled. It matters profoundly not only for Spain but for mankind that the fascist aggression of which Franco is the nominal and brutal leader be defeated. Persons who believe this must support the gallant resistance of the workers and other loyalists."

The presence of fascism was making itself felt across Europe, and abroad. To many people it looked worse than war.

In 1934 A. A. Milne wrote his book *Peace with Honour*. He was determined to destroy the "conventional belief that war was an honourable way of settling international disputes." Six years later he felt different: "If anybody reads *Peace with Honour* now, he must read it with that one word *Hitler* scrawled across every page." *

Many people in the peace movement looked to Gandhi for the answer.

"Can the Jews resist this organized and shameless persecution?" Gandhi asked. "I am convinced that if someone with courage and vision can arise among them to lead them in nonviolent action, the winter of their despair can in the twinkling of an eye be turned into the summer of hope. And what has today become a degrading man-hunt can be turned into a calm and determined stand offered by unarmed men and women possessing the strength of suffering given to them by Jehovah."

But he disturbed pacifists who were looking for ways to justify the war they saw coming, when he said, "If ever there could be a justi-

* A. A. Milne, *War with Honour*, introduction.

fiable war in the name of and for humanity, a war against Germany, to prevent the wanton persecution of a whole race, would be completely justified. But I do not believe in any war. A discussion of the pros and cons of such a war is therefore outside my horizon and province." *

In anguish, Rabbi Judah Magnes wrote a letter to Gandhi from the Hebrew University in Jerusalem. "Your statement is a challenge, particularly to those of us who had imagined ourselves your disciples," he said. But the pros and cons of such a war disturbed him deeply. He asked Gandhi's guidance. "The question gives me no rest, and I am sure there are many like myself. Like you, I do not believe in any war. I have pledged myself never to take part in a war. I spoke up for pacifism in America during the [First] World War, alongside of many whose names are known to you. That war brought the 'peace' of Versailles and the Hitlerism of today. But my pacifism, as, I imagine, the pacifism of many others, is passing through a pitiless crisis.

"I ask myself: Suppose America, England, France are dragged into a war with the Hitler bestiality, what am I to do and what am I to teach? This war may destroy the life of a large part of the youth of the world, and force those who remain alive to lead the lives of savages. Yet I know I would pray with all my heart for the defeat of the Hitler inhumanity; and am I to stand aside and let others do the fighting? During the last war I prayed for peace without defeat or victory." †

Hayem Greenburg, writing in the *Jewish Frontier*, commented: "A Jewish Gandhi in Germany, should one arise, could 'function' for about five minutes—until the first Gestapo agent would lead him, not to a concentration camp, but directly to the guillotine."

Gandhi answered that this "will not disprove my case or shake my belief in the efficacy of *ahimsa* [nonviolence]." He admitted that "it is highly probable" that this would happen to a Jewish Gandhi in Germany. "I can conceive the necessity of the immolation of hundreds, if not thousands, to appease the hunger of dictators who have no belief in *ahimsa*. Indeed the maxim is that *ahimsa* is the most efficacious in front of the greatest *himsa*. Its quality is really tested only in such cases. Sufferers need not see the result during their lifetime. They must have faith that, if their cult survives, the result is a certainty. The method of violence gives no greater guarantee than that of nonviolence. It gives infinitely less. For the faith of the votary of *ahimsa* is lacking." ‡

The case was being prepared for another "just" war, at best a

* M. K. Gandhi, *Non-Violent Resistance*, pp. 348, 349.

† Judah L. Magnes, *In the Perplexity of the Times*, pp. 117, 122-23.

‡ M. K. Gandhi, *Non-Violence in Peace and War*, pp. 235-36.

"necessary" war. Perhaps no war has ever produced so many individuals who at one time or another in their lives had vowed never to fight again, and then with the first trumpets found reasons as to why *this* war was different.

The voices opposing the Second World War were far scarcer than those that had spoken out against World War I. Old-time pacifists who had withstood the crisis of 1917 were now "reluctantly" fighting a war against aggression and savagery. Bertrand Russell, for example, who favored conscientious objection to military service in the first war, supported his government in World War II.

But there were some who maintained their nonviolent outlook; they served in prisons, in various service camps, and proudly wore the Conscientious Objector label. Many of these came from historic peace churches; others from the secular pacifists: socialists, anarchists, war resisters.

For those who served in the prisons, those who opposed the war, the Hiroshima bomb only fortified the conviction that war is not the answer to the settlement of international tension.

Arthur Wiser

explains why he walked out of Civilian Public Service camp No. 94

ARTHUR WISER [1920-   ] *was born and schooled in India, where his parents were American missionaries. In the United States during the Second World War, Wiser refused the draft and was put in Civilian Public Service camp. After thirty-two months in three different camps, he and three others who felt the loss of the driving spirit that had made them useful, walked out of CPS camp in protest. Wiser was arrested on the day of Hiroshima and was sentenced to eighteen months' imprisonment. On October 19, 1945, he read the following statement to the judge.*

I appear in court for breaking a regulation of the Selective Service System by "walking out" of Civilian Public Service Camp No. 94 at Trenton, North Dakota.

As you can see from a letter which I sent to the Attorney General at the time I left camp, I left intentionally for what I consider moral reasons and am aware that I have violated federal law. I am not acquainted with legal method, but do not request legal assistance, largely because I am not appealing to the laws or the Constitution of the United States in defense of my action, but rather to a consideration of the needs of our time and necessary steps toward meeting them. My action is an application of the same principles of human responsibility and individual freedom that, I believe, were in the minds of those who framed the Constitution.

In my evaluation of the problems of our time, it had seemed to me that my greatest contribution could be made by healthful family living as a responsible citizen in close neighborly relationships with common folk. At the same time I would attempt to work out patterns for applying a philosophy of interdependence to local and world problems. I was gradually deciding to settle in Macedonia Cooperative Community in the hills of northeastern Georgia and had spent about fifteen months there, largely in contributed labor.

When the war came, I accepted induction into Civilian Public Service as inevitable for a pacifist. I was confused by such concepts as "this is an improvement in recognition for Conscientious Objectors over that in the last war," "in Civilian Public Service, pacifists can do constructive work in time of war," and "the majority of the people have the right to demand national service, either military or civilian, of the citizens of the country."

With only slight protest I sacrificed the things which I had thought fundamental in my own living—healthful family living, neighborliness to common folk, and the working out of new patterns of living—out of belief in the above concepts. I worked hard at the projects assigned me and spent altogether thirty-one months in the CPS program.

I now feel that CPS, as the internment of Conscientious Objectors by a wartime government, exists only to assert the state's authority to final jurisdiction over the individual to direct his living, even though professing to recognize a particular scruple of conscience. It was a serious mistake to abandon the constructive way of living which I felt would be my contribution to solving the complex problems facing us. It is in an attempt to rectify that mistake that I have left CPS to resume normal constructive living.

I am convinced that the work I am doing managing a dairy in a cooperative community and delivering milk to children as a part of a hot-lunch program is far more important than any work I've done in CPS, and am confident that anyone making a careful comparison would reach the same conclusion. While getting milk to children who did not have it before, some of whom could not secure it from any other source, I am at the same time assisting in the establishment of an agricultural pattern in the region which conserves the resources, am helping to demonstrate a more abundant economic method, am cooperating with county, state and national agencies to improve the region, and am establishing a family where our children will have sound values and a sense of security. In CPS I was doing few of these things and was chiefly a laborer without responsibility following the orders of government men above me. Perhaps the chief difference is that now as a husband and citizen I am working with my fellows using local resources to better our locality and in that way our part of the world, while in CPS as a conscript I was furthering reliance on government direction. The judgment of most people, I believe, would concur with mine with respect to the comparative value of the work I have just been doing and that which I left in CPS.

Though my position seems absolute, I think of my relation to the government in relative terms. Regulations vary in nature. When the regulations concern sanitary measures and traffic codes, for example, I often accede to the judgment of others even though it differs from mine. But such regulations do not require me to do something which I consider seriously harmful: they are in considerable contrast to the regulations demanding that I compromise my basic philosophy.

More important, the function of government itself is involved. Government can be defined as the organization of people for their mutual benefit, and much of our government activity is of that nature. In modern history, however, the chief function of the nation-state seems to be becoming one of preparation for and prosecution of war to the end of increasing its power relative to that of other nation-states. National conscription and heavy armament programs are becoming typical of the modern state. Instead of the state's being organized for the good of the people, the people are being organized for the good of the state. I believe that those parts of our government that are carrying us in that direction should be opposed rather than supported. I consider Selective Service to be such a part.

Since CPS is directed by the Selective Service System, I found myself participating in a program to which I was opposed on principle. It raised in my mind the question, Have the representatives of the government the right to demand that a person do something against his best judgment? Clearly they believed they had the right or even the responsibility to order me into CPS, regardless of my judgment—and their belief has been supported by the opinion of the Supreme Court with respect to assignment to CPS.

Legally, I am aware, I will be held at fault for disrespect to the law of the United States. I should like to pose for your consideration, however, the ethical problem which confronts me. The government's representatives have directed me to abandon what I consider my chief contribution to society in order to accept a pattern of activity (Civilian Public Service) and an assumption underlying it (the individual is at the government's disposal) which I consider ominously fascist. Am I to be responsible to the standards of action actively required by some and passively accepted by others in the country, or to my own judgment and standards of action?

This is a personal problem, but it is significant in relation to current world problems. It seems clear that one of the chief contributions to the crisis in Western civilization is the diminishing of individual responsibility and in its place the substitution of state direction and control. While it seems difficult to see this in our own country, it is easy enough to see in the Nazi and fascist developments in Germany and Italy. While the dangers of "anarchy" are easily seen and quickly mentioned, the dangers in conscript uniformity are obscured and little considered.

Lao-Tse says, "When people lost sight of the way to live came codes of love and honesty. . . ." So it seems to me that while our problems arise from individual exploitation, confusion and irresponsibility, people look to the state and compliance to the state's regulations for their solution. This serves to increase rather than solve the problems. In an essay, "The Responsibility of Peoples," Dwight MacDonald quotes a correspondent interviewing an official of a death camp captured by the Russian Army from the Germans.

> "*Q. Did you kill people in the Camp?*
> *A. Yes.*
> *Q. Did you poison them with gas?*
> *A. Yes.*
> *Q. Did you bury them alive?*
> *A. It sometimes happened.*
> *Q. Did you personally kill people?*
> *A. Absolutely not. I was only paymaster of the camp.*
> *Q. What did you think of what was going on?*
> *A. It was bad at first, but we got used to it.*
> *Q. Do you know the Russians will hang you?*
> *A. (Bursting into tears) Why should they? What have I done?"*

And MacDonald comments, "*What have I done?* These words ring true. One feels the worthy paymaster . . . is sincerely outraged by the proposal to hang him for his part in killing several million human beings. What had he done indeed? Simply obeyed orders and kept his mouth shut. It was what he had *not* done that shocks our moral sensibilities."

We can say that the paymaster was obligated to humanity above his obligation to his superiors and that he should have died, if need be, before he followed his orders. Yet how quickly we say that an individual has no right to make his own decisions when he opposes the opinion of the majority or the regulation of the United States government.

The paymaster's acquiescence to orders that at first repelled him made possible in part the functioning of the death camp. Even so, I believe, war and fascism are made possible by the acquiescence of large numbers of people to things to which they are at first opposed.

It has become clear to me that I am obligated to live in the manner which I believe right and to refuse to participate in any program or activity which I believe wrong. This may lead me into conflict with the contemporary government, but I believe it to be best in the long run for the people as a whole.

Evan Thomas

explains that peace can be demanded only on the basis of conscience

EVAN W. THOMAS [1890-   ], *the brother of Norman Thomas and now a well-known physician, was sentenced to life imprisonment for his refusal to serve in the United States armed forces during World War I. His sentence was commuted after the war. During the Second World War, he was national chairman of the War Resisters League. When Thomas refused to register for the draft at the age of fifty-one, he was indicted, but the indictment was later dropped. As spokesman for the rights of conscientious objectors, Dr. Thomas worked to convince the United States government that it should accept political and philosophical objections to war as well as those based on religious grounds.*

The witnessing to truth which forms the basis of conscience cannot justify itself merely by appealing to the authority of some sect or organization. Those who think in such terms have yet to understand the meaning of conscience. A young man once interviewed me because he claimed conscientious objection to war solely on the grounds of opposition to vaccination. He believed this was a religious conviction because of the teachings of his sect. He himself had not attempted to verify the teachings of his sect that vaccination did more harm than good in protecting society against certain diseases. Nor was he willing to risk prison for his faith. There was no use reasoning with him because he was not interested in facts but only in the theories of his sect. One could sympathize with his predicament but hardly justify it socially as conscience. The same is true of the conscientious objector to war on any other grounds if he refuses to verify available facts and if his conscience is based merely on the authority of others. Had the youth who was opposed only to vaccination been willing to investigate facts one might have disagreed with him but still respected his conscience. It is barely possible that he might in the course of time prove that he was right and the medical profession wrong about vaccination.

The genuine conscientious objector to war refuses to give war his active support because he believes that it is absolutely wrong. He believes that war is wrong not only for him but for society as a whole. He respects the conscience of those who disagree with him but insists on his own moral integrity for the sake of proving to others the truth as he sees it. He is not running away from facts nor indifferent to them. In war he sees for millions of people lies, waste, hunger, starvation and death. These are verifiable facts. The theorists are those who tell him he must kill for some abstraction like freedom, patriotism or democracy. These remain theories unless one is enjoying them now in the conduct of the war.

The function of conscience is to be realistic about facts and to hold fast to the faith which sees truth in truthfulness. But is it always wise to be truthful? With respect to individuals, kindly lies may be excused, but where society is concerned they are inexcusable. The physician who withholds scientific facts from a discussion in a medical society for sentimental reasons is condemned by his colleagues.

The Selective Service Act in our country limits conscience to religion. Yet science demands conscience even more rigidly than the Church. The method on which all science rests is nothing more than truthfulness. In science ends and means cannot be separated as is so universal in human thinking elsewhere. Scientific experiments are planned in accordance with known facts. Imagination and theory are important to the scientist but hard experience has taught him to rebel at the idea of using methods which will prevent the ascertaining of the truth. So important is truthfulness to science that frequently ends are achieved which were not foreseen or expected. In this manner truth and knowledge are obtained scientifically. Religion and politics might learn much from the scientific method because it demands first of all conscientiousness. Without conscientiousness science deteriorates back to witchcraft and magic. Religion has no monopoly on conscience, the Selective Service Act to the contrary notwithstanding.

The exact sciences, we are told, are not comparable to life, which demands faith of a different kind. Certainly the exact sciences are limited to an objectivity that no man can achieve in the business of living, but this does not alter the fact that moral integrity is the foundation upon which all culture and social welfare rest. We deny it at our peril. The faith which alone can be ultimately accepted must be verified in experience. The vision of Christianity as given by its Master is limitless in its possibilities. It is never attained entirely and it affords a goal for society which will always demand continuous struggle with no place for smug complacency. The most important truth for the individual with respect to this goal is that the Kingdom of God lies within him. That is the place it must begin if society as a whole is to profit. This means that the individual must live his faith as best he can. Though we fail as we all do in any absolute sense, faith becomes a mockery and a sham when it denies its own principles and betrays itself. Only through faith checked by honesty can man escape the determinism of the economic struggle.

Among the things which are Caesar's are taxes. No individual can control how taxes are to be spent. Every individual owes a fair share of whatever wealth he possesses to the community which must spend it as the majority sees fit. But when it comes to a man's life and conduct, the individual is responsible for what he does and no state or human power has the right to force dishonesty on any man. By doing so it condemns itself finally to the death it decreed for others. That is a moral law which is verified in the history of the struggle for power.

By far the greatest obstacle to freedom today is war and the fear of war. The unexpressed but genuine desire for peace which fills the hearts of most people can be fulfilled only when this desire is linked with conscience. Until this is done all plans for peace based on the complete collapse of Germany and Japan or on negotiations are unrealistic and futile in the prevention of totalitarianism. There is no guarantee whatever that the defeat of Germany will end this war, or that another will not follow after a brief breathing spell. "A negotiated peace" is a meaningless phrase unless we can see our way through the almost impenetrable complexities which negotiations at the present time would involve. To secure peace, negotiations must be founded on the demand of people that militarism be abandoned, and the negotiating governments must be convinced that the people mean what they say. This is merely another way of saying that peace depends on conscience. Any settlement of the present war which leaves militarism still in the saddle and military conscription an accepted institution is a snare and a delusion. There is a growing realization among the people that such a peace cannot last.

In reality, if peace is our desire, the choice available to us as I write is limited to one of two practical possibilities. One is to continue the present war in the hope that the side we favor can win, and impose a temporary cessation of hostilities. The logic of this position leads inevitably to totalitarianism with probable permanent conscription and increased armaments for America. The other choice is the bold and definite decision that the institution of war must go because it is intellectually and morally wrong, utterly destructive of the well-being of man. For the individual under existing conditions either decision requires the willingness to pay a price for his convictions. Reason and conscience alike are on the side of the latter of the two choices. If even 10 per cent of the adult population throughout the world would listen to the voice of reason and conscience, war would end. To demand peace on any other basis is unrealistic.

The most obvious fact in power politics is that no world organization or balance of power can prevent war as long as people believe that their interests can be advanced by armed conflict. This belief is the root of all war and until it is recognized as the tragic sham it is, wars will continue or we shall have a world totalitarianism in which people no longer care about freedom. Those who understand something about the principles on which freedom is founded can create free institutions. But no organization founded on power politics can make men free. Freedom cannot be bestowed upon us by a royal decree or even by a constitution. We must be worthy of freedom or we won't find it.

A sizable minority of individuals who are honest and know what they are about can end the sordid evil of war. This is true because the majority of people now hate war and are only waiting the courageous example of enough individuals to show them the way to something better. Peace will be possible when a sufficient number of people demand it on the basis of conscience, and not before. That is why nothing is more important in our time than the demand for freedom of conscience. It is worth the price that must be paid vastly more than that of the gamble of war, which is now a gamble no longer because its inevitable evil results are apparent.

Millions of men today, if they were really honest with themselves and true to the principles which they profess, would lay down their arms and quit the senseless business of killing. Their failure to accept this solution which is dictated by the laws of nature as well as of the spirit, lies in its simplicity. Propaganda and public pressure have so confused people that they dare not trust their own inclinations or inner sense of decency. So they fight for freedom with the methods of their enemies knowing full well that such methods contradict the values they are fighting for. In doing so they hope for the best in spite of the logic of reason. By accepting this course they have embarked on an adventure so complex that no man can see his way through it, least of all the leaders at whose bidding they fight. Within his own mind, every sane and reasonably intelligent individual knows that evil can be resisted by refusing to co-operate with it. One can die, if necessary, for principle without killing the other fellow. In doing so one not only upholds the principle but to some extent lessens the power for evil in society. Once again, this solution is too simple for most people to grasp. The penalty paid for this scorn of simple honesty is death for millions, starvation and hunger for many more millions and the loss of freedom for all.

If the United Nations in the present war were sincere in their claims about democracy and freedom, no individual would be in prison today for conscience' sake. The nation loses by this even more than the conscientious objectors, most of whom desire to cooperate in every way that does not deny the principles at stake.

As long as conscription for war purposes continues, every freedom-loving nation will have conscientious objectors to militarism, some of whom will go to prison and to death itself, if necessary. They thus serve a society bent upon its destruction. Forgotten though the objectors in prison may be at the present time, the moral drive which sent them there is still functioning in society. Such men do not go to jail for themselves but for mankind—their fellows on the firing line, millions of little children who are starving physically and spiritually, and for their own enemies at home and abroad. Believing that no government should conscript anyone against his will because a nation is at war, they deliberately accept the punishment and guilt which actually belong to the society that imprisons them. If people realized what the conscientious objectors are doing, this sacrifice by individuals would be unnecessary.

The most distasteful task of all for the objector to war conscription is to object. One does not live to become an objector but to create a society where such disagreeable conduct will not be necessary. Desiring above all things to cooperate with his fellow men, the conscientious objector to war is forced to refuse his cooperation and endure the resulting isolation. This may seem sheer waste and folly to the pragmatist, pacifist or not, but these practical people forget that the individual involved knows that his conduct is significant because of the principle behind it.

Conscientious objectors in prison today are pointing the way to salvation for society, whatever happens to them. This is salvation enough for them, and in that faith they live and die as free souls, unafraid and undismayed. Life can hold no more disillusionment for them. They have tasted of the bitter and faced facts as they were confronted by them. No power on earth can confute that spirit or faith without itself dying. In whatever words the conscientious objectors may couch their convictions, here is a faith which understands the meaning of sacrifice, the essence of Christianity, and the moral foundation of freedom for all.

Henry Miller

says: "Murder the murderer."

HENRY MILLER [1891-   ], *American novelist and widely known iconoclast, has never been a member of any group, organization, cult, or ism, nor has he been active in the peace movement. He thinks "men war—and women too—because they are really not peaceable, do not desire peace deeply enough," and he believes that "making war, as a member of a group or nation, or league of nations, is murder, the worst kind of murder because it is senseless mass murder." Murder the Murderer, from which this selection comes, was originally written (but never sent) as a letter to a friend who had joined the British Pioneer Corps. The date was 1941.*

DEAR FRED,

. . . I have always doggedly maintained the notion that if freedom cannot be had in times of peace there is little chance of obtaining it by going to war. I have always thought of freedom, moreover, as something that one earns rather than as something conferred upon one by a benevolent government. Once again we are being told that freedom and liberty are at stake, threatened this time by those monsters, Hitler and Mussolini. Those who have the audacity or foolhardiness to voice their dissent with this view of things are confronted with the loss of what little liberty they possess. The difference between being out of step with a dictator and being out of step with the democratic majority is practically negligible. The important thing is to be in step. You know me well enough to realize that I have always been out of step, even with those who agree with me.

You admit somewhere in your letter that you have never been fond of war, though at present reconciled to it. The truth is that nobody is really fond of war, not even the military-minded. And yet, throughout the short history of the human race, there have been only a few breathing spells of peace. What are we to conclude from this seeming paradox? My own conclusion is the simple, obvious one that, though fearing war, men have never truly and ardently desired peace. I do earnestly desire peace, and what intelligence I have tells me that peace is not attained by fighting but by acting peaceably. If one were to make this statement to the draft board, on being called to the colors, one would be clapped in jail. Such a statement would not be considered bona fide unless one happened to be a Quaker or a member of some other religious sect recognized as being sincere in the belief that men should not kill one an-other. Yet, as you know, all the Christian sects throughout the world have incorporated in their doctrine the Mosaic law which says, "Thou shalt not kill!" To confront our Christian libertarians with this particular Biblical commandment at this time is to enrage them, curiously enough. This is no time for hair-splitting, they say. But nothing could be less hair-splitting than these brief unequivocal words. . . .

With each day we live, a greater area of the world is engulfed in the madness of war. War is the most hideous expression of inner con-flict. We know from previous experience that all the nations now engaged in this war will emerge from it defeated. We are not even clear as to the issue involved, though it is said, as so often in the past, that it is civilization which is at stake. You know as well as I that this is not true. However much we may detest the German way of life, as exemplified by the Nazi regime, we cannot in all honesty pretend that ours is the only true way of civilization. The whole civilized world, from one end of the globe to the other, is rotten and must fall apart either now or later. I don't believe in bolstering up something which is falling apart. I don't believe that the preservation of the British Empire or any other empire, or any present system of government, for that matter, involves the preservation of humanity. The forces which brought about the war are bound up in the erroneous doctrines and beliefs which animate all members of civilized society. Civilization itself is in question. But the Germans, the Italians, the Japanese are just as much a part of this civili-zation as the English, the French, the Americans et alia. To prove by force of arms that one side or the other of these civilized nations now aligned in conflict is right or wrong will contribute nothing to the under-standing of the meaning of civilization. Whether it be true or not, civiliza-tion has come to stand for something in the nature of a continuous ad-vance, something ineradicable in the human scheme of things underlying the ephemeral birth and death of cultures. Is this advance maintained by war? If not, why should one take up arms, even though the aggressor be obviously in the wrong? Are those of us who believe in the efficacy of truth to be treated as cowards and traitors because we refuse to act except in ac-cordance with the dictates of our conscience? Are we to pretend, for the sake of convenience, that we are willing to put the voice of a government above the voice of our own conscience?

I have nothing to say to those who believe in fighting for their rights. For one like yourself, who has come to a decision on his own and voluntarily elected to sacrifice his life, there are ten thousand who are incapable of making a decision, and ten thousand more who will abide by any decision so long as it is not of their own making. To say nothing of those who, realizing the misery of their plight, demand that the rest of the world keep them company. Nations make war upon one another on the assumption that the views of the people and those who govern them are one. The moment war is declared it is impossible to dissent. The man who yesterday might have been regarded as the greatest single contributor to the nation's happiness may find himself in disgrace, if not in jail, should he happen not to believe in making war. He may have declared his stand on this subject his whole life long, but that will make no difference. He is regarded as an enemy of society just as much as the lowest criminal, more of an enemy in fact than the man who stays at home and makes a fortune selling the instruments of destruction. People are almost never unanimously in favor of making war, especially in modern times. It is the minority which sponsors war, and this minority always represents the vested interests. No government ever has the courage or the honesty to put the question of war up to the people. Nor is there ever the remotest possibility of establishing a situation whereby those in favor of war go to war and those not in favor remain passive. The unanimity of a nation, in times of war, is brought about by coercion pure and simple. You are one of the rare few in this present conflict who enjoyed the privilege of deciding your own fate. You had to be a man without a country in order to have this privilege. An ironical situation! . . .

I remember well the long discussions we had in Paris about the economic condition of the world. Even such nonpolitically-minded people as you and I could see that a drastic change had to come about, that there could be no talk of peace until there was real equality, real brotherhood. The war would seem to have killed that hope for a long time. Yet, who can say that the way may not serve a greater purpose than is now apparent? Beneath the reluctance and hesitancy of the democracies to wage war lies the fear of unloosing a more devastating evil: worldwide revolution. That most likely will be the result of the present conflict, and in bringing it about, the Germans, the Italians, the Japanese are playing just as important and valuable a role as the Allies. When nations resort to war they blind themselves to the real forces at work; by opposing one another they make themselves the instruments of a force which is superior to their antagonistic aims. They stage a drama for an invisible audience—the men and women of the future. The participants of the drama receive their reward in suffering, not in realization. Conflict engenders conflict, war creates war, ad infinitum. Even if tomorrow world revolution is ushered in, the conflict will not cease. But without going too far afield, what I wish to point out is that the result of the war will probably be quite different from the hopes or desires of either side. Though outwardly enemies, both sides are blindly collaborating to bring about a new world order. I do not say a better world order. I say merely a necessary one. We have outlived the present pattern and we have not had the wisdom to create a new one peaceably. We learn through suffering. War is not necesary; it is an expression of our crude and stupid way of seeking experience. It comes as a blow of fate because we refuse to pursue our own destinies. The hatred that has been engendered brings together in a death-lock those who were sundered; admiration, sympathy, love follow in the wake of death. When the supreme sacrifice has been made there comes the moment of understanding, of recognition. Wisdom, however, does not demand such bloody heroism; nor does it entail the disillusioning aftermath which makes these sacrifices appear hollow. Wisdom consists in perceiving the real trend of the world and living one's life in accordance with it. When the whole world blindly rushes to arms it may be well that a few men remain aloof to guide those to come with a clear mind. For, one thing is certain—the men who are directing this war will not be at the helm when peace is declared. . . .

Harry Emerson Fosdick

explains why he cannot participate in the war even if the United States is drawn into it

REV. HARRY EMERSON FOSDICK [1878-   ] *was a pastor of the Riverside Church, New York, from 1925 to 1946. He is known as a liberal, and as a "fighting" minister. This is Dr. Fosdick's answer to a question which was posed in* The Christian Century *in 1940-41, to a group of leading Americans: "If America is drawn into the war, can you, as a Christian, participate in it, or support it?"*

In replying to the question proposed by *The Christian Century,* "If America is drawn into the war, can you, as a Christian, participate in it, or support it?" my answer must be, "No!"

As I understand the matter, this inquiry is to be taken as intimate and personal. I am not asked to discuss in the abstract "absolute" and "doctrinaire" pacifism, concerning which I should have to be critical. I am not asked what I would do were I a Chinese or an Englishman, although the answer may be implied in what I say. I am not asked what

I would do were I a layman of draft age. If I understand myself, I should be a conscientious objector asking for alternative civilian service, the harder the better. The question proposed faces me, a minister of Christ in the United States today, with the practical inquiry: If this nation now becomes an active belligerent, will I support the war?

In answering I propose mainly to present my minimal position, the place where, no matter how urgent the national necessities may seem to be, I know I must take my stand. That minimal position seems clear: I can never use my Christian ministry in the support and sanction of war.

During the last war I did so use my ministry. I was ready to declare war, as some of my brethren are today, even before the nation was. I, a minister of Christ, went all out for the backing of the fray, and was proud when, in France, after an address to the troops, an officer told me I was worth a battalion. To be sure, it cost a struggle. The whole business of war, the causes that produce it, the processes that characterize it, the moral consequences that accompany it, are too obviously the denial of everything that Jesus taught, for a minister easily to fit Christ into a military uniform. I twisted and turned every which way to harmonize war and the Christian ethic, preaching against hate, praying for the Germans, and arguing beautifully about the way we could slaughter them in the spirit of love. My rationalizations in trying to make that oil and water mix arouse my wonder at their ingenuity and my shame at their futility, and the crux of my regret is that I so used my Christian ministry, as though such halloaing after the dogs of war were the function of the Church of Christ.

Today when I picture Christ in this warring world I can see him in one place only, not arrayed in the panoply of battle on either side, but on his judgment seat, sitting in condemnation on all of us—aggressor, defender, neutral—who by our joint guilt have involved ourselves in a way of life that denies everything he stood for. The function of the church is to keep him there, above the strife, representing a manner of living, the utter antithesis of war, to which mankind must return if we are to have any hope. But the Christian ministry does not keep him there by throwing itself, generation after generation, into the support and sanction of the nation's wars. Rather it drags him down, until the people, listening, can feel little if any difference between what Christ says and what Mars wants. It is not the function of the Christian church to help win a war. A church that becomes an adjunct to a war department has denied its ministry. The function of the church is to keep Christ where he belongs, upon his judgment seat, condemner of our joint guilt, chastener of our impenitent pride, guide to our only hope.

This does not mean that in the present worldwide conflict I am neutral. These last months I have sometimes thought I lived more in

Britain and China than at home, so keen have been my sympathies, so deep my apprehensions, so desperate my hopes. Obviously it makes a difference to us which side wins. The Christian minister, maintaining the position for which I plead, lives in no ivory tower apart from the realistic facts, but under terrific tension, with a warring world on one side, in which his personal emotions and his nation's interests are involved, and with Christ on the other; but he accepts the *tension,* and does not try to resolve it by reducing Christ to the level of the warring world.

This does not mean that I am uncritical of pacifism as it sometimes is presented. Some pacifists seem to me to drift unwittingly into philosophical anarchism, denying the rightful functions of the state, blind to the incalculable benefits that arise when private force is supplanted by public force for the good of all, falsely resting their case on opposition to all force rather than on a distinction between salutary and diabolical uses of it, and unrealistic about the necessities of social coercion, whether through municipal police or through international police when a world government has been created. Some pacifism seems to me merely individualistic and negative, as though a few individuals, refusing the fight, were the solution of the peace problem, when only a federation of the nations, a unified world order, can present an ultimate substitute for war.

Some pacifists seem to me far too complacent, as though by refusing any part in war themselves, they washed their hands of the common guilt that involves us all, from the burden of whose consequence the conscientious soldier feels he cannot ask exemption. And some pacifism becomes mere passiveness, as though one who let himself be a doormat for aggressive evil to wipe its feet on were really a peacemaker, whereas to be *that* always involves a whole battery of positive moral qualities issuing from creative good will, and commonly involves obdurate, sacrificial resistance to evil, even if violent means are eschewed.

Yet, while I am neither neutral nor a contented absolutist in my pacifism, I come back to my position, sure that I must maintain it: I will not prostitute the ministry of Jesus Christ to the sanction and support of war. . . .

My personal judgment is that for the United States to become a belligerent in this conflict would be a colossal and futile disaster and, along with millions of others, I should hold that judgment, pacifist or no pacifist. What if, however, the United States were invaded? That, I think, is not a practical possibility and never has been, but it is continually presented as a test case to those who do not propose to use their ministry in support of war. What would we do in case of invasion? My own answer is clear: resist, whether by violent or nonviolent means.

The identification of pacifism with mere submissiveness is a familiar

misunderstanding. . . . Nonviolent resistance—tireless, incorrigible refusal of participation in tyranny and of subjection to it—is today one
of the major hopes of Europe in countries like Norway, Holland, Belgium. At least when military resistance breaks down and a nation faces
the choice between submission on the one side and, on the other, the
pacifist method—obstinate, courageous, nonviolent resistance—the latter
can determine the course of history, and those who are at work on its
basic ideas and practical methods are about important business.

If our country were invaded, therefore, I should say resist, each
according to his best conscience, by violent or nonviolent means. . . .

Nevertheless, even in case of invasion, I should hold to my position.
Honoring the consciences of all who resist aggressive evil whether by
violent or nonviolent means, trying in the church I serve to minister
alike to the needs of the conscientious objector and the conscientious
soldier, all the more in such a crisis I should try to keep Christ where
he belongs—on his judgment seat, above the strife, standing for a way
of life that condemns both aggressor and defender, and offers the only
hope of salvation from their joint guilt and their insensate brutality.
I will not use my Christian ministry to bless war.

To be sure, I distrust the judgment of any man so contented with
his attitude in this complicated crisis that he thinks he has escaped inconsistency. We pacifists need humbly to confess that we are deeply
involved in the war system and cannot pretend that we purely wash our
hands of it. Like a socialist fighting the profit system who is at leisure
to do so because he owns stock on whose profits he can live, so, like
everyone else, we are inextricably entangled in the very war system we
disclaim and are trying to displace.

We say we will not support war, but we do support it in every
tax we pay, and we have no intention of imitating Thoreau's inane
refusal. We know that vast armaments are essentially anti-Christian,
and yet we know too that disarmament can never be unilateral, that
when disarmament comes it must come by mutual international agreement, and so we have habitually taken our national Army and Navy
for granted and now take for granted their inevitable enlargement. We
see clearly that a war for democracy is a contradiction in terms, that war
itself is democracy's chief enemy, and that after every World War, whoever wins it, there is bound to be less democracy than there was before;
yet we see too that the military victory of Hitler is the worse of two
evils, that American bombing planes going to Britain may give democracy at least a breathing space, and may conceivably save us here
from plunging into active belligerency.

Moreover, sure as we are that we stand for convictions which in
the long run are the world's hope, we nonetheless recognize that in the

immediate emergency were our attitude to become predominant and controlling on one side of the battle line and not on the other, the worse of two evils might temporarily be strengthened by the very stand that so conscientiously we take.

If the pacifist finds himself so involved in difficulty, the Christian who supports war, and especially the Christian minister who throws his influence as Christ's representative into the waging of war, seems to me utterly distraught by self-contradiction. Christ and the bombing of civilians, the Sermon on the Mount and the starving of whole populations, every essential element in the gospel on one side, and on the other every "diabolical outrage against human personality"—it may be difficult to choose between them, but what can one say about trying to amalgamate them?

Let the Christian nonpacifist get this matter down out of the abstract into the concrete, stripped of the sentimental romanticism with which once more the "glory of war" is being clothed, and let him see war as it actually is! In the last war an officer drilling a group of boys in the use of the bayonet said this: "You've got to get down and hook them out with a bayonet; you will enjoy that, I assure you. Get sympathy out of your head. We go out to kill. We don't care how so long as they are killed. . . . And I say to you, if you see a wounded German, shove him out and have no nonsense about it. . . . Kill them, every mother's son of them. Remember that your job is to kill them—that is the only way —exterminate the vile creatures." That, along with innumerable things like that, on a scale more terrible than any previous conflict knew, *is* war, and when a minister of Christ supports war, that is what he is supporting.

Well aware of the difficulties of my own position, I watch with deep concern the endeavors of Christian ministers to subsume war under Christian categories. A sermon lies before me in which the preacher urges that because God sends men to hell—an obviously coercive process! —therefore Christians may use violence in war. All the way from *that* the devious arguments range to and fro, and up and down, until I find one eminent and fine-spirited preacher, laboring with the text, "God is love," who concludes that bombing planes can be one expression of the divine compassion and that "men may be forced at times, *in the service of love* [the italics are his], to use weapons which strike down the innocent as well as the guilty." Am I wrong in being horrified at that?

Whichever side a man espouses, let him not suppose he can extricate himself from inconsistency! Humility becomes us all. Nevertheless, facing the choice between the two, I think I see where the clearer ground is and the better hope of maintaining our Christian testimony unimpaired.

Meanwhile, to the limit of our ability, let us keep our Christian fellowship intact! Dr. Tittle is right: "Christian fellowship cannot survive internationally unless it survives locally. It cannot possibly be maintained in the ends of the earth unless it is maintained in the church on the corner." As the crisis thickens this will grow more difficult; in some cases it will doubtless be impossible; some churches will be torn asunder by the war psychosis and some ministers will lose their pulpits. Hard as it is to discover the truly Christian position in this crisis, it is often harder to maintain it in a Christian spirit when one thinks one has found it. I see letters written by Christian pacifists to their nonpacifist brethren that for bitterness, acrimony, venom and dogmatism pass all decent bonds; and I see statements made by Christian nonpacifists about their pacifist fellows that for scorn, misrepresentation, rancor and contemptuousness are appalling. There is no hope in such a spirit. Unless we Christians can maintain humility, a joint penitence, good will, and a sincere respect for one another's consciences within our churches, we cannot help the world much in mainstaining such attitudes, without which we and the world alike are doomed.

Nevertheless, if the issue is drawn, some of us will have to abide by the consequences. We will not use our Christian ministry to support war. As for myself, I am essentially a Quaker, and my convictions belong in what seems to me the great tradition of the Society of Friends.

Ernest Fremont Tittle
states the case for Christian pacifism

DR. ERNEST FREMONT TITTLE [1885-1949], *minister of the First Methodist Church in Evanston, Illinois, for almost thirty years, was an outspoken pacifist. The honor of preaching the baccalaureate sermon at Northwestern University was denied him in 1924. Members of the class had objected to Dr. Tittle because he had permitted a World War I "slacker" (who had served a term in a Federal penitentiary) to speak before the church's Sunday night youth group. When during World War II The Christian Century asked ten prominent clergymen "If America is drawn into the war, can you, as a Christian, participate in it, or support it?" Dr. Tittle answered, "No."*

In 1917 I believed that war was the only means of preserving a humane and civilized culture. In that conviction, I left a wife and three children and went to France. I undertook to promote a fighting morale. I did what little I could, at a first-aid dressing station, to relieve the suffering of wounded men. On the way to the front, I came upon a poem that deeply moved me. It was found on the body of a dead and unidentifiable Australian, who had written:

> Rejoice, whatever anguish rend the heart,
>   That God has given you a priceless dower
> To live in these great times and have your part
> In freedom's crowning hour,
> That ye may tell your sons, who see the light
>   High in the heavens, their heritage to take,
> I saw the powers of darkness put to flight,
>   I saw the morning break.

But the powers of darkness were not put to flight. Men were killed, millions of them, including promising young writers and artists and musicians and scientists and philosophers. Women were desolate, multitudes of them. Wealth was destroyed. Hunger stalked and pestilence raged over vast areas of the earth. Thirty million civilians were liquidated. The world was set on the road to an economic debacle. But justice was not achieved. Liberty was not secured. The rights and liberties of small nations were not guaranteed. Brute force was not banished from international affairs. The world was not made safe for democracy or for morality or for Christianity or for anything else that decent men care for and would be glad to die for. A heritage there was for the sons of men who died in the First World War, but it was not light "high in the heavens" or anywhere else. It was the descending darkness of the present war.

I am now convinced that war, being, as the Oxford Conference said, "a defiance of the righteousness of God as revealed in Jesus Christ and him crucified," cannot serve the ends of freedom and justice but is certain to defeat them. So, if the United States becomes a belligerent in Europe or in Asia, I shall undertake to contribute in some way to the good of my country, but I shall not "support" the war.

The present war in Europe is not only a clash of imperialism; it is also a conflict of ideologies and ways of life. There is now far more at stake than there was in 1917. Prussianism threatened the world with whips; Hitlerism threatens it with scorpions. It is now all-essential to the welfare and progress of humanity that Hitlerism be overcome. On this point American Christians are agreed. The point on which they are not agreed is the means by which Hitlerism *can be* overcome. Christian pacifists do not proclaim that tyranny is better than war; they proclaim that tyranny cannot be overcome by war. They believe with the late Lord Lothian that "the triumph of Hitler grew out of the despair that settled on central Europe in the years of war, defeat, inflation and revolutionary propaganda." And they believe that this war is now producing political, economic and psychological conditions that make for the survival and spread of Hitlerism.

1. I believe that war as we now know it cannot pave the way for the doing of good. When the fighting ends, who makes the peace? Not the man who actually fought the war, nor the parsons who blessed it, nor the professors who glorified it. When the fighting ends, the people who make the peace are the same people whose ambitions and practices created the situation which bred the war. It is they who, behind the scenes if not at the peace table, decide what is to be done. It is their interests that are considered, their ideas that prevail. Idealists may fight or bless a war, but they, when the fighting ends, have little voice in the making of peace. This is inevitable; for war, being what it is, plays into the hands of unreason and reaction. It provides a field day for the munitions industry, for the jingoistic press, for every kind of industry that is antisocial and reckless in the pursuit of private gain. It provides a sounding board for politicians and other persons who have the deadly gifts of the demagogue. Inevitably, war strengthens the forces of darkness and destruction. . . .

It has been said of the pacifist that he has "a confidence in human nature that human nature cannot support." As a matter of fact, it is the nonpacifist, not the pacifist, who believes that after a long-drawn-out orgy of indiscriminate killing and wholesale destruction people may be expected to think rationally and act justly. The pacifist has no such confidence in human nature.

2. I believe that war as we now know it cannot even hold evil in check. Total war is itself a most active and destructive evil. It knows no distinction of guilty and innocent or even of combatant and noncombatant. It has no "reverence for personality." It treats human beings as if they were things. It demands the distortion of truth. It knows no distinction of right and wrong but only military necessity. It requires men to believe that the end for which they are fighting is so important that it justifies the use of any means. It is now persuading men that a food blockade, although it may bring starvation, disease and death to innocent aged persons and women and children, is justified on the ground that it is essential to the preservation of civilization!

Can war, nevertheless, be made to hold evil in check? I have no confidence in attempts to preserve civilization by means that are themselves a denial and betrayal of everything that is essential to a humane and civilized culture. When men do evil that good may come, what they get is not the good they seek but the evil they do. History joins the New Testament in saying, "Be not deceived; God is not mocked: for whatsoever a man soweth, that shall he also reap." . . .

I am convinced that the doing of good is the only way to put an end to aggression. Under present conditions, aggression may not be wholly unprovoked. It may be provoked by fear of future aggression on the part of some other nation. It may be provoked by bitter belief, not wholly unwarranted, that there is now no peaceful way of solving a desperate economic problem. It may be provoked by a stinging sense of inferiority in a world where certain other nations are now in a position to gather wealth from the ends of the earth and to lord it over others. To say this is by no means to condone aggression, which in any case is an infamous thing; it is only to face the fact that, rooted in historical events and psychological situations, aggression is seldom unprovoked. Nations that benefit from a world situation which denies equality of opportunity may view with abhorrence any attempt to change it by force. But if they themselves refuse to consent to peaceful change through discussion and negotiation, their refusal may be as immoral as the aggression it provokes.

In a world that is suffering from injustice piled upon injustice, the immediate overcoming of evil may be impossible. There may be no escape from the wages of sin. The question then is: What course, if faithfully followed, would eventually lead to a better state of affairs? War, I am convinced, is not the answer. War can overcome a dictator; it cannot rid the world of dictatorship. It can stop an aggressor; it cannot put an end to aggression. On the contrary, it can only provide new soil for the growth of dictatorship and aggression. The answer, I believe, is the persistent doing of good. Injustice breeds injustice. Hatred breeds hatred. Cruelty breeds cruelty. War breeds war. And no less surely does good beget good.

If the United States were invaded I should feel called upon to resist the invader by refusing to become his accomplice in the doing of evil. Both in South Africa and in India this kind of resistance has produced notable results. (To say that it can be effective only when the aggressor is an Anglo-Saxon is to invite the charge of dogmatism, if not of self-righteousness.) It produces a situation which the aggressor is unprepared to handle. Air raid for air raid, blockade for blockade, evil for evil—this he has been taught to expect, and when it occurs he knows what to do. But what is he to do when the pastors of all the Protestant churches of the Netherlands read from their pulpits a vigorous protest, in the name of Christ, against any attempt to force upon their country an anti-Jewish program? Nonviolent resistance forces the aggressor to think, which he can hardly do without a disastrous loss of military morale. It forces him to think because, although it refuses to become his accomplice, it does not seek to hurt him.

Pacifists do not suppose that nonviolent resistance can be offered without risk of arrest, imprisonment and death. There would doubtless be many casualties, just as in war. Yet the end result, pacifists believe, would be far different; for war produces in victor and vanquished alike a state of mind that forbids the making of a just and durable peace, whereas nonviolent resistance, which appeals to the best in the aggressor and calls forth the best in his victim, may hope to be redemptive. Of course, nonviolent resistance to evil is not enough. It must be accompanied by a positive program of good which seeks long-range objectives.

I believe that Christian pacifism has relevance to the relations between nations as well as to the relations of the individual to his fellows. The doing of good is not only the way of life for the individual; it is also the way of life for society. This way the pacifist is obligated both to take for himself and to advocate for his nation.

What would pacifism as our national policy require? . . . As a national policy, pacifism would require the United States to set its own house in order. It would seek a real solution (which peacetime conscription is not) for the problem of unemployment and equality of opportunity for all Americans, including Negroes. It would require the repeal of the Oriental exclusion act and the placing of Orientals on the quota basis which now governs immigration from other countries. It would call upon the United States to abrogate its present unequal treaties with China and to establish its relations with China on a basis of complete equality and reciprocity. It would require the United States, in the formation of its domestic policies, to have a lively and continuing regard for the welfare of the rest of mankind. . . . It would lead the United States to become indeed a good neighbor, concerned that all nations should have equal access to raw materials and needed markets for their industrial goods.

In the present crisis, pacifism as a national policy would constrain the United States to announce to the world (1) its readiness to associate itself with other nations in the building of a new world order; (2) its determination in any case to order its own life with a sensitive regard for the well-being of other peoples; (3) its desire to contribute to the relief of human suffering in war-stricken regions, through gifts of food, clothing and medical supplies; and (4) its readiness at the war's end to make loans for economic rehabilitation, if convinced of the desirability of the projects for which the money was sought. This foundation of justice being laid, pacifism would constrain the United States to appeal for an armistice and for an earnest attempt through discussion and negotiation to find a fundamental solution of world problems in a just peace.

The pacifist well knows the objections which are now being offered to the idea of a negotiated peace. He also knows that the same objections were offered when Woodrow Wilson, in his address to the Senate (and to the people of the warring nations) on January 22, 1917, made his earnest plea for "a peace without victory." With high purpose and political realism he declared that "upon a triumph which overwhelms and humiliates cannot be laid the foundations of peace and equality and good will"; that a dictated peace would "leave a sting, a resentment, a bitter memory upon which terms of peace would rest not permanently but only as upon quicksand." These words were not heeded. There could be no hope, it was then said, of a just and durable peace until Germany was brought to her knees. The idea of a negotiated peace was scorned and rejected; the result was Versailles—and the present war. What reason is there to believe that the result would be greatly different if the present conflict should be decided by slow attrition and ultimate exhaustion or by a knockout blow?

Pacifism as a national strategy would pursue a policy not of appeasement but of reconciliation. Between these policies there is a vast range of difference. Appeasement is concerned only to safeguard individual and national self-interest at whatever cost to others; reconciliation seeks to promote fellowship through justice and good will. Pacifism finds the surest grounds of security not in concession or in conquest but in confidence. "Good will" is a recognized asset in business; it is equally crucial in the affairs of nations. To seek good will is not impractical idealism; it is the most hard-headed realism.

But would it not be an act of insanity to trust Hitler? Yes, under present conditions. It is a fact, however, that Hitler has power only so long as the German army chooses to support him. And it is *not* a fact that the German people are wholly devoid of human decency or that they have no appreciation of the things which make for peace. To say that the Germans have ceased to be a civilized people is to reveal oneself a victim of war-born bitterness and confusion. It would not, in my judgment, be an act of insanity to seek an official statement of peace aims, a reasonable basis for the cessation of hostilities, and opportunity through discussion and negotiation to find a fundamental solution of world problems in a just peace. On the contrary, it would be an act of high statesmanship which would indicate that the responsible leadership of the United States had decided to trust in God and in the power of justice and good will, not merely in human cunning and brute force.

War is an attempted short cut to the solution of terrific social problems, which it does not solve but only makes more difficult of solution. It is thought to be, but never is, a relatively quick way out of an intolerable situation. I can see only ruin ahead if the United States becomes a belligerent in Europe or in Asia—ruin for us and for all mankind. The only way out of the world's misery is, I believe, the doing of good. That way I feel bound to take and to advocate for my country.

Arle Brooks
defends his refusal to register for the draft

ARLE BROOKS .[1910-   ] *refused to register under the Selective Service Training Act of 1940. Though he had no church, he was an ordained minister of the Disciples of Christ. In the year before his conviction on the charge of refusing to register, Brooks was employed by the Work Camp Committee of the American Friends Service Committee. In passing sentence, Judge George A. Welsh, a member of the Society of Friends himself, told Brooks: "This is your conscience and it is your duty to obey it, even if it brings physical pain or death, when it comes to a real matter of conscience." The judge sentenced him to a year and a day. But before sentence was pronounced, Brooks gave this address to the court.*

My conscience forbade me to register under the Selective Service Training Act of 1940.

The present wars are the natural product of our economic system and our way of living. Preparation for war is easier than going through the painful process of reconstructing our social and economic system and improving our own lives.

Wars destroy human lives. Individuals have the right to give their lives for a cause. They have no right to take the life of another. Wars are destructive, futile and immoral. Wars have failed to solve the basic problems of the world. Participation in war to settle international or national differences does not do justice to man's intelligence.

The people of America are filled with fear of an invasion. Are we so morally weak that the power of one man could control 130,000,000 free people? Free people cannot be enslaved unless they allow it. Are we too lethargic to find a better method of settling international affairs? The people of India have almost won their freedom from Great Britain without firing a shot. They are willing to give their lives but refuse to take the lives of the British soldiers.

Democracy does not mean a blind following of the will of the majority. In a democracy the minority has a right and a duty to follow its ideals. Sometimes the ideals of the minority have eventually been adopted by the majority. Gandhi said: "We are sunk so low that we fancy that it is our duty and our religion to do what the law lays down. If man will only realize that it is unmanly to obey laws that are unjust no man's tyranny will enslave him. . . . It is a superstition and an ungodly thing to believe that an act of a majority binds a minority."

I believe in and have worked for the brotherhood of man, which is the highest form of democracy and which recognizes no national boundaries. I have worked with children of the slums of Chicago, with transients, relief people, prisoners in Texas, and with sharecroppers in Mississippi.

Conscription is a denial of the democracy for which I have worked. Under conscription the individual is required blindly to obey his superior officer even when the superior officer is wrong. Hitler could not wage his war if the people of Germany had not granted him the power to conscript them. The United States is adopting a system of conscription which may produce tyranny instead of freedom.

I cannot agree with those who believe that registration is a mere census. Registration is the first and necessary step in conscription. My conscience will not permit me to take this first step.

As a minister I could have received complete exemption. I felt it my moral duty to do all within my power to protest against conscription which will eventually weaken and destroy democracy. I am not evading the draft. I am opposing it. I am defending democracy.

Richard B. Gregg

assures pacifists that the sacrifice of oneself is an affirmation of a greater unity

RICHARD B. GREGG [1885-   ] *was an American lawyer who worked in labor relations, but he left his practice to go to India. He has lived there for several periods and has written extensively on India and on nonviolence. His book* The Power of Non-Violence *is an important contribution to that subject. The selection here is from a booklet by Gregg published in 1939: "The Pacifist Program in Time of War, Theatened War, or Fascism."*

If war comes, the first clear negative duty of the absolute pacifist male citizen, if he be of military age, is to refuse to join the Army, Navy, or Air Force, or to serve in them if he is conscripted. This is his major act of nonviolent resistance. To this he has pledged himself.

He should be willing to endure the opprobrium and punishment resulting from such refusal, even death. All that he values in life has been made possible by adherence to principle. Our lives are held together by the loyalty of our forefathers and of our contemporaries to truth, human unity, cooperation, nonviolence and love. If we give our suffering or our lives for those things, we are simply paying a debt that we owe. Truth, human unity, nonviolence and love outlast any individual or nation. Therefore they are more important than I am. Therefore, if it is a choice whether those things are to suffer or I am to suffer, it must be I. Or to put it in another way: The chief and ultimate insecurity is division, disunity, separation from our fellow men and from God. Hence unity is the greatest security, and unity is immensely important to live for, or, if need be, to die for. Unity must be unlimited by national boundaries or ideological distinctions. Or again, as an English writer has recently stated it in *Peace News:* "Safety lies neither in my possession nor in yours. It lies forever between us. Hence, if either of us seeks it for himself, both of us must miss it. Could we but see that each of us is desirous of the same thing, and could we but restrain the childish desire to snatch it for ourselves alone, then we should experience the security that comes of mutual trust." Since security does not lie in our possessions but in the quality of our relationship, and I, by the right kind of persistent effort can make that relationship better, it would be utter folly for me to go to war. The quickening and spreading of moral sensitiveness elevates society and is a service to the state.

It might be pertinent here to mention one explanation of the paradox that "he that loseth his life . . . shall find it." Evolution consists in the gradual formation of progressively subtler, more complex, and more delicately poised integrations. The molecule of organic protein is much more complex than that of any inorganic compound. How vastly more complex and marvelously balanced is the body of a man than that of an amoeba! How much more complex is modern society than a primitive tribe! In view of that principle of evolution, to take a risk for the sake of human ideals, to be a peacemaker, is a way of saying and meaning that you trust life, that you are not afraid. Since fear is born of a sense of separateness and is itself still further divisive, such denial of fear affirms human unity or harmony of relationships, making possible a closer and more complex integration. All life responds to that principle and rallies to its support, for it is the principle underlying the evolution of all organisms. Hence the risk of pacifism is not so great as it seems at first, and the chance of success is greater than seems probable at first. It seems too great a risk only when we forget the imponderables which are steadily pressing toward a higher, subtler, closer, more inclusive organization, an organization which, although more sensitive and delicately poised than those which preceded it, is, like man himself, richer in resources because inclusive of more forces, and therefore more adaptable and more enduring.

The willingness to sacrifice one's individual self is the affirmation of the greater unity, and therefore attracts the support of many forces, by themselves subtle and seemingly weak but together in organized unity immensely strong. Thus the giving up of the smaller original self is the first necessary step toward the creation of a richer, more inclusive and more permanent self.

There is still another consideration for those who may say, "How can my one little insignificant effort or life affect the movement of this tremendous belligerence? This urge to fight has the momentum of ages of human life, it is a biological urge." Such a doubt overlooks the principle of summation of stimuli, so immensely potent in all growth processes, the power of example and imitation in the strengthening of ideals. It overlooks the historical instances of righting such great wrongs as the subjection of women and legal slavery. The very fact that the government is so set against conscientious objectors proves that their refusal is not futile.

Whether the conscientious objector should make his refusal as soon as the draft law becomes effective or should wait to be conscripted, and whether the refusal should be made to the civil or military authorities, are matters which may depend on considerations of conscience and social wisdom as well as law. Probably the earlier the refusal, the better. An immediate refusal would probably be tried in the civil courts and be likely to get publicity which would help the cause; while if refusal is postponed, the person summoned in the draft would come before a court martial which would be secret. . . .

Women would probably not be drafted into fighting services, but might be ordered to register and be liable to service in industry or nursing. Those who are pacifists should, I believe, refuse to do nursing under military or semimilitary orders or to work in munitions plants or factories doing war work, for the same reasons as apply to refusals by men.

Suppose a person who works in a munitions factory becomes converted to pacifism. What should he or she do? Or suppose a pacifist works in a mill which ordinarily makes peaceful products but begins to make goods for the Army, Navy or Air Force. What should such a pacifist employee do? Or suppose a pacifist is unemployed and receiving government relief money or work provided by a government agency. He is told that he must accept work in a nearby munitions factory or he will be deprived of his relief. This last is not a purely imaginary problem. It was actually hinted to unemployed people at Yarrow, England, about two years ago. What should such a pacifist be advised to do?

If he is without family responsibilities, his conduct will depend on the depth of his conviction, his courage and resourcefulness. He may seek other work which does not aid the military establishment. If he has a wife and children depending on him, the wife's attitude will count heavily. If she agrees with his pacifist beliefs, they may together take the risk of finding other work or subsisting on private charity. If she disagrees, his problem is more difficult. In every case the decision must be made by the person himself. Only he can judge his inner strength or weakness and take the responsibility for action. Just as a general takes responsibility for the death of his troops in battle, so a pacifist in his struggle may have to do this in regard to his dependents. Leaders like Jesus and George Fox, the Quaker, risked their followers' lives when they risked their own.

If the pacifist parent feels that he must, despite his convictions, take munitions work in order to provide for his family, let him at least engage in as much humanitarian service to others as possible. Let him read pacifist literature, avoid hatred of opponents, adhere strictly to the truth, join or form a small pacifist group or "seed," strive to become nonviolent in all his relationships. Thus he may, as the Chinese say, be like a bamboo, bending before the storm but not breaking. To the extent that he expresses love and a sense of unity with his fellow men he is reducing the poison of his compromise and generating in himself courage and power for further advance and ultimate complete refusal to serve war.

Milton S. Mayer

announces he is "going to sit this one out"

MILTON S. MAYER [1908-   ] *is a newspaperman, magazine writer and a former member of the University of Chicago faculty. He has been a visiting professor at a number of European institutions, including Frankfurt University in Germany and Comenius Theological Faculty in Prague. During World War II he was a conscientious objector. He has lectured for the Friends Service Committee, the Fellowship of Reconciliation and the Jewish Peace Fellowship. This article, originally called "I Think I'll Sit This One Out," appeared in* The Saturday Evening Post *in October 1939.*

When I was in college, ten years ago, the bright young men were taking the Oxford oath. I was one of the bright young men, but I didn't take the Oxford oath. Of course I wasn't going to fight in any more imperialist wars, but something told me that the rest of the boys were. Something told me that these peacetime pacifists were bad company. Something told me that they wouldn't fight in any more imperialist wars except the next one. So I didn't take the Oxford oath.

Sure enough, I'm all alone now, as I was then. Of a dozen college friends, all of them the noisiest kind of slackers back in 1929, only one of them isn't itching to get his hands on a gun. He says he's going underground when we enter the war, and he's going to work for the revolution, and he wants to know if I'm with him. No, I'm against him, and it isn't because I've fallen for the democracy bunk again. It's because I haven't fallen for the democracy bunk or the revolution bunk either. I'm going to sit this one out for reasons all my own.

I think I know what brought the rest of the peacetime pacifists around, and I'm not sure that another batch of Hun atrocities—beg pardon, Nazi atrocities—won't bring me around. I'm afraid that when the bands start playing I'll get in line. I'm afraid that when the heat is on me, when the finger points, when "America calls," I'll grab a gun, and the girls will throw roses and the home folks will say, "There's Mayer; right there in the front."

I can make my decision now, to go or not to go, and, as in any prejudgment, take the chance of having decided wrong. Or I can postpone my decision as events move closer and closer. Today I have the prudence essential to making a choice. Will I have it tomorrow, a month from now, six months from now, as the war fever rises around me? I know, of course, that I can't really make a choice until I meet the problem face to face. But I know, too, that as the war fever rises, as the emotional sweep of events rolls up, there comes a time when I can no longer exercise the prudence that enables me to choose. When that time comes I may still think I am choosing, but my choice will be dictated by my hysteria.

I do not face this problem, now or when we enter the war, by thanking God that I am overage or flat-footed. I do not face this problem by announcing that because of religious or conscientious scruples I will sing psalms or empty bedpans behind the lines. I do not face this problem by getting a bombproof job in Washington while the goofs go out and stop the bullets. There is only one way to face this problem, and that is to face it. I have to decide, now or when we enter the war, to stand up and fight or to stand up and oppose the war.

And so I exercise such prudence as the unpredictable future permits and I make my decision now. I make my decision to oppose this war, to oppose it now and when America enters it, and I make that decision despite my horror of "the Berchtesgaden maniac" and my disinclination to set myself up as martyr to my ideals. I oppose the current war for three reasons. I think it will destroy democracy. I think it will bring no peace. And I think it will degrade humanity. . . .

I do not want Hitler to rule the world, and if he wins this war he will. The trouble is that if we win it he will rule the world anyway. "Autocracy" and "Prussianism" were crushed twenty years ago with the lives of millions of men and the money that reduced the world to poverty. And the map of the world today shows us how well they were crushed.

Of course it won't be Hitler twenty years from now. Hitler will have been retired to Doorn. But Hitlerism, Prussianism, or whatever you want to call it, will be as much closer to ruling the world of 1960 as it is closer today than in 1920.

I am trying to keep my eye on the ball in spite of my hatred of a man called Hitler. Who is this Hitler, anyway? A man, like the rest of us, a man capable, like the rest of us, of acting like a man; but a man brutalized, as the rest of us may be, by war and the poverty of war and the animal degradation of war—a man, in short, behaving like an animal. Fascism is animalism. The wolves are fascists; the bees have the perfect fascist state. It is not Hitler I must fight, but fascism. And I know, from philosophy and from science, from the Bible and from Freud, that it is not the sinner I must exorcise, but the sin. If I want to beat fascism, I cannot beat it at its own game. War is at once the essence and the apotheosis, the beginning and the triumph, of fascism, and when I go to war I join "Hitler's" popular front against the man in men. I cannot fight animals their way without turning animal myself. . . .

Society may make many demands on me, as long as it keeps me out of the cave. It may take my property. It may take my life. But when it puts me back into the cave I must say, politely but firmly, to hell with society. My ancestors were cannibals without benefit of parliaments.

My friends conclude that I can't be "reasoned with," and they agree to gang up on me with one last *ad hominem* appeal. "What good can you do in jail?" they ask. "A Debs, yes. But who ever heard of Mayer? Who cares if Mayer opposes the war?" And my answer is that Mayer is indeed inconsequential, but a thousand Mayers, a million Mayers, ten million Mayers, may prove to be too many to ignore. And if there are only a hundred Mayers this time, their example may produce a thousand Mayers next time. That will mean a lot of wars before the Mayers are heard, but I can wait.

And if there is only one Mayer, his case against this war remains the same. That one Mayer will have to take his kicking around like the man he claims to be, and he may not get a chance to open his mouth, much less build a better world. But he will have taken his stand, not because he thinks God or the big battalions are with him but because he can take no other. And he will have to say, with William the Silent, that it is not necessary to hope in order to undertake, nor to succeed in order to persevere.

George Lansbury

calls on all European nations to abolish war

THE RIGHT HONORABLE GEORGE LANSBURY, M.P. [1859–1940] *was born in Suffolk, England. Educated in the public schools, he became a printer and then a politician, working his way up in the ranks to cabinet member in the Labor government. He was called "Britain's Number One Pacifist" for his lifelong agitation against war. In his campaign for peace, he was in touch with most of the world's rulers, including Pope Pius XII, President Roosevelt, Hitler and Mussolini, to plead for "one more supreme effort." He argued that war came from economic causes and could be averted if people cared enough. In 1935 he resigned his post as leader of the British Labor Party in protest against the party's support of rearmament. This is from a talk given to the Kulturbund in Vienna in December 1937.*

I come to you as a pacifist Socialist, a member of the British House of Commons elected to oppose violence and war of every kind, and to work for the establishment of peace and security through international cooperation between all peoples.

We pacifists possess no more courage, no more virtue than other people; neither are we cowards—as many prisons in the world testify at this moment. We make no claim to be able to cure the ills of the world by the use of smooth words, excusing evil, or by any means other than those associated with the two words "common sense." Religion is applied common sense. When Jesus bid men and women to pray to be forgiven their sins, and to forgive others as they hoped to be forgiven; to love their enemies and to do to others as they would be done unto, he was not talking sentimental nonsense, but telling people in a simple, realist manner that all of us need forgiveness because all of us, individuals and nations, have sinned against the light, and are continually doing so. And of this there will be no end until we are willing to accept the simple truth that we have all sinned and come short of the glory of God.

May I, at this point, make it quite clear that I am not speaking on behalf of any political or trade unionist organization; I am speaking on behalf of the world pacifist movement comprising Christian pacifist churchmen, members of the Society of Friends, and men and women pacifists who belong to no religious denomination. The active group is known as Embassies of Reconciliation.

We are strengthened in our faith because our own life experience and the history of the world have demonstrated the final and complete futility of war. This is a fact that I would respectfully drive home to all who listen to me or may later read what I say. Twenty-three years have passed since August, 1914; nineteen years since Armistice Day of 1918; and now Europe is once again an armed camp and the civilized world from pole to pole is again preparing for mass suicide.

Every statesman to whom I have spoken asserts that his country is arming for defense. Every statesman of any authority in every land declares that another great war will result in the destruction of civilization and in chaos. During the last war the youth of the world was enlisted to save democracy and destroy militarism: neither objective was accomplished. The war which the world is now preparing for must take as its slogan—"Join up and fight to make the world safe for barbarism." War cannot be destroyed by war. We shall kill the war spirit when we substitute cooperation for competition and are willing to be partners in a world commonwealth within which peoples will live at peace, because collective justice has taken the place of violence and war.

Make no mistake: these warnings about barbarism are not made by pacifists alone. We agree with those who make them, all of whom are men holding leading positions in all the governments of the world. These men tell the world that another great war will result in neither victors nor defeated; that all will face ruin. The infliction of fearful agony on the peoples of Spain and China is condemned by everybody. The awful suffering and slaughter are a blasphemy against God and humanity. There are many pacifists who would willingly sacrifice their lives if by so doing these frightful happenings could by stopped; but we all know that neither pacifists nor those opposed to them can settle those wars by an extension of the fighting. And no government is as yet sufficiently free of self-interest to act alone the part of peacemaker.

The world situation is seen on a small scale in these lands, and I appeal to any who disagree with me to think for a moment what is going on in other countries described as civilized. Everywhere towns are being blacked out at night for the purpose of trying out defensive measures against air attack; gas masks by the million are being manufactured, to be worn by newborn babies, aged and sick persons, and whole populations in all lands. This means that all those nations who condemn bombing in Africa, Spain and China, and all who denounce the slaughter of women and children and men, are themselves preparing to use the same hell-begotten, devastating methods whenever another war breaks out. Defenses against aerial warfare, we are told by some authorities, are being perfected. Governments know, however, quite certainly that "bombers" will get through. If this were not so, these same governments would not be manufacturing millions of gas masks and organizing schemes for the removal of whole populations from what are described as danger zones.

I confess to a feeling almost of despair as I write these words. But somehow the conviction strengthens and deepens within me that the peoples of the world will rise up in their millions and refuse to allow themselves to be destroyed in this barbarous manner. Thousands of women in all countries are now refusing to bear children; they will not go through the trouble of childbirth knowing the horrible future which governments are planning for these children. They will not accept the hideous dilemma, "Choke or be choked," which is what aerial bombing has brought to us. No, women understand the meaning of international and national affairs more clearly than ever before. But in spite of all the propaganda and the devilish efforts made in a few quarters to keep the hate fires burning, most people desire peace with those called enemies, rather than war.

We must not allow our minds to be swamped by a recital of the horrors of war, although it is of supreme importance that we should keep in mind the fact that all beneficial advance in scientific and inventive knowledge may be lost if once the world's devilish machinery for slaughter is set in motion. . . .

We are living in a world which in many ways appears more marvelous than in any previous period in the history of man. I met Senator Marconi during my visit to Rome. Although he was terribly depressed when speaking of the danger of war, he was cheerful and confident that ultimately mankind would use the great inventions which men like Edison, himself and many others had given to the world, not for destruction, but for the purpose of bringing peace, happiness and good will to the nations of the world.

I cannot think otherwise. Men and women are as brave and courageous, as adventurous and unselfish in the pursuit of knowledge and power which will benefit mankind as others are in the desperate gamble of war. It is really nonsensical to talk as if our children must be trained to fight if we are to retain the great virtues of chivalry and disinterested sacrifice for great ideals. In the past, ordinary seamen, without knowledge of whither they were sailing, found their way across the great water spaces and opened up the seven seas, for the service, not of a nation, but for the whole human race. These adventurers came from many lands. In the same manner brilliant men and women of all races are today conquering the air. Who is there who does not feel a thrill of downright pride and admiration for those who, braving all danger, are able to demonstrate that mountain ranges and ocean barriers will very soon no longer be obstacles to free intercourse between nations? . . .

My main point . . . in these remarks concerning new conditions, is to emphasize the fact that this generation is rapidly conquering space, has overcome all difficulties of direct communication between nations— by the spoken word across the air—and is able to do so even in the midst of what is said to be widespread hatred between nations. The nations of the world are now at this moment cooperating for mutual service. The principle and practice are established. Our task is to extend what is now being practiced so that all the economic and territorial difficulties which confront us can be peaceably settled. . . .

What then shall we do to save ourselves from the calamity which all statesmen say threatens us? The simple straightforward way is for the masses in all countries to make their voices heard in such a manner as will compel each government to adopt a complete change of policy and accept as the foundation of their relationships with other nations the basic principle of Christ's teaching—that all mankind is one family and that in this world there is room enough and cooperative power enough to enable all the children of men to enjoy the good gifts nature has given us, and the enormous scientific and other results of invention that the world now possesses. It is impossible for any of us to live in isolation, although it is equally true that we shall not for many centuries to come, if ever, be able to live under one rule. But it is possible to organize international relationships in such a way as will ensure, through cooperative sharing of territories, natural resources and markets, the peaceful solution of the present economic plight of the world. . . .

There is truth in the saying that though evil may seem to prosper for a time, there is a Nemesis in the world which in the end destroys it. But I am here pleading for a peace of understanding based on good will and cooperation. Governments win the support of their people in war by declaring that the war they are undertaking is forced upon them and necessary for the defense of their interests and territory. There is, however, a growing intelligence among the masses of all classes which is enabling them to realize that once ordinary people refuse to consider as their enemies people whose language, religion and culture are different from their own, we shall soon secure peace. This is also true of national government. There is no reason in the assumption that because I am a Socialist I should want to kill a Tory or a fascist. It is my right and my duty to do my utmost by reason and argument to counter the opinions of those who disagree with me, and for them to have the same rights. We do not convert people to our point of view by persecution, imprisonment or slaughter. Murder is murder whenever murder takes place, no matter what excuse the murderer may make. It is possible for us to kill one another but impossible to destroy truth: for truth is eternal.

I have no intention of discussing any particular form of government. My own political home is in socialism, a socialism established by consent and not by bloody revolution or violence. Neither fascism, socialism, Communism nor any other form of government will last if based on force; all history teaches this truth. Theories change, but experience gained through the centuries contains unanswerable truths. How can we boast of progress if we continue to try and defend greed and selfishness, and imperialist nationalism, with the use of the most diabolical methods of destruction? Some form of government always arises out of disorder; but true government of the people, by the people, for the people, can be permanently established by only good will, cooperation and peaceful means. Nowhere in the world has force proved itself capable of giving prosperity and peace to any nation.

All peoples, within their own borders, must be free to live their own lives in their own way. In the United States of America people belonging to nearly every race in the world live side by side with a minimum of disorder and discontent, except the discontent which prevails in all countries where life is organized for private profit and not for social service. It does not at present seem possible for Europe immediately to redistribute territories and move frontiers. It is, however, possible for Britain, France, Russia, Germany and Italy to unite in a great crusade with all other peoples to establish an economic unity throughout the whole European continent.

Both inside and outside our own nations we must accept as a law of our being that all must rise together or ultimately face ruin together. This new world cannot hold together as competitive units. We must cooperate with each other in order to ensure that mankind as a whole shall benefit and enjoy all the abundant blessings that God, nature and science give us for our use and service. . . .

So far my talk has been on a variety of subjects which have occupied my thoughts when going round the world advocating peace. May I now, in bringing this paper to a conclusion, again say that we are living in an entirely new world of opportunity? Within a few years the powers which men possess for world development have expanded at a very great rate. The old saying, "You cannot put new wine into old bottles," is a very simple truth, and very applicable to our present-day requirements. It is not now possible for any of us to live in isolation. Pure and simple individualism must now find its fulfillment in association with those among whom we live. Communal service will alone enable us to give into the common pool of helpfulness what is needed to assist in the development of that form of life expressed in the words "each for all and all for each." This old Cornish motto is possible of realization in every land, because everywhere with good will, the knowledge we now possess, if used cooperatively, will enable us to live as brothers and sisters. The form of government and administration, once this is understood, will be very simple and understandable, and will be based on a true fraternity, because each one will for the first time be doing his utmost for the good of all, confident that in doing so he too will share in the fuller and nobler life which will follow such a change.

If Jesus Christ came through that door with Julius Caesar and Napoleon beside him, to whom would you kneel? You know, as I do, that we should kneel to Jesus Christ. And so I appeal that we make up our minds tonight to reject violence and accept the way of love, and become citizens of the kingdom of heaven.

Lord Ponsonby
insists that teaching hate is a crime

ARTHUR AUGUSTUS WILLIAM HARRY PONSONBY [1871-1946] *was trained in the diplomatic service. It was while he was principal private secretary to Premier Campbell-Bannerman that he first became conscious of the extremes of luxury and poverty existing in England. He became a liberal member of Parliament, but after ten years joined the Labor Party. During World War I he urged a negotiated peace. He resigned as a leader of the Labor opposition in the House of Lords in 1935 because of his pacifist convictions, asserting that force of arms cannot at any time serve world peace. His only public appearances after his resignation were at peace rallies. This is an address he gave in 1937.*

On behalf of the War Resisters International I desire to express our grateful thanks to our Danish Section for all the arrangements they have made to enable us to meet here in Copenhagen, the capital of a country which we regard as one of the most hopeful and advanced nations in a troubled world.

I would extend greetings to the representatives we have here of twenty-one nations. Our meetings and consultations together can do nothing but good. I am sure you will allow me to pick out for special greeting and congratulation our Spanish comrades. While their country is still torn by a terrible and cruel fratricidal conflict, while the lives of their fellow countrymen are being sacrificed or constantly in danger and their cities are being devastated, they have with remarkable courage and without betraying the convictions they hold in common with us, devoted their energies to alleviating the suffering of the civil population and saving more especially the children, as far as they possibly can, from the miseries and torture which civil war involves. They give us a fine example of how war resisters should behave in face of a hideous and uncontrollable outbreak of violence.

The War Resisters International is, as you know, also carrying out to the best of its ability relief work in Spain, without neglecting our main work, and without forgetting those, nearly 500 in number, who are being punished and imprisoned in Europe for their resistance to military service. In some cases we have been able to secure the release of such victims, or to give them help and encouragement.

This is not my first visit to Copenhagen. Nearly forty years ago I came here with my wife, a fortnight after our marriage, and I remained here as Secretary to the British Legation for two years. I have retained a happy and unfaded memory of those two years during which I learned something of the friendliness and efficiency and the high political, scientific and artistic standard of the Danish people; and I was able from that time onward to recognize that size, power and riches were, in nations as in individuals, no necessarily true sign of an enlightened civilization.

I am afraid I have forgotten the little Danish I even knew, although I can still read it. One short sentence, however, has remained in my memory—*Det er ikke sand*—"It is not true," a very useful phrase, and one that if you will allow me I will apply to some of the considerations which I will bring before you today.

Det er ikke sand—it is not true that armaments mean security.

While it would be an impertinence for me to discuss the disputes which have taken place in the Danish parliament during this century on the subject of armaments, I may say that Denmark has the reputation in the world of having attempted to advance closer to the idea of complete disarmament, so far as international war is concerned, than any other nation. I would add that the first nation that disarms and refuses to participate in any international conflict will find that it has thereby obtained complete security. But more than that, it will have sent out a message to the nations of the world so well-founded both in morality and common sense, and so completely in accord with the wishes of the common people all the world over, that it is bound to have widespread influence in checking the possible destruction of modern civilization, with which the piling up of armaments we see today constantly threatens us. This mistaken confidence in force with which the governments of nations appear to be obsessed today is a legacy from the war of 1914-1918, and it requires courage on the part of some statesman or nation to proclaim to the world that since violence is no cure for any evil, that since violence never solves any dispute, and that since violence sows the seeds of hatred and revenge, advance toward a better civilization can only be pursued by refusing to yield to the temptation of joining with others in preparing for war, and by turning back from the downward path which leads to misery and chaos and taking the new path which leads to national well-being and international conciliation.

Det er ikke sand—it is not true that you can defend your people from the terrible destruction and ravages of modern warfare. It cannot be done, even if you have a superiority over the enemy in numbers and equipment. If your armaments are small they are worse than useless, because they only give the enemy the excuse for saying that just because you are armed you must be destroyed. But if a nation is unarmed, then I maintain that, low as international morality may be, there is no government which would attack a completely unarmed nation.

Det er ikke sand—it is not true that you can crush fascism, Communism or any other creed by force of arms—any more than it was possible for the Allies and associated powers to crush German militarism in the war twenty years ago. Ideas, if they are wrong, can only be crushed by allowing ideas which are right to prevail in the country itself.

Let me say here that while we detest some of the policies and ideas adopted by the governments of several of the nations in the world today, we have no quarrel with the peoples, and we should therefore waste less time in criticizing and abusing the governments and emphasizing all the things which they do that we think wrong, thereby increasing ill feeling. Let us rather seize on every sign of friendliness and good will which any government or dictator may offer, and encourage a sympathy which will make them develop their policy along better lines.

Det er ikke sand—it is not true that the League of Nations, as at present constituted, can check an aggressor by force of arms without greatly extending the area of warfare. The influence of the League can be greatly strengthened and its membership increased if its authority rests on a moral basis and the element of force is taken out of the Covenant altogether. As long as it is the ultimate basis of League action, those who have the biggest armaments will dominate the League. Wisdom, whether it comes from a big nation or a small nation, is of infinitely greater value for an international body whose main purpose is conciliation than any number of ships, guns or airplanes.

To put it shortly, we in the War Resisters International want the complete abolition of the thing we are resisting, namely, war. We do not believe in any halfway house, in proposals for limiting armaments or in trying to humanize the barbarities of modern warfare. We do not want a crack of the door to be left open. We want to bolt and bar the door against war as a method of attempting to settle international disputes.

We believe, therefore, not in accentuating differences of ideas and of governmental methods in various countries, but in cooperation all together. We are convinced that by international conference alone can such disputes as may exist be settled. Not after a bloody conflict, but before it can arise. We want our governments to think less of thwarting, correcting and punishing others and to concentrate more on concilating, encouraging and cooperating with the better elements which exist in every nation. We have no use for threats. We know that the world cannot remain carved up as it is today for all time. Necessary changes can be brought about by agreement, whereas changes effected by force must, as they have invariably in the past, sow the seeds of future conflict.

I venture to think that more people agree with us now than ever before. Some may be frightened to say so because of the pressure of the old false form of patriotism. Others may find it still difficult to believe that you are safer unarmed than well armed. But all except a few madmen and profiteers are desperately anxious to avoid war. The conflict in Spain shows what terrible injury and destruction even very inferior equipment may inflict.

We must continue to lead and show the way. Our position is based on the good that exists in mankind which we believe to be far stronger than the evil. To teach people to hate one another is a crime—a crime which the governments of the nations are preparing to commit again today.

Let us stand out. In every country the peoples are yearning for permanent peace. We are voicing their view, and by our deliberations we hope to send out a message of encouragement to the great human family who with us believes the path of violence means race suicide and the downfall of civilization.

Gerald Heard

diagnoses war as a symptom of a diseased civilization

GERALD HEARD [1889-   ] *has written on religion, mysticism and science. As a writer of mysteries under the name of H. F. Heard, he won the Ellery Queen Award in 1946 for the best mystery story of the year. He was born and educated in England and came to America in 1937. For a time he participated in a monastic community life near Laguna Beach, California, where members spend hours in meditation and silence and work is done on a communal basis. The remarks here were part of a speech Heard made in 1935 at a meeting in London on peace and internationalism.*

Social diagnosis today shows war to be only a symptom of a diseased individualized civilization. But, equally, that diseased individualism and egotism—the fundamental appeal to greed and fear as the two sole compelling motives of man—that can only be lived down by a conviction equal to its own force. The appeal to "mutual self-interest" to stop war is like relieving a dysenteric patient's sense of deadly weakness by giving him a square meal. We all live in a civilization, sociology makes us now realize, in which certain group suggestions dominate. To lift over the social organism onto other beliefs, to swing the ship onto another tack, needs intense experience of, and so conviction of, another way of living, a true way of life because it is creative and not destructive.

The new friendship aims, then, at having every pacifist trained in the initiative of social creativeness. It aims at so doing by every member joining a cell, or team, club or group in which he will constantly renew that direct sense of unlimited liability and psychological communism which make war and competition irrelevant. Then he will have the absolute assurance of "the excellent way," because he has actually experienced it, and that experience will make him not only able to resist the countersuggestion of those masses which cannot believe because they have not experienced anything but greed and fear, but will also call out (Lazarus-like) the ceremented soul in each and make it have the faith that it, too, can live and so civilization be saved.

War has, we now know, a triple root. It springs from political problems and diplomatic disingenuousness, from patriotic prestige and that love of scoring over or deceiving an antagonist, which frame of mind becomes a second nature to those who have won to national power by the exercise of such emotions and exclusive reflection on such thoughts. War, however, also springs from economic problems and financial devices. Third, it springs from those unresolved and unconscious neuroses, those profound inner conflicts which if we do not know how to cure we project on the world, assuaging our misery by blaming and finally assaulting others. War cannot, then, be really cured unless all these three sources of conflict are dried up. Its causes can be eliminated only by creating neutralizing causes. Such causative action can be generated in a small group of like-minded people who are agreed—as is every modern peace lover—on these three sources of war. For in such cells or teams active peace lovers can have a realization of kinship which will cure their own inner conflict, permit them to live a life of unlimited liability with their company—a true cooperative commonwealth based surely on psychology, which is the only sure foundation on which a just economy can rest—and give the world a demonstration of how free from anxiety and all psychoses, how sanely economic and how free of all necessity for coercion such a social life can be. Of the early Christians it was said that they had two irresistible advertisements, love ("See how these Christians love one another") and joy, the freedom and more than freedom from the anxiety, resentment and depression that are the by-products of the ego which can find no goal but itself. We now know from history that small units of like-minded people not only keep each other up to their first enthusiasm but help each other over times of individual discouragement. These are conscious things and, like giving each other fresh argumentative reasons for the faith that is in them, in helping each other to know the full strength of their case and the difficulties of hesitants, they are useful. They are, however, secondary to the unconscious forces which a group like-minded and regularly gathered together can and does release.

It is clear no individual can stand by himself against the invincible ignorance and the blind belief in greed and fear as the only social forces which still dominate our society today. He must gain practical actual reassurance that this belief is only a deadly half-truth which vanishes when the light of actual devotion is kindled against it. He can, however, no more do this by himself than a traveler who has tumbled into a bog in the dark can strike a light to see his way out. His matches are damp. Only in the group-field of fellow believers can he rekindle his light. That, however, is itself only half a truth. History shows that small groups meeting once a week for meditation, if each member is every day meditating by himself (and by meditation is meant the spiritual exercise every sincerely religious mind recognizes as essential to the spirit) do have experience of precipitated power. This is not only uniquely restorative, bodily as well as mentally, not only makes the members capable of real cooperative behavior and unlimited liability toward each other, but also gives each a power to deal generously and with creative initiative with all outside. Further, by all outside it is recognized as a power of sanity, happiness and good will which they they too would wish to share, and which they are ready to meet, if not halfway, at least far farther than they would have gone to with any other approach or appeal. The new attitude to this power is empirical. It is recognized as uniquely valuable for all pacific work. Without it we can do nothing. At the same time it is also recognized as an empirical fact that this power works under definite limits which we have not discovered how to transcend. It depends for its effectiveness on: (1) the degree that the constituents *are* of one mind, have the same goal; (2) the degree that they believe that this power of dynamic affection *and no other way* is the approach to and power over all human beings and all conscious creatures (to mix this method with any form of violence is to water gasoline); (3) the degree that they have learned how to meditate (and to use silence); (4) the degree that they find time daily to meditate by themselves and the regularity with which they meet to meditate together; and, finally, a queer but distinctive limitation which empiricists can only recognize and obey; (5) the degree to which the numbers are kept to a sum not exceeding a dozen.

Following this method, this praxis, there seems clear historical evidence (and indeed everyone may try it out for himself will he but find a handful of others to help) that the life of activism which eliminates self-conflict, class conflict and nation conflict can be lived. It is not easy, but it is no more exacting and far more interesting than any military discipline, and it is, of course, far more effective. It is a form of training, and so undertaking it people naturally are not afraid of discarding impediments, and as they advance such obstacles are more easily discarded. That is a reciprocal process. At the same time we must walk before we can run, and empiricism in this matter warns itself (from the sad experience of centuries) against imagining its first draft of this power as conferring either plenary inspiration or miraculous accomplishments. That is not to say such things can never be bestowed. It is only to point out that they only come after extreme training so that much work can be done even with the first yields and that nothing is gained, indeed often all lost, by rashly claiming privileges and powers, which humility would soon discover had in fact not yet been delegated. What is clear beyond a doubt is that in the "field" of a small like-minded group trained in meditation are the powers essential to curing conflict in the self, in society and between humanity.

Aldous Huxley

shows that peace is a by-product of a certain way of life

ALDOUS HUXLEY [1894-   ], *novelist and essayist, was born in England, educated at Eton, and came to the United States in the 1930's. His early novels were satirical discussions of contemporary English society. Pacifist ideas appear time and again in Huxley's writings—most noticeably in* Ends and Means, An Encyclopaedia of Pacifism *and in the pamphlet* "What Are You Going to Do About It?" *In 1935 Huxley spoke at a Peace and International meeting sponsored by the London and Middlesex Quarterly Peace Committee and the London Center of Friends Service Council. The following was part of his address, which was called* "Pacifism and Philosophy."

The warlike passions burn most fiercely in minds which think about the problems of peace and war in terms of generalizations and abstractions. To bring oneself to kill individual human beings is not easy; but when those human beings are thought of merely as members of a class which has previously been defined as evil, then killing becomes a simple matter. Brown, Jones and Robinson must not be thought of as Brown, Jones and Robinson, but as heretics, enemies of God, gentiles, non-Aryans, niggers, barbarians, Huns, fascists, Communists, capitalists, whichever the case may be. When they have been called such names and assimilated to the accursed class to which these names apply, Brown, Jones and Robinson cease to be regarded as human beings and become vermin or devils whom one is justified in exterminating in the most painful way possible. All war propaganda consists, in the last resort, in substituting diabolical abstractions for human beings. Similarly, those who defend war have invented a pleasant-sounding vocabulary of abstractions in which to describe the process of mass murder.

Consider the phrase which was on everybody's lips in 1917—the phrase "war of attrition." Nothing could be more genteel, less calculated to shock the sensibilities. For what is "attrition"? A mere process of rubbing. The word suggests the delicate polishing of a telescope lens. There is no hint of individuals suffering pain, going mad, being killed. All writings on the art of war are a tissue of such abstract or elegantly figurative phrases. (Coleridge called them "Our dainty terms for fratricide.") It is a most salutary exercise to go through such treatises translating each phrase as it occurs into other phrases expressing the individual reality of the situation under discussion. In general, no pacifist can permit himself to think in terms of abstractions. The abstractions in terms of which strategists describe war are meant to conceal the fact that war is a process of large-scale murder. The abstractions in terms of which propagandists describe the enemy are meant to conceal the fact that the hostile nation consists of individual men and women, having the same potentialities for good and evil as ourselves. Similarly abstractions such as "the state," and "the nation" should constantly be retranslated into terms descriptive of concrete individual reality. If this is not done, state and nation may easily come to be regarded as self-subsisting, divine entities which it is our duty to worship.

Abstractions are indispensable instruments of thought. Without them it would be impossible for us to think clearly or rapidly about the immensely complex world in which we live. But, though useful, abstractions are also dangerous. If we think only in terms of abstractions we shall go astray—go astray not only intellectually, but also emotionally and conatively. At any and every moment we must be prepared to see the individual realities behind our abstractions and generalizations. If we do this we shall retain our sanity, not only of intellect, but also—and this is more important in the circumstances—of feeling and of will. Abstractions and generalizations are symbols. Realities are individual.

The final question with which I shall deal is this: Which is the most propitious metaphysical environment for pacifism—a humanistic philosophy, or a philosophy which recognizes the existence of more than human spiritual realities?

History seems to show that many kinds of belief in spiritual powers are not only compatible with war, but that they also actively encourage the warlike passions of the believer. Thus any belief in an exclusive deity attached to a particular place or belonging to a particular community must inevitably make for war. Again, the deity may be theoretically universal, the father of all men; but particular groups may believe that their own views of the deity's nature and their own magical devices for enter-ing into touch with him are the only correct views and the only effective devices. Strong in this belief, they proceed to classify all those who think differently as "heretics" or "miscreants." Heretics can be thought of ab-stractly, not as human beings, but as representatives of a principle which is by definition a principle of evil. They are devils whom it is a duty to destroy. Belief in more than human spiritual realities has been in the past more often the enemy of pacifism than its friend. It can become its friend only on one condition: that the doctrine of the essential spiritual unity of man be taken seriously; that God be regarded, and if possible, experienced as a psychological fact, present at least potentially in every human being.

Let us now consider humanism. This philosophy of man for man's sake emerges at the Renaissance and becomes gradually more explicit during the seventeenth and eighteenth centuries. Humanism starts as the revolt against a Christianity in which belief in the universal fatherhood of God and consequent unity of men is purely theoretical, a Christianity not only compatible with war, but also directly responsible for wars. At first humanism reveals itself as the friend of pacifism. Wars are still freely waged during the eighteenth century, but are waged with a decency un-paralleled in earlier or later history. Then something strange, something utterly unanticipated by any of the great eighteenth-century humanists, takes place. There is a religious revival. This is partly a revival in terms of the old religion; but mainly and much more significantly a revival in terms of new, humanistic, mundane religions: the religions of nationalism and—a much less powerful creed—socialism. During the nineteenth cen-tury these religions (and especially the religion of nationalism) grow more and more powerful. Humanism, reinforced on its doctrinal side by the spectacular advances of science, makes it ever more difficult for ever increasing numbers of Europeans to accept the theologies of the old religion. But the desire to worship, to devote oneself and make sacrifices persists. To whom shall the sacrifices be made? Transcendental deities are out of the question. Finding themselves unable to believe in anything that they cannot see, men bow down to mundane gods. Superstition be-comes positivistic. A new idolatry appears. Instead of God, men adore the Nation, the State, the Class, the Leader. All history takes an undula-tory course. Religion has always had its ups and downs. A period of fervor and self-discipline is followed by one of slackness and self-indul-gence. In recent years this undulatory movement has shown itself most clearly in the history of the essentially humanistic religion of nationalism. Periods of slackness, during which people have thought only of money and what is called a good time, have alternated with periods of intense devotion—not to God, for humanism and science have made it difficult for the masses to believe in God, but to the local idols, Nation, State and Leader. We are living at the moment in a period of extreme idolatrous fervor.

Humanism has as its principal end-product the religion of nationalism. This religion, it is sufficiently obvious, is wholly incompatible with pacifism and can never be anything else. For nationalism marks a retreat from monotheism toward tribal gods, from beliefs in the essential unity of man to belief in his essential diversity. Significantly enough, our contemporary emperor-worship differs from that established by Augustus in being, not a unifying religion, but a separating and divisive one. Today there is not one emperor for many peoples; there is a whole pantheon of local emperors, each worshiped by his own people.

Humanism was once a favorable environment for pacifism. It has now become wholly inimical. Merely on grounds of utility we are justified in rejecting humanism. The tree is known by its fruits and in this case the fruits are bad. Humanism doesn't work and so is pragmatically untrue. There are, of course, other grounds for regarding humanism as an unsatisfactory doctrine and for believing in the existence of a spiritual reality at once transcendent and immanent, in which all human beings are united. I have no time, nor in the present talk is it my business, to set forth these grounds. Suffice it to say that, so far as pacifism is concerned, humanism has not in the long run shown itself propitious. Equally unpropitious is any kind of superhumanism that lends itself to exclusiveness and division. There is left the belief in a spiritual reality to which all men have access and in which they are united. Such a belief is the best metaphysical environment for pacifism; and if enough people address themselves to living up to this belief, if enough people set out to experience the spiritual reality in which men are united, then there will be peace; for peace is, so to speak, the by-product of a certain way of life—a way of life that is not only the outcome and practical illustration of the philosophy I have described, but is also, and at the same time, a device for advancing farther into the knowledge of the realities with which that philosophy is concerned.

Sherwood Eddy

explains how he made his decision for peace

SHERWOOD EDDY [1871-1963], *a world leader of the Y.M.C.A., studied theology and began his career in India as a missionary. He founded the American Seminar, which was an experiment in international education sponsored by the Y.M.C.A. He had a passion for social justice. As a result of his experience during World War I, Eddy became an absolute pacifist. But when Mussolini took over Abyssinia, when Hitler invaded the Rhineland, and World War II was in the making, he decided that the "absolute ethic" was an "impossible possibility." Commenting on the challenge of a nuclear war, Dr. Eddy asserted that to accomplish world peace, "on one hand we need at least a few pacifists as absolute idealists, and on the other hand many realists and relativists." The selection here is from* A Pilgrimage of Ideas, *published in 1934.*

It was the war which showed me the doom of the old competitive world of strife which often led to class war at home and to world war abroad. War was logically and vitally part and parcel of our competitive system. . . .

I had to face the question of war not only as a stubborn fact in experience, but as a challenge in my pilgrimage of ideas. Unless I was to be an unthinking robot, an automaton, a witless superpatriot, ready to respond to every slogan of easy propaganda, I was forced to take some final attitude with regard to war. Some things were not in my power, such as the vast social systems of slavery, capitalism and war; but some things were in my power, such as the attitude I should personally hold and the action I should take with regard to these systems. Here I was morally responsible, knowing that a small moral minority has led in every reform and every revolution in history.

In my long pilgrimage of ideas the war brought me face to face with one of the supreme moral problems of my life and of our generation. Whatever my preconceptions had been, I had lived through one war and had seen it in all its stark reality. What was I to do about war in the future? Was it for me a necessary or an unnecessary evil? Would I take part in such a slaughter again or break with the whole war system?

Temperamentally I could not remain in pale neutrality, nor postpone judgment in academic detachment till the bands would be playing again, the streets resounding to the tread of marching men, and the whole herd of us would be swept upon an emotional tidal wave into the next war, as we had been into the last.

By temperament and training I had not a pacifist bone in my body. The traditions in my family of fighting for the free soil of Kansas, of hunting and shooting, and the overcompensation for my early physical weakness and timidity, all weighed down the scale on the side of war. I had an abhorrence of "pacifism" and of everything passive. A militant crusade appealed to me more than *"passive* resistance," or any negative protest. During the war I had written *The Right to Fight,* defending America's entry into the world conflict with her high motives and ends, and making a tenfold indictment of Prussian militarism.

I had been deeply ashamed of America's failure to enter the war long before she did. Before I saw it at the front in all its ghastly reality the war had seemed to me to be a holy crusade, a half-divine crucifixion of humanity for the saving of the world. Germany was the personified devil incarnate and we were the self-appointed divine saviors of humanity. Such was our comforting, oversimplified misinterpretation of this moral problem.

But even during the war I began to be troubled by grave doubts and misgivings of conscience. I witnessed at the front a daily attrition of 25,000 in killed, wounded and prisoners. When I went to speak at Bradford, England, on an occasion when the Princess Marie Louise also spoke on behalf of the men at the front, they told us that the favorite sons of that city in a battalion of the "Bradford Pals" had been mowed down by machine-gun fire in a recent battle in France until there was not a man left on his feet. The whole battalion on that day had been swept into the categories of killed or wounded. We could not tell those parents much about the war. They knew far more than we did.

I can remember pacing up and down within sound of the guns on the sands of the seashore in the great base camps of France, deeply troubled in conscience and wrestling with the most difficult moral problem of my life up to that time. Here was a sharp conflict of duties. Could I be at once loyal to my country and to Christ? Could I serve both Caesar and God, or must I choose between two masters? The panorama of the war, like the reel of a moving picture, passed vividly before me: "A picture of a leprous earth, scattered with the swollen and blackening corpses of hundreds of young men. The appalling stench of rotting carrion, mingled with the sickening smell of exploded lyddite and ammonal. Mud like porridge, trenches like shallow and sloping cracks in the porridge—porridge that stinks in the sun. Swarms of flies and bluebottles clustering on pits of offal. Wounded men lying in the shell holes among decaying corpses, helpless under the scorching sun and bitter nights, under repeated shelling. Men with bowels dropping out, lungs shot away, with blinded, smashed faces, or limbs blown into space. Men screaming and gibbering, wounded men hanging in agony on the barbed wire until a friendly spout of liquid fire shrivels them up like a fly in a candle."

Some of my difficulties were caused by confusion of thought and of terminology. War, police, the use of force, the defense of one's family, the killing of a mad dog, Christ's cleansing the temple of the money changers—were all indiscriminately confused. The whole question was settled for some by a simple illustration or a supposed analogy: Would I kill a mad dog? Would I defend my wife against a violator? To which I would reply that of course I would kill a mad dog; that I would certainly defend my wife or child against a murderer or violator, and that I believed in an adequate police force under judicial sanction. None of these was war, nor had they anything to do with war. The police is a neutral third party for bringing the criminal to a judicial trial, based not upon force but upon law; it deals specifically with guilty criminal individuals, while war represents inevitable mass destruction of innocent and guilty alike; and finally the police is ideally, and in large measure actually, redemptive while war is inevitably destructive. Where the police exists to protect life and property, war represents the boundless maximum destruction of life and property. While the police force can be controlled, and acts as a voluntary body under judicial sanction, a modern army is drafted by compulsion, it cannot be morally controlled but is unleashed like a cyclone or an earthquake, for boundless mass destruction.

For myself, I must take the position of absolute pacifism as regards both world war and civil war. I will not hate and I will not kill. I think I have found a better weapon than a machine gun. I would try to use the same creative and constructive weapon which Gandhi wields today and which was wielded by Jesus of Nazareth centuries ago. I realize that this is most difficult. It is at the farthest remove from passive inertia or mere negative protest. It belongs to the imponderables which are not seen. It is always easier to go with the crowd, to fall in behind the band, to be swept by the mob orator and the mass appeal to "patriotism." But that course has become for me morally impossible. As once we put an end to slavery, so now we must stop war or war will destroy us. Faith, at least, can see a better way. And after all the strife of tongues and the academic debates of reason, faith must make the decision and take the plunge. My decision has been made for peace. Whether or not we can stop a world war, that decision has resulted personally in coming to rest in great peace of mind. It is one of the clearest convictions and surest satisfactions of my life.

Ernst Toller

offers a program for teaching the love of peace

ERNST TOLLER [1893-1939] *was a German dramatist who wrote in one of his plays, "Violence is always reactionary." He was born in Prussia and raised in a bourgeois and complacent world. He enlisted in the German army during World War I and was wounded. He turned to pacifism and organized the Student League for Peace in Heidelberg. He joined the Socialist movement, which aimed at overthrowing the Kaiser. He participated in the various revolutionary strikes and became head of the Council of Workers, Peasants, and Soldiers in the revolutionary government in Bavaria. When the revolutionary movement was suppressed, he was sentenced to five years in prison. During the twenties, he became a mystical preacher of nonviolence, and wrote revolutionary dramas and poetry. With the rise of Hitler, Toller left Germany, first living in Spain, and later in the United States. "Fight for Peace" was an article that appeared in 1934.*

That state which fires the first shot is not the breaker of the peace.

The peace-breaker is the state which teaches its people to glorify war; which teaches its children not the commandment of loving one's neighbor but the art of destroying one's neighbor; which instructs them in the handiwork of the soldier; which lets them play an inhuman game with those hellish productions of our time, poison gases and gas masks.

The word is stronger than weapons. For that reason we need:

The banishment of the spirit of war from school and universities.

The banishment of the spirit of war from all history books.

The banishment of the spirit of war from all newspapers, films and plays.

The banishment of the spirit of war from word and image and deed.

But this banishment of the spirit of war is only a beginning. Youth does not merely want to know what ought not to be; it wants to know what ought to be.

Teach them that peace is not a state but a risk.

Teach them peace as a dangerous and an adventurous task.

Teach them peace as the revolutionary activity of man.

Teach them that a hero's death is a small thing in comparison with a heroic life for great moral aims, which daily and hourly demand renunciation and manliness, a daring and strong spirit.

Teach them that the senseless adventure of war is nothing beside the adventures of rational life. Peace, as we know it today, is no ideal; it is poisoned by social injustice; it is a mere semblance of that peace which, with the strength of our reason, with the strength of our hearts, we can plan and build.

That peace in which the ideas of human and social justice, the ideas of spiritual freedom, the ideas of the true development of all citizens shall penetrate the work of all nations.

Teach them to love this adventure, and they will turn with contempt from the cannibal customs of degenerate tribes.

Guglielmo Ferrero
finds war nothing but a form of collective suicide

GUGLIELMO FERRERO [1871-1942], *an Italian journalist, author and historian, was born in Portici, near Naples. Because he strongly opposed the fascist regime in Italy, he moved to Switzerland where he could teach at the Geneva University and continue to speak out against fascism. Mussolini called him "an anti-Italian, anti-Roman, anti-fascist, anti everything alive and strong in this Italy." The following comes from Ferrero's book* Peace and War, *which came out in 1933.*

The history of mankind is nothing but a succession of great catastrophes. Why? Because such catastrophes are necessary to free the world from the monstrosities that periodically torment it. Powerful as he is, man is an imperfect and unbalanced creature, and he always ends by exaggerating the principles, aspirations and needs most in keeping with his nature to such a monstrous pitch that they become unbearable afflictions. The most splendid civilizations have perished either directly through the action of these insufferable miscreations or indirectly through man's desperate efforts to get rid of them. Ancient civilization accomplished marvels, but it had stretched the hierarchical principle so far as to divide mankind into two classes, gods and brutes. The members of the ruling aristocracies or monarchies were not made of the same clay as the miserable rabble who existed but to obey—they were divided beings. The only service done by the immense upheaval which demolished almost the whole of ancient civilization—arts, literature, schools of philosophy, law, religions, institutions—was to blot out this enormity finally and forever and to lead back kings and nobles to the fold of poor mortal humankind. Almost everything that had been destroyed was made anew—art, literature, philosophy, law, institutions; but gods of flesh and blood were no longer to be seen seated on their thrones or stalking past with sword in hand. Freed from this monstrous notion, the Mediterranean world created a new and marvelous civilization, founded on a new principle— the supremacy of the spiritual over the temporal. It was a sublime principle, but man contrived to push even this too far, and to evolve from it a theocracy which likewise in due course became unbearable. Its overthrow cost three centuries of strife and the destruction of part of the wonderful civilization of the Middle Ages. For the last century we have been trying to reconstruct, as best we can, as much of this as can still be rebuilt.

The monstrous thing that threatens Western civilization is "super"-war, waged without any definite reason, with aims that continually shift and expand, and with no possible conclusion but revolution on the weaker side. As a morbid exaggeration of the human agencies in war, it is doomed to disappear. Mankind will rid itself of it as it has rid itself of all the bloated growths that have endangered its existence. The question is, whether it will be swept away by some brutal onslaught of material forces upon our sluggish passivity in the course of a series of disasters which will destroy the very foundations of the new powers that mankind is beginning to misuse; or whether it will be abolished by some reaction of our moral sense and an act of the human will prompted by the first such disaster. In the first case many things that deserve to survive, and that will have to be laboriously refashioned, will perish at the same time. Russia offers for our contemplation the initial stages of what might be, within a few degrees more or less, the future existence of all Western civilization if it does not find in itself the strength to solve the problem. *De te fabula narratur.*

Are we still masters of our fate? The great riddles of our age are not in our heads, but in our hearts. What are we? Pagans or Christians? Civilized people or barbarians? Masters or slaves? We do not know. All is mist and confusion in our souls. What has happened in our conscience to our two great legacies from the past—the humanitarianism of the eighteenth century, which was the secular form of Christianity; and Christianity itself, the religious sublimation of all the highest aspirations of mankind of old, or at least of its noblest peoples? Are they still alive in our conscience or have they been gradually withered up by wealth, power, knowledge, pride, the distracting influences of endless activity, ambition, envy, and the thirst for pleasure? Can we have become just clever barbarians, without admitting it, without knowing it, without noticing it?

The heart and not the head will decide our future. If the deep springs of Christianity and humanitarianism have dried up in our souls, if, among the peoples who are responsible for leading Western civilization, the ruling classes and the masses do not feel it to be the universal duty to rest from bloodshed after the last great massacre, if we submit ourselves to destiny in face of the problem of war and the difficulties we have gradually allowed to accumulate in it and around it, our civilization will one day or other be the victim of that nightmare outburst of violence we now vaguely dread. We shall only reach salvation by way of a new Middle Age, brought into being by the loosing of the monstrous power we have created and no longer know how to control; a Middle Age—alas!—of high explosives, with no Giotto, with no Dante, with no Christ.

Simone Weil

asks if a revolution can be accomplished without war

SIMONE WEIL [1909-1943], *was born in Paris of Jewish parents, but she rejected Judaism and became sympathetic to the Catholic Church. She belonged to no political party, but identified herself with the poor and the suffering. She left her job as a teacher in a university to work in factories. At the outbreak of the Spanish Civil War, she joined the Spanish Loyalists in a position where she did not have to use weapons. She volunteered for the French resistance to Hitler, but was rejected because of poor health. Simone Weil was only twenty-four years old when she wrote "Reflections on War." It originally appeared in 1933 in* La Critique Sociale, *a magazine published in Paris.*

Revolutionary war is the grave of revolution. And it will be that as long as the soldiers themselves, or rather the armed citizenry, are not given the means of waging war without a directing apparatus, without police pressure, without courts-martial, without punishment for deserters. Once in modern history was a war carried on in this manner—under the Commune. Everybody knows with what results. It seems that revolution

engaged in war has only the choice of either succumbing under the murderous blows of counterrevolution or transforming itself into counterrevolution through the very mechanism of the military struggle.
The perspectives of a revolution seem therefore quite restricted.
For can a revolution avoid war? It is, however, on this feeble chance that we must stake everything or abandon all hope. An advanced country will not encounter, in case of revolution, the difficulties which in backward Russia served as a base for the barbarous regime of Stalin. But a war of any scope will give rise to others as formidable.

For mighty reasons a war undertaken by a bourgeois state cannot but transform power into despotism and subjection into assassination. If war sometimes appears as a revolutionary factor, it is only in the sense that is constitutes an incomparable test for the functioning of the state. In contact with war, a badly organized apparatus collapses. But if the war does not end soon, or if it starts up again, or if the decomposition of the state has not gone far enough, the situation results in revolutions, which, according to Marx's formula, perfect the state apparatus instead of shattering it. That is what has always happened up to now.

In our time the difficulty developed by war to a high degree is especially that resulting from the ever growing opposition between the state apparatus and the capitalist system. The Briey affair during the last war provides us with a striking example. The last war brought to several state apparatuses a certain authority over economic matters. (This gave rise to the quite erroneous term of "war socialism.") Later the capitalist system returned to an almost normal manner of functioning, in spite of custom barriers, quotas and national monetary systems. There is no doubt that in the next war things will go a little farther. We know that quantity can transform itself into quality. In this sense, war can constitute a revolutionary factor in our time, but only if one wants to give the term "revolution" the meaning given to it by the Nazis. Like economic depression, a war will arouse hatred against capitalists, and this hatred, exploited for "national unity," will benefit the state apparatus and not the workers. Furthermore, to realize the kinship of war and fascism, one has but to recall those fascist tracts appealing to "the soldierly spirit" and "front-line socialism." In war, as in fascism, the essential "point" is the obliteration of the individual by a state bureaucracy serving a rabid fanaticism. Whatever the demagogues may say, the damage the capitalist system suffers at the hands of either of these phenomena can only still further weaken all human values.

The absurdity of an antifascist struggle which chooses war as its means of action thus appears quite clear. Not only would this mean to fight barbarous oppression by crushing peoples under the weight of even more barbarous massacre. It would actually mean spreading under an-

other form the very regime that we want to suppress. It is childish to suppose that a state apparatus rendered powerful by a victorious war would lighten the oppression exercised over its own people by the enemy state apparatus. It is even more childish to suppose that the victorious state apparatus would permit a proletarian revolution to break out in the defeated country without drowning it immediately in blood. As for bourgeois democracy being annihilated by fascism, a war would not do away with this threat but would reinforce and extend the causes that now render it possible.

It seems that, generally speaking, history is more and more forcing every political actor to choose between aggravating the oppression exercised by the various state apparatuses and carrying on a merciless struggle against these apparatuses in order to shatter them. Indeed, the almost insoluble difficulties presenting themselves nowadays almost justify the pure and simple abandonment of the struggle. But if we are not to renounce all action, we must understand that we can struggle against the state apparatus only inside the country. And notably in case of war, we must choose between hindering the functioning of the military machine of which we are ourselves so many cogs and blindly aiding that machine to continue to crush human lives.

Thus Karl Liebknecht's famous words, "The main enemy is at home," take on their full significance and are revealed to be applicable to all wars in which soldiers are reduced to the condition of passive matter in the hands of a bureaucratic and military apparatus. This means that as long as the present war technique continues, these words apply to any war, absolutely speaking. And in our time we cannot foresee the advent of another technique. In production as in war, the increasingly collective manner with which forces are operated has not modified the essentially individual functions of decision and management. It has only placed more and more of the hands and lives of the mass at the disposal of the commanding apparatuses.

Until we discover how to avoid in the very act of production or of fighting, the domination of an apparatus over the mass, so long every revolutionary attempt will have in it something of the hopeless. For if we do know what system of production and combat we aspire with all our heart to destroy, we do not know what acceptable system could replace it. Furthermore, every attempt at reform appears puerile in face of the blind necessities implied in the operation of the monstrous social machine. Our society resembles an immense machine that ceaselessly snatches and devours human beings and which no one knows how to master. And they who sacrifice themselves for social progress are like persons who try to catch hold of the wheels and the transmission belts in order to stop the machine and are destroyed in their attempts.

But the impotence one feels today—an impotence we should never consider permanent—does not excuse one from remaining true to one's self, nor does it excuse capitulation to the enemy, whatever mask he may wear. Whether the mask is labeled fascism, democracy, or dictatorship of the proletariat, our great adversary remains The Apparatus—the bureaucracy, the police, the military. Not the one facing us across the frontier or the battle lines, which is not so much our enemy as our brothers' enemy, but the one that calls itself our protector and makes us its slaves. No matter what the circumstances, the worst betrayal will always be to subordinate ourselves to this Apparatus, and to trample underfoot, in its service, all human values in ourselves and in others.

3
THE WAR TO END WARS

[1914-1932]

In 1914 Europe was armed to the teeth and playing with intrigue. It was one of these intrigues, the assassination of the Archduke Francis Ferdinand at Sarajevo, that kindled World War I.

War took the peace movement by surprise.

In Germany, the prewar peace movements were virtually silenced. In France, pacifist publications were banned, and within the peace societies themselves a militant patriotism took over, making any talk of pacifism suspect, if not treasonable.

The peace society in England remained passive. In May 1915, the London *Herald of Peace* commented that "the pacifist has no chance when his country is at war. . . . Strict personal neutrality becomes imperative."

British pacifists set up a twofold duty for themselves during the war: One, to seek its end by mediation at the first opportunity, with the United States acting as mediator; and two, to aid the wounded and the victims of battle. Many of the British pacifists, like their American counterparts later in the war, opposed conscription.

The government of the United States had taken a position of neutrality and demanded of the Central Powers respect for the rights of a neutral on the high seas. When the war began, Woodrow Wilson, at one time a member of the American Peace Society, was President. William Jennings Bryan, an avowed Christian pacifist and an admirer of Tolstoy, was his Secretary of State. Wilson was re-elected in 1916 on a platform stressing that "he kept us out of war," in spite of American outrage after the *Lusitania*, with 114 American citizens aboard, was sunk by a German submarine.

In April 1917 the United States abandoned its neutrality and declared war on Germany. Nearly all of the country rallied behind its President. Even Bryan, who had pleaded that the U.S. should not "get down and wallow in the mire of human blood," was now ready to support his country in war. President Wilson called for a war to make the world "safe for democracy." "This," he told Congress in January 1918, "is the culminating and final war for human liberty."

The American Peace Society supported the government in the war effort, though it kept pointing out in *Advocate of Peace*, its publication, that the society was "opposed to any war. . . . The abolition of war is an international job. Were we to stop this war today, it would not mean that the disease of war would be cured, or even ameliorated. . . . We must now end this war by winning it. There can be no end of war until after the collapse of the existing German Imperial Government."

But still there were dissenters. The American Friends Service Committee in a letter to Friends of draft age expressed the hope that "you are so deeply grounded in the principles of Friends that your conscience will lead you to act consistently with these principles." The historically peaceful religious sects issued proclamations. Some of their members went to prison for their stands, but their numbers were small. Most church leaders were carried away by the war cry. In the academic world, the pacifist voice was generally silenced, too. Only a few people remained strong and uncompromising.

The most outspoken antagonists of war in the United States came from the Socialists, the Anarchists, and the Industrial Workers of the World, although most of their counterparts in Europe forgot the international solidarity they had been preaching.

Eugene V. Debs spoke for the majority of American Socialists when he said, "Let us swear by all that is dear to us and all that is sacred to the cause, never to become soldiers and never to go to war." His party, in its famous St. Louis declaration, stated: "Our entrance into the European war was instigated by the predatory capitalists in the United States. . . . The working class of the United States has no quarrel with the working class of Germany or of any other country." They pledged "continuous, active, and public opposition to the war, through demonstrations, mass publications, and all other means within our power."

The Industrial Workers of the World sang Joe Hill's song— "Don't take my papa away from me"—and scorned church support of the war by singing, "Onward Christian soldiers, duty's way is plain: slay your Christian neighbors, or by them be slain." At its 1916 general convention, the IWW adopted a resolution which openly declared the group to be "determined opponents of all nationalistic sectionalism, or patriotism, and the militarism preached and supported by our enemy, the capitalist class. . . . We condemn all wars, and for the prevention of such, we proclaim the antimilitarist propaganda in time of peace, thus promoting class solidarity among the workers of the entire world, and, in time of war, the general strike in all industries."

After the armistice in 1918 came a flood of antiwar books—among them John Dos Passos' *Three Soldiers* and Erich Maria Remarque's *All Quiet on the Western Front*. In France, Barbusse and Rolland wrote against war. Poets and writers, students and workers marched, sang, proclaimed "never again."

The International Congress of Women held at Zurich in 1919 lamented the terms of the Versailles Treaty, which it charged "seriously violates the principles upon which alone a just and lasting peace can be secured, and which the democracies of the world have come to accept." They objected that "the terms of peace tacitly sanction secret diplomacy, deny the principles of self-determination, recognize the right of the victors to the spoils of war, and create all over Europe discords and animosities, which can only lead to future wars."

The peace movement had undergone a change because of the First World War. It ceased to talk simply about the evils of war; it began looking for plausible solutions through international law and political bonds. And it began to attract all kinds of authoritative support.

The American bar and bench, for example, cooperated in the erection of a memorial to Hugo Grotius, the father of international law, on the three-hundredth anniversary of his *De Jure Belli ac Pacis*. Many organizations apart from the Nobel board were awarding peace prizes: the Filene Award, for the best proposal for peace and prosperity through international cooperation; the Raphel Herman prize for the best educational plan to aid in maintaining world peace. The Carnegie Endowment was a rich source of funds—and respectability. Nicholas Murray Butler, the president of Columbia University, lent invaluable support to efforts for international peace.

The churches went on with their campaigns. The Committee on World Friendship Among Young People, which was an affiliate of the Federal Council of Churches, proposed what they called "A Peace Creed for Youth." In it they said, "We believe: that the supreme task of the rising generation is the abolition of war. We believe: that the Church of Jesus Christ is the only institution capable of generating the will-to-peace. If war is to be outlawed it will be because the Christian church has summoned the nations to sheathe their swords and live at peace with one another."

While the peace movement was again gathering momentum, the Indian National Congress was held, and there Mahatma Gandhi proposed his program of nonviolent resistance as a weapon for his people against British rule. "The lawbreaker breaks the law surreptitiously and tries to avoid the penalty," Gandhi explained; "not so the civil resister. He ever obeys the laws of the state to which he belongs, not out of fear of the sanctions but because he considers them to be good for the welfare of society. But there come occasions, generally rare, when he considers certain laws to be so unjust as to render obedience to them a dishonour. He then openly and civilly breaks them and quietly suffers the penalty for their breach. And in order to register his protest against the action of the law givers, it is open to him to withdraw his cooperation from the state by disobeying such other laws whose breach does not involve moral turpitude." *

In 1932 Henri Barbusse and Romain Rolland invited peace groups and labor unions to a Congress Against War. The Socialist Second International and certain pacifist groups called the congress a Communist front and refused to participate. In fact, the congress did have the support of the Communist Third International and the Red International of Labor Unions. The accusation of "Communist front" was to become more acute in later years as the Communists attempted more and more to dominate such organizations.

It was also in 1932 that the Women's International League for Peace printed slips of paper with the declaration: "That part of the income tax which is levied for preparation for war is paid only under protest and duress." The slips were designed to be pasted to the individual income-tax return.

In the same year, Adolf Hitler's Nazi Party won its first majority in the German Reichstag.

* M. K. Gandhi, *Non-Violent Resistance*, p. 7.

Stephen Wise

*warns his congregation against supporting the deepest
and most terrible sin of men*

RABBI STEPHEN S. WISE [1874-1949] *was born in Budapest and
brought to the United States at the age of one. He was president of
the American Jewish Congress and chairman of the executive committee
of the World Jewish Congress. He actively championed the peace cause
before World War I, but when the United States entered the war, he
gave full support to the war effort. In 1932, on the twenty-fifth anniversary of the founding of The Free Synagogue in New York City, and the
quarter-century anniversary of his rabbinate at that temple, Dr. Wise
pledged that he would not support war again. But with the rise of Hitler,
he could see no other way of defeating Nazism, and he reluctantly accepted war as the lesser evil. This is part of his 1932 speech.*

We might go on in forecast of the problems which are bound to face us
and our successors. I shall limit myself to one which, it appears to me, lies
at the heart of all other problems, and is bound up with them. I single it
out for the special and personally grievous reason that in relation thereto
I have failed more completely than in any other phase of my life's ministry.
And it behooves me to set down my failures with something of the vigor
with which I have outlined the cause of my unchanging adherence. Like
most teachers of religion, Jewish or Christian, I was, prior to the World
War, a more or less active champion of the peace cause. The war came,
and to my everlasting regret, I took sides. I gave my public and private
support to that which I still impenitently believed to have been the less
guilty of the two groups of warring nations. I believed at the time that the
war would prove to be the last war, and that it should and must be entered
by our nation as the war to end war. I was not deceived herein by the
leader of the nation. I knew him well enough to be justified in saying that
he truly though erringly believed that this war would with our help end
wars. He did not, perhaps could not, foresee what we have come to know,
that the World War could not end war, because war never did end war,
because war never will end war. War breeds war and not peace. The war
to end war can never be. It is not contriteness alone that moves me to
make this confession. I make it because it leads to consequences which
are of the largest import to me and may prove, in time, to be deeply
important to my people.

Without reservation or equivocation, I herewith affirm that the pulpit of the Free Synagogue, while I stand in it, will never give its support to war, to any war whatsoever, to war with any other people or nation. I would as little support a war to crush Hitlerism as a war for the strengthening of Jewish claims in Palestine. Though I bore no arms, I gave the fullest measure of my private and public support, that is to say, my material and moral support to the United States and the Allied Nations in the World War. I will never do so again.

But why speak of this now, seeing that there is no war nor likelihood of war? Because there is no war or seeming likelihood thereof! If war should come, as it may come, I do not wish my people to be justified in saying they had no knowledge of the pacifist principles of their pulpit. If the day should come when our nation goes to war, it would be understood that I could have no part therein, that not only would I refuse to give moral support, but I would not directly or indirectly give aid and furtherance to them that have part therein. Whenever that eventuality arises, I should be prepared, as I am today, to face the consequences of my refusal, within the law if possible, outside it if necessary, to support my country in time of war. And one of the consequences of my refusal might well be the necessity of withdrawing from the pulpit of the Free Synagogue, if any number of my people believed it desirable that I should withdraw.

Far off though the day of war may be for us, it cannot be too soon to make one pertinent observation. If war should come and I find it necessary to utter my unyielding opposition thereto, not a few of you, my people, would share my conviction and still imagine that as Jews you could not afford to take a stand as pacifists. Without discussing the rights and wrongs of war at this time, I feel justified in warning my fellow Jews against the harm they do themselves and their country by foreswearing a conviction the moment it becomes inconvenient or difficult or unpopular to hold it. Whatever of moral greatness inheres in the history of Israel arises out of the truth that our people were ever content to be a people of hopeless minorities and lost causes. Whether Christendom is to prove faithful or faithless to the teaching of its great founder, "They that take up the sword shall perish by the sword," we of the Jewish brotherhood know that every command of our faith runs counter to war, that war is the supreme repudiation and negation of religion forasmuch as war commands man to kill, to hate, to lie, to covet, to steal, and that, until war goes, the prophecy and faith of our fathers cannot be fulfilled: "and no man shall slay his brother." I dwell on this, because at any hour war may come, and I wish my beloved people to know that far from giving support to war, any war, this pulpit will lift up its voice against the godlessness of the deepest and most terrible sin of men.

Lately, a Jew, the foremost living scientist, addressed a public appeal to his fellow scientists, urging them to refuse to cooperate in creating new terrors for warfare, with a view to maintaining world peace. The message was addressed to the International Conference of War Resisters. But it was an appeal to scientists to stop scientific research for war purposes. Scientists not a few will doubtless demur, maintaining that their first duty is to their respective countries. And it will be bombastically averred that science and its achievements must always be at the command of national interests. And there will be Jews in all lands who will, Bernard Shaw to the contrary notwithstanding, lament that this most distinguished of Jews, this "universe maker," has entered upon courses which will prove seriously harmful to Jews in many lands. I venture to say that this word of Einstein and his founding of the War Resisters' League may prove to have a more enduring effect upon the moral and spiritual development of mankind than the propounding of the doctrine of relativity will have upon the progress of physical science. The German scientist takes his place by the side of the Hebrew prophets. Man may resist and deny and banish and smite the prophet for an hour, but the future belongs to him. If we are to be fearful of hurt which courage and nobility may do us, then we do not deserve to go on as a people.

Roderick Seidenberg

describes the prison life of conscientious objectors

RODERICK SEIDENBERG [1889-   ], *an architect and writer, was born in Schwetzinger near Heidelberg; four years later he came to the United States with his family. When World War I began, Seidenberg registered as an absolute conscientious objector. In May 1918 he was drafted—and refused service. Two days after the armistice was declared, Seidenberg was tried at Fort Riley, Kansas, on the technical charge of having refused to help clean up the parade grounds. He was sentenced to life imprisonment at hard labor, but after one and a half years he was discharged. His article called "I Refuse to Serve" first appeared in* The American Mercury *in 1932.*

... To steal, rape or murder, to slap an officer's face and call him a son of a bitch—these are the standard peacetime entrance requirements to the Disciplinary Barracks. But in time of war too firm a belief in the words of Christ, too ardent a faith in the brotherhood of man, is even more acceptable. But prisons are democratic institutions, and no matter how one entered, one's number was stencilled on one's trousers and the back of one's shirt in white to mark a new beginning. One might rise and receive a white star as a trusty, but it was just as likely that one would sink, first into the red-numbered lock-step gang and finally into solitary, where the digits in yellow marked the lowest depths of the vast military hierarchy. We sank to the yellow bottom, for our offense was the gravest one can commit—in prison. Even the murder gang, who had trampled to death an unfortunate "rat," enjoyed the comparative freedom of wandering about in a basement cell-block when they were not exercising in the sunlight of the yard. Our case was different; we had offended military pride. We must be broken.

The first to arrive at Leavenworth who refused to work were six stalwart Molokans, true Christians if ever there were any. They went cheerfully into the "hole," each one in a pitch-dark cell on bread and water, manacled standing to the bars of their cells for nine hours every day—to sleep, exhausted, on the bare cement floor. Others followed. . . .

Leavenworth was taken by surprise. There were not enough dark cells. The officers had never before encountered a like demonstration. Each morning the executive officer inquired of our health and smilingly offered us the rock pile. Each morning we declined. Two weeks passed, and the executive officer no longer smiled. We had broken not only the rules of the institution, but its traditions as well. No one had ever stood this treatment for more than a few days. . . .

. . . If we could not be overwhelmed, perhaps we could be undermined. Psychiatry was brought into action as a form of depth-bombery. With infinite tact and a judicious show of esteem, we were invited to realize that our position as political objectors was altogether untenable. We were not a bad lot, but we were sadly misguided. It appeared, indeed, that we were intelligent. This was not to be inferred from our actions; it had simply been established by the Army intelligence tests. But if we were intelligent, we were all the more guilty of a deplorable lack of judgment.

This lack of judgment was due not to our attitude toward war, but to our method of expressing it. We had obviously not stopped the war. We were not merely in the minority; we were ludicrously alone. It appeared that the acknowledged leader of the American intelligentsia, Professor John Dewey, had analyzed our attitude and found us wanting. We were the victims of moral futility, of an egocentric lack of judgment that was close to being culpable. Our conscience was largely self-conceit. If

Professor Dewey's participation in the war enterprise had no other effect, it at least allayed the last doubts of the more liberal-minded officials about condemning us. His utterances were retailed with unction, and we were reminded of the high source whence they came.

Having staked all upon a war to end war, the liberal people were not above trick questions, false appeals and spurious arguments. Under the impact of such tactics the simplicity of our position gave way; we were forced to make elaborate efforts to define our principles and to draw, with ever minuter distinctions, the nature of our stand. Our sincerity, it is true, was no longer in question. That had been officially conceded months ago, though no one knew, upon examining the question, precisely what sincerity might mean. Our lapses from rectitude, it was apparent, were of a subtler order; they arose from defections that only psychiatry could reveal.

We had refused to participate in organized slaughter; we were considered insensitive and unfeeling toward the higher causes of humanity. We had thought to stand aloof from the madness of war; we were antisocial and doctrinaire. We had taken what appeared to us the one direct and positive and unarguable position for peace; we were negative obstructionists. We had refrained from any propaganda, we believed in freedom of conscience; we were egocentric heretics. We thought ourselves tolerably sane; we were psychopathic.

. . . Here were men from all quarters and from all walks of life: religious farmers from the Middle West who alone seemed capable of community living, I.W.W.'s from the Far West, Socialists from the East Side of New York; men from Chicago, from the South; men who had been sailors, carpenters, college students, tailors. One was a statistician, one a prize-fighter from Philadelphia, one a music teacher. . . . I missed a few of the older friends who were no longer with us—Evan Thomas, with whom I could talk of philosophy and a *Weltanschauung;* Maurice Hess, a Dunkard, now a college professor, a man of exceptional erudition and amazing courage behind the mildest exterior.

But most of all, in a way, I missed my friend Sam Solnitski. His racy, ironic humor helped many an hour along. In the guardhouse at Fort Riley, while we awaited trial, he would pace up and down with me, telling of his life in Poland, of his escape to America to avoid military service, of his days in this country as a skilled worker on the uppers of women's shoes—the very finest—for prostitutes! Best of all, however, he had read, it seemed to me, all of literature—in Yiddish. Now he told the grand stories of Maupassant, of Balzac, of Anatole France, in a mixture half-English, half-Yiddish, which made these tales of elegant ladies and Parisian life more real than ever. Solnitski had distinguished himself at his court-martial. In his own way he had attempted to explain to the twelve precise majors of the court the reasons for his opposition to military service—but in vain. He broke off in despair: "Ow, shucks, what's the use!" The court stenographer immortalized the words. . . .

Sigmund Freud
examines the nature of man's aggressive instincts

SIGMUND FREUD [1856-1939], *the founder of psychoanalysis, was raised and educated in Vienna, where he became a doctor of medicine in 1881. In 1930 Germany awarded him one of its highest honors when the city of Frankfort presented him with the Goethe Prize. Only a few years later, the Hitler government confiscated and destroyed his books and property. He left Austria for London in 1938. In July 1932 Dr. Albert Einstein had written to Freud inviting him to a frank exchange of views on the question "Why war?" The exchange came from a proposal of the League of Nations and its International Institute of Intellectual Cooperation. This was Freud's reply.*

Vienna, September 1932

DEAR PROFESSOR EINSTEIN,

When I learned of your intention to invite me to a mutual exchange of views upon a subject which not only interested you personally but seemed deserving, too, of public interest, I cordially assented. I expected you to choose a problem lying on the borderland of the knowable, as it stands today, a theme which each of us, physicist and psychologist, might approach from his own angle, to meet at last on common ground, though setting out from different premises. Thus the question which you put me —what is to be done to rid mankind of the war menace?—took me by surprise. And, next, I was dumbfounded by the thought of my (of *our,* I almost wrote) incompetence; for this struck me as being a matter of practical politics, the statesman's proper study. But then I realized that you did not raise the question in your capacity of scientist or physicist, but as a lover of his fellow men, who responded to the call of the League of Nations much as Fridtjof Nansen, the Polar explorer, took on himself the task of succoring homeless and starving victims of the World War. And, next, I reminded myself that I was not being called on to formulate practical proposals, but, rather, to explain how this question of preventing wars strikes a psychologist.

But here, too, you have stated the gist of the matter in your letter—and taken the wind out of my sails! Still, I will gladly follow in your wake and content myself with endorsing your conclusions, which, however, I propose to amplify to the best of my knowledge or surmise.

You begin with the relations between Might and Right, and this is assuredly the proper starting point for our inquiry. But, for the term "might," I would substitute a tougher and more telling word: "violence." In right and violence we have today an obvious antinomy. It is easy to prove that one has evolved from the other and, when we go back to origins and examine primitive conditions, the solution of the problem follows easily enough. I must beg your indulgence if in what follows I speak of well-known, admitted facts as though they were new data; the context necessitates this method.

Conflicts of interest between man and man are resolved, in principle, by the recourse to violence. It is the same in the animal kingdom, from which man cannot claim exclusion; nevertheless men are also prone to conflicts of opinion, touching, on occasion, the loftiest peaks of abstract thought, which seem to call for settlement by quite another method. This refinement is, however, a late development. To start with, brute force was the factor which, in small communities, decided points of ownership and the question which man's will was to prevail. Very soon physical force was implemented, then replaced, by the use of various adjuncts; he proved the victor whose weapon was the better, or handled the more skillfully. Now, for the first time, with the coming of weapons, superior brains began to oust brute force, but the object of the conflict remained the same: one party was to be constrained, by the injury done him or impairment of his strength, to retract a claim or a refusal. This end is most effectively gained when the opponent is definitively put out of action—in other words, is killed. This procedure has two advantages; the enemy cannot renew hostilities, and, secondly, his fate deters others from following his example. Moreover, the slaughter of a foe gratifies an instinctive craving—a point to which we shall revert hereafter. However, another consideration may be set off against this will to kill: the possibility of using an enemy for servile tasks if his spirit be broken and his life spared. Here violence finds an outlet not in slaughter but in subjugation. Hence springs the practice of giving quarter; but the victor, having from now on to reckon with the craving for revenge that rankles in his victim, forfeits to some extent his personal security.

Thus, under primitive conditions, it is superior force—brute violence, or violence backed by arms—that lords it everywhere. We know that in the course of evolution this state of things was modified, a path was traced that led away from violence to law. But what was this path? Surely it issued from a single verity; that the superiority of one strong man can be overborne by an alliance of many weaklings, that *l'union fait la force.* Brute force is overcome by union, the allied might of scattered units makes good its right against the isolated giant. Thus we may define "right" (i.e., law) as the might of a community. Yet it, too, is nothing else than violence, quick to attack whatever individual stands in its path, and it employs the selfsame methods, follows like ends, with but one difference; it is the communal, not individual, violence that has its way. But, for the transition from crude violence to the reign of law, a certain psychological condition must first obtain. The union of the majority must be stable and enduring. If its sole *raison d'être* be the discomfiture of some overweening individual and, after his downfall, it be dissolved, it leads to nothing. Some other man, trusting to his superior power, will seek to reinstate the rule of violence and the cycle will repeat itself unendingly. Thus the union of the people must be permanent and well organized; it must enact rules to meet the risk of possible revolts; must set up machinery ensuring that its rules—the laws—are observed and that such acts of violence as the laws demand are duly carried out. This recognition of a community of interests engenders among the members of the group a feeling of unity and fraternal solidarity which constitutes its real strength.

So far I have set out what seems to me the kernel of the matter: the suppression of brute force by the transfer of power to a larger combination, founded on the community of sentiments linking up its members. All the rest is mere tautology and glosses. Now, the position is simple enough so long as the community consists of a number of equipollent individuals. The laws of such a group can determine to what extent the individual must forfeit his personal freedom, the right of using personal force as an instrument of violence, to ensure the safety of the group. But such a combination is only theoretically possible; in practice the situation is always complicated by the fact that, from the outset, the group includes elements of unequal power, men and women, elders and children, and very soon, as a result of war and conquest, victors and the vanquished—i.e., masters and slaves—as well. From this time on the common law takes notice of these inequalities of power, laws are made by and for the rulers, giving the servile classes fewer rights. Thenceforward there exist within the state two factors making for legal instability, but legislative evolution, too: First, the attempts by members of the ruling class to set themselves above the law's restrictions and, secondly, the constant struggle of the ruled to extend their rights and see each gain embodied in the code, replacing legal disabilities by equal laws for all. The second of these tendencics will be particularly marked when there takes place a positive mutation of the balance of power within the community, the frequent outcome of certain historical conditions. In such cases the laws may gradually be adjusted to the changed conditions or (as more usually ensues) the ruling class is loath to reckon with the new developments, the result being insurrections and civil wars, a period when law is in abeyance and force once more the arbiter, followed by a new regime of law. There is another factor of constitutional change, which operates in a wholly pacific manner, viz.: the cultural evolution of the mass of the community; this factor, however, is of a different order and can only be dealt with later.

Thus we see that, even within the group itself, the exercise of violence cannot be avoided when conflicting interests are at stake. But the common needs and habits of men who live in fellowship under the same sky favor a speedy issue of such conflicts and, this being so, the possibilities of peaceful solutions make steady progress. Yet the most casual glance at world history will show an unending series of conflicts between one community and another, or a group of others, between large and smaller units, between cities, countries, races, tribes and kingdoms, almost all of which were settled by the ordeal of war. Such wars end either in pillage or in conquest and its fruits, the downfall of the loser. No single all-embracing judgment can be passed on these wars of aggrandizement. Some, like the war between the Mongols and the Turks, have led to unmitigated misery; others, however, have furthered the transition from violence to law, since they brought larger units into being, within whose limits a recourse to violence was banned and a new regime determined all disputes. Thus the Roman conquests brought that boon, the *pax romana,* to the Mediterranean lands. The French kings' lust for aggrandizement created a new France, flourishing in peace and unity. Paradoxical as it sounds, we must admit that warfare well might serve to pave the way to that unbroken peace we so desire, for it is war that brings vast empires into being, within whose frontiers all warfare is proscribed by a strong central power. In practice, however, this end is not attained, for as a rule the fruits of victory are but short-lived, the new-created unit falls asunder once again, generally because there can be no true cohesion between the parts that violence has welded. Hitherto, moreover, such conquests have only led to aggregations which, for all their magnitude, had limits, and disputes between these units could be resolved only by recourse to arms. For humanity at large the sole result of all these military enterprises was that, instead of frequent not to say incessant little wars, they had now to face great wars which, for all they came less often, were so much the more destructive.

Regarding the world of today the same conclusion holds good, and you, too, have reached it, though by a shorter path. There is but one sure way of ending war and that is the establishment, by common consent, of a central control which shall have the last word in every conflict of interests. For this, two things are needed: first, the creation of such a supreme court of judicature; secondly, its investment with adequate executive force. Unless this second requirement be fulfilled, the first is unavailing. Obviously the League of Nations, acting as a Supreme Court, fulfills the first condition; it does not fulfill the second. It has no force at its disposal and can only get it if the members of the new body, its constituent nations, furnish it. And, as things are, this is a forlorn hope. Still we should be taking a very shortsighted view of the League of Nations were we to ignore the fact that here is an experiment the like of which has rarely —never before, perhaps, on such a scale—been attempted in the course of history. It is an attempt to acquire the authority (in other words, coercive influence), which hitherto reposed exclusively in the possession of power, by calling into play certain idealistic attitudes of mind. We have seen that there are two factors of cohesion in a community: violent compulsion and ties of sentiment ("identifications," in technical parlance) between the members of the group. If one of these factors becomes inoperative, the other may still suffice to hold the group together. Obviously such notions as these can only be significant when they are the expression of a deeply rooted sense of unity, shared by all. It is necessary, therefore, to gauge the efficacy of such sentiments. History tells us that, on occasion, they have been effective. For example, the Panhellenic conception, the Greeks' awareness of superiority over their barbarian neighbors, which found expression in the Amphictyonies, the Oracles and Games, was strong enough to humanize the methods of warfare as between Greeks, though inevitably it failed to prevent conflicts between different elements of the Hellenic race or even to deter a city or group of cities from joining forces with their racial foe, the Persians, for the discomfiture of a rival. The solidarity of Christendom in the Renaissance age was no more effective, despite its vast authority, in hindering Christian nations, large and small alike, from calling in the sultan to their aid. And, in our times, we look in vain for some such unifying notion whose authority would be unquestioned. It is all too clear that the nationalistic ideas, paramount today in every country, operate in quite a contrary direction. Some there are who hold that the Bolshevist conceptions may make an end of war, but, as things are, that goal is very far away and, perhaps, could only be attained after a spell of brutal internecine warfare. Thus it would seem that any effort to replace brute force by the might of an ideal is, under present conditions, doomed to fail. Our logic is at fault if we ignore the fact that right is founded on brute force and even today needs violence to maintain it.

I now can comment on another of your statements. You are amazed that it is so easy to infect men with the war fever, and you surmise that man has in him an active instinct for hatred and destruction, amenable to such stimulations. I entirely agree with you. I believe in the existence of this instinct and have been recently at pains to study its manifestations. In this connection may I set out a fragment of that knowledge of the instincts, which we psychoanalysts, after so many tentative essays and gropings in the dark, have compassed? We assume that human instincts are of two kinds: those that conserve and unify, which we call "erotic" (in the meaning Plato gives to *Eros* in his *Symposium*), or else "sexual" (explicitly extending the popular connotation of "sex"); and, secondly, the instincts to destroy and kill, which we assimilate as the aggressive or destructive instincts. These are, as you perceive, the well-known opposites, Love and Hate, transformed into theoretical entities; they are, perhaps, another aspect of those eternal polarities, attraction and repulsion, which fall within your province. But we must be chary of passing overhastily to the notions of good and evil. Each of these instincts is every whit as indispensable as its opposite and all the phenomena of life derive from their activity, whether they work in concert or in opposition. It seems that an instinct of either category can operate but rarely in isolation; it is always blended ("alloyed," as we say) with a certain dosage of its opposite, which modifies its aim or even, in certain circumstances, is a prime condition of its attainment. Thus the instinct of self-preservation is certainly of an erotic nature, but to gain its ends this very instinct necessitates aggressive action. In the same way the love instinct, when directed to a specific object, calls for an admixture of the acquisitive instinct if it is to enter into effective possession of that object. It is the difficulty of isolating the two kinds of instinct in their manifestations that has so long prevented us from recognizing them.

If you will travel with me a little further on this road, you will find that human affairs are complicated in yet another way. Only exceptionally does an action follow on the stimulus of a single instinct, which is *per se* a blend of Eros and destructiveness. As a rule several motives of similar composition concur to bring about the act. This fact was duly noted by a colleague of yours, Professor G. C. Lichtenberg, sometime Professor of Physics at Göttingen; he was perhaps even more eminent as a psychologist than as a physical scientist. He evolved the notion of a "Compass-card of Motives," and wrote: "The efficient motives impelling man to act can be classified like the 32 Winds, and described in the same manner, e.g. *Food-Food-Fame* or *Fame-Fame-Food*." Thus, when a nation is summoned to engage in war, a whole gamut of human motives may respond to this appeal; high and low motives, some openly avowed, others slurred over. The lust for aggression and destruction is certainly included; the innumerable cruelties of history and man's daily life confirm its prevalence and strength. The stimulation of these destructive impulses by appeals to idealism and the erotic instinct naturally facilitates their release. Musing on the atrocities recorded on history's page, we feel that the ideal motive has often served as a camouflage for the lust of destruction; sometimes, as with the cruelties of the Inquisition, it seems that, while the ideal motives occupied the foreground of consciousness, they drew their strength from the destructive instinct submerged in the unconscious. Both interpretations are feasible.

You are interested, I know, in the prevention of war, not in our theories, and I keep this fact in mind. Yet I would like to dwell a little longer on this destructive instinct, which is seldom given the attention that its importance warrants. With the least of speculative efforts we are led to conclude that this instinct functions in every living being, striving to work its ruin and reduce life to its primal state of inert matter. Indeed it might well be called the "death instinct"; whereas the erotic instincts vouch for the struggle to live on. The death instinct becomes an impulse to destruction when, with the aid of certain organs, it directs its action outward, against external objects. The living being, that is to say, defends its own existence by destroying foreign bodies. But, in one of its activities, the death instinct is operative *within* the living being and we have sought to trace back a number of normal and pathological phenomena to this *introversion* of the destructive instinct. We have even committed the heresy of explaining the origin of human conscience by some such "turning inward" of the aggressive impulse. Obviously, when this internal tendency operates on too large a scale, it is no trivial matter, rather a positively morbid state of things; whereas the diversion of the destructive impulse toward the external world must have beneficial effects. Here is, then, the biological justification for all those vile, pernicious propensities which we now are combating. We can but own that they are really more akin to nature than this our stand against them, which, in fact, remains to be accounted for.

All this may give you the impression that our theories amount to a species of mythology and a gloomy one at that! But does not every natural science lead ultimately to this—a sort of mythology? Is it otherwise today with your physical science?

The upshot of these observations, as bearing on the subject in hand, is that there is no likelihood of our being able to suppress humanity's aggressive tendencies. In some happy corners of the earth, they say, where nature brings forth abundantly whatever man desires, there flourish races whose lives go gently by, unknowing of aggression or constraint. This I can hardly credit; I would like further details about these happy folk. The Bolshevists, too, aspire to do away with human aggressiveness by ensuring the satisfaction of material needs and enforcing equality between man and man. To me this hope seems vain. Meanwhile, they busily perfect their armaments, and their hatred of outsiders is not the least of the factors of cohesion among themselves. In any case, as you, too, have observed, complete suppression of man's aggressive tendencies is not in issue; what we may try is to divert it into a channel other than that of warfare.

From our "mythology" of the instincts we may easily deduce a formula for an indirect method of eliminating war. If the propensity for war be due to the destructive instinct, we have always its counteragent, Eros, to our hand. All that produces ties of sentiment between man and man must serve us as war's antidote. These ties are of two kinds. First, such relations as those toward a beloved object, void though they be of sexual intent. The psychoanalyst need feel no compunction in mentioning "love" in this connection; religion uses the same language: Love thy neighbor as thyself. A pious injunction easy to enounce, but hard to carry out! The other bond of sentiment is by way of identification. All that brings out the significant resemblances between men calls into play this feeling of community, identification, whereon is founded, in large measure, the whole edifice of human society.

In your strictures on the abuse of authority I find another suggestion for an indirect attack on the war impulse. That men are divided into leaders and the led is but another manifestation of their inborn and irremediable inequality. The second class constitutes the vast majority; they need a high command to make decisions for them, to which decisions they usually bow without demur. In this context we would point out that men should be at greater pains than heretofore to form a superior class of independent thinkers, unamenable to intimidation and fervent in the quest of truth, whose function it would be to guide the masses dependent on their lead. There is no need to point out how little the rule of politicians and the Church's ban on liberty of thought encourage such a new creation. The ideal conditions would obviously be found in a community where every man subordinated his instinctive life to the dictates of reason. Nothing less than this could bring about so thorough and so durable a union between men, even if this involved the severance of mutual ties of sentiment. But surely such a hope is utterly utopian, as things are. The other indirect methods of preventing war are certainly more feasible, but entail no quick results. They conjure up an ugly picture of mills that grind so slowly that, before the flour is ready, men are dead of hunger.

As you see, little good comes of consulting a theoretician, aloof from worldly contacts, on practical and urgent problems! Better it were to tackle each successive crisis with means that we have ready to our hands. However, I would like to deal with a question which, though it is not mooted in your letter, interests me greatly. Why do we, you and I and many another, protest so vehemently against war, instead of just accepting it as another of life's odious importunities? For it seems a natural thing enough, biologically sound and practically unavoidable. I trust you will not be shocked by my raising such a question. For the better conduct of an inquiry it may be well to don a mask of feigned aloofness. The answer to my query may run as follows: Because every man has a right over his own life and war destroys lives that were full of promise; it forces the individual into situations that shame his manhood, obliging him to murder fellow men, against his will; it ravages material amenities, the fruits of human toil, and much besides. Moreover wars, as now conducted, afford no scope for acts of heroism according to the old ideals and, given the high perfection of modern arms, war today would mean the sheer extermination of one of the combatants, if not of both. This is so true, so obvious, that we can but wonder why the conduct of war is not banned by general consent. Doubtless either of the points I have just made is open to debate. It may be asked if the community, in its turn, cannot claim a right over the individual lives of its members. Moreover, all forms of war cannot be indiscriminately condemned; so long as there are nations and empires, each prepared callously to exterminate its rival, all alike must be equipped for war. But we will not dwell on any of these problems; they lie outside the debate to which you have invited me. I pass on to another point, the basis, as it strikes me, of our common hatred of war. It is this: we cannot do otherwise than hate it. Pacifists we are, since our organic nature wills us thus to be. Hence it comes easy to us to find arguments that justify our standpoint.

This point, however, calls for elucidation. Here is the way in which I see it. The cultural development of mankind (some, I know, prefer to call it civilization) has been in progress since immemorial antiquity. To this process we owe all that is best in our composition, but also much that makes for human suffering. Its origins and causes are obscure, its issue is uncertain, but some of its characteristics are easy to perceive. It well may lead to the extinction of mankind, for it impairs the sexual function in more than one respect, and even today the uncivilized races and the backward classes of all nations are multiplying more rapidly than the cultured elements. This process may, perhaps, be likened to the effects of domestication on certain animals—it clearly involves physical changes of structure —but the view that cultural development is an organic process of this order has not yet become generally familiar. The psychic changes which accompany this process of cultural change are striking, and not to be gainsaid. They consist in the progressive rejection of instinctive ends and a scaling down of instinctive reactions. Sensations which delighted our forefathers have become neutral or unbearable to us; and, if our ethical and aesthetic ideals have undergone a change, the causes of this are ultimately organic. On the psychological side two of the most important phenomena of culture are, firstly, a strengthening of the intellect, which tends to master our instinctive life, and, secondly, an introversion of the aggressive impulse, with all its consequent benefits and perils. Now, war runs most emphatically counter to the psychic disposition imposed on us by the growth of culture; we are therefore bound to resent war, to find it utterly intolerable. With pacifists like us it is not merely an intellectual and affective repulsion, but a constitutional intolerance, an idiosyncrasy in its most drastic form. And it would seem that the aesthetic ignominies of warfare play almost as large a part in this repugnance as war's atrocities.

How long have we to wait before the rest of men turn pacifist? Impossible to say, and yet perhaps our hope that these two factors—man's cultural disposition and a well-founded dread of the form that future wars will take—may serve to put an end to war in the near future, is not chimerical. But by what ways or by-ways this will come about we cannot guess. Meanwhile, we may rest on the assurance that whatever makes for cultural development is working also against war.

With kindest regards and, should this *exposé* prove a disappointment to you, my sincere regrets.

Yours,

Sigmund Freud

Mahatma Gandhi
describes his means of battle

MOHANDAS K. GANDHI [1869-1948] *was educated in London and practiced law in Bombay. In 1893 he went to South Africa on a legal matter for an Indian firm, and became deeply involved in the plight of the oppressed Indian community. It was there that he developed Satyagraha, his conception of nonviolent resistance. From Christ, Gandhi maintained, he learned passive resistance and nonviolence, from Tolstoy noncooperation, from Thoreau disobedience. Satyagraha was the foundation of Gandhi's long battle for India's freedom, which was won in 1947. The first of the two articles here appeared as "My Faith in Nonviolence" in 1930; the second, as "The Future" in 1940.*

I have found that life persists in the midst of destruction and, therefore, there must be a higher law than that of destruction. Only under that law would a well-ordered society be intelligible and life worth living. And if that is the law of life, we have to work it out in daily life. Wherever there are jars, wherever you are confronted with an opponent, conquer him with love. In a crude manner I have worked it out in my life. That does not mean that all my difficulties are solved. I have found, however, that this law of love has answered as the law of destruction has never done. In India we have had an ocular demonstration of the operation of this law on the widest scale possible. I do not claim therefore that nonviolence has necessarily penetrated the three hundred millions, but I do claim that it has penetrated deeper than any other message, and in an incredibly short time. We have not been all uniformly nonviolent; and with the vast majority, nonviolence has been a matter of policy. Even so, I want you to find out if the country has not made phenomenal progress under the protecting power of nonviolence.

It takes a fairly strenuous course of training to attain to a mental state of nonviolence. In daily life it has to be a course of discipline, though one may not like it—like, for instance, the life of a soldier. But I agree that, unless there is a hearty cooperation of the mind, the mere outward observance will be simply a mask, harmful both to the man himself and to others. The perfect state is reached only when mind and body and speech are in proper coordination. But it is always a case of intense mental struggle. It is not that I am incapable of anger, for instance, but I succeed on almost all occasions to keep my feelings under control. Whatever may be the result, there is always in me a conscious struggle for following the law of nonviolence deliberately and ceaselessly. Such a struggle leaves one stronger for it. Nonviolence is a weapon of the strong. With the weak it might easily be hypocrisy. Fear and love are contradictory terms. Love is reckless in giving away, oblivious as to what it gets in return. Love wrestles with the world as with the self and ultimately gains a mastery over all other feelings. My daily experience, as of those who are working with me, is that every problem lends itself to solution if we are determined to make the law of truth and nonviolence the law of life. For truth and nonviolence are, to me, faces of the same coin.

The law of love will work, just as the law of gravitation will work, whether we accept it or not. Just as a scientist will work wonders out of various applications of the law of nature, even so a man who applies the law of love with scientific precision can work greater wonders. For the force of nonviolence is infinitely more wonderful and subtle than the material forces of nature, like, for instance, electricity. The men who discovered for us the law of love were greater scientists than any of our modern scientists. Only our explorations have not gone far enough and so it is not possible for everyone to see all its workings. Such, at any rate, is the hallucination, if it is one, under which I am laboring. The more I work at this law the more I feel the delight in life, the delight in the scheme of this universe. It gives me a peace and a meaning of the mysteries of nature that I have no power to describe.

. . . But I may state my own individual view of the potency of non-violence. I believe that a state can be administered on a nonviolent basis if the vast majority of the people are nonviolent. So far as I know, India is the only country which has a possibility of being such a state. I am conducting my experiment in that faith. Supposing, therefore, that India attained independence through pure nonviolence, India could retain it too by the same means. A nonviolent man or society does not anticipate or provide for attacks from without. On the contrary, such a person or society firmly believes that nobody is going to disturb them. If the worst happens, there are two ways open to nonviolence. To yield possession but noncooperate with the aggressor. Thus, supposing that a modern edition of Nero descended upon India, the representatives of the state will let him in but tell him that he will get no assistance from the people. They will prefer death to submission. The second way would be nonviolent resist-ance by the people who have been trained in the nonviolent way. They would offer themselves unarmed as fodder for the aggressor's cannon. The underlying belief in either case is that even a Nero is not devoid of a heart. The unexpected spectacle of endless rows upon rows of men and women simply dying rather than surrender to the will of an aggressor must ultimately melt him and his soldiery. Practically speaking there will be probably no greater loss in men than if forcible resistance was offered; there will be no expenditure in armaments and fortifications. The non-violent training received by the people will add inconceivably to their moral height. Such men and women will have shown personal bravery of a type far superior to that shown in armed warfare. In each case the bravery consists in dying, not in killing. Lastly, there is no such thing as defeat in nonviolent resistance. That such a thing has not happened before is no answer to my speculation. I have drawn no impossible picture. History is replete with instances of individual nonviolence of the type I have mentioned. There is no warrant for saying or thinking that a group of men and women cannot by sufficient training act nonviolently as a group or nation. Indeed the sum total of the experience of mankind is that men somehow or other live on. From which fact I infer that it is the law of love that rules mankind. Had violence, i.e., hate, ruled us, we should have become extinct long ago. And yet the tragedy of it is that the so-called civilized men and nations conduct themselves as if the basis of society was violence. It gives me ineffable joy to make experiments proving that love is the supreme and only law of life. Much evidence to the contrary cannot shake my faith. Even the mixed nonviolence of India has supported it. But if it is not enough to convince an unbeliever, it is enough to incline a friendly critic to view it with favor.

Toyohiko Kagawa
says violence is its own destruction

TOYOHIKO KAGAWA [1888-1960] *was a Japanese social worker, reformer, novelist, and pacifist. Born in Kobe of a wealthy Buddhist family, Kagawa was converted to Christianity at fifteen. He gave away his wealth and went to live in the slum section of Kobe and work among the poor. He was active in the organization of cooperatives, and also helped to win universal male suffrage in Japan. He received his divinity degree from Princeton University in 1915. Returning to Japan he became active in the labor movement, and in 1921 helped to organize the first labor union in that country. He opposed both the war with China and World War II; before Pearl Harbor he led a delegation of Japanese Christians to the United States to try to prevent a break between the two nations. He was jailed several times by Japanese authorities for his pacifist views, and by 1941 he was forbidden to speak or write on the subject of war. After 1945 he devoted himself to working with various groups for peace. In 1946 he was named to the House of Peers. The following excerpt is from his book* Love—the Law of Life, *published in 1929.*

I stand against all learning, all institutions, all governments, all arts, all religions, which reject love. I protest against every so-called church which preaches faith and fails to love. I oppose the politicians who rely on force and know nothing about love. If I have to be arrested for saying this, let me be handcuffed, for I had rather die quickly by the sword than die of thirst in a loveless desert.

Nonresistance does not mean cowardice. Some misunderstand the meaning of nonresistance and take it to signify nonrejection of evil. But that is a gross error. For since it fundamentally rejects evil, it tells men to cease their petty interference.

Love evolves perennially, never grudging sacrifice. Since love has never abhorred matyrdom, it perceives that in the process of evolution it is more effective to be killed than to kill.

Men who fear to make the sacrifice of love will have to fight. Those who believe in the sacrifice through love believe in the principle of non-injury.

For those who eternally evolve there is an eternal cross.

Love is basic for the birth of a true society, while violence has in it the essence of antisociality.

Love is positive; violence is negative.

Love injures none, is eternal. Violence is degeneracy: it is its own destruction.

John Haynes Holmes

sees pacificism taking hold in personal relationships

J O H N   H A Y N E S   H O L M E S   [1879-   ], *clergyman and lifelong abso-lute pacifist, was born in Philadelphia and raised in Boston. He became a Unitarian minister in 1904, but fifteen years later he withdrew from the ministry and reorganized his church as a free society rather than a sec-tarian church. Dr. Holmes was one of the founders of the American Civil Liberties Union, which started during World War I as the Ameri-can Union Against Militarism. He has been associated with this organi-zation ever since, as well as with the National Association for the Advancement of Colored People, of which he was also a founder. The article here appeared in 1929.*

It is an easy and pleasant task to discuss pacifism in personal relations. For it is precisely in these relations that pacifism has won its victory—a victory so complete and final that it is difficult now to conceive that it was ever in doubt.

In international relations force still rules the world, and the program of pacifism is regarded by practical men as a foolish and on occasion

dangerous dream of amiable because weak fanatics. In economic relations
the jungle law prevails between competing capitalists and between similarly competing capitalists and laborers, and constant strife, both horizontal
and vertical, reveals with lurid glare "the good old plan" that

> *They should take who have the power*
> *And they should keep who can.*

In social relations we have our prisons, our police, our constabulary,
our whole vast system of repression, punishment and death imposed upon
the weak by the sheer physical power of the strong; and any proposal
that there may be another and better way of keeping order in society is
scorned as inexcusable levity when not denounced as mild insanity. Yet
the very men who accept force and violence as the divinely ordered
method of controlling and directing human affairs are most of them
exemplifying in their personal relations the program of pure pacifism!
In this most intimate, delicate and difficult of all phases of human conduct,
which once was ruled, like other relations between human beings, by the
dominance of physical power, these men are dispensing with force and
violence altogether. They have found this better way of which we have
spoken—a way itself so simple, beautiful and effective that it has been
forgotten that there was ever any other.

Yesterday, in our relations as individuals, we were all of us brutes
whose reliance was on "tooth and claw," just as we are still such brutes in
our relations as members of the social order; today, in these personal relations, however, we are most of us men who have discovered reason and
good will. In that one field of experience, in other words, wherein we
are able to exert direct personal control over events, we have established
life on an out-and-out pacifist basis. And this achievement, so hardly won,
and now so quietly and happily accepted, is the prophecy of the coming
victory of pacifism in those more remote international, industrial and
social fields which men have yet to reclaim from the jungle to civilization.

The most primitive and intimate of all personal relations is the sex
relation between man and woman. So far as we can make out, one of the
earliest forms of marriage was "marriage by capture." The man went out
and seized by force the woman with whom he had chosen to consort.
The helpmate thus seized by force must of course be held by force; and
thus for ages the basis of the marital relation was accepted without question as the superior physical strength of the male. Long after "marriage by
capture" had been succeeded by "marriage by purchase," and still later
by other more civilized methods of acquisition, the laws and customs of
society sustained the husband in the forceful possession of the wife. If
defeated in war, for example, his wife became a part of the booty of the

conqueror, to be held by him in perpetuity as wife or concubine. Euripides' *Trojan Women* shows how obediently, if tragically, this convention was accepted by women as well as men.

In the ordinary relations of daily life the rule of the husband over the wife ran all the way from the ancient power of life and death to the modern power of rebuke and chastisement. As late as the early decades of the nineteenth century in England, the right of a husband to beat his wife was duly established in the statute laws of the kingdom. The growing humanity of the times imposed a limit, to be sure, upon the pain and injury which could be inflicted—the rod of his anger must not be thicker than the man's thumb! But the right itself to beat into submission was incontestable. How could it be otherwise? For a man must keep order in his household; he must hold his wife fast to the stern duties of "bed and board." And how can this be done save by the rule of force? As well expect a slave to labor without the overseer's lash, as the wife to serve without the husband's fist or stick.

But all this is now a part of the barbarism of the past. No longer is marriage established and maintained upon the basis of the physical power of the male. There is compulsion still, but it is the compulsion of love and not of force. If a man is to win a woman today he must stir her compassion for his need and her admiration for his virtue. If a man is to hold a woman he must bind her to him by the compelling power of pure affection. The faithful wife now stands by her husband not because she fears his strength, but because she adores his devotion. She loves him, that is all! And "love is enough." Thus slowly through the ages has the marital relation been lifted from the low plane of physical force to the high plane of "soul force," to use Gandhi's great phrase. If husband and wife hold together today it is because they are "kindly affectioned one toward another, tender hearted, forgiving one another." Marriage, in other words, to the exact degree of its real success, is a purely pacifist institution.

What is true of the relation of husband and wife is true as well of the relation of parent and child. For centuries it was believed, and among multitudes of men is still believed, that children must be disciplined by force. "Spare the rod and spoil the child" is an adage not of one language but of many. In ancient times the father had frequently the power to slay his child on an occasion of extremity. This barbaric right has been tempered in our time to various forms of corporal punishment. But at the bottom of the latter as of the former is the conviction that a natively incorrigible boy or girl must be controlled, and that control must be compassed by the threat or use of force. The superior physical power of the adult is the guarantee of order in the household. How otherwise can a child be disciplined to that capacity of self-control and self-direction which is the essence of character?

But corporal punishment, the use of force in the handling of a child, is in our time utterly discredited. In no enlightened household is the hand of the father or mother even so much as lifted against their offspring. Whipping, slapping, shutting in closets, denial of food, all penalties successfully visited upon children because the parents have the physical power to enforce their will, are now seen to be, like all use of violence, an indulgence of the primitive within us, and thus a breakdown of the very character which we would create in the child. They are above all, like all use of violence again, a resort of desperation on the part of those who know no better way.

But this better way exists—and has been found and is now being practiced in many homes. To understand a child, to respect a child, to love a child—this is all that is necessary to control a child. Nay, this very word "control" is inaccurate, a survival of the old and horrid days of physical compulsion! We do not "control" children any more; rather do we liberate them into a favorable environment created and sustained by the wisdom of enlightened minds and the peace of loving hearts. Our task as parents is to discipline, not our children but ourselves, and thus to make a world in which they may grow like flowers in the sun. . . .

In our wider personal relations, as between man and man, the same truth holds. In earlier days the individual citizen went armed upon the street by day, and hid himself away at night in a home which was at once a fort and an arsenal. The sword or stave was as much a part of the personal equipment of a man three centuries ago as the fountain pen or match box is a part of the equipment of the modern man. Security of property and person demanded, according to the practice of the time, that force be ready for instant and effective use.

But we have a different practice today. The old convention still endures, rather foolishly, in the case of certain men who carry revolvers on their persons or keep them handy in their bedrooms. But most men today are emancipated from this personal bondage to the rule and armament of force. My own experience, I imagine, is typical of millions of men and women in our time. I was brought up in a household wherein firearms were taboo. I never saw a pistol or a gun except in places altogether removed from my immediate experience. For many years my father was regularly away from home for periods varying from one to three weeks, or even a month. This left my mother and the three younger children alone, to guard our property and protect our lives as best we could. But we never had firearms, most of the time not even a dog, to resist a possible intruder. Now the custom of the family has descended to me. My home is as defenseless against attack as a paper box. Neither bolts nor bars, pistols nor swords, have any place in my household economy. As for myself, I have traveled far, been in dark places in strange cities at unseemly hours, hiked 'cross country as a stranger in a strange land, but have never carried so much as a stick to defend myself from molestation. And this is a commonplace of experience today, is it not? The armed man is disappearing from contemporary life. The armored home is as antiquated as a medieval castle. We no longer live together as citizens on the basis of force. Slowly but surely, through centuries of evolution in social contacts, we have been learning to substitute for force the intangible but substantial virtues of trust, good will, and fair play one with another; until the weapons which were yesterday regarded as necessary to security are now actually regarded as a menace to security and, in a city like New York, for example, are prohibited by law. So far have we gone in shifting the daily routine of life to a pacifist basis that I am today, as a citizen of New York, actually guilty of a crime under the laws of the state if I have a revolver on my person or in my home.

But, it may be argued, this change in social custom does not mean that force has disappeared as the sanction of order and security in personal relations. It simply means that force has changed its form, or rather its place. Weapons are carried just as much today as they ever were, only they have been transferred from the possession of the single citizen as a law unto himself to the possession of official police as the representative of the citizen. We do not undertake today to arm ourselves for defense at home and abroad for the obvious reason that there are armed men on every street corner charged professionally with this task. What we cannot do now, policemen will do for us with precisely the same weapons that our fathers used in the good old days of private arms. Behind the defense-less citizen, in other words, there stands the whole vast machinery of the police. Society exists today, as it has always existed, on the basis of force. Not so conspicuous as it used to be, this force is now infinitely more effec-tive, since it is no longer distributed among myriad amateurs, but concen-trated in the hands of professionals trained, like soldiers, to the job of shooting and killing.

To such plea of avoidance there are two answers. First, the police system is nothing new or unique in our time. Rome was superbly policed in the classic days of her imperial power. Yet her citizens felt it as neces-sary to be armed as to be decently clothed and shaved. In the Middle Ages there were wide areas where law of the king or the duke was imposed upon the people with a rigor unmatched in most areas of social life today. Yet every burgher went armed, and every traveler on the highways had his armed retainers. *Per contra,* in certain cities, not altogether unknown in our time, the police power has disintegrated under the corrosive influ-ence of political and commercial corruption, and insecurity, so far as public control is concerned, has become rife throughout the community. But there has been no general arming of the populace, and few individual householders have felt it necessary to turn their domiciles into citadels. Such collapse of the police power, it may be said incidentally, is coincident with veritable orgies of violence upon the part of the uniformed officers of law. In Chicago, for example, which is as near to a condition of primitive anarchy as any city in this country, the police are frequently armed with rifles as well as revolvers, and patrol the streets in armored automobiles equipped, like tanks on a battlefront, with machine guns. In London, on the other hand, long famous for the orderliness of its streets and the security of its homes, the police have no weapons at all. As a matter of fact, there is little causal relation between the phenomena of unarmed citizenry and an armed police. So far have we gone in the direction of pure pacifism in our civic life that we are actually in sight of disarming the state as well as the individual in the routine associations of our daily affairs.

A second answer to our opponent's plea is found in the fact that men in all ages have explored and traveled through areas of the world which were unorganized socially, or were inhabited by savage tribes, and yet have found arms unnecessary. Most men, to be sure, have relied in such regions upon physical force for their security. They have met the spear with the sword, the arrow with the bullet. But others have gone unarmed and unafraid, on the simple basis of manly confidence in men, and have not had their trust betrayed. In the absence, in other words, of all force, save that wielded menacingly by the strange barbarians among whom they have moved, these gallant adventurers have not only survived, but have enjoyed a security and happiness unknown to those who have come breathing bloodshed and slaughter. The Quakers have given us the supreme examples of this pacifist achievement in modern times. William Penn, in his Pennsylvania experience, answered conclusively and forever the claim that there is no ultimate security in our contacts with our fellow men, especially those of inferior culture, except in the control and exercise of superior physical force. Arms are necessary only when "hatred, variance, emulations, wrath, strife, seditions, envyings, murders, and such like" are present in the heart. Displace these sentiments with "love, joy, peace, long-suffering, gentleness, goodness, faith, meekness, temperance" —and weapons of wood and steel may safely be put away. "Walk in the spirit," said Paul, "and ye shall not fulfill the lusts of the flesh."

No, there is more, far more, in this matter of pacifism in our civic contacts as individuals than the mere transfer of arms from the citizen to the state. There is something deeper here in our peaceful relationships as citizens than reliance upon force remote and organized. What we really have today is not a new police but a new psychology, a new inward mental habit projecting itself outwardly in the form of a new social convention. Today we trust our neighbors, instead of distrusting them. We take it for granted that the great mass of our fellow men in our community, even in our nation, are friendly, and establish our individual conduct upon this basis. Consciously or unconsciously we breathe the air of fellowship, and therewith find the whole temper of our lives transformed. The use of force as the sanction of personal life is disappearing. Already, in this our time, has pacifism become the law of men if not of nations.

Thus is pacifism coming into its own in our personal relations. This rule and discipline of action, so feverishly denounced, is nothing new or strange. Least of all is it anything quixotic, fanatical, mad. On the contrary, it is today the basis of the life we live in all the most intimate and difficult relationships of our human experience. The very men who clamor for ever greater armies and navies as the sole condition of national survival, and who rage at every suggestion of preparedness for peace instead of for war, are themselves the living witnesses, in their personal relations with their wives, their children, and their fellow citizens, of the practicability and beauty of that law of love which some of us would now extend to all the world. Pacifism has been proved. Wherever applied, it has stood trial. Like the discovered cure of a disease, it needs only to be extended from individual test cases in the laboratory to all cases in the world at large, to bring universal healing unto men.

For human nature, in things spiritual as in things material, is everywhere the same. Two men in contact present largely the same psychological problem as two million men in contact, just as two cells in contact present largely the same biological problem as two million cells in contact. Indeed, these personal relations of which we have been speaking are at bottom social relations. Every contact between individuals transforms itself at once into a social institution. The love of husband and wife creates the home. The care of parent for child creates the school. The life of neighbor with neighbor creates the community; the life of citizen with citizen creates the state. Our pacifism, therefore, is already prevailing, not only in individual experience but in social experience. Here are great institutions, formed by the relationships of individuals in daily contacts, dominated and glorified by the rule of peace. In the home, the school, the community, the nation, physical force has gone, and "soul force" is come. What has been done and is being done on this smaller scale can also be done on a vastly larger scale. The same gravitation that binds two dust grains in the soil binds as well two planets in the sky. So the same love that binds two brothers in the home may bind as well two nations on far-sundered continents. The law of life is one. Its fulfillment anywhere is the promise, prophecy, and pledge of its fulfillment everywhere.

Rosika Schwimmer

petitions for naturalization

ROSIKA SCHWIMMER [1877-1948] *was an active feminist as well as a pacifist. In 1915 she was a delegate from Hungary to the International Conference of Women at The Hague, where she proposed a "Conference of Neutral Nations for Mediation." That same year, she was the moving force behind the ill-fated Ford Peace Ship. She became one of the first women to hold a diplomatic post when she was appointed Hungarian Minister to Switzerland in 1918. All her life she campaigned for a people's world constitution. In 1921 Mrs. Schwimmer moved to the United States, and six years later she applied for citizenship. Because she refused to swear that she would bear arms in defense of this country, citizenship was denied her as we see in this official court record. When her case was appealed, the United States Supreme Court upheld the earlier decision, with Justice Holmes and Associate Justice Brandeis dissenting.*

ROSIKA SCHWIMMER,

the petitioner herein, called as a witness in her own behalf, having been first duly sworn, was examined by Mr. Jordan, and testified as follows:

Q. What is your full name, please?
A. Rosika Schwimmer.
Q. You were born in Hungary?
A. Hungary, Budapest. . . .
Q. Is it your intention to remain in the United States permanently?
A. It is.
Q. Is there anything in our form of government that you are not in sympathy with?
A. Nothing.
Q. You have read the oath of allegiance?
A. I did.
Q. Are you able to take that oath without any reservations?
A. I am.
Q. I would like for you to inform the court that this is the information sheet you filled out in connection with your application for citizenship (*handing document to the witness*).
A. Yes.

Q. And in answer to question 22, "If necessary, are you willing to take up arms in defense of this country?" You have answered, "I would not take up arms personally."

A. Yes.

Q. And that is correct, is it?

A. Yes.

Q. Now, on January 11, 1927, Mr. Schlotfeldt wrote you a letter, didn't he?

A. Yes.

Q. About some statement you had made to Colonel Stone?

A. Well, it wasn't a statement. It was part of a letter. It wasn't a statement at all.

Q. And in that you also reiterated to Mr. Schlotfeldt to this effect: "I am an uncompromising pacifist for whom even Jane Addams is not enough of a pacifist. I am an absolute atheist. I have no sense of nationalism."

A. Yes.

Q. Is that correct?

A. Yes, that is correct.

THE COURT: What do you mean by "no sense of nationalism?"

A. I mean that if I had a sense of nationalism I could not want to leave the Hungarian nationality into which I was born.

Q. This has nothing to do with war. I am asking you what you mean when you say you have no sense of nationalism, because nationalism is a very comprehensive term and includes more than war.

A. I didn't speak now of war. Perhaps I didn't express myself well enough, Your Honor. I say I meant when I said this, if I had a feeling of nationalism, then being born a Hungarian, I would have such a feeling of Hungarian nationality that I would not want to leave that nationality, whatever the things are that are displeasing me.

Q. In other words, if something came up between Hungary and the United States, your sympathies would still be with Hungary?

A. No, to the contrary they would not be. I said I have no sense of nationality that would bind me to Hungary.

Q. Of course, I do not believe the time is ever coming when this country, this government, is going to send its women to fight. We have not as yet a regiment of Amazons.

A. I hope you don't have.

Q. But we may have to send them as nurses to look after our fighters. We may have to send them in the various religious organizations, like the Y.M.C.A. or the Knights of Columbus, to give succor and aid to our fighters. Now, are you willing to be sent on missions of that sort by this government to look after the boys that are fighting for this country?

A. I am willing to do everything that an American citizen has to do, except fighting.

Q. Well, our women do not fight. We do not expect you to shoulder a musket.

A. Oh, I am willing to obey every law that the American government compels its citizens to do.

Q. Are you willing to do anything that an American woman is called upon to do? I mean an American citizen, a woman of this country.

A. Yes, I am, because I have not found that anything was asked that was against—I mean it is only the fighting question. That is, if American women would be compelled to do that, I would not do that.

Q. You say you are an uncompromising pacifist?

A. Yes.

Q. How far does that go? Does it refer only to yourself?

A. Yes.

Q. That you are not going to use your fists on somebody?

A. Yes.

Q. Or that you disapprove of the government fighting?

A. It means that I disapprove of the government asking me to fight.

Q. You mean fight personally?

A. Yes, physically.

Q. Carrying a gun?

A. Yes.

Q. Is that as far as it goes?

A. That is as far as it goes.

Q. Or is it more deep-seated?

A. No.

Q. Really, of course, none of us wants war—

A. Yes.

Q. But there are a great many of us when war comes and our country is in danger who get our backs to the wall—

A. Yes.

Q. And we fight until there is nothing but the wall left.

A. Yes.

Q. Now, are you willing to do that?

A. I am afraid, Your Honor, I did not catch the point of the question. I am awfully sorry.

Q. I don't mean to bear arms for the country.

A. Yes.

Q. The time will never come, I venture to say, when the women of the United States will have to bear arms.

A. Well, I am not willing to bear arms. In every other single way, civic way, I am ready to follow the law and do everything that the law compels American citizens to do. I am willing to do that. That is why I say I can take the oath of allegiance because as far as I, with the able help of my lawyers, could find out there is nothing that I could be compelled to do that I could not do.

Q. Your lawyer can't search into your heart any more than I can. You are the only one that can answer these questions.

A. I am opening my heart very frankly because there is nothing to hide. As I said when the question came up, if it is a question of fighting, as much as I desire American citizenship I would not seek the citizenship.

Q. Now, is it a question of fighting personally?

A. Yes.

Q. You yourself?

A. Myself.

Q. You do not care how many other women fight?

A. I don't care because I consider it a question of conscience. If there are women fighters, it is their business.

Q. Do you expect to spread this propaganda throughout this country with other women?

A. Which propaganda, may I ask?

Q. That you are an uncompromising pacifist and will not fight.

A. Oh, of course, I am always ready to tell that to anyone who wants to hear it.

Q. What is your occupation, madam?

A. I am a writer and lecturer.

Q. And in your writings and in your lectures you take up this question of war and pacifism?

A. If I am asked for that, I do.

Q. You know we have a great deal to give—at least we think so—

A. I think so, too.

Q. —when we confer citizenship upon people of other countries.

A. I think so, too.

Q. And we expect when we do that they come in on an equal footing, and out of regard to the other stockholders in this great united corporation we have to see to it that any partners or stockholders coming in are willing to do what those who are already here are willing to do. Now, it seems that your general views—

Now, I am not at all against people writing. There are a great many American citizens who are now decrying the possibility of the occurrence of war. They are against it. We have a great many pacifists in this country, but when the time comes, and they are called out for the country, they forget all their views, all of the things they have been talking about, and start in on the defense of the home.

Now, you can't come in halfway. You must come in the whole distance, because there you are and under that flag is our country, and you can't get under that flag unless you promise to do every single thing that the citizens of this country not only have permission to do, but are willing to do.

A. Well, I can only repeat what I said: that I am willing to do everything that, to my knowledge to this day, American women are asked to do.

THE COURT: Well, can we ask anything more than that?

MR. JORDAN: I would just like, Your Honor, to bring out a few things in Madame Schwimmer's letter to Mr. Schlotfeldt, and also excerpts from one of her radio speeches.

In the letter here, "My answer to question 22 in my petition for final examination demonstrated that I am an uncompromising pacifist." A little further down: "Highly as I prize the privilege of American citizenship, I could not compromise my way into it by giving an untrue answer to question 22, though for all practical purposes I might have done so."

Then there are a few little excerpts here from the radio talks I would like the court to hear: "I cannot see that a woman's refusal to take up arms is a contradiction to the oath of allegiance, promising to support and defend the Constitution and laws of the United States of America. I have for the fulfillment of this duty other ways and means in mind."

MRS. RABE: Would you mind reading the rest of that statement right there?

MR. JORDAN: That finishes that paragraph, I believe.

MRS. RABE: Oh, does it? I thought she spoke about having written in favor of our Constitution.

THE COURT: Let me ask you this one question—

A. Yes, sir.

Q. If you were called to the service, and the kind of work that women usually can perform better than the men can—say as a nurse or as someone to give cheer to the soldiers—and you were at some place in a war, which I hope never will come, and you saw someone coming in the headquarters or the barracks, wherever it was, with a pistol in his hand to shoot the back of an officer of our country, and you had a pistol handy by, would you kill him?

A. No, I would not.

THE COURT: The application is denied.

MR. GEMMILL: Just a moment, Your Honor. We would like to perfect our record. We expect to go up on this case, Your Honor. . . .

MR. GEMMILL: I would like to ask Mrs. Schwimmer one question.

Q. What do you mean, Mrs. Schwimmer, when you say you can take the oath and you are willing to support and defend the Constitution and the laws of the United States?

A. I mean the things that I have practically already done; that I was in many meetings in which it was said that it would be far better to have a Soviet regime—"that is a far better kind of regime"—and myself having lived under Soviet regime in Hungary, I could get up and tell the people —as I have practically done—"Don't think you change to something better." To this day there is no better form of government than that of the United States, which is by the people, for the people, as the great saying is, and that Sovietism is nothing but tyranny under another name —old-fashioned tyranny under a new name; and I wrote these things, and I said these things, and I can prove it by writings which I can get from Hungary; so that is what I meant; that there are other means to defend the Constitution and the institutions of this country.

Q. Is it your belief, Mrs. Schwimmer, your own personal belief, that you would not take the life of anyone?

A. Yes.

Q. Of any animal?

A. Animals, no. I have no objections against taking the life of animals. I personally wouldn't shoot, but I have no objections against that; but I would not shoot. Even if a pistol was pointed to me, I would not shoot.

Q. Is that what you had in mind when you answered the court's last question—

A. Yes.

Q. —relative to the shooting of the officer?

A. Yes, of course, I couldn't.

THE COURT: What do you mean by that?

MR. GEMMILL: I mean to say, Your Honor, I am trying to explain her answer. It wasn't the cold-blooded murder of the United States officer that Mrs. Schwimmer had in mind. It was her feeling against the killing of anyone.

THE WITNESS: Yes.

THE COURT: I raised a question that might arise in any war, and asked her what she would do if in order to save the life of an officer of this country, whether it was a general officer or the lowest man in the ranks, and she had the opportunity to kill the enemy before he killed our soldier would she do it, and she said "no."

THE WITNESS: Yes.

MR. GEMMILL: May I ask one or two more questions?

THE COURT: Yes.

MR. GEMMILL: Under that same case, Mrs. Schwimmer, would you have given the officer any warning, if it was posible?

A. Certainly.

Q. So that he could defend himself?

A. Certainly.

THE COURT: That is, you would have given him—

A. I would try to hit the pistol out of the man's hand who tries to shoot. That is what I would try to do.

Q. Let me ask you this: Would you have thrown yourself on the assailant?

A. Yes, I might do that.

Q. And run the risk of being shot yourself?

A. Yes, I might do that. Yes.

MR. JORDAN: You say you might do that?

A. Well, I speak of a possibility. I can't say I would do that. We speak of hypothetical things. I can't say I "will" do that, because there is no occasion for it.

THE COURT: One never can tell until the occasion arises what will be done.

THE WITNESS: If it would happen this moment I would do it.

THE COURT: But my first question referred not to your trying to stop the man from reaching the American soldier.

THE WITNESS: I understand.

THE COURT: —because he may have been ten feet off—

THE WITNESS: I understand.

THE COURT: —and the American soldier would have been killed before you could have reached his assailant.

THE WITNESS: Yes.

THE COURT: I am asking if you had the weapon, if it were handy by—

THE WITNESS: Yes.

THE COURT: —would you have killed the assailant—

THE WITNESS: No.

THE COURT: —before he reached the American soldier?

THE WITNESS: No.

THE COURT: Then I am of the same opinion.

MR. GEMMILL: Supposing that pistol had been pointed at you and you had a pistol?

A. I would not defend myself. I mean I wouldn't take a pistol to defend myself even if you handed it to me; under no circumstances.

THE COURT: That question is not involved at all. This is a very close question, gentlemen, and I am really refusing this because the government, I think, has no appeal, but it is an attitude—the attitude of the applicant—that I think is not common with the women of this country.

Is there anything more, gentlemen?

MR. GEMMILL: I just want to be a little careful about this record.

THE COURT: Suppose it is written up and then we will reduce it to an agreed statement of facts?

MR. GEMMILL: That is satisfactory.

MR. JORDAN: Do you care, Your Honor, to take the statements of the witnesses so that they will not be required further?

THE COURT: Oh, yes. Let both witnesses step forward, please. . . .

THE COURT: Both of the witnesses believe that the applicant is a thoroughly good woman.

MR. BIRD: Yes.

MISS HOLBROOK: Yes, I do.

THE COURT: That is all. That is what we want to know.

MR. JORDAN: The witnesses may be excused then.

MR. GEMMILL: I suppose in this kind of a case a motion for a new trial first should be made.

THE COURT: No, I think not.

MR. GEMMILL: Motion in arrest, or pray an appeal then. . . .

THE COURT: . . . You understand, madam, that while the court may have said some things that shock, perhaps, your views of nationalism, we are here to administer the law as we see it. We have taken an oath for that purpose and we try to live up to it. There is nothing personal about it all.

MADAME SCHWIMMER: I realize that, Your Honor.

Judah Magnes
supports the right of all men to speak freely

DR. JUDAH L. MAGNES [1877-1948] *was ordained a rabbi in 1900. He resigned as rabbi of a Brooklyn temple when his congregation objected to his appearing at the head of a parade down Fifth Avenue in protest of the pogroms in Czarist Russia. In 1922 he moved to Palestine and began to work for the establishment of the Hebrew University, of which he became the first chancellor and first president. A Zionist for forty years, Dr. Magnes believed that the Jewish people must, and can, live together with the Arabs in the Holy Land, and he advocated a binational state. Dr. Magnes was an outspoken pacifist during the First World War, but during World War II he was faced with an anguished choice and relinquished his pacifist stand to support the war effort. The speech here represents his stand in 1920.*

I abhor bloodshed. I believe that human life and the human personality are sacred, and that human life may not be taken at any time. I do not believe in war between one people and another, and I did not believe in this past war, and I do not believe in the next. I recount these personal items because, as a pacifist, I may differ greatly from this or that radical group. I stand nevertheless for the right of every man and every group to advocate any and every governmental, political, economic, spiritual change, no matter what be the doctrines they preach and no matter what be the methods they talk and write about. I am as much opposed to the use of machine guns and bombs and hand grenades and poison gas by the workers, by the proletariat, as to the use of these instruments of hatred and murder by organized governments. But I believe that every man and every political and economic organization have the right to formulate their doctrines in speech and in writing freely. Only when speech and writing are left in the background and actual overt acts of physical violence and bloodshed are committed has a people's government the right to intervene. Under all circumstances we must maintain the right of free speech, without qualification and without let or hindrance.

Government has no right to interfere with ideas, with programs, with opinions formulated in speech or in writing, no matter what these ideas and opinions may be. If men wish to advocate the use of force and violence in the change and overthrow of government, let them advocate it openly, above ground, frankly. Then let you and me meet them by reason if we can, by argument, by free discussion. Prove them wrong, if we can, by trying to remove the underlying causes of their impatience and their skepticism. It is injustice, cruelty, terrorization of the weak by the strong, spiritual and physical slavery which they wish to force out of existence. Can we show by precept and by example that these age-long iniquities can be removed from the lives of men in other ways than through force and violence? If even then men wish to take upon themselves the burden and the odium of writing or talking in advocacy of force and violence, let them. It is old American doctrine that freedom of discussion, the conflict of ideas, debate, argument, will bring out the true and will suppress the false. It is old American faith that the masses of the people are sound at heart and in mind, and that it is possible to reason with them, to convince them through information, through candor, through mental integrity. It is an old American idea that government is based upon free consent, and that it is perpetuated or changed through an informed and honest public opinion.

Scott Nearing

shows war to be a social curse

SCOTT NEARING [1883-   ] *is an American Socialist, scholar and writer who has spent his life agitating for the Socialist philosophy and for world peace. In 1917 he had to resign from the Toledo University because of his pacifist viewpoint. Nearing, along with the American Socialist Society, was indicted in 1918 because of a pamphlet he wrote called "The Great Madness." The case was tried in February 1919; it was charged that the pamphlet attempted to cause insubordination, disloyalty, mutiny and refusal of duty in the armed services, and obstructed recruitment and enlistment. Nearing was found not guilty, the American Socialist Society guilty and fined $3,000 on the last count. Nearing did not defend himself at the trial, but he did explain to the court the philosophy of socialism as he saw it.*

I told the District Attorney on the stand that I was opposed to all wars. I regard war as a social disease, something that afflicts society, that curses people. I do not suppose three people in a hundred like war. I do not suppose that three people in a hundred want war. There are some people who are pugnacious, and who love to fight, for the sake of a fight, and they might like war, but I do not believe there are three people in a hundred, certainly not five in a hundred, that do.

I believe the great majority of people agree with me that war is a curse, an unmitigated curse. All the things that come out of war come out in spite of war and not because of it.

The democracy that has come into Europe, whatever it is called, has come in spite of the war and not because of it. That would have come out in any case, and we would have had it without the expenditure of twenty million lives and a hundred and eighty billions of wealth.

I regard war as a social disease, a social curse, and I believe that we should stamp war out. To my mind the great curse of war is not that people are killed and injured, not that property is destroyed. That happens every day in peace times as well as in war times. To my mind the great curse of war is that it is built on fear and hate.

Now, fear and hate are primitive passions; the savages in the woods are intimidated by fear and hate. They do not belong in civilized society. In civilized society, for fear and hate we substitute constructive purposes and love. It is their positive virtues. When we fear things, we draw back from them. When we hate things, we want to destroy them.

In civilized society, instead of drawing away from things, and wanting to destroy them, we want to pull things together and build them up. Fear and hate are negatives. Peace and love are positives, and form the forces upon which civilization is built. And where we have collectively fear and hate, it is a means of menace to the order of the world.

Furthermore, during war, we ask people to go out and deliberately injure their fellows. We ask a man to go out and maim or kill another man against whom he has not a solitary thing in the world—a man who may be a good farmer, a good husband, a good son, and a good worker, and a good citizen. Another man comes out and shoots him down; that is, he goes out and raises his hand against his neighbor to do his neighbor damage. That is the way society is destroyed. Whenever you go out to pull things to pieces, whenever you go out to injure anybody, you are going out to destroy society. Society can never be built up unless you go out to help your neighbors.

The principle "each for all and all for each" is the fundamental social principle. People must work together if they are going to get anywhere. War teaches people to go out and destroy other people and to destroy other people's property.

And when Sherman said that war was hell, I believe that he meant, or at least to me that means, that war creates a hell inside of a man who goes to war. He is going to work himself up into a passion of hatred against somebody else, and that is hell.

The destruction of life and property is incidental. The destructive forces that that puts into a man's soul are fundamental. That is why I am opposed to all wars, just as I am opposed to all violence. I don't believe in any man having the right to go out and use violence against another man. That is not the right of one human being to have against the other, that is not the way you get brotherhood. That is the reason I told the District Attorney on the stand that I was against all wars. I am against dueling; I am against all violence of man against man, and war is one of those methods of violence.

I believe war is barbaric, I believe it is primitive, I believe it is a relic of a bygone age; I believe that society will be destroyed if built up that way. That is, I believe that they that take the sword must perish by the sword; just as they that set out to assist their neighbors are bound to build up a strong, cohesive, united society. That is the field over which I went in my direct testimony and in the cross-examination.

I have been a student of public affairs. I am a Socialist. I am a pacifist. But I am not charged with any of these things as offenses. On the other hand I believe that as an American citizen I have a right to discuss public questions. I think the judge will charge you so. I have a right to oppose the passage of a law. I think the judge will charge you so. I have a right under the law, after the law is passed, to agitate for a development of public sentiment that will result in a repeal of that law. I think the judge will charge you so.

In other words, as I said in the beginning, in a democracy, if we are to have a democracy, as a student of public affairs and as a Socialist and as a pacifist, I have a right to express my opinions. I may be wrong, utterly wrong, and nobody listen to me, nobody pay any attention to me. I have a right to express my opinions.

Gentlemen, I have been throughout my life as consistent as I could be. I have spoken and written for years, honestly and frankly. I went on the stand and I spoke to you as honestly as I know how. I answered the District Attorney's questions as honestly and as frankly as I could. I stand before you today as an advocate of economic justice and world brotherhood, and peace among all men.

Eugene V. Debs
offers his defense to the court

EUGENE VICTOR DEBS [1855-1926] *was an American labor leader and four-time presidential candidate on the Socialist ticket. He started his career in the labor movement with the Brotherhood of Loco-motive Firemen; he was president of the American Railway Union and later a founder of the Industrial Workers of the World. In 1896, while he was president of the ARU, the famous Pullman strike took place. Debs was indicted and convicted for contempt as a result of the strike. While serving the sentence, he became a Socialist. In his fourth nomi-nation, he ran for President from jail, where he was Convict No. 9653 serving a jail term for violating the Espionage Act. The following is part of Debs's speech to the court before he was sentenced in 1918.*

Gentlemen of the jury, you have heard the report of my speech at Canton on June 16, and I submit that there is not a word in that speech to warrant the charges set out in the indictment. I admit having delivered the speech. I admit the accuracy of the speech in all of its main features as reported in this proceeding.

In what I had to say there my purpose was to have the people understand something about the social system in which we live and to prepare them to change this system by perfectly peaceable and ordely means into what I, as a Socialist, conceive to be a real democracy.

From what you heard in the address of the counsel for the prosecution, you might naturally infer that I am an advocate of force and violence. It is not true. I have never advocated violence in any form. I have always believed in education, in intelligence, in enlightenment, and I have always made my appeal to the reason and to the conscience of the people.

I admit being opposed to the present social system. I am doing what little I can, and have been for many years, to bring about a change that shall do away with the rule of the great body of the people by a relatively small class and establish in this country an industrial and social democracy. . . .

Gentlemen of the jury, I am accused of having obstructed the war. I admit it. Gentlemen, I abhor war. I would oppose the war if I stood alone. When I think of a cold, glittering steel bayonet being plunged in the white, quivering flesh of a human body, I recoil with horror.

Men talk about holy wars. There are none. War is the trade of unholy savages and barbarians. . . .

Gentlemen of the jury, I am accused of being unpatriotic. I object to that accusation. It is not true. I believe in patriotism. I have never uttered a word against the flag. I love the flag as a symbol of freedom. . . .

I believe, however, in a wider patriotism. Thomas Paine said, "My country is the world. To do good is my religion." That is the sort of patriotism I believe in. I am an internationalist. I believe that nations have been pitted against nations long enough in hatred, in strife, in warfare. I believe there ought to be a bond of unity between all of these nations. I believe that the human race consists of one great family. I love the people of this country, but I don't hate a human being because he happens to be born in some other country. Why should I? Like myself, he is the image of his Creator. I would infinitely rather serve him and love him than to hate him and kill him. . . .

Yes, I am opposed to killing him. I am opposed to war. I am perfectly willing on that account to be branded as a traitor. And if it is a crime under the American law to be opposed to human bloodshed, I am perfectly willing to be branded as a criminal and to end my days in a prison cell. . . .

From the beginning of the war to this day I have never by word or by act been guilty of the charges embraced in this indictment. If I have criticized, if I have condemned, it is because I believed it to be my duty, and that it was my right to do so under the laws of the land. I have had ample precedents for my attitude. The country has been engaged in a number of wars and every one of them has been condemned by some of the people, among them some of the most eminent men of their time. . . .

The revolutionary fathers who had been oppressed under king's rule understood that free speech, a free press and the right of free assemblage by the people were fundamental principles in democratic government. The very first amendment to the Constitution reads:

Congress shall make no law respecting an establishment of religion, or prohibiting the free exercise thereof; or abridging the freedom of speech, or of the press; or the right of the people peaceably to assemble, and to petition the Government for a redress of grievances.

That is perfectly plain English. It can be understood by a child. I believe the revolutionary fathers meant just what is here stated—that Congress shall make no law abridging the freedom of speech or of the press, or of the right of the people to peaceably assemble, and to petition the government for a redress of their grievances.

That is the right I exercised at Canton on the sixteenth day of last June; and for the exercise of that right, I now have to answer to this indictment. I believe in the right of free speech, in war as well as in peace. I would not under any circumstances gag the lips of my bitterest enemy. I would under no circumstances suppress free speech. It is far more dangerous to attempt to gag the people than to allow them to speak freely what is in their hearts. . . .

If I believed in the war I could not be kept out of the first-line trenches. I would not be patriotic at long range. I would be honest enough, if I believed in bloodshed, to shed my own. But I do not believe that the shedding of blood bears any actual testimony to patriotism, to lead a country to civilization. On the contrary, I believe that warfare, in all of its forms, is an impeachment of our social order, and a rebuke to our much vaunted Christian civilization. . . .

Gentlemen, I am the small part of this trial. I have lived long enough to appreciate my own personal insignificance in relation to a great issue that involves the welfare of the whole people. What you may choose to do to me will be of small consequence. After all, I am not on trial here. There is an infinitely greater issue that is being tried in this court, though you may not be conscious of it. American institutions are on trial here before a court of American citizens. The future will render the final verdict.

I am prepared for your verdict.

G. F. Nicolai

shows that morality and humanity are inseparable

G. F. NICOLAI [1872-   ] *was a leading German heart specialist and had attended the German empress before the outbreak of World War I. He opposed militarism, and when Germany violated Belgian neutrality, he protested. Because of his pacifist teachings, Dr. Nicolai's professorship was withdrawn, his property confiscated, and he was imprisoned. The Biology of War, from which the selection below is taken, was written while he was in the fortress and was published in Zurich in 1918. Dr. Nicolai eventually escaped to Denmark. After the German revolution, he was again going to teach at Berlin University, but protests from Junker students prevented it.*

Whoever would fain have a real religion must base it in the reality of man and not on visionary ideals. The natural result of this ever-changing human reality, which in the course of time becomes ever more and more perfect, is that the future will seem to us an ever higher reality, in which we can believe, on which we may legitimately set our affections, and to which we must pin our hopes. The three cardinal virtues of Christianity are in truth the main supports of every true religion; but we must not believe in anything unreal, nor set our affections on anything past, or our hopes on any mere visions.

It may be asked, Do such views deserve to be called a religion?

They do and they do not. In actual truth they do, for they mean nothing more or less than that we feel ourselves inseparably bound up with that with which we are, after all, inseparably bound up; that is, with our bodies and their sensations. But, after all, this is so obvious, or at any rate ought to be so obvious, as to need no special name. . . .

To be humane . . . simply means that we have comprehended the history of the evolution of mankind; that we know whence we come; that we have an inkling of whither we are going; and that we are accordingly trying to conform to the general scheme of nature, which for us means the progress of human evolution. We believe in this progress of evolution; we love mankind, and we hope for further progress; in other words, for that superman who is daily and hourly slowly coming into being. This recognition of self-evident facts embraces every moral law. . . .

How we formulate our morality, however, is no matter; all that matters is that we should bethink ourselves of ourselves and understand that man is an individual unit and at the same time a part of a superordinate organism. Whosoever knows this, and realizes it not merely as a truth which can be acquired, but as a living law in him and a feeling, is a human being indeed and in truth. But whosoever does not realize this is no true human being, no matter how much he may resemble one, or, as Kant puts it, how civilized he may be; for he lacks that essential thing which differentiates man from all other living beings—the feeling of belonging to the *genus humanum*.

> *Scio et sento genus humanum esse simplex et unum,*
> *Scio et volo me esse hominem,*
> *Scio et spero nunquam oblivisci.*

Whoever is a human being at all is also a moral human being. In face of this truth no isolated occurrences have any importance save as phenomena, and so it is with war. If humanity wins, the death-knell of war will have sounded, but only then; for man cannot and will not break his sword in sunder so long as he does not know that a sword has neither part nor lot in the conception of mankind, but is merely a tool to be laid aside like any other.

Roger Baldwin
refuses to obey the draft

ROGER N. BALDWIN [1884-   ] *was a founder, and for many years executive director, of the American Civil Liberties Union. He was an early member of the Fellowship of Reconciliation, and today he is a consultant to the United Nations on human rights. When the Japanese government recently awarded him the Order of the Rising Sun and cited him for services to humanity, Baldwin remarked wryly, "My earlier activities have not been distinguished by the appreciation of governments." During World War I, Baldwin declared himself a conscientious objector. He was tried for violation of the Selective Service Act in 1918, and in spite of his moving address to the court, he was sentenced and served a year in prison.*

I am before you as a deliberate violator of the Draft Act. . . . The compelling motive for refusing to comply with the Draft Act is my uncompromising opposition to the principle of conscription of life by the state for any purpose whatever, in time of war or peace. I not only refuse to obey the present conscription law, but I would in future refuse to obey any similar statute which attempts to direct my choice of service and ideals. I regard the principle of conscription of life as a flat contradiction of all our cherished ideals of individual freedom, democratic liberty, and Christian teaching.

I am the more opposed to the present act, because it is for the purpose of conducting war. I am opposed to this and all other wars. I do not believe in the use of physical force as a method of achieving any end, however good. . . . My opposition is not only to direct military service, but to any service whatever designed to help prosecute the war. I could accept no service, therefore, under the present act, regardless of its character. . . . I am fully aware that my position is extreme, that it is shared by comparatively few, and that in the present temper it is regarded either as unwarranted egotism or as a species of feeble-mindedness. I cannot, therefore, let this occasion pass without attempting to explain the foundations on which so extreme a view rests.

I have had an essentially American upbringing and background. Born in a suburb of Boston, of the stock of the first settlers, I was reared in the public schools and at Harvard College. Early my mind was caught by the age-old struggle for freedom; America meant to me a vital new experiment in free political institutions; personal freedom to choose one's way of life and service seemed the essence of the liberties brought by those who fled the medieval and modern tyrannies of the Old World. But I rebelled at our whole autocratic industrial system—with its wreckage of poverty, disease, and crime, and childhood robbed of its right to free growth. So I took up social work upon leaving college, going to St. Louis as director of a settlement and instructor in sociology at Washington University. For ten years I have been professionally engaged in social work and political reform, local and national. . . .

Personally I share the extreme radical philosophy of the future society. I look forward to a social order without any external restraints upon the individual, save through public opinion and the opinion of friends and neighbors. I am not a member of any radical organization, nor do I wear any tag by which my views may be classified. I believe that all parts of the radical movement serve the common end—freedom of the individual from arbitrary external controls.

When the war came to America, it was an immediate challenge to me to help protect those ideals of liberty which seemed to me not only the basis of the radical economic view, but of the radical political view of the founders of this republic, and of the whole medieval struggle for religious freedom. Before the war was declared I severed all my connections in St. Louis, and offered my services to the American Union Against Militarism to help fight conscription. Later that work developed into the National Civil Liberties Bureau, organized to help maintain the rights of free speech and free press, and the Anglo-Saxon tradition of liberty of conscience, through liberal provisions for conscientious objectors. This work has been backed both by pro-war liberals and so-called pacifists. It is not antiwar in any sense. It seemed to me the one avenue of service open to me, consistent with my views, with the country's best interest, and with the preservation of the radical minority for the struggle after the war. Even if I were not a believer in radical theories and movements, I would justify the work I have done on the ground of American ideals and traditions alone—as do many of those who have been associated with me. They have stood for those enduring principles which the revolutionary demands of war have temporarily set aside. We have stood against hysteria, mob violence, unwarranted prosecution, the sinister use of patriotism to cover attacks on radical and labor movements, and for the unabridged right of a fair trial under war statutes. We have tried to keep open those channels of expression which stand for the kind of world order for which the President is battling today against the tories and militarists.

Now comes the government to take me from that service and to demand of me a service I cannot in conscience undertake. I refuse it simply for my own peace of mind and spirit, for the satisfaction of that inner demand more compelling than any considerations of punishment or the sacrifice of friendships and reputation.

I seek no martyrdom, no publicity. I merely meet as squarely as I can the moral issue before me, regardless of consequences. . . . I am not complaining for myself or others. I am merely advising the court that I understand full well the penalty of my heresy, and am prepared to pay it. The conflict with conscription is irreconcilable. Even the liberalism of the President and Secretary of War in dealing with objectors leads those of us who are "absolutists" to a punishment longer and severer than that of desperate criminals.

But I believe most of us are prepared even to die for our faith, just as our brothers in France are dying for theirs. To them we are comrades in spirit—we understand one another's motives, though our methods are wide apart. We both share deeply the common experience of living up to the truth as we see it, whatever the price.

Though at the moment I am of a tiny minority, I feel myself part of a great revolt surging up from among the people—the struggle of the masses against the rule of the world by the few—profoundly intensified by the war. It is a struggle against the political state itself, against exploitation, militarism, imperialism, authority in all forms. It is a struggle to break in full force only after the war. Russia already stands in the vanguard, beset by her enemies in the camps of both belligerents; the Central Empires break asunder from within; the labor movement gathers revolutionary force in Britain; and in our own country the Nonpartisan League, radical labor, and the Socialist Party hold the germs of a new social order. Their protest is my protest. Mine is a personal protest at a particular law, but it is backed by all the aspirations and ideals of the struggle for a world freed of our manifold slaveries and tyrannies.

I ask the court for no favor. I could do no other than what I have done, whatever the court's decree. I have no bitterness or hate in my heart for any man. Whatever the penalty, I shall endure it, firm in the faith that whatever befalls me, the principles in which I believe will bring forth out of this misery and chaos a world of brotherhood, harmony and freedom for each to live the truth as he sees it.

Siegfried Sassoon
speaks for the soldiers

SIEGFRIED SASSOON [1886-   ] *is an English writer best known for the bitter poetry he wrote during and after the First World War. In the hospital after he was wounded on the field, Sassoon decided that the war must end. He announced that he would no longer serve in the army, and he threw his military cross into the sea. He hoped to be courtmartialed so he could make a public pronouncement of his position. Instead, the War Office declared him "temporarily insane" and hospitalized him. After his confinement, Sassoon was shipped to Palestine and then again to the French front. When the war was over, he supported the pacifist platform in the general elections.*

I am making this statement as an act of willful defiance of military authority, because I believe that the war is being deliberately prolonged by those who have the power to end it. I am a soldier, convinced that I am acting on behalf of soldiers. I believe that this war, upon which I entered as a war of defense and liberation, has now become a war of aggression and conquest. I believe that the purposes for which I and my fellow soldiers entered upon this war should have been so clearly stated as to have made it impossible to change them, and that, had this been done, the objects which actuated us would now be attainable by negotiation. I have seen and endured the sufferings of the troops, and I can no longer be a party to prolong these sufferings for ends which I believe to be evil and unjust. I am not protesting against the conduct of the war, but against the political errors and insincerities for which the fighting men are being sacrificed. On behalf of those who are suffering now I make this protest against the deception which is being practiced on them; also I believe that I may help to destroy the callous complacency with which the majority of those at home regard the continuance of agonies which they do not share, and which they have not sufficient imagination to realize.

John Reed

asks, "Whose war?"

JOHN REED [1887-1920] *was a radical American journalist who opposed war and was a political agitator against social ills. He edited* The Masses, *a radical magazine, and when it was suppressed for its antiwar stand, Reed was indicted under the Sedition Act. The charges were dropped and Reed went to Russia, where he wrote his famous book* Ten Days that Shook the World. *He died in Moscow and was buried in the Kremlin. The article here appeared in* The Masses *in April 1917.*

By the time this goes to press the United States may be at war. The day the German note arrived, Wall Street flung the American flag to the breeze, the brokers on the floor of the Stock Exchange sang "The Starspangled Banner" with tears rolling down their cheeks, and the stock market went up. In the theaters they are singing "patriotic" ballads of the George M. Cohan-Irving Berlin variety, playing the national anthem, and flashing the flag and the portrait of long-suffering Lincoln—while the tired surburbanite who has just been scalped by a ticket speculator goes into hysterics. Exclusive ladies whose husbands own banks are rolling bandages for the wounded, just like they do in Europe; a million-dollar Fund for Ice in Field-hospitals has been started; and the Boston Budget for Conveying Virgins Inland has grown enormously. The directors of the British, French and Belgian Permanent Blind Relief Fund have added "American" to the name of the organization, in gruesome anticipation. Our soldier boys, guarding the aqueducts and bridges, are shooting each other by mistake for Teutonic spies. There is talk of "conscription," "war brides," and "on to Berlin." . . .

I know what war means. I have been with the armies of all the belligerents except one, and I have seen men die, and go mad, and lie in hospitals suffering hell; but there is a worse thing than that. War means an ugly mob-madness, crucifying the truth-tellers, choking the artists, side-tracking reforms, revolutions, and the working of social forces. Already in America those citizens who oppose the entrance of their country into the European melée are called "traitors," and those who protest against the curtailing of our meager rights of free speech are spoken of as "dangerous lunatics." We have had a forecast of the censorship—when the naval authorities in charge of the Sayville wireless cut off American news from Germany, and only the wildest fictions reached Berlin via London, creating a perilous situation. . . . The press is howling for war. The church is howling for war. Lawyers, politicians, stock brokers, social leaders are all howling for war. Roosevelt is again recruiting his thrice-thwarted family regiment.

But whether it comes to actual hostilities or not, some damage has been done. The militarists have proved their point. I know of at least two valuable social movements that have suspended functioning because no one cares. For many years this country is going to be a worse place for free men to live in; less tolerant, less hospitable. Maybe it is too late, but I want to put down what I think about it all.

Whose war is this? Not mine. I know that hundreds of thousands of American workingmen employed by our great financial "patriots" are not paid a living wage. I have seen poor men sent to jail for long terms without trial, and even without any charge. Peaceful strikers, and their wives and children, have been shot to death, burned to death, by private detectives and militiamen. The rich have steadily become richer, and the cost of living higher, and the workers proportionally poorer. These toilers don't want war—not even civil war. But the speculators, the employers, the plutocracy—they want it, just as they did in Germany and in England; and with lies and sophistries they will whip up our blood until we are savage—and then we'll fight and die for them.

I am one of a vast number of ordinary people who read the daily papers, and occasionally *The New Republic,* and want to be fair. We don't know much about international politics; but we want our country to keep off the necks of little nations, to refuse to back up American beasts of prey who invest abroad and get their fingers burned, and to stay out of quarrels not our own. We've got an idea that international law is the crystallized common sense of nations, distilled from their experiences with each other, and that it holds good for all of them, and can be understood by anybody.

We are simple folk. Prussian militarism seemed to us insufferable; we thought the invasion of Belgium a crime; German atrocities horrified us, and also the idea of German submarines exploding ships full of peaceful people without warning. But then we began to hear about England and France jailing, fining, exiling and even shooting men who refused to go out and kill; the Allied armies invaded and seized a part of neutral Greece, and a French admiral forced upon her an ultimatum as shameful as Austria's to Serbia; Russian atrocities were shown to be more dreadful than German; and hidden mines sown by England in the open sea exploded ships full of peaceful people without warning.

Other things disturbed us. For instance, why was it a violation of international law for the Germans to establish a "war zone" around the British Isles, and perfectly legal for England to close the North Sea? Why is it we submitted to the British order forbidding the shipment of noncontraband to Germany, and insisted upon our right to ship contraband to the Allies? If our "national honor" was smirched by Germany's refusal to allow war materials to be shipped to the Allies, what happened to our national honor when England refused to let us ship noncontraband food and even *Red Cross hospital supplies* to Germany? Why is England allowed to attempt the avowed starvation of German civilians, in violation of international law, when the Germans cannot attempt the same thing without our horrified protest? How is it that the British can arbitrarily regulate our commerce with neutral nations, while we raise a howl whenever the Germans "threaten to restrict our merchant ships going about their business?" Why does our government insist that Americans should not be molested while traveling on Allied ships armed against submarines?

We have shipped and are shipping vast quantities of war materials to the Allies, we have floated the Allied loans. We have been strictly neutral toward the Teutonic powers only. Hence the inevitable desperation of the last German note. Hence this war we are on the brink of.

Those of us who voted for Woodrow Wilson did so because we felt his mind and his eyes were open, because he had kept us out of the mad-dog-fight of Europe, and because the plutocracy opposed him. We had learned enough about the war to lose some of our illusions, and we wanted to be neutral. We grant that the President, considering the position he'd got himself into, couldn't do anything else but answer the German note as he did—but if we had been neutral, that note wouldn't have been sent. The President didn't ask us; he won't ask us if we want war or not. The fault is not ours. It is not our war.

Max Eastman
challenges conscription

MAX EASTMAN [1883-   ] *was born in New York State of parents who were both Congregational ministers. Eastman organized the first Men's League for Woman's Suffrage in the United States. He was an editor of* The Masses *from 1913, when it was founded, until its suppression for antiwar attitudes in 1917, and later he founded and edited* The Liberator. *When* The Masses *was suppressed, Eastman, together with John Reed and Floyd Dell, was indicted under the Sedition Act. They were brought to trial twice; each time the jury disagreed, and finally the indictment was dropped. In recent years, Eastman has been a roving editor for the* Reader's Digest. *"Conscription for What?" was published in* The Masses, *July 1917.*

President Wilson has to breathe an atmosphere of optimistic emotion. He always automatically idealizes a bad business, and he generally does this with skill and plausibility. But in declaring that his selective draft is "in no sense a conscription of the unwilling; it is, rather, selection from a nation which has volunteered in mass," he builds himself up to a height of casuistic complaisance from which the fall may be tragic and terrible.

If anything is true, it is true that this nation has not volunteered either in mass or any other way. The people here, happy in their geographic security and divided in their reminiscent patriotisms, have long and deeply abhorred the idea of carrying war into Europe. So universal is this abhorrence that every tradition and prediction of political history was overthrown last fall, and Woodrow Wilson elected to the White House as a peace President, in the face of stalwart Republicanism, Rooseveltism, and Wall Street united in a solemn compact of blood to beat him.

During the time of this event and after, this peace President, under influences perhaps too subtle for political analysis, appears to have changed into a man of the Army and Navy. He has declared a European war, in face of the people's manifest will that he refrain—in face even of the will of a majority of the House of Representatives, if that house had possessed the courage to make its will known. Acknowledging that to this war, undesired by the people, he could not raise a volunteer army of 500,000 free citizens, he has forced upon Congress the principle of conscriptive draft—a principle which even when adopted for military purposes within the boundaries of the United States, and for the very defense of the Union, and at the hands of Abraham Lincoln, met riotous resistance from the devotees of individual liberty. He has forced this principle upon them for a war of offense, to be waged wholly on the continent of Europe and the contiguous ocean, and waged against a country which has so far declined to retaliate, or recognize that there is either war or the cause of war between us. He proposes to gather the free citizens of this country who have expressed their abhorrence of this act at the polls, into small squares, and ship them over a bloody sea to Europe, to be slaughtered in a war waging between other countries than their own. It requires no vision to predict that some of the brave among these free will conscientiously object to this deed of violence against their elementary liberties.

They would object even if their intelligence had been respected, and the purpose for which they are to be shipped and delivered to Europe, had been explained to them. But up to the present moment (May 16), with preparations for the exportation under way, the President has not even deigned to announce to his victims the end for which they are to march into the pens. At a moment of sacred, if now very distant memory, in last January, he did announce that the United States would stand for a "League of the Nations" based upon "Peace Without Victory." And he is reported vaguely to have stated that since then the diplomatic aims of the United States have not changed. But inasmuch as German high officials have given more endorsement to the League of Nations than the officials of England, and inasmuch as the President has now definitely declared a war for victory over Germany, the statement seems to have even less validity than it has clearness of meaning.

We have joined the war of the British against Germany, a war which is affirmed by the British king, among others, to be a war for the sacred principles of democracy. But fortunately for those of us who know that war impulses are never, and never can be, either so simple or so spiritual as that, it has also been declared (January 10, 1917), by the official British government and her allies, to be a war for the following concrete and specified ends:

"In all necessity and in the first instance, the restitution of Belgium, of Serbia and of Montenegro, and the indemnities which are due them; the evacuation of the invaded territories of France, of Russia and of Roumania, with just reparation. The reorganization of Europe, guaranteed by a stable regime and founded as much upon respect of nationalities and full security and liberty of economic development, which all nations, great or small, possess, as upon territorial conventions and international agreements, suitable to guarantee territorial and maritime frontiers against unjustified attacks. The restitution of provinces and territories wrested in the past from the Allies by force or against the will of their populations; the liberation of Italians, of Slavs, of Roumanians, and of Tcheco-Slovaques from foreign domination; the enfranchisement of populations subject to the bloody tyranny of the Turks; the expulsion from Europe of the Ottoman Empire."

If the British Empire and its allies, boasting a war for democracy, brackets under the general slogan of democracy these various specific and largely irrelevant nationalistic purposes, which Germany declares to mean a dismemberment of her empire, must we not, in absence of any pronouncement to the contrary, assume that the United States, joining the British Empire under the same slogan, endorses the same purposes? Or if we must not assume that, are we not at least entitled by our ancient liberties to ask the President, and expect an answer to our question:

For what specific purposes are you shipping our bodies, and the bodies of our sons, to Europe?

For my part I do not recognize the right of a government to draft me to a war whose purposes I do not believe in. But to draft me to a war whose purposes it will not so much as communicate to my ear, seems an act of tyranny, discordant with the memory even of the decent kings. . . .

Randolph Bourne

takes the American intellectuals to task for their lack of thinking

RANDOLPH BOURNE [1886-1918] *found his first cause in progressive education as exemplified in the philosophy of John Dewey. When he decided that Dewey's pragmatism would not meet the issues of the time, Bourne became a radical pacifist; his was one of the vigorous voices protesting World War I. He attacked America's part in the war in the various magazines for which he wrote. When* Seven Arts *and* The Masses *were suppressed by the government in 1917, he was left with no forum for his opinions, because the remaining magazines closed their doors to him. The article here was published in* Seven Arts, June 1917.

To those of us who still retain an irreconcilable animus against war, it has been a bitter experience to see the unanimity with which the American intellectuals have thrown their support to the use of war technique in the crisis in which America found herself. Socialists, college professors, publicists, *New-Republicans,* practitioners of literature, have vied with each other in confirming with their intellectual faith the collapse of neutrality and the riveting of the war mind on a hundred million more of the world's people. And the intellectuals are not content with confirming our belligerent gesture. They are now complacently asserting that it was they who effectively willed it, against the hesitation and dim perceptions of the American democratic masses. A war made deliberately by the intellectuals! A calm moral verdict, arrived at after a penetrating study of inexorable facts! Sluggish masses, too remote from the world conflict to be stirred, too lacking in intellect to perceive their danger! An alert intellectual class, saving the people in spite of themselves, biding their time with Fabian strategy until the nation could be moved into war without serious resistance! An intellectual class gently guiding a nation through sheer force of ideas into what the other nations entered only through predatory craft or popular hysteria or militarist madness! A war free from any taint of self-seeking, a war that will secure the triumph of democracy and internationalize the world! This is the picture which the more self-conscious intellectuals have formed of themselves, and which they are slowly impressing upon a population which is being led no man knows whither by an indubitably intellectualized President. And they are right, in that the war certainly did not spring from either the ideals or the prejudices, from the national ambitions or hysterias, of the American people, however acquiescent the masses prove to be, and however clearly the intellectuals prove their putative intuition.

Those intellectuals who have felt themselves totally out of sympathy with this drag toward war will seek some explanation for this joyful leadership. They will want to understand this willingness of the American intellect to open the sluices and flood us with the sewage of the war spirit. We cannot forget the virtuous horror and stupefaction which filled our college professors when they read the famous manifesto of their ninety-three German colleagues in defense of their war. To the American academic mind of 1914 defense of war was inconceivable. From Bernhardi it recoiled as from a blasphemy, little dreaming that two years later would find it creating its own cleanly reasons for imposing military service on the country and for talking of the rough rude currents of health and regeneration that war would send through the American body politic. They would have thought anyone mad who talked of shipping American men by the hundreds of thousands—conscripts—to die on the fields of France. Such a spiritual change seems catastrophic when we shoot our minds back to those days when neutrality was a proud thing. But the intellectual progress has been so gradual that the country retains little sense of the irony. The war sentiment, begun so gradually but so perseveringly by the preparedness advocates who came from the ranks of big business, caught hold of one after another of the intellectual groups. With the aid of Roosevelt, the murmurs became a monotonous chant, and finally a chorus so mighty that to be out of it was at first to be disreputable and finally almost obscene. And slowly a strident rant was worked up against Germany which compared very creditably with the German fulminations against the greedy power of England. The nerve of the war feeling centered, of course, in the richer and older classes of the Atlantic seaboard, and was keenest where there were French or English business and particularly social connections. The sentiment then spread over the country as a class phenomenon, touching everywhere those upper-class elements in each section who identified themselves with this eastern ruling group. It must never be forgotten that in every community it was the least liberal and least democratic elements among whom the preparedness and later the war sentiment was found. The farmers were apathetic, the small businessmen and workingmen are still apathetic toward the war. The election was a vote of confidence of these latter classes in a President who would keep the faith of neutrality. The intellectuals, in other words, have identified themselves with the least democratic forces in American life. They have assumed the leadership for war of those very classes whom the American democracy has been immemorially fighting. Only in a world where irony was dead could an intellectual class enter war at the head of such illiberal cohorts in the avowed cause of world liberalism and world democracy. No one is left to point out the undemocratic nature of this war liberalism. In a time of faith, skepticism is the most intolerable of all insults.

Our intellectual class might have been occupied, during the last two years of war, in studying and clarifying the ideals and aspirations of the American democracy, in discovering a true Americanism which would not have been merely nebulous but might have federated the different ethnic groups and traditions. They might have spent the time in endeavoring to clear the public mind of the cant of war, to get rid of old mystical notions that clog our thinking. We might have used the time for a great wave of education, for setting our house in spiritual order. We could at least have set the problem before ourselves. If our intellectuals were going to lead the administration, they might conceivably have tried to find some way of securing peace by making neutrality effective. They might have turned their intellectual energy not to the problem of jockeying the nation into war, but to the problem of using our vast neutral power to attain democratic ends for the rest of the world and ourselves without the use of the malevolent technique of war. They might have failed. The point is that they scarcely tried. The time was spent not in clarification and education, but in a mulling over of nebulous ideals of democracy and liberalism and civilization which had never meant anything fruitful to those ruling classes who now so glibly used them, and in giving free rein to the elementary instinct of self-defense. The whole era has been spiritually wasted. The outstanding feature has been not its Americanism but its intense colonialism. The offense of our intellectuals was not so much that they were colonial—for what could we expect of a nation composed of so many national elements?—but that it was so one-sidedly and partisanly colonial. The official, reputable expression of the intellectual class has been that of the English colonial. . . .

The American's training was such as to make the fact of war almost incredible. Both in his reading of history and in his lack of economic perspective he was badly prepared for it. He had to explain to himself something which was too colossal for the modern mind, which outran any language or terms which we had to interpret it in. He had to expand his sympathies to the breaking point, while pulling the past and present into some sort of interpretative order. The intellectuals in the fighting countries had only to rationalize and justify what their country was already doing. Their task was easy. A neutral, however, had really to search out the truth. Perhaps perspective was too much to ask of any mind. Certainly the older colonials among our college professors let their prejudices at once dictate their thought. They have been comfortable ever since. The war has taught them nothing and will teach them nothing. And they have had the satisfaction, under the rigor of events, of seeing prejudice submerge the intellects of their younger colleagues. And they have lived to see almost their entire class, pacifists and democrats too, join them as apologists for the "gigantic irrelevance" of war. . . .

An intellectual class that was wholly rational would have called insistently for peace and not for war. For months the crying need has been for a negotiated peace, in order to avoid the ruin of a deadlock. Would not the same amount of resolute statesmanship thrown into intervention have secured a peace that would have been a subjugation for neither side? Was the terrific bargaining power of a great neutral ever really used? Our war followed, as all wars follow, a monstrous failure of diplomacy. Shamefacedness should now be our intellectuals' attitude, because the American play for peace was made so little more than a polite play. The intellectuals have still to explain why, willing as they now are to use force to continue the war to absolute exhaustion, they were not willing to use force to coerce the world to a speedy peace. . . .

The case of the intellectuals seems, therefore, only very speciously rational. They could have used their energy to force a just peace or at least to devise other means than war for carrying through American policy. They could have used their intellectual energy to insure that our participation in the war meant the international order which they wish. Intellect was not so used. It was used to lead an apathetic nation into an irresponsible war, without guarantees from these belligerents whose cause we were saving. The American intellectual, therefore, has been rational neither in his hindsight nor his foresight. To explain him we must look beneath the intellectual reasons to the emotional disposition. It is not so much what they thought as how they felt that explains our intellectual class. Allowing for colonial sympathy, there was still the personal shock in a world war which outraged all our preconceived notions of the way the world was tending. It reduced to rubbish most of the humanitarian internationalism and democratic nationalism which had been the emotional thread of our intellectuals' life. We had suddenly to make a new orientation. There were mental conflicts. Our latent colonialism strove with our longing for American unity. Our desire for peace strove with our desire for national responsibility in the world. That first lofty and remote and not altogether unsound feeling of our spiritual isolation from the conflict could not last. There was the itch to be in the great experience which the rest of the world was having. Numbers of intelligent people who had never been stirred by the horrors of capitalistic peace at home were shaken out of their slumber by the horrors of war in Belgium. Never having felt responsibility for labor wars and oppressed masses and excluded races at home, they had a large fund of idle emotional capital to invest in the oppressed nationalities and ravaged villages of Europe. Hearts that had felt only ugly contempt for democratic strivings at home beat in tune with the struggle for freedom abroad. All this was natural, but it tended to overemphasize our responsibility. And it threw our thinking out of gear. The task of making our own country detailedly fit for peace was abandoned in favor of a feverish concern for the management of the war, advice to the fighting governments on all matters, military, social and political, and a gradual working up of the conviction that we were ordained as a nation to lead all erring brothers toward the light of liberty and democracy. The failure of the American intellectual class to erect a creative attitude toward the war can be explained by these sterile mental conflicts which the shock to our ideals sent raging through us. . . .

With how many of the acceptors of war has it been mostly a dread of intellectual suspense? It is a mistake to suppose that intellectuality necessarily makes for suspended judgments. The intellect craves certitude. It takes effort to keep it supple and pliable. In a time of danger and disaster we jump desperately for some dogma to cling to. The time comes, if we try to hold out, when our nerves are sick with fatigue, and we seize in a great healing wave of release some doctrine that can be immediately translated into action. Neutrality meant suspense, and so it became the object of loathing to frayed nerves. The vital myth of the League of Peace provides a dogma to jump to. With war the world becomes motor again and speculation is brushed aside like cobwebs. The blessed emotion of self-defense intervenes too, which focused millions in Europe. A few keep up a critical pose after war is begun, but since they usually advise action which is in one-to-one correspondence with what the mass is already doing, their criticism is little more than a rationalization of the common emotional drive.

The results of war on the intellectual class are already apparent. Their thought becomes little more than a description and justification of what is going on. They turn upon any rash one who continues idly to speculate. Once the war is on, the conviction spreads that individual thought is helpless, that the only way one can count is as a cog in the great wheel. There is no good holding back. We are told to dry our unnoticed and ineffective tears and plunge into the great work. Not only is everyone forced into line, but the new certitude becomes idealized. It is a noble realism which opposes itself to futile obstruction and the cowardly refusal to face facts. This realistic boast is so loud and sonorous that one wonders whether realism is always a stern and intelligent grappling with realities. May it not be sometimes a mere surrender to the actual, an abdication of the ideal through a sheer fatigue from intellectual suspense? The pacifist is roundly scolded for refusing to face the facts, and for retiring into his own world of sentimental desire. But is the realist, who refuses to challenge or criticize facts, entitled to any more credit than that which comes from following the line of least resistance? The realist thinks he at least can control events by linking himself to the forces that are moving. Perhaps he can. But if it is a question of controlling war, it is difficult to see how the child on the back of a mad elephant is to be any more effective in stopping the beast than is the child who tries to stop him from the ground. The ex-humanitarian, turned realist, sneers at the snobbish neutrality, colossal conceit, crooked thinking, dazed sensibilities, of those who are still unable to find any balm of consolation for this war. We manufacture consolations here in America while there are probably not a dozen men fighting in Europe who did not long ago give up every reason for their being there except that nobody knew how to get them away.

But the intellectuals whom the crisis has crystallized into an acceptance of war have put themselves into a terrifyingly strategic position. It is only on the craft, in the stream, they say, that one has any chance of controlling the current forces for liberal purposes. If we obstruct, we surrender all power for influence. If we responsibly approve, we then retain our power for guiding. We will be listened to as responsible thinkers, while those who obstructed the coming of war have committed intellectual suicide and shall be cast into outer darkness. Criticism by the ruling powers will only be accepted from those intellectuals who are in sympathy with the general tendency of the war. Well, it is true that they may guide, but if their stream leads to disaster and the frustration of national life, is their guiding any more than a preference whether they shall go over the right-hand or the left-hand side of the precipice? Meanwhile, however, there is comfort on board. Be with us, they call, or be negligible, irrelevant. Dissenters are already excommunicated. Irreconcilable radicals, wringing their hands among the debris, become the most despicable and impotent of men. There seems no choice for the intellectual but to join the mass of acceptance. But again the terrible dilemma arises— either support what is going on, in which case you count for nothing because you are swallowed in the mass and great incalculable forces bear you on; or remain aloof, passively resistant, in which case you count for nothing because you are outside the machinery of reality.

Is there no place left, then, for the intellectual who cannot yet crystallize, who does not dread suspense, and is not yet drugged with fatigue? The American intellectuals, in their preoccupation with reality, seem to have forgotten that the real enemy is war rather than imperial Germany. There is work to be done to prevent this war of ours from passing into popular mythology as a holy crusade. What shall we do with leaders who tell us that we go to war in moral spotlessness, or who make "democracy" synonymous with a republican form of government? There is work to be done in still shouting that all the revolutionary by-products will not justify the war, or make war anything else than the most noxious complex of all the evils that afflict men. There must be some to find no consolation whatever, and some to sneer at those who buy the cheap emotion of sacrifice. There must be some irreconcilables left who will not even accept the war with walrus tears. There must be some to call unceasingly for peace, and some to insist that the terms of settlement shall be not only liberal but democratic. There must be some intellectuals who are not willing to use the old discredited counters again and to support a peace which would leave all the old inflammable materials of armament lying about the world. There must still be opposition to any contemplated "liberal" world order founded on military coalitions. The "irreconcilable" need not be disloyal. He need not even be "impossiblist." His apathy toward war should take the form of a heightened energy and enthusiasm for the education, the art, the interpretation that make for life in the midst of the world of death. The intellectual who retains his animus against war will push out more boldly than ever to make his case solid against it. The old ideals crumble; new ideals must be forged. His mind will continue to roam widely and ceaselessly.

The thing he will fear most is premature crystallization. If the American intellectual class rivets itself to a "liberal" philosophy that perpetuates the old errors, there will then be need for "democrats" whose task will be to divide, confuse, disturb, keep the intellectual waters constantly in motion to prevent any such ice from ever forming.

Norman Thomas
makes a plea for the conscientious objector

NORMAN THOMAS [1884-   ], six times Socialist candidate for President of the United States, was one of a small group of Protestant ministers who opposed World War I. During the war Mr. Thomas, with Roger Baldwin and John Haynes Holmes, helped form the American Union against Militarism. When Baldwin was sent to jail for opposing the war, Thomas carried on much of the work of the group, which eventually became the American Civil Liberties Union. Before World War II, he was chairman of the Keep America Out of War Committee, but after the United States entered the war he became a "critical supporter." He was one of the founders of the National Committee for a Sane Nuclear Policy.

Any effort to think intelligently about a war avowedly waged for human liberty brings one face to face with the problem of the conscientious objector. Undoubtedly he is an irritant to the whole-souled patriot. His very existence seems a piece of inconsiderate egotism and annoyingly interrupts us in the midst of our enthusiasms for a war fought "by no compulsion of the unwilling" "to make the world safe for democracy." So newspapers, orators and Colonel Roosevelt call him slacker, coward or pro-German; philosophers gravely pronounce him antisocial, and scientists like Dr. Paton analyze him from a study chair with a truly Teutonic subjectivity and heaviness. Meanwhile his defenders and comrades are a bit embarrassed because he is not of one type or philosophy, but of many. Even the name "conscientious objector" is most unwelcome to some moderns among them to whom the phrase has an "archaic flavor," an objective quality, "like a godly grandmother," which hardly fits into their scheme of life. They are not, then, overly sympathetic with the defense which is entirely satisfactory to the man to whom conscience is the real norm of life and "thou shalt not kill" a complete statement of its law.

Therefore it is with some diffidence that I, a conscientious objector, undertake to speak for my brethren and to appeal even in the heat of war for some measure of understanding—not so much for our own sakes as in the interest of sound public policy and ultimately of democracy itself.

As a starting point we can define conscientious objectors as men who are absolutely persuaded that enforced participation in this war is so opposed to their deepest convictions of right and wrong for themselves or for society that they must refuse conscription at least for combatant service. If they know themselves they will hold this position whatever it may cost. This attitude springs from no insufferable priggishness. The objector does not primarily seek to judge others; he may heartily admire the heroism which leads his friends into battle, he may admit the idealism of their ends, only he cannot agree with them as to the method they use.

How many such folk there are in the United States no one knows. Naturally, the government will not permit an aggressive attempt to discover and organize all conscientious objectors. There are, however, many societies, local and national, whose members are avowed conscientious objectors, and there are many more unorganized individuals who hold such convictions. Again, it is uncertain how many of the thousands of objectors will be drawn in the first group called to report under the draft law.

It is natural to think of conscientious objectors as essentially religious, and the government showed a certain deference to religious liberty in exempting from combatant service members of well-recognized religious organizations whose creed or principles are opposed to war. Of course this is illogical in theory, for conscience is an individual and not a corporate matter. Not all conscientious objection is avowedly religious, nor is religious conscientious objection confined to the relatively small sects which have incorporated it in their creeds. Within the last generation there has been a wide growth of peace sentiment in the churches, not all of which is as amenable to conversion to war as the average ecclesiastical organization or that erstwhile prophet of the Prince of Peace, William J. Bryan. You have to reckon with it. Then you have young idealists among the intellectuals to whom humanity is a reality never served by the stupid horrors of war, and the very much larger group of workingmen who have learned too well the doctrine of the solidarity of the working class to believe that the organized destruction of their brethren who march under a different national banner will hasten the dawn of real liberty and fraternity.

In short, conscientious objectors include Christians, Jews, agnostics and atheists; economic conservatists and radicals; philosophic Anarchists and orthodox Socialists.

It is not fair, therefore, to think of the conscientious objector simply as a man who with a somewhat dramatic gesture would save his own soul though liberty perish and his country be laid in ruins. I speak with personal knowledge when I say that such an attitude is rare. Rightly or wrongly, the conscientious objector believes that his religion or his social theory in the end can save what is precious in the world far better without than with this stupendously destructive war. He is a pacifist but not a passivist. . . .

We are lovers of America because we believe she still strives for democracy. It is the essence of democracy to believe that the state exists for the well-being of individuals; it is the essence of Prussianism to believe that individuals exist for the service of some unreal metaphysical entity called the state. True, the individual exists and finds his complete self-realization only in society—an immeasurably greater concept than the state. Democracy means, of course, mutual accommodation of individuals and social control. In proportion as the state is the effective agent of such control its power should grow but never should it grow to a control over men's convictions. It then becomes as dangerous to society as to the individual. When the state seeks to compel a man who believes that war is wrong, not merely to abstain from actual sedition, as is its right, but to participate in battle, it inevitably compels him, however deep his love of country, to raise once more the cry, "we ought to obey God rather than men." He acknowledges with Romain Rolland that he is the citizen of two fatherlands and his supreme loyalty is to the City of God, of which he is a builder. Some conscientious objectors may substitute mankind or humanity for God, but their conviction remains the same; only the free spirit can finally determine for a man the highest service he can render. Compulsory service rendered against one's conscience is genuinely antisocial. The deep principles which guide a man's life are not formed or suddenly altered by any act of Congress whatsoever. There is a region in human life where the commandment of the state does not run. On this very issue Christianity long withstood the whole might of the Roman Empire, and wherever she is strong it is because of her assertion of the responsibility of conscience to God. In the long run that state is most secure which recognizes this truth.

We are not now pleading that our critics recognize that conscientious objectors are right in their opposition to war. We are not claiming a monopoly of idealism for ourselves or denying that men may seek our name from unworthy motives. Our interest is deeper than securing justice for ourselves. We are pleading for recognition of the social value of heresy. Every movement worth while began with a minority. Democracy degenerates into mobocracy unless the rights of the minority are respected. The Church of the Middle Ages made the sincerest, most magnificent effort in history to coerce the individual's conscience for the sake not only of the eternal welfare of his soul, but of the church universal. At last she recognized her failure, but not until she had done incalculable damage. Her own sons rejoice in that failure. Now the state, less universal in its outlook, less definite in its dogma, sets itself up as a secular deity and demands not the outward conformity which usually satisfied the Church, but active participation in doing that which is to its heretic sons the supreme denial of their sense of righteousness. It deliberately thinks it can save democracy by this final act of autocracy. Gone is our belief in the power of ideas, in the might of right. America, founded by exiles for conscience's sake, their refuge in all generations, gives her sons the option of service in the trenches or imprisonment and thereby wounds her very soul as no outward victory of Prussian power can do. The heretic may be very irritating, he may be decidedly wrong, but the attempt to choke heresy or dissent from the dominant opinion by coercing the conscience is an incalculable danger to society. If war makes it necessary, it is the last count in the indictment against war.

I have chosen to dwell on the recognition of conscientious objection as a matter of democratic right rather than a matter of expediency or of sound public policy because this aspect is the more fundamental and because a nation that sees the importance of the issue involved will discover the statesmanship to give justice expression in law.

In point of fact we might make a case on the question of policy. The conscientious objector in prison adds no strength to the nation, nor does he commend our brand of democracy to the German people for whose freedom we are fighting. If the conscientious objector is cowardly enough to be intimidated into the ranks he is the last man to help win the war. This is no time for the government to indulge in a petty fit of exasperation at the conscientious objector who oftentimes is quite willing to give some real nonmilitary service to his country. The problem of giving effect to a policy of fair treatment for conscientious objectors is not without its difficulties. Real freedom of conscience is impossible under conscription partly because of the practical difficulty of framing an exemption clause and partly because some coercion upon the unformed conscience inconsistent with genuine liberty is inevitable in any system of conscription of young men. This is one of the reasons why so many lovers of liberty were steadfast opponents of the passage of the draft law.

But even under our present system exemption can be granted on the basis of the individual, as in England, and he can be at least allowed to take alternative service which may not violate his conscience. It is entirely possible to copy the general principles of the British system and avoid certain of its stupid brutalities of administration.

But behind any change in the law or its administration must lie the far more fundamental matter of a public opinion not swayed by false and prejudiced statements against conscientious objectors but informed as to their real position and attitude, and above all aroused to the desperate urgency that, in a war for democracy, America shall not kill at home that "privilege of men everywhere to choose their way of life and obedience" which she seeks to secure for the world. If this is indeed a people's war for freedom the people can be trusted to see it through, without any coercion of conscience. To deny this is either to distrust democracy or to doubt the validity of war as its instrument. Justice to the conscientious objector secures, not imperils, the safety of the democratic state.

Norman Angell

answers the question, "If a German attacked your wife . . ."

SIR NORMAN ANGELL [1874-   ] *is a British economist and writer who has devoted his life to the cause of international peace. He was a Labor member of Parliament from 1929 to 1931, and for several years editor of* Foreign Affairs. *In 1931 he was knighted, and in 1933 he won the Nobel Peace Prize. He has never been an absolutist, and here he defends a conscientious objector's right to protect himself against attack without jeopardizing his beliefs. The article appeared in 1917.*

"If a German attacked your mother"—or wife or sweetheart or grandmother as the case may be—"would you not defend her?"

The question may be heard any day at one of the tribunals created in England under the new conscription law to hear claims for exemption from military service. It is asked, of course, of the applicant who bases his claim upon a conscientious objection to war, and is part of the means by which the tribunal decides whether his conscience is the real thing. Should the questionee—usually some nervous, stammering and inarticulate workman of prolonged religious feeling belonging to one of the small bodies of Christians who make a refusal to kill in war one of their tenets—appear to admit that he would defend his mother, or if he should lack glibness or precision in his reply, the tribunal is pretty certain to decide that his conscience is not genuine: that if he would defend his mother he cannot have any conscientious objection to killing Arabs in Mesopotamia or Bulgarians in the Balkans (none of whom was exactly threatening his mother) in order that Russia's claims to Constantinople may be made entirely secure.

Once you have admitted that you would defend your wife, this new Inquisition into conscience will prove to you not only that you cannot logically or justly object to being compelled to kill or be killed on behalf of any foreign policy which the government may decree, but that you cannot resist its right to prohibit your discussion of the subject; or to lock up Mr. Bertrand Russell, who might mention the matter in his lectures; or to refuse him a passport to America; and so forth. You would defend your mother? Then, of course, the authorities must have power to prevent the advocacy of a patched-up peace, or the Germans will attack us again. The "competent military authority" must be judge of how much foreign policy common folk will be allowed to know, just as they have become judges, under the Defense of the Realm Act, of how far Mr. Russell shall be allowed to go in discussing political ideals.

You object that the continuation of this sort of thing, by depriving a people of any real freedom to discuss the foundations of their policy, will produce a public opinion so passionate and ill informed as to be unable to distinguish between good and bad policy, between defense and aggression? Then obviously you don't mind if Huns ravish your sister.

Is this logical chain quite as complete as the elderly tradesmen who sit in judgment upon men's lives and consciences in the new English tribunals would have us believe? If I have a moral objection to tearing off a man's face with a piece of hot metal because his government has disagreed with mine as to whether Austrian or Russian influence shall dominate in the Balkans, must I also stand aside when some drunken savage attacks a child?

Is the choice really between these two absolutes? If we undertake to defend our lives and our womenfolk by force, shall we be dragged by an unbreakable chain to war and militarism? Must we choose between nonresistance and Prussianism?

Mr. John Haynes Holmes in his book *New Wars for Old* says, in effect, Yes. Self-defense, he says, can be made to justify anything. "To resort to force from motives of self-defense is as perilous as to resort to force from motives of liberation" (p. 63), and he gives instances from Marcus Aurelius to the Kaiser in justification. And to this extent he is in agreement with the chairman of the conscription tribunal: once admit that you must defend your mother by force, and you admit the right of the state to ask of you anything it pleases in what it considers some necessary part of that object—like the annexation of Egypt or of Mesopotamia.

It is because Mr. Holmes has accepted the premises of the tribunal —they are indeed the usual assumptions of most discussions of the place of force in human affairs—that his book, able, persuasive and arresting as it is, will not have upon prevailing ideas on the subject the effect that it might have otherwise. For while a useful and noteworthy contribution to this very difficult problem—the most difficult and the most important problem now confronting organized society—and worth reading from the first page to the last, it does not, alas, answer that question about the Hun and the grandmother in any way that would enable the conscientious objector rationally to explain and define his objection; or to protect himself from impalement on one or other of the horns of that dilemma which the chairman of the tribunal presents to him. Mr. Holmes cites a large number of cases where nonresistance, or moral resistance, or passive resistance have been successful. But he has not said—any more than the conscientious objector is able to say—what he would do in the case of the assault on his mother; and why, if he would justify her defense by force, he condemns the defense of his country by force: he has not shown by what clearly defined principle the English or German Socialist who refuses to take part in his country's wars, however "defensive," can be justified in defending his own person or that of his dependents or neighbors from bodily assault.

I suppose that question about the Hun and the grandmother has been asked some hundreds, perhaps thousands, of times in the English tribunals. Not once, so far as I am aware, has a conscientious objector pointed out that though Belgium (say) in refusing to resist the Germans might have committed a monstrous and despicable crime, she would at least by that means have rendered her women and children as safe as have been those of Luxemburg, which did not resist. If England had refused to enter the war and had induced France to refuse, we might have had a German domination of Europe, the end of liberty, the passing of democracy, anything you please; but there would have been no slaughter of English or French populations.

This, of course, does not make out a case for political nonresistance, but it does indicate that the grandmother argument, far from telling against such nonresistance, is perhaps the very strongest argument for it.

It is very difficult, as we know, and some of us almost give up the task in despair (though there is nothing upon which Shaw's "average stockbroker" is more dogmatic!) to know why great states go to war, why countries like England and France have during the last few centuries fought one another and every great state in the world. But of the struggles between them—whatever may be true of the wars of conquest of such territories as India or Mexico—we can at least with absolute dogmatism say this: They have not been from any need of protecting their citizens from outrage. Yet that one reason, which on examination we must realize to be either the grossest kind of pretense or the most hopeless befuddlement, is the one reason paraded in nationalist oratory, recruiting posters, or "Battle Cry of Peace" films. And to that befuddlement I am afraid the advocates of nonresistance have themselves contributed by this implication that the same reasons which impel you to use force to defend your wife or children, also justify your using force to defend your country against foreign rule.

Common thought on this matter confuses two entirely distinct problems: that of protecting national sovereignty, or asserting political power to nationalist ends—with which all war between great states is closely concerned; and that of the maintenance of social order, or protection of the person and property as that term is understood in the Western world—with which object war between Western powers has nothing whatever to do. New York would be as well policed under German as under Tammany rule. Not that political nonresistance necessarily implies submission to foreign rule. When the Germans, having completely smashed all French resistance in 1872, having imposed their power upon the whole country, then completely evacuated it (except for the German-speaking portions), what must we assume to have been the objects of German policy? The actual reduction of France to a German province? Then why was it not accomplished, since the German rulers must have known that never again would German action be likely to have so free a hand for such a policy?

What was aimed at, of course, was the destruction of French power, the removal of France as a political rival in Europe. Supposing that France had accepted that position and said: "After this we shall have no army." Obviously, in view of the German evacuation when France *had* no army, her soil and autonomous government would have been safe. Have then the forty-four years of labor and the present sacrifice of what promises to be her entire youth, been for mere political glory, for the conquests in Africa and Asia?

We cannot say with any certainty. Frenchmen themselves do not know. For, owing precisely to the confusions just indicated, the difference between a struggle for political power or expansion, and the defense of the French folk from personal outrage by Germans, has never been cleared up. The two things are still identified in the mind of the average European.

Push the inquiry a little further. We talk of the defense of French culture, but has French expansion in Africa, in the Sahara, into Tunis, into Madagascar, into equatorial swamps, into Morocco—with which, after all, the war was more concerned than with French literature or drama —advanced that culture? Would its influence have been less if France, first of all the great states, had surrendered the scramble for political power? What really is the relation of military force to those things? May it not be that we are misconceiving that relationship as grossly as in the past we mistook the need of defending our religious faiths by force?

I am not urging that this makes a case for nonresistance. I do not believe it does. For the purpose of resistance to foreign rule, it may be worth while to subject our women and children to the danger and hardship to which they are usually subject in war. I am not challenging that for a moment. But the everlasting confusion between the two objects in popular discussion is of the very essence of those misunderstandings out of which wars arise; and it should be cleared up.

In that task the advocacy of political nonresistance might play a useful role if only it could get away from those absolutes by which it seems to be dominated. Even then of course it would not win the nations to nonresistance as a practical policy; but the discussion which it would provoke might so clear political thought as to render it capable of policies a little less disastrous than those now adopted. That is the service which the advocacy of "extreme views" usually performs.

At this moment the whole course of Allied policy rests far more upon the fashion in which the great mass will answer a simple question of human psychology than upon any question of politics. Will Germans be less or more inclined to "do it again" if they are now "punished" by a "fight to a finish"? You have there a question upon which an observant woman who has brought up half a dozen children and kept her temper is as able to pronounce as the most experienced statesman. It is the average Englishman's ideas as to the efficacy of force and punishment, the extent to which his own ordinary judgment has survived the temper of war, and not any expert decision in the intricacies of Balkan politics that will decide the question of continuing the war.

It is obvious that the millions who in the last resort make up national feeling and determine the general line of national policy will never be expert in political, historical and geographical technicalities. Nor is it necessary that they should be. If the temper and atmosphere which arise out of the general attitude to the more elementary issues are of the right kind, difficulties of detail will almost settle themselves. If that temper and atmosphere are wrong, then some small defect of detail against which no cleverness of the expert can protect us will suffice once more to set the world ablaze. In the fundamental problems of human relationship—in those of conscience and morals—the bootblack is as well fitted to judge as the bishop. Indeed, as a matter of simple historical fact (as the political record, for instance, of the Bench of Bishops in the British House of Lords will show) the bootblack has generally been right and the bishop wrong. And this, of course, is because the data for judgment are the common facts of daily life concerning which the bootblack is probably better informed than any bishop could be.

It is by right reasoning through these common facts that we shall find salvation.

Hermann Hesse

challenges a minister of state to end the dilemma of war

HERMANN HESSE [1877-1962] *was a German novelist and poet who won the 1946 Nobel Prize for Literature. He left Germany during World War I, decrying its bloodshed, hatred and violence, and moved to Switzerland, where he became a citizen. "I was not susceptible to nationalistic sentiments," Hesse wrote. "I have twice changed my nationality, and am today a Swiss citizen without considering Swiss people a nation of half-gods." He wrote poetry attacking Hitler, and during their rule in Germany the Nazis banned and burned his books. He wrote the letter here in 1917.*

Tonight, after a strenuous work day, I asked my wife to play a Beethoven sonata for me. This music recalled me from the tension of my business affairs into the only reality we possess, that which causes us pleasure and torment, in which and for which we are living.

Later, I read a few lines in the Book that contains the Sermon on the Mount and the great age-old basic words: "Thou shalt not kill."

But I found no rest. I could neither go to bed nor continue my reading. I was filled with unrest and fear. While I was thinking and searching for the cause, I suddenly remembered a few sentences from a speech of yours, Mr. Minister, which I read during the last few days. Your speech was sophisticated, but it was not especially new, important or provocative. Condensed to its most important, it said about the same that all speeches of governing members have said for a long time: That we do not wish for anything more fervently than for peace, a new unity, and fruitful work for the future of the people; that we neither want to enrich ourselves nor do we desire to satisfy a lust for murder; that, however, "the moment for negotiations" has not yet arrived. And so for the time being, we must continue bravely to go to war. Any minister of any warring people could give a similar talk—maybe tomorrow or the day after tomorrow.

This speech did not let me sleep tonight, although I have often read similar speeches with the same sad finale and I have slept well afterward. I am sure now that it was the Beethoven sonata—it, and that Book I later read where the wondrous commandments of Sinai and the enlightening words of Christ are written.

Beethoven's music and the words of the Bible said exactly the same to me. It was water from One Source, the only Source from which good comes to man. And suddenly I felt that your speech, Mr. Minister, and the speeches of your governing colleagues, now and then do not stem from this Source; they lack that which makes words valuable and meaningful. Your words lack love; they lack humanity.

Your speech shows a deep feeling of concern and responsibility for your people, for the army of your people, for the honor of your people. But it does not show a feeling for mankind. It means, in brief, a few ten thousand new human sacrifices.

You may possibly call my memories of Beethoven a sentimentality. The words of Christ and of the Bible you will, at least in public, regard with certain reverence. But if you believe in only one of the ideals for which you are fighting this war—be it freedom of countries or of the seas, be it the political progress or the rights of the small nations—if you believe in only one of these ideals, in one of these nonegotistical thoughts in your soul—then, while reading your speech, you must recognize that it has not served this ideal. It has not served any ideal at all. It is not expression and result of a belief, of a feeling, of a humane need. But, unfortunately, it is only an expression and the result of a dilemma. An understandable dilemma, to be sure, for nothing might be more difficult than to admit a certain disappointment over the results of the war, and to search for the next road to peace—now, today.

Meanwhile, a dilemma, may it be one of ten governments, is something that cannot endure. Over the dilemmas, the necessities will triumph. Somehow, once, it will become necessary for you and all your hostile colleagues—it will be inevitable—to confess the dilemma and to determine to make an end to it.

For the results of the war are disappointing to all war lords—today and for some time. No matter who was the victor—here or there—no matter how many prisoners were taken or lost, how much territory was occupied and how much was lost—the result has not been what was expected of war. No solution, no clarity, no decision has come, and none seems to be forthcoming.

To conceal a great dilemma for the time being, for yourself and your people, to postpone great and important decisions (which always demand sacrifices)—that's why you gave your speech, and that's why the other ruling parties give theirs. It's understandable. It is easier for a revolutionary or for a writer than it is for a responsible statesman to recognize the human in a world situation and to draw conclusions from it. It is easier for one of us because we are not responsible for the tremendous depression which grips a people when it realizes that it has not reached its war aim, and it may possibly have sacrificed hundreds of thousands of people and milliards of "values."

But not only for this is it more difficult to admit embarrassment and to foster the end of the war through decisions. It is more difficult for you because you don't listen enough to music, and because you don't read enough in the Bible or the great poets.

This makes you smile. Maybe you also say that you as a private individual have a very close relationship to Beethoven and to everything beautiful and noble. And perhaps you really do. But I really wish that one of these days you would listen to fine music, and suddenly hear the voices that come from these holy sources! I wish that one of these days in a moment of peace you would read a profile of Christ, a poem by Goethe, a saying by Lao-tse.

The moment in which you would do it could become extremely important for the world. Possibly you would find inner freedom. It could be that your eyes and ears would suddenly be opened. Your eyes and ears, Mr. Minister, have been trained for years to see theoretical goals instead of reality, they are—true, it was necessary!—long since used to not seeing a great many of the things of reality, to overlook them, to deny them to yourself.

You know what I mean? Yes, you know. But the voice of a great poet, the voice of the Bible, the eternally clear voice of humanity that speaks to you from this art, maybe it will make you for a moment really see and hear. Ah, what you would see and hear! Nothing any more of a dearth of work and the prices of coal. Nothing any more of tonnage and of pacts, of loans and all the things which have long since become the realities for you. In their place you would see the world, our old patient world, as it lies strewn with corpses and dying, as it is torn and ruined, burnt and defiled. You would see soldiers who lie between the frontiers for days, and how they cannot chase away with their shattered hands the flies from the wounds from which they perish. You would hear the voices of the wounded, the cries of the insane, the clamor and accusations of mothers and fathers, of brides and sisters, the cry of hunger in the people.

If you would hear all this again—what conveniently you were not permitted to hear for months and years—maybe then, with new thoughts, you would comprehend your war aims, your ideals and theories, and test them, and you would really seek to weigh its actual value against the misery of one single month of war, of one single day of war.

If it were only possible to achieve this! This hour of music, this return to the true reality! I know you would hear the voice of humanity, I know you would lock yourself in and cry. And the next day you would go and do what is your duty to humanity. You would forsake a few millions or milliards of money, you would consider a small loss of prestige, you would blow to the winds the thousands of things (things for which in reality you are still fighting alone), if necessary even your seat of Ministry. For it you would do what humanity is pleading for and hopes for from you in untold anguish and misery—you would be the first among the reigning to condemn this lamentable war. You would be the first among the responsible to express what secretly all are already feeling: that a half year, that a month of war, is costlier than all it can gain in return.

Then, Mr. Minister, we would never forget your name, and your deed would mean more to humanity than the deeds of all who have ever led and won the wars.

Meyer London

speaks in Congress against declaring war on Germany

MEYER LONDON [1871-1926] *was an American labor leader, a founder of the Socialist Party of America and of The Workmen's Circle, a Socialist fraternal organization. He was born in Russia and came to the United States at the age of twenty. He served three terms in the United States Congress as a representative from New York. He was an outspoken opponent of warfare and went to Congress with the intention of making "war on war." He advocated forcing Europe to come to terms by refusing food and war materials to warring nations. He made the speech here in the 65th Congress, in 1917.*

MR. LONDON. Mr. Chairman and gentlemen, I am sorry that I could not get myself to prepare a speech. I have spoken so often on the subject that my mind has stopped creating. I cannot argue with a man who favors war. War is incomprehensible to me. Nor do I hope that it will be possible at this moment to convert anybody. I feel, however, that I owe an obligation to myself to again state my position.

The greatest service to democracy that could be rendered by this Congress would be to refuse to endorse the request for war. This is the only parliament in the world to which the question of war or peace has been submitted. No other parliament has had an opportunity to vote on the question of war or peace. The German Reichstag, the British Parliament, the French Chamber of Deputies, the Russian Duma were all confronted with an accomplished fact. War had either taken place when they were called upon to vote for the military budget or the representatives of the people were told so.

MR. QUIN. Will the gentleman yield?

MR. LONDON. No; I cannot. I am sorry, but I have not enough time. This is the only parliament, the only congress, where the representatives of the people are called upon to act. They are invited to search their minds and their consciences. Will they throw away that opportunity? If this representative body endorses the idea of war, then all hope for international peace may as well be abandoned.

Only six weeks ago the Members of this Congress had an opportunity to express themselves on the subject of war during the discussion of the armed-neutrality bill. Almost every man who favored armed neutrality argued that it excluded the idea of war; that war was inconceivable, impossible, unimaginable.

Now, the very same men who only six or eight weeks ago declared that war was inconceivable are ready to vote for war because the President asks for it. In six weeks you are invited to reverse a policy as old as this republic; you are invited not only to defend the territory of the United States and the territorial waters of the United States as is your sworn obligation to do, but you are invited to fight for rights admitted to be disputable within the war zone thousands of miles away. You are invited within six weeks to change a policy as old as the Republic, to enter into all sorts of alliances, into all sorts of partnerships with kings, rulers by divine right, with monarchs of all sorts. Congress is vested by the Constitution with the power to declare war. Is it a mere clerical duty that we are to perform? It may be true that in the past Congresses have acted this way. Shall we now, when we are called upon to fight for democracy abroad, surrender all democracy here?

The President says we have no war with the German people. Of course we have not. The very same words were uttered by the British premier in the parliament of England; and the British premier meant it, and he was sincere about it; and the President meant what he said, and he was sincere about it. But, while you have no war today with the German people, and while the nations of Europe had no war in their hearts in July 1914, and while the war was originally a war of capitalists, plutocrats, expansionists, and kings, it became a war of the people, a war of the nations themselves. With every fresh grave, with the crippled, the mutilated, and the sightless returning home, hatreds grew, bitterness grew, until men became beasts. They ceased being Germans, they ceased being Frenchmen, they ceased to be Britishers. Through hatred they reverted to the brutal instinct of the savage, and the worst animal of all animals is the human being who hates.

Of course we have no hatred of the German people, but with the first victim of the war hatred will grow and we will be at war, not with the Kaiser but with the German people. We will be at war with the people who have built up a glorious civilization, with a people among whom there are millions of social democrats, the most advanced democracy of the world, whose hearts beat in unison with ours, whose souls crave for communion with the democratic elements throughout the world. . . .

The question was asked here: How do we know that the people are opposed to war? Of course, we know that the people are opposed to war, and I hate to say I am afraid the President himself doubts whether the people favor war. I should hate to say so, but it is the only implication which his recommendation for compulsory military service carries. In the Spanish-American War the martyred President McKinley had no difficulty in getting volunteers. There was an ideal presented to the American young man, the delivery of an oppressed people, and 225,000 young men responded in less than six weeks to the call of the President. There was no talk of conscription then. A spiritual thing was conjured up which demanded of men to sacrifice their lives. But now nobody dares speak of volunteers. In order that we should be able to get volunteers there must be a desire in the hearts of the people to fight, to fight for the things for which the President asks us now to fight. Not on February 26, not on January 22, but now on April 2 he determined the destiny of this republic. On April 2 he told the great mass of the American people what they should fight for—for a new idea—not to improve this republic, not that the American people may rise to greater heights, but to change the forms of government in Turkey, in Austria, and Germany. No wonder he is compelled to recommend compulsory military service. Australia has been generous to her mother country. So has the Dominion of Canada, but neither the Dominion of Canada nor Australia has tolerated the idea of compulsory service. On the contrary, when that issue was presented to the people of Australia they voted down compulsory service after two years of war.

MR. AUSTIN. Mr. Chairman, will the gentleman allow me to ask him a question?

MR. LONDON. No, please do not interrupt me now.

MR. AUSTIN. It is a question on volunteer and compulsory service.

MR. LONDON. I have so much material I desire to incorporate in my remarks I cannot yield, and I have just a few more moments.

MR. AUSTIN. I will yield the gentleman time myself.

MR. LONDON. Pardon me. We may as well frankly admit that the great mass of the American people do sympathize with the Allies. It is but natural. Every American loves France. France has exercised a noble influence upon the course of America. In the Declaration of Independence you will find the very language of the French encyclopedists and of the liberal philosophers of that day. In turn the American Declaration of Independence and the successful American Revolution have reacted upon France. It is the only great sister republic.

This is an Anglo-Saxon country, with the great heritage of English literature, of English political institutions, and the English system of jurisprudence. Besides these spiritual causes, there are strong economic reasons why the friendship of the great naval power should be more valuable than the friendship of the central powers on the continent of Europe. But if we are to render aid to the Allies, why necessarily in the form of war? Why has no one thought of suggesting noncombatant aid? Why should we use the last and most desperate method, the unspeakable method of war, before we have tried other expedients? Why has not the President of the United States, in view of the great wave of democratic thought upon the continent of Europe, again made his offer of peace? Why has not the President now again asked that the nations of the world make an effort to get together? Why should we not suggest a truce; why should we not suggest a three or four months' stoppage of this slaughter, so that the representatives of the free people of the free democracies of which he speaks, should have an opportunity to get together and take up the question of peace and war? But I fear that the average Member of Congress will against his own convictions and against his own judgment vote as the President asks him to vote. This talk that every vote against the resolution will be helpful to Germany and the German emperor is cheap, vulgar nonsense. That is all right on the platform before an irresponsible mob, near the door of a saloon.

The elected representatives of the people should speak their minds freely. Our newspapers have not always reported the facts, but in the French Chamber of Deputies, in the English Parliament, in the German Reichstag, in the Austrian Reichsrath, and in the Russian Duma there have been minorities all the time during the war. Here an attempt is being made to suppress every free expression of opinion before a declaration of war.

MR. AUSTIN. Where is the attempt made to suppress the expression of opinion?

THE CHAIRMAN. Does the gentleman yield?

MR. LONDON. Not to the gentleman from Tennessee, unless he will interrupt no more. It is an extremely ungrateful task for me to take the stand that I am taking now, but I would have no respect for myself unless I voted against the resolution. The issue is not between Germany and America. The issue is between two Americas—between those who believe that it is the mission of America to influence the world for the better by being a free democracy, by growing into a genuine democracy, by marching unhindered on the road toward nobler and more beautiful ideals, and the group of men who believe that the United States must follow in the footsteps of the European countries and adopt the jargon of European diplomacy about national honor and national dignity. There is no national honor in superior physical force, there is no national honor in whipping a weaker fellow, there is no national honor in a combination with other military and naval forces to crush a weaker military or naval force. This country has suffered from the inroads of the imperial German government upon the rights of the American people. . . .

The President, one arm of the government, has made a request upon the elected representatives of a free people to endorse the idea of war, and every elected representative of the people should say, "No; I shall not kill; I shall not vote to kill; I am ready to suffer injury rather than kill; I shall not permit anyone to vote that my arm should be stretched to kill a fellow human being." Mr. Chairman, war is wrong, inexcusable, indefensible. Let us be strong men; let us throw away our political ambitions; let us throw away our chances of reelection. The people will ultimately do right; they will ultimately stand by every man who will show courage in this moment of crisis, a crisis not only for the American people but for the whole world. Let us be free, strong men, and do as men should do in momentous times like these.

Alfred H. Fried

predicts that pacifism will survive its failure to prevent the First World War

ALFRED H. FRIED [1864-1921] *was a writer and a leader in the German peace movement. He was interested not only in the condemnation of war, but in the need for cooperation between independent states, and to give voice to his conviction he founded several periodicals concerned with international understanding. He attacked the German and Austrian empires for their medievalism and militarism, and he helped form the German Peace Society. In 1911 Fried received the Nobel Peace Prize. During World War I he was an exile in Switzerland. The selection here came out in 1916.*

There are two books whose titles hamper the progress of pacifism. The titles only are dangerous—not the books. Just because Kant's *Eternal Peace* and Bertha von Suttner's *Lay Down Your Arms* have had so wide a circulation, many have thought it unnecessary to know their contents, and have been content to accept the wording of their titles as the program of pacifism. Accordingly eternal peace and general disarmament appeared to be our program. This has hurt the pacifist movement, but it has hurt even more those who have been misled by such superficiality. It kept them from appreciating those demands of the age to which we called their attention.

When, then, the war broke out, such superficial and infatuated thinkers held but *one* opinion: that pacifism had failed and was proved an illusion. To have disarmed would have been madness, and the dream of eternal peace was ended. As if we had ever dreamed such a dream, or had ever pleaded for disarmament! Such people were not disturbed by the facts of the case; there were the two titles! A person who defined Darwinism today as the descent of man from the ape, or who defined socialism as the redistribution of all property, would hardly be called educated. But a similar pronouncement about pacifism, eternal peace and disarmament does not yet carry the same stigma. There are still people with high-sounding scientific titles who believe that there is such a pacifism, who *so* explain its aims, and undertake to refute it with such cheap allegations.

The war has brought no collapse of pacifism. It is the collapse of that "practical" policy which scorned to accept the pacifists' suggestions for self-preservation. It is European diplomacy and the apostles of force, the fanatics of preparedness and the Utopians of world domination, who are bankrupt—they who before had to wait for the war accepting the cold hard facts. They are bankrupt . . . they who lived in the belief that peace could be secured by preparing for war and only by preparing for war; they who thought that a sharp sword and dry powder outweighed all the instruments of reconciliation and peaceful settlement. Rivers of blood and the desolation of war have proved this philosophy unfitted for the age.

The opponents and critics who thought pacifism was living in the clouds were mistaken. To pacifists the war brought no disillusionment. Just because they had seen it coming, they had struggled to prevent it, and sounded the warning. They indicated the path of reason which might have avoided it. Had they been as sure of world peace as these others believed them to be, they would have ceased their agitation. It would have been superfluous. Pacifists never indulged in the dream that they who fed the fires of national hatred would escape without war. They merely demanded that the instruments of compromise and conciliation be strengthened, so that hate and jingoism might be stifled and disputes be settled by the instruments of reason. They failed in their endeavor; but the results of their failure are the proof that the salvation of the future lies in the success of their program. . . .

No, the war was *no surprise* to us. We knew that it might have been avoided, and we struggled loyally for that end. Our ideas had begun to influence politics, and the achievements of international reconciliation grew every day. The hope arose that the great crisis might be passed, and that the people of Europe might without a bloody struggle arrive at a settlement promising peace and harmony for the future. But the forces of international anarchy were too strong. The war came before our ideas had won full sway. Now it must complete what we had not yet achieved. Its brutal method of instruction may perhaps be more successful.

We pacifists were misrepresented both in regard to the extent of our hopes and to the instruments by which we hoped to attain them. We were accused of the crudest attitude toward the complicated problem of *disarmament*—the first impulse to the investigation and study of which had been given by us. It was said that we sought disarmament, even one-sided disarmament of our own people, while the other nations were still in armor. Disarmament was made to appear the fundament of our teachings. Such is the curse of those familiar titles, *Lay Down Your Arms* and *Eternal Peace*. Nothing was further from our minds than such an attempt to begin a house with the roof. We looked forward to a general and simultaneous relief from the burden of armaments as the final consequence of that reorganization of international relations which we urged.

We were misrepresented on other subjects as well. We were said to regard *arbitration* as a universal remedy, which would solve the most difficult problems. In reality we looked upon it as only one among many peaceful methods of adjustment. This was another case where a problem, the study of which had developed into a great science, was stated with the crudest simplicity. It was not we who were guilty of that misrepresentation, but the naiveté of our opponents who did not observe that we understood that not all international conflicts were capable of legal solution, and that the character of these disputes would have to be changed before they would be capable of such solution. Our critics had no conception of the problem of transforming international anarchy into international organization, or of the change in the character of international disputes thus to be effected. They knew nothing of the fundamental problem of pacifism. In their heads buzzed only the two phrases, "disarmament" and "eternal peace."

They were equally ignorant of the *extent of pacifism*. They had no fineness of perception; they could only see things in lumps: here an evil, there a remedy. Of the great work of education, of the gradual diffusion of ideas with the purpose of gradual transformation of an evil into a rational state of affairs, they noticed nothing. In how many fields of human activity pacifism makes itself felt today—often without its agents being aware of the pacifist origin or the pacifist purpose of their activity! Has not every political party, every religious confession, every school of thought, accepted at least a part of the pacifist program or in some fashion undertaken pacifist activities—often indeed so unconsciously that they thought that they were opposing organized pacifism? Has not all the work of the world become pacifist in purpose, do not the sciences of international law, economics and sociology emphasize their pacifist elements, have not entirely new sciences such as the science of internationalism (*Internationalogie*) and the economics of human life (*Menschenökonomie*) arisen as a result of the pacifist movement? Its radius of action is far greater than the horizon of those who scorn and misunderstand it. Its teachings permeate every field of human activity, and every kind of activity serves its purposes. In roundabout ways, but comprehensively and certainly, it draws near its goal.

In the turmoil of the war we are told to unlearn and learn anew. It will be easier to renounce old errors when to have believed them carries no stigma. Good! Let us revise our views, adapt them to reality, and then meet life with them. Pacifism expects such a revision on the part of its opponents who have been so guilty of misunderstanding and misrepresentation. Pacifism does not need to unlearn. Perhaps alone in this time of general collapse, it needs no such revision. *Its great hour has come.* When humanity awakens from this bloody hallucination, when it sees and counts and realizes the cost of all the harvest of war, when it is able coolly to distinguish between cause and effect, means and end—then humanity will and must return to the doctrines offered it so long ago by this despised pacifism.

The hour draws near. In millions of minds the world over the thought arises, and the fateful question is put: Was it inevitable? Must it be thus eternally? And the answer swells to an iron echo, awakening and sweeping the world: NO!

Floyd Dell

explains his special brand of nonresistance

FLOYD DELL [1887-   ], *essayist, playwright, novelist, and a Socialist for many years, was associate editor of* The Masses *from 1914-1917, and of* The Liberator *from 1918-24. Together with Max Eastman and John Reed, he was a defendant when the editors of* The Masses *were charged with violation of the Espionage Act during World War I. The indictment was dismissed after two trials when the jury could not agree. Here is an article of his published in 1916.*

How ironic it is to have a belief which can be expressed only in ridiculous language! I have recently become a convert to the theory of nonresistance. "Nonresistance"—what a foolish sound the phrase has. As if I did not resist something or other every day of my life! "Passive resistance" is scarcely better: there is nothing passive about my resistance. "The law of love"—a maudlin phrase!

Some day—soon, I hope—somebody will invent a new terminology for this theory, and the comic, sentimental old phrases can be chucked aside—as the terminology of the alchemists was thrown aside with the advent of the science of chemistry. For the theory of nonresistance is the prescientific phase of a new kind of knowledge, the knowledge—to put it vaguely—of relationships. Here is a field as yet unexplored save by the seers and the poets. Its laws are as capable of being discovered as those of astronomy or botany; and the practical application of this knowledge is capable of effecting far greater social changes than the invention of the steam engine. At present, however, we have only rhapsodies and maxims, the biography of an Oriental god—and a few contemporary anecdotes. For, as there were wizards before wizardry became science, there are scattered about, here and there, people who make some use of this knowledge, intuitively or empirically, in business, in friendship, in politics, in administration—with results that seem miraculous. Thus a man who has had his house robbed many times takes the locks off the doors—and remains unmolested. Another goes unarmed into the midst of savage and bloodthirsty tribes—and returns safely. Another takes the leg irons off a prisoner with a notorious record for attempted escapes—and the prisoner stays faithfully to serve out his sentence. A merchant, finding that a clerk has stolen from him, lends him the money to pay back—and gets a devoted and honest employee. We do not burn these people at the stake, but we do generally fear and hate them. And when a man is found willing to treat the enemies of his country in a similar fashion, he is usually stood up against a wall and shot.

The principle involved in such actions has no adequate name as yet. "Love," "charity," "tolerance," "returning good for evil"—these terms are not much better than the ones applied to it by way of insult—"sentimental folly," "milk-and-water humanitarianism," "mollycoddling" and "insanity." The principle, however, is the same as was involved in the two great achievements of early mankind, the taming of animals and the domestication of plants. Do you imagine that it was by force that the wild horse, the wolf, the wildcat, became the friends and servants of men? It was rather by a patient and passionate sympathy, half understanding and half affection, for which "love" is not, after all, a bad term. There are a few people who can tame even tigers and snakes; and they are precisely the persons who like tigers and snakes. Anybody can catch fish with a hook; but Thoreau could pick them up in his hand; and if you think it was by force, you are mistaken. And what is the patient and passionate understanding of growing things, half understanding and half affection, by which Burbank produces new species, but a new manifestation of an ancient love which transformed the wilderness of the world into orchards and fields and gardens? The earth itself—does force get better crops out of it than love and understanding? Tools—is he the worse carpenter who, as we say, loves his tools? Is he a bad sailor who loves his boat? Is he the poorest writer who loves words? The very instruments of death—Rudyard Kipling uttered an extremely "nonresistant" sentiment when he advised:

When 'arf of your bullets fly wide in the ditch,
Don't call your Martini a cross-eyed old bitch.

She's human as you are—you treat her as sich,
And she'll fight for the young British soldier.

Ask the cowboy who conquers a bucking bronco whether he hates that horse or not. Ask the captain of ships that have been overwhelmed by storms whether he hates the sea. Ask the man to whom life has brought many heartaches and disappointments and pains, if he hates life. It is possible, it is even customary, to love such enemies. And, not to overlook anything, let us add' that soldiers sometimes, in fact as well as in fiction, love war. "Return good for evil, and do good unto them that hate you" is in the light of these instances revealed as a maxim of efficiency. Thoroughly understood and broadly applied, it means that our blundering and stupid humanity will at last succeed in managing its affairs.

Hitherto, humanity has been too easily scared into the use of force. Like the man I read about in the paper the other day, it shoots first, and discovers afterward that the supposed burglar is a darling son. It does, to be sure, require some spiritual courage to treat something which may be a burglar as if it were a darling son—and no wonder scary people like Colonel Roosevelt want conscription! But if the wolf hadn't been treated like a dog he never would have turned into one: and men have made fortunes precisely by treating scoundrels as if they were honest. Nothing is so disarming, burglars say, as to be treated like a darling son. They may resist it once or twice and carry off your silver, but if you keep it up long enough they can't stand it; they give up their profession, and become plumbers.

But, as the conscription boards are in the habit of asking nonresistants in England, "What would you do if a German soldier were to ravish your wife and kill your child before your eyes?" The answer is that I am so weak in faith that even a smaller thing—the asking of such a foolish question, for instance—would make me want to commit murder; even though sober reason told me that the killing of one member of a conscription board would be as irrelevant to human progress as the killing of one German soldier.

In fact, speaking for myself as a nonresistant, I have no particular desire to abolish murder. A little murder now and then, of a passionate and unreasoned sort, will do society little harm. It is the reasoned belief in murder, and in the other forms of force, that I object to. A great war is now being waged on the theory that international relations can be arranged satisfactorily by the use of force. Well, the theory is wrong. The device of force in international, social and personal relations is ineffective and wasteful. As a method of progress it is a tragic and terrible failure. It leads only to cynicism and despair. And it can and must be abandoned. There will be violence, and crimes of violence, as long as man is man;

but violence will not be the deliberately chosen Way of Life for mankind.
I am moved to these reflections by John Haynes Holmes' *New Wars for Old*. It belongs, like these reflections, to the utopian stage of the non-resistant theory. It concerns itself, among many other things, with just what Jesus meant when he said, "I came not to send peace, but a sword." But it is an eloquent, keenly argued, splendidly sincere and extraordinarily interesting discussion of the gospel of force versus the gospel of love. If you believe in 'force—and of course you do—I dare you to read it!

Mark Twain
foresees war a million years ahead

MARK TWAIN [1835-1910], *American novelist and humorist, was born Samuel Langhorne Clemens. In 1899, after he had created the two unforgettable characters of Tom Sawyer and Huckleberry Finn, he started to write a bitter book called* The Mysterious Stranger. *The final chapter was not found until after Twain's death, and not until six years later was the book published. The selection here is taken from Chapter Nine.*

There has never been a just one, never an honorable one—on the part of the instigator of the war. I can see a million years ahead, and this rule will never change in so many as half a dozen instances. The loud little handful—as usual—will shout for the war. The pulpit will—warily and cautiously—object—at first; the great, big, dull bulk of the nation will rub its sleepy eyes and try to make out why there should be a war, and will say, earnestly and indignantly, "It is unjust and dishonorable, and there is no necessity for it." Then the handful will shout louder. A few fair men on the other side will argue and reason against the war with speech and pen, and at first will have a hearing and be applauded; but it will not last long; those others will outshout them, and presently the antiwar audiences will thin out and lose popularity. Before long you will see this curious thing: the speakers stoned from the platform, and free speech strangled by hordes of furious men who in their secret hearts are still at one with those stoned speakers—as earlier—but do not dare to say so. And now the whole nation—pulpit and all—will take up the war cry, and shout itself hoarse, and mob any honest man who ventures to open his mouth; and presently such mouths will cease to open. Next the statesmen will invent cheap lies, putting the blame upon the nation that is attacked, and every man will be glad of those conscience-soothing falsities, and will diligently study them, and refuse to examine any refutations of them; and thus he will by and by convince himself that the war is just, and will thank God for the better sleep he enjoys after this process of grotesque self-deception.

Emma Goldman

calls "preparedness" the road to universal slaughter

E M M A G O L D M A N [1869-1940] *was an antimilitarist and anarchist who was deported from the United States in 1919 for obstructing conscription. She came to the United States from Russia at seventeen and worked in a dress shop, where she gained her first knowledge of labor problems. After the Haymarket anarchists were hanged, she joined the anarchist movement, in which she remained until her death. She believed that through education man could attain a society in which he could govern himself. She opposed state coercion. Back in Russia after 1919, Emma Goldman and her lifelong friend Alexander Berkman found disillusionment there. They believed that Lenin and Trotsky were betrayers of the revolution.*

Ever since the beginning of the European conflagration, the whole human race almost has fallen into the deathly grip of the war anesthesis, overcome by the mad teeming fumes of a blood-soaked chloroform, which has obscured its vision and paralyzed its heart. Indeed, with the exception of some savage tribes, who know nothing of Christian religion or of brotherly love, and who also know nothing of dreadnaughts, submarines, munition manufacture and war loans, the rest of the race is under this terrible narcosis. The human mind seems to be conscious of but one thing, murderous speculation. Our whole civilization, our entire culture is concentrated in the mad demand for the most perfected weapons of slaughter.

Ammunition! Ammunition! O Lord, thou who rulest heaven and earth, thou God of love, of mercy and of justice, provide us with enough ammunition to destroy our enemy. Such is the prayer which is ascending daily to the Christian heaven. Just like cattle, panic-stricken in the face of fire, throw themselves into the very flames, so all of the European people have fallen over each other into the devouring flames of the furies of war, and America, pushed to the very brink by unscrupulous politicians, by ranting demagogues, and by military sharks, is preparing for the same terrible feat.

In the face of this approaching disaster, it behooves men and women not yet overcome by the war madness to raise their voice of protest, to call the attention of the people to the crime and outrage which are about to be perpetrated upon them.

America is essentially the melting pot. No national unit composing it is in a position to boast of superior race purity, particular historic mission, or higher culture. Yet the jingoes and war speculators are filling the air with the sentimental slogan of hypocritical nationalism, "America for Americans," "America first, last, and all the time." This cry has caught the popular fancy from one end of the country to another. In order to maintain America, military preparedness must be engaged in at once. A billion dollars of the people's sweat and blood is to be expended for dreadnaughts and submarines for the Army and the Navy, all to protect this precious America.

The pathos of it all is that the America which is to be protected by a huge military force is not the America of the people, but that of the privileged class; the class which robs and exploits the masses, and controls their lives from the cradle to the grave. No less pathetic is it that so few people realize that preparedness never leads to peace, but that it is indeed the road to universal slaughter.

With the cunning methods used by the scheming diplomats and military cliques of Germany to saddle the masses with Prussian militarism, the American military ring with its Roosevelts, its Garrisons, its Daniels, and lastly its Wilsons, are moving the very heavens to place the militaristic heel upon the necks of the American people, and, if successful, will hurl America into the storm of blood and tears now devastating the countries of Europe.

Forty years ago Germany proclaimed the slogan: "Germany above everything. Germany for the Germans, first, last and always. We want peace; therefore we must prepare for war. Only a well armed and thoroughly prepared nation can maintain peace, can command respect, can be sure of its national integrity." And Germany continued to prepare, thereby forcing the other nations to do the same. The terrible European war is only the culminating fruition of the hydra-headed gospel, military preparedness.

Since the war began, miles of paper and oceans of ink have been used to prove the barbarity, the cruelty, the oppression of Prussian militarism. Conservatives and radicals alike are giving their support to the Allies for no other reason than to help crush that militarism, in the presence of which, they say, there can be no peace or progress in Europe. But though America grows fat on the manufacture of munitions and war loans to the Allies to help crush Prussians the same cry is now being raised in America which, if carried into national action, would build up an American militarism far more terrible than German or Prussian militarism could ever be, and that because nowhere in the world has capitalism become so brazen in its greed and nowhere is the state so ready to kneel at the feet of capital.

Like a plague, the mad spirit is sweeping the country, infesting the clearest heads and staunchest hearts with the deathly germ of militarism. National security leagues, with cannon as their emblem of protection, naval leagues with women in their lead have sprung up all over the country, women who boast of representing the gentler sex, women who in pain and danger bring forth life and yet are ready to dedicate it to the Moloch War. Americanization societies with well-known liberals as members, they who but yesterday decried the patriotic claptrap of today, are now lending themselves to befog the minds of the people and to help build up the same destructive institutions in America which they are directly and indirectly helping to pull down in Germany—militarism, the destroyer of youth, the raper of women, the annihilator of the best in the race, the very mower of life.

Even Woodrow Wilson, who not so long ago indulged in the phrase "A nation too proud to fight," who in the beginning of the war ordered prayers for peace, who in his proclamations spoke of the necessity of watchful waiting, even he has been whipped into line. He has now joined his worthy colleagues in the jingo movement, echoing their clamor for preparedness and their howl of "America for Americans." The difference between Wilson and Roosevelt is this: Roosevelt, a born bully, uses the club; Wilson, the historian, the college professor, wears the smooth polished university mask, but underneath it he, like Roosevelt, has but one aim, to serve the big interests, to add to those who are growing phenomenally rich by the manufacture of military supplies.

That which has driven the masses of Europe into the trenches and to the battlefields is not their inner longing for war; it must be traced to the cutthroat competition for military equipment, for more efficient armies, for larger warships, for more powerful cannon. You cannot build up a standing army and then throw it back into a box like tin soldiers. Armies equipped to the teeth with weapons, with highly developed instruments of murder and backed by their military interests, have their own dynamic functions. We have but to examine into the nature of militarism to realize the truism of this contention.

Militarism consumes the strongest and most productive elements of each nation. Militarism swallows the largest part of the national revenue. Almost nothing is spent on education, art, literature and science compared with the amount devoted to militarism in times of peace, while in times of war everything else is set at naught; all life stagnates, all effort is curtailed; the very sweat and blood of the masses are used to feed this insatiable monster—militarism. Under such circumstances, it must become more arrogant, more aggressive, more bloated with its own importance. If for no other reason, it is out of surplus energy that militarism must act to remain alive; therefore it will seek an enemy or create one artificially. In this civilized purpose and methods, militarism is sustained by the state, protected by the laws of the land, is fostered by the home and the school, and glorified by public opinion. In other words, the function of militarism is to kill. It cannot live except through murder.

But the most dominant factor of military preparedness and the one which inevitably leads to war, is the creation of group interests, which consciously and deliberately work for the increase of armament whose purposes are furthered by creating the war hysteria. This group interest embraces all those engaged in the manufacture and sale of munitions and in military equipment for personal gain and profit. For instance, the family Krupp, which owns the largest cannon-munition plant in the world; its sinister influence in Germany, and in fact in many other countries, extends to the press, the school, the church and to statesmen of highest rank. Shortly before the war, Karl Liebknecht, the one brave public man in Germany now, brought to the attention of the Reichstag that the family Krupp had in its employ officials of the highest military position, not only in Germany, but in France and in other countries. Everywhere its emissaries have been at work, systematically inciting national hatreds and antagonisms. The same investigation brought to light an international war supply trust who cares not a hang for patriotism, or for love of the people, but who uses both to incite war and to pocket millions of profits out of the terrible bargain.

It is not at all unlikely that the history of the present war will trace its origin to this international murder trust. But is it always necessary for one generation to wade through oceans of blood and heap up mountains of human sacrifice that the next generation may learn a grain of truth from it all? Can we of today not profit by the cause which led to the European war, can we not learn that it was preparedness, thorough and efficient preparedness on the part of Germany and the other countries for military aggrandizement and material gain; above all can we not realize that preparedness in America must and will lead to the same result, the same barbarity, the same senseless sacrifice of life? Is America to follow suit, is it to be turned over to the American Krupps, the American military cliques? It almost seems so when one hears the jingo howls of the press, the blood and thunder tirades of bully Roosevelt, the sentimental twaddle of our college-bred President.

The more reason for those who still have a spark of libertarianism and humanity left to cry out against this great crime, against the outrage now being prepared and imposed upon the American people. It is not enough to claim being neutral; a neutrality which sheds crocodile tears with one eye and keeps the other riveted upon the profits from war supplies and war loans, is not neutrality. It is a hypocritical cloak to cover the countries' crimes. Nor is it enough to join the bourgeois pacifists, who proclaim peace among the nations, while helping to perpetuate the war among the classes, a war which in reality is at the bottom of all other wars.

It is this war of the classes that we must concentrate upon, and in that connection the war against false values, against evil institutions, against all social atrocities. Those who appreciate the urgent need of cooperating in great struggles must oppose military preparedness imposed by the state and capitalism for the destruction of the masses. They must organize the preparedness of the masses for the overthrow of both capitalism and the state. Industrial and economic preparedness is what the workers need. That alone leads to revolution at the bottom as against mass destruction from on top. That alone leads to true internationalism of labor against Kaiserdom, kingdom diplomacies, military cliques and bureaucracy. That alone will give the people the means to take their children out of the slums, out of the sweatshops and the cotton mills. That alone will enable them to inculcate in the coming generation a new ideal of brotherhood, to rear them in play and song and beauty; to bring up men and women, not automatons. That alone will enable woman to become the real mother of the race, who will give to the world creative men, and not soldiers who destroy. That alone leads to economic and social freedom, and does away with all war, all crimes, and all injustice.

Romain Rolland

calls for an end to the homicidal fury in Europe

ROMAIN ROLLAND [1866-1944], *winner of the Nobel Prize for Literature in 1915, was a French idealist and pacifist. He was a great admirer of Gandhi. During the First World War, Rolland had attempted to unite the intellectuals of Europe against the war.* Above the Battle, *a series of articles he published in the* Journal de Genève *in 1914, made him highly unpopular with the belligerents. He foresaw World War II and warned against it, but when it actually came he abandoned his pacifist stand. "In these decisive days," Rolland wrote to Premier Daladier of France, "when the French Republic is rising to bar Nazi tyranny from overrunning Europe, please allow a veteran fighter for peace to declare his devotion to the cause."*

Is our civilization so solid that you do not fear to shake the pillars on which it rests? Can you not see that all falls in upon you if one column be shattered? Could you not have learned if not to love one another, at least to tolerate the great virtues and the great vices of the other? Was it not your duty to attempt—you have never attempted it in sincerity—to settle amicably the questions which divided you—the problem of peoples annexed against their will, the equitable division of productive labor and the riches of the world? Must the stronger forever darken the others with the shadow of his pride, and the others forever unite to dissipate it? Is there no end to this bloody and puerile sport, in which the partners change about from century to century—no end, until the whole of humanity is exhausted thereby?

The rulers who are the criminal authors of these wars dare not accept the responsibility for them. Each one by underhanded means seeks to lay the blame at the door of his adversary. The peoples who obey them submissively resign themselves with the thought that a power higher than mankind has ordered it thus. Again the venerable refrain is heard: "The fatality of war is stronger than our wills." The old refrain of the herd that makes a god of its feebleness and bows down before him. Man has invented fate, that he may make it responsible for the disorders of the universe, those disorders which it was his duty to regulate. There is no fatality! The only fatality is what we desire; and more often, too, what we do not desire enough. Let each now repeat his *mea culpa*. The leaders of thought, the Church, the Labor Parties, did not desire war. . . . That may be. . . . What then did they do to prevent it? What are they doing to put an end to it? They are stirring up the bonfire, each one bringing his faggot.

The most striking feature in this monstrous epic, the fact without precedent, is the unanimity for war in each of the nations engaged. An epidemic of homicidal fury, which started in Tokyo ten years ago, has spread like a wave and overflowed the whole world. None has resisted it; no high thought has succeeded in keeping out of the reach of this scourge. A sort of demoniacal irony broods over this conflict of the nations, from which, whatever its result, only a mutilated Europe can emerge. For it is not racial passion alone which is hurling millions of men blindly one against another, so that not even neutral countries remain free of the dangerous thrill, but all the forces of the spirit, of reason, of faith, of poetry and of science, all have placed themselves at the disposal of the armies in every state. There is not one amongst the leaders of thought in each country who does not proclaim with conviction that the cause of his people is the cause of God, the cause of liberty and of human progress. And I, too, proclaim it.

Strange combats are being waged between metaphysicians, poets, historians—Eucken against Bergson; Hauptmann against Maeterlinck; Rolland against Hauptmann; Wells against Bernard Shaw. Kipling and D'Annunzio, Dehmel and de Régnier sing war hymns, Barrès and Maeterlinck chant paeans of hatred. Between a fugue of Bach and the organ which thunders *Deutschland über Alles,* Wundt, the aged philosopher of eighty-two, calls, with his quavering voice, the students of Leipzig to the holy war. And each nation hurls at the other the name "Barbarians." . . .

Come friends! Let us make a stand! Can we not resist this contagion, whatever its nature and virulence be—whether moral epidemic or cosmic force? Do we not fight against the plague, and strive even to repair the disaster caused by an earthquake? Or must we bow ourselves before it, agreeing with Luzzatti in his famous article that "In the universal disaster, the nations triumph"? Shall we say with him that it is good and reasonable that "the demon of international war, which mows down thousands of beings, should be let loose," so that the great and simple, "love of our country," be understood? It would seem, then, that love of our country can flourish only through the hatred of other countries and the massacre of those who sacrifice themselves in the defense of them. There is in this theory a ferocious absurdity, a Neronian dilettantism which repels me to the very depths of my being. No! Love of my country does not demand that I shall hate and slay those noble and faithful souls who also love theirs, but rather that I should honor them and seek to unite with them for our common good.

You Christians will say—and in this you seek consolation for having betrayed your Master's orders—that war exalts the virtue of sacrifice. And it is true that war has the privilege of bringing out the genius of the race in the most commonplace of hearts. It purges away, in its bath of blood, all dross and impurity; it tempers the metal of the soul; of a niggardly peasant, of a timorous citizen it can make a hero of Valmy. But is there no better employment for the devotion of one people than the devastation of another? Can we not sacrifice ourselves without sacrificing our neighbors also? I know well, poor souls, that many of you are more willing to offer your blood than to spill that of others. . . . But what a fundamental weakness! Confess, then, that you who are undismayed by bullets and shrapnel yet tremble before the dictates of racial frenzy—that Moloch that stands higher than the Church of Christ—the jealous pride of race. You Christians of today would not have refused to sacrifice to the gods of Imperial Rome; you are not capable of such courage! Your Pope Pius X died of grief to see the outbreak of this war—so it is said. And not without reason. The Jupiter of the Vatican who hurled thunderbolts upon those inoffensive priests who believed in the noble chimera of modernism—what did he do against those princes and those criminal rulers whose measureless ambition has given the world over to misery and death? May God inspire the new Pontiff who has just ascended the throne of St. Peter with words and deeds which will cleanse the Church from the stain of this silence.

As for you Socialists who on both sides claim to be defending liberty against tyranny—French liberty against the Kaiser, German liberty against the czar, is it a question of defending one despotism against another? Unite and attack both. . . .

When the war is over! The evil is done now, the torrent let loose and we cannot force it back into its channel unaided. Moreover, crimes have been committed against right, attacks on the liberties of peoples and on the sacred treasuries of thought, which must and will be expiated. Europe cannot pass over unheeded the violence done to the noble Belgian people, the devastation of Malines and Louvain, sacked by modern Tillys. . . . But in the name of heaven let not these crimes be expiated by similar crimes! Let not the hideous words "vengeance" and "retaliation" be heard; for a great nation does not revenge itself, it re-establishes justice. But let those in whose hands lies the execution of justice show themselves worthy of her to the end.

It is our duty to keep this before them; nor will we be passive and wait for the fury of this conflict to spend itself. Such conduct would be unworthy of us who have such a task before us.

Our first duty, then, all over the world, is to insist on the formation of a moral High Court, a tribunal of consciences, to watch and pass impartial judgment on any violations of the laws of nations. And since committees of inquiry formed by belligerents themselves would be always suspect, the neutral countries of the Old and New World must take the initiative. . . .

But for us, the artists and poets, priests and thinkers of all countries, remains another task. Even in time of war it remains a crime for finer spirits to compromise the integrity of their thought; it is shameful to see it serving the passion of a puerile, monstrous policy of race, a policy scientifically absurd—since no country possesses a race wholly pure. Such a policy, as Renan points out in his beautiful letter to Strauss, "can only lead to zoological wars, wars of extermination, similar to those in which various species of rodents and carnivorous beasts fight for their existence. This would be the end of that fertile admixture called humanity, composed as it is of such various necessary elements." Humanity is a symphony of great collective souls; and he who understands and loves it only by destroying a part of those elements, proves himself a barbarian and shows his idea of harmony to be no better than the idea of order another held in Warsaw.

For the finer spirits of Europe there are two dwelling places: our earthly fatherland, and that other City of God. Of the one we are the guests, of the other the builders. To the one let us give our lives and our faithful hearts; but neither family, friend nor fatherland, nor aught that we love has power over the spirit. The spirit is the light. It is our duty to lift it above tempests, and thrust aside the clouds which threaten to obscure it; to build higher and stronger, dominating the injustice and hatred of nations, the walls of that city wherein the souls of the whole world may assemble. . . .

Karl Liebknecht
votes "no" in the Reichstag

KARL LIEBKNECHT [1871-1919] *served in the German Reichstag in 1912 and was the first Social Democratic deputy to vote against military credit for World War I. He wrote a pamphlet attacking the military and because of it, served 18 months in prison. He was expelled from the Socialist Party because of his antiwar stand. When he shouted*

"Down with war!" to a group of soldiers on a Berlin street, he was arrested, charged with treason, and sentenced to thirty months' imprisonment. After the collapse of the German empire, Liebknecht was freed, and then arrested by the provisional government headed by some of his former comrades. He and Rosa Luxemburg, both members of the revolutionary Spartacus Party, were murdered by soldiers who were charged with their custody.

My vote against the War Credit Bill of today is based on the following considerations. This war, desired by none of the people concerned, has not broken out in behalf of the welfare of the German people or any other. It is an imperialist war, a war over important territories of exploitation for capitalists and financiers. From the point of view of rivalry in armaments, it is a war provoked by the German and Austrian war parties together, in the obscurity of semifeudalism and of secret diplomacy, to gain an advantage over their opponents. At the same time the war is a Bonapartist effort to disrupt and split the growing movement of the working class.

The German cry "Against czarism!" is invented for the occasion—just as the present British and French watchwords are invented—to exploit the noblest inclinations and the revolutionary traditions and ideals of the people in stirring up hatred of other peoples.

Germany, the accomplice of czarism, the model of reaction until this very day, has no standing as the liberator of the peoples. The liberation of both the Russian and the German people must be their own work.

The war is no war of German defense. Its historical basis and its course at the start make unacceptable the pretense of the capitalist government that the purpose for which it demands credits is the defense of the fatherland.

A speedy peace, a peace without conquests, this is what we must demand. Every effort in this direction must be supported. Only by strengthening jointly and continuously the currents in all the belligerent countries which have such a peace as their object can this bloody slaughter be brought to an end.

Only a peace based upon the international solidarity of the working class and on the liberty of all the peoples can be a lasting peace. Therefore it is the duty of the proletariat of all countries to carry on during the war a common socialistic work in favor of peace.

I support the relief credits with this reservation: I vote willingly for everything which may relieve the hard fate of our brothers on the battlefield as well as that of the wounded and sick, for whom I feel the deepest compassion. But as a protest against the war, against those who are responsible for it and who have caused it, against those who direct it, against the capitalist purposes for which it is being used, against plans of annexation, against the violation of the neutrality of Belgium and Luxemburg, against unlimited rule of martial law, against the total oblivion of social and political duties of which the government and classes are still guilty, I vote against the war credits demanded.

4

ORGANIZING FOR PEACE

[1815-1913]

The nineteenth century was the flowering era of peace societies. Before then, peace had been an ideal preached by individuals and religious groups; now it was taken up by organizations specifically formed to promote and encourage peace. The end of the Napoleonic Wars and the War of 1812 acted as catalysts to the formation of these organizations, and the movement was born simultaneously in North America and Europe.

In New York a merchant named David Low Dodge published a pamphlet denouncing all war as contrary to Christian teaching. He wanted to form a society whose principles would reflect his thinking, but the War of 1812 interrupted his plans. He published a second pamphlet, called "War Inconsistent with the Religion of Jesus Christ," and in 1815 he organized the first peace society in America.

Without any knowledge of this activity in New York, Dr. Noah Worcester published his "Solemn Review of the Custom of War," and the Peace Society of Massachusetts was formed. Worcester did not claim to be a nonresistant, whereas Dodge did; but their arguments against war were virtually identical.

In the meantime an Englishman named William Allen, unaware of what was happening on the other side of the Atlantic, invited some friends to his home for a discussion of peace. Three years later, the Society for the Promotion of Permanent and Universal Peace was organized in England. The members were nonresistants: they opposed not only offensive, but defensive wars as well. The society's purpose was "to print and circulate tracts and to diffuse information showing that war is inconsistent with the spirit of Christianity and the true interests of mankind, and to point out the means best calculated to maintain permanent and universal peace upon the basis of Christian principles." Thus, divided by thousands of miles of ocean and without knowledge of each other, the first peace societies began independently to put forth their principles in language surprisingly similar.

As the peace groups burgeoned in the United States, a man named William Ladd decided to bring them all together to form the American Peace Society. To encompass the ideas of all its members, the society was founded on very broad principles. Its general credo did not specifically denounce defensive wars. Some of its members objected to this reservation and demanded an uncomprising stand denouncing war of any kind and for whatever motive. In 1837 the society revised its constitution to conform with this demand, declaring itself opposed to *all* wars. But again there was a difference of opinion, with several members pressing for an endorsement of nonresistance. Since they could not claim a majority, they decided to leave and form their own group, the Non-Resistance Society, which registered its "testimony not only against all wars, whether offensive or defensive, but all preparation for war. . . ."

In spite of minor dissension, the peace movement was full of vitality; some of the works published from its ranks in this period remain classics. The groups were broadening their principles all the time. Although their formation had been inspired mainly by religious conviction, they began to show the marked influence of humanitarian idealism and extended their cause to such areas as the emancipation of women and opposition to capital punishment and slavery. As Charles Sumner said, the cause of peace "embraces all the causes of human benevolence."

By the mid-nineteenth century, the peace movement had become organized enough to conduct a series of peace conferences in Europe—at Brussels in 1848, Paris in 1849 and Frankfurt in 1850. Elihu Burritt, the American "learned blacksmith," was the backbone of these conferences, and in Brussels he urged the approval of a congress of nations. At the 1849 conference, Victor Hugo proposed a United States of Europe. A year later at militaristic Frankfurt, the delegates voted not only against war, dueling and the intervention of one state in the affairs of another, but also against loans to warring countries. The same meeting approved a resolution favoring arbitration, disarmament and the codification of international law.

"These peace congresses," says Merle Curti, "clarified the issues in resolutions demanding the simultaneous reduction of armaments, a congress of nations and court of arbitration, permanent and obligatory treaties for arbitration, boycotts on the sale of war materials and the lending of money to belligerents, and the organization of public opinion in the interest of peace." *

* Merle Curti, *Peace or War: The American Struggle 1636-1936*, p. 39.

But war was not held at bay for long. The Crimean War came in 1854, Sardinia's war against Austria in 1859; then the Civil War in the United States, the Austro-Prussian War, the Franco-Prussian War. The peace societies could do nothing to stop these wars; they simply continued with their organizations and published their newspapers, their tracts, their manifestoes.

In America, the Mexican War was the first to bring a crisis into the peace movement. Should a man support his country or his principles? Henry David Thoreau went to jail for refusing to pay taxes to perpetuate the war. Ralph Waldo Emerson visited him there. "David, what are you doing here?" Emerson is said to have asked, and Thoreau made his famous answer: "Waldo, what are you doing out *there?*"

The American Peace Society divided into factions. At its 1846 convention, a resolution was introduced "that we deeply lament, not only the actual collision of our republic with Mexico, but also the outbursts of the war spirit in so many parts of our land, and the obvious, deplorable tendency of the existing war excitement to demoralize, more or less, the general mind of the nation, especially the lower classes and the rising generations." Another resolution proposed to announce that "all good men should repudiate the doctrine which requires us to support our government, right or wrong, in any war it may choose to undertake. . . ."

The majority of the members voted against these resolutions. Instead they approved: (1) "That the society in accordance with its constitution as it has ever done, will confine itself strictly to the single object of abolishing international war," and (2) "That the society be so managed as to be kept entirely distinct from antigovernment, from the question of capital punishment, and all other extraneous subjects, as it has heretofore been."

When the Civil War came, the society was faced with an even graver crisis. Most of the members felt that slavery was worse than war; there could be no compromise with it. Many influential members, men like Charles Sumner and Amos Walker, said nothing. It was a "just" war. The society commented in its publication, *Advocate of Peace*, "We cannot for a moment countenance or tolerate rebellion. . . . It is not strictly war, but a legitimate effort by the government for the enforcement of its laws."

From England, a peace advocate commented: "Infinite as is the iniquity of slavery, the attempt to abolish it by war is only an attempt to cast out devils by Beelzebub the prince of devils. . . . We must say candidly we are not prepared to buy the freedom of slaves at so tremendous a cost." But other Englishmen in the peace movement felt that war was the only way out for the United States.

Elihu Burritt was among the few Americans who did not follow the clamor of patriotism during either the Mexican War or the Civil War. He had formed the League of Universal Brotherhood in 1846. Members of the league pledged: "Believing all war to be inconsistent with the spirit of Christianity, and destructive of the best interests of mankind, I do hereby pledge myself never to enlist or enter into any army or navy, or to yield any voluntary support or sanction to any war, by whomsoever or for whatsoever proposed, declared, or waged. . . ."

At the end of the Civil War there were efforts to revitalize the organized peace movement. The American Peace Society attempted to recruit educators, the press and the clergy. The clergy and educators responded well; the press generally was uninterested or scornful.

In 1866 a new and militant group under the leadership of Alfred Love was formed in the United States—the Universal Peace Union, whose program was "to remove the causes and abolish the causes of war, to discountenance all resorts to deadly force between individuals, states or nations, never acquiescing in present wrongs." It called for "immediate disarmament"; it denounced imperialism and advocated a boycott of war taxes. It further concerned itself with labor problems, advocating arbitration during strikes. From its initial meeting, the union condemned capital punishment.

The peace societies, of course, were not the only pacifist voices in the nineteenth century. Other groups, both political and religious, favored peace as a natural concomitant to their beliefs. But they were no more immune to dissension over specific wars than were the peace societies. Among the churches that traditionally stood for peace, there was a difference of opinion over the American Civil War. The Quakers held to their "peace testimony," but individuals among them found justification for supporting the struggle between the states.

The Socialist movement, too, heartily opposed war. Socialists in all countries stressed their bond with the working class everywhere, rather than any national allegiance to their capitalist rulers. They insisted that the basic causes of war were economic and resulted from the capitalist system, but when they were faced with particular wars their principles often gave way to nationalism.

The first peace societies had been confined mainly to the United States, Britain, Switzerland, and France. Now came the organizations in Italy, Denmark, Holland; in Germany, Austria, Japan and South America. A series of international peace congresses was held between 1889 and 1908 in Paris, London, Rome, Berne, Chicago and Antwerp. France, Great Britain, Italy, Scandinavia, Germany and the United States held national peace congresses during the early years of the twentieth century. For the peace movement, the biggest news of this period had come in August 1898 when the Russian czar called for a conference to discuss armaments and their ever-growing burdens. He invited twenty-six powers to attend. Skepticism greeted the invitation, and a second notice was sent out four months later. On May 18, 1900, the first Hague Conference was convened at the House in the Woods, with 101 representatives from twenty-six countries present. They were in session for nine weeks, striving to set up the machinery for better international understanding and the limitation of armaments. When the meeting disbanded, they recommended that another meeting be called.

This conference "broke the ice of national isolation; but it amounted to little in terms of peace; its labors were primarily devoted to making war polite. . . . The Conference did, however, promote the procedure of mediation, conciliation and inquiry, and established the Hague Tribunal. . . ." *

A Universal Peace Congress was held in Geneva and resolved: "Every pacifist ought to regard it as his sacred duty to oppose any war of conquest undertaken by the government of his country." Peace workers were optimistic about the situation in Europe. In 1911 one of their publications assured its readers that "the nations are moving toward world peace." Three years later, when World War I began, the movement was faced with a greater crisis than any it had seen yet.

Abdu'l-Bahá

deplores man's descent to slaying

A B D U ' L - B A H Á [1844-1921] *was the third prophet of the Baha'i Faith, and the only one who ever visited the West. His father was a Persian nobleman (Bahá'u'lláh) who had proclaimed himself to be "the Mes-*

* Devere Allen, *The Fight for Peace*, p. 131.

*senger of God" whom Ba'b (founder of the faith) had told his followers
to await. Abdu'l-Bahá was named by his father as his successor and interpreter of his word. "The Pitiful Causes of War and the Duty of Everyone
to Strive for Peace" was an address delivered in Paris on October 21,
1911.*

I hope you are all happy and well. I am not happy, but very sad. The
news of the Battle of Benghazi grieves my heart. I wonder at the human
savagery that still exists in the world! How is it possible for men to fight
from morning until evening, killing each other, shedding the blood of
their fellow men! And for what object? To gain possession of a part
of the earth! Even the animals, when they fight, have an immediate and
more reasonable cause for their attacks! How terrible it is that men, who
are of the higher kingdom, can descend to slaying, and bringing misery
to their fellow beings, for the possession of a tract of land!

The highest of created beings fighting to obtain the lowest form of
matter, earth! Land belongs not to one people, but to all people. This
earth is not man's home, but his tomb. It is for their tombs these men are
fighting. There is nothing so horrible in this world as the tomb, the abode
of the decaying bodies of men.

However great the conqueror, however many countries he may reduce to slavery, he is unable to retain any part of these devastated lands but
one tiny portion—his tomb! If more land is required for the improvement of the condition of the people, for the spread of civilization (for the
substitution of just laws for brutal customs)—surely it would be possible
to acquire peaceably the necessary extension of territory.

But war is made for the satisfaction of men's ambition; for the sake
of worldly gain to the few, terrible misery is brought to numberless
homes, breaking the hearts of hundreds of men and women!

How many widows mourn their husbands, how many stories of
savage cruelty do we hear! How many little orphaned children are crying for their dead fathers, how many women are weeping for their slain
sons!

There is nothing so heartbreaking and terrible as an outburst of
human savagery!

I charge you all that each one of you concentrate all the thoughts of
your heart on love and unity. When a thought of war comes, oppose it by
a stronger thought of peace. A thought of hatred must be destroyed by a
more powerful thought of love. Thoughts of war bring destruction to all
harmony, well-being, restfulness and content.

Thoughts of love are constructive of brotherhood, peace, friendship,
and happiness.

When soldiers of the world draw their swords to kill, soldiers of God clasp each other's hands! So may all the savagery of man disappear by the mercy of God, working through the pure in heart and the sincere of soul. Do not think the peace of the world an ideal impossible to attain! Nothing is impossible to the divine benevolence of God.

If you desire with all your heart friendship with every race on earth, your thought, spiritual and positive, will spread; it will become the desire of others, growing stronger and stronger, until it reaches the minds of all men.

Do not despair! Work steadily. Sincerity and love will conquer hate. How many seemingly impossible events are coming to pass in these days! Set your faces steadily towards the light of the world. Show love to all—"Love is the Breath of the Holy Spirit in the Heart of Man." Take courage! God never forsakes his children who strive and work and pray! Let your hearts be filled with the strenuous desire that tranquillity and harmony may encircle all this warring world. So will success crown your efforts, and with the Universal Brotherhood will come the kingdom of God in peace and good will.

In this room today are members of many races, French, American, English, German, Italian brothers and sisters, meeting in friendship and harmony! Let this gathering be a foreshadowing of what will, in very truth, take place in this world, when every child of God realizes that they are leaves on one tree, flowers in one garden, drops in one ocean, and sons and daughters of one Father, whose name is Love!

Havelock Ellis

predicts that peace will offer great scope for daring and adventure

HAVELOCK ELLIS [1859-1939], *born in England, became a physician and made a lifetime study of sexual behavior. His writings dispelled the taboo around sex and made it a legitimate subject of everyday parlor conversation. He was a pacifist, and shortly before he died, reiterated his belief that peace "is our next upward movement." "The War Against War" appeared in the* Atlantic Monthly, *June 1911.*

It is not alone the future of civilization which is forever menaced by the possibility of war: the past of civilization, with all the precious embodiments of its traditions, is even more fatally imperiled. As the world grows older and the ages recede, the richer, the more precious, the more fragile become the ancient heirlooms of humanity. They constitute the final symbols of human glory; they cannot be too carefully guarded, too highly valued. But all the other dangers that threaten their integrity and safety, if put together, do not equal war. No land that has ever been a cradle of civilization but bears witness to this sad truth. All the sacred citadels, the glories of humanity—Jerusalem and Athens, Rome and Constantinople—have been ravaged by war, and in every case the ruin has been a disaster that can never be repaired. If we turn to the minor glories of more modern ages, the special treasure of England has been its parish churches, a treasure of unique charm in the world and the embodiment of the people: today in their battered and irreparable condition they are the monuments of a civil war waged all over the country with ruthless religious ferocity. Spain, again, was a land which had stored up, during long centuries, nearly the whole of its accumulated possessions in every art, sacred and secular, of fabulous value, within the walls of its great fortresslike cathedrals; Napoleon's soldiers overran the land and brought with them rapine and destruction; so that in many a shrine, as at Montserrat, we still can see how in a few days they turned a paradise into a desert. It is not only the West that has suffered. In China the rarest and loveliest wares and fabrics that the hand of man has wrought were stored in the Imperial Palace of Pekin; the savage military hordes of the West broke in less than a century ago, and recklessly trampled down and fired all that they could not loot. In every such case the loss is final; the exquisite incarnation of some stage in the soul of man that is forever gone, is permanently diminished, deformed or annihilated.

At the present time all civilized countries are becoming keenly aware of the value of their embodied artistic possessions. This is shown in the most decisive manner possible by the enormous prices placed upon them. Their pecuniary value enables even the stupidest and most unimaginative to realize the crime that is committed when they are ruthlessly and wantonly destroyed. Nor is it only the products of ancient art which have today become so peculiarly valuable. The products of modern science are scarcely less valuable. So highly complex and elaborate is the mechanism now required to ensure progress in some of the sciences that enormous sums of money, the most delicate skill, long periods of time, are necessary to produce it. Galileo could replace his telescope with but little trouble; the destruction of a single modern observatory would be almost a calamity to the human race.

Such considerations as these are, indeed, at last recognized in all civilized countries. The engines of destruction now placed at the service of war are vastly more potent than any used in the wars of the past. On the other hand, the value of the products they can destroy is raised in a correspondingly high degree. But a third factor is now intervening. And if the museums of Paris, or the laboratories of Berlin, were threatened by a hostile army it would certainly be felt that an international power, if such existed, should be empowered to intervene, at whatever cost to national susceptibilities, in order to keep the peace. Civilization, we now realize, is wrought out of inspirations and discoveries which are forever passed and repassed from land to land; it cannot be claimed by any individual land. A nation's art products and its scientific activities are not mere national property: they are international possessions, for the joy and service of the whole world. The nations hold them in trust for humanity. The international force which will inspire respect for that truth it is our business to create.

The only question that remains—and it is a question the future alone will solve—is the particular point at which this ancient and overgrown stronghold of war, now being invested so vigorously from so many sides, will finally be overthrown—whether from within or from without, whether by its own inherent weakness, by the persuasive reasonableness of developing civilization, by the self-interest of the commercial and financial classes, or by the ruthless indignation of the proletariat. That is a problem still insoluble, but it is not impossible that some already living may witness its solution.

Two centuries ago the Abbé de Saint-Pierre set forth his scheme for a federation of the states of Europe, which meant, at that time, a federation of all the civilized states of the world. It was the age of great ideas scattered abroad to germinate in more practical ages to come. The amiable abbé enjoyed all the credit of his large and philanthropic conceptions. But no one dreamed of realizing them, and the forces which alone could realize them had not yet appeared above the horizon. In this matter, at all events, the world has progressed, and a federation of the states of the world is no longer the mere conception of a philosophic dreamer. The first step will be taken when two of the leading countries of the world —and it would be most reasonable for those which have the closest community of origin and language to take the initiative—resolve to submit all their differences, without reserve, to arbitration. As soon as a third power of magnitude joined this federation the nucleus would be constituted of a world state. Such a state would be able to impose peace on even the most recalcitrant outside states, for it would furnish that "visible power to keep them in awe" which Hobbes rightly declared to be indispensable: it could even in the last resort, if necessary, enforce peace by war. There are no other methods than war of enforcing peace, and these such a federation of great states would be easily able to bring to bear on even the most warlike of states, but the necessity of a mighty armed international force would remain for a long time to come. To suppose, as some seem to suppose, that the establishment of arbitration in place of war means immediate disarmament is an idle dream. At the recent conference of the English Labor Party on this question, the most active opposition to the proposed strike method for rendering war impossible came from the delegates representing the workers in arsenals and dockyards. But there is no likelihood of arsenals and dockyards closing in the lifetime of the present workers; and though the establishment of peaceful methods of settling international disputes cannot fail to diminish the number of the workers who live by armament, it will be long before they can be dispensed with altogether.

It is feared by some that the reign of universal peace will deprive them of the opportunity of exhibiting daring and heroism. Without inquiring too carefully what use has been made of their present opportunity by those who express this fear, it must be said that such a fear is altogether groundless. There are an infinite number of positions in life in which courage is needed, as much as on a battlefield, although, for the most part, with less risk of that total annihilation which in the past has done so much to breed out the courageous stocks. Moreover, the certain establishment of peace will immensely enlarge the scope for daring and adventure in the social sphere. There are departments in the higher breeding and social evolution of the race—some perhaps even involving questions of life and death—where the highest courage is needed. It would be premature to discuss them, for they can scarcely enter the field of practical politics until war has been abolished. But those persons who are burning to display heroism may rest assured that the course of social evolution will offer them every opportunity.

William James

proposes a moral equivalent of war

WILLIAM JAMES [1842-1910] *started his professional career as a zoologist, but turned to medicine. At about the same time he received his medical degree, he began his studies of "physiological psychology."*

He became an authority in the field of psychology, and a philosopher as well. He believed in pragmatism—i.e., that knowledge is based on experience and observation. Among his essays was this one in which he proposed "The Moral Equivalent of War." It was originally published in McClure's Magazine, August 1910.

Pacifists ought to enter more deeply into the aesthetical and ethical point of view of their opponents. So long as antimilitarists propose no substitute for war's disciplinary function, no *moral equivalent* of war, analogous, as one might say, to the mechanical equivalent of heat, so long they fail to realize the full inwardness of the situation. And as a rule they do fail. The duties, penalties, and sanctions pictured in the utopias they paint are all too weak and tame to touch the military-minded. Tolstoy's pacifism is the only exception to this rule, for it is profoundly pessimistic as regards all this world's values, and makes the fear of the Lord furnish the moral spur provided elsewhere by the fear of the enemy. But our socialistic peace advocates all believe absolutely in this world's values; and instead of the fear of the Lord and the fear of the enemy, the only fear they reckon with is the fear of poverty if one be lazy. This weakness pervades all the socialistic literature with which I am acquainted. Even in Lowes Dickinson's exquisite dialogue,* high wages and short hours are the only forces invoked for overcoming man's distaste for repulsive kinds of labor. Meanwhile men at large still live as they always have lived, under a pain-and-fear economy—for those of us who live in an ease economy are but an island in the stormy ocean—and the whole atmosphere of present-day utopian literature tastes mawkish and dishwatery to people who still keep a sense for life's more bitter flavors. It suggests, in truth, ubiquitous inferiority.

Inferiority is always with us, and merciless scorn of it is the keynote of the military temper. "Dogs, would you live forever?" shouted Frederick the Great. "Yes," say our utopians, "let us live forever, and raise our level gradually." The best thing about our "inferiors" today is that they are as tough as nails, and physically and morally almost as insensitive. Utopianism would see them soft and squeamish, while militarism would keep their callousness, but transfigure it into a meritorious characteristic, needed by "the service," and redeemed by that from the suspicion of inferiority. All the qualities of a man acquire dignity when he knows that the service of the collectivity that owns him needs them. If proud of the collectivity, his own pride rises in proportion. No collectivity is like an army for nourishing such pride; but it has to be confessed that the only sentiment which the image of pacific cosmopolitan industrialism is ca-

Justice and Liberty, New York, 1909.

pable of arousing in countless worthy breasts is shame at the idea of belonging to *such* a collectivity. It is obvious that the United States of
America as they exist today impress a mind like General Lea's as so
much human blubber. Where is the sharpness and precipitousness, the
contempt for life, whether one's own or another's? Where is the savage
"yes" and "no," the unconditional duty? Where is the conscription?
Where is the blood tax? Where is anything that one feels honored by belonging to?

Having said thus much in preparation, I will now confess my own
utopia. I devoutly believe in the reign of peace and in the gradual advent
of some sort of a socialistic equilibrium. The fatalistic view of the war
function is to me nonsense, for I know that warmaking is due to definite
motives and subject to prudential checks and reasonable criticisms, just
like any other form of enterprise. And when whole nations are the armies, and the science of destruction vies in intellectual refinement with the
sciences of production, I see that war becomes absurd and impossible
from its own monstrosity. Extravagant ambitions will have to be replaced by reasonable claims, and nations must make common cause
against them. I see no reason why all this should not apply to yellow as
well as to white countries, and I look forward to a future when acts of
war shall be formally outlawed as between civilized peoples.

All these beliefs of mine put me squarely into the antimilitarist
party. But I do not believe that peace either ought to be or will be permanent on this globe, unless the states pacifically organized preserve some
of the old elements of army discipline. A permanently successful peace
economy cannot be a simple pleasure economy. In the more or less socialistic future toward which mankind seems to be drifting we must still
subject ourselves collectively to those severities which answer to our real
position upon this only partly hospitable globe. We must make new
energies and hardihoods continue the manliness to which the military
mind so faithfully clings. Martial virtues must be the enduring cement;
intrepidity, contempt of softness, surrender of private interest, obedience
to command, must still remain the rock upon which states are built—unless, indeed, we wish for dangerous reactions against commonwealths
fit only for contempt and liable to invite attack whenever a center of crystallization for military-minded enterprise gets formed anywhere in their
neighborhood.

The war party is assuredly right in affirming and reaffirming that
the martial virtues, although originally gained by the race through war,
are absolute and permanent human goods. Patriotic pride and ambition
in their military form are, after all, only specifications of a more general
competitive passion. They are its first form, but that is no reason for supposing them to be its last form. Men now are proud of belonging to a

conquering nation, and without a murmur they lay down their persons and their wealth, if by so doing they may fend off subjection. But who can be sure that *other aspects of one's country* may not, with time and education and suggestion enough, come to be regarded with similarly effective feelings of pride and shame? Why should men not someday feel that it is worth a blood tax to belong to a collectivity superior in *any* ideal respect? Why should they not blush with indignant shame if the community that owns them is vile in any way whatsoever? Individuals, daily more numerous, now feel this civic passion. It is only a question of blowing on the spark till the whole population gets incandescent, and on the ruins of the old morals of military honor, a stable system of morals of civic honor builds itself up. What the whole community comes to believe in grasps the individual as in a vise. The war function has grasped us so far; but constructive interests may someday seem no less imperative, and impose on the individual a hardly lighter burden.

Let me illustrate my idea more concretely. There is nothing to make one indignant in the mere fact that life is hard, that men should toil and suffer pain. The planetary conditions once for all are such, and we can stand it. But that so many men, by mere accidents of birth and opportunity, should have a life of *nothing else* but toil and pain and hardness and inferiority imposed upon them, should have *no* vacation, while others natively no more deserving never get any taste of this campaigning life at all—*this* is capable of arousing indignation in reflective minds. It may end by seeming shameful to all of us that some of us have nothing but campaigning, and others nothing but unmanly ease. If now—and this is my idea—there were, instead of military conscription a conscription of the whole youthful population to form for a certain number of years a part of the army enlisted against *nature,* the injustice would tend to be evened out, and numerous other goods to the commonwealth would follow. The military ideals of hardihood and discipline would be wrought into the growing fiber of the people; no one would remain blind as the luxurious classes now are blind, to man's relations to the globe he lives on, and to the permanently sour and hard foundations of his higher life. To coal and iron mines, to freight trains, to fishing fleets in December, to dishwashing, clothes-washing and window-washing, to road-building and tunnel-making, to foundries and stokeholes, and to the frames of skyscrapers, would our gilded youths be drafted off, according to their choice, to get the childishness knocked out of them, and to come back into society with healthier sympathies and soberer ideas. They would have paid their blood tax, done their own part in the immemorial human warfare against nature; they would tread the earth more proudly, the women would value them more highly, they would be better fathers and teachers of the following generation.

Such a conscription, with the state of public opinion that would have required it, and the many moral fruits it would bear, would preserve in the midst of a pacific civilization the manly virtues which the military party is so afraid of seeing disappear in peace. We should get toughness without callousness, authority with as little criminal cruelty as possible, and painful work done cheerily because the duty is temporary, and threatens not, as now, to degrade the whole remainder of one's life. I spoke of the "moral equivalent" of war. So far, war has been the only force that can discipline a whole community, and until an equivalent discipline is organized, I believe that war must have its way. But I have no serious doubt that the ordinary prides and shames of social man, once developed to a certain intensity, are capable of organizing such a moral equivalent as I have sketched, or some other just as effective for preserving manliness of type. It is but a question of time, of skilful propagandism, and of opinion-making men seizing historic opportunities.

The martial type of character can be bred without war. Strenuous honor and disinterestedness abound elsewhere. Priests and medical men are in a fashion educated to it, and we should all feel some degree of it imperative if we were conscious of our work as an obligatory service to the state. We should be *owned,* as soldiers are by the army, and our pride would rise accordingly. We could be poor, then, without humiliation, as army officers now are. The only thing needed henceforward is to inflame the civic temper as past history has inflamed the military temper.

Charles E. Jefferson

urges Christians to batter down institutions that make war

REV. CHARLES E. JEFFERSON [1860-1937] *was pastor of the Broadway Congregational Tabernacle Church in New York City, and was among the most influential clergymen of his time. In 1906 he helped organize the New York Peace Society. "Militarism and the Church" is a sermon he preached at the Broadway Tabernacle Church on May 3, 1908.*

Throw yourself against militarism, I beg you, with all your might. Do not be afraid of pushing too hard. You will not push it over. Do not be afraid of being too radical. There are enough conservatives to render your radicalism harmless. You need not fear that anything which you may say or do will sweep all the armies from the land or the navies from the sea. They will survive and flourish long after you are dead. The friends of Caesar are so numerous and so mighty that the friends of Jesus need not be afraid of banishing too precipitately the ideals of militarism from the earth.

Militarism is a growth of many generations. It is entrenched in national traditions, its roots run down deep into the selfish heart of vested interests and into the vanities and ambitions of ancient aristocracies—and into the lowest deeps of hell. Do not be afraid of overturning the system too suddenly. Hosts of men are on hand ready to see that no sudden or sweeping change is made. Why then should you do anything at all? Because if one man throws himself against a thing against which the heart of God is beating in quenchless opposition, he will by his example inspire some brother man to hurl himself also against the same evil thing, and this second man will inspire another and he another, and all these many others, until at last—it may be generations off—the number shall be sufficient to bring the accursed thing to the dust. When I meet the God of love I do not want to say: "I saw the burden, I realized the weight of it, I heard the sighs of women, the sobs of children and the groans of men, I saw nations distracted, despondent, bleeding, I saw the pictures of the poor peasants in their comfortless huts, but I did nothing against the cause of all this trouble because the forces against me were too mighty. I knew that many of the men to whom I preached would not believe me. I knew my labor would be in vain."

Rather do I pray that God will give me grace and strength to fight unceasingly and with every ounce of energy of brain and heart against everything which my own conscience tells me is contrary to the will of God and the happiness of men, no matter what forces are arrayed against me and how utterly hopeless the outcome of my labor seems. Paul failed to overturn the throne of Caesar, but he fought a good fight, he finished the course, he kept the faith and—he won the crown.

Jane Addams

observes the passing of the war virtues

JANE ADDAMS [1860-1935], *founder of the world-famous Hull House in Chicago, pioneered in establishing many early welfare laws affecting labor, women and children. She was an ardent pacifist. In 1915 she presided over the International Congress of Women at The Hague, Netherlands, and she was the first international president of the newly formed Women's International League for Peace and Freedom, which was organized after World War I. In 1931 she won the Nobel Peace Prize. She was sensitive always to the cries of the underprivileged. The following is from "Newer Ideals of Peace," published in 1907.*

It is quite possible that we have committed the time-honored folly of looking for a sudden change in men's attitude toward war, even as the poor alchemists wasted their lives in searching for a magic fluid and did nothing to discover the great laws governing chemical changes and reactions, the knowledge of which would have developed untold wealth beyond their crude dreams of transmuted gold.

The final moral reaction may at last come, accompanied by deep remorse, too tardy to reclaim all the human life which has been spent and the treasure which has been wasted, or it may come with a great sense of joy that all voluntary destruction of human life, all the deliberate wasting of the fruits of labor, have become a thing of the past, and that whatever the future contains for us, it will at least be free from war. We may at last comprehend the truth of that which Ruskin has stated so many times, that we worship the soldier not because he goes forth to slay, but to be slain.

That this world peace movement should be arising from the humblest without the sanction and in some cases with the explicit indifference, of the church founded by the Prince of Peace, is simply another example of the strange paths of moral evolution.

To some of us it seems clear that marked manifestations of this movement are found in the immigrant quarters of American cities. The previous survey of the immigrant situation would indicate that all the peoples of the world have become part of the American tribunal, and that their sense of pity, their clamor for personal kindness, their insistence upon the right to join in our progress, can no longer be disregarded. The burdens and sorrows of men have unexpectedly become intelligent and urgent to this nation, and it is only by accepting them with some magnanimity that we can develop the larger sense of justice which is becoming world-wide and is lying in ambush, as it were, to manifest itself in governmental relations. Men of all nations are determining upon the abolition of degrading poverty, disease and intellectual weakness, with their resulting industrial inefficiency, and are making a determined effort to conserve even the feeblest citizen to the state. To join in this determined effort is to break through national bonds and to unlock the latent fellowship between man and man. In a political campaign men will go through every possible hardship in response to certain political loyalties; in a moment of national danger men will sacrifice every personal advantage. It is but necessary to make this fellowship wider, to extend its scope without lowering its intensity. Those emotions which stir the spirit to deeds of self-surrender and to high enthusiasm, are among the world's most precious assets. That this emotion has so often become associated with war by no means proves that it cannot be used for other ends. There is something active and tangible in this new internationalism, although it is difficult to make it clear, and in our striving for a new word with which to express this new and important sentiment, we are driven to the rather absurd phrase of "cosmic patriotism." Whatever it may be called, it may yet be strong enough to move masses of men out of their narrow national considerations and cautions into new reaches of human effort and affection. Religion has long ago taught that only as the individual can establish a sense of union with a power for righteousness not himself can he experience peace; and it may be possible that the nations will be called to a similar experience.

The International Peace Conference held in Boston in 1904 was opened by a huge meeting in which men of influence and modern thought from four continents gave reasons for their belief in the passing of war. But none was so modern, so fundamental and so trenchant as the address which was read from the prophet Isaiah. He founded the cause of peace upon the cause of righteousness, not only as expressed in political relations, but also in industrial relations. He contended that peace could be secured only as men abstained from the gains of oppression and responded to the cause of the poor; that swords would finally be beaten into plowshares and pruning hooks, not because men resolved to be peaceful, but because all the metal of the earth would be turned to its proper use when the poor and their children should be abundantly fed. It was as if the ancient prophet foresaw that under an enlightened industrialism peace would no longer be an absence of war, but the unfolding of world-wide processes making for the nurture of human life. He predicted the moment which has come to us now that peace is no longer an abstract dogma but has become a rising tide of moral enthusiasm slowly engulfing all pride of conquest and making war impossible.

Bertha von Suttner

explains how she came to write Lay Down Your Arms

BARONESS BERTHA VON SUTTNER [1843-1914] *was an Austrian writer who became famous for her novel* Lay Down Your Arms. *The book was translated into almost every known language. Before it was published, she had not been an active peace worker, but afterward she devoted the rest of her life to the cause of peace. A year after its publication, she founded the Austrian Peace Society. She was honorary president of the International Peace Bureau at Berne, and as a peace crusader she attended every Universal Peace Congress until she died.*

It was toward the end of the year 1880, when I had already reached a mature age and was in the midst of zealous studies in science, philosophy and history, that the idea dawned on me and soon became a deep-set conviction, that war was an institution handed down to us by the barbarians, and to be removed by civilization. At this same moment I learned by accident that a society existed in England based on this same idea and aiming to influence public opinion in favor of the creation of a court of arbitration. So I hastened to write to this "Peace and Arbitration Association" and asked for information. The now venerable Hodgson Pratt, who is the founder and president of that organization, forthwith sent me the bylaws and publications of the society, and thenceforth kept up an active correspondence with me. Thus it was that I learned all that had been done and all that remained to be done in this important field of work.

The more I looked into the question the more I became absorbed by it and the more eager I was to do what little I could to advance the cause of peace. As I had had some experience in authorship, I felt that it was in the department of literature that I could do the most good. My idea was, at first, to write a little story in which I would describe a young woman who had lost her beloved husband on the battlefield, and who then, as it had happened to me, suddenly awoke to the condemnation of war. In my own case, however, my convictions were based only on theories, whereas my heroine was to be converted through dire experience.

While I was engaged in gathering materials for my little tale, so much accumulated on my hands and my mind was so teeming with my subject that from a novelette my plan grew into a two-volume novel. Not satisfied with superficial information, I now began to consult recognized authorities, to study the campaigns of 1859, 1864, 1866 and 1870-71, to read the memoirs of different generals, to examine the reports of army sur geons and the Red Cross Society, to rummage in libraries and archives, among the diplomatic dispatches exchanged during those periods and among the orders given the various armies. Provided with this data, I set to work on the historical scaffolding of my book and the development of my plot, whose foundation was, of course, the ardent condemnation of war; and when I could write on the last page of my manuscript "The End," and put at the head of the first page, *Lay Down Your Arms,* I felt that now I really was in a position to do something for the cause so near my heart. I was armed!

Full of confidence, I sent my manuscript to the Stuttgart [magazine] editor who had always heretofore accepted what I offered him and who had recently asked me for a fresh one. But it was promptly returned to me with this message: "We regret it, but this novel we cannot use." So I tried other editors, but all declined it with the remarks: "This does not interest our public," or "It would offend many of our readers," or "It is impossible to publish this in the present military state of affairs." Such were the opinions of the leading editors of German periodicals.

I next turned toward the [book] publishers, and first sent the manuscript to my habitual publisher, Pierson, of Dresden. He kept it a long time and then advised me to change the title, which he found too aggressive, and to submit the manuscript to a competent public man for revision, who would suppress or modify the passages which could give offense in military and political circles. This I, of course, utterly refused to permit. The title of the book expressed clearly the purpose I had in writing it, and told the reader, without any subterfuge, just what he was to expect between the covers, while the passages which it was proposed to cut out because they would excite disapproval in certain quarters were the very essence of the book, what gave it its *raison d'être.* So I would consent to no change, either in title or text.

As I afterward took part in the peace movement, it has been thought in some quarters that I wrote this book as a consequence of that movement. But the facts are exactly the contrary. My book made me a peace advocate, but it did not spring from my participation in that reform. This is how it happened.

In the spring of 1891, about fifteen months after the publication of *Lay Down Your Arms,* I and my husband were stopping in Venice. One afternoon somebody knocked at the door, and the servant being absent, my husband himself opened it. An elderly, well-dressed gentleman was standing on the landing.

"Does the Baroness von Suttner live here?" he asked.

"Yes; she is my wife," was the answer.

"What! You are the husband of Madame von Suttner—Bertha von Suttner?"

"I certainly am."

"You are not dead, then?"

"With your permission, I am still living."

"But were you not shot in Paris?"

"It seems not."

In the meantime I stepped forward and led our guest into the drawing room, when he presented himself to us and told us the object of his visit. We soon learned that we had before us Mr. Felix Moscheles, son of the celebrated composer, Ignąz Moscheles, and godson of Felix Mendelssohn, he himself a painter, an earnest peace advocate and vice-president of the London Peace and Arbitration Association. He told us he had been ill during a pleasure trip in Egypt, and his wife, to amuse him, had given him a copy of *Lay Down Your Arms* to read. He began the book rather against his will, he went on to tell us, for he does not care for fiction. But when he saw the nature of the volume he hurried through to the end with feverish interest, because here were all his own views against war condensed in a living and possible story. "I must make the acquaintance of the author of this volume," he then and there said, and forthwith decided to journey home via Vienna. He had intended simply to pass through Venice, but while telling one of his friends why he was going to Vienna, learned that the person sought for was at that moment in Venice, and that she even lived in the Palazzo Dario, just opposite his lodgings. So he started out immediately to make the personal acquaintance of the unhappy widow, the expounder of all his cherished ideas, when lo! her lawful husband himself opens the door. Thus the widowhood was found to be fiction, while the communion of ideas is still a living thing; and during that first hour was formed a friendship between us three which has lasted without a cloud from that time to this, and whose first act, on the evening of that same day, was the laying of the foundations of a new work which was to have an important influence on the peace movement.

At that time there lived in Venice, where he kept open house, Marquis Beniamino Pandolfi and his wife, who had been a friend of my childhood. I knew that Pandolfi, who was a member of the Italian Parliament, was a supporter of peace ideas, and as he was giving a reception that evening, I suggested to Mr. Moscheles that he seize the occasion to speak with him about the movement in England, and that he urge him to secure, among his colleagues in the Italian Parliament, adherents to the Inter-Parliamentary Union, which was at that time a very small body. It was especially important to strengthen this organization at that moment, for in November of that year the union was to meet at Rome. This association had been founded in 1888 by William R. Cremer, M.P., of London, and Frédéric Passy, of Paris, then member of the Chamber of Deputies, and it was at the French capital, during the International Exhibition of 1889, that the first Inter-Parliamentary Conference was held, France and England alone being represented. The second meeting was held in London, with a few more parliaments represented, and now the third meeting was to take place in Rome.

The result of the advent of Mr. Felix Moscheles at the Palazzo Bianca Capello, Pandolfi's home, was that, while the elegant society of Venice and its gay youth were dancing and eating in the big dining room, a long conversation took place in the host's study, in which the Marquis, Mr. Moscheles and we two participated. The upshot of it all was that not only did Pandolfi promise to aid in the organization of the approaching conference, but invitations and circulars were prepared on the spot looking to the foundation in Venice of a peace society. The plan succeeded, and some of the most prominent men of the town came into the movement.

Clarence Darrow
decries violence and force as punishment

CLARENCE DARROW [1857-1938] *was an internationally famous defense attorney who became known as a defender of unpopular causes. He was an uncompromising foe of capital punishment. For a time he considered himself a pacifist, but when World War I began, he became convinced that "man can never reach a state of nonresistance." Years later, however, he could still write, "What we know as moral forces are much more important than guns and battleships." "The Right Treatment of Violence" is a chapter from* Resist Not Evil, *published in 1903.*

Sentimental and humane thoughts and purposes are often, perhaps generally, based on real life, and have a natural reason for their being. To "turn the other cheek" or to "resist not evil" may seem at first glance to have no support in the facts of life, but after all that which makes for a higher humanity, a longer life and a more vigorous community is the true philosophy. To use violence and force upon the vicious and the weak must produce the evil that it gives. Like produces like. Clubs, jails, harsh language, brutal force inevitably tend to reproduce the same state of mind in the victim of the assault. This is not merely a fact in human nature. It is a fact in all nature, plant and animal and man. So long as the gentle springtime rather than the cruel winter brings vegetable and animal life to an awakening earth, just so long will kindness and love triumph, produce joy and life, where force and violence bring only evil and death. Harsh treatment kills plant life, and kind treatment builds it up. Violence and brutality produce their like in animal life, and kindness tames and subdues. With gentleness and kindness a swarm of wild bees may be handled and controlled, but approach them with violence and force and each bee is converted into a criminal whose only purpose is to destroy.

With all animal life the same rule exists; even those beasts whose nature calls for a diet of flesh and blood may be subdued in time by gentleness and love. Man with his higher intellect and better developed moral being is much more susceptible to kindness and love. Likewise he more easily learns to fear and hate. Man readily discerns the feelings and judgment of his fellows, and as readily renders judgment in return. The outcast and abandoned form not the slightest exception to the rule—they know and understand the ones who meet them with gentleness and love, for these they make sacrifices, to these they are faithful, to these they exhibit the higher qualities that show the possibilities of the soul. Cases where one convicted of crime comes from a place of safety and risks his liberty and life to help save his friend are not rare in the least. True comradeship and loyalty is met quite as often here as in the higher walks of life. Nothing is more common in ordinary selfish society than to see one man refuse all aid and help to another in financial need. Many convicts and outcasts could teach a much needed lesson of loyalty and generosity to the exemplary man.

No amount of treatment can reclaim an evil heart if the treatment is administered without love. As children at school we knew with our young natural instincts the teacher who loved us and the teacher who despised us—the one awoke feelings of love and kindness, the other hatred and revenge. No heart is so pure that it may not be defiled and hardened by cruelty, hatred and force, and none so defiled that it may not be touched and changed by gentleness and love. Unless this philosophy of life is true the whole teaching of the world has been a delusion and a snare. Unless love and kindness tend to love, then hatred and violence and force should be substituted and taught as the cardinal virtues of human life.

The mistake and evil of society is in assuming that love is the rule of life, and at the same time that large classes of people are entirely outside its pale. No parent ever teaches his child any other philosophy than that of love. Even to quarrelsome playmates they are taught not to return blows and harsh language, but to meet force with kindness and with love. The parent who did not depend on love to influence and mold the character of the child rather than force would be regarded not as a real parent but a brute. Force is worse than useless in developing the conduct of the child. It is true that by means of force the little child may be awed by superior brute power, but he gives way only under protest, and the violence that he suppresses in his hand or tongue finds refuge in his heart. Violent acts are not evil—they are a manifestation of evil. Good conduct is not goodness. It is but a manifestation of goodness. Evil and goodness can only be the conditions of the inmost life, and human conduct, while it generally reflects this inmost life, may be so controlled as not to manifest the real soul that makes the man.

Every child needs development, needs training to fit him to live in peace and right relations with his fellow man. Every intelligent and right-thinking person knows that his development must be through love, not through violence and force. The parent who would teach his child to be kind to animals, not to kill and maim ruthlessly, would not teach this gentleness with a club. The intelligent parent would not use a whip to teach a child not to beat a dog. The child is not made into the good citizen, the righteous man, by pointing out that certain conduct will lead to punishment, to the jail or the gallows. The beneficence of fear was once considered a prime necessity in the rearing of the child, and this theory peopled the earth with monsters and the air with spooks ready to reach down and take the helpless child when he wandered from the straight and narrow path; but this method of rearing children does not appeal to the judgment of humanity today. The conduct of children can only be reached for good by pointing to the evil results of hatred, of inharmony, of force, by appealing to the higher and nobler sentiments which, if once reached, are ever present, influencing and controlling life.

The code of hatred, of violence and force, too, is a negative code. The child is given a list of the things he must not do, exactly as the man is furnished a list of the acts forbidden by the state. At the best, when the limits of this list are reached and the forbidden things are left undone, nothing more is expected or demanded. But no code is long enough to make up the myriad acts of life. Kindness or unkindness can result in a thousand ways in every human relationship. If the child or the man observes the written code through fear, the unwritten moral code, infinitely longer and more delicate, will be broken in its almost every line. But if the child or the man is taught his right relations to the world and feels the love and sympathy due his fellow man, he has no need of written codes; his acts, so far as those of morals can be, will be consistent with the life and happiness of his fellow man. And this not through fear, but because he bears the highest attitude toward life.

With our long heredity and our imperfect environment, even if the organized force of the state should disappear, even if the jails and penitentiaries should close their doors, force would only completely die in course of time. Evil environment and heredity may have so marked and scarred some men that kindness and love could never reach their souls. It might take generations to stamp out hatred or destroy the ill effects of life; but order and kindness most surely would result, because nature demands order and tolerance, and without it man must die. No doubt here and there these so-called evil ones would arouse evil and hatred in return, and some sudden act of violence would for a time occasionally be met with violence through mob law in return. But uncertain and reprehensible as mob law has ever been it is still much more excusable and more certain than the organized force of society operating through the criminal courts. Mob law has the excuse of passion, of provocation, not the criminal nature of deliberation, coldness and settled hate. Mob law, too, generally reaches the objects of its wrath, while evidence is fresh and facts are easily understood and unhampered by those rules and technical forms which ensnare the weak and protect the strong. And unjust and unwise as the verdicts of mob law often are, they are still more excusable, quicker, more certain and less erring than the judgments of the criminal courts.

But neither civil law nor mob law is at all necessary for the protection of individuals. Men are not protected because of their strength or their ability to fight. In the present general distribution of weapons, in one sense, every man's life is dependent on each person that he meets. If the instinct was to kill, society as organized presents no obstacle to that instinct. When casual violence results it is not the weakest or most defenseless who are the victims of the casual violence of individuals. Even the boy at school scorns to war upon a weaker mate. The old, the young, the feeble, children and women are especially exempt from violent deeds. This is because their condition does not call for feelings of violence, but rather awakens feelings of compassion, and calls for aid and help. The nonresistant ever appeals to the courageous and the manly. Without weapons of any kind, with the known determination to give no violence in return, it would be very rare that men would not be safe from disorganized violence. It is only that state that ever lays its hands in anger on the nonresistant.

Neither would nonresistance in the state or individual indicate cowardice or weakness or lack of vital force. The ability and inclination to use physical strength is no indication of bravery or tenacity to life. The greatest cowards are often the greatest bullies. Nothing is cheaper and more common than physical bravery. In the lower animals it is more pronounced than in man. The bulldog and the fighting cock are quite as conspicuous examples of physical bravery as the prize fighter or the soldier. The history of all warfare shows either that physical bravery is not an indication of great excellence or that supreme excellence is very common, in fact almost a universal possession. Under the intoxication of patriotism, or the desire for glory, or the fear of contempt, most men will march with apparent willingness into the face of the greatest danger. Often it requires vastly more courage to stay at home than to enlist— more courage to retreat than to fight. Common experience shows how much rarer is moral courage than physical bravery. A thousand men will march to the mouth of the cannon where one man will dare espouse an unpopular cause. An army well equipped and ready for action has less terror for the ordinary man than the unfavorable comment of the daily press. True courage and manhood come from the consciousness of the right attitude toward the world, the faith in one's own purpose, and the sufficiency of one's own approval as a justification for one's own acts. This attitude is not that of the coward, for cowardice is really disapproval of self, a consciousness of one's own littleness and unworthiness in the light of one's own soul, which cannot be deceived.

Intelligent men are willing to accept many truths that they believe are not fitted for the universal acceptance of mankind, and however they may feel that punishment is wrong they still urge that it will not do to teach this doctrine to the great mass of men and to carry its practice into daily life. But sooner or later all conduct and all life must rest on truth. It is only fact that can form a basis for permanent theories that tend to the preservation of the race. No one is too poor, or too young, or too vicious to know the truth, for the truth alone is consistent with all the facts of life, and this alone can furnish any rule of life. The truth alone can make free. When society is taught the truth that it is wrong to punish, to use force, to pass judgment on man, it will have no need for jails. The man who really knows and understands this truth can have no malice in his heart, can use no force and violence against his fellow, but will reach him with love and pity. The name or society that understands this truth will know that so-called crime is only so-called crime; that human conduct is what the necessities of life make of the individual soul. Then in reality, as now only partially, men will turn their attention to the causes that make crime. Then will they seek to prevent and cure, not to punish and destroy. Then man will learn to know that the cause of crime is the unjust condition of human life; that penal laws are made to protect earth's possessions in the hands of the vicious and the strong. Man will learn that poverty and want are due to the false conditions, the injustice which looks to human law and violence and force for its safeguard and protection. Man will learn that crime is but the hard profession that is left open to a large class of men by their avaricious fellows.

When new opportunities for life are given, a fairer condition of existence will gradually be opened up and the need for violence and the cause of violence will disappear.

Instead of avenging a murder by taking a judge, sheriff, jurors, witnesses, jailer, hangman, and the various appendages of the court, by taking these and staining their hands with blood and crime, the world will make the original murder impossible, and thus save the crimes of all. Neither will the vicious control without the aid of law. Society ever has and must ever have a very large majority who naturally fall into order, social adjustment and a rational, permissible means of life. The disorganized vicious would be far less powerful than the organized vicious, and would soon disappear.

Punishment to terrorize men from violating human order is like the threat of hell to terrorize souls into obedience to the law of God. Both mark primitive society, both are degrading and debasing, and can only appeal to the lower instincts of the lower class of men. Most religious teachers have ceased to win followers by threats of hell. Converts of this sort are not generally desired. The religion that does not approach and appeal to men along their higher conduct is not considered worthy to teach to man. And those souls who cannot be moved through the sentiments of justice and humanity, rather than threats of eternal fire, are very, very rare, and even should such a soul exist the fear of hell would cause it still further to shrivel and decay.

Hatred, bitterness, violence and force can bring only bad results— they leave an evil stain on everyone they touch. No human soul can be rightly reached except through charity, humanity and love.

Frédéric Passy

salutes the future of arbitration

FRÉDÉRIC PASSY [1822-1912] *was a French economist and pacifist, and the first recipient—with M. Henry Dunant, Swiss founder of the Red Cross—of the Nobel Prize for Peace. He was educated as a lawyer and entered the government service as an auditor in the state council. He later became a member of the Chamber of Deputies in France. He was one of the founders in 1867 of the Société Française des Amis de la Paix, and was president of the French Arbitration Society. In his will and last testament, Passy warned that "the world will only be saved on that day when it shall be penetrated with the necessity of self-respect, mutual love, and the necessity of helping in the common struggle against all forms of error and vice."*

I am asked to give my opinion, in a few pages, on the future of arbitration. To do so is not an easy matter, especially under the conditions imposed, but I will nevertheless try.

The first question that naturally occurs to one's mind is whether it can be said that arbitration has a future.

Not long ago great hopes were entertained of it, which have been doomed to disappointment. The Hague Conference seemed to announce the dawn of a new era. It was asserted to mean an almost immediate reduction of the various military armaments, with the charges involved by them, and, at the same time, the introduction into international law of judicial settlements in national quarrels, such introduction to be accompanied by a fixed code of procedure. Recent experience has shown how powerless the jurisdiction of the court established by the plenipotentiaries is, when appeals have been made to it, to prevent conflicts from breaking out or to bring them to a conclusion. "So far from The Hague Conference being a consecration of arbitration," say the skeptics, "it has proved to be its condemnation."

And yet the skeptics are wrong. If The Hague Conference has not yielded all that was expected from it, a fact which is only too evident, the reason lies partly in this—viz., that more was required from it than it was able to give. It is not in a single day, however solemn the declaration of purpose, that the habits, ideas and sentiments of nations can be changed, or of the individuals that compose them. Moreover, mistakes were made both in the constitution and in the carrying on of the conference. Without any slur on the good intentions of the plenipotentiaries, it may be said that some of them had not a sufficiently clear idea of the greatness of the work in which they were called to participate, or yet an adequate faith in the efficacy of their decisions. They feared that if they adopted too direct a course they would be abandoned by their colleagues. "If you insist," it was objected, "on the conference being open unreservedly to all who may wish to attend it, and if you try to frame a general law binding on all, with a view to arbitration being universally adopted, you will most likely bring about the failure of the generous scheme your mission is to promote; for either there will be no conference at all, or the sittings will be rendered practically inoperative by the public withdrawal, at a certain stage, of some of its members."

Well! This might have happened. And, no doubt, the scandal would have been great. But, at least, light would have been thrown on the real motives of all; equivocation would have been impossible; and thus some good would have been obtained. Moreover, all excuses for persisting in following old political methods must have necessarily been taken away or at any rate have lost their force, and a step further been made toward their definite condemnation.

Alas! It is not the first time that mistakes of a similar kind have turned against the intentions of those who committed them.

When, a hundred and twenty-five years ago, the young republic of the United States was formed, slavery existed only as an exception in one or two parts of the Union; and the number of Negroes in bondage was exceedingly small. In abstaining from an immediate abolition of the slave system it was thought that a slight concession only was made and that it would be wiser to avoid offending the few whom this system concerned. But the bane spread and invaded other colonies, and the private institution, which it would have been so easy to abolish as such, finally became a general one and prevailed to the extent that the master's right prevailed to seize the fugitive slave in a place where servitude did not exist and whither the poor wretch had fled believing himself to be in safety. The upshot of all this was that, nearly a century later, it needed, in order to destroy the bane which a little energy at the beginning would have been sufficient to do, a waste of blood and of gold. And today, still, after the terrible crisis of the secession, the Negro question continues to be one of the difficulties of the great American nation.

There was the same lack of firmness at The Hague. It was thought that to adjourn difficulties was to avoid them; and, lest the cooperation of one or another of the principal parties interested should be lost, half measures were accepted. Then, almost immediately after, but when it was already too late, it was perceived that by the very terms of the convention agreed on the work of the conference would have no practical result.

Such being the case, one may be permitted to think that, in this matter as in many others, the prudence of diplomatists has not been very clearsighted, and that an exceptional occasion has been missed of making a definite and decisive advance in the path leading to international concord.

It cannot, however, be denied that a great effort was made, and that something still remains. A good example has been set, and set in a high quarter. A cry of alarm has been uttered, and not only its sound, but its importance, has been recognized. A solemn engagement has been entered into, and the world has taken note of it. A great hope has swept over the globe.

Despite ourselves, toward the skies
We are constrained to raise our eyes

says Alfred de Musset in lines that have become celebrated.

In spite of yourselves, politicians of the old school, adorers of force
and disbelievers in equity, yes, in spite of yourselves, you are constrained
to raise your eyes toward peace; that is, toward the means which are
capable of procuring and preserving it; toward arbitration, toward mediation, toward justice, liberty, mutual respect, and joint action in work
and the exchange of its products. For the peoples of the earth have learned
from you, from your words if not from your actions so far, after learning
it to their cost from the divisions into which you have involved them, by
what considerations of interest, as also of morality, they ought to detest
war; they have learned, too, how easy it will be, whenever you shall seriously try, either to prevent war's outbreak or else to appease its strife.

For example, in a war which is being carried on in a far part of the
world, and in which it would seem that Europe and America are in no
wise concerned, notice to what an extent public opinion has been moved.
The reason is, notwithstanding all that shortsighted statesmen and
wrongheaded patriots say to prove that recourse to arbitration and mediation is inadmissible, the reason is that everybody feels, knows and sees
that nothing would have been easier and more honorable than to prevent,
by an arrangement advantageous to both sides, this disastrous war.

Moreover, at the present time, with the improved means of information and communication that have in a manner annihilated space and
time, all that takes place in any part of the globe is perceived at our doors,
beneath our windows, and we see with our eyes, we hear with our ears,
the tumult and horror of the battlefield; we are present with those that
are dying, we feel the heat of conflagrations, we breathe the odor of
charnel houses. This being so, we are seized with disgust, and we are no
longer content, as of old, the few that were wise, to curse, from the midst
of our apparent security, the tempest that rages afar off; we spurn it as a
shame in which we share and the approach of which we dread.

The world is sick of war, and shows it; for, while in South Africa
we have pointed out to us, as a proof of the eternal impotency of our efforts, the war fiend raging in all his fury, elsewhere, in South and Central America, we see him chained and muzzled. The Argentine and
Chilean Republics, which were on the verge of hostilities, have had the
good sense to pause and to entrust the settlement of their dispute to the
decision of a foreign sovereign. In addition to this, the Pan-American
Congress of Mexico has adopted for the new hemisphere the resolutions
voted at The Hague; and the code of international law is able to count
another victory.

What is the meaning of all this, if not that, in spite of its occasional recrudescences, nay, even by reason of these recrudescences, war is losing its prestige, and is being relegated to limbo?

This latter result is not altogether attained, and perhaps never will be; but, at any rate, the action of war is even now considerably restricted. When the tide has reached its highest point, and is beginning to recede, it sometimes happens that from the retiring mass of waters a stray wave will fling its foam far enough up the beach for a momentary impression to be created that the tide is coming in again. But this stray wave is soon seen to be only a last effort against the irresistible force which is drawing back the sea from the land.

This is what war is doing just now. After flooding, during the past century, with its tide of blood the shores that work and peace had toiled to fertilize, it is gradually retiring from them, regretfully, no doubt, but still it is retiring. And, in vain, as it withdraws, it hurls on our shores, protestingly and defiantly, some of its most raging billows; it is none the less compelled to recede and spends itself uselessly to regain the ground it has lost. The future, if only we can learn to will, shall belong to neither war, nor division, nor hatred. It shall belong to peace, to work, and—to arbitration. Instead of devastating the earth while quarreling for it, peoples shall learn, as indeed they are beginning now, to render it fruitful for each other. Commerce, the great conqueror, which costs neither tears nor blood, shall achieve for each, by opening to him the riches scattered in earth's varied regions, the pacific and beneficent conquest of the whole globe. Blessed are the peacemakers, for they shall inherit the earth.

Pacifici hereditabunt terram.

Jean de Bloch

describes the burdens of "armed peace"

JEAN DE BLOCH [1836-1902] *was born Ivan Stanislavovich Blioch in Radom, Poland. He worked as a peddler to get enough money for his education at the University of Berlin. He later became the leading banker of Poland and acquired a reputation as a sociologist and economist. He was a critical student of military affairs, and in 1898 he published the seven-volume* Future of War. *It was criticized for being "too radical in its demands for arbitration and international peace." But it was this book which influenced the czar to call the International Peace Conference at The Hague in 1899.*

It must be admitted that to decide the question whether militarism is inevitable or not is no easy task. We constantly hear the argument adduced that there always have been wars and always will be, and if in the course of all the centuries recorded in history, international disputes were settled only by means of war, how can it be possible to get along without it in the future? To this we might reply that not only the number, equipment, training, and technical methods of armies, but the very elements from which they are constructed have essentially changed.

The relations of the strength of armies in time of war to their strength in time of peace in former times was very different. Wars formerly were carried on by standing armies consisting mainly of long-service soldiers. The armies employed in future wars will be composed mainly of soldiers taken directly from peaceful occupations. Among the older soldiers will be vast numbers of heads of families torn from their homes, their families and their work. The economic life of whole peoples will stand still, communications will be cut, and if war be prolonged over the greater part of a year, general bankruptcy, with famine and all its worst consequences, will ensue. To cast light on the nature of a prolonged war from all sides, military knowledge alone is not enough. The study and knowledge of economic laws and conditions which have no direct connection with military specialism is no less essential.

Consideration of the question is made all the more difficult by the fact that the direction of military affairs belongs to the privileged ranks of society. The opinions expressed by nonspecialists as to the improbability of great wars in the future, are refuted by authorities simply by the declaration that laymen are ignorant of the subject. Military men cannot admit to be unnecessary that which forms the object of their activity in time of peace. They have been educated on the history of warfare, and practical work develops in them energy and capacity for self-sacrifice. Nevertheless, such authorities are not in a position to paint a complete picture of the disasters of a future war. Those radical changes which have taken place in the military art, in the composition of armies, and in international economy, are so vast that a powerful imagination would be required adequately to depict the consequences of war, both on the field of battle and in the lives of peoples.

Yet it cannot be denied that popular discontent with the present condition of affairs is becoming more and more keenly noticeable. Formerly only solitary voices were raised against militarism, and their protests were platonic. But since the adoption of conscription, the interests of society, and the disasters which must be expected under modern conditions, have been better appreciated by the people.

It is impossible, therefore, not to foresee the constant growth of the antimilitary propaganda, the moral foundations of which were not so indisputable in the past as they are today. To this moral sentiment has lately been added a consciousness of the complexity of the business relations threatened by war, of the immense increase of means of destruction, and of the deficiency of experienced leadership and the ignorance and cloudiness now prevailing on the subject of war.

All these tend to make the people see in war a misfortune truly terrifying. And if, even in the past, it was found that the sentiments of peoples are more powerful than any force, how much more so now, when in the majority of states the masses indirectly share in the government, and when everywhere exist strong tendencies threatening the whole social order. How much more significant now are the opinions of the people both directly as to the system of militarism and in their influence on the spirit of armies themselves!

It is impossible here even to outline the energetic struggle against militarism which is being carried on in the West. It is true that the advocates of the settlement of international disputes by peaceful means have not attained any tangible success. But success, it must be admitted, they have had if the fact is taken into account that the necessity of maintaining peace has been recognized by governments, and that dread of the terrible disasters of war has been openly expressed by statesmen, and emphasized even from the height of thrones.

As a chief factor tending to preserve the system of militarism the existence of a professional military class must be considered. It is true that the changes which have taken place under the influence of conscription and short service have given to armies a popular character. On the mobilization of armies a considerable proportion of officers will be taken from the reserve: these officers cannot be considered professional. Nevertheless, a military professional class continues to exist, consisting mainly of officers serving with the colors.

It is natural that the existence of such a numerous and influential class, which—in Prussia, for instance—is partly hereditary, a class in which are found many men of high culture, should be one of the elements supporting the system of militarism, even independently of its other foundations. Even if the conviction were generally accepted that it is impossible to carry on war with modern methods of destruction and in view of the inevitable disasters, yet disarmament would be somewhat delayed by the existence of the military caste, which would continue to declare that war is inevitable, and that even the decrease of standing armies would be accompanied by the greatest dangers. . . . The times are past when officers rushing on in advance led their men in a bold charge against the enemy, or when squadrons seeing an ill-defended battery galloped up to it, sabered the gunners, and spiked the guns or flung them into ditches. Courage now is required no less than before, but this is the courage of restraint and self-sacrifice and no longer scenic heroism. War has taken a character more mechanical than knightly. Personal initiative is required not less than before, but it is no longer visible to all.

It is true that warfare and the military profession will continue to preserve their attractions for such restless, uncurbed natures as cannot reconcile themselves to a laborious and regular life, finding a charm in danger itself. But even these will find that the stormy military life and feverish activity of battle are no more surrounded by the aureole which once set them above the world of work.

It is notable that the younger and the better educated they are, the more pessimistically do officers look on war. And although military men do not speak against warfare publicly, for this would be incompatible with their calling, it cannot escape attention that every year fewer and fewer stand up in defense of its necessity or use. . . .

In our time both military and political affairs have ceased to be high mysteries accessible only to the few. General military service, the spread of education, and wide publicity have made the elements of the polities of states accessible to all. All who have passed through the ranks of an army have recognized that with modern weapons whole corps and squadrons may be destroyed in the first battle, and that in this respect the conquerors will suffer little less than the conquered.

Can it be possible that the growth of expenditure on armaments will continue forever? To the inventiveness of the human mind and the rivalry between states no limits exist. It is not surprising therefore that the immense expenditure on military aims and the consequent growth of taxation are the favorite arguments of agitators, who declare that the institutions of the Middle Ages—when from thousands of castles armed knights pounced upon passing merchants—were less burdensome than modern preparations for war.

The exact disposition of the masses in relation to armaments is shown by the increase in the number of opponents of militarism and preachers of the Socialist propaganda. In Germany in 1893, the opponents of the new military project received 1,097,000 votes more than its supporters. Between 1887 and 1893 the opposition against militarism increased more than seven times. In France the Socialist party in 1893 received 600,000 votes, and in 1896 1,000,000.

Thus, if the present conditions continue, there can be but two alternatives, either ruin from the continuance of the armed peace, or a veritable catastrophe from war.

The question is naturally asked: What will be given to the people after war as compensation for their immense losses? The conquered certainly will be too exhausted to pay any money indemnity, and compensation must be taken by the retention of frontier territories which will be so impoverished by war that their acquisition will be a loss rather than a gain.

With such conditions can we hope for good sense among millions of men when but a handful of their former officers remain? Will the armies of western Europe, where the Socialist propaganda has already spread among the masses, allow themselves to be disarmed, and if not, must we not expect even greater disasters than those which marked the short-lived triumph of the Paris Commune? The longer the present position of affairs continues the greater is the probability of such convulsions after the close of a great war. It cannot be denied that conscription, by taking from productive occupations a greater number of men than the former conditions of service, has increased the popularity of subversive principles among the masses. Formerly only Socialists were known; now anarchism has arisen. Not long ago the advocates of revolution were a handful; now they have their representatives in all parliaments, and every new election increases their number in Germany, in France, in Austria, and in Italy. It is a strange coincidence that only in England and in the United States, where conscription is unknown, are representative assemblies free from these elements of disintegration. Thus side by side with the growth of military burdens rise waves of popular discontent threatening a social revolution.

Such are the consequences of the so-called armed peace of Europe —slow destruction in consequence of expenditure on preparations for war, or swift destruction in the event of war—in both events convulsions in the social order.

Leo Tolstoy

pleads for each man to follow his own reason and conscience

COUNT LEO TOLSTOY [1828-1910], *the great Russian writer, was the son of a wealthy nobleman. He was accustomed to the splendid social life of his class, but when he was in the army Tolstoy became aware of the contrast between the "battle casualties and victory balls." He freed his own slaves long before their general emancipation in Russia. He found orthodox religion too formal and ritualistic and evolved his own form of Christianity based on the principle of "Resist not evil." He was a Christian anarchist who opposed all forms of violence. Just as his novels were enormously influential in world literature, so was his Christian philosophy an influence on men like Gandhi, who freely acknowledged his debt to Tolstoy's ideas.*

Two wars are at the present time being waged in the Christian world. One, it is true, has been ended, while the other is still going on; but they were waged at one and the same time, and the contrast between the two is striking. The first, now ended, was an old, vainglorious, stupid, cruel, untimely, obsolete, pagan war, the Spanish-American War, which by the murder of one set of men decided how and by whom another set of men was to be ruled. The second war, which is still going on, and which will be ended only when all wars shall end, is a new, self-sacrificing, sacred war, which is based on nothing but love and reason, the war against war, which (as Victor Hugo expressed it at one of the congresses) the best, most advanced part of the Christian humanity declared long ago against the other, the coarse and savage part of the same humanity, and which a handful of Christian men, the Dukhobors of the Caucasus, have of late waged with particular force and success against the powerful Russian government.

The other day I received a letter from Colorado, from a Mr. Jesse Glodwin, who asks me to send him "a few words or thoughts, expressive of my sentiments, in regard to the noble work of the American nation and the heroism of her soldiers and sailors." This gentleman is, with the vast majority of the American nation, fully convinced that the action of the Americans, which is, that they beat a few thousands of almost unarmed men (in comparison with the armament of the Americans the Spaniards were almost unarmed), is unquestionably a "noble work," and that those people who, having killed a large number of their neighbors, for the most part survived and were well and fixed themselves comfortably in life, were heroes.

The Spanish-American War, to say nothing of the horrible things which the Spaniards had done in Cuba, and which served as the pretext for the war, resembles this:

A decrepit and doting old man, who was brought up in the traditions of false honor, to settle a misunderstanding that arose between him and a young man, challenges this young man, who is in the full possession of his strength, to fisticuffs; and the young man, who, to judge from his past and from what he has said more than once, ought to stand incomparably higher than such a settlement of the question, accepts the challenge with knuckles in his clenched fist, jumps upon the decrepit and doting old man, knocks out his teeth, breaks his ribs, and then ecstatically tells his exploits to a vast public of just such young men as he is, and this public rejoices and praises the hero who has maimed the old man.

Such is the one war which occupied the minds of all in the Christian world. Nobody speaks of the other war; hardly anyone knows anything about it. The other war is like this:

All the states deceive the people, saying: "All of you who are ruled by me are in danger of being conquered by other nations; I look after your well-being and security, and so demand that you shall annually give me millions of rubles, the fruits of your labors, which I am going to use for rifles, cannon, powder, ships for your defense; I demand, besides, that you shall enter the organizations instituted by me, where they will make of you senseless particles of an immense machine—the army—which I manage. While connected with this army you will cease being men and having your own will, but will do everything I want you to do. What I want to do first of all is to rule, and the means I use for ruling is murder; and so I am going to teach you to commit murder."

In spite of the obvious insipidity of the assertion that men are in danger from the attack of the governments of other states, which assert that they, in spite of their desire for peace, are in the same danger; in spite of the degradation of that slavery to which men are subjected when they enter the army; in spite of the cruelty of the business to which they are called, men submit to the deception, give up their money for their own enslavement, and themselves enslave one another.

And here there appear people who say:

"What you say of the threatening danger and of your concern about protecting us against it is a deception. All the states affirm that they want peace, and at the same time arm themselves against one another. Besides, according to the law which you profess, all men are brothers, and it makes no difference whether we belong to this state or to another, and so the attack of other states upon us, with which you frighten us, has no terror and no meaning for us. But the main thing is this, that, according to the law which was given to us by God, and which you, too, profess, who demand of us a participation in murder, we are clearly forbidden to commit murder or even any acts of violence, and so we cannot and will not take part in your preparations for murder, will not give you any money for the purpose, and will not join the gangs established by you, where you corrupt the reason and the conscience of men, by changing them into instruments of violence, who are submissive to every evil man taking this instrument into his hands."

In this consists the second war, which has for a long time been waged with the representatives of rude force, and which of late has burned up with particular virulence between the Dukhobors and the Russian government. The Russian government has brought out against the Dukhobors all those instruments with which it can fight. These instruments are: the police measures of arrests, the prohibition of leaving the place of abode, the prohibition of intercommunication, the seizure of letters, espionage, the prohibition of printing in the newspapers any information on matters pertaining to the Dukhobors, calumny of them, printed in the periodicals, bribery, flogging, prisons, deportation, the ruin of families. But the Dukhobors, on their side, have put forth nothing but their own religious instrument, meek reasonableness and long-suffering firmness, and say: "We must not obey men more than God, and no matter what they may do, we cannot and will not obey them."

They praise the Spanish and American heroes of that savage war, who, wishing to distinguish themselves in the eyes of men and to receive rewards and glory, have killed a very large number of men, or themselves have died in the process of slaying their neighbors. But no one speaks or knows of these heroes of the war against war, who are not seen and heard by anyone, who have died under rods or in stinking cells, or in oppressive exile, and still to their very last breath remain true to the good and to truth.

I know of dozens of these martyrs who have died, and hundreds who, scattered over the whole world, continue this martyrs' profession of the truth.

I know Drózhzhin, a peasant teacher, who was tortured to death in the disciplinary battalion; I know another, Izyumchénko, Drózhzhin's companion, who was kept awhile in the disciplinary battalion and then was sent away to the end of the world; I know Olkhóvik, a peasant, who refused to do military service, was for this sentenced to be sent to the disciplinary battalion, and on the boat converted his guard, Seredá. Seredá, who understood what Olkhóvik said about the sin of military service, came to the authorities and said, as the ancient martyrs said: "I do not want to be with the tormentors, join me to the martyrs," and they began to torture him, sent him to the disciplinary battalion, and then to Yakútsk Territory. I knew dozens of Dukhobors, many of whom have died or grown blind, who none the less do not submit to the demands which are contrary to the law of God.

The other day I read a letter about a young Dukhobor who was sent by himself, without any companions, to a regiment stationed in Samarkand. Again the same demands on the part of the authorities, and the same simple, unswerving answers: "I cannot do what is contrary to my faith in God." "We will torture you to death." "That is your business. You do your business, and I will do mine."

And this twenty-year-old boy, cast by himself into a foreign country, amidst hostile people, strong, rich, cultured people, who direct all their forces to conquering him, does not succumb and does his great work.

They say: "These are useless sacrifices. These men will perish, but the structure of life will remain the same." Even thus, I think, people spoke of the uselessness of Christ's sacrifice and of the sacrifice of all the martyrs for the sake of truth. The people of our time, especially the scholars, have become so gross that they do not understand, and in their grossness cannot even understand, the significance and the influence of spiritual force. A charge of ten thousand pounds of dynamite sent into a crowd of living men—that they understand, and in that they see strength; but an idea, truth, which has been realized, has been introduced into life to the point of martyrdom, has become accessible to millions—that is according to their conception not force, because it does not boom, and you do not see broken bones and puddles of blood. Scholars (it is true, bad scholars) use all the power of their erudition to prove that humanity lives like a herd, which is guided only by economic conditions, and that reason is given to it only for amusement; but the governments know what it is that moves the world, and so unerringly, from a sense of self-preservation, look most zealously upon the manifestation of spiritual forces, on which depends their existence or their ruin. For this reason all the efforts of the Russian government have been directed upon making the Dukhobors harmless, upon isolating them and sending them abroad.

But, in spite of all their efforts, the struggle of the Dukhobors has opened the eyes of millions.

I know hundreds of old and young military men who, thanks to the persecutions of the meek, industrious Dukhobors, have had misgivings as to the legality of their own activity; I know people who for the first time reflected upon life and the significance of Christianity, when they saw the life of these people or heard of the persecutions to which they have been subjected.

And the government, which rules over millions of people, knows this and feels that it has been struck at its very heart.

Such is the second war, which is being waged in our time, and such are its consequences. Its consequences are of importance, and not for the Russian government alone. Every government which is based on the army and on violence is struck in the same way by this weapon. Christ said, "I have conquered the world." He has really conquered the world, if people will only believe in the power of this weapon which is given to them.

This weapon is, for each man to follow his own reason and conscience.

This is so simple, so indubitable and obligatory for every single man. "You want to make me a participant in murder. You demand of me money for the preparation of the implements of murder, and you want me to become a participant in the organized gathering of murderers," says a rational man, who has not sold or dimmed his conscience. "But I confess the same law with you, in which not only murder, but even every hostility, has long ago been forbidden, and so I cannot obey you."

It is this means, which is so simple, that conquers the world.

Herbert Spencer

deplores the cry of "Our country, right or wrong!"

HERBERT SPENCER [1820-1903] *was an influential English philosopher interested in psychology and the natural sciences, and particularly in the theory of evolution, which he saw as the unifying principle of knowledge. He did not address himself to metaphysical abstractions. His philosophy has been summarized as "individualistic, anti-military, anticoercive, evolutionary, and materialistic." The first of his writings was a series of letters that appeared in* The Nonconformist.

Were anyone to call me dishonest or untruthful he would touch me to the quick. Were he to say that I am unpatriotic, he would leave me unmoved. "What, then, have you no love of country?" That is a question not to be answered in a breath.

The early abolition of serfdom in England, the early growth of relatively free institutions, and the greater recognition of popular claims after the decay of feudalism had divorced the masses from the soil, were traits of English life which may be looked back upon with pride. When it was decided that any slave who set foot in England became free; when the importation of slaves into the Colonies was stopped; when twenty millions were paid for the emancipation of slaves in the West Indies; and when, however unadvisedly, a fleet was maintained to stop the slave trade, our countrymen did things worthy to be admired. And when England gave a home to political refugees and took up the causes of small states struggling for freedom, it again exhibited noble traits which excite affection. But there are traits, unhappily of late more frequently displayed, which do the reverse. Contemplation of the acts by which England has acquired over eighty possessions—settlements, colonies, protectorates, etc.—does not arouse feelings of satisfaction. The transitions from missionaries to resident agents, then to officials having armed forces, then to punishments of those who resist their rule, ending in so-called "pacification"—these processes of annexation, now gradual and now sudden, as that of the new Indian province and that of Baretziland, which was declared a British colony with no more regard for the wills of the inhabiting people than for those of the inhabiting beasts—do not excite sympathy with their perpetrators.

Love of country is not fostered in me on remembering that when, after our Prime Minister had declared that we were bound in honor to the khedive to reconquer the Soudan, we, after the reconquest, forthwith began to administer it in the name of the queen and the khedive—practically annexing it; nor when, after promising through the mouths of two colonial ministers not to interfere in the internal affairs of the Transvaal, we proceeded to insist on certain electoral arrangements, and made resistance the excuse for a desolating war.* Nor does the national character shown by a popular ovation to a leader of filibusters, or by the according of a university honor to an arch-conspirator, or by the uproarious applause with which undergraduates greeted one who sneered at the "unctuous rectitude" of those who opposed his plans of aggression, appear to me lovable. If because my love of country does not survive these and many other adverse experiences I am called unpatriotic—well, I am content to be so called.

To me the cry "Our country, right or wrong!" seems detestable. By association with love of country the sentiment it expresses gains a certain justification. Do but pull off the cloak, however, and the contained sentiment is seen to be of the lowest. Let us observe the alternative cases.

Suppose our country is in the right—suppose it is resisting invasion. Then the idea and feeling embodied in the cry are righteous. It may be effectively contended that self-defense is not only justified but is a duty. Now suppose, contrariwise, that our country is the aggressor—has taken

* We continue to hear repeated the transparent excuse that the Boers commenced the war. In the far west of the U.S., where every man carries his life in his hand and the usages of fighting are well understood, it is held that he is the aggressor who first moves his hand toward his weapon. The application is obvious.

possession of others' territory, or is forcing by arms certain commodities on a nation which does not want them, or is backing up some of its agents in "punishing" those who have retaliated. Suppose it is doing something which, by the hypothesis, is admitted to be wrong. What is then the implication of the cry? The right is on the side of those who oppose us; the wrong is on our side. How in that case is to be expressed the so-called patriotic wish? Evidently the words must stand, "Down with the right, up with the wrong!" Now, in other relations this combination of aims implies the acme of wickedness. In the minds of past men there existed, and there still exists in many minds, a belief in a personalized principle of evil—a being going up and down in the world everywhere fighting against the good and helping the bad to triumph. Can there be more briefly expressed the aim of that being than in the words "Up with the wrong and down with the right"? Do the so-called patriots like the endorsement?

Some years ago I gave expression to my own feeling—antipatriotic feeling, it will doubtless be called—in a somewhat startling way. It was at the time of the second Afghan war, when, in pursuance of what were thought to be "our interests," we were invading Afghanistan. News had come that some of our troops were in danger. At the Athenaeum Club a well-known military man—then a captain but now a general—drew my attention to a telegram containing this news, and read it to me in a manner implying the belief that I should share his anxiety. I astounded him by replying, "When men hire themselves out to shoot other men to order, asking nothing about the justice of their cause, I don't care if they are shot themselves."

I foresee the exclamation which will be called forth. Such a principle, it will be said, if accepted, would make an army impossible and a government powerless. It would never do to have each soldier use his judgment about the purpose for which a battle is waged. Military organization would be paralyzed and our country would be a prey to the first invader.

Not so fast, is the reply. For one war an army would remain just as available as now—a war of national defense. In such a war every soldier would be conscious of the justice of his cause. He would not be engaged in dealing death among men about whose doings, good or ill, he knew nothing, but among men who were manifest transgressors against himself and his compatriots. Only aggressive war would be negatived, not defensive war.

Of course it may be said, and said truly, that if there is no aggressive war there can be no defensive war. It is clear, however, that one nation may limit itself to defensive war when other nations do not. So that the principle remains operative.

But those whose cry is "Our country, right or wrong!" and who would add to our eighty-odd possessions others to be similarly obtained, will contemplate with disgust such a restriction upon military action. To them no folly seems greater than that of practicing on Monday the principles they profess on Sunday.

Alfred Love

urges a friend not to serve as a chaplain in the Civil War

ALFRED H. LOVE [1830-1913] *was among the few men in the American peace movement who opposed the Civil War. When he was drafted in 1863, he refused to serve or to exercise his privilege of producing a substitute to serve in his place. The Universal Peace Society—a group of nonresistants who left the American Peace Society when it acquiesced in the Civil War—chose Love as its first president. He not only urged arbitration in international affairs, he was also a pioneer in the idea of using arbitration in disputes between labor and capital, and he acted as a mediator in strikes.*

Riverton, 8th mo. 22d, 1861

William J. Mullen:

MY GOOD AND ESTEEMED FRIEND:

The accidental turn of our conversation, a few evenings since, was remarkable, and must prove full of meaning. Returning from a meeting of the Philadelphia Society for Alleviating the Miseries of Public Prisons, the philanthropic objects of which enlist our attention, and of which I find thee its active and indefatigable agent, gaining so much merited praise and popularity by thy full appreciation of the sufferings of the unfortunate and needy, and thy self-sacrificing life service in ameliorating their condition; returning from this meeting I was, indeed, astonished at the announcement of thy abandoning thy peace principles for the present, owing to the peculiar demands of the war for the government and the

Union, and accepting a position as chaplain of a body of soldiers. It seems strange that such a one can be found countenancing war under any circumstances, especially when impressed with proclivities so philanthropic and humanitarian.

Excuse me if I reflect too severely. But thy having been associated with the Peace Society of Pennsylvania, and for several years its treasurer; having been imbued with the importance of pure peace principles, and even now acknowledging their virtue; unwilling to recall a single word of thy testimonies against war, and intending, when this war is over, to espouse again those principles, render thee far more recreant to the trust imposed by our Father, than one who has not advanced to this high moral standard. There is far more reproach deserved by thee, than one whose conscience has not been thus touched, and whose time and talents have been differently directed.

Holding a position so responsible and enviable, such a one as but few men are competent to occupy, when accepting a level with fighting men, thy fall becomes a melancholy one indeed. As a light in the world, thy good services have caused thee to be respected, and followed by those less gifted and favored. Be careful then and do not deceive them. Acknowledging war a horrible evil, and yet accepting it on account of the cause, seemingly so just, is not calculated to lessen its enormity, nor elevate thee in the estimation of those poor, unfortunate people who so readily spring to arms at the least provocation. Nor can the evils be mitigated by saying "there are some more horrible." The proposition, "of two evils choose the lesser," is fallacious. The moment we recognize the evils, we presuppose the right; therefore of two evils choose neither—choose the right, for it admits of no comparative degree—no alternative. The positive admission of its being an evil, should, therefore, deter thee from taking any part, or encouraging others to do so. It seems almost unnecessary to weigh war in the scale of horrible evils. Where is the evil that is parent to more sin and crime than this, and more fully superinduces a transgression of every one of the ten commandments; in short, ignores virtue, morality and a Christlike life. Still, I am willing to leave the portentousness of the evil to every one's estimate, sufficient it certainly is, that it is an evil—then reject it! Although a pure nonresistance by carnal weapons politically considered, may seem at this time impracticable, yet as Christians, we must know nothing of expediency, for that presupposes a palliation of evil; we must know nothing of compromises, for that mediates an agreement with wickedness; we must know nothing of majorities or minorities, for that engenders fear, and a reliance upon others, rather than ourselves. All we should know is our duty guided by the conscientious and revealed right. Procrastination should not be in the vocabulary of the friend of man. Admitting my premises are right, why say it is too late to talk peace and irresistance; that it may do hereafter; that this is not the millennium? Why do we make milleniums! They are the highest development of our spiritual nature, attainable only by lives of purity and virtue, by abjuring the use of carnal weapons and adopting a system of universal benevolence and love to mankind. Why defer, and yet be conscious of thy error? It is never too late to do right. Life is short, uncertain and transitory, and often enfeebled by sickness and obstructed with cares. No! "Act in the living present." Procrastination has been called "the thief of time." It is so, and more, it is the thief of duty. . . . Procrastination murders the outbursting of the Divine Spirit, which ought to act promptly when the cause is presented. It kills ambition, deadens enterprise and destroys true manhood. Surely this trait should receive no encouragement from one, who so boldly proclaims, that when this war is over, he will espouse again former peace principles and testimonies. . . .

Think of the possibility of thy not living till the war is over. I find thee in the full vigor of life and health, and yet next week we may be in our graves. Do not defer then thy noble intentions! We must begin sometime, and that time is when the spirit prompts and the exigency arises.

Recollect that life is a test, we are placed here for trial, well fortified by examples, revelation, reason and conscience, for a higher state of existence in the future. The test of the present is probably one of the severest that could be presented to the American citizen. But we have been boastful of our enlightenment and morality, and require severe tests. Our feelings are at once enlisted, and our impulses are to rush to arms in the defense of our rights and the support of our government. But where do we weigh the heaviest? Where is thy influence the greater? In the army and on the battlefield, or in thy God-given round of duties—in the prison and on the streets of a crowded city? Why, in the former position, the first fire of the enemy may take thy life; in the latter, thy services cease only with sickness, accident, the infirmities of age or thy natural demise. In the one case, thy life is subjected to destruction, and in the other it is reserved for thy Creator, for the fulfillment of the mission of its creation.

Mark the effect of thy encouraging war, *this or any other*. Those who look up to thee—follow. Becoming absorbed in the enthusiasm of the hour, we float along on the swelling tide, forgetful that popular movements always should be carefully watched, often even doubted. Let us heed that we do not become driftwood. The rushing tide has overleaped its banks, driftwood will not dam it—will not control it—rock masonry will. Stay this flood of waters, and it will deepen and compose; and its great powers, instead of dashing along uncontrolled, to waste, devastating all in its course, may be used to turn the glorious machinery of the world, the grist mills and the sawmills—the wheels of thought and action, of utility and morality!

Thou kindly handed me a report of thy speech made at the late sword presentation, soliciting a reply; and in a deep impressive wood, at sunrise, upon a summer's morning of smiles and cheer, I have read and conned it over. Seated near the Delaware, an unromantic stream just here, yet hallowed by the example of William Penn, who without a precedent in history, and against the advice of worldly men, settled in the midst of savages on principles of nonresistance; this river seems to have received the kiss of Divinity, and to mirror back a lesson for all future time, and its ebbing and flowing seem to me a kind of re-echo from the great founder, in the very city in which I find thee living and fulfilling thy beautiful mission.

Heed then, my friend, this spirit! The government of Penn existed in its purity and unimpaired, the same length of time as that of the United States—a strange coincidence! It would have continued, but for the adoption of carnal weapons as a means of defense, by those who succeeded to the government, after the death of Penn and his immediate followers. The type that I read is this river, the composure of these woods, the serenity of sky, the harmony of all around me, the matins of birds, the glow of sun—all these types are large and can be read by old eyes and young eyes—yes, educated and uneducated, and they mean peace, utility and purity. Conning thy address in such a place, surrounded by such divine influences and stimulated by the warmest friendship and concern for thee, excuse me if I condemn rather than commend that which, rhetorically considered, I so much admire and the sentiment of which many, from their own standpoints, will very much applaud. I regret it was ever made.

"Having been requested by members of the church to present a sword as a testimonial of their attachment to the cause for which it is destined to be used." To me it is a sad commentary upon the church, which should be the synonym of godliness teaching the fatherhood of God and the brotherhood of man, to present a weapon of revenge and death. This very church, professedly, has been promulgating the "golden rule" of "Do unto others as you would have them do unto you," and that other rule, of doubly refined gold, "Love your enemies." It has been urging "Love thy neighbor as thyself"; "Return good for evil"; "Whosoever smiteth thee upon one cheek, turn to him the other also"; "Overcome evil with good"; "Resist not evil" and all the precepts of love, meekness, peace and submission. Take the Sermon on the Mount as an instance. How strange then is it, that for the church, the sword is presented. What are its principles worth, if when the time comes to try them, they are laid aside? What is the example of the "meek and lowly Jesus" worth, if it is followed and recommended until the test of all comes, and then is rejected? What is our conscience worth, if when we consult it we find it points to our responsibility as children of an impartial and loving

Father, and reveals our highest duty to Him, rather than an imagined duty to country?

Deep indeed are the sensibilities of our countrymen, and when touched are quickly moved. How unfortunate is it that we should be under the war power. If we were as easily moved by the peace motive, the result would be enduring. We find our people in the midst of military training, learning the *arts of war*. Enthusiasm leads—we blindly follow.

From 50,000 churches the cry goes forth for war, and thou endorses it, in accepting thy present position. Even in our public schools the lesson seems taught, and legislatures have proposed the establishment of military professorships in our colleges and schools. Let Americans pause ere they take this step, or there may be a reaction dreadful to realize.

Rather let our halls, churches and parks be thrown open to teach the *arts of peace*. They never yet have been fully developed.

They are not confined merely to education and prayer, but comprehend proper amusements, mutual sympathy, cheer and social life—pure and liberal—the development of freedom, the exclusion of caste and the guaranties of the rights of man. These will draw us together most securely. . . .

Patriotism used to mean love of country, and was then a virtue; but now it seems to be a love to have our own way, in our country, and is now ambition. The true patriot is one who loves to develop the highest excellence of his Father's bounty-land, and comprehends soil, institutions and his fellow men, untrammeled by geographical or genealogical lines. We forget that God is above country, and while the latter may do to live by, he alone will do to die by. Love of liberty, of life, family and home, are all virtues; but we must be watchful that the means used to protect them subserve the highest moral authority. The patriotism which says, I do not know how to fight—I will not learn—I would not fight if I knew how, nor aid others in doing so—a patriotism which elevates the spiritual above the animal nature; which regards the slaveholder less an enemy than an unfortunate, misguided and erring brother, who requires even more love and solicitude; which does not call him brute or savage, though facts might justify such expression; that metes out, the more he errs, kindness and goodness, with an earnest vindication of all the rights of humanity, an advanced civilization and the love of the whole country, with the love of its countrymen—such patriotism opens up the duties of the true citizen and patriot, and fears no peril to self or nation.

This sword is presented for the church, and for the past services therein of the recipient. Art thou not, on the one hand, desecrating the spirit of the church, and he, on the other, proving recreant to its teachings?

Why ask him to accept this sword "to be drawn in the defense of our holy religion"? A religion that needs the defense of the sword is not holy, nor worth defending. The moment it demands such protection, it ceases to be acceptable to our Father, who taught a religion in the example of his beloved Son, of meekness with firmness, submission with persuasion, martyrdom with resurrection.

"If we triumph in this struggle, our posterity will be favored with freedom." Was there ever a perfect, satisfactory and permanent freedom secured by successful war? "The world's history is the world's judgment doom," and the annals of history prove that war begets war, as evil begets evil. It is so demoralizing that it seems to live in the very vitals of the nation, permeating the institutions of the country, and cramping the full development of that freedom, which knows no sect, color or condition, restrained alone by strict justice and pure virtue. No! Freedom is not secured by the sword—military despotism, oppression and contention are to be feared continually.

"But I should be a traitor to my country were I to refuse to take part in this contest." Is there but one way to take part? Is the spirit of nonresistance by force of arms such a cushioned-pew, easy rocking-chair or feather-bed existence that it demands no action; and are all who decline to join the army, or aid others in doing so, traitors? No! The work that opens to the nonresistant at this time is immense. It consists in arguing and appealing, petitioning and protesting, in demanding and prayerfully desiring—using the great levers of an enlightened age; these moral forces of action and example that are truly difficult, yet invincible. No! Thou wouldst be far from traitor by grasping with these difficulties on the purest peace basis, with a view to develop the highest claims of morality, by a long, anxious, unremitted, even if unpopular, effort. By testimonies that would bear trial and even martyrdom; and all for the love of our country, our fellow men, and our Creator.

"Under our national government the oppressed and down-trodden of every land on earth have found and may find a safe refuge." Forget not the African and the Indian! Thou dost not seem to forget the former, but alludes to the 4,000,000 enslaved, and yet this boastful North is verily guilty of the curse to a very great extent. I know thy sympathies are deeply moved in their behalf, but should we be so well satisfied that this war is the "death blow to slavery"? I mean slavery in its widest sense. There may open opportunities when slaves will be liberated, and how eager some will be to shield their war doctrines by proclaiming it the good work of war; unwilling to give credit, where it properly belongs, to the long, anxious and earnest efforts, of the purest *moral forces,* rather than the direct agency of the sword.

Should such glorious results, however, be accomplished, by other means than the pressure of moral sentiment, beware that it does not give a significance to war that will react; and hereafter, when any object is desired, this power will be adopted with the word: Oh! It achieved victories for the government and the slave, in days gone by, *we* will use it now, for our purposes. Thus we will be under the oppression of military power—standing armies—the slavery of the sword! Then, too, we may fear the slavery of caste—the exclusion of a portion of God's children from equal rights, because of some imagined disqualification of color. Be careful then and do not use *wicked* means even to free the slave!

Some, indeed, may be influenced by the injunction "Thou shalt let the oppressed go free"; but this does not comprehend, and cannot be construed, to mean, Thou shalt *compel* the oppressor to let the oppressed go free. Can so sublime a virtue as perfect freedom, a child so pure, a consummation so devoutly desired, be the offspring of so corrupt a parentage as war? Is it possible that a people so diverted from the even tenor of their way, and so demoralized by war, should not imbibe an irritability of spirit, and disposition for contention that will undervalue real worth, cheapen life and give a sway to evil passions, that when the war is over, and perhaps while it lasts, may be demonstrated against those who have urged, and still urge the abolition of slavery as the greatest boon to humanity and the whole-country? We see it already in our midst—the spirit of dissatisfaction is madly on the increase. We well know that many who are engaged in the war are opposed to the abolitionists, and it is not likely they can be changed from hatred and opposition to love and cooperation. If they were to, I should have little faith in such "eleventh hour" conversions, for they would be the conversions of the bullet, rather than the heart, and not reliable; beyond all—the plain, uphill tug of moral force is to be depended upon. Patience, with unremitted moral effort, will secure devout ends.

The idea that this is a war for the rights and liberties of the Negro, north and south—is it not illusory? It has never been proclaimed by government or permitted by generals. So far, indeed, is such an expression from the heads of the movement that to breathe it would seem to them (strangely deceived as they are) certain defeat, loss of forces and a deadening of the enthusiasm. I fear a cause that will not bear the fullest exposure, and rejects a volunteer on account of his color. I fear a treaty made under such auspices, for it is not impossible, or improbable, that not a single word will be uttered relative to the cause. The history of treaties proves this: take the Madison treaty at Ghent as an example.

The shout is, "The Union, the Constitution and the enforcement of the laws." A political trinity, which under immoral influences, resolves itself into a Union of greatest discord, and held together by other laws than those of attraction; but which in its *purity* comprehends the fullest concord, obedience and the recognition of all the inalienable rights of the people. We have not had such since the birth of the nation, and it is scarcely to be expected, when we started with slavery, and promulgated in our Declaration of Independence a monstrous falsehood. The American citizen seems to want no higher motive than this trinity; but he needs the purest means, and he should have the highest aims. What a sad commentary upon our age and country, if after the war is over, the unfortunate compromises with slavery and wrong should be reaffirmed, the old Union with all its oppressions re-established, and the influence of our choicest spirits wasted. Such is not the mission of America! Whereas, what a splendid achievement it would be to find our countrymen, whether in victory or defeat, masters throughout of themselves, contending unflinchingly with brain, with tongue, with pen and example, for the abolition of slavery, the purity of government and the rights of man, from the very requirements of morality. Such appeals are not lost upon mankind. . . .

Suppose the three-quarters of a million of northern men now enrolled for war were to present themselves in plain citizen's dress, without the sword and trappings of war, to the South, as their brothers and friends, with the word: We will not fight; if blood is to be shed to consecrate our cause, it will have to be ours—we will not take your lives—we will love you and will aid you for all moral ends—we appeal to your best natures for our rights and the welfare of the whole human family. Grant our request, and you shall not regret it! If you force us to submission, we submit, rather than engage in war. We can make no compromise with injustice and inhumanity, as we will resort to no inhumanity for expediency. We will make use of all the *moral forces* in our power for the *right,* whatever be our condition, and will never deny our Lord and Master!

With such a course I cannot believe a single hair of the head would be harmed. No army, especially no American army, would sacrifice many lives, but eventually grant all the rights that could be conquered by the victorious sword. And this without the horrors of bloodshed, the legalized robbery, the profuse drunkenness, profanity and demoralization which are the concomitants of war. Without, too, the immense debt which we are imposing upon ourselves and our posterity, at the rate of $2,000,000 per day. Why, if this investment of money, of brain and muscle, were appropriated to removing the *cause* of our difficulties, and converting and cementing our countrymen, we would achieve permanent victories, and transmit to our children an inestimable legacy. I do not pretend that this course would be feasible under *all* circumstances in the midst of wicked and unreflective war, excepting by an entire revolution of sentiment. It would be like calling in a physician expecting him to cure a dying patient when improper remedies had been administered. Still, if *politically* impracticable at present, I know it is *morally* right, and mean to offer it as a preventive and as a duty—a course eminently calculated for an enlightened age and republican government, and the surest manner of establishing it for any future time, is to begin *now*. Hence, I repeat, let the testimony of a pure nonresistance be the germ of an honorable plan to settle difficulties. If for nothing else, I respect our Constitution because it is an amendable document, and we cannot too soon amend it, and place our government upon such a moral basis as will relieve our President, our Cabinet, our Congress and ourselves from what are regarded as political obligations. It is our duty to assimilate the law of the land with the immaculate law of our Father in heaven.

What a sublime spectacle it would be to find a people willing to relinquish their artificial claims of country for the sake of peace and carrying out the great principles of Christ. There never has been a nation willing to relinquish a single inch of territory. Why not part with discordant members for the sake of Union, which means harmony; why not be willing to retreat and retire into such a domain as would be harmonious, and where the rights of all of God's creatures would be recognized? This would, indeed, be an example of purity and morality challenging respect, and worthy of imitation. As there was free will in the formation of the Union, for mutual benefit, let it be maintained upon this free-will policy, which has been the admiration of the world. . . .

Thine, hopefully and fraternally,

ALFRED H. LOVE

Elihu Burritt

proposes a working man's strike against war

ELIHU BURRITT [1810-1879] *worked as a blacksmith and taught himself almost all the European and Asiatic languages. From 1844-51, he published* The Christian Citizen, *a weekly newspaper devoted to temperance, antislavery and world peace. While he was in England in 1846, he founded the League of Universal Brotherhood. Burritt was one of the first to support a congress of nations as a means against war, and in 1848 he organized the Brussels Congress of Friends of Peace. He was instrumental in bringing the American antiwar movement together with European peace groups.*

Nations, like individuals, often come to junctures in their lives where two if not four roads meet, and one of these they must take with all the hazards of the choice. The world has seen pretty clearly the road which all the nations of Europe have been traveling for the last quarter of a century. The world sees now what their armed-peace system has brought them to. For all this period they have been running neck and neck in this costly and perilous race of war armaments. This delusion has grown by what it fed upon. Every additional regiment on land, or ironclad put on the sea by one, has created more suspicion in the other, and that suspicion has reproduced its kind in *defenses* against the increased danger. Thus, while all these nations have been stoutly protesting against an intention to invade or injure a neighbor *offensively,* their *defenses* have been steadily growing from year to year until they have reached that point and peril of magnitude at which Disraeli has called them "bloated armaments."

This, then, is the juncture at which two roads meet on the highway thus far traveled by the nations of Europe. They are now to determine whether they will go straight forward in the old beaten track, or diverge into a new path. At this junction point there are several finger posts of much significance, and a milestone covered with deeply engraved figures relating to the periodical totals of past experience. All these should be like warning voices before and behind them at the opening of the new road, saying, "This is the way; walk ye therein." With all these voices from before and behind them, will they take the new road? If they do, they must first hold a council at the junction. We cannot expect that one of them will be brave enough to enter it alone. They must hold a congress to agree upon taking step and keeping step in this new march in another direction.

There is no time to lose in this decision. The great, honest, toiling masses of the world have waited for them long to take this new road. These masses are beginning to feel a strength that their governments would do well to heed now, before it takes an inconvenient direction for the powers that be. They have been feeling for some time past the strength of a common sentiment, interest and experience and inheritance. They are beginning to get their eyes open to some of the wicked delusions that have victimized them in past generations. They begin to see whither they have been led, and how they have been cheated, by the siren lights and siren songs of a false patriotism. And while this deceptive music was still in their ears, they have shaken hands with each other across the boundaries that once made them enemies. And the hands they interfolded in friendly grasp felt very much alike each other, hard and horny with their common lot. And they have compared the blisters and callous ridges made on their hands by "foreign policies." They have weighted and compared the burdens put upon them by their governments, and found and said that the most crushing of them all was the armed-peace system of Christendom.

And their governments, at the junction of the two roads, will do well to heed now, and honestly, what these workingmen, in congress assembled, feel, and say, and determine in regard to this system. Their feeling and meaning grow stronger and louder on the subject every time they meet in their international assembly; and, doubtless, they will meet every year, and their annual parliaments will begin soon to legislate for the great democracy of labor throughout the civilized world. And "the great powers," at the junction of the two roads, will do well to heed this habit of their workingmen of sending their representatives, chosen at primary meetings, to these annual parliaments. It is a very significant and portentous habit in itself. And their *agenda* and *facienda* are more portentous still to the powers that be. If they work out their program, it will upset the classic poetry of that malignant patriotism which worships silken rags covered with beastial emblems, and sacrifices to the idolatry more human blood than all the pagan altars of this wide world ever drank this side of the murder of Abel. It is very rude, very unsentimental, and unpatriotic for them to say and purpose these things when they come together in this way. It will doubtless shock the sensibilities of the whole military aristocracy of Christendom, and of all the students, professors and amateurs of the school and history of military glory, to hear what these workingmen will say in the next session of their parliament. They have said strong things before about war and its burdens upon them. But this time their representatives will have to pass to their assembly half a million of fresh graves in France and Germany, wherein lie, like buried dogs, half a million of their own fraternity of toil, taken from honest labor to mutual butchery on the field of battle. They will see a million of blackened, blasted homes on their way, and widows and orphans trying to quench the still red ashes of those homes with their own tears. They will see wan, armless or legless men by the ten thousands begging on crutches, by the roadside, for the bread they once earned and ate by the sweat of the brow. Now, these sights and the low, faint voices of woe they will see and hear on their way to their parliament will very sensibly affect their discussions, and give an utterance and a character to their resolutions which their governments, at the junction of the two roads, will do well to heed in advance, anticipate and supersede by their own action. Such action, honest and effective and immediate, is their only alternative, if they would evade or check the rising of a power too strong for their old "foreign policy."

What is asked of the great powers, at the junction of the two roads, is a very simple, straightforward matter. It is the step proposed to them, before these late and bloody wars, by Louis Napoleon; to convene a congress of nations to agree upon a *ratio* of general and simultaneous disarmament. The idea was not original with him, for it had been developed and propounded by eminent philosophers and philanthropists for two hundred years. But he was the first reigning sovereign in the world that ever proposed the measure to the nations. We may justly say that for him in his prison, which he would never have seen had the other great powers accepted his proposition.

The toiling, patient masses of the great commonwealth of labor do not ask a great deal of these powers; they do not say how far in the new road they shall reach at the first step, but that they shall make one, however small. They know what a thorny crop of suspicions the armed-peace system has grown among them. Therefore they will be contented with a very short step that brings their faces and feet in the right direction. Even if they should only venture to reduce their standing armies by sending home to the plow or hammer, one man in five, they would be satisfied with the installment, knowing that it would be followed by larger reductions. Even a reduction of one-fifth of the present armed-peace expenditure, to begin with, would so lighten the burden upon the masses of the people of Christendom that they would feel the relief at every meal and at every hour of their toil. Just think what that small, tentative reduction would do. In the first place it would send back to peaceful and reproductive labor nearly a million of picked, stalwart men from the armies of Europe. See what it would do for England, who does not pretend to be a military power in the French or German sense. One-fifth taken from the expense of her armed peace establishment for 1870 would be £5,600,000. Think what taxes might be lifted from the people by that small *ratio* of reduction. But the workingmen and women in France, Germany, Italy and other continental countries would be more relieved still by this reduction, because their wages do not average, in the gross, more than half what their English brethren receive for their labor.

Now, if the press, the platform and the pulpit of these Christian countries have any power with their governments, every consideration that should move them ought to enlist their best influence in behalf of a congress of nations for this one object to begin with, whatever other measures it might subsequently accomplish. The necessity is very pressing for such a congress to be convened before the next parliament of the workingmen of Christendom. Their national organizations, represented in these parliaments, are growing more and more powerful. And when they meet next time, they will see the condition and prospects of their class in a new light, and feel them with a new sensibility. They may not strive to alter the past, but they will grasp at their future with a rough strength of heart and hand which the great powers, at the junction of the two roads, will do well to anticipate and avoid. Poor, patient masses! Thousands and tens of thousands of them have fought, bled and died for national territory who could not buy enough in that or their own land to make their graves in. They cannot change this new and horrible past of one year's length. This huge abomination of desolation wrought upon the late peaceful and sunny bosom of Europe, will fall upon their industry and life of toil and trial with a burden they never bore before. As the yoke upon the necks of two working oxen presses upon each with equal weight, so the yoke of this great war's burden will bear with equal weight upon the raw necks of the French and German working classes. They will have to work out the damages done to each other by this war. The yoke will gall and bend alike victors and vanquished; and the weight will tell on every plow, sickle and spindle in Europe, and on every meal earned by these honest tools.

This is the new weight that the armed-peace system has just now added to the burdens it had before put upon the working classes of Europe. Now then, if the great powers, at the junction of the two roads, do not say to this destroying angel, begotten and winged of their madness and folly, "It is enough," its millions of patient victims, even without a Moses, may break the bondage and find on their side and behalf the same God who led an equal number of workingmen, more lightly taxed, to a better land and condition. It may appear unnatural and unseemly for an edge-tool to rebel and turn against the hand that wields it. It will doubtless spoil the romance of modern chivalry, and many martial songs of military glory, if the "food for powder" should rebel at the cannon's mouth. It may even disgust the classic predilections of the great class of hero worshipers and hero makers if the workingmen of Christendom venture to put an end to such pretentious valuations upon their earthly possibilities as to believe they are worth more for producing food for man and beast, than for feeding with their own flesh and blood the hungry maws of mortar and *mitrailleuses* on fields of human slaughter.

But the great powers, at the junction of the two roads, must face the alternative before them. These workingmen have been practicing for several years on "strikes," organized to affect their condition throughout large sections of their country. They have been perfecting the machinery and the forces of these combinations for a wider field of action, and in their last parliament they decided upon the field for employing their co-operative forces; they proposed a strike against war, and the whole armed-peace system, when they last met. If they had motive then for this resolution, what a trebled one will they have at their next session to carry out that resolution! This, then, is the alternative: either a congress of nations for simultaneous and proportionate disarmament, or an organized strike of the workingmen of Christendom against war, root and branch. The great powers, at the junction of the two roads, must choose without delay which of these two measures they will adopt.

William Lloyd Garrison
denies that nonresistance is a state of "passivity"

WILLIAM LLOYD GARRISON [1805-1879] *was born in Newburyport, Massachusetts. He became a newspaper writer, and in 1831 began publication of the* Liberator, *a newspaper devoted to agitating against slavery, war, liquor and capital punishment. He founded the first anti-slavery society in 1832. Three years later he was mobbed and almost lynched in Boston by antiabolitionists. Though he fought for years to abolish slavery on moral grounds, in 1856 he said: "Peace or war is a secondary consideration in view of our present perils. Slavery must be conquered—peaceably if we can, forcibly if we must." "The Practical Working of Non-Resistance" was published in 1852.*

An esteemed correspondent expresses a doubt as to the practical working of nonresistance, as applied to the case of Austrian despotism, for example. But is that despotism the result of an adoption, or of a rejection of the principle of nonresistance? Clearly the latter. Is the principle, then, to be discarded, in order to put down that which it radically condemns and utterly repudiates? Is this philosophical? Can Beelzebub cast out Beelzebub? Is evil to be overcome with evil? True, the cause of justice and liberty must eventually triumph, whether by or without a resort to murderous weapons; but it will not be because of those weapons, but because of its inherent goodness, and the transitory nature of tyranny. There will be no real freedom or security among mankind until they beat their swords into plowshares, and their spears into pruning hooks, and learn war no more.

We grant that every successful struggle for freedom on the part of the oppressed, even with the aid of cannon and bombshells, is to be hailed with rejoicing; but simply in reference to its object, and not to the mode of its accomplishment. That a people sufficiently enlightened to be conscious of their degradation, yet far from being morally and spiritually regenerated, should take up arms against their merciless oppressors, is not surprising—nay, it is inevitable, in their condition; but this is no real justification of revenge or murder on their part. If they were truly pure and good, theirs would be the course of Jesus and his apostles, of prophets and "the noble army of martyrs and confessors," in maintaining the right and in confronting the wrong—a course attended by no crime, stained by no blood excepting their own freely shed for their enemies, divinely magnanimous, and "mighty through God to the pulling down of strong holds"—a course which wholly eclipses, in power and glory, any ever pursued by blood-spilling revolutionists.

Our correspondent burns with indignation in view of Austrian tyranny; so do we. He rejoices to see its victims rising against it; so do we. He is in doubt whether the principle of nonresistance, if adopted by them, would procure for them the deliverance they seek; we are not. A people able to adopt that principle in theory and practice cannot possibly be enslaved, any more than the angels of God; and no form of despotism can make them servile. They do not fear the face of the tyrant, and it is their mission to "beard the lion in his den." They may be burnt to ashes, but they can never be conquered. Theirs is the "unresistible might of weakness" (to borrow the expressive language of Milton), and no weapon used against them shall prosper. But no people, constituting a nation, has reached this sublime state of moral exaltation; all are more or less brutal, eager for revenge in case of suffering, and incapable of understanding how they who take the sword shall perish with the sword. This is to be lamented; but it is history. Surely it is no reason why those who are "under grace" should abandon their position, and discard Jesus, the nonresistant, for Moses or Joshua, the warrior.

Our correspondent is greatly in error in speaking of nonresistance as a state of "passivity." On the contrary, it is a state of activity, ever fighting the good fight of faith, ever foremost to assail unjust power, ever struggling for "liberty, equality, fraternity," in no national sense, but in a world-wide spirit. It is passive only in this sense—that it will not return evil for evil, nor give blow for blow, nor resort to murderous weapons for protection or defense. In its purity it is the blending of the gentleness and innocency of the Lamb of God with the courage and strength of the Lion of the tribe of Judah.

Victor Hugo
calls on all nations to hasten the day of international unity

VICTOR HUGO [1802-1885], *the great French poet, dramatist and novelist, was for a long time the leader of the romantic school of writing in Europe. He was born in Besançon, where his father was an officer with Napoleon, and though he had only sporadic schooling, he was a writer from his early boyhood. By the time he was nineteen he had won two prizes for his poetry. Hugo lived in a privileged position under Louis Philippe, but he became a republican and was forced to flee the country during the reign of Napoleon III. Just two years before that, at the International Conference for Peace in Paris in 1849, Hugo proposed a United States of Europe.*

Gentlemen: Many of you have come from the most distant points of the globe, your hearts full of holy and religious feelings. You count in your ranks men of letters, philosophers, ministers of the Christian religion, writers of eminence, and public men justly popular for their talents. You, gentlemen, have wished to adopt Paris as the center of this meeting, whose sympathies, full of gravity and conviction, do not merely apply to one nation, but to the whole world. You come to add another principle of a still superior—of a more august kind—to those that now direct statesmen, rulers and legislators. You turn over, as it were, the last page of the gospel—that page which imposes peace on the children of the same God; and in this capital, which has as yet only decreed fraternity among citizens, you are about to proclaim the brotherhood of mankind.

Gentlemen, we bid you a hearty welcome! In the presence of such a thought and such an act, there can be no room for the expression of personal thanks. Permit me, then, in the first words which I pronounce in your hearing, to raise my thoughts higher than myself, and, as it were, to omit all mention of the great honor which you have just conferred upon me, in order that I may think of nothing else than the great thing which we have met to do.

Gentlemen, this sacred idea, universal peace, all nations bound together in a common bond, the gospel for their supreme law, mediation substituted for war—this holy sentiment, I ask you, is it practicable? Can it be realized? Many practical men, many public men grown old in the management of affairs, answer in the negative. But I answer with you, and I answer without hesitation, Yes! And I shall shortly try to prove it to you. I go still further. I do not merely say it is capable of being put into practice, but I add that it is inevitable, and that its execution is only a question of time, and may be hastened or retarded. The law which rules the world is not, cannot be different from the law of God. But the divine law is not one of war—it is peace. Men commenced by conflict, as the creation did by chaos. Whence are they coming? From wars—that is evident. But whither are they going? To peace—that is equally evident. When you enunciate those sublime truths, it is not to be wondered at that your assertion should be met by a negative; it is easy to understand that your faith will be encountered by incredulity; it is evident that in this period of trouble and of dissension the idea of universal peace must surprise and shock, almost like the apparition of something impossible and ideal; it is quite clear that all will call it utopian; but for me, who am but an obscure laborer in this great work of the nineteenth century, I accept this opposition without being astonished or discouraged by it. Is it possible that you can do otherwise than turn aside your head and shut your eyes, as if in bewilderment, when in the midst of the darkness which still envelops you, you suddenly open the door that lets in the light of the future?

Gentlemen, if four centuries ago, at the period when war was made by one district against the other, between cities, and between provinces— if, I say, someone had dared to predict to Lorraine, to Picardy, to Normandy, to Brittany, to Auvergne, to Provence, to Dauphiny, to Burgundy, "A day shall come when you will no longer make wars—a day shall come when you will no longer arm men one against the other—a day shall come when it will no longer be said that the Normans are attacking the Picards, or that the people of Lorraine are repulsing the Burgundians. You will still have many disputes to settle, interests to contend for, difficulties to resolve; but do you know what you will substitute instead of armed men, instead of cavalry and infantry, of cannon, of falconets, lances, pikes and swords? You will select, instead of all this destructive array, a small box of wood, which you will term a ballot box, and from which shall issue—what?—an assembly—an assembly in which you shall all live—an assembly which shall be, as it were, the soul of all—a supreme and popular council, which shall decide, judge, resolve everything —which shall make the sword fall from every hand, and excite the love of justice in every heart—which shall say to each, 'Here terminates your right, there commences your duty: lay down your arms! Live in peace!' And in that day you will all have one common thought, common interests, a common destiny; you will embrace each other, and recognize each other as children of the same blood, and of the same race; that day you will no longer be hostile tribes, you will be a people; you will no longer be Burgundy, Normandy, Brittany or Provence—you will be France! You will no longer make appeals to war—you will do so to civilization."

If, at the period I speak of, someone had uttered these words, all men of a serious and positive character, all prudent and cautious men, all the great politicians of the period, would have cried out, "What a dreamer! What a fantastic dream! How little this pretended prophet is acquainted with the human heart! What ridiculous folly! What an absurd chimera!" Yet, gentlemen, time has gone on and on, and we find that this dream, this folly, this absurdity, has been realized! And I insist upon this, that the man who would have dared to utter so sublime a prophecy would have been pronounced a madman for having dared to pry into the designs of the Deity.

Well, then, you at this moment say—and I say it with you—we who are assembled here, say to France, to England, to Prussia, to Austria, to Spain, to Italy, to Russia—we say to them, "A day will come when from your hands also the arms you have grasped will fall. A day will come when war will appear as absurd, and be as impossible, between Paris and London, between St. Petersburg and Berlin, between Vienna and Turin, as it would be now between Rouen and Amiens, between Boston and Philadelphia. A day will come when you, France—you, Russia—you, Italy —you, England—you, Germany—all of you, nations of the Continent, will, without losing your distinctive qualities and your glorious individuality, be blended into a superior unity, and constitute a European fraternity, just as Normandy, Brittany, Burgundy, Lorraine, Alsace have been blended into France. A day will come when the only battlefield will be the market open to commerce and the mind opening to new ideas. A day will come when bullets and bombshells will be replaced by votes, by the universal suffrage of nations, by the venerable arbitration of a great Sovereign Senate, which will be to Europe what the Parliament is to England, what the Diet is to Germany, what the Legislative Assembly is to France. A day will come when a cannon will be exhibited in public museums, just as an instrument of torture is now, and people will be astonished how such a thing could have been. A day will come when those two immense groups, the United States of America and the United States of Europe, shall be seen placed in presence of each other, extending the hand of fellowship across the ocean, exchanging their produce, their commerce, their industry, their arts, their genius, clearing the earth, peopling the deserts, improving creation under the eye of the Creator, and uniting, for the good of all, these two irresistible and infinite powers, the fraternity of men and the power of God." Nor is it necessary that four hundred years should pass away for that day to come. We live in a rapid period, in the most impetuous current of events and ideas which has ever borne away humanity; and at the period in which we live, a year suffices to do the work of a century.

But French, English, Germans, Russians, Slavs, Europeans, Americans, what have we to do in order to hasten the advent of that great day? We must love each other! To love each other is, in this immense labor of pacification, the best manner of aiding God! God desires that this sublime object should be accomplished. And to arrive at it you are yourselves witnesses of what the Deity is doing on all sides. See what discoveries are every day issuing from human genius—discoveries which all tend to the same object—peace! What immense progress! What simplification! How nature is allowing herself to be more and more subjugated by man! How matter every day becomes still more the handmaid of intellect, and the auxiliary of civilization! How the causes of war vanish with the causes of suffering! How people far separated from each other so lately, now almost touch! How distances become less and less and this rapid approach, what is it but the commencement of fraternity? Thanks to railroads, Europe will soon be no larger than France was in the Middle Ages. Thanks to steamships, we now traverse the mighty ocean more easily than the Mediterranean was formerly crossed. Before long, men will traverse the earth, as the gods of Homer did the sky, in three paces! But yet a little time, and the electric wire of concord shall encircle the globe and embrace the world. And here, gentlemen, when I contemplate this vast amount of efforts and of events, all of them marked by the finger of God—when I regard this sublime object, the well-being of mankind—peace—when I reflect on all that Providence has done in favor of it, and human policy against it, a sad and bitter thought presents itself to my mind. It results, from a comparison of statistical accounts, that the nations of Europe expend each year for the maintenance of armies a sum amounting to 2,000,000,000 francs, and which, by adding the expense of maintaining establishments of war, amounts to 3,000,000,-000. Add to this the lost produce of the days of work of more than 2,000,000 men—the healthiest, the most vigorous, the youngest, the elite of our population—a produce which you will not estimate at less than 1,000,000,000 francs, and you will be convinced that the standing armies of Europe cost annually more than 4,000,000,000 francs.

Gentlemen, peace has now lasted thirty-two years, and yet in thirty-two years the enormous sum of 128,000,000 francs has been expended during a time of peace on account of war! Suppose that the people of Europe, in place of mistrusting each other, entertaining jealousy of each other, hating each other, had become fast friends—suppose they had said that before they were French, or English, or German, they were men, and that if nations form countries, the human race forms a family; and that enormous sum of 128,000,000 francs, so madly and so vainly spent in consequence of such mistrust, let it be spent in acts of mutual confidence—these 128,000,000 francs that have been lavished on hatred, let them be bestowed on love—let them be given to peace, instead of war—give them to labor, to intelligence, to industry, to commerce, to navigation, to agriculture, to science, to art; and then draw your conclusions.

If for the last thirty-two years this enormous sum had been expended in this manner, America in the meantime aiding Europe, know you what would have happened? The face of the world would have been changed. Isthmuses would be cut through, channels formed for rivers, tunnels bored through mountains. Railroads would cover the two continents; the merchant navy of the globe would have increased a hundredfold. There would be nowhere barren plains, nor moors, nor marshes. Cities would be found where there are now only deserts. Ports would be sunk where there are now only rocks. Asia would be rescued to civilization; Africa would be rescued to man; abundance would gush forth on every side, from every vein of the earth, at the touch of man, like the living stream from the rock beneath the rod of Moses. Misery would be no longer found; and with misery, what do you think would disappear? Revolutions. Yes, the face of the world would be changed! In place of mutually destroying each other, men would pacifically extend themselves over the earth. In place of conspiring for revolution, men would combine to establish colonies! In place of introducing barbarism into civilization, civilization would replace barbarism.

You see, gentlemen, in what a state of blindness war has placed nations and rulers. If the 128,000,000 francs given for the last thirty-two years by Europe to the war which was not waged had been given to the peace which existed, we positively declare that nothing of what is now passing in Europe would have occurred. The Continent in place of being a battlefield would have become a universal workshop, and in place of this sad and terrible spectacle of Piedmont prostrated, of the Eternal City given up to the miserable oscillations of human policy, of Venice and noble Hungary struggling heroically, France uneasy, impoverished and gloomy; misery, mourning, civil war, gloom in the future—in place, I say, of so sad a spectacle, we should have before our eyes hope, joy, benevolence, the efforts of all toward the common good, and we should everywhere behold the majestic ray of universal concord issue forth from civilization.

And this fact is worthy of meditation—that revolutions have been owing to those very precautions against war. All has been done, all this expenditure has been incurred, against an imaginary danger. Misery, which was the only real danger, has by these very means been augmented. We have been fortifying ourselves against a chimerical peril; our eyes have been turned to all sides except to the one where the black spot was visible. We have been looking out for wars when there were none, and we have not seen the revolutions that were coming on. Yet, gentlemen, let us not despair. Let us, on the contrary, hope more enthusiastically than ever. Let us not allow ourselves to be daunted by momentary commotions—convulsions which, peradventure, are necessary for so mighty a production. Let us not be unjust to the time in which we live—let us not look upon it otherwise than as it is. It is a prodigious and admirable epoch after all; and the nineteenth century will be, I do not hesitate to say, the greatest in the page of history. As I stated a few minutes since, all kinds of progress are being revealed and manifested almost simultaneously, the one producing the other—the cessation of international animosities, the effacing of frontiers on the maps, and of prejudices from the heart—the tendency toward unity, the softening of manners, the advancement of education, the diminution of penalties, the domination of the most literary languages—all are at work at the same time—political economy, science, industry, philosophy, legislation; and all tend to the same object—the creation of happiness and of good will, that is to say—and for my own part, it is the object to which I shall always direct myself—the extinction of misery at home, and the extinction of war abroad.

Yes, the period of revolutions is drawing to a close—the era of improvements is beginning. The education of people is no longer of the violent kind; it is now assuming a peaceful nature. The time has come when Providence is about to substitute for the disorderly action of the agitator the religious and quiet energy of the peacemaker. Henceforth the object of all great and true policy will be this—to cause all nationalities to be recognized, to restore the historic unity of nations, and enlist this unity in the cause of civilization by means of peace—to enlarge the sphere of civilization, to set a good example to people who are still in a state of barbarism—to substitute the system of arbitration for that of battles—and, in a word—and all is comprised in this—to make justice pronounce the last word that the old world used to pronounce by force.

Gentlemen, I say in conclusion, and let us be encouraged by this thought, mankind has not entered on this providential course today for the first time. In our ancient Europe, England took the first step, and by her example declared to the people, "You are free!" France took the second step, and announced to the people, "You are sovereigns!" Let us now take the third step, and all simultaneously, France, England, Germany, Italy, Europe, America—let us proclaim to all nations, "You are brethren!"

Henry David Thoreau
calls men to the duty of civil disobedience

HENRY DAVID THOREAU [1817-1862], *a New England essayist and poet, was graduated from Harvard but would not accept his diploma. "Let every sheep keep its own skin," he is reported to have said. His best-known book is the journal he kept during his experiment in living at Walden Pond. When the Mexican War came, Thoreau thought it was wrong and refused to pay his taxes. He was imprisoned. The essay "On the Duty of Civil Disobedience" sums up his feeling about the state and his rebellion against it.*

Under a government which imprisons any unjustly, the true place for a just man is also a prison. The proper place today, the only place which Massachusetts has provided for her freer and less desponding spirits, is in her prisons, to be put out and locked out of the state by her own act, as they have already put themselves out by their principles. It is there that the fugitive slave, and the Mexican prisoner on parole, and the Indian come to plead the wrongs of his race, should find them; on that separate but more free and honorable ground, where the state places those who are not *with* her but *against* her—the only house in a slave state in which a free man can abide with honor.

If any think that their influence would be lost there, and their voices no longer afflict the ear of the state, that they would not be as an enemy within its walls, they do not know by how much truth is stronger than error, nor how much more eloquently and effectively he can combat injustice who has experienced a little in his own person.

Cast your whole vote, not a strip of paper merely, but your whole influence. A minority is powerless while it conforms to the majority; it is not even a minority then; but it is irresistible when it clogs by its whole weight.

If the alternative is to keep all just men in prison, or give up war and slavery, the state will not hesitate which to choose. If a thousand men were not to pay their tax bills this year, that would not be a violent and bloody measure, as it would be to pay them, and enable the state to commit violence and shed innocent blood.

This is, in fact, the definition of a peaceful revolution, if any such is possible. If the tax gatherer or any other public officer asks me, as one has done, "But what shall I do?" my answer is, "If you really wish to do anything, resign your office." When the subject has refused allegiance, and the officer has resigned his office, then the revolution is accomplished.

But even suppose blood should flow. Is there not a sort of blood shed when the conscience is wounded? Through this wound a man's real manhood and immortality flow out, and he bleeds to an everlasting death. I see this blood flowing now. . . .

Must the citizen ever for a moment, or in the least degree, resign his conscience to the legislator? Why has every man a conscience, then? I think that we should be men first, and subjects afterwards. It is not desirable to cultivate a respect for the law so much as for the right. The only obligation which I have a right to assume is to do at any time what I think right. It is truly enough said, that a corporation has no conscience; but a corporation of conscientious men is a corporation *with* a conscience.

Law never made men a whit more just; and, by means of their respect for it, even the well-disposed are daily made the agents of injustice. A common and natural result of an undue respect for law is that you may see a file of soldiers, colonel, captain, corporal, privates, powder-monkeys, and all, marching in admirable order over hill and dale to the wars, against their wills, aye, against their common sense and consciences, which make it very steep marching indeed, and produces a palpitation of the heart. They have no doubt that it is a damnable business in which they are concerned; they are all peaceably inclined. Now, what are they? Men at all? or small movable forts and magazines, at the service of some unscrupulous man in power. . . .

The mass of men serve the state thus, not as men mainly, but as machines, with their bodies. They are the standing army, the militia, jailers, constables, posse comitatus, etc. In most cases there is no free exercise whatever of the judgment or of the moral sense; but they put themselves on a level with wood and earth and stones; and wooden men can perhaps be manufactured that will serve the purpose as well. Such command no more respect than men of straw or a lump of dirt. They have the same sort of worth only as horses and dogs. Yet such as these even are commonly esteemed good citizens.

Others—as most legislators, politicians, lawyers, ministers and office holders—serve the state chiefly with their heads; and, as they rarely make any moral distinctions, they are as likely to serve the devil, without *intending* it, as God.

A very few, as heroes, patriots, martyrs, reformers in the great sense, and *men,* serve the state with their consciences also, and so necessarily resist it for the most part; and they are commonly treated as enemies by it.

A wise man will only be useful as a man, and will not submit to be "clay," and "stop a hole to keep the wind away," but leave that office to his dust at least:

I am too high-born to be propertied,
To be secondary at control,
Or useful serving man and instrument
To any sovereign state throughout the world.

Theodore Parker
protests against the Mexican War

DR. THEODORE PARKER [1810-1860] *was a Unitarian minister, transcendentalist and social reformer, whose grandfather led the Minutemen at Lexington. Parker strongly advocated Negro freedom: he assisted in the escape of fugitive slaves, and he lent his support to John Brown. From his pulpit he continually appealed to his congregation in the cause of emancipation. Some historians feel that Parker did more to enlighten the conscience of the North than any other individual. The following is from an address delivered at an antiwar meeting in Boston on February 4, 1847.*

Mr. Chairman: We have come here to consult for the honor of our country. The honor and dignity of the United States are in danger. I love my country; I love her honor. It is dear to me almost as my own. I have seen stormy meetings in Faneuil Hall before now, and am not easily disturbed by a popular tumult. But never before did I see a body of armed soldiers attempting to overawe the majesty of the people, when met to deliberate on the people's affairs. Yet the meetings of the people of Boston have been disturbed by soldiers before now, by British bayonets; but never since the Boston Massacre on the fifth of March, 1770! Our fathers hated a standing army. This is a new one, but behold the effect! Here are soldiers with bayonets to overawe the majesty of the people! They went to our meeting last Monday night, the hireling soldiers of President Polk, to overawe and disturb the meetings of honest men. Here they are now, and in arms!

We are in a war; the signs of war are seen here in Boston. Men needed to hew wood and honestly serve society are marching about your streets; they are learning to kill men, men who never harmed us nor them; learning to kill their brothers. It is a mean and infamous war we are fighting. It is a great boy fighting a little one, and that little one feeble and sick. What makes it worse is, the little boy is in the right, and the big boy is in the wrong, and tells solemn lies to make his side seem right. He wants, besides, to make the small boy pay the expenses of the quarrel.

The friends of the war say, "Mexico has invaded our territory!" When it is shown that it is we who have invaded hers, then it is said, "Aye, but she owes us money." Better say outright, "Mexico has land, and we want to steal it!"

This war is waged for a mean and infamous purpose, for the extension of slavery. It is not enough that there are fifteen slave states, and 3,000,000 men here who have no legal rights—not so much as the horse and the ox have in Boston; it is not enough that the slaveholders annexed Texas, and made slavery perpetual therein, extending even north of Mason and Dixon's line, covering a territory forty-five times as large as the State of Massachusetts. Oh, no; we must have yet more land to whip Negroes in!

The war had a mean and infamous beginning. It began illegally, unconstitutionally. The Whigs say, "The President made the war." Mr. Webster says so! It went on meanly and infamously. Your Congress lied about it. Do not lay the blame on the Democrats; the Whigs lied just as badly. Your Congress has seldom been so single-mouthed before. Why, only sixteen voted against the war, or the lie. I say this war is mean and infamous, all the more because waged by a people calling itself democratic and Christian. I know but one war so bad in modern times, between civilized nations, and that was the war for the partition of Poland. Even for that there was more excuse.

We have come to Faneuil Hall to talk about the war; to work against the war. It is rather late, but "better late than never." We have let two opportunities for work pass unemployed. One came while the annexation of Texas was pending. Then was the time to push and be active. Then was the time for Massachusetts and all the North to protest as one man against the extension of slavery. Everybody knew all about the matter, the Democrats and the Whigs. But how few worked against that gross mischief! One noble man lifted up his warning voice [this refers to John Quincy Adams]; a man noble in his father—and there he stands in marble; noble in himself—and there he stands yet higher up; and I hope time will show him yet nobler in his son—and there he stands, not in marble, but in man! He talked against it, worked against it, fought against it. But Massachusetts did little. Her tonguey men said little; her handy men did little. Too little could not be done or said. True, we came here to Faneuil Hall and passed resolutions; good resolutions they were, too. Daniel Webster wrote them, it is said. They did the same in the State House; but nothing came of them. They say "Hell is paved with resolutions"; these were of that sort of resolutions, which resolve nothing, because they are of words, not works!

Well, we passed the resolutions; you know who opposed them; who hung back and did nothing—nothing good I mean; quite enough not good. Then we thought all the danger was over; that the resolution settled the matter. But then was the time to confound at once the enemies of your country; to show an even front hostile to slavery.

But the chosen time passed over, and nothing was done. Do not lay the blame on the Democrats; a Whig Senate annexed Texas, and so annexed a war. We ought to have told our delegation in Congress, if Texas were annexed, to come home, and we would breathe upon it and sleep upon it, and then see what to do next. Had our resolutions, taken so warmly here in Faneuil Hall in 1845, been but as warmly worked out, we had now been as terrible to the slave power as the slave power, since extended, now is to us!

Why was it that we did nothing? That is a public secret. Perhaps I ought not to tell it to the people. [Cries of "Tell it."]

The annexation of Texas, a slave territory big as the kingdom of France, would not furl a sail on the ocean; would not stop a mill wheel at Lowell! Men thought so.

That time passed by, and there came another. The government had made war; the Congress voted the dollars, voted the men, voted a lie. Your representative men of Boston voted for all three—the lie, the dollars, and the men; all three, in obedience to the slave power! Let him excuse that to the conscience of his party; it is an easy matter. I do not believe he can excuse it to his own conscience. To the conscience of the world it admits of no excuse. Your President called for volunteers, 50,000 of them. Then came an opportunity such as offers not once in one hundred years, an opportunity to speak for freedom and the rights of mankind! Then was the time for Massachusetts to stand up in the spirit of '76, and say, "We won't send a man, from Cape Ann to Williamstown— not one Yankee man, for this wicked war." Then was the time for your merchants to say, "Not a ship, not a dollar, for this wicked war"; for your manufacturers to say, "We will not make you a cannon, nor a sword, nor a kernel of powder, nor a soldier's shirt, for this wicked war." Then was the time for all good men to say, "This is a war for slavery, a mean and infamous war; an aristocratic war, a war against the best interests of mankind. If God please, we will die a thousand times, but never draw blade in this wicked war." [Cries of "Throw him over," etc.] Throw him over, what good would that do? What would you do next, after you have thrown him over? ["Drag you out of the hall!"] What good would that do? It would not wipe off the infamy of this war!—would not make it less wicked!

That is what a democratic nation, a Christian people ought to have said, ought to have done. But we did not say so; the Bay State did not say so, nor your governor, nor your merchants, nor your manufacturers, nor your good men; the governor accepted the President's decree, issued his proclamation calling for soldiers, recommended men to enlist, appealing to their "patriotism" and "humanity."

Governor Briggs is a good man; and so far I honor him. He is a temperance man, strong and consistent; I honor him for that. He is a friend of education; a friend of the people. I wish there were more such. Like many other New England men, he started from humble beginnings; but unlike many such successful men of New England, he is not ashamed of the lowest round he ever trod on. I honor him for all this. But that was a time which tried men's souls, and his soul could not stand the rack. I am sorry for him. He did as the President told him. . . .

I think there is a good deal to excuse the volunteers. I blame them, for some of them know what they are about. Yet I pity them more, for most of them, I am told, are low, ignorant men; some of them drunken and brutal. From the uproar they make here tonight, arms in their hands, I think what was told me is true! I say, I pity them. They are my brothers; not the less brothers because low and misguided. If they are so needy that they are forced to enlist by poverty, surely I pity them. If they are of good families, and know better, I pity them still more! I blame most the men that have duped the rank and file! I blame the captains and colonels, who will have least of the hardships, most of the pay, and all of the "glory." I blame the men that made the war; the men that make money out of it. I blame the great party men of the land. Did not Mr. Clay say he hoped he could slay a Mexican? [Cries, "No, he didn't."] Yes, he did; said it on Forefather's Day! Did not Mr. Webster, in the streets of Philadelphia, bid the volunteers, misguided young men, go and uphold the stars of their country? [Voices, "He did right!"] No; he should have said the stripes of his country, for every volunteer to this wicked war, is a stripe on the nation's back! Did not he declare this war unconstitutional, and threaten to impeach the President who made it, and then go and invest a son in it? Has it not been said here, "Our country, howsoever bounded," bounded by robbery or bounded by right lines! Has it not been said, all round, "Our country, right or wrong!"

I say, I blame not so much the volunteers as the famous men who deceived the nation! [Cries of "Throw him over; kill him, kill him!" and a flourish of bayonets.] Throw him over! You will not throw him over. Kill him! I shall walk home unarmed and unattended, and not a man of you will hurt one hair of my head. . . .

It is time for the people of Massachusetts to instruct their servants in Congress to oppose this war; to refuse all supplies for it; to ask for the recall of the army into our own land. It is time for us to tell them that not an inch of slave territory shall ever be added to the realm. Let us remonstrate; let us petition; let us command. If any class of men have hitherto been remiss, let them come forward now and give us their names—the merchants, the manufacturers, the Whigs and the Democrats. If men love their country better than their party or their purse, now let them show it.

Let us ask the General Court of Massachusetts to cancel every commission which the governor has given to the officers of the volunteers. Let us ask them to disband the companies not yet mustered into actual service; and then, if you like that, ask them to call a convention of the people of Massachusetts, to see what we shall do in reference to the war; in reference to the annexation of more territory; in reference to the violation of the Constitution. [Loud groans from crowds of rude fellows in several parts of the hall.] That was a Tory groan; they never dared groan so in Faneuil Hall before; not even the British Tories, when they had no bayonets to back them up! I say, let us ask for these things!

Your President tells us it is treason to talk so! Treason, is it? Treason to discuss a war which the government made, and which the people are made to pay for? If it be treason to speak against the war, what was it to make the war, to ask for 50,000 men and $74,000,000 for the war? Why, if the people cannot discuss the war they have got to fight and to pay for, who under heaven can? Whose business is it, if it is not yours and mine? If my country is in the wrong, and I know it, and hold my peace, then I am guilty of treason, moral treason. Why, a wrong—it is only the threshold of ruin. I would not have my country take the next step. Treason is it, to show that this war is wrong and wicked? Why, what if George III, any time from '75 to '83, had gone down to Parliament and told them it was treason to discuss the war then waging against these colonies! What do you think the Commons would have said? What would the Lords say? Why, that king, foolish as he was, would have been lucky, if he had not learned there was a joint in his neck, and, stiff as he bore him, that the people knew how to find it.

I do not believe in killing kings, or any other men; but I do say, in a time when the nation was not in danger, that no British king, for two hundred years past, would have dared call it treason to discuss the war— its cause, its progress, or its termination!

Now is the time to act! Twice we have let the occasion slip; beware of the third time! Let it be infamous for a New England man to enlist; for a New England merchant to loan his dollars, or to let his ships in aid of this wicked war; let it be infamous for a manufacturer to make a cannon, a sword, or a kernel of powder to kill our brothers with, while we all know that they are in the right, and we in the wrong.

I know my voice is a feeble one in Massachusetts. I have no mountainous position from whence to look down and overawe the multitude; I have no background of political reputation to echo my words. I am but a plain, humble man; but I have a background of truth to sustain me, and the justice of heaven arches over my head! For your sakes, I wish I had that oceanic eloquence whose tidal flow should bear on its bosom the driftweed which politicians have piled together, and sap and sweep away the sand hillocks of soldiery blown together by the idle wind; that oceanic eloquence which sweeps all before it, and leaves the shore hard, smooth and clean! But feeble as I am, let me beg of you, fellow citizens of Boston, men and brothers, to come forward and protest against this wicked war, and the end for which it is waged. I call on the Whigs, who love their country better than they love the tariff of '42; I call on the Democrats, who think justice is greater than the Baltimore Convention—I call on the Whigs and Democrats to come forward and join with me in opposing this wicked war! I call on the men of Boston, on the men of the old Bay State, to act worthy of their fathers, worthy of their country, worthy of themselves! Men and brothers, I call on you all to protest against this most infamous war, in the name of the state, in the name of the country, in the name of man—yes, in the name of God; leave not your children saddled with a war debt, to cripple the nation's commerce for years to come. Leave not your land cursed with slavery, extended and extending, palsying the nation's arm and corrupting the nation's heart. Leave not your memory infamous among the nations, because you feared men, feared the government; because you loved money got by crime, land plundered in war, loved land unjustly bounded; because you debased your country by defending the wrong she dared to do; because you loved slavery, loved war, but loved not the eternal justice of all-judging God. If my counsel is weak and poor, follow one stronger and more manly. I am speaking to men; think of these things, and then act like men!

Thomas Cooper
says the regeneration of the world depends on moral resistance

THOMAS COOPER [1805-1892] *was born in England. He educated himself and gave up cobbling to become first a schoolteacher, then a Methodist preacher. In 1840 he joined the staff of the Leicester* Mercury. *He became a Chartist, organized the Leicester workers into a Chartist "army," and led a general strike there in 1842. He was imprisoned for two years on a charge of sedition. During his term he saw six persons hanged in front of the Stafford Gaol, and this experience made a pacifist of him. When he was released from prison, he spoke several times against the Chartist error of physical force.*

To attempt to correct force by force—to prevent injury by injury—murder by murder—is a blunder so many thousand years old that we ought to have learned, ere this, to shake our heads at it in pity, and to abandon it. Opposite principles—new, regenerating principles—must be brought to bear on the world: new not because they have only just been discovered, but because the world at large has not hitherto acted on them. These principles only can change the world, can banish the evil competitive state, and bring about the establishment of the universal brotherhood.

"And is this principle of nonresistance what you would recommend as the great agent in true civilization?" It is; but I beg you will consider what is meant by it. I beg you will not believe that it has been properly represented as "beastly, slavish, cowardly, unmanly," and so on. Although it forbids its disciples to shed blood even in self-defense, it does not inculcate a resignation of body and soul to the power of tyrants. It arrests the hand of violence in every man, because it teaches that a higher power than force exists: that truth is omnipotent, and is sure to prevail if maintained: the truth has *not* prevailed solely because she has not been consistently maintained by her advocates, who have either committed the absurdity of resorting to the weakness of force, or the crookedness of cunning, or have deserted her altogether, through cowardice, or for self and world honor: that truth's battle is to be won with her own weapons only, and it may be truly said that "the weapons of her warfare are not carnal, though mighty": that truth's warfare is to be maintained in her own armor; and the warrior, in the panoply of truth, is to be, most characteristically, a true man: *always opposed to error.*

Need words be multiplied to show, then, that what some have named "nonresistance," is really moral resistance? That the principles of the true civilization consist not in indolence and supineness, but in a more unwearied watchfulness against the encroachments of error, than ever characterized the soldier of force?

Moral resistance, then—moral resistance is the true word for the world's regenerators. Our work is not to "stand at ease" mentally—nor in speech; no, nor even in act. Remember, my brother, you are not to take that flattering unction to your soul, that since you have avowed your conviction that bloodshedding and violence are wrong; and since you have virtuously cried, "I stand at ease!" when the weapon of blood was offered, or attempted to be forced into your hands, or when an act of violence was proposed: remember, I say, that you are not to take that flattering unction to your soul—that you have fully done your part as a man, that you have wholly discharged your duty as a member of the human family. No! You may not sit down, tongue-stricken and nerveless, and sinewless, and let the unenlightened and the mistaught be trepanned into the league for evil, and so let wrong wax strong. You are to cry out against wrong, until the wrongdoer be paralyzed with the shout. You are to stand in the gap, and morally oppose yourself to the enemies of right, and urge and entreat others to unite with you. Dream not, I say again, that you have done your part by refusing to participate in the doing of one wrong in order to put down another. Think not that there is, thenceforth, nothing left for you to do. You are to "gird up the loins of your mind," like a true man, for the better fight—for the moral death struggle. Not a day of your life, not an hour of your existence, but must be devoted, in thought or wish, in intent or resolve, in speech or act, to the grand moral warfare against wrong.

Who has done what he might, in moral or intellectual effort, for the enterprise of seeking to make right triumphant? Who has tried all his powers of suasion, who hath fully essayed his gift of head-and-heart logic to convince, and to win toward the phalanx of right, his friend, or his neighbor—not to speak of the greater moral glory of winning over an enemy to the cause of truth and right? Know you not that complaint of others' apathy is worse than folly, in the man who has not used all the appliances of explication and argument that he can muster, in order to win another from the active ranks of wrong, or from the couch of indifference? Do you reflect how deep is your own share of the blame you cast on the wrongdoer, or the moral slumberer, if you have never discharged your own duty by endeavoring to proselyte him? Do you reflect how much you are involved in the guilt of your brethren's suffering, of your own wife's want, of your own children's tears, under the system of wrong—by your supineness? Brother, do you know how far the suffering you endure—the deprivation you complain of—is of your own agency, by your indifference and inertion? Bear with me, my brethren, and hear me speak the truth even in its strictest severity! Do you reflect how truly even the most active and persevering among us may be charged with sinking into seasons of supineness and unmanly discouragement at difficulties? How truly many among us may be affirmed to have aided, by guilty sloth, the manacling of their own limbs—the riveting of their own chains and fetters?

And then our part to others. Can we pass life in guiltless indifference to the sufferings and wrongs of our brethren? Is, then, our being so entirely void of responsibility, that when we see wrong there is no crime in passing it by, silently—that there is nothing censurable in neglecting to end the wrong, when, for aught we know, we have the power to end it? Who hath been sufficiently impressed with the grandeur of the martyr spirit—the highest nobility of being ever foremost in the lists of right—to struggle against wrong, and to peril health and wealth, and liberty, aye, and life itself, in grappling with it? Who sufficiently weighs the transcendent maxim—who rivets his gaze upon it—who fastens heart and brain upon it—till the mighty energy of brotherhood it enshrines penetrates his whole being, and renders his entire life an act of philanthropy —"Be not overcome of evil—but overcome evil with good?"

What sayest thou, priest? It was the tent-maker—the working-man missionary—who wrote that sentence! I believe it; for there never was one of thy sleek class who had a soul large enough to breathe such a thought!

"Be not overcome of evil—but overcome evil with good!"—*that* is the philanthropist's golden rule of action. It expresses the essence of moral resistance. I care not who wrote the sentence—or whether I can approve all the sentences the writer wrote, by the exercise of that private judgment I claim, and the right of which I assert for every man. Were he Jew or Egyptian, Greek or Roman—I care not. His life proved him a sincere man, a real hero, and a transcendent philanthropist. He labored with his own hands, and endured poverty, and toil, and sickness, and peril, and shipwreck and chains—and, it is but too probable, death itself, in teaching what he believed to be right. He, and his heroic coadjutors, the poor fishermen of Galilee—aye, and their all-glorious Master, the carpenter's son of Nazareth, never rode idly in pompous carriages amid the splendor of equipage—they were not do-nothings, who were called lords, and right reverends—nor sought they thirstlessly for riches while the poor starved! My brothers, they belonged to our order—to the spurned, and degraded and ill-treated working class. Tell us not, priests, of your reverence for them, while you mock your own souls, as well as the poor, by violating the precepts they taught, and the worth of which they sealed with their heart's blood! We reverence them more truly than you. We are not the dupes of the superstition you would mix up with their veritable history —but we love the unsubduable and persevering philanthropy that characterized them; and we wish you would become what they were. We would hail your conversion to the right as real—even if you fell far behind the martyr spirits you profess to homage—and merely employed your authority to denounce wrong in earnest, by modernizing His language who spake out, and said, "Woe unto you, scribes and Pharisees, hypocrites! for ye devour widows' houses, and for a pretense make long prayer . . . ye bind heavy burdens and grievous to be borne, and lay them on men's shoulders, [and] will not move them with one of your fingers —ye make clean the outside of the cup and of the platter, but within you are full of extortion and excess!"

Alas! We call in vain to the richly paid, well endowed, beneficed, honored, educated, titled, mitred or surpliced class, to help us to the true civilization by example. No, my brothers, nor will the robed and coroneted class help us either. We will not waste time in waiting for them: we will not waste our strength in calling on Hercules: we will set our own shoulder to the wheel.

"Be not overcome of evil—but overcome evil with good." This is the precept of that future life of energy to which, I trust, we are all now ready to bind ourselves. Let the covenant be complete! Let the glorious federation of goodness be sworn to tonight! Let us now resolve to breathe the great martyr spirit: the spirit which saith, "Imprison me if you will—persecute me if you will—take my life if you will—but I will cry out against your wrong to me and to my fellows, while my mind can think, while my tongue can utter an accent! The world shall be made better in some small degree, if the little effort that I can display can serve to make it better."

My fellow working man, whose soul is now enkindled by thought, quail not at the expectation of sneers and mockery, while thou art half resolving to become a hero in the strife against wrong! Remember that every truly good and great cause commenced with one who encountered sneers and scoffs, but valued them not—because he was conscious of uprightness. Countest thou on loss, aye, and on suffering, while exposing wrong, and confronting it, and while championing the right. Remember how the truly brave and high-souled have endured, in ages past, the chain, the dungeon, the scaffold, the flame—and exulted in the midst of privation and torture. Thinkest thou that one hour of such endurance brings not an ecstasy of self-approval that is a millionfold more worth than threescore years and ten of sloth, and sensuality, and self-indulgence, and listless no-life? Dare to encounter an evil alone—if there be none to help; and have all the glory of thy great deed. Yet, call aloud for help: seek for union, even with the weak and the oppressed—and ye may become mighty with the consciousness of right against the wrongdoer, whose self-conviction of wrong will, perchance, benumb him.

And if no success crown thy struggle—if thy life be the forfeit of thy moral heroism— Oh! I know it is much to say, and may be met with ridicule: I know it may be asked of me what good a man shall gain who exposes his life with the certitude that he shall lose it: but there have been glorious martyrdoms for truth, and philanthropy, and science, and for the right to think untrammeled by despotism, and we know not but there may be such again, and many martyrdoms too! Then welcome the martyr's death, rather than the world should become stagnant with abuse; rather than wrong should grow gigantic till it dwarfs all right, and vice obscures all virtue, and misery claims the world for its cesspool that shall swallow up all happiness. My brother, cleave to the resolve to abide by truth, however fatal the consequences to thy own life. The self-approval—the consciousness of right, even for an hour, is worth a million of years passed in mere animal enjoyment. Go on to cry out that men must cease to take life even in self-defense, if they expect the age of brotherhood to come. Go on to urge it, to argue for it, to maintain it—to be "instant in season," aye, or out of season, in advocating it. If it be truth it *will* prevail—it *will* change the world. My brethren, let us have faith in it! We shall be instrumental in making the world a happy world—a world of brothers!

Charles Sumner

declares the victories of peace to be higher than the triumphs of war

CHARLES SUMNER [1811-1874] *was a United States Senator from Massachusetts who involved himself deeply in the fight against slavery and against laws that obstructed equal rights for Negroes. His work was in great part responsible for preparing a public opinion favorable to the Emancipation Proclamation, and after the Civil War he favored harsh reconstruction measures. He was also a member of the American Peace Society. Because of his statements against the Mexican War, the Social Registry of Boston declared Sumner to be "outside the pale of society."*

And now, if it be asked why, in considering the true grandeur of nations, I dwell thus singly and exclusively on war, it is because war is utterly and irreconcilably inconsistent with true greatness. Thus far, man has worshiped in military glory a phantom idol, compared with which the colossal images of ancient Babylon or modern Hindustan are but toys; and we, in this favored land of freedom, in this blessed day of light, are among the idolaters. The heaven-descended injunction *Know thyself* still speaks to an unheeding world from the far-off letters of gold at Delphi: *Know thyself; know that the moral is the noblest part of man,* transcending far that which is the seat of passion, strife, and war—nobler than the intellect itself. And the human heart, in its untutored, spontaneous homage to the virtues of peace, declares the same truth—admonishing the military idolater that it is not the bloody combats, even of bravest chiefs, even of gods themselves, as they echo from the resounding lines of the great poet of war, which receive the warmest admiration, but those two scenes where are painted the gentle, unwarlike affections of our nature, the "Parting of Hector from Andromache" and the "Supplication of Priam." In the definitive election of these peaceful pictures, the soul of man, inspired by a better wisdom than that of books, and drawn unconsciously by the heavenly attraction of what is truly great, acknowledges, in touching instances, the vanity of military glory. The Beatitudes of Christ, which shrink from saying "Blessed are the warmakers," inculcate the same lesson. Reason affirms and repeats what the heart has prompted and Christianity proclaimed. Suppose war decided by *force,* where is the glory? Suppose it decided by *chance,* where is the glory? Surely, in other ways true greatness lies. Nor is it difficult to tell where.

True greatness consists in imitating, as nearly as possible for finite man, the perfections of an Infinite Creator—above all, in cultivating those highest perfections, justice and love: justice, which, like that of St. Louis, does not swerve to the right hand or to the left; love, which, like that of William Penn, regards all mankind as of kin. "God is angry," says Plato, "when anyone censures a man like himself, *or praises a man of an opposite character:* and the godlike man is the good man." Again, in another of those lovely dialogues precious with immortal truth: "Nothing resembles God more than that man among us who has attained to the highest degree of justice." The true greatness of nations is in those qualities which constitute the true greatness of the individual. It is not in extent of territory, or vastness of population or accumulation of wealth—not in fortifications, or armies or navies—not in the sulphurous blaze of battle—not in Golgothas, though covered by monuments that kiss the clouds; for all these are creatures and representatives of those qualities in our nature which are unlike anything in God's nature. Nor is it in triumphs of the intellect alone—in literature, learning, science or art. The polished Greeks, our masters in the delights of art, and the commanding Romans, overawing the earth with their power, were little more than splendid savages. And the age of Louis the Fourteenth, of France, spanning so long a period of ordinary worldly magnificence, thronged by marshals bending under military laurels, enlivened by the unsurpassed comedy of Molière, dignified by the tragic genius of Corneille, illumined by the splendors of Bossuet, is degraded by immoralities that cannot be mentioned without a blush, by a heartlessness in comparison with which the ice of Novaya Zemlya is warm, and by a succession of deeds of injustice not to be washed out by the tears of all the recording angels of heaven.

The true greatness of a nation cannot be in triumphs of the intellect alone. Literature and art may enlarge the sphere of its influence; they may adorn it; but in their nature they are but accessories. *The true grandeur of humanity is in moral elevation, sustained, enlightened and decorated by the intellect of man.* The surest tokens of this grandeur in a nation are that Christian beneficence which diffuses the greatest happiness among all, and that passionless, godlike justice which controls the relations of the nation to other nations, and to all the people committed to its charge.

But war crushes with bloody heel all beneficence, all happiness, all justice, all that is godlike in man—suspending every commandment of the Decalogue, setting at naught every principle of the gospel, and silencing all law, human as well as divine, except only that impious code of its own, the *laws of war.* If in its dismal annals there is any cheerful passage, be assured it is not inspired by a martial fury. Let it not be forgotten, let it be ever borne in mind, as you ponder this theme, that the virtues which shed their charm over its horrors are all borrowed of peace —that they are emanations from the spirit of love, which is so strong in the heart of man that it survives the rudest assault. The flowers of gentleness, kindliness, fidelity, humanity, which flourish unregarded in the rich meadows of peace, receive unwonted admiration when we discern them in war—like violets shedding their perfume on the perilous edge of the precipice, beyond the smiling borders of civilization. God be praised for all the examples of magnanimous virtue which he has vouchsafed to mankind! God be praised that the Roman emperor, about to start on a distant expedition of war, encompassed by squadrons of cavalry, and by golden eagles swaying in the wind, stooped from his saddle to hear the prayer of a humble widow, demanding justice for the death of her son! God be praised, that Sidney, on the field of battle, gave with dying hand the cup of cold water to the dying soldier! That single act of self-forgetful sacrifice has consecrated the deadly field of Zutphen, far, oh, far beyond its battle; it has consecrated thy name, gallant Sidney, beyond any feat of thy sword, beyond any triumph of thy pen! But there are lowly suppliants in other places than the camp; there are hands outstretched elsewhere than on fields of blood. Everywhere is opportunity for deeds of like charity. Know well that these are not the product of war. They do not spring from enmity, hatred, and strife, but from those benign sentiments whose natural and ripened fruit of joy and blessing are found only in peace. If at any time they appear in the soldier, it is less *because* than *notwithstanding* he is the hireling of battle. Let me not be told, then, of the virtues of war. Let not the acts of generosity and sacrifice sometimes blossoming on its fields be invoked in its defense. From such a giant root of bitterness no true good can spring. The poisonous tree, in Oriental imagery, though watered by nectar and covered with roses, produces only the fruit of death.

Casting our eyes over the history of nations, with horror we discern the succession of murderous slaughters by which their progress is marked. Even as the hunter follows the wild beast to his lair by the drops of blood on the ground, so we follow man, faint, weary, staggering with wounds, through the Black Forest of the past, which he has reddened with his gore. Oh, let it not be in the future ages as in those we now contemplate! Let the grandeur of man be discerned, not in bloody victory or ravenous conquest, but in the blessings he has secured, in the good he has accomplished, in the triumphs of justice and beneficence, in the establishment of perpetual peace!

As ocean washes every shore, and with all-embracing arms clasps every land, while on its heaving bosom it bears the products of various climes, so peace surrounds, protects and upholds all other blessings. Without it, commerce is vain, the ardor of industry is restrained, justice is arrested, happiness is blasted, virtue sickens and dies.

Peace, too, has its own peculiar victories, in comparison with which Marathon and Bannockburn and Bunker Hill, fields sacred in the history of human freedom, lose their luster. Our own Washington rises to a truly heavenly stature not when we follow him through the ice of the Delaware to the capture of Trenton, not when we behold him victorious over Cornwallis at Yorktown, but when we regard him, in noble deference to justice, refusing the kingly crown which a faithless soldiery proffered, and at a later day upholding the peaceful neutrality of the country, while he met unmoved the clamor of the people wickedly crying for war. What glory of battle in England's annals will not fade by the side of that great act of justice, when her Parliament, at a cost of one hundred million dollars, gave freedom to eight hundred thousand slaves? And when the day shall come (may these eyes be gladdened by its beams!) that shall witness an act of larger justice still—the peaceful emancipation of three million fellow men "guilty of a skin not colored as our own," now, in this land of jubilant freedom, bound in gloomy bondage—then will there be a victory by the side of which that of Bunker Hill will be as the farthing candle held up to the sun. That victory will need no monument of stone. It will be written on the grateful hearts of countless multitudes that shall proclaim it to the latest generation. It will be one of the famed landmarks of civilization—or, better still, a link in the golden chain by which humanity connects itself with the throne of God.

As man is higher than the beasts of the field, as the angels are higher than man, as Christ is higher than Mars, as he that ruleth his spirit is higher than he that taketh a city—so are the victories of peace higher than the victories of war.

William Jay
insists that man is not compelled to do evil

WILLIAM JAY [1789-1858] *was an American judge and a crusader for liberal reform. He founded the New York City Anti-Slavery Society in 1833, and in 1843 he was removed from the bench in the court of Westchester County through the influence of pro-slavery Democrats. Jay was president of the American Peace Society for ten years. He advocated the use of arbitration to settle international disputes, and when his pamphlet called "War and Peace" was published in 1842, the first campaign for "stipulated arbitration" began. The pamphlet was reprinted as "a timely contribution" to the peace discussions of 1919.*

But after all that can be said against war, and after the fullest admission of its folly, cruelty and wickedness, still the question recurs, how can it be prevented? It would be an impeachment of the divine economy to suppose that an evil so dreadful was inseparably and inevitably connected with human society. We are informed by divine authority that wars proceed from our lusts, but our lusts, although natural to us, are not unconquerable. He who admits the free agency of man will not readily allow that either individuals or nations are compelled to do evil. The general prevalence of Christian principles must necessarily exterminate wars, as well as all other national crimes, and hence we are informed by revelation, that when righteousness shall cover the earth, "the nations shall learn war no more."

And are we to wait, it will be inquired, till this distant and uncertain period, for the extinction of war? We answer that revelation affords us no ground to expect that all mankind will be previously governed by a sense of justice, but that, on the contrary, there is abundant reason to believe that the regeneration of the world will be a gradual and progressive work. Civilization and Christianity are diffusing their influence throughout the globe, mitigating the sufferings and multiplying the enjoyments of the human family. Free institutions are taking the place of feudal oppressions; education is pouring its light upon minds hitherto enveloped in all the darkness of ignorance; the whole system of slavery, both personal and political, is undermined by public opinion, and must soon be prostrated; and the signs of the times assure us that the enormous mass of crime and wretchedness, which is the fruit of intemperance, will at no very remote period disappear from the earth. And can it be possible that of all the evils under which humanity groans, war is the only one which religion and civilization and the active philanthropy of the present age can neither remove nor mitigate? Such an opinion, if general, would be most disastrous to the world, and it will now be our endeavor to prove that it is utterly groundless.

Individuals possess the same natural right of self-defense as nations, but the organization of civil society renders its exercise, except in very extreme cases, unnecesary, and therefore criminal. A citizen is injured in his person or property—were he to attempt to redress his wrong, a forcible contest would ensue, and as the result would be uncertain, the injury he had already sustained might be greatly aggravated. Instead therefore of resorting to force, he appeals to the laws. His complaint is heard by an impartial tribunal, his wrongs are redressed, he is secured from further injury, and the peace of society is preserved.

No tribunal, it is true, exists for the decision of national controversies; but it does not, therefore, follow that none can be established.

We have often seen extensive national alliances for the prosecution of war, and no sufficient reason can be assigned why such alliances might not also be formed for the preservation of peace. It is obvious that war might instantly be banished from Europe, would its nations regard themselves as members of one great society, and, by mutual consent, erect a court for the trial and decision of their respective differences. But such an agreement, we are told, is impossible. That the immediate or early establishment of such a court is impossible we are not disposed to deny, since time would be necessary to enlighten and direct public opinion, and produce general acquiescence in the plan, as well as to arrange the various stipulations and guarantees that would be requisite. It is not surprising that those who suppose such a tribunal can be established only by a simultaneous movement among the nations who are to continue warring with each other till the signal is given for universal peace, should be startled at the boldness and absurdity of the project.

Of such a project we are wholly guiltless. We have no hope or expectation, in the present state of the world, of a general and simultaneous negotiation throughout Christendom in behalf of a tribunal for the decision of national differences and the suppression of war. Such a movement can only be expected after an extensive although partial abandonment of the military policy; and must be demanded and effected by the pacific sentiments of mankind. We have no hesitation, therefore, in avowing our belief that, under existing circumstances, the idea of a congress of nations for the extinction of war is utterly chimerical. But both reason and experience warrant the hope that some one nation may set an example which, through the blessing of Providence, may be made instrumental in ushering in the reign of universal peace.

William E. Channing
asks, "Has the duty of obeying government no bounds?"

WILLIAM ELLERY CHANNING [1780-1842] *was a Unitarian minister whose work has been described as attempting "the conversion of the Christian church to Christian principles." He was opposed to slavery but his strong feelings against war led him to think that the Negro problem "could be solved by moral reform rather than by forcible means." Channing, who was a pioneer of the modern peace movement, helped to found the Massachusetts Peace Society. Although he admitted a nation's right to fight a defensive war, he asked for a clear-cut definition of such self-defense.*

I know it will be asked, "And is not the citizen bound to fight at the call of his government? Does not his commission absolve him from the charge of murder or enormous crime? Is not obedience to the sovereign power the very foundation on which society rests?" I answer, "Has the duty of obeying government no bounds? Is the human sovereign a God? Is his sovereignty absolute? If he command you to slay a parent, must you obey? If he forbid you to worship God, must you obey? Have you no right to judge his acts? Have you no self-direction? Is there no unchangeable right which the ruler cannot touch? Is there no higher standard than human law?" These questions answer themselves. A declaration of war cannot sanction wrong, or turn murder into a virtuous deed. Undoubtedly, as a general rule, the citizen is bound to obey the authorities under which he lives. No difference of opinion as to the mere expedience of measures will warrant opposition. Even in cases of doubtful right he may submit his judgment to the law. But when called to do what his conscience clearly pronounces wrong, he must not waver. No outward law is so sacred as the voice of God in his own breast. He cannot devolve on rulers an act so solemn as the destruction of fellow beings convicted of no offense. For no act will more solemn inquisition be made at the bar of God.

I maintain that the citizen, before fighting, is bound to inquire into the justice of the cause which he is called to maintain with blood, and bound to withhold his hand, if his conscience condemn the cause. On this point he is able to judge. No political question, indeed, can be determined so easily as this of war. War can be justified only by plain, palpable necessity; by unquestionable wrongs, which, as patient trial has proved, can in no other way be redressed; by the obstinate, persevering invasion of solemn and unquestionable rights. The justice of war is not a mystery for cabinets to solve. It is not a state secret which he must take on trust. It lies within our reach. We are bound to examine it.

We are especially bound to this examination because there is always a presumption against the justice of war; always reason to fear that it is condemned by impartial conscience and God. This solemn truth has peculiar claims on attention. It takes away the plea that we may innocently fight because our rulers have decreed war. It strips off the most specious disguise from the horrors and crimes of national hostilities. If hostilities were, as a general rule, necessary and just, if an unjust war were a solitary exception, then the citizen might extenuate his share in the atrocities of military life by urging his obligation to the state. But if there is always reason to apprehend the existence of wrong on the part of rulers, then he is bound to pause and ponder well his path. Then he advances at his peril, and must answer for the crimes of the unjust, unnecessary wars in which he shares.

The presumption is always against the justice and necessity of war. This we learn from the spirit of all rulers and nations toward foreign states. It is partial, unjust. Individuals may be disinterested; but nations have no feeling of the tie of brotherhood to their race. A base selfishness is the principle on which the affairs of nations are commonly conducted. A statesman is expected to take advantage of the weaknesses and wants of other countries. How loose a morality governs the intercourse of states! What falsehoods and intrigues are licensed diplomacy! What nation regards another with true friendship? What nation makes sacrifices to another's good? What nation is as anxious to perform its duties as to assert its rights? What nation chooses to suffer wrong rather than to inflict it? What nation lays down the everlasting law of right, casts itself fearlessly on its principles, and chooses to be poor or to perish rather than to do wrong?

Can communities so selfish, so unfriendly, so unprincipled, so unjust, be expected to wage righteous wars? Especially if with this selfishness are joined national prejudices, antipathies and exasperated passions, what else can be expected in the public policy but inhumanity and crime? An individual, we know, cannot be trusted, in his own cause, to measure his own claims, to avenge his own wrongs; and the civil magistrate, an impartial umpire, has been substituted as the only means of justice. But nations are even more unfit than individuals to judge in their own cause; more prone to push their rights to excess, and to trample on the rights of others; because nations are crowds, and crowds are unawed by opinion, and more easily inflamed by sympathy into madness. Is there not, then, always a presumption against the justice of war?

This presumption is increased when we consider the false notions of patriotism and honor which prevail in nations. Men think it a virtuous patriotism to throw a mantle, as they call it, over their country's infirmities, to wink at her errors, to assert her most doubtful rights, to look jealously and angrily on the prosperity of rival states; and they place her honor not in unfaltering adherence to the right, but in a fiery spirit, in quick resentment, in martial courage, and especially in victory; and can a good man hold himself bound and stand prepared to engage in war at the dictate of such a state?

The citizen or subject, you say, may innocently fight at the call of his rulers; and I ask, who are his rulers? Perhaps an absolute sovereign, looking down on his people as another race, as created to toil for his pleasure, to fight for new provinces, to bleed for his renown. There are indeed republican governments. But were not the republics of antiquity as greedy of conquest, as prodigal of human life, as steeled against the cries of humanity, as any despots who ever lived? And if we come down to modern republics, are they to be trusted with our consciences? What does the Congress of these United States represent? Not so much the virtue of the country as a vicious principle, the spirit of party. It acts not so much for the people as for parties; and are parties upright? Are parties merciful? Are the wars to which party commits a country generally just?

Unhappily, public men under all governments are, of all moral guides, the most unsafe, the last for a Christian to follow. Public life is thought to absolve men from the strict obligations of truth and justice. To wrong an adverse party or another country is not reprobated as are wrongs in private life. Thus duty is dethroned; thus the majesty of virtue insulted in the administration of nations. Public men are expected to think more of their own elevation than of their country. Is the city of Washington the most virtuous spot in this republic? Is it the school of incorruptible men? The hall of Congress, disgraced by so many brawls, swayed by local interest and party intrigues, in which the right of petition is trodden under foot, is this the oracle from which the responses of justice come forth? Public bodies want conscience. Men acting in masses shift off responsibility on one another. Multitudes never blush. If these things be true, then I maintain that the Christian has not a right to take part in war blindly, confidingly, at the call of his rulers. To shed the blood of fellow creatures is too solemn a work to be engaged in lightly. Let him not put himself, a tool, into wicked hands. Let him not meet on the field his brother man, his brother Christian, in a cause on which heaven frowns. Let him bear witness against unholy wars as his country's greatest crimes. If called to take part in them, let him deliberately refuse. If martial law seize on him, let him submit. If hurried to prison, let him submit. If brought thence to be shot, let him submit. There must be martyrs to peace as truly as to other principles of our religion. The first Christians chose to die rather than obey the laws of the state which commanded them to renounce their Lord. "Death rather than crime"; such is the good man's watchword, such is the Christian's vow. Let him be faithful unto death.

Undoubtedly it will be objected that if one law of the state may in any way be resisted, then all may be, and so government must fall. This is precisely the argument on which the doctrine of passive obedience to the worst tyrannies rests. The absolutist says, "If one government may be overturned, none can stand. Your right of revolution is nothing but the right of anarchy, of universal misrule." The reply is in both instances the same. Extreme cases speak for themselves. We must put confidence in the common sense of men, and suppose them capable of distinguishing between reasonable laws and those which require them to commit manifest crimes. The objection which we are considering rests on the supposition that a declaration of war is a common act of legislation, bearing no strong marks of distinction from other laws, and consequently to be obeyed as implicitly as all. But it is broadly distinguished. A declaration of war sends us forth to destroy our fellow creatures, to carry fire, sword, famine, bereavement, want'and woe into the fields and habitations of our brethren; whilst Christianity, conscience and all the pure affections of our nature call us to love our brethren, and to die, if need be, for their good.

And from whence comes this declaration of war? From men who would rather die than engage in unjust or unnecesary conflict? Too probably, from men to whom Christianity is a name, whose highest law is honor, who are used to avenging their private wrongs and defending their reputations by shedding blood, and who, in public as in private life, defy the laws of God. Whoever, at such men's dictation, engages in war without solemnly consulting conscience, and inquiring into the justice of the cause, contracts great guilt, nor can the "right of war," which such men claim as rulers, absolve him from the crimes and woes of the conflict in which he shares.

Adin Ballou

charts a course for nonresistants

ADIN BALLOU [1803-1890] *was an American Universalist clergyman who founded the Hopedale community, a nineteenth-century Christian utopian colony. He spent his life fighting war, slavery and intemperance. His work was "met by a conspiracy of silence" during his lifetime, but he undoubtedly had an influence on Universalist and Unitarian thinking. The selection here is part of a speech he made in Boston at the first annual meeting of the Nonresistance Society in 1839.*

We expect to do as much toward keeping the world in order by a straightforward, consistent, exemplary practice of our principles, nay more, than by voting, office-holding, legislating, or punishing criminals. A truly good man wields an influence on our ground great and salutary wherever he is known. It is not by the poor test of numbers that righteousness can gain its deserved respect in the world. It is not by getting into places of worldly power and emolument, that Christians are to promote human welfare. It is not by fighting with carnal weapons, and wielding the instruments of legal vengeance, that they can hope to strengthen the bonds of moral restraint. Majorities often decree folly and iniquity. Power oftener corrupts its possessor than benefits the powerless. The real power which restrains the world is moral power, acting silently and unostentatiously within and upon the soul. He therefore, who has the fewest outward ensigns of authority, will, if wise and holy, contribute most to the good order of mankind.

Besides, even unprincipled men in office are compelled to bow to a strong public sentiment, superinduced by the efforts of good men in private life. They are not wanting in vanity to be esteemed the friends of virtue, and from this motive generally conform their laws and proceedings more or less to a right general opinion. If we can do anything toward promoting a sound morality, as we hope to do, we shall make our influence felt without envy, not only in the lowest depths of society, but in the high places of political power. I expect, if true to my sense of duty, to do as much in my town and community toward preserving wholesome moral order as if clothed with the official dignity of a first selectman, a representative to General Court, a justice of the peace, or even a member of Congress. Whatever my natural ambition might have coveted in the blindness of unchastened nature, I now envy not governors, presidents or monarchs their stations of usefulness and glory; but feel that in humble obscurity I have a higher mission assigned to me, in the faithful fulfillment of which it may be my privilege to do more for my race than if elevated to either of their world-envied seats. Every true nonresistant will be a great conservator of public as well as private morals. Away then with the intrigues and tricks of political ambition, the petty squabbles of partisans and office holders, the hollow bluster of demagogues, and the capricious admiration of a tickled multitude. Let us obey God, declare the truth, walk in love and deserve the gratitude of the world, though we never receive it.

"But should nonresistants ever become the great majority in any community, pray, how would they get on with public affairs? There must be highways, and bridges and schoolhouses, and education and almshouses, and hospitals." Very well; nothing easier than for communities of Christian nonresistants to get along with all these matters. Suppose them to meet, in those days, from time to time within each town, or more general community, voluntarily, just as we are here assembled.

Suppose them all anxious to know their duty, and ready to do it, as soon as clearly pointed out. Then of course the wisest will speak to attentive ears and upright minds. They will propose measures, discuss them in friendship, and come to a conclusion in favor of the best—without wounding personal vanity, or breeding a quarrel with each other's selfishness. The law of love and the counsels of wisdom will prevail without strife, and all be eager to contribute their full share of expense and effort to the object. Instead of the leading few striving, as now, who shall be the first and greatest, the strife will then be, who shall have the least authority. And among the mass, instead of the strife, as now, who shall bear the lightest burden, the only strife will be—who shall do most for the promotion of every good work.

Happy days, whenever they arrive! If there shall be any poor in those days, or any insane, or any unlettered, or unaccommodated travelers, they will soon be abundantly provided for, without the aid of physical force, pains of penalties. God hasten that blessed era of love and peace, and grant success to all our well directed efforts in this holy cause. Thus finally may all human governments be superseded by the divine government, and the kingdoms of this world be swallowed up in the one all-glorious kingdom of our Lord Jesus Christ.

And now, having freely expressed my views and feelings on the subject of the resolution presented, I submit them to the consideration of the friends, hoping that they will receive into good and honest hearts whatever is worth retaining, and the worthless cast away.

Ralph Waldo Emerson

declares that the cause of peace is not the cause of cowardice

RALPH WALDO EMERSON [1803-1882] *was an essayist and poet, known in his time as the "Sage of Concord" because an important group of American thinkers known as transcendentalists gathered around him there. He had been educated for the Unitarian ministry, but he gave up formal preaching and became famous as a lecturer. He favored social and political reforms, and when the Civil War began he joined with the*

Abolitionists. Emerson talked about nonresistance in his early writings, and his essay called "War," taken from a lecture he delivered in Boston in 1838, is considered a peace classic.

That the project of peace should appear visionary to great numbers of sensible men; should appear laughable, even, to numbers; should appear to the grave and good-natured to be embarrassed with extreme practical difficulties, is very natural. "This is a poor, tedious society of yours," they say; "we do not see what good can come of it. Peace! Why, we are all at peace now. But if a foreign nation should wantonly insult or plunder our commerce, or, worse yet, should land on our shores to rob and kill, you would not have us sit, and be robbed and killed? You mistake the times; you overestimate the virtue of men. You forget that the quiet which now sleeps in cities and in farms, which lets the wagon go unguarded and the farmhouse unbolted, rests on the perfect understanding of all men that the musket, the halter and the jail stand behind there, ready to punish any disturber of it. All admit that this would be the best policy, if the world were all a church, if all men were the best men, if all would agree to accept this rule. But it is absurd for one nation to attempt it alone."

In the first place, we answer that we never make much account of objections which merely respect the actual state of the world at this moment, but which admit the general expediency and permanent excellence of the project. What is the best must be the true; and what is true—that is, what is at bottom fit and agreeable to the constitution of man—must at last prevail over all obstruction and all opposition. There is no good now enjoyed by society that was not once as problematical and visionary as this. It is the tendency of the true interest of man to become his desire and steadfast aim.

But, further, it is a lesson which all history teaches wise men, to put trust in ideas, and not in circumstances. We have all grown up in the sight of frigates and navy yards, of armed forts and islands, of arsenals and militia. The reference to any foreign register will inform us of the number of thousand or million men that are now under arms in the vast colonial system of the British Empire, of Russia, Austria and France; and one is scared to find at what a cost the peace of the globe is kept. This vast apparatus of artillery, of fleets, of stone bastions and trenches and embankments; this incessant patrolling of sentinels; this waving of national flags; this reveille and evening gun; this martial music and endless playing of marches and singing of military and naval songs seem to us to constitute an imposing actual, which will not yield in centuries to the feeble, deprecatory voices of a handful of friends of peace.

Thus always we are daunted by the appearances; not seeing that their whole value lies at bottom in the state of mind. It is really a thought that built this portentous war establishment, and a thought shall also melt it away. Every nation and every man instantly surround themselves with a material apparatus which exactly corresponds to their moral state, or their state of thought. Observe how every truth and every error, each a *thought* of some man's mind, clothes itself with societies, houses, cities, language, ceremonies, newspapers. Observe the ideas of the present day— orthodoxy, skepticism, missions, popular education, temperance, anti-masonry, antislavery; see how each of these abstractions has embodied itself in an imposing apparatus in the community; and how timber, brick, lime and stone have flown into convenient shape, obedient to the master idea reigning in the minds of many persons.

You shall hear, someday, of a wild fancy which some man has in his brain, of the mischief of secret oaths. Come again one or two years afterwards, and you shall see it has built great houses of solid wood and brick and mortar. You shall see a hundred presses printing a million sheets; you shall see men and horses and wheels made to walk, run and roll for it: this great body of matter thus executing that one man's wild thought. This happens daily, yearly about us, with half thoughts, often with flimsy lies, pieces of policy and speculation. With good nursing they will last three or four years before they will come to nothing. But when a truth appears—as, for instance, a perception in the wit of one Columbus that there is land in the Western Sea; though he alone of all men has that thought, and they all jeer, it will build ships; it will build fleets; it will carry over half Spain and half England; it will plant a colony, a state, nations and half a globe full of men.

We surround ourselves always, according to our freedom and ability, with true images of ourselves in things, whether it be ships or books or cannon or churches. The standing army, the arsenal, the camp and the gibbet do not appertain to man. They only serve as an index to show where man is now; what a bad, ungoverned temper he has; what an ugly neighbor he is; how his affections halt; how low his hope lies. He who loves the bristle of bayonets only sees in their glitter what beforehand he feels in his heart. It is avarice and hatred; it is that quivering lip, that cold, hating eye, which built magazines and powder houses.

It follows of course that the least change in the man will change his circumstances; the least enlargement of his ideas, the least mitigation of his feelings in respect to other men; if, for example, he could be inspired with a tender kindness to the souls of men, and should come to feel that every man was another self with whom he might come to join, as left hand works with right. Every degree of the ascendancy of this feeling would cause the most striking changes of external things: the tents would be struck; the men-of-war would rot ashore; the arms rust; the cannon would become streetposts; the pikes, a fisher's harpoon; the marching regiment would be a caravan of emigrants, *peaceful* pioneers at the fountains of the Wabash and the Missouri. And so it must and will be: bayonet and sword must first retreat a little from their ostentatious prominence; then quite hide themselves, as the sheriff's halter does now, inviting the attendance only of relations and friends; and then, lastly, will be transferred to the museums of the curious, as poisoning and torturing tools are at this day.

War and peace thus resolve themselves into a mercury of the state of cultivation. At a certain stage of his progress, the man fights, if he be of a sound body and mind. At a certain higher stage he makes no offensive demonstration, but is alert to repel injury, and of an unconquerable heart. At a still higher stage he comes into the region of holiness; passion has passed away from him; his warlike nature is all converted into an active medicinal principle; he sacrifices himself, and accepts with alacrity wearisome tasks of denial and charity; but, being attacked, he bears it and turns the other cheek, as one engaged, throughout his being, no longer to the service of an individual but to the common soul of all men.

Since the peace question has been before the public mind, those who affirm its right and expediency have naturally been met with objections more or less weighty. There are cases frequently put by the curious —moral problems, like those problems in arithmetic which in long winter evenings the rustics try the hardness of their heads in ciphering out. And chiefly it is said, Either accept this principle for better, for worse, carry it out to the end, and meet its absurd consequences; or else, if you pretend to set an arbitrary limit, a "Thus far, no farther," then give up the principle, and take that limit which the common sense of all mankind has set, and which distinguishes offensive war as criminal, defensive war as just. Otherwise, if you go for no war, then be consistent, and give up self-defense in the highway, in your own house. Will you push it thus far? Will you stick to your principle of nonresistance when your strongbox is broken open, when your wife and babes are insulted and slaughtered in your sight? If you say yes, you only invite the robber and assassin; and a few bloody-minded desperadoes would soon butcher the good.

In reply to this charge of absurdity on the extreme peace doctrine, as shown in the supposed consequences, I wish to say that such deductions consider only one half of the fact. They look only at the passive side of the friend of peace, only at his passivity; they quite omit to consider his activity. But no man, it may be presumed, ever embraced the cause of peace and philanthropy for the sole end and satisfaction of being plundered and slain. A man does not come the length of the spirit of martyrdom without some active purpose, some equal motive, some flaming love. If you have a nation of men who have risen to that height of moral cultivation that they will not declare war or carry arms, for they have not so much madness left in their brains, you have a nation of lovers, of benefactors, of true, great and able men. Let me know more of that nation; I shall not find them defenseless, with idle hands springing at their sides. I shall find them men of love, honor and truth; men of an immense industry; men whose influence is felt to the end of the earth; men whose very look and voice carry the sentence of honor and shame; and all forces yield to their energy and persuasion. Whenever we see the doctrine of peace embraced by a nation, we may be assured it will not be one that invites injury; but one, on the contrary, which has a friend in the bottom of the heart of every man, even of the violent and the base; one against which no weapon can prosper; one which is looked upon as the asylum of the human race and has the tears and the blessings of mankind.

In the second place, as far as it respects individual action in difficult and extreme cases, I will say, such cases seldom or never occur to the good and just man; nor are we careful to say, or even to know, what in such crises is to be done. A wise man will never impawn his future being and action, and decide beforehand what he shall do in a given extreme event. Nature and God will instruct him in that hour.

The question naturally arises, How is this new aspiration of the human mind to be made visible and real? How is it to pass out of thoughts into things?

Not, certainly, in the first place, *in the way of routine and mere forms*—the universal specific of modern politics; not by organizing a society, and going through a course of resolutions and public manifestoes, and being thus formally accredited to the public and to the civility of the newspapers. We have played this game to tediousness. In some of our cities they choose noted duelists as presidents and officers of antidueling societies. Men who love that bloated vanity called public opinion think all is well if they have once got their bantling through a sufficient course of speeches and cheerings, of one, two or three public meetings; as if *they* could do anything: they vote and vote, cry hurrah on both sides, no man responsible, no man caring a pin. The next season, an Indian war, or an aggression on our commerce by Malays; or the party this man votes with have an appropriation to carry through Congress: instantly he wags his head the other way, and cries, Havoc and war!

This is not to be carried by public opinion, but by private opinion, by private conviction, by private, dear and earnest love. For the only hope of this cause is in the increased insight, and it is to be accomplished by the spontaneous teaching, of the cultivated soul, in its secret experience and meditation, that it is now time that it should pass out of the state of beast into the state of man; it is to hear the voice of God, which bids the devils that have rended and torn him come out of him and let him now be clothed and walk forth in his right mind.

Nor, in the next place, is the peace principle to be carried into effect by fear. It can never be defended, it can never be executed, by cowards. Everything great must be done in the spirit of greatness. The manhood that has been in war must be transferred to the cause of peace, before war can lose its charm, and peace be venerable to men. . . .

The cause of peace is not the cause of cowardice. If peace is sought to be defended or preserved for the safety of the luxurious and the timid, it is a sham, and the peace will be base. War is better, and the peace will be broken. If peace is to be maintained, it must be by brave men, who have come up to the same height as the hero, namely, the will to carry their life in their hand, and stake it at any instant for their principle, but who have gone one step beyond the hero, and will not seek another man's life; men who have, by their intellectual insight or else by their moral elevation, attained such a perception of their own intrinsic worth that they do not think property or their own body a sufficient good to be saved by such dereliction of principle as treating a man like a sheep.

If the universal cry for reform of so many inveterate abuses, with which society rings; if the desire of a large class of young men for a faith and hope, intellectual and religious, such as they have not yet found, be an omen to be trusted; if the disposition to rely more in study and in action on the unexplored riches of the human constitution; if the search of the sublime laws of morals and the sources of hope and trust, in man, and not in books, in the present, and not in the past, proceed; if the rising generation can be provoked to think it unworthy to nestle into every abomination of the past, and shall feel the generous darings of austerity and virtue, then war has a short day, and human blood will cease to flow.

It is of little consequence in what manner, through what organs, this purpose of mercy and holiness is effected. The proposition of the congress of nations is undoubtedly that at which the present fabric of our society and the present course of events do point. But the mind, once prepared for the reign of principles, will easily find modes of expressing its will. There is the highest fitness in the place and time in which this enterprise is begun. Not in an obscure corner, not in a feudal Europe, not in an antiquated appanage where no onward step can be taken without rebellion, is this seed of benevolence laid in the furrow, with tears of hope; but in this broad America of God and man, where the forest is only now falling, or yet to fall, and the green earth opened to the inundation of emigrant men from all quarters of oppression and guilt; here, where not a family, not a few men, but mankind, shall say what shall be; here, we ask, Shall it be war, or shall it be peace?

Thomas Carlyle
describes the soldiers of Dumdrudge

THOMAS CARLYLE [1795-1881], *the well-known essayist and historian, was born in Ecclefechan, Scotland. He studied for the ministry and then the law, and after a period of teaching he began to write. He believed that it is in society's nature to change and that it must be made to do so intelligently. Carlyle's writings made him a leading social critic of his time.* Sartor Resartus, *published in 1833, from which the following selection is taken, is a kind of spiritual autobiography in which he puts forth his views and opinions.*

What, speaking in quite unofficial language, is the net purport and upshot of war? To my own knowledge, for example, there dwell and toil, in the British village of Dumdrudge, usually some five hundred souls. From these, by certain "natural enemies" of the French, there are successfully selected, during the French war, say, thirty able-bodied men: Dumdrudge, at her own expense, has suckled and nursed them: she has, not without difficulty and sorrow, fed them up to manhood, and even trained them to crafts, so that one can weave, another build, another hammer, and the weakest can stand under thirty stone avoirdupois. Nevertheless, amid much weeping and swearing, they are selected; all dressed in red, and shipped away, at the public charges, some 2,000 miles, or say only to the south of Spain; and fed there until wanted. And now at that same spot, in the south of Spain, are thirty similar French artisans, from a French Dumdrudge, in like manner wending; till at length, after infinite effort, the two parties come into actual juxtaposition, and Thirty stands fronting Thirty, each with a gun in his hand. Straightway the word "Fire!" is given and they blow the souls out of one another, and in the place of sixty brisk, useful craftsmen, the world has sixty dead carcasses, which it must bury, and anew shed tears for. Had these men any quarrel? Busy as the Devil is, not the smallest! They lived far enough apart; were the entirest strangers; nay, in so wide a universe, there was even, unconsciously, by commerce, some mutual helpfulness between them. How then? Simpleton! Their governors had fallen out; and, instead of shooting one another, had the cunning to make these poor blockheads shoot. Alas, so is it in Deutschland, and hitherto in all other lands; still as of old, "what devilry soever kings do, the Greeks must pay the piper!" In that fiction of the English Smollett, it is true, the final cessation of war is perhaps prophetically shadowed forth; where the two natural enemies, in person, take each a tobacco pipe, filled with brimstone; light the same, and smoke in one another's faces, till the weaker gives in: but from such predicted peace era, what blood-filled trenches, and contentious centuries, may still divide us!

Thomas Grimke

calls the law of violence the law of murder

THOMAS SMITH GRIMKE [1786-1834] *was a Connecticut lawyer and a pioneer for the cause of temperance. He belonged to the American Peace Society and argued that there was nothing in the Scriptures which admitted the legality of war. He objected to Connecticut's preparation for military resistance- during the nullification controversy, but at the same time he disapproved of Federal coercion. The address here was one he delivered in 1832 at the request of the Connecticut Peace Society during a session of the state legislature.*

War is the law of violence, *peace* the law of love. That law of violence prevailed without mitigation, from the murder of Abel to the advent of the Prince of Peace. During all that period of forty centuries, war appeared to be the great end of all the institutions of society. Governments seemed to be successfully organized only when strong for the destruction of others. Rulers appeared to be fortunate in their administration and illustrious in their achievements, only when marches and battlefields, burning cities and shattered navies were the trophies of their renown. The warrior was the great man of those ages, for his art presented the chief means of aggrandizement, with nations and individuals, at home and abroad. Peace, the natural state of man, whether he consults his duties, his interests or his happiness, was regarded as worthy only of the vulgar, ignorant multitude: and as the natural state, *not of the free, but of the slave.*

The spirit of all those ages was embodied in the sentiment of Cleomenes: Homer is the poet of the Spartans, because he sings of war, Hesiod of the Helots, because agriculture is his theme. War, the unnatural state of man if he respects his obligations, welfare and improvement, was considered as the only natural state of government in all its forms of despotism, oligarchy and democracy. Even in the comparatively free states of Greece and Italy, amidst their hideous compounds of despotic aristocracy and turbulent licentious democracy, *war was the master passion of the people, the master spring of government.* The republicans of antiquity appear to have lived in vain unless they died in battle; and all the vital powers of their government were so entirely military that they perished as soon as they lost the capacity to make war successfully.

Such institutions and states of society present one of the most remarkable proofs of the folly and depravity of man. In them we behold the singular and revolting spectacle of *the people* constructing their governments and administering their public concerns on the cruel, unjust and ruinous maxims of tyrants and conquerors. With war as the prevailing spirit of all their institutions, the republics of antiquity have demonstrated *how utterly unfit the people are to govern themselves, if the law of violence be the fundamental law of their social compact.* They have demonstrated that if nations, though comparatively free and enlightened, live by the sword, they shall perish by the sword: *that the law of violence is the law of murder to others, of suicide to ourselves.*

There was a time when the distinguishing mark of Christians was, that they would not bear arms. But, for more than sixteen hundred years, peace has been the lost Pleiad in the constellation of Christian virtues. From the commencement of the history of Christian nations and governments they have ceased to bear that mark, and more than sixteen centuries have recorded their inextinguishable wars. O! that Christians had persevered in the primitive spirit, *which regarded the character of a soldier as pagan, not Christian!* O! that they had abided inflexibly by the rule never to bear arms! Then would the primitive church have bequeathed an illustrious, invaluable example to all posterity. Then pagan, not Christian, governments would have been overturned. Then the northern invaders, after conquering the monarchs and armies of heathenism, would themselves have been subdued and civilized by the all prevailing law of Christian peace and love. But unfortunately, Christianity was first enslaved by the warlike character of classic paganism, and afterward by the martial spirit of the barbarous heathen. Had its disciples inflexibly resisted the first, they never would have dishonored their founder and his church by the last.

Their maxims, from the moment the Redeemer ascended, should have been these, "Let the heathen take arms against each other and even against us, but come what may, Christians never will bear arms against each other, or against them. Christianity never shall be defended or spread abroad by force of arms. Christians never shall employ the sword to protect property, character, liberty, or life. Let the heathen rule us with a rod of iron. Let them insult, persecute, oppress, torment, slay us. Let them confiscate property, slander character, cast us into prison, strip us of life itself. Let them separate husband and wife, parent and child; let them seduce the brother to betray the brother, and the friend the friend. Let them poison the comfort and happiness of private and social life, and heap on us all the enormities and cruelties that malice can suggest and tyranny execute. Still we will bear it all; nor shall the sword ever be employed to deliver, much less to avenge us. Be it our duty to exhibit the consistence and beauty, the unconquerable strength, the inflexible constancy, of Christian love, humility and forgiveness. Cost what it may, we will return good for evil, and blessing for cursing; we will love them that hate, and pray for such as persecute and oppress us. Thus and thus only will we conquer our enemies, and convert the heathen to Christianity." Then would they indeed have conquered, for the law of love and humility and forgiveness is invincible in the hands of faith and hope. Thus would the whole Roman empire, and all the barbarian hordes that overran it, have been subdued by the pure and holy religion of peace; not by that misnamed Christian church with the warrior's helmet on her head, with his sword in her right hand, and a bloody cross in the left, as her battle ensign.

Joshua P. Blanchard
envisions a patriotism based on pacific principles

JOSHUA P. BLANCHARD [1782-1868], *a Boston merchant, was one of the most important of the nonclerical members in the American peace movement in his time. He condemned all forms of war, defensive and offensive, and therefore refused to serve in the militia. He opposed the War of 1812, the Mexican War, and the Civil War. His writings appeared in Garrison's* Liberator *and Burritt's* Bond of Brotherhood. *The following is Blanchard's address before the Massachusetts Peace Society on December 25, 1828.*

Do I say there should be no patriotism? Far from it. Let our country receive all the attachment which can be spared from the paramount love of God, and our domestic affections; but let it, like those affections, be directed to the moral worth of the object beloved, and not to a mischievous celebrity. Let the love of country be shown, not by guarding it with a fence of terror, which shall repel the goodwill as well as the assaults of foreigners, but by striving to invest it with those characters of true greatness and goodness which shall render it venerable and amiable and happy; not by extending its political power and magnifying its martial renown, but by acquiring for it the far better renown of justice, forbearance, benevolence and moral purity. Could I look forward to the day when the land in which I have been nurtured, and to which I owe my dearest political affection, shall be pervaded by pacific principles and, relying on the protecting arm of omnipotence and its own impartial justice, shall cast its vain armaments and warlike preparations and its proud menaces to the winds, and magnanimously devote its abundant resources and mighty energies to the diffusion of its own comforts and improvements and liberty and religion, through a suffering and darkened world—what brighter vision could patriotism unfold?

Fear not that you would be laid open to unresisted aggression. The spectacle of an upright, forbearing, beneficent magnanimity would be more dignified and appealing than uncounted hosts. The nations who perceived your disinterestedness and experienced your kindness would stretch out to you the open arms of grateful friendship and strive to imitate your example. In the noble course which religious charity and enlarged philanthrophy would dictate, you would find a surer safeguard than could be procured for you by fleets which should whiten your seas or fortresses which should line your coasts, a higher renown than could be purchased by conquests which should carry you on to unbounded empire.

I hear it said that this is all an utopian imagination, the dream of a purer world not to be realized in this. To those who look on the vices, the prejudices, the corrupt customs of men as natural and irremovable, the idea of the departure of so vast and deep-rooted a custom as war, and the existence of a state of universal peace and charity, seems a chimerical expectation. But it should be recollected that we have the sure word of a prophecy which we dare not call "utopian" that there shall be a period on the earth when "nation shall not lift up sword against nation; neither shall they learn war any more." Nor will this appear improbable to those who attend to the rapid diffusion of light through the world. Will it be said that the impetus, which through the mediums of art and science, and especially the press, is carrying an intellectual and moral renovation into all countries and conditions, is to be suddenly checked in its course? And if not, who shall mark the limits or determine its direction in the conversion and amelioration of man?

But the celerity of this progress, let it be remembered, must still depend on individual exertion, and this is a cause in which none can be neutral. You passively obstruct when you do not aid the great cause of virtue and harmony of the world, and although your supineness may not prevent the ultimate arrival of this result, yet to yourselves the part you take in it may be all-important. The true religion of the gospel, and unbroken peace and holiness, will indeed pervade the whole earth and present a scene delightful even to angelic eyes. And if your departed spirits still cling with fond interest to their infant home and are permitted to behold the felicity of your improved posterity, with what feelings will your past agency in its production come home upon the conscience? Then the thought that to you it owes no part of its advancement will be indeed a bitter mortification, or then the remembrance and reputation of anxieties, labors and sacrifices in this sacred cause will be a glory compared to which all the plaudits of warring myriads would be poor and worthless, a glory which will shine with unfading luster on your brows when the gaudy diadem of the monarch and the blood-stained decorations of the warrior shall be sunk in the contempt of ages.

William Ladd

urges men to give public testimony for peace

WILLIAM LADD [1778-1841] *was a New Hampshire sea captain— and a graduate of Harvard University. He had been ordained a Congregational minister, and from his pulpit he advocated a world organization of nations. He was the man chiefly responsible for consolidating a number of peace groups in this country into the American Peace Society. Although at first he sanctioned defensive wars, he later took an uncompromising attitude against war in all its forms. In the history of the American peace movement, Ladd is one of the most important figures in the early era of organization. The following is one of the essays written by Ladd under the pseudonym of Philanthropos. It was published in the* Christian Science Monitor *on May 11, 1827.*

There is a loud call on all orders and conditions of men to seize with avidity the present favorable season for disseminating the principles of peace. Let us not wait until the angry passions of mankind are excited by designing men; until the alarm of war shall be sounded, and the remonstrances of reason and religion drowned in "the confused noise of the warrior." Then,

> *You might as well go stand upon the beach,*
> *And bid the sea to 'bate its wonted roar;*
> *You might as well plead pity with the wolf.*

In the present quiet state of the world, no age, sex or condition is exempted from the imperious duty of endeavoring to make "our peace like a river," gently flowing and widening, until it becomes "a sea without a shore."

Are you a legislator? Use every means in your power to encourage a pacific disposition toward other nations. The late arrangement between this country and Great Britain, by which privateering against each other is abolished, is a glorious victory of the principles of peace. The mutual right of searching vessels suspected of being engaged in the slave trade is another victory: for slavery and war are almost synonymous.* Abolish slavery, and many wars in Africa will cease. Abolish war, and much slavery in Europe will cease.

Are you a private citizen? Make the most of your suffrage in favor of peace. Never cast a vote in favor of a man who has been guilty of private war, or an encourager of public hostilities. Seek those *men,* as well as things, that make for peace—considering that "righteousness exalteth a nation: but sin is a reproach to any people." Can you conscientiously vote for one who has broken the laws of his country by private revenge, and imbrued his hands in the blood of a fellow citizen, and who *glories* in it? Or can you support a man for office who is for settling every trivial difference with a foreign nation by the sword, regardless of the misery he brings on his own country, and the danger to which he exposes your property, liberty, morals and eternal salvation? Bear in mind that the reformation of a nation from warlike to peaceable habits, like all other reformations, must begin with *the people.* Rulers, under every form of government, are inclined to war, because it strengthens their hands, increases their power, flatters their ambition, enlarges their patronage, and fills their pockets.

Are you an author?—a poet?—a man of letters? Your influence on public opinion is great. It was said by an Athenian that he cared not who made the laws, so that he made the music, intimating that music had

---

* These arrangements, which were in progress when this essay was written, we have reason to lament, have not yet taken effect; Great Britain having neglected to confirm one and the Senate of the United States the other.—W.L.

more influence on popular opinion than the laws had. If this is the case with bare sound, how much more when sound is accompanied with sentiment! The effect of "national airs," as they were called, in arousing a bloodthirsty spirit, was witnessed in the French Revolution. The verses of Homer and Virgil, and the prose of Xenophon and Livy, have done much to keep up a war spirit in the world; and it is not to be doubted that an opposite character of their works would have had a contrary effect. A pastoral song representing the happy life of a Swiss peasant, and imitating the mooing of cows, when sung among the Swiss soldiers in the French army, had such an effect as to make them desert in great numbers so that the French officers prohibited the singing of it on pain of death. If then you are an author, and a friend of peace, you ought not to omit any opportunity of giving your testimony in its favor; and whenever you are called on to describe the circumstances of a battle, or the character of a warrior by profession, it is your duty to put both in a proper point of view; that the tender minds of youth, which are just taking their bent, may not receive from you a wrong direction. Charles XII of Sweden, while studying Latin in his youth, had his mind influenced by reading the life of Alexander the Great by Quintus Curtius, so that the Roman historian became accessory to all the murders which Charles committed in Europe.

Are you a soldier by profession? Remember the injunction of John the Baptist, the forerunner of our Saviour: "Do violence to no man." Examine the principles of the Christian religion with impartiality, and then if you can conscientiously follow your trade—do it. If not, seriously ask yourself this question: "What shall it profit a man to gain the whole world and lose his own soul?" . . .

There is no station in society in which a man may not be useful in disseminating the principles of peace. And if he does no more than barely give his testimony in favor of peace principles by joining a peace society, and purchasing and distributing peace tracts, it will not lose its effect, nor will he lose his reward.

In conversing a few days ago with a gentleman of talents and influence, and also a professor of religion, I asked him if he belonged to the peace society. No. I expressed my surprise. "I have not the least doubt," said he, "that the custom of war is in direct opposition to the Christian religion; and I am so fully convinced that I have no occasion for reading anything further on the subject." He might as well have said that as he was perfectly well convinced of the truth of the Christian religion, he had no occasion for a Bible. It is as much the duty of every friend of peace to give public testimony in favor of it, as it is of a Christian to make a profession of religion. By becoming a member of a peace society, a man puts the weight of his character into the scale of peace. By buying their publications, he increases their funds. By reading them, he strengthens his principles; fills his mouth with arguments; learns the most effectual way of furthering the cause of peace, and how to act in concert with others. By circulating them, he serves the cause of peace by making known its principles, and very probably will make converts. I speak from experience, for it was by reading a few numbers of the *Friend of Peace,* casually lent me by a friend, that my attention was called to the subject, and I renounced my former sentiments, and became an advocate for peace. . . .

When wars shall become unpopular, they must cease in free countries, and they cannot long continue even in absolute monarchies —but the world will never be free until "wars and fightings" cease. It is, therefore, the imperious duty of the republican, the philanthropist, and the Christian, to do all they can to disseminate the principles of peace. I have been actuated by these motives, to cast my "mite" into the scale of peace. If it has any effect, I shall be thankful. If it has not, I shall still have the satisfaction of having "done what I could."

But there has been an evident and general change in public opinion, respecting the custom of war; and the principles of peace are steadily and constantly progressing. What if the present generation does not see the full accomplishment of God's promise—is that a reason for despair? "Though it tarry, wait for it: because it will surely come." What if we cannot accomplish all we wish—is that a reason why we should do nothing? If all the exertions of all the peace societies and philanthropists in the world should prevent one war, or even one battle—in which thousands of immortal souls are precipitated into a miserable eternity, and as many thousands bereaved of near and dear relatives—the reward would infinitely exceed the labor.

I now take my leave of the public. If I have hurt the feelings of any individual, I am sorry for it. It has not been my intention, for having no personal antipathies to indulge, none of my remarks have been made for personal application. I am an enemy to no one, except so far as he is an enemy to my brethren of the human family. I wish temporal and eternal happiness to all; and if I know my own heart, I have been influenced to write these essays by a love of "peace on earth and good will to men."

Thomas Hancock
condemns "necessity" as an excuse for war

THOMAS HANCOCK [1783-1849] *was a Quaker physician who practiced in London and Liverpool and was a part of the English peace movement. In his tract called* Principles of Peace, *Hancock held up the behavior of the Society of Friends during the Irish Rebellion in 1798 as an excellent implementation of peaceful principles.*

The word "necessity," when applied to the moral conduct of free agents, implies nothing more than duty, and in the case of war it involves two considerations: first, the duty of preserving our existence; and second, obedience to moral or divine requisition.

It is plain that in all cases in which these duties may seem to interfere, the first must yield to the last. For the promise or assurance of immortal felicity to all who obey the divine commands cuts off the justification that would lean upon self-preservation as a paramount duty; and by making *temporal* concerns of little account in the scale, whether they be possessions, privileges, rights or the endearments of kindred, it enhances the value of the *eternal,* and therefore exacts unconditional submission to the divine law. If these principles did not hold, no man would ever have been a martyr to the convictions of his conscience.

Necessity cannot surely imply that when life appears to be in danger, every other consideration is to be set aside in order to preserve it. This is not the doctrine of Scripture: it is not even the doctrine of heathen philosophy.

It was an old saying among those who were but partially enlightened respecting a future state, *Fiat justitia, ruat coelum*—Let man do his duty, whatever extremity may happen; and it was consistently held that, in some cases when pressed by violence, men ought rather to surrender their lives than submit to any act of turpitude or ignominy, for the sake of prolonging their existence. So then, the preservation of life was not to be regarded as the only end and object of rational beings. For virtue required that life itself should be undervalued when placed in competition with duty and true honor. If a man were reduced to the supposed necessity of telling a falsehood to save his life, would he be justified in violating the truth, when he felt persuaded that there is a God in heaven to reward the upright? If he were reduced to the supposed necessity of killing another to save himself, would he be justified in breaking the Christian injunction "not to resist evil," when he entertained a religious confidence that mercy would hereafter be extended to all that show mercy?

But it might happen, as it often has happened, that the necessity of violent resistance might not be real, and that in the very crisis of alarm, by some unforeseen incident, life might be preserved with honor. How lamentable, then, must be the reflection to a Christian that by yielding to revenge, he had cut off a fellow creature in the midst of his crimes, who by a little kindness and persuasion, from an enemy, might have been made a friend, and, who, by means of salutary discipline, might have been turned from a course of wickedness to a state of acceptance with his Maker!

The argument which supports the necessity of force being opposed to force, assumes that, nations or individuals being threatened, and life or liberty or property being in consequence endangered, arms must be resorted to for the purpose of affording protection: therefore, that those who meditate or offer violence are to be resisted with brute violence, as a matter of course, and if possible put to death.

Now, who is competent to judge of the necessity and the danger, supposing the plea to be admitted? Is he who is impelled by fear or anger? Or the sensitive politician, who weaves his web at every court, and is tremblingly alive to each of its vibrations? Or is the weaker state when threatened by the stronger?

There is no one, surely, more unfit for judging dispassionately of what is right to be done in cases of imminent peril, than the fearful. Fear pictures imaginary dangers. It excludes all reliance upon Providence. It therefore moves the mind from the settled resting place of fortitude, in which it is best prepared to meet and to overcome danger by moral intrepidity. Hence fear ought not to govern a rational being in the midst of peril, either as a motive or a guide. What has the man of integrity to fear?

With respect to the quick and headlong impulse of anger, he that seeks to attain any rational end while under its influence, instead of waiting for a calm, "puts to sea in the violence of a storm." As the instinctive principles which comprehend the appetites and desires must be restrained, so nothing is more true than that moral and intellectual beings are not to suffer the animal principle of resentment to hurry them indiscriminately and without deliberation into action.

If it be said that in well-disciplined armies there is neither fear nor anger, but a courageous and manly spirit, and therefore that these strictures do not apply, we grant the objection may be true, as far as it refers to these as instruments. But the case is widely different with those who make use of them. The soldier, being reduced, by a voluntary act, to the state of passive obedience, makes a conscience of submitting his will in everything to that of his superior; whether he be commanded to shoot his fellow soldier, or to destroy his enemy and burn his habitation, or to seize the property of his countrymen, or to expose his own life to certain destruction; and if he conscientiously believes this duty to be paramount, far be it from us to condemn him. We have not to do with the different degrees of light in the minds of men, but with the light of Scripture—the clear and explicit commands of Christ. When it can be proved from these that a man *may resist evil, may pursue his revenge with the sword, may hate his enemy and take away his life,* then we will give up the argument. But we think there would be more honesty in avowing that the yoke of Christian discipline is too hard for us to bear than in attempting to reconcile the duty of forbearance with revenge, the love of our enemies with their destruction, and the peaceable character with the warlike.

Christian laws have respect to the highest degree of human excellence: they admit no inferior standard of virtue; they will have men to be Christians in deed and in truth. They do not insist upon precise conformity in some, and allow partial conformity in others, merely because the latter choose a path for themselves not quite so straight. There is but one pattern of excellence proposed to all for imitation. All may fall short in degree: but no man is allowed to content himself with a relaxed discipline, or to fix any inferior rule. If so, the rule might vary in every community. And at last the conqueror might be esteemed more noble than the martyr; and the warlike Mahomet be set up as a more worthy example for men to follow than the peaceful Messiah.

Whatever allowance therefore may be made in the case of the hired soldier, to those at the helm of Christian states, as lawgivers and counselors, who send him upon his commission, and give the impulse to his movements, upon Christian principles, the same indulgence cannot be extended. Whether these may call it honor or national independence for which they have recourse to arms, it cannot be doubted that the true motives for organizing armies arise from fear, jealousy, or resentment.

Now, these are motives which ought not to enter into the mind of a Christian, much less to influence his conduct. With respect indeed to resentment, it would be more creditable at least to humanity that men should go forward to the work of death under this animal influence—because brute passion extinguishes for the time what is generous and amiable—than under the factitious and delusive influence of any other principle which has acquired a specious name among men, and which seems to permit the growth of good and evil together, one of the most dangerous kinds of union, because they are then so apt to be confounded, such as honor, glory and love of country. Human nature, the more it is refined and enlightened, the more it ought to possess of the milk of human kindness, and the less of a thirst for blood. True honor, true glory, true love of country, if the terms were rightly understood, would effectually restrain the inhabitants of any nation, who knew their real interests, from engaging in conflicts that must tend unavoidably to demoralize their countrymen, to waste their strength and resources and to subject themselves to reprisals from their enemies.

But honor, glory and love of country, by means of capricious and false associations, which artfully cover a deformity that could not be endured if the veil were removed, have long been prostituted to ends alike derogatory to reason, and abhorrent from the meek spirit of Christianity, which cannot therefore in any way be supposed to exalt the dignity of human nature. If they could have this effect, the world ought to be used as a great arena on which contending armies should be perpetually struggling for the support and exercise of the *military virtues,* instead of a theater for the display of benevolence, the diffusion of knowledge, the propagation of truth, the improvement and happiness of the human race, and the universal spread of peace and righteousness.

Some of the cases of presumed necessity, which have been urged by politicians, for embroiling two nations in war, are almost calculated to excite a smile—if it were possible to excite a smile on such a subject. The reasons have been so puerile, and the causes of difference so easy to have been removed by a little mutual concession, that it is marvelous that any stresss should have been laid on such pretended justifications; for these are seen by the dispassionate observers at a distance, in their true light, as unworthy of the least consideration in the scale of humanity and true national glory. The sensitive jealousy of politicians toward rival nations is always rankling as in a state of feverish excitement. To them "trifles light as air" are strong confirmations of intended coolness and hostility. They raise the phantom and they pursue it. Hence a political necessity for war has been urged on account of an obsolete claim of some insignificant portion of territory, or an alleged insult offered to a flag or an ambassador, or a breach of some state punctilio, or the exclusive monopoly of some article of commerce, or some private pique between rulers or ministers, or the fancied undue preponderance in the scale of balanced power, or some other of the many bubbles blown by secret ambition and constantly floating in the fluctuating element of diplomatic intrigue. It is manifest that every one of these causes could really have no more to do with *necessity* than the appearance of a comet; which in times of superstition it was imagined *did* exert some *necessary* influence in producing war—

> . . . *The Comet from its flaming hair,*
> *Shakes down diseases, pestilence and war.*

(Pope's "Homer")

When a weak state is menaced by one that is powerful, there is *prima facie* a strong justification for taking up arms to defend what are called its rights. The cause is supposed to be one which heaven must approve. The love of liberty natural to man awakes enthusiasm; the God of justice is invoked in aid of the enterprise: and, as if to encourage and embolden, the secret prayers of the friends of civil liberty in all countries *who look at the object without regarding the means,* are put up for its success. And what are the usual consequences? As if the Almighty Controller of human events designed to show his creature, man, that in this age of the world it is not by savage contention that the ends of his sovereign justice should be attained in the earth, the weak state is overthrown; wickedness is triumphant; thousands perhaps are slain; and the remainder reduced to a condition far more abject and degraded than if they had submitted peaceably to the aggression, with no other appearance of resistance than that moral sting which an unoffending and peaceable state throws against its adversary, when it protests firmly and energetically, with reason and justice on its side, against wanton and unprincipled aggression. In so hard a case as the latter, as human nature is constituted, the very agents would be ashamed of the commission they had undertaken; and they would be disposed, as far as lay in their power, to lessen the weight of oppression upon the innocent, instead of adding to the burden.

Of all the reasonings in favor of the use of arms, there is none which comes home more closely to flesh and blood, or is more triumphantly urged against the disciple of peace, than that which supposes the circumstance of a civil war and of a murderer at our own houses. In civil wars, it is well known that violence, as in the contentions of kindred, rages with unnatural fury; for men will bear oppression from strangers better than from their own countrymen; so that he who professes to be neutral, instead of being regarded as a friend, is commonly looked upon as an enemy by both parties.

And when the peace of a family circle is invaded, and instant destruction seems to be impending over our dearest connections, all that is human within us is roused by the argument in question, to justify the immediate attempt to destroy the guilty, for the purpose of defending the innocent.

Abstractedly viewing the two cases, there could scarcely be a difference of opinion respecting the course a man of common worldly prudence would adopt.

In the one case he would connect himself with one side or the other, as well to secure his safety as to fulfill what he might consider a point of duty. In the other, he would obey the impulse of his sensitive nature, and would pursue the first bent of his mind, not only in resisting the meditated wrong, but in taking the life of his opponent. With those to whom this world is everything, and father, mother, wife, children, friends, riches, possessions, privileges and life are dearer than the cross of Christ, with the promises of a blessed immortality annexed, it is perfectly clear that it would be nugatory to argue in this matter. But with any who place their hopes in heaven, and their reliance upon Providence, and who would rather surrender the object most dear to them than violate the least of the commands of the Prince of Peace, a momentary inquiry at least might be admitted:

Will heaven, indeed, permit the arm of violence to rob me of my friends or property, and perhaps my life? Shall I obey the commands of Christ in pursuing my enemy even to death? Shall I hurry an assassin to the grave in the midst of his crime, who may possibly become my friend, and sincerely repent of his wicked design? Shall I resist the violent on his own ground, with his own weapons, and on his own principles—those of violence? If I do, how then is the standard of peace to be supported in the world? How is the example of Christ himself imitated and recommended to others by such conduct?

If the first impulse is right and must be obeyed, these questions are not appropriate. If these questions strike the sincere Christian with any weight, and cannot be answered without serious misgivings, it is most probable that the first impulse is wrong, or at least is to be restrained by a higher principle.

After all, therefore, that can be said on either side, we must at last come to this question, whether the Lord's devoted followers, the peacemakers on whom Christ pronounced his blessing, not Christians by name and tradition only, not those who would cement the interest of two worlds together, which are incompatible—are to rely upon his Providence in their extremity, or on the use of means which seem directly to involve a breach of his divine laws, and to foster the indulgence of propensities entirely opposed to the enlargement of his peaceful kingdom. It is impossible to argue the case upon Christian principles without distinct reference to the immediate care of Providence. Unless this be taken for granted, all human reasoning is against the principles we defend.

If this be admitted, with those proper limitations which man's free agency requires, the cause of truth and innocence and justice must be the cause of God himself, and defensible only by moral weapons. He that proceeds to violence in the support of moral order usurps the scepter of the Sovereign Ruler, and employs the thunder, and the earthquake, and the flood, and the lightning against his fellow creature. But there is this essential difference: in the hands of the Almighty, the elemental conflict is succeeded by a state of calm, and it contributes to some good natural design, bringing things into harmony; whereas in the hands of man, when he attempts to wield these instruments of vengeance, in other words, of physical power, against his enemy, whatever calm may ensue, it is not the quiet of harmony but of smothered hate, ready, on the first slight occasion, to burst into fury.

In the one case, there is only a deformity of the natural world, which is slight and transient and salutary in its effects; in the other, a state of moral disorder, which the conflict does not terminate, but heartburnings and misery, and the various forms of moral evil, are left behind. For it must be confessed that war puts in operation a more demoralizing, inhuman and unchristian machinery than was ever devised by the perverted ingenuity of man. Its causes and its effects go hand in hand, and like the tree and its fruits, betray their affinity. On one side we may see the lust of dominion and of military fame, with its aspiring notions: on the other, fear and revenge, with its low, degrading passions, all alike antichristian, entering into the motives. As to the effects, we shall scarcely err in affirming that few conquerors ever yet returned from battle without some secret stings of conscience, nor armies, without more or less moral corruption; nor has any nation ever withdrawn itself from a contest without paying a severe and bloody price for all its victories.

Cicero would not have declared that he preferred the most unjust and disadvantageous peace to the justest war—*"iniquissimam pacem justissimo bello antefero"*—if his experience had not proved this to be the case. It cannot be doubted that he deduced this conclusion from facts more than from theory. And Tacitus, another enlightened Roman, takes it for granted, as a thing in itself obvious, that it was infinitely better for a nation to cultivate peace than to perplex itself with war—*"Quis ignorat satius ac melius esse pace frui quam bello vexari?"*

It is not to be supposed that heathen statesmen would have established principles like these in direct opposition to fact and expediency. How strong, then, must be the ground taken by the Christian statesman in advocating peace, when he finds that the principles of that religion which was sent to lead human nature to its highest perfection confirm the practical conclusions of the wise heathen! No man can be so bold as to argue that any one of the precepts of Christ, or any part of his conduct, can be construed into a direct or indirect vindication of war. On the other hand, the positive injunctions to maintain peace, and to subdue the elements of war, are numerous and unequivocal. And the same thing may be said of the apostles, with the casual exception of Peter, who met with a signal reproof at the time, strong enough to establish the law of peace forever: "Put up thy sword into the sheath: for all they that take the sword shall perish with the sword."

Jonathan Dymond

suggests that civil disobedience is the final duty of Christians

JONATHAN DYMOND [1796-1828] *was a leading Quaker intellectual of the early nineteenth century in England. The atrocities of the Napoleonic Wars strengthened his hatred of war, and as early as 1819 he was writing against it. He founded an auxiliary peace society in Exeter, England, in 1825. His "Inquiry into the Accordancy of War" presented the orthodox Quaker attitude of that era.*

It will perhaps be asked, what then are the duties of a subject who believes that all war is incompatible with his religion, but whose governors engage in a war and demand his service? We answer explicitly, *It is his duty, mildly and temperately, yet firmly, to refuse to serve.*

There are some persons, who, without any determinate process of reasoning, appear to conclude that responsibility for national measures attaches solely to those who direct them; that it is the business of *governments* to consider what is good for the community, and that, in these cases, the duty of the subject is merged in the will of the sovereign. Considerations like these are, I believe, often voluntarily permitted to become opiates of the conscience. "I have no part," it is said, "in the government, and am not therefore responsible for its crimes." We are, indeed, not responsible for the crimes of our rulers, but we are responsible for our own; and the crimes of our rulers *are* our own if whilst we believe them to be crimes we promote them by our cooperation. "It is at all times," says Gisborne, "the duty of an Englishman, steadfastly to decline obeying any orders of his superiors, which his conscience should tell him were in any degree impious or unjust."

The apostles, who instructed their converts to be subject to every ordinance of man for conscience' sake, and to submit themselves to those who were in authority, and who taught them that whoever resisted the power resisted the ordinance of God, made one necessary and uniform provision—*that the magistrate did not command them to do what God had commanded them to forbear.* With the regulations which the government of a country thought fit to establish, the apostles complied, whatever they might think of their wisdom or expediency, provided, and only provided, they did not, by this compliance, abandon their allegiance to the Governor of the world. It is scarcely necessary to observe in how many cases they refused to obey the commands of the governments under which they were placed, or how openly they maintained the duty of re-fusal, whenever these commands interfered with their higher obligations. It is narrated very early in the Acts that one of their number was im-prisoned for preaching, that he was commanded to preach no more, and was then released. Soon afterward all the apostles were imprisoned. "Did we not straitly command you," said the rulers, "that ye should not teach in this name?" The answer which they made is in point: "We ought to obey God rather than men." And this system they continued to pursue. If Caesar had ordered one of the apostles to be enrolled in his legions, does anyone believe that he would have served?

But those who suppose that obedience in all things is required, or that responsibility in political affairs is transferred from the subject to the sovereign, reduce themselves to a great dilemma. It is to say that we must resign our conduct and our consciences to the will of others, and act wickedly or well as their good or evil may preponderate, without merit for virtue or responsibility for crime. If the government directs you to fire your neighbor's property, or to throw him over a precipice, will you obey? If you will not, there is an end of the argument; for if you may reject its authority in one instance, where is the limit to rejection? There is no rational limit but that which is assigned by Christianity, and that is both rational and practicable. If anyone should ask the meaning of the words, "whoso resisteth the power resisteth the ordinance of God" —we answer that it refers to *active* resistance; *passive* resistance, or non-compliance, the apostles themselves practiced. On this point we should be distinctly understood. We are not so inconsistent as to recommend a civil war in order to avoid a foreign one. *Refusal to obey* is the *final* duty of Christians.

We think, then, that it is the business of every man who believes that war is inconsistent with our religion, respectfully but steadfastly to refuse to engage in it. Let such as these remember that an honorable and an awful duty is laid upon them. It is upon their fidelity, so far as human agency is concerned, that the cause of peace is suspended. Let them then be willing to avow their opinions and to defend them. Neither let them be contented with words, if more than words, if suffering also, is required. It is only by the unyielding perseverance of good that corruption can be extirpated. If you believe that Jesus Christ has prohibited slaughter, let not the opinion or the commands of a world induce you to join in it. By this "steady and determinate pursuit of vir-tue," the benediction which attaches to those who hear the sayings of God and do them will rest upon you, and the time will come when even the world will honor you, as contributors to the work of human refor-mation.

Noah Worcester
shows that war is the effect of a popular delusion

NOAH WORCESTER [1758-1837] *was an American clergyman, editor of the* Friend of Peace, *and the founder and secretary of the Massachusetts Peace Society. His* Solemn Review of the Custom of War, *which was published under the name of* Philo Pacificus, *is considered a classic in the history of peace literature. It was one of the first treatises to suggest the formation of what we might call modern peace societies. Worcester made personal sacrifices and deprived himself of the necessities of life to keep the Peace Society alive.*

The question to be considered is this: Cannot the state of society and the views of civilized men be so changed as to abolish so barbarous a custom, and render wars unnecessary and avoidable?

If this question may be answered in the affirmative, then we may hope that "the sword will not devour forever."

Some may be ready to exclaim, "None but God can produce such an effect as the abolition of war; and we must wait for the millennial day." We admit that God only can produce the necessary change in the state of society, and the views of men; but God works by human agency and human means. None but God could have produced such a change in the views of the British nation as to abolish the slave trade; yet the event was brought about by a long course of persevering and honorable exertions of benevolent men.

When the thing was first proposed, it probably appeared to the majority of the people as an unavailing and chimerical project. But God raised up powerful advocates, gave them the spirit of perseverance, and finally crowned their efforts with glorious success. Now, it is probable, thousands of people are wondering how such an abominable traffic ever had existence in a nation which had the least pretensions to Christianity or civilization. In a similar manner God can put an end to war, and fill the world with astonishment that rational beings ever thought of such a mode of settling controversies.

As to waiting for the millennium to put an end to war, without any exertions on our own part, it is like the sinner's waiting God's time for conversion, while he pursues his course of vice and impiety. If ever there shall be a millennium, in which the sword will cease to devour, it will probably be effected by the blessing of God on the benevolent exertions of enlightened men. Perhaps no one thing is now a greater obstacle in the way of the wished-for state of the church than the spirit and custom of war which is maintained by Christians themselves. Is it not then time that efforts should be made to enlighten the minds of Christians on a subject of such infinite importance to the happiness of the human race?

That such a state of things is desirable no enlightened Christian can deny. That it can be produced without expensive and persevering efforts is not imagined. But are not such efforts to exclude the miseries of war from the world as laudable as those which have for their object the support of such a malignant and desolating custom?

The whole amount of property in the United States is probably of far less value than what has been expended and destroyed within two centuries by wars in Christendom. Suppose, then, that one-fifth of this amount had been judiciously laid out by peace associations in the different states and nations, in cultivating the spirit and art of peace, and in exciting a just abhorrence of war; would not the other four-fifths have been in a great measure saved, besides many millions of lives, and an immense portion of misery? Had the whole value of what has been expended in wars been appropriated to the purpose of peace, how laudable would have been the appropriation and how blessed the consequences! . . .

If the eyes of people could be opened in regard to the evils and delusions of war, would it not be easy to form a confederacy of nations, and organize a high court of equity, to decide national controversies? Why might not such a court be composed of some of the most eminent characters from each nation, and a compliance with the decision of the court be made a point of national honor, to prevent the effusion of blood, and to preserve the blessings of peace? Can any considerate person say that the probability of obtaining right in such a court would be less than by an appeal to arms? When an individual appeals to a court of justice for the redress of wrongs, it is not always the case that he obtains his right. Still, such an appeal is more honorable, more safe, and more certain, as well as more benevolent, than for the individual to attempt to obtain redress by his pistol, or his sword. And are not the reason for avoiding an appeal to the sword, for the redress of wrongs, always great in proportion to the calamities, which such an appeal must naturally involve? If this be a fact, then there is infinitely greater reason why two nations should avoid an appeal to arms, than usually exists against a bloody combat between two contending individuals. . . .

The impression that aggressive war is murderous is general among Christians, if not universal. The justness of the impression seems to be admitted by almost every government in going to war. For this reason each of two governments endeavors to fix on the other the charge of aggression, and to assume to itself the ground of defending some right, or avenging some wrong. Thus each excuses itself, and charges the other with all the blood and misery which result from the contest.

These facts, however, are so far from affording a plea in favor of the custom of war that they afford a weighty reason for its abolition. If, in the view of conscience, the aggressor is a murderer, and answerable for the blood shed in war; if one or the other must be viewed by God as the aggressor; and if such is the delusion attending war that each party is liable to consider the other as the aggressor, surely there must be serious danger of a nation's being involved in the guilt of murder, while they imagine they have a cause which may be justified.

So prone are men to be blinded by their passions, their prejudices and their interests that in most private quarrels, each of two individuals persuades himself that he is in the right, and his neighbor in the wrong. Hence the propriety of arbitrations, references and appeals to courts of justice, that persons more disinterested may judge, and prevent that injustice and desolation which would result from deciding private disputes by single combats or acts of violence.

But rulers of nations are as liable to be misled by their passions and interests as other men; and when misled, they are very sure to mislead those of their subjects who have confidence in their wisdom and integrity. Hence it is highly important that the custom of war should be abolished, and some other mode adopted, to settle disputes between nations. In private disputes there may be cause of complaint on each side, while neither has reason to shed the blood of the other: much less to shed the blood of innocent family connections, neighbors and friends. So, of two nations, each may have cause of complaint, while neither can be justified in making war; and much less in shedding the blood of innocent people, who have had no hand in giving the offense.

It is an awful feature in the character of war, and a strong reason why it should not be countenanced, that it involves the innocent with the guilty in the calamities it inflicts, and often falls with the greatest vengeance on those who have had no concern in the management of national affairs. It surely is not a crime to be born in a country which is afterwards invaded; yet in how many instances do warmakers punish, or destroy, for no other crime than being a native or resident of an invaded territory! A mode of revenge or redress which makes no distinction between the innocent and the guilty ought to be discountenanced by every friend to justice and humanity.

Besides, as the rulers of a nation are as liable as other people to be governed by passion and prejudice, there is as little prospect of justice in permitting war for the decision of national disputes as there would be in permitting an incensed individual to be, in his own cause, complainant, witness, judge, jury and executioner.

5

THE RISE OF PROTESTANT PACIFISM

[1400-1814]

By the beginning of the fifteenth century, already well into the Renaissance, the monastic pacifism of the Middle Ages gave way to the teaching of nonviolence by various nonorthodox religious sects. Individuals
too made important contributions to pacifist ideals. The Dutch humanist Erasmus consistently opposed war and violence throughout the late
fifteenth and early sixteenth century. Two of the most important religious leaders of the Protestant movement, Martin Luther and John
Calvin, were individual advocates of pacifist principles during their early
years. But both of them discarded these principles later in life: Luther
during the Peasant Revolt in 1524, when he urged the nobles to be
merciless in their suppression of the peasants (although his own writings
on Christian liberty had inspired the revolt); and Calvin when the
Spanish heretic theologian Michael Servetus was seized by Calvin's own
order and burned at the stake.

Most of the churches that preached pacifist ideas were Protestant
sects breaking away from the Catholic orthodoxy. Among them the
Mennonites, who were an Anabaptist sect, became the first of what have
been described as the historic peace churches. They taught nonviolence
and held to it in their daily lives. The sect originated in Switzerland as
the Swiss Brethren. In 1524 one of their early leaders said that true
Christians "are sheep among wolves, sheep for the slaughter, who must
be baptized in anxiety and need, tribulation, persecution, suffering and
death, who must be tested in the fire, and who must find the homeland
of eternal rest not by the means of killing but by spiritual means. They
use neither worldly sword nor war, for among them killing is done away
with altogether." * A century later, Mennonites in their Dortrecht Confession reiterated this early principle: "Regarding revenge, whereby we

* Harold S. Bender, *Conrad Grebel*, p. 179.

resist our enemies with the sword, we believe and confess that the Lord Jesus has forbidden his disciples and followers all revenge and resistance, and has thereby commanded them not to 'return evil for evil, nor railing for railing'; but to 'put up the sword into the sheath,' or, as the prophets foretold, 'beat them into ploughshares.' " *

Since its founding in the seventeenth century, the Society of Friends has been the religious group most consistent in its testimony against war. From the beginning they maintained that it was possible for states to deal with each other according to the same Christian principles that governed the relationships of individuals. George Fox, an Englishman who founded the society, made one of the first Quaker testimonies against war in 1650 from prison, where he had been sent for blasphemy. Toward the end of his term, Fox was offered release if he would take up arms for the Commonwealth against the king. "I told them I knew from whence all wars arose," he said; "even from the lust, according to James's doctrine, and that I lived in the virtue of that life and power that took away the occasion of all wars." †

The Quakers have always cooperated with their respective governments unless the government's will violated their belief in peace; and at such times they have offered passive resistance and civil disobedience to any attempt to involve them in war.

Like the Society of Friends and the Mennonites, the Church of the Brethren has upheld the Biblical doctrine of nonviolence. Their earliest meetings dealt with nonresistance. "They have been a nonresistant people, choosing rather to suffer wrongs than, by physical force, to oppose them. They have always opposed war, and as a church have refused any active, voluntary participation therein. On all questions consistent with their religious convictions they have given loyal support to the government, but cannot permit their members to learn the art of war." ‡

A number of other religious sects that were formed between the fifteenth and late seventeenth centuries spoke out against war. Among them were the Collegiants, a movement of Dutch origin, who believed in religion without dogma, who opposed the taking of oaths and agitated against all war; the Schwenkfelders, followers of Kaspar Schwenkfeld, a Silesian nobleman, whose views were almost identical with the Mennonites' (in a *Candid Declaration* published in 1777, they stated that their conscience forbade them to take up arms and kill their fellow men); the

---

* Guy Franklin Hershberger, *War, Peace, and Nonresistance,* p. 371.
† *Journal of George Fox,* Vol. I.
‡ Otho Winger, *History and Doctrines of the Church of the Brethren,* p. 213.

Shakers, whose fundamental precepts were nonresistance and nonparticipation in government affairs; the Dukhobors, Russian Slavs who won Leo Tolstoy to their cause when they came into conflict with the czar's government over conscription. They believed that man, who is endowed with a conscience and reason, need not resort to the use of physical force.

These religious groups were the real pacifists of their time, but they were by no means the only people who talked about peace. To many thinkers, peace seemed a reasonable ideal for secular reasons, and a number of them outlined plans for preventing war. The authors were not necessarily pacifists, but they all agreed that war was folly, and offered their plans in the hope of perpetuating peace. In the fourteenth century, Dante had proposed a world empire in *De Monarchia*. Pierre Dubois, an adviser to King Philip le Bel of France, called for a federation of sovereign Christian states in *On the Recovery of the Holy Land*.

Most schemes proposed between the sixteenth and eighteenth centuries called for some form of federation of sovereign European states. The Great Design of Henry IV and the Duke of Sully suggested the division of Europe into fifteen equal parts with an international army, as a way of maintaining a balance of power; a similar proposal made by Éméric Crucé suggested a kingdom of all Europe and called for arbitration. "The evil passions of princes are the real causes of wars," Crucé said. "Human society is a body all of whose members have a common sympathy, so that it is impossible for the sickness of one not to be communicated to the others." *

The Abbé Charles Irénée Castel de Saint-Pierre proposed a twenty-four-delegate Senate of Europe; and William Penn wrote an "Essay Towards the Present and Future Peace of Europe by the Establishment of an European Diet, Parliament, or Estates." Penn's idea was based on Christian ethics. Through his treaty with the American Indians, he had set up an unarmed government in Pennsylvania. "We meet on the broad pathway of good faith and good will," Penn said. "No advantage shall be taken on either side, but all shall be openness and love. . . ."

And Hugo Grotius laid the basis for a code of international law with *De Jure Belli ac Pacis*, published in 1625. Like many others, Grotius suggested congresses and courts of arbitration; but he also included in his scheme the regulation and humanizing of war.

Neither these proposals nor the work of the pacifist sects could prevent war and revolution during these 400 years as Europe was making the transition to the modern period. But, conversely, the trumpets of

* Quoted in A. C. F. Beales, *The History of Peace*, p. 29.

war never silenced the talk of peace. Even when peace seemed an impossible vision, men dreamed of it—the dream of Isaiah, the dream of the new peace societies.

Immanuel Kant
outlines the basis of perpetual peace

IMMANUEL KANT [1724-1804], *the great German philosopher, was born in Prussia and subjected to a strict Pietist religion at an early age. He was not a churchgoer but he retained the stamp of German Puritanism.* Critique of Pure Reason, *his* magnum opus, *startled the philosophic world and influenced all philosophic thought that followed it. Most teachers in Prussian universities supported the monarchy, but Kant hailed the French Revolution. He was reprimanded by the Prussian king because "you misuse your philosophy to undermine and destroy many of the most important and fundamental doctrines of the Holy Scripture and of Christianity." Kant's work* Perpetual Peace *was published in 1795. Under its title the author wrote: "These words were once put by a Dutch innkeeper on his signboard as a satirical inscription over the representation of a chuchyard cemetery."*

> *Standing armies* (miles perpetuus) *shall be abolished in course of time.*

For they are always threatening other states with war by appearing to be in constant readiness to fight. They incite the various states to outrival one another in the number of their soldiers, and to this number no limit can be set. Now, since owing to the sums devoted to this purpose, peace at last becomes even more oppressive than a short war, these standing armies are themselves the cause of wars of aggression, undertaken in order to get rid of this burden. To which we must add that the practice of hiring men to kill or to be killed seems to imply a use of them as mere machines and instruments in the hand of another (namely, the state) which cannot easily be reconciled with the right of humanity in our own person.* The matter stands quite differently in the case of voluntary periodical military exercise on the part of citizens of the state, who thereby seek to secure themselves and their country against attack from without. The accumulation of treasure in a state would in the same way be regarded by other states as a menace of war, and might compel them to anticipate this by striking the first blow. For of the three forces, the power of arms, the power of alliance and the power of money, the last might well become the most reliable instrument of war, did not the difficulty of ascertaining the amount stand in the way. . . .

No state shall violently interfere with the constitution and administration of another.

For what can justify it in so doing? The scandal which is here presented to the subjects of another state? The erring state can much more serve as a warning by exemplifying the great evils which a nation draws down on itself through its own lawlessness. Moreover, the bad example which one free person gives another (as *scandalum acceptum*) does no injury to the latter. In this connection, it is true, we cannot count the case of a state which has become split up through internal corruption into two parts, each of them representing by itself an individual state which lays claim to the whole. Here the yielding of assistance to one faction could not be reckoned as interference on the part of a foreign state with the constitution of another, for here anarchy prevails. So long, however, as the inner strife has not yet reached this stage, the interference of other powers would be a violation of the rights of an independent nation which is only struggling with internal disease. It would therefore itself cause a scandal and make the autonomy of all states insecure.

The law of nations shall be founded on a federation of free states.

Nations, as states, may be judged like individuals who, living in the natural state of society—that is to say, uncontrolled by external law—injure one another through their very proximity. Every state, for the sake of its own security, may—and ought to—demand that its neighbor should submit itself to conditions similar to those of the civil society where the right of every individual is guaranteed. This would give rise to a federation of nations which, however, would not have to be a state of nations. That would involve a contradiction. For the term "state" implies the relation of one who rules to those who obey—that is to say, of lawgiver to the subject people: and many nations in one state would constitute only one nation, which contradicts our hypothesis, since here we have to consider

* A Bulgarian Prince thus answered the Greek emperor who magnanimously offered to settle a quarrel with him, not by shedding the blood of his subjects, but by a duel: "A smith who has tongs will not take the red-hot iron from the fire with his hands."

the right of one nation against another, in so far as they are so many separate states and are not to be fused into one.

The attachment of savages to their lawless liberty, the fact that they would rather be at hopeless variance with one another than submit themselves to a legal authority constituted by themselves, that they therefore prefer their senseless freedom to a reason-governed liberty, is regarded by us with profound contempt as barbarism and uncivilization and the brutal degradation of humanity. So one would think that civilized races, each formed into a state by itself, must come out of such an abandoned condition as soon as they possibly can. On the contrary, however, every state thinks rather that its majesty (the "majesty" of a people is an absurd expression) lies just in the very fact that it is subject to no external legal authority; and the glory of the ruler consists in this, that, without his requiring to expose himself to danger, thousands stand at his command ready to let themselves be sacrificed for a matter of no concern to them. The difference between the savages of Europe and those of America lies chiefly in this, that, while many tribes of the latter have been entirely devoured by their enemies, Europeans know a better way of using the vanquished than by eating them; and they prefer to increase through them the number of their subjects, and so the number of instruments at their command for still more widely spread war.

The depravity of human nature shows itself without disguise in the unrestrained relations of nations to each other, while in the law-governed civil state much of this is hidden by the check of government. This being so, it is astonishing that the word "right" has not yet been entirely banished from the politics of war as pedantic, and that no state has yet ventured to publicly advocate this point of view. For Hugo Grotius, Puffendorf, Vattel and others—Job's comforters, all of them—are always quoted in good faith to justify an attack, although their codes, whether couched in philosophical or diplomatic terms, have not—nor can have—the slightest legal force, because states as such are under no common external authority; and there is no instance of a state having ever been moved by argument to desist from its purpose, even when this was backed up by the testimony of such great men. This homage which every state renders—in words at least—to the idea of right, proves that, although it may be slumbering, there is, notwithstanding, to be found in man a still higher natural moral capacity by the aid of which he will in time gain the mastery over the evil principle in his nature, the existence of which he is unable to deny. And he hopes the same of others; for otherwise the word "right" would never be uttered by states who wish to wage war, unless to deride it like the Gallic prince who declared: "The privilege which nature gives the strong is that the weak must obey them."

The method by which states prosecute their rights can never be by process of law—as it is where there is an external tribunal—but only by war. Through this means, however, and its favorable issue, victory, the question of right is never decided. A treaty of peace makes, it may be, an end to the war of the moment, but not to the conditions of war which at any time may afford a new pretext for opening hostilities; and this we cannot exactly condemn as unjust, because under these conditions everyone is his own judge. Notwithstanding, not quite the same rule applies to states according to the law of nations as holds good of individuals in a lawless condition according to the law of nature, namely, "that they ought to advance out of this condition." This is so because, as states, they have already within themselves a legal constitution, and have therefore advanced beyond the stage at which others, in accordance with their ideas of right, can force them to come under a wider legal constitution. Meanwhile, however, reason, from her throne of the supreme lawgiving moral power, absolutely condemns war as a morally lawful proceeding, and makes a state of peace, on the other hand, an immediate duty.

Without a compact between the nations, however, this state of peace cannot be established or assured. Hence there must be an alliance of a particular kind which we may call a covenant of peace (*foedus pacificum*), which would differ from a treaty of peace (*pactum pacis*) in this respect, that the latter merely puts an end to one war, while the former would seek to put an end to war forever. This alliance does not aim at the gain of any power whatsoever of the state, but merely at the preservation and security of the freedom of the state for itself and of other allied states at the same time. The latter do not, however, require, for this reason, to submit themselves like individuals in the state of nature to public laws and coercion. The practicability or objective reality of this idea of federation, which is to extend gradually over all states and so lead to perpetual peace, can be shown. For if fortune ordains that a powerful and enlightened people should form a republic—which by its very nature is inclined to perpetual peace—this would serve as a center of federal union for other states wishing to join, and thus secure conditions of freedom among the states in accordance with the idea of the law of nations. Gradually, through different unions of this kind, the federation would extend further and further.

It is quite comprehensible that a people should say, "There shall be no war among us, for we shall form ourselves into a state, that is to say, constitute for ourselves a supreme legislative, administrative and judicial power which will settle our disputes peaceably." But if this state says, "There shall be no war between me and other states, although I recognize no supreme lawgiving power which will secure me my rights and whose rights I will guarantee," then it is not at all clear upon what grounds I could base my confidence in my right, unless it were the substitute for that compact on which civil society is based—namely, free federation which reason must necessarily connect with the idea of the law of nations, if indeed any meaning is to be left in that concept at all.

There is no intelligible meaning in the idea of the law of nations as giving a right to make war; for that must be a right to decide what is just, not in accordance with universal, external laws limiting the freedom of each individual, but by means of one-sided maxims applied by force. We must then understand by this that men of such ways of thinking are quite justly served when they destroy one another, and thus find perpetual peace in the wide grave which covers all the abominations of acts of violence as well as the authors of such deeds. For states, in their relation to one another, there can be, according to reason, no other way of advancing from that lawless condition which unceasing war implies than by giving up their savage lawless freedom, just as individual men have done, and yielding to the coercion of public laws. Thus they can form a state of nations (*civitas gentium*), one, too, which will be ever increasing and would finally embrace all the peoples of the earth. States, however, in accordance with their understanding of the law of nations, by no means desire this, and therefore reject *in hypothesi* what is correct *in thesi*. Hence, instead of the positive idea of a world republic, if all is not to be lost, only the negative substitute for it, a federation averting war, maintaining its ground and ever extending over the world may stop the current of this tendency to war and shrinking from the control of law. But even then there will be a constant danger that this propensity may break out. *"Furor impius intus—fremit horridus ore cruento"* (Virgil).

Job Scott

shows war to be incompatible with Christianity

JOB SCOTT [1751-1793] *was an American Quaker and extreme mystic. Personal experience was the essence of his religion: "If thou dost not feel it, it is nothing." He emphasized the spiritual nature of life. During the American Revolution he suffered privation because he did not want to accept paper currency, which had been issued to finance the war. His pamphlet "War Inconsistent with the Doctrine and Example of Jesus Christ" was a letter to a friend, and was "recommended to the perusal of the professors of Christianity."*

DEAR SIR,

When I saw you lately, you may remember a part of our conversation turned on war—and perhaps you thought me singular in some of my sentiments, as controverting the received opinion of men in general. I have therefore devoted an hour or two to state further to you my particular views on this subject.

It is really astonishing to observe with how much composure mankind, and many persons acknowledged to be among the best men living, admit the propriety of war; and while they in general terms deplore the misery of it, maintain its necessity in some shape or other; for the most part, in that of defense. Under this mask, the great adversary of men has so imposed on them that they do not even think of discussing the lawfulness of war in any case, though they profess to act on Christian principles. For my own part, I cannot help wishing to see it become a subject of universal discussion, till the renunciation of the tenet shall spread itself as wide as the misery it has produced.

War, however dreadful in its progress, and awful in its consequences, has always been pleaded for as necessary. Time would be lost in endeavoring to prove what scarcely anyone will deny, namely, "the unlawfulness of *offensive wars,*" even on moral, much less on Christian principles. The most thorough-paced politician, to the existence of whose power and dominion war is necessary, will always produce acts of aggression on the part of his adversaries, and justify his measures as defensive, on the ground of necessity. How liable such reasoning is to objection will be evident when it is considered that under this plea, the most ambitious and arbitrary tyrants have justified their vilest atrocities; and if war be convenient, and promise a partial gain, an argument in justification will always be too readily found, although one certain consequence of war is a *"general loss"*—the gain only accruing to an inconsiderable number of individuals.

In these sentiments, then, I have not merely to contend with men who oppose all the order of society, by committing depredation and offense universally; but with those also who interweave the system of bloodshed with the profession of Christianity.

And here it is necessary to observe that all war, even admitting an aggression, goes on the principle of rendering evil for evil. And how difficult is it, even politically, to decide where the aggression begins, or how one nation possesses a right to call in question what to another nation seems an equal right of theirs; yet in questions of this kind frequently originate the most bloody, destructive and unnatural wars. And even admitting the case to be clearly made out, how often does the retaliation of the injured party exceed the offense! In which case, in a moral point of view, they certainly change ground, and the original aggressors become the injured party. Many instances of this kind might be stated, but I shall name one only—the late contest between Great Britain and America. America had chartered rights, which she supposed were infringed by the parent state; she remonstrated and petitioned; the parent state resisted, and refused her demands. America resisted again. Great Britain exercised coercion and sent over an army. America raised a counter army to defend her rights, and was finally successful. And yet how often in that contest did the parties change ground, and each act offensively as well as defensively? And who can state precisely where the act of aggression began, or where retaliation ought to have ceased? Indeed, the subject seems involved in all this intricacy and these evil consequences, as if, by a special intervention of Providence, the rash steps of man should be restrained from going to the extreme bounds of right, lest they should overleap those bounds and enter upon the territory of wrong. In some cases the right will seem more clear; and perhaps on certain principles, may be made out; but as the question is, not whether morality, but whether Christianity allow of war on such occasions, I am bound no further than to the consideration of the latter part of the question. I therefore state the following proposition, as a truth intimately connected with the nature of Christianity, and as a sentiment which will finally prevail.

That war in every shape is incompatible with the nature of Christianity; and that no persons professing that religion, and under the full and proper inflence of the temper and mind of Christ, can adopt, pursue or plead for it. . . .

I have sometimes given scope to my imagination and fancied myself engaged in war, in the defense of the best cause for which the sword was ever drawn—civil liberty, and the deliverance of the oppressed from the hand of tyranny; and have, for the moment, supposed it to be lawful; I have anticipated the sound of the trumpet leading on to the charge, and then have plunged amidst the roaring of cannon, or the clangor of arms in the heat of action—either leading on or led, my bosom swelling with the importance of the cause, my heart beating high, I looked on death with defiance, and on my foes with disdain, determining to conquer or perish in the attempt. All fresh from this bloody scene, I have brought my temper, my bosom, my heart, to the great Exemplar of Christian perfection, and shame has covered me. What trait of the mind of Christ did I follow when I defied death? Did I do it as a Christian? Ah, no! Could my hopes of endless glory be certain during the eventful and bloody scene? Did the spirit of the Christian religion, or the pattern of the holy Jesus, inspire me with disdain for my enemies, while piercing their vitals, and sending their souls into the shades of death? No; he commanded me to love my enemies, but I have been destroying them: he has enjoined submission and suffering, but I have sought for superiority, victory and conquest. On the whole, let that man stand forth, if earth can produce him, who can say he goes into action and engages in the heat of war in that spirit which he is conscious will be approved and owned by the Judge of all the earth, when all our subterfuges and self-impositions must be renounced; and if such a one should arise, and declare that he could do so, I for my own part should infer that a depraved heart had perverted his judgment. But if it be admitted that the temper of mind necessary for the action of war is inconsistent with Christianity, I have all I ask; and those who argue for war have to support an allowed indefensible scheme. But let professing Christians beware how they support it, for in proportion as they give their aid to it, they impede the real progress of Christ's religion.

I shall now notice, and endeavor to answer, some of the most popular objections in favor of the fighting system. It is said that if any nation were to adopt the pacific conduct I have recommended, the surrounding nations of the world would beset and swallow it up. But be it remembered that I expect this conduct only to proceed from the effects of Christianity;* and this, if real and effectual, supposes a degree, a large degree, of confidence and dependence upon God; and were I to bring Scripture, or matter of fact, to prove that such a people were never forsaken nor confounded, it would be like holding a taper to the sun. Who ever trusted in God, and were confounded? Who ever depended on his aid, and were not delivered? Who, in the exercise of obedience to his precepts, were ever forsaken? The annals of time cannot produce an instance—the annals of time can produce thousands against it.

Let facts speak; the man, the family, the society, the nation, who live in obedience to his commands, have God's peculiar attention: his arm is an invincible shield; and when a man's ways please the Lord, he marketh even his enemies to be at peace with him. But if, in the wise and inscrutable ways of his Providence, he permits some to suffer, in order to excite stronger zeal in others, and to spread truth by their sufferings, this is no argument in favor of resistance by violence; nor should we impute their sufferings merely to the conquest and superiority of their enemies, but to divine permission, that thousands may be won by the firmness and constancy, the patience and exalted piety with which they meet the terrors of their persecutors. The conquest is on their side, and they go by the very means of persecution (however evil the intention) from an inferior to a superior enjoyment, from earth to heaven: in this, Christianity at first triumphed; not by the law of retaliation, or force, but by a constant, faithful adherence to the law of Christ.

And, oh! had reformers and their followers stopped there, instead of endeavoring to support the cause of piety by temporal power and the

* Let it not be forgotten that we are a *professing* Christian nation.

secular arm, the spirit of Christ had still been seen triumphant. But the idea of maintaining true religion, pure and undefiled religion, by pomp and splendor, by power and the sword, is like death in the pot, destructive of the true notion and spirit of Christianity: in false apprehensions of external glory and worldly splendor lay the ground of this error, which the Scriptures, the example of Christ himself, and the experience of good men, uniformly combat. The idea of a temporal Messiah, says a good writer, is mean and carnal: this mean idea hath possessed the minds of the professed disciples of Christ in all ages. The apostles indeed soon struggled through such low secular notions; but a very large succession of their pretended followers have expired incurable under this disease.

That the Christian Church is not indebted for its existence and success, even in this age of the world, to the sword has lately been instanced in the history of the Quakers, and of the Moravians, whose example in this respect, it is much to be regretted, is so little followed.

Another argument which I have heard, and am grieved that I do not wrong human nature in reporting it, is that were it not for the intervention of wars, the inhabitants of the earth would be too numerous; and that wars therefore are necessary to prevent a pressure which the earth could not sustain. Providence, say some, ordains or permits the continuance of war to thin the ranks of life, and take the superfluous out of the way. Humanity, to say nothing of religion, shudders at such an argument! It might suit a Nero, an Attila, or a Tamerlane, but only with wretches of that sanguinary cast can the argument have any weight. For an answer to this I would only refer its advocates to their own bosom: to the terrors, the consciousness, the horror, which must shortly awaken the keen sensations of the guilt of bloodshed, and condemn them at that bar where hypocrisy shall lose its mask, and the cruel meet with a full reward. The argument can have no weight with a heart susceptible of human sensibility; much less with those persons who study and imitate the compassion of the Lord and Saviour Jesus Christ.

Another objection is founded on the argument of natural or civil right, and infers the justice of resistance, in defense of those rights and liberties, which are by many esteemed dearer than life itself, and to maintain which thousands have died.

This objection has a degree of weight and may be tenable on the score of natural religion. It was under this case that the Jews often fought, and had the divine command; and under this case also many of the Gentile nations have resisted the invasions of tyrants and oppressors, and a system of human policy may justify such resistance to the oppressions of tyranny. It has indeed been lauded under the name of patriotism; but Christianity calls on us to renounce it for submission, for suffering for Christ's sake, and for the exercise of patience and endurance. To make it lawful for Christians to wage war, some abatement must necessarily be made, from the positive commands of Christ to "love our enemies," to "do good to them that hate us," to "return good for evil"—commands of equal import with those which instituted all the ordinances of the gospel, and, deserving of no less regard. To what a wonderful degree of prejudice then must the minds of professing Christians have risen to question these commands, or rob them of their effect! You see I take the liberty of differing from the general sentiments of allowed good men on this subject; but remember, I am accountable to none but God. No human tribunal can with justice interfere with the rights of conscience; and I have a hope that if an interchange on sentiments were possible, I should find thousands and millions who think with me; and although I infer nothing from multitude, yet I think the hope is not vain. The dreadful avidity with which war has been pursued of late by the French nation, by the Continental allies, and the deep, affecting and determined part which our own country has taken in it, will, I trust, arouse professing Christians to a consideration of their ways, and to think seriously of discussing the lawfulness of war, and the nature of those arguments by which it is supported; which could not fail, in some degree, to remove from before the minds of men the veil which has so long and so unhappily obscured their moral vision. This must be the case before obedience to Christ is much more prevalent, or before it becomes universal; a blessing which we have reason to expect, and confidence to pray for, supported as we are by many of the prophetic promises of Scripture, which remain yet to be fulfilled.

It were to be wished that this might be made the subject for some academic or scholastic prize. If treated in a proper manner, it could not fail to make the question more popular, and the subject better understood. The miseries of war, its expenses, the national losses and the immoral effects caused by it, furnish matter too copious for me to urge within my present compass and design; and they are worthy of much abler and more minute discussion than mine. With a hope, and some degree of expectation, that such a discussion may hereafter prevail, I daily use that petition of my Master—"Thy kingdom come."

I am, dear Sir,

Yours, etc.

Anthony Benezet

warns that the consequences of war are timeless

ANTHONY BENEZET [1713-1784] *was born in St.-Quentin, France, of Huguenot parents, who moved to England to escape religious persecution. Benezet joined the Society of Friends, and in 1731 went to Philadelphia, where he taught in a Friends school, and then founded a school for girls. In 1755 he was one of a group of Friends who protested the Militia Bill. They warned that they would not pay war taxes and demanded "measures consistent with our peaceable principles." In 1774 Benezet pleaded with representatives of the Continental Congress for abolition of slavery and the maintenance of peace. Even after the Revolutionary War began, he published pamphlets preaching peace. "Serious Considerations on Several Important Questions" was published in 1778.*

War, considered in itself, is the premeditated and determined destruction of human beings, of creatures originally *formed after the image of God,* and whose preservation, for that reason, is secured by heaven itself within the fence of this righteous law, that *at the hand of every man's brother, the life of man shall be required.* And though this created image of our holy God must be owned to have been so wretchedly defaced as to retain but a very faint resemblance of its divine original, yet as the highest enforcement of that heavenly law which was published for the security of life, it is most graciously renewed by the incarnation of the son of God, and the indwelling of the Holy Ghost. . . .

War, like all other evils, is described as centering in itself; and the end of it is declared to be gratification of those very appetites and passions from which it derives its birth; for in this unhappy circle, which is indeed the great circle of the history of man, the fatal mischief proceeds. *War is the inseparable union between the sensual and malignant passions; war protracted to a certain period necessarily compels peace; peace revives and extends trade and commerce; trade and commerce give new life, vigor and scope to the sensual and malignant passions, and these naturally tend to generate another war.*

The disorders of nature and of life are wholly the effects of sin, of a voluntary aversion and alienation from the life, light and love of God, in perfect union, with which perfect peace and happiness are only to be found; hence that discordance of the outward elements, which brings forth pestilence, famine, earthquakes, storms and tempests; hence, in the corporal part of the human frame, pain, sickness and death; in the mental, sensuality, pride and malignity, including all the selfish and wrathful passions, that between individuals engender envy, hatred, injury, resentment and revenge; and between nations, a peculiar kind of enmity and wrong, that issues in war. Surrounded with evil as men are, and full of evil themselves, what would become of the whole wretched race at any given instant of time, at this very moment, for example, if the effect of that evil were not continually suspended, and directed by infinite power; so as to become continually subservient to the purposes of infinite wisdom, righteousness and love.

It would be needless to mention the nature of that universal redemption which is proposed by the gospel if in this age of levity we were not so apt to forget it. It is, in general, a full restoration of the life of God in the soul; the life of the Father, Son and Holy Spirit, which was once the life and perfection of fallen man, which the Son of God, the bruiser of the serpent, has by his suffering been restoring to human nature from the time in which Adam fell.

When the Son of God became incarnate, what was implied in this restoration as the effect of its influence upon man was fully evident from our blessed Saviour's doctrine and his life; namely, the conquest and renunciation of the world, the death of the will and of all the appetites and passions of fallen animal nature, through faith in his name—not a historical and speculative faith, a mere rational assent to the truth of a well attested history of facts and doctrines, but a full, ardent, continual desire of the *life of Christ,* as begotten and formed in the soul, by the continual operation of the Holy Ghost. Thus it was that at first the personal duties of single Christians, when they were scattered over the face of the earth and were only parts of different nations, became afterward national duties, when whole nations became Christians. If, therefore, *to love our enemy, to forgive him, to do him good, and pray for him;* if to *overcome the world,* whose power consists in *the lust of the flesh, the lust of the eye, and the pride of life,* are Christian personal duties, if to *love the Lord our God with all our heart, with all our soul, with all our mind, and with all our strength, and our fellow creatures as ourselves,* is the purity and perfection of the Christian personal life, the same must also be true of a Christian national duty; for a Christian nation differs no otherwise from a Christian person than as the whole differs from one of the parts of which it essentially consists.

It would be needless to propose this subject to the consideration of experimental Christians, who know with certainty that human nature, left to itself, has no power but that of producing mere evil, and that everything within it and without it that is either great or good, is the free gift of grace, the unmerited bounty of redeeming love. But the true Christian spirit being much departed from the earth, true Christian knowledge, as its inseparable companion, is departed with it, and men seem to be gone back again to their old animal life; and though in speculation and idea they profess an assent to the truths of revelation, yet in heart and practice they are apt to consider the course of all things as connected only with temporal good and evil, and themselves as the center and circumference, the first cause, and the last end of all, ascribing *to human understanding designs which only infinite Wisdom can form, and to human power events which Omnipotence only can produce.* If the Christian, however, recollects himself, he will find *war* to be a sad consequence of the apostacy and fall of man, when he was abandoned to the fury of his own lusts and passions,* as the natural and penal effects of breaking loose from the divine government, the fundamental law of which is LOVE; *thou shall love the Lord thy God with all thy heart, with all thy soul, with all thy mind, with all thy strength, and thy fellow creatures as thyself.*

The consequences of war, when impartially examined, will be found big, not only with outward and temporal distress, but also with an evil that extends itself (where in the darkness and tumult of human passions, it is by many neither expected nor conceived to reach) even into the regions of eternity. That property is confounded, scattered, and destroyed; that laws are trampled under foot, government despised, and the ties of all civil and domestic order broken into pieces; that fruitful countries are made deserts, and stately cities a heap of ruins, that matrons and virgins are violated; and neither the innocence of unoffending infancy nor the impotence of decrepit age afford protection from the rage and thirst for blood; this is but the mortal progeny of this teeming womb of mischief; the worst, even the dreadful effect it has upon the immortal soul, is still behind; and though remote from those senses and passions that are exercised only by present good and evil, must yet, upon the least recollection, impress with horror every mind that believes there is a righteous God, and a state of retribution, that is to last forever.

Under these considerations, what must the real Christian feel; he who is fully convinced that the fall of man is a fall from meekness, purity and love, into sensuality, pride and wrath; that the Son of God became incarnate, and suffered and died to restore that first life of meekness, purity and love; and that for these in whom the restoration of that life is not begun, in the present state the Son of God incarnate, it is to be feared, suffered and died in vain. What must he feel for those immortal spirits who in the earliest dawn of their day of purification, are by hundreds and thousands driven into eternity—some inflamed with drunkenness, some fired with lust, and all stained with blood? In those direful conflicts, which are maintained with so much rage that when the van-

---

* Wars, says Augustine, are spectacles by which the devil cruelly sports with mankind.

quished at last retreats with the loss of *twenty thousand human beings,* the victor finds he has purchased some little advantage, at the expense of more than half that number. Heaven and earth! What a possibility is here of a sacrifice made to the *prince of darkness,* the first and chief apostate, who rejoices in beholding men, through the abuse of those benefits which undeserved mercy has conferred upon them, transformed into enmity and hatred of God and their brethren; forsaken by God, and destroying one another, and thus hastening once more into his horrid society; that having been accomplices in his rebellion, they may become partakers of his misery and torment.

Now, if the man of valor, whom consenting nations have dignified with the title of *hero,* and *the man devoted to the world,* are asked from whence this immortal mischief, that may thus extend its influence into the regions of eternity, can proceed, what must they answer? Indeed, what can they answer but that it is engendered by the love of human glory—as vain a phantom as ever played before *a madman's eye;* by the lust of dominion, the avarice of wealth, or some other pursuit that centers in this present life. May all those who are called to be the followers of Christ be preserved from these *earthly,* these *sensual* and *malignant motives,* so repugnant to the generous, compassionate and forgiving temper, which, through the influence of redeeming mercy, is concomitant with the pure beams of heavenly light, that light which is intended to remove all the darkness of human corruption, and transform selfish, sensual, proud spirits into angels of patience, humility, meekness, purity and love, *the children and heirs of God, the brethren and joint heirs of Christ.*

All external blessings, whether national or personal, are curses, when they become the fuel of the sensual and malignant fire in corrupt nature, when they not only alienate the mind from *the Lord that reigneth,* but madden it to impious rebellion and defiance against him. "If ye will not lay it to heart, to give glory unto my name, saith the Lord of Hosts, I will even send a curse upon you, and I will curse your blessings" (Malachi 2:2). From the foregoing it is evident that Christians can have no interest in war, they cannot derive blessings from its success, nor triumph and exult, when to the shortsighted view of the human mind, the appearance of success presents itself; these know that the means are infinitely disproportionate to the end, and our Redeemer himself, in the revelation of his future judgments, upon a fallen and obstinate evil world, has declared that "he that leadeth into captivity shall go into captivity, and he that killeth with the sword must be killed with the sword" (Rev. 13:10). Here is the trial of the faith, and patience of the saints, who being called to a state of suffering, and treading in the footsteps of their great exemplar, *when they are reviled, revile not again. When they suffer, threaten not, but commit themselves to the Lord that reigneth to him that judgeth righteously* (Peter 2:23). And to this solemn declaration of righteous judgment the penman of that awful book calls upon all mankind to attend, and says, *If any man have an ear, an ear* that is not totally deafened by the tumultuous passions of nature, separated from God, and turned wholly to itself, *let him now hear;* let him now repent, and forsaking his own sensual and malignant will, seek after the God of peace and love, and live.

William Penn

demonstrates that peace is not merely the end of war

WILLIAM PENN [1644-1718] *was the Quaker founder of Pennsylvania. He had been imprisoned in England several times for his philosophy and preaching, and he turned to America as a refuge for himself and his fellow Quakers. In Pennsylvania he set up a model government, particularly in his peaceable dealings with the Indians. His "Essay Towards the Present and Future Peace of Europe" was written and published in 1693. Penn wanted to show "the desirableness of peace and the truest means of it."*

As Justice is a Preserver, so it is a better Procurer of Peace than War. Though *Pax quoeritur bello* be a usual Saying, Peace is the end of War, and as such it was taken up by O.C. for his Motto. Yet the Use generally made of that expression shows us that properly and truly speaking, Men seek their Wills by War rather than Peace, and that as they will violate it to obtain them, so they will hardly be brought to think of Peace unless their Appetites be some Way gratified. If we look over the Stories of all Times, we shall find the Aggressors generally moved by Ambition; the Pride of Conquest and Greatness of Dominion more than Right. But as those Leviathans appear rarely in the World, so I shall anon endeavor to make it evident they had never been able to devour the Peace of the World, and engross whole Countries as they have done, if the Proposal I have to make for the Benefit of our present Age had been then in Practice. The Advantage that Justice has upon War is seen by the Success of Embassies, that so often prevent War by hearing the Pleas and Memorials of Justice in the Hands and Mouths of the Wronged Party. Perhaps it may be in a good Degree owing to Reputation or Poverty, or some Particular Interest or Conveniency of Princes and States, as much as Justice; but it is certain that as War cannot in any Sense be justified, but upon Wrongs received, and Right, upon Complaint, refused; so the Generality of Wars have their Rise from some such Pretension. This is better seen and understood at Home; for that which prevents a Civil War in a Nation is that which may prevent it Abroad, viz., Justice; and we see where that is notably obstructed, War is kindled between the Magistrates and People in particular Kingdoms and States; which, however it may be unlawful on the side of the People, we see never fails to follow, and ought to give the same Caution to Princes as if it were the Right of the People to do it: though I must needs say, the Remedy is almost ever worse than the Disease: the Aggressors seldom getting what they seek, or performing, if they prevail, what they promised: and the Blood and Poverty that usually attend the Enterprise, weigh more on Earth, as well as in Heaven, than what they lost or suffered, or what they get by endeavoring to mend their Condition, comes to: which Disappointment seems to be the Voice of Heaven, and Judgment of God against those violent Attempts. But to return, I say, Justice is the Means of Peace, betwixt the Government and the People, and one Man and Company and another. It prevents Strife, and at last ends it: for besides Shame or Fear, to contend longer, he or they being under Government, are constrained to bound their Desires and Resentment with the Satisfaction the Law gives. Thus Peace is maintained by Justice, which is a Fruit of Government, as Government is from Society, and Society from Consent.

There is another manifest Benefit which redounds to Christendom, by this Peaceable Expedient: the Reputation of Christianity will in some Degree be recovered in the Sight of Infidels; which, by the many Bloody and unjust Wars of Christians, not only with them, but one with another, hath been greatly impaired. For, to the Scandal of that Holy Profession, Christians that glory in their Saviour's Name have long devoted the Credit and Dignity of it, to their wordly Passions, as often as they have been excited by the Impulses of Ambition or Revenge. They have not always been in the Right: nor has Right been the Reason of War: and not only Christians against Christians but the same Sort of Christians have embrewed their Hands in one another's Blood: Invoking and Interesting, all they could, the Good and Merciful God to prosper their Arms to their Brethren's Destruction: yet their Saviour has told them that he came to save, and not to destroy the Lives of Men: to give and plant Peace among Men: and if in any Sense he may be said to send War, it is the Holy War indeed; for it is against the Devil, and not the Persons of Men. Of all his Titles this seems the most Glorious as well as comfortable for us, that he is the Prince of Peace. It is his Nature, his Office, his Work, and the End and excellent Blessing of his Coming, who is both the Maker and Preserver of our Peace with God. And it is very remarkable that in all the New Testament he is but once called Lion, but frequently the Lamb of God; and that those who desire to be the Disciples of his Cross and Kingdom, for they are inseparable, must be like him, as St. Paul, St. Peter and St. John tell us. Nor is it said the Lamb shall lie down with the Lion, but the Lion shall lie down with the Lamb. That is, War shall yield to Peace, and the Soldier turn Hermit. To be sure, Christians should not be apt to strive, not swift to Anger against anybody, and less with one another, and least of all for the uncertain and fading Enjoyments of this Lower World: and no Quality is exempted from this Doctrine. Here is a wide Field for the Reverend Clergy of Europe to act their Part in, who have so much the Possession of Princes and People too. May they recommend and labor this pacific Means I offer, which will end Blood, if not Strife; and then Reason, upon free Debate, will be Judge, and not the Sword. So that both Right and Peace, which are the Desire and Fruit of wise Governments, and the choice Blessings of any Country, seem to succeed the Establishment of this Proposal.

Robert Barclay
cites the Christian roots of nonviolence

ROBERT BARCLAY [1648-1690], born in Scotland, was the son of Col. David Barclay, a Protestant soldier of fortune. The colonel fell under suspicion during the Restoration, and was jailed. In prison, he converted to Quakerism under the influence of a fellow prisoner. Young Barclay, while visiting his father, became interested in attending meetings of the Society of Friends and subsequently, in 1667, he joined them. He devoted the rest of his life to preaching the "Divine Truth." He was nominal governor of the province of East New Jersey, a Quaker settle-

ment, from 1682 to 1688. In his Apology, *written in 1676, Barclay explained the basic principles of his religion and what he considered the means for abolishing war.*

The last thing to be considered is *Revenge* and *War,* an Evil as opposite and contrary to the Spirit and Doctrine of Christ as *Light* to *Darkness.* For, as is manifest by what is said, through contempt of Christ's Law, the whole World is filled with various *Oaths, Cursings, blasphemous Profanations,* and *horrid Perjuries;* so likewise through contempt of the same Law, the World is filled with *Violence, Oppression, Murders, Ravishing* of *Women* and *Virgins, Spoilings, Depradations, Burnings, Devastations,* and all manner of *Lasciviousness* and *Cruelty:* so that it is strange that Men, made after the Image of *God,* should have so much degenerated that they rather bear the Image and Nature of Roaring Lions, Tearing Tigers, Devouring Wolves and Raging Boars, than Rational Creatures endued with Reason. And is it not yet much more admirable that this *horrid Monster* should find place, and be fomented among those Men, that profess themselves *Disciples* of our *Peaceable Lord* and *Master* Jesus Christ, who by *Excellency* is called the *Prince of Peace,* and hath expressly prohibited his Children all Violence; and on the contrary, commanded them that according to his Example, they should follow Patience, Charity, Forbearance and other Virtues worthy of a Christian?

Hear then what this great Prophet saith, whom every Soul is commanded to hear, under the pain of being cut off, *Matthew 5,* from verse 38 to the end of the Chapter. For thus he saith: "Ye have heard that it hath been said, An eye for an eye, and a tooth for a tooth: But I say unto you, That ye resist not evil; but whosoever shall smite thee on thy right cheek, turn to him the other also. And if any man will sue thee at the law, and take away thy coat, let him have thy cloke also. And whosoever shall compel thee to go a mile, go with him twain. Give to him that asketh thee, and from him that would borrow of thee turn not thou away. Ye have heard that it hath been said, Thou shalt love thy neighbour, and hate thine enemy. But I say unto you, Love your enemies, bless them that curse you, do good to them that hate you, and pray for them which despitefully use you, and persecute you; That ye may be the children of your Father which is in Heaven: for he maketh his sun to rise on the evil and on the good, and sendeth rain on the just and the unjust. For if ye love them which love you, what reward have ye? do not even the publicans the same? And if ye salute your brethren only, what do ye more than others? Do not the publicans so? Be ye therefore perfect, even as your Father which is in heaven is perfect."

These words, with a respect to *Revenge,* as the former in the case of *Swearing,* do forbid some things which were formerly lawful to the *Jews,* considering their Condition and Dispensation; and Command unto such as will be the Disciples of Christ a more perfect, eminent and full Signification of Charity, as also Patience and Suffering than was required of them in that Time, State and Dispensation, by the Law of *Moses.* This is not only the Judgment of most, if not all, the *Ancient Fathers* (so called) of the first Three Hundred Years after Christ, but also of many others; and in general of all those, who have rightly understood and propagated the Law of Christ concerning *Swearing.* . . .

From hence it appears that there is so great a Connection betwixt these two Precepts of *Christ* that as they were uttered and commanded by him at one and the same time, so the same way they were received by Man of all Ages, not only in the first Promulgation, by the little number of the Disciples, but also after the Christians increased in the first Three Hundred Years. Even also in the *Apostasy,* the one was not left and rejected without the other; and now again in the *Restitution,* and renewed Preaching of the *Eternal Gospel,* they are acknowledged as Eternal and Unchangeable Laws, properly belonging to the *Evangelical State* and *Perfection* thereof: from which if any withdraw, he falls short of the Perfection of a *Christian Man.*

And truly, the words are so clear in themselves that (in my Judgment) they need no illustration to explain their Sense: for it is as easy to reconcile the greatest Contradictions as these Laws of our Lord Jesus Christ, with the wicked Practices of *Wars;* for they are plainly inconsistent. Whoever can reconcile this, *Resist not Evil,* with *Resist Violence by Force;* again, *Give also thy other Cheek* with *Strike again;* also, *Love thine Enemies* with *Spoil them, make a Prey of them, pursue them with Fire and Sword;* or, *Pray for those that persecute you, and those that calumniate you,* with *persecute you by Fines, Imprisonments and Death itself;* and not only such as do not *persecute you,* but *who heartily seek and desire your Eternal and Temporal Welfare:* whoever, I say, can find a Means to reconcile these things, may be supposed also to have found a way to reconcile *God* with the *Devil, Christ* with *Antichrist, Light* with *Darkness,* and *Good* with *Evil.* But if this be impossible, as indeed it is, so will also the other be impossible; and Men do but deceive themselves and others while they boldly adventure to establish such absurd and impossible things.

James Nayler

exalts peace on his deathbed

JAMES NAYLER [1618-1660], *a quartermaster in the Parliamentary army, joined the Quakers in 1651. Gradually he became convinced that "Christ was in him." He had a devoted following who were extravagant in their worship of him. But he was convicted of "horrid blasphemy" in 1656, whipped through the streets of Bristol, his tongue pierced with a hot iron, his forehead branded with "B" for blasphemer, and imprisoned at the Bridewell in London. He made a public confession in 1659.*

There is a Spirit which I feel, that delights to do no Evil, nor to revenge any Wrong, but delights to endure all things, in hope to enjoy its own in the End: its hope is to outlive all Wrath and Contention, and to weary out all Exaltation and Cruelty, or whatever is of a Nature contrary to itself. It sees to the End of all Temptations: as it bears no Evil in itself, so it conceives none in Thoughts to any other: if it be betrayed it bears it; for its Ground and Spring is the Mercies and Forgiveness of God: its Crown is Meekness, its Life is Everlasting Love unfeigned, and takes its Kingdom with Entreaty, and not with Contention, and keeps it by Lowliness of Mind. In God alone it can rejoice, though none else regard it, or can own its Life. It's conceived in Sorrow, and brought forth without any to pity it; nor doth it murmur at Grief and Oppression. It never rejoiceth but through Sufferings; for with the World's Joy it is murdered. I found it alone, being forsaken; I have Fellowship therein, with them who lived in Dens, and desolate Places in the Earth, who through Death obtained this Resurrection and Eternal Holy Life.

George Fox

swears to Oliver Cromwell that he will do no violence

GEORGE FOX [1624-1691], *founder of the Society of Friends, believed that man could reach God through "inward light" and not through organized religion. He was frequently imprisoned for his unorthodox preaching. During one of his prison terms he was offered his freedom and a high position in Cromwell's army if he agreed to renounce publicly his pacifist ideals and urge his Quaker followers to do the same. He refused, saying, "I told them I knew from whence all wars arose even from the lust, according to James's doctrine; and that I lived in the virtue of that life and power that took away the occasion of all wars." This excerpt from his journal for January 5, 1654 is reproduced verbatim.*

I (who am of the-world called George ffox) doe deny the carrying or drawing of any carnall sword against any, or against thee Oliver Crumwell or any man in the presence of the lord god I declare it (god is my wittnesse, by whom I am moved to give this forth for the truthes sake, from him whom the world calls George ffox, who is the son of God), who is sent to stand A wittnesse against all violence & against all the workes of darkenesse, & to turne people from the darkenesse to the light, & to bring them from the occassion of the warre, & from the occassion of the Magistrates sword, which is A terrour to the evill doers (which actes contrary to the light of the lord Jesus Christ, which is A praise to them that doe well, and not the evill and such souldiers that are putt in that place no false accussers must bee, no violence must doe, but bee content with their wages, and that Magistrate beares not the sword in vaine, from under the occassion of that sword I doe seeke to bring people, my weapons are not carnall but spirituall. And my kingdome is not of this world, therefore with the carnall weapon I doe not fight, but am from those things dead, from him who is not of the world, called of the world by the name George ffox, and this I am ready to seale with my blood, and this I am moved to give forth for the truthes sake, who A wittnesse stands against all unrighteousnesse, and all ungodlynesse, who A sufferer is for the righteous seed sake, waiteing for the redemption of it, who A crowne that is mortall seekes not for, that fadeth away, but in the light dwells, which comprehends that Crowne, which light is the condemnacon of all such. In which Light I wittnesse the Crowne that is Immortall that fades not away, from him who to all your soulls is A friend, for establishing of righteousnesse and cleansseing the Land of evill doers, and A wittnesse against all wicked inventions of men & murderous plotts, which Answered shall bee with the Light in all your Consciences, which makes no Covenant with death, to which light in you all I speake, and am clear.

ff. G.

who is of the world called George ffox
who A new name hath which the world knowes not.

Hugo Grotius
points out that in the conflict of arms, laws are silent

HUGO GROTIUS [1583-1645], *born Huig de Groot in Delft, Holland, was a statesman, jurist, and the founder of international law. At twelve he attended the University of Leyden, at fifteen he edited the encyclopedic work of Martianus Capella. He practiced law at The Hague, then entered public life. Grotius wrote* De Jure Belli ac Pacis *originally in 1604, but it was not published until 1625, when it immediately became the standard authority on international law.*

But still rights, even unsupported by force, are not destitute of all effect; for justice, the observance of rights, brings security to the conscience, while injustice inflicts on it tortures and wounds such as Plato describes as assaulting the bosoms of tyrants. The conscience of honest men approves justice, condemns injustice. And, what is the greatest point, injustice has for its enemy, justice, has for its friend, God, who reserves his judgments for another life, yet in such a manner that he often exhibits their power in this life, of which we have many examples in history.

The reason why many persons, while they require justice as necessary in private citizens, commit the error of thinking it superfluous in a people or the ruler of a people, is this: in the first place, that in their regard to rights they look at nothing but the utility which arises from rights, which in the case of private citizens is evident, since they are separately too weak to protect themselves; while great states, which seem to embrace within them all that is requisite to support life in comfort, do not appear to have need of that virtue which regards extraneous parties, and is called justice.

But, not to repeat what I have already said, that rights are not established for the sake of utility alone, there is no state so strong that it may not, at some time, need the aid of others external to itself either in the way of commerce or in order to repel the force of many foreign nations combined against it. And hence we see that leagues of alliance are sought even by the most powerful peoples and kings, which can have no force according to the principles of those who confine rights within the boundary of the state alone. It is most true (as Cicero says) that everything loses its certainty at once if we give up the belief in rights.

If no society whatever can be preserved without the recognition of mutual rights, which Aristotle (rather Plato—*Barbeyrac*) proves by the strong instance of a society of robbers, assuredly that society which includes the whole human race, or at any rate the greater part of nations, has need of the recognition of rights, as Cicero saw when he said that some things are so bad that they are not to be done even for the sake of saving our country. . . . Aristotle speaks with strong condemnation of those who, while they will allow no one to hold rule among themselves except him who has the right to do so, yet in their dealings with strangers have no care of rights or the violation of rights.

A little while ago we quoted Pompey for his expression on the other side; yet, on the other hand, when a certain Spartan king had said, "Happy that republic which has for its boundaries the spear and the sword," Pompey corrected him and said, "Happy rather that which has justice for its boundary." And to this effect he might have used the authority of another Spartan king, who gave justice the preference over military courage on this ground—that courage is to be regulated by justice, but, if all men were just, they would have no need of courage. Courage itself was defined by the Stoics—virtue exercised in defense of justice. Themistius, in an oration to Valens, eloquently urges that kings, such as the rule of wisdom requires them to be, ought not to care for the single nation only which is committed to them, but for the whole human race. They should be, as he expresses it, not *philo-Macedonian* only, or *philo-Roman,* but *philanthropic.* The name of Minos became hateful to posterity in no other way than this, that he terminated his equity at the boundaries of his own government.

It is so far from being proper to admit, what some choose to say, that in war all rights cease, that war is never to be undertaken except to assert rights, and, when undertaken, is never to be carried on except within the limits of rights and of good faith. Demosthenes well said that war was the mode of dealing with those who could not be kept in order by judicial proceedings. For judicial proceedings are of force against those who feel themselves to be the weaker party; but, against those who make themselves or think themselves equals, war is the proceeding; yet this, too, in order to be justifiable, to be carried on in a no less scrupulous manner than judicial proceedings are.

Be it so, then, that, in the conflict of arms, laws must be silent; but let this be understood of laws civil, judicial, proper to peace, not of those laws which are perpetual and accommodated to all time. For it is excellently said by Dio Prusaeensis that between enemies written laws— that is, civil laws—are not in force, but that unwritten laws are; namely, those which nature dictates or the consent of nations institutes. We may learn this from the old formula of the Romans: "I decide that those things may be sought by a pure and pious war." The same old Romans, as Varro remarked, undertook war tardily, and without allowing themselves any license, because they thought that no war except a pious one ought to be undertaken. Camillus said that wars were to be carried on no less justly than bravely. Africanus said that the Romans began just wars and ended them. Again in Livy we read, "War has its laws no less than peace." And Seneca admires Fabricius as a great man, and, what is most difficult, a man innocent even in war and who thought that there were wrongs even toward an enemy.

How great the power of the conscience of justice is the writers of histories everywhere show, often ascribing victory to this cause mainly. Hence have arisen these proverbs: that it is the cause which makes the soldier brave or base; that he rarely comes safe back who goes out on the bad side; that hope is the ally of the good cause; and others to the same effect. Nor ought any persons to be moved by the occasional success of unjust designs; for it is enough if the equity of the cause has an efficacy, and that a great one, in action, even though this efficacy, as happens in human affairs, is often prevented from taking effect, being counteracted by other causes. And, further, in conciliating friendships, which nations, as well as individuals, need on many accounts, a great effect must be assigned to an opinion that we do not hastily or unjustly undertake war and that we carry it on religiously; for no one readily joins himself to those whom he believes to think lightly of right laws and good faith.

I, for the reasons which I have stated, holding it to be most certain that there is among nations a common law of rights which is of force with regard to war and in war, saw many and grave causes why I should write a work on that subject. For I saw prevailing throughout the Christian world a license in making war of which even barbarous nations would have been ashamed, recourse being had to arms for slight reasons or no reason; and, when arms were once taken up, all reverence for divine and human law was thrown away, just as if men were thenceforth authorized to commit all crimes without restraint.

And the sight of these atrocities has led many men, and these, estimable persons, to declare arms forbidden to the Christian whose rule of life mainly consists in love to all men. And to this party sometimes John Ferus and our countryman Erasmus seem to approximate—men much devoted to peace, both ecclesiastical and civil. But they take this course, as I conceive, with the purpose with which, when things have been twisted one way, we bend them the other, in order to make them straight. But this attempt to drive things too far is often so far from succeeding that it does harm, because the excess which it involves is easily detected, and then detracts from the authority of what is said, even within the limits of truth. We are to provide a remedy for both disorders, both for thinking that nothing is allowable and that everything is.

Moreover, having practiced jurisprudence in public situations in my country with the best integrity I could give, I would now, as what remains to me, unworthily ejected from that country graced by so many of my labors, promote the same subject, jurisprudence, by the exertion of my private diligence. Many, in preceding times, have designed to invest the subject with the form of an art or science; but no one has done this. Nor can it be done except care be taken in that point which has never yet been properly attended to—to separate instituted law from natural law. For natural law, as being always the same, can be easily collected into an art, but that which depends upon institution, since it is often changed and is different in different places, is out of the domain of art, as the perceptions of individual things in other cases also is.

If, then, those who have devoted themselves to the study of true justice would separately undertake to treat of separate parts of natural and permanent jurisprudence, omitting all which derives its origin from the will of man alone; if one would treat of laws, another of tributes, another of the office of judges, another of the mode of determining the will of parties, another of the evidence of facts, we might, by collecting all these parts, form a complete body of such jurisprudence.

For in the First Book (after a preface concerning the origin of rights and laws) we have examined the question whether any war be just. Next, in order to distinguish between public and private war, we have to explain the nature of sovereignty—what peoples, what kings, have it entire, what partial, who with a right of alienation, who otherwise; and afterward we have to speak of the duty of subjects to superiors.

Erasmus

questions whether man was shaped to war

DESIDERIUS ERASMUS [1465-1536], *born in Rotterdam, at the age of thirteen was compelled by his guardian to enter a monastery, and later was ordained a priest. He devoted his time to study and writing, and sought reform within the Catholic Church. It is said of him that he "helped to scatter the darkness of the Middle Ages and to bring the wonders of the Renaissance." Erasmus opposed the whole concept of war and violence, and preached the contradictions between war and Christianity. "Against War" was published in 1514.*

If one would consider well but the behavior and shape of man's body shall he not forthwith perceive that nature, or rather God, hath shaped this creature, not to war, but to friendship, not to destruction, but to health, not to wrong, but to kindness and benevolence? For whereas nature hath armed all other beasts with their own armor, as the violence of the bulls she hath armed with horns, the ramping lion with claws; to the boar she hath given the gnashing tusks; she hath armed the elephant with a long trump snout, besides his great huge body and hardness of skin; she hath fenced the crocodile with a skin as hard as a plate; to the dolphin fish she hath given fins instead of a dart; the porcupine she defendeth with thorns; the ray and thornback with sharp prickles; to the cock she hath given strong spurs; some she fenceth with a shell, some with a hard hide, as it were thick leather, or bark of a tree; some she provideth to save by swiftness of flight, as doves; and to some she hath given venom instead of a weapon; to some she hath given a much horrible and ugly look, she hath given terrible eyes and grunting voice; and she hath also set among some of them continual dissension and debate—man alone she hath brought forth all naked, weak, tender, and without any armor, with most soft flesh and smooth skin. There is nothing at all in all his members that may seem to be ordained to war, or to any violence. I will not say at this time that where all other beasts, anon as they are brought forth, they are able of themselves to get their food, man alone cometh so forth that a long season after he is born, he dependeth altogether on the help of others. He can neither speak nor go, nor yet take meat; he desireth help only by his infant crying: so that a man may, at the least way, by this conject that this creature alone was born all to love and amity, which specially increaseth and is fast knit together by good turns done eftsoons of one to another.

And for this cause nature would that a man should not so much thank her for the gift of life which she hath given unto him as he should thank kindness and benevolence, whereby he might evidently understand himself, that he was altogether dedicate and bounden to the gods of graces, that is to say, to kindness, benevolence and amity. And besides this, nature hath given unto man a countenance not terrible and loathly, as unto other brute beasts; but meek and demure, representing the very tokens of love and benevolence. She hath given him amiable eyes, and in them assured marks of the inward mind. She hath ordained him arms to clip and embrace. She hath given him the wit and understanding to kiss: whereby the very minds and hearts of men should be coupled together, even as though they touched each other. Unto man alone she hath given laughing, a token of cheer and gladness. To man alone she hath given weeping tears, as it were a pledge or token of meekness and mercy. Yea, and she hath given him a voice not threatening and horrible, as unto other brute beasts, but amiable and pleasant. Nature not yet content with all this, she hath given unto man alone the commodity of speech and reasoning: the which things verily may specially both get and nourish benevolence, so that nothing at all should be done among men by violence. . . .

What in all this world is more sweet or better than amity or love? Truly nothing. And I pray you, what other thing is peace than amity and love among men, like as war on the other side is naught else but dissension and debate of many men together? And surely the property of good things is such that the broader they be spread, the more profit and commodity cometh of them. Farther, if the love of one singular person with another be so sweet and delectable, how great should the felicity be if realm with realm and nation with nation were coupled together, with the band of amity and love? On the other side, the nature of evil things is such that the farther they sprawl abroad, the more worthy they are to be called evil, as they be indeed. Then if it be a wretched thing, if it be an ungracious thing, that one man armed should fight with another, how much more miserable, how much more mischievous is it, that the selfsame thing should be done with so many thousands together? By love and peace the small things increase and wax great, by discord and debate the great things decay and come to naught. Peace is the mother and nurse of all good things. War suddenly and at once overthroweth, destroyeth and utterly fordoeth everything that is pleasant and fair, and bringeth in among men a monster of all mischievous things.

In the time of peace (none otherwise than as if the lusty springtime should show and shine in men's businesses) the fields are tilled, the gardens and orchards freshly flourish, the beasts pasture merrily; gay manors in the country are edified, the towns are builded, where as need is reparations are done, the buildings are heightened and augmented, riches increase, pleasures are nourished, the laws are executed, the commonwealth flourisheth, religion is fervent, right reigneth, gentleness is used, craftsmen are busily exercised, the poor men's gain is more plentiful, the wealthiness of the rich men is more gay and goodly, the studies of most honest learnings flourish, youth is well taught, the aged folks have quiet and rest, maidens are luckily married, mothers are praised for bringing forth of children like to their progenitors, the good men prosper and do well and the evil men do less offense.

Ye say ye make war for the safeguard of the commonweal; yea, but noway sooner nor more unthriftily may the commonweal perish than by war. For before ye enter into the field, ye have already hurt more your country than ye can do good getting the victory. Ye waste the citizens' goods, ye fill the houses with lamentations, ye fill all the country with thieves, robbers and ravishers. For these are the relics of war. And whereas before ye might have enjoyed all France, ye shut yourselves from many regions thereof. If ye love your own subjects truly, why revolve you not in mind these words: Why shall I put so many, in their lusty, flourishing youth, in all mischiefs and perils? Why shall I depart so many honest wives and their husbands, and make so many fatherless children? Why shall I claim a title I know not, and a doubtful right, with spilling of my subjects' blood? We have seen in our time that in war made under color of defense of the Church, the priests have been so often pillaged with contributions that no enemy might do more.

So that while we go about foolishly to escape falling in the ditch, while we cannot suffer a light injury, we afflict ourselves with most grievous despites. While we be ashamed of gentleness to bow to a prince, we be fain to please people most base. While we indiscreetly covet liberty, we entangle ourselves in most grievous bondage. While we hunt after a little lucre, we grieve ourselves and ours with inestimable harness. It had been a point of a prudent Christian man (if he be a true Christian man) by all manner of means to have fled, to have shunned, and by prayer to have withstood so fiendish a thing, and so far both from the life and doctrine of Christ. But if it can by no means be eschewed, by reason of the ungraciousness of many men, when ye have essayed every way, and that ye have for peace sake left no stone unturned, then the next way is that ye do your diligence that so ill a thing may be gested and done by them that be evil, and that it be achieved with as little effusion of man's blood as can be.

Menno Simons
condemns the use of carnal weapons

MENNO SIMONS [1492-1559] *was born in the Dutch province of Friesland and at the age of twenty-eight was ordained a Catholic priest. He renounced Catholicism in 1536 and became an Anabaptist minister. He and his followers, a moderate Anabaptist sect called the Mennonites, espoused a doctrine of nonresistance; they practiced adult baptism and silent prayer, and they opposed war, oaths and capital punishment.*

These regenerated people . . . are the children of peace who have beaten their swords into plowshares and their spears into pruning hooks, and know war no more.

Our weapons are not weapons with which cities and countries may be destroyed, walls and gates broken down, and human blood shed in torrents like water. . . . Christ is our fortress; patience our weapon of defense; the word of God our sword. . . . And iron and metal spears and swords we leave to those who, alas, regard human blood and swine's blood about alike.

Murder is unknown to us, much less inculcated and permitted, for we believe of a truth that a murder has neither lot nor part in the Kingdom of God.

I say, in an evangelical manner, for to aid with the sword is forbidden to all true Christians. In the New Testament all true believers should suffer patiently and not fight and do battle with swords and muskets.

I am aware, my dear friends, that these Scriptures have reference for the most part to the inward peace which comes through Christ. Yet whoever has this inward Christian peace in his heart will never more be found guilty before God and the world of turmoil, treason, mutiny, murder, theft, or of consenting to or taking part in them.

We do not contend with carnal, but with spiritual weapons, with patience and the word of God, against all flesh, the world, and the devil, trusting in Christ. Nor shall there ever be found any other weapons with us. . . .

All Christians are commanded to love their enemies; to do good unto those who abuse and prosecute them; to give the mantle when the cloak is taken, the other cheek when one is struck. Tell me, how can a Christian defend Scripturally retaliation, rebellion, war, striking, slaying, torturing, stealing, robbing and plundering and burning cities, and conquering countries?

Our weapons are not swords and spears, but patience, silence, and hope, and the word of God. With these we must maintain our heavy warfare and fight our battle.

6

BEFORE GUNS

[Sixth century B.C. — 1400 A.D.]

The ideal of peace runs through antiquity; it can be found in the Old and the New Testaments, in the philosophy of Buddha and the writings of Lao-Tse. No one can know, of course, who the very first pacifist may have been. But one of the first pacifists in recorded history lived a thousand years before Buddha. He was Ikhnaton, a pharaoh who ruled Egypt for seventeen years (c. 1375-c. 1358 B.C.), and until 1907 he lay in an unknown tomb in Egypt. He lived in a bellicose society, but "when the world reverberated with the noise of war, he preached the first known doctrine of peace; when the glory of martial pomp swelled the hearts of his subjects, he deliberately turned his back upon heroics. He was the first man to preach simplicity, honesty, frankness and sincerity, and he preached it from a throne." *

Motse, in the fifth century B.C., wrote of the need for "equal love to all" above war and injustice. Mencius, who lived in the third century B.C., proclaimed: "When one by force subdues men, they do not submit to him in heart; when he subdues them by virtue in the heart's core they are pleased, and sincerely submit."

The Greeks and Romans were not pacifists, but the Jews considered peace a gift of Yahweh. Micah and Isaiah were the foremost Jewish exponents of pacifism and nonviolence. There is no consistent tradition of nonviolence in Judaism, but the sacred literature of the Jews has in it distinct elements of pacifism—in the Bible, the Talmud, the Midrash. And in their history, elements of pacifism emerge: the Essenes, a Jewish sect in the second century B.C., proclaimed their resolve "to hurt no man voluntarily or at the command of another"; and Hillel, a Jewish scholar and leader of the Pharisees in the first century B.C., said, "Be of the disciples of Aaron, loving peace and pursuing peace, loving thy fellow crea-

* Arthur E. P. Weigall, *The Life and Times of Akhnaton*, p. 283.

tures, and drawing them close to the Torah." He explained the principles of Judaism thus: "Do not unto your neighbor what you would not have him do unto you; this is the whole law, the rest is commentary."

Even the pagans had gods of peace, though they worshiped gods of war as well. The writings of some of the most sophisticated pagans— Seneca, Marcus Aurelius, Zeno—show pacifist thinking.

In antiquity just as in modern times, men who did not necessarily pursue peace spoke against war for various reasons: its costliness, its irrationality, its immorality.

Herodotus, Greek historian of the fifth century B.C., pointed to the irrationality of war by putting these words in Croesus' mouth: "No one is so foolish as to prefer war to peace, in which instead of sons burying their fathers, fathers bury their sons." But Croesus adds: "God willed it so."

In the fourth century B.C. a Greek lyric poet showed up the costliness of war when he said: "Even by the feeble, a city may be shaken to its foundation, but to set it up again is a sore struggle."

The Roman satirical poet Juvenal, who exposed the vices of Roman society in the first and second centuries A.D., questioned the rationality of war among men when even animals of the lower kingdom do not hurt creatures of their own species. In one of his satires Juvenal asks when "did a lion with a lion's blood imbrue the sand, or scandalize the wood?" But

> . . . *man is not content to make*
> *The deadly sword for murder's impious sake:*
> *(Though ancient smiths knew only to produce*
> *Spades, rakes, and mattocks, for the rustic's use,*
> *And guiltless animals, in those early times,*
> *Were not subservient to the soldier's crimes).*
> *Murder is nothing in our latter age,*
> *And too humane to glut Egyptian rage,*
> *That scorns to let resentment die with death,*
> *And tears the slaughtered foe with feates teeth.*

The basis of pacifism in the New Testament, and in Christian pacifism thereafter, is primarily the Sermon on the Mount, where Christ proclaimed, "Ye have heard that it hath been said, An eye for an eye, and a tooth for a tooth: but I say unto you, That ye resist not evil: but whosoever shall smite thee on thy right cheek, turn to him the other also."

Christian pacifists cite the sermon not only as a pacifist doctrine regarding war between nations, but also as a statement against the use of force and coercion by civil and judicial authorities.

For almost three hundred years after Christianity began, Christian writers were generally agreed that war was unlawful and immoral. Tertullian felt that it was. Lacantius (c. 260-325) wrote in *The Divine Institutes*: "When God forbids us to kill, he not only prohibits us from open violence, which is not even allowed by public laws, but he warns us against the commission of those things which are esteemed lawful among men. Thus it can never be lawful for a righteous man to go to war, since his warfare is in righteousness itself; nor to accuse anyone of a capital charge, since it makes no difference whether you put a man to death by word or by sword, since it is the act of putting to death which is prohibited. Therefore, with regard to this precept of God, there can be no exception at all . . . it is always unlawful to put a man to death."

Both Justin Martyr and Tatian made distinctions between soldiers and Christians; Origen said that Christians "no longer take up 'sword against nation,' nor do we 'learn war any more,' having become children of peace, for the sake of Jesus, who is our leader."

But even before the conversion of Constantine, Christians began to compromise in their outlook on war, and especially on the issue of joining the army. During the fourth and fifth centuries the Christians evolved a philosophy to explain what has ever since been described as the "just" war.

With the union of church and state after the conversion of Constantine in the fourth century A.D., protests against war by the Christian fathers generally ceased. Now guideposts were needed to tell what part Christians could take in war. St. Augustine provided such guidance by dividing wars into the just and unjust ones, with "the unjust represented by the contemporary barbarian onslaughts on the Empire, the just by the efforts of the Empire to defend itself and the cause of civilization." Augustine felt that peace should be the goal of both church and state, but he considered war to be a necessary police action against evildoers. He maintained that the Christian's obligation is to both church and state; thus if the state is engaged in war, the Christian is obliged to carry out his responsibility to the state by lending support. But Augustine left no doubt about what he thought of the humanitarian aspects of the issue: "He who can think of war without feeling some pain must have lost all feeling for humanity."

But the Middle Ages began with a wave of wars, and for the next ten centuries there was fighting between imperial dynasties and among lords; there were civil wars, the Hundred Years' War between England and France, and struggles between kings and feudal aristocracies. Religious motives caused yet more wars: Islamic armies marched into Europe, and Christianity sent its Crusaders into long and bloody battle for the Holy Land. The Treuga Dei (Truce of God) was proclaimed by the Christian bishops and church councils, declaring certain days sacred from bloodshed. But Christians were not forbidden warfare, they were simply required to lay down their weapons for a given period.

The idea of the "just" war that Augustine had proposed was further developed in the writings of St. Thomas Aquinas. He defined a just war as "War waged by a state in a just cause with the approval of the Church." If the Church approved the cause, so did God. What made a war legitimate? "First," said Aquinas, "the authority of the sovereign by whose command the war is to be waged. . . . The natural order conducive to peace among mortals demands that the power to declare and counsel war should be in the hands of those who hold the supreme authority.

"Secondly, a just war requires, namely that those who are attacked should be attacked because they deserve it on account of some fault. . . . (A just war is wont to be described as one that avenges wrongs, when a nation or state has to be punished for refusing to make amends for the wrongs inflicted by its subjects, or to restore what it has seized unjustly.)

"Thirdly, it is necessary that the belligerents should have a rightful intention, so that they intend the advancement of good, or the avoidance of evil. . . . (True religion looks upon as peaceful those wars that are waged not for motives of aggrandizement, or cruelty, but with the object of securing peace, of punishing evildoers, and of uplifting the good.)"

Until this time the Christian doctrine of nonresistance had been carried on only by certain monastic orders and some heretical sects. St. Francis of Assisi spoke out against the compromises of the Church, and the Third Franciscan Order was explicit in its instructions against war: "Let them not take up the arms of death against anybody or bear such themselves."

Among the heretical sects that kept alive the doctrine of nonresistance through the Middle Ages were the Albigenses, or Cathari. They did not resist violence, they would only suffer it; and their members were not allowed to kill any beast. The Waldenses, followers of Peter Waldo, based their nonresistance not only on Christ's principles, but also on the Mosaic law "Thou shalt not kill." They turned away from war and rejected capital punishment. A poem of Waldensian teaching called "The Noble Lesson" says:

The Old Law commands to fight against enemies and render evil for
*   evil;*
But the New says, Avenge not thyself,
But leave vengeance to the heavenly King,
And let those live in peace who do thee harm;
And thou shalt find pardon with the heavenly King.
The Old Law says, Thou shalt love thy friend, and hate thy enemy;
But the New says, Thou shalt no more do this;
But love your enemies, and do good to those who hate you,
And pray for them who persecute you, and seek occasion against you;
That ye may be the children of your Father who is in heaven.
The Old Law commands to punish malefactors;
But the New says, Pardon all people,
And thou shalt find pardon with the father almighty;
For if thou dost not pardon thou shalt not be saved.

With such teachings, the Waldenses upheld nonresistance.

Another of these sects was the Lollards, founded in the mid-fourteenth century by John Wycliffe, the English Biblical scholar and reformer. He insisted that "Christ taught not his apostles to fight with the sword of iron, but with the sword of God's word, which standeth in meekness of heart and in the prudence of man's tongue." A Lollard tract, *The Sum of the Scriptures*, said, "Men of war are not allowed by the Gospel; the Gospel knoweth peace and not war."

But in general for many, many years Christianity supported war and waged battle itself. Only after the beginning of the Renaissance did pacifist thinking gain a strong position again, coming out of the monastaries and into more general acceptance.

Saint Martin

withdraws from Julian's army

SAINT MARTIN [c. 316-c. 397], *bishop of Tours, was responsible for establishing what became probably the first monastary in the West. He had been born of heathen parents in Pannonia (now Hungary), and his father was a military tribune. When he was ten years old Martin became a catechumen; at fifteen he reluctantly entered the Roman army. He was baptized, and two years later was freed from the army. Sulpitius Severus wrote the following piece about Martin's retirement from military service.*

In the meantime, as the barbarians were rushing within the two divisions of Gaul, Julian the Apostate, bringing an army together at the city of the Vaugiones, began to distribute a donative to the soldiers. As was the custom in such a case, they were called forward, one by one, until it came to the turn of Martin. Then, indeed, judging it a suitable opportunity for seeking his discharge—for he did not think it would be proper for him, if he were not to continue in the service, to receive a donative—he said to Caesar, "Hitherto I have served *you* as a soldier: allow me now to become a soldier to God: let the man who is to serve thee receive thy donative: I am the soldier of Christ: it is not lawful for me to fight." Then truly the tyrant stormed on hearing such words, declaring that from fear of the battle, which was to take place on the morrow, and not from any religious feeling, Martin withdrew from the service. But Martin, full of courage, yea, all the more resolute from the danger that had been set before him, exclaimed, "If this conduct of mine is ascribed to cowardice, not to faith, I will take my stand unarmed before the line of battle tomorrow, and in the name of the Lord Jesus, protected by the sign of the cross, and not by shield or helmet, I will safely penetrate the ranks of the enemy." He is ordered, therefore, to be thrust back into prison, determined on proving his words true by exposing himself unarmed to the barbarians. But, on the following day, the enemy sent ambassadors to treat about peace and surrendered both themselves and all their possessions. In these circumstances who can doubt that this victory was due to the saintly man? It was granted him that he should not be sent unarmed to the fight. And although the good Lord could have preserved his own soldier, even amid the swords and darts of the enemy, yet that his blessed eyes might not be pained by witnessing the death of others, he removed all necessity for fighting. For Christ did not require to secure any other victory in behalf of his own soldier than that, the enemy being subdued without bloodshed, no one should suffer death.

Maximilian

refuses to be conscripted into the Roman army

MAXIMILIAN OF THEBESTE [274-295] *was a young Numidian who would not join the Roman army when he was commanded to do so. He was brought before a Roman proconsul in a North African court, where he declared: "I cannot fight; I am a Christian." He was beheaded. It is said that his father returned home "giving thanks to God that he had been able to bring such a present to the Lord." When Maximilian had been brought before the tribunal to be enrolled as a soldier, Dion, the proconsul, asked his name. This was his reply.*

Maxmilian having been brought before the tribunal, in order to be enrolled as a soldier, Dion, the proconsul, asked him his name. Maxmilian, turning to him, replied, "Why wouldst thou know my name? *I am a Christian, and cannot fight."*

Then Dion ordered him to be enrolled, and when he was enrolled it was recited out of the register that he was five feet ten inches high. Immediately after this Dion bade the officer mark him. But Maximilian refused to be marked, still asserting that he was a Christian; upon which Dion instantly replied, "Bear arms, or thou shalt die."

To this Maxmilian answered, *"I cannot fight if I die; I am not a soldier of this world,* but a soldier of God." Dion then said, "Who has persuaded thee to behave thus?" Maximilian answered, "My own mind, and he who called me." Dion then spoke to his father, and bade him persuade his son. But his father observed that his son knew his own mind, and what it was best for him to do.

After this had passed, Dion addressed Maximilian, again in these words, "Take thy arms, and receive the mark." "I can receive," said Maximilian, "no such mark. I have already the mark of Christ;" upon which Dion said, "I will send thee quickly to thy Christ." "Thou mayest do so," said Maximilian, "but the glory will be mine."

Dion then bade the officer mark him. But Maximilian still persisted in refusing, and spoke thus: "I cannot receive the mark of this world, and if thou shouldst give me the mark, I will destroy it. It will avail nothing. I am a Christian, and it is not lawful for me to wear such a mark about my neck, when I have received the saving mark of the Lord Jesus Christ, the Son of the living God, whom thou knowest not, who died to give us life, and whom God gave for our sins. Him all we Christians obey. Him we follow, as the Restorer of our life, and the Author of our salvation."

Dion instantly replied to this, "Take thy arms, and receive the mark, or thou shalt suffer a miserable death." "But I shall not perish," said Maximilian: "My name is already enrolled with Christ—*I cannot fight.*"

Dion said, "Consider then thy youth, and bear arms. The profession of arms becomes a young man." Maximilian replied, *"My arms are with the Lord. I cannot fight for any earthly consideration. I am now a Christian."*

Dion, the proconsul, said, "Among the life guards of our masters, Diocletian and Maximian, and Constantius and Maximus, there are Christian soldiers, and they fight." Maximilian answered, "They know best what is expedient for them; *but I am a Christian, and it is unlawful to do evil.*"

Origen

says Christians need not fight for their kings

ORIGEN [c. 185-c. 254], *a Christian theologian and probably the most prolific writer of the ancient Church, was born in Alexandria of Christian parents. His father was martyred in the Severan persecutions of 203. Origen headed the catechetical school in Alexandria and eventually was raised to priesthood, but Bishop Demetrius, one of his early sponsors, had him deposed. He accused Origen of castrating himself early in his teaching career and of promulgating objectionable doctrines. The sentence was ignored in Palestine, where Origen taught for nineteen years and had his most famous disciples. He died four years after being imprisoned and tortured in the Decian persecutions.*

In the next place, Celsus urges us "to help the king with all our might, and to labor with him in the maintenance of justice, to fight for him; and if he requires it, to fight under him, or lead an army along with him." To this our answer is that we do, when occasion requires, give help to kings, and that, so to say, a divine help, "putting on the whole armor of God." And this we do in obedience to the injunction of the apostle, "I exhort, therefore, that first of all, supplications, prayers, intercessions, and giving of thanks, be made for all men, for kings, and for all that are in authority"; and the more anyone excels in piety, the more effective help does he render to kings, even more than is given by soldiers, who go forth to fight and slay as many of the enemy as they can.

And to those enemies of our faith who require us to bear arms for the commonwealth, and to slay men, we can reply: "Do not those who are priests at certain shrines, and those who attend on certain gods, as you account them, keep their hands free from blood, that they may with hands unstained and free from human blood offer the appointed sacrifices to your gods; and even when war is upon you, you never enlist the priests in the army. If that, then, is a laudable custom, how much more so that while others are engaged in battle, these too should engage as the priests and ministers of God, keeping their hands pure, and wrestling in prayers to God on behalf of those who are fighting in a righteous cause, and for the king who reigns righteously, that whatever is opposed to those who act righteously may be destroyed! And as we by our prayers vanquish all demons who stir up war, and lead to the violation of oaths, and disturb the peace, we in this way are much more helpful to the kings than those who go into the field to fight for them. And we do take our part in public affairs, when along with righteous prayers we join self-denying exercises and meditations, which teach us to despise pleasures, and not to be led away by them. And none fight better for the king than we do. We do not indeed fight under him, although he require it; but we fight on his behalf, forming a special army—an army of piety—by offering our prayers to God."

Tertullian

asks if it is lawful to make an occupation of the sword

TERTULLIAN [c. 160-c. 230] *was born in Carthage, the son of a cen-turio proconsularis, or military leader. He was educated in Greek and*

Latin, studied law and became an eminent jurist. Around 192 A.D. Tertullian was converted to Christianity, and in later years he was one of the most able and zealous of the Christian leaders of his time. He was an extreme antimilitarist, and to some of his pagan critics who accused Christians of the "crime" of nonresistance, he replied: "Shall it be held lawful to make an occupation of the sword, when the Lord proclaimed that he who takes the sword shall also perish by the sword?"

To begin with the real ground of the military crown, I think we must first inquire whether warfare is proper at all for Christians. What sense is there in discussing the merely accidental, when that on which it rests is to be condemned? Do we believe it lawful for a human oath to be superadded to one divine, and for a man to come under promise to another master after Christ, and to abjure father and mother and all nearest kinsfolk, whom even the law has commanded us to honor and love next to God himself, to whom the gospel, too, holding them only of less account than Christ, has in like manner rendered honor?

Shall it be held lawful to make an occupation of the sword, when the Lord proclaims that he who uses the sword shall perish by the sword? And shall the son of peace take part in the battle when it does not become him even to sue at law? And shall he apply the chain, and the prison, and the torture, and the punishment, who is not the avenger even of his own wrongs? Shall he, forsooth, either keep watch-service for others more than for Christ, or shall he do it on the Lord's day, when he does not even do it for Christ himself? And shall he keep guard before the temples which he has renounced? And shall he take a meal where the apostle has forbidden him? (I Corinthians 8:10.) And shall he diligently protect by night those whom in the daytime he has put to flight by his exorcisms, leaning and resting on the spear the while with which Christ's side was pierced? Shall he carry a flag too, hostile to Christ? And shall *he* ask a watchword from the emperor who has already received one from God? Shall *he* be disturbed in death by the trumpet of the trumpeter, who expects to be aroused by the angel's trump?

And shall the Christian be burned according to camp rule, when he was not permitted to burn incense to an idol when to him Christ remitted the punishment of fire? Then how many other offenses there are involved in the performance of camp offices, which we must hold to involve a transgression of God's law, you may see by a slight survey. The very carrying of the name over from the camp of light to the camp of darkness is a violation of it. Of course, if faith comes later, and finds any preoccupied with military service, their case is different, as in the instance of those whom John used to receive for baptism, and of those most faithful centurions—I mean the centurion whom Christ approves, and the centurion whom Peter instructs; yet, at the same time, when a man has become a believer, and faith has been sealed, there must be either an immediate abandonment of it, which has been the course with many; or all sorts of quibbling will have to be resorted to in order to avoid offending God, and that is not allowed even outside of military service; or, last of all, for God the fate must be endured which a citizen-faith has been no less ready to accept. For neither does military service hold out escape from punishment of sins, or exemption from martyrdom. Nowhere does the Christian change his character. There is one gospel, and the same Jesus, who will one day deny everyone who denies, and acknowledge everyone who acknowledges God—who will save, too, the life which has been lost for his sake; but, on the other hand, destroy that which for gain has been saved to his dishonor. With him the faithful citizen is a soldier, just as the faithful soldier is a citizen.

Agrippa
urges the Jews not to undertake
war against the Romans

HEROD AGRIPPA II [28-c. 100] *was the son of Herod Agrippa I, who is mentioned with favor in the Talmud and the Midrash. The Roman emperor Claudius gave Agrippa II the Kingdom of Chalcis. When the Jews rose against the Romans in 66, Agrippa attempted to prevent the uprising. He believed that submission to the Romans might be the way to save the Jews. His passionate plea was in vain, and after the fall of Jerusalem he went to Rome.*

If I had known that all of you were resolved to maintain a war against the Romans, neither that the more sound and sincere part among you was inclined to cultivate peace, and preserve harmony, I had never appeared thus before you, or presumed to give you my advice; for all words are needless, and all language superfluous, to point out those things which ought to be done; when all who hear me are with a unanimous consent hurried away to obey precepts of worse consequence than mine. But because some of you may be so young as not to know the misfortunes that war produces, some of you may entertain rash and ill-concerted hopes of liberty, and some of you may be desirous of adding more to your present acquisitions, and making advantage of the weaker side, if things should come to be in confusion: I have considered the means of instilling into such persons' minds notions of better use, that may make them recant their resolutions, and free themselves from the dangers to which they expose themselves by following the pernicious advice of a few; being now, as you are all assembled together, minded to explain those circumstances to you which I am persuaded are for your common interest and advantage.

But let no one exclaim against me while I am speaking, if he happens to hear anything that he cannot relish; for they who are resolved upon a defection are still at liberty, for me, after my exhortation, to continue in the same sentiments as before. Neither will my words avail anything with those who are desirous to hear me unless everyone preserve silence. I am sensible, indeed, that many exaggerate the injuries they have received from several procurators, and very much amplify and increase the commendations of liberty. But before I enter into any examination, who you are, and against whom you maintain a war, I will first of all lay open, and separate one from another, the different pretenses you urge for it: for if you go about to revenge yourselves on those who have injured you, to what end do you so much boast of your liberty? If you are of opinion that your slavery is not to be borne with, then the complaints you bring against your governors are of no moment. For though they should govern mildly, yet the notion of servitude will still present terrible ideas.

Consider things separately by themselves, how ridiculous is the reason for fomenting a war; but chiefly how far those things go which you lay at the door of the Roman procurators. It is your business to gain the affections of those in power by friendly offices, and not strive to vex and irritate them with words. For when you charge them with crimes of slight consequence, and make those crimes of the most flagrant nature, you are all the time heaping the guilt upon your own heads, which you endeavor to lay upon others: so that the injuries they do you will no longer be committed in secrecy, but your losses will be open, and acted above board: for nothing so much mitigates and alleviates an hardship as patiently to bear it, and submissively to receive the injuries done one; for ofttimes shame and delay are impediments in the way of those who do them.

But let it be so indeed that the Roman governors are so troublesome as not to be borne with; yet all the Romans do not injure you, nor Caesar, against whom you are going to undertake a war. There are no commands issued out by them, I apprehend, to send any bad governor, nor is it possible that they should cast their eyes from the west to the east: but neither is it an easy matter that what is transacted here should immediately be known there. It is ridiculous to pretend to fight with so many because of one, with so great a people, because of such trifling reasons, and with those who know nothing of what we complain of. Besides, a sudden remedy will be applied to the crimes which we charge them with. Neither will the same governor always continue in his post, and probably others of a more gentle behavior may come and succeed him. When the war is once set on foot, it will be found no easy matter to lay it aside, nor will such a proceeding be carried on or sustained without losses and hardships. But now it is unseasonable to harbor sentiments of liberty, when your business should have been before now valiantly to have fought to have maintained, and not lost it.

The experience of slavery is a very great hardship, and the endeavor to shake off the yoke is just and honorable; but he who is once subdued, and afterwards revolts, is deemed more a contumacious slave than a lover of liberty. When Pompey first made his entrance into this country, every measure ought then to have been taken that the Romans were not admitted; but our ancestors, and their kings, who had more money, larger bodies and braver souls than you, were not able to hold out against a small portion of the Roman power. But you, who are accustomed to obey the Romans, and so much inferior in every circumstance to those who first submitted to them, presume to withstand the whole Roman empire. The Athenians, who, to purchase the Grecian liberty, laid their city in ashes, who, when Xerxes, the proudest man upon earth, failed through the land, and marched through the sea, and whom the ocean could not confine, and led an army broader than Europe itself; the Athenians, I say, pursued him as he fled in one ship, and broke to pieces that formidable power of Asia near the small town of Salamis: they now are slaves to the Romans, and Italy imposes laws upon, and governs that city which was once the mistress of all Greece. Also, the Lacedemonians, after the famous battles of Thermopylae and Plataea, and having such a general as Agefilaus, who penetrated throughout all Asia, now acquiesce under the Romans as their masters. The Macedonians too, gazing still on the picture of Philip, and casting their eyes with Alexander on him who promises them the empire of the world, quietly sustain their change, and reverence those to whom fortune hath allotted them. And there are innumerable other nations, who, puffed up with an elevated desire of liberty, yet submit to the Romans.

You are the only people who cannot vouchsafe to obey them, who have jurisdiction over everything. Upon what armies, or upon what arms is it that you depend? Where are your fleets to possess themselves of the

Roman seas? Where is the sum of money sufficient to defray the expense
of so grand an undertaking? Do you suppose to maintain a war against
the Egyptians or the Arabians? Will not you consider a little what a
leviathan the empire of the Romans is? Will you not reflect a moment or
two on your own imbecility and weakness? Have you not several times
been conquered and defeated by the nations that dwell around you? And
yet their strength hath remained insuperable over all the world, more
than which they have made acquisitions. The whole Euphrates, to the
east, the Ifther to the north, and the ransacking of Lybia, as far as the
desert, to the south, and the Gades to the west, were not sufficient to
humor their ambition. But they carried their arms beyond the ocean to
another world, and to the Britons, unknown to them before. What then?
Are you wealthier than the Gauls? Are you more valiant than the Germans? Are you more wise than the Grecians? Or are you more in number
than the inhabitants of the whole world? What confidence is this that
prompts you against the Romans?

It will be objected and said, perhaps, that it is a hardship to be
slaves; but how much more reason have the Grecians to complain of
this hardship, who are more dignified than any other nation the sun
shines upon, and possess so large a tract of land, and now pay obedience
to six faces of the Romans. The Macedonians too obey the same number,
who have abundantly more reason on their sides to push for their liberty.
What should the five hundred cities of Asia do? Do not they, without
any garrison, submit to the ordinances of one governor, and give reverence to the faces of consuls? Why should I mention that the Heniochians,
the Colchians, and the nation of the Tauri, the inhabitants of Bosporus,
the people of Pontus, and the nations of the Maeotis, who formerly did
not acknowledge a master of them, are now kept within the bounds of
their duty by 300 soldiers; and 400 long ships make that sea secure and
peaceful, which before was unnavigable, and full of pirates. How much
have the Bithynians, and Cappadocians, and Pamphylians, Lycians, and
Cilicians to urge for regaining their liberty, and yet pay tribute without
being compelled to it by force of arms? Why should I produce the example of the Thracians, who inhabit a region of five days' journey in
breadth, and seven days' journey in length; a country much more inaccessible, and better fortified, than yours is; and, by reason of its penetrating cold, unfit to make an expedition into, yet these Thracians live
under the subjection of 2,000 Romans garrisoned among them? And the
Illyrians, their next neighbors, who inhabit a country reaching as far as
Dalmatia and the Ifther, are under the obedience of two legions only, by
whose authority the inroads of the Daci are restrained. The Dalmatians
too, who have so often risen up to vindicate their liberty, and been only
so far defeated as always to endeavor at regaining it, and rebel by sup-

plies of fresh forces, are now content to pursue a quiet life under the command of one legion of Romans. But if great opportunities were sufficient to induce any to a revolt, certainly it is chiefly the business of the Gauls to bring about a defection; who are so fortified by the natural strength of the places they inhabit, having the lofty mountains of the Alps on the east, the Rhine on the north, the Pyraenean hills on the south, and the ocean on the west.

But though they have these strong barriers to oppose, and stand against their enemies, and are 305 nations, and, if I may be allowed the liberty to say so, have fountains within themselves that supply them with all the conveniences of life, and water the whole world with their produce, nevertheless submit to be tributaries of the Romans, and to own the happiness they enjoy as a gift from them: and this submission can never be imputed to any effeminacy of theirs, or any degeneracy in their courage, having for fourscore years maintained several successive battles to recover their liberty. But it must be confessed that their obedience was the pure result of the surprise and admiration they had of the Roman courage, as well as fortune, which had a more powerful effect upon them than the force of arms. For which reason they patiently abide under the dominion of 1,200 Roman soldiers, when they have almost a larger number of cities within the confines of their country.

Neither could all the gold that was dug out of the earth avail the Spaniards anything in the battle they undertook to make a path for their liberty; neither their being separated from the Romans by such a vast space of land and sea, nor the warlike nations of the Lusitanians and Cantabrians, nor the bordering sea, which looks dreadful to the natives with its raging and boiling tide. But the Romans carried their arms beyond the Pillars of Hercules, and passed the Pyraenean mountains through the clouds, which they subdued. And though of exceeding great difficulty to penetrate, and placed at so great a distance, yet one legion is sufficient to keep these countries in due obedience.

Who among you hath not heard of the prodigious multitude of the Germans? For I suppose you have frequently been eyewitnesses how much they excel in strength, and the magnitude of their bodies, since the Romans have garrisons of them in most parts of the world. But though the country they inhabit is of such vast extent, their bravery and spirits much superior to their bodies, their souls above the apprehensions of death, and their fury crueler than the most savage beasts, and have the Rhine for the boundary of their incursions, yet eight legions were found sufficient to enslave them. As many as are taken are forced to the Roman obedience; and all the rest of the nation is obliged to preserve its safety by living a vagabond sort of life. Besides, think a little on the wall of the Britains, you who confide so much in the walls of Hierosolyma. For the

Romans, notwithstanding their being hemmed in with the sea, and inhabiting an island almost as large as the world we live in, crossed the ocean and made slaves of them, and now retain an island of such magnitude, within the bounds of its duty, with no more than four legions.

Last, what need have I to produce more examples, since the Parthians, the most warlike people upon the earth, and under whose dominion so many people are subject, and whose great multitude of martial forces is such, send hostages to Rome? And you may see that the pride and glory of the east, under color of preserving peace, remain slaves in Italy. Will you then be the only nation to maintain a war with the Romans, when almost all the nations which the sun shines upon submit to their victorious arms? Neither considering the melancholy fate of the Carthaginians, who, boasting of their great Hannibal, and their illustrious race from the Phoenicians, fell under the triumphant arm of Scipio. But neither have the Cyrenaeans, the descendants of the Lacedaemonians, nor the Marmaridae, a nation stretching themselves to the barren and unwatery deserts, nor the Syrtes, Nasamones, Mauri, and the innumerable multitudes of the Numidians—terrible names to those that hear them mentioned—made any resistance against the Roman valor. And more than all these, their victorious arms won all the third part of the world, the many nations whereof are hard to be enumerated, which is bounded with the vast Atlantic sea, and the Pillars of Hercules, and which to the Red Sea produces and feeds innumerable numbers of Aethiopians; and besides the annual exportation of corn made to Rome, which supplies the inhabitants of that city full eight months, the nations of this immense tract of land pay all other sorts of taxes, and afford, by the tributes levied among them, a seasonable supply to the necessities of the empire, and count it no dishonor, as you do, to perform the commands which are laid upon them, although but one legion resides among them.

But what reason have I to cite further examples to unfold the great power of the Romans, when you yourselves can be sufficient witnesses of it in Egypt, a country that borders upon you? Which being bounded with Ethiopia, and Arabia Faelix, and bordering on Judea, supports with provisions, exclusive of the inhabitants of Alexandria, 1,050,000 souls, as may be calculated from the tax imposed on every head; and yet thinks not much to live under the Roman obedience, though it has one of the strongest inducements in the world to revolt: I mean Alexandria, with regard to the prodigious number of its inhabitants, and its exceeding great wealth; not to mention its magnitude, which stretches full thirty furlongs in length, and no less than ten in breadth.

And the taxes they pay in one month exceed all that is exacted of you in a whole year; and, setting aside the money raised among them, they supply Rome with provisions for four months. Besides, the town is defended on every side, either with walls or some part of the inaccessible desert, or with the sea, or with rivers or marshes: yet none of these are found to prevail so much as the fortunate success of the Romans; two legions that reside there in garrison being sufficient to keep Egypt, so vast a tract of land, within the bounds of its obedience, and restrain the aspiring aims of the Macedonian.

Whom then will you take as confederates, in the war you are going to undertake, out of a country that is uninhabited, if it so be that all, where the world is peopled, stand on the side of the Romans? Probably some may convey your hopes beyond the Euphrates, and have confidence to believe that your countrymen will bring you assistance out of Adiabene. Let me tell you, they will never suffer themselves to be drawn into a war of such great consequence upon a frivolous reason, nor, should they go about to act anything in consequence of ill-concerted schemes, will the Parthian suffer it. For it is his interest to preserve, inviolated, the alliance made with the Romans; and should anyone in his dominions presume to take up arms against the Romans, he will determine such an one as an infringer of the truce.

Your recourse, then, is to rely on some divine assistance. But this is too visibly seen on the Roman side; for it is not possible that an empire of such greatness could arrive to its present height without the immediate assistance of God. Consider the difficulty, even supposing the battle was to be fought with an enemy less powerful than you are: you would have to perform the exact and necessary parts of your religion, and should necessity force you to do things quite contrary to those from which you expect his assistance, probably you may turn the presence of the Almighty from you; for if you keep sacred the seventh days, and move your hands, during those seasons, to no manner of work, your captivity then is easy, and will be attended with the same consequences as when your ancestors submitted to Pompey, who chiefly made his most obstinate attacks on those days wherein the besieged took rest. And if you transgress the laws of your country in the prosecution of a war, I am plainly at a loss to know what can be the next thing that can induce you to go out to battle.

This one article ought to be well considered, not to be yourselves the instruments of ruining your country. But if you are voluntarily resolved to abandon the service and observance you owe to God, what assurance have you to implore his assistance? For everyone undertakes the carrying on of a war either through a reliance on God or a dependence on some human means. But if your own contentions deprive you of either of these assistances, you may depend upon it that your enemies will make themselves your masters. But what impediment lies in the way that hinders you from cutting the throats of your wives and children with your own hands, and laying this beautiful country of yours in ashes? This seasonable piece of rage will be of advantage to you, and save you from the dishonorable treatment of your conquerors.

It is prudent, my friends, it is prudent, while the ship remains in the harbor, to ward against the coming storm, and not fail out of port in the midst of a furious tempest (for they who unwarily fall into dangers which they did not foresee are worthy of our compassion and pity, but he who throws himself into a calamity which he might have seen and avoided, his fate is to be branded with reproach) unless some would have it be thought that there had been an agreement to maintain the war on both sides, and that the Romans, proving victorious, would make a moderate use of their conquest, and deal gently with you; and not, to give other nations a lesson in it, destroy the sacred city with fire, and quite root out all your nation. Neither, supposing you should have the fortune to survive their arms, can you hope to find any place of refuge, since all at this time of day obey the Romans as their masters, or are in expectation to have them as such. Nor will the calamity fall upon only your heads, but as many as have habitations in other cities will fall a sacrifice; for there is no nation, wheresoever dispersed over the face of the whole world, but among whom you make a three; wherefore your revolt will bring all under condemnation, and your enemies dispatch every soul among them, and the pernicious counsels of a few men will prove the fatal cause to make every city swim in Jewish blood. And yet they who shall commit these scenes of bloodshed will be idemnified in their actions. But allowing they should neglect to put them in execution, yet consider the impiousness of the action in taking up arms against such bountiful friends; probably you may have reason to pity this mother of cities, and this sacred enclosure, though you may entertain no bowels of compassion for your wives and children.

Be compassionate to the temple, and endeavor to preserve that house with yourselves and the sanctified things in it. For the Romans, becoming conquerors, will not any longer refrain their hands from them, since they made no advantage when they first spared them. For my part, I take all your solemn things to witness, and call upon the holy angels of God, and my country, that I have passed by nothing that any ways concerns your welfare and safety; and as for you, if you are resolved to act in concert in those things which are absolutely necessary to be done, you will live peaceably with me; but if you are bent to pursue the dictates of your inveteracy and furious passion, you will then explode yourselves to numberless calamities, which I shall have no hand in.

The Bible

Old Testament

Thou shalt not kill.   —*Exodus 20:13*

Say not thou, I will recompense evil; but wait on the Lord, and he shall save thee.   —*Proverbs 20:22*

If thine enemy be hungry, give him bread to eat; and if he be thirsty, give him water to drink.   —*Proverbs 25:21*

If thou meet thine enemy's ox or his ass going astray, thou shalt surely bring it back to him again. If thou see the ass of him that hateth thee lying under his burden, and wouldest forbear to help him, thou shalt surely help with him.   —*Exodus 23:4, 5*

And Abram said unto Lot, Let there be no strife, I pray thee, between me and thee, and between my herdmen and thy herdmen; for we be brethren. Is not the whole land before thee? separate thyself, I pray thee, from me: if thou wilt take the left hand, then I will go to the right; or if thou depart to the right hand, then I will go to the left.
                               —*Genesis 13:8, 9*

And the herdmen of Gerar did strive with Isaac's herdmen, saying, The water is ours: and he called the name of the well Esek; because they strove with him. And they digged another well, and strove for that also: and he called the name of it Sitnah. And he removed from thence, and digged another well; and for that they strove not: and he called the name of it Rehoboth; and he said, For now the Lord hath made room for us, and we shall be fruitful in the land.   —*Genesis 26:20-22*

And he shall judge among the nations, and shall rebuke many people: and they shall beat their swords into plowshares, and their spears into pruning hooks: nation shall not lift up sword against nation, neither shall they learn war any more.   —*Isaiah 2:4*

Woe to them that go down to Egypt for help; and stay on horses, and trust in chariots, because they are many; and in horsemen, because they are very strong; but they look not unto the Holy One of Israel, neither seek the Lord! . . . Now the Egyptians are men, and not God; and their horses flesh, and not spirit. When the Lord shall stretch out his hand, both he that helpeth shall fall, and he that is holpen shall fall down, and they all shall fail together.

—Isaiah 31:1, 3

But God said unto me, Thou shalt not build an house for my name, because thou hast been a man of war, and hast shed blood.

—I Chronicles 28:3

New Testament

From whence come wars and fightings among you? come they not hence, even of your lusts that war in your members? Ye lust, and have not: ye kill, and desire to have, and cannot obtain: ye fight and war, yet ye have not, because ye ask not.

—James 4:1, 2

Whosoever hateth his brother is a murderer: and ye know that no murderer hath eternal life abiding in him.

—I John 3:15

Jesus said unto him, Thou shalt love the Lord thy God with all thy heart, and with all thy soul, and with all thy mind. This is the first and great commandment. And the second is like unto it, Thou shalt love thy neighbour as thyself. On these two commandments hang all the law and the prophets.

—Matthew 22:37-40

Love worketh no ill to his neighbour. . . . Owe no man any thing, but to love one another.

—Romans 13:10, 8

A new commandment I give unto you, That ye love one another; as I have loved you, that ye also love one another.

—John 13:34

Ye have heard that it hath been said, An eye for an eye, and a tooth for a tooth: but I say unto you, that ye resist not evil: but whosoever shall smite thee on thy right cheek, turn to him the other also. And if any man will sue thee at the law, and take away thy coat, let him have thy cloke also.

—Matthew 5:38-40

Ye have heard that it hath been said, Thou shalt love thy neighbour, and hate thine enemy. But I say unto you, Love your enemies, bless them that curse you, do good to them that hate you, and pray for them which despitefully use you, and persecute you; that ye may be the children of your Father which is in heaven: for he maketh his sun to rise on the evil and on the good, and sendeth rain on the just and on the unjust. For if ye love them which love you, what reward have ye? do not even the publicans the same? And if ye salute your brethren only, what do ye more than others? do not even the publicans so? Be ye therefore perfect, even as your Father which is in heaven is perfect. —*Matthew 5:43-48*

Then said Jesus unto him, Put up again thy sword into his place: for all they that take the sword shall perish with the sword.
—*Matthew 26:52*

Recompense to no man evil for evil. Provide things honest in the sight of all men. If it be possible, as much as lieth in you, live peaceably with all men. Dearly beloved, avenge not yourselves, but rather give place unto wrath: for it is written, Vengeance is mine; I will repay, saith the Lord. Therefore if thine enemy hunger, feed him; if he thirst, give him drink: for in so doing thou shalt heap coals of fire on his head. Be not overcome of evil, but overcome evil with good. —*Romans 12:17-21*

See that none render evil for evil unto any man; but ever follow that which is good, both among yourselves, and to all men.
—*I Thessalonians 5:15*

Asoka

proclaims no living beings are to be killed

ASOKA [c. 264-227 B.C.] *was emperor of the Maurya empire, whose dominion extended from Afghanistan to Madras. He was converted to Buddhism, which reached its height in India under his rule. After his successful invasion of Kalinga he became disgusted with the cruelties and horrors of war and declared that henceforth if there were to be conquest, it would be by religion rather than warfare. He forbade animal sacrifice and stressed the sanctity of all life. He was noted for his religious tolerance. His edicts on the practical morality of Buddhism are engraved on pillars and rocks which have survived in various parts of India. The ones that follow were written about 256 B.C.*

This Dharma rescript has been caused to be written by the Beloved of the gods, King Priyadarśin.

Here [in my dominion] no living beings are to be killed and offered in sacrifice.

The Kalingas were conquered by the Beloved of the gods, King Priyadarśin, [when he was] crowned eight years.

One hundred and fifty thousand in number [were] the men who were carried away from there; one hundred thousand in number were slain there; and nearly as many died.

Thereafter, when the Kalingas had been newly conquered, the Beloved of the gods felt a strong inclination for Dharma, desire for Dharma and instruction in Dharma.

Now, it is repentance that the Beloved of the gods felt on conquering the Kalingas.

Indeed, the slaughter or death or deportation of the people [that take place] there when an unconquered country is conquered, is considered very painful and serious by the Beloved of the gods.

And this is considered even more serious than that by the Beloved of the gods [viz.]—

Those who live there—Brāhmanas or ascetics or other sects or householders—among whom are practiced these [viz.]—respectfulness toward superiors, respectfulness toward mother and father, respectfulness toward elders, proper behavior toward [and] firm devotion to friends, acquaintances, companions, relatives, slaves and servants—to them thereby is caused injury or slaughter or the going away of [their] beloved ones.

Again, of those even who are [themselves] of good conduct [and] whose affection [for their beloved ones] is undiminished—the friends, acquaintances, companions and relatives suffer misfortunes, [and] thereby that too becomes an injury to themselves.

And these [misfortunes] fall to the lot of all men and are considered serious by the Beloved of the gods.

And, there is no country—except among the Yonas—where do not exist these classes [of religious people, viz.,] the Brāhmanas and the ascetics.

And there is no country where men are not attached to all, to one or other [religious] sect.

Therefore, even a hundredth part of a thousandth part of the number of men who were slain, who died or were carried away at that time when the Kalingas were conquered, is now considered serious indeed by the Beloved of the gods.

And even if one does harm, he whom it is possible to forgive, the Beloved of the gods thinks, should be forgiven.

And even the forest dwellers that are in the dominion of the Beloved of the gods—they too are entreated and reasoned with, and they are told of the might of the Beloved of the gods in spite of [his] remorse, in order that they may feel ashamed and be not killed.

Indeed, the Beloved of the gods wishes all beings noninjury, restraint [and] impartiality, [even] in case of offensive conduct.

And this is considered by the Beloved of the gods as the best conquest, viz., conquest by the Dharma. . . .

And for this purpose is this Dharma rescript written, that my sons [and] great-grandsons [that there] may be, may not consider new conquests worth making; that [even] in conquests by arms—if such are at all undertaken by them—mercy and light punishments may please them; and that they may consider that alone as conquest which is Dharma-conquest—[for] it bears fruit in this world [as also] in the next world.

And may all [their] intense devotion be the devotion to exertion [in practicing the Dharma]—[for] that bears fruit indeed in this world, [as also] in the next world.

Whatever I consider [to be good], in [respect of] that I desire that I may carry it out by deeds and may accomplish [it] by [various] means.

And this is considered by me the principal means for [accomplishing] this object, viz., [to give] instructions to you.

All men are my children. As for [my own] children, I desire that they may be provided by me with all the welfare and happiness of this world and of the next world; likewise is my desire toward all men.

Perhaps to [my] unconquered Borderers may occur [this thought, viz.,] "What may the king's intentions be toward us?"

These alone are my wishes that should be [made] known to the Borderers, viz.—

"The king desires thus, viz.—that they may be without fear in respect of me, and that they may have confidence in me; and [that they may] obtain only happiness from me, [and] not sorrow."

And they should [also] understand thus, viz.—"that the king will forgive those who can be forgiven; and, that they may be induced by me to practise the Dharma; and, that they may attain [the happiness of] this world and of the next world."

And for this purpose I am instructing you [that] I may discharge the debts [which I owe to the Borderers] by this alone, [viz.,] by instructing you and by informing [you] of my intentions, [that is to say, of] what [is] my will and firm determination.

Therefore, in such manner have [your] duties to be performed and they are to be inspired with confidence, that they may feel [thus], viz. —"As [one's] father, so toward us is the king; as he feels for himself, so he feels for us; [and] as [his own] children [are to him], so are we to the king."

By instructing you and by informing [you] of my intentions, [that is to say, of] what [is] my will and firm determination, I shall be applying myself in complete fullness to [the accomplishment of] this object.

You are able indeed to inspire them with confidence and to secure their welfare and happiness in this world and in the next world.

By acting thus, you will attain heaven as well as discharge the debts [which you owe] to me.

And for this purpose is this rescript written here that the Mahāmā-tras may devote themselves at all, times to inspiring the Borderers with confidence and to inducing them to practise the Dharma.

And this rescript is to be listened to [by all] every four months on [the day of] Tiṣya. And it should be listened to also between [the days of Tiṣya]. On [suitable] occasions, [it] should be listened to even by a single person.

And acting thus, you will be able to perform [your duties] rightly.

The Beloved of the gods said:
Wherever there are either stone pillars or stone slabs, thereon this Dharma rescript is to be engraved, so that it may long endure.

Now, for this purpose has this been engraved that it may last as long as [my] sons and great-grandsons [shall live and] as long as the moon and the sun [shall shine], and that men may practice [it] as instructed.

By practicing [it] thus, [happiness] in this and in the next [world] is indeed attained.

This Dharma rescript has been caused to be written by me [when] crowned twenty-seven years.

Aristophanes
Lysistrata strikes for peace

ARISTOPHANES [c. 448-385 B.C.], *author of the greatest Greek comedies that have survived, was an Athenian of the tribe of Pandion. Athens awarded him the Crown of the Wild Olive in appreciation of his effective satire. In politics he was a conservative, and he consistently favored peace with Sparta on reasonable terms. Lysistrata was first produced in Athens in 411 B.C.*

LYSISTRATA: I'll tell you now: 'tis meet ye all should know.
O ladies! Sisters! If we really mean
To make the men make peace, there's but one way,
We must abstain—

MYRRHINA: Well! Tell us.

LYSISTRATA: Will ye do it?

MYRRHINA: Do it? Aye, surely, though it cost our lives.

LYSISTRATA: We must abstain—each—from the joys of love.
How! What! Why turn away? Where are ye going?
What makes you pout your lips, and shake your heads?
What brings this falling tear, that changing color?
Will ye, or will ye not? What mean ye, eh?

MYRRHINA: I'll never do it. Let the war go on.

CALONICE: Zeus! Nor I either. Let the war go on.

LYSISTRATA: You, too, Miss Turbot? You who said just now
You'd cleave, for peace, your very self in twain?

CALONICE: Ask anything but this. Why, if needs be,
I'd walk through fire: only, not give up love.
There's nothing like it, dear Lysistrata.

LYSISTRATA: And why say you?

MYRRHINA: I'd liefer walk through fire.

LYSISTRATA: O women! Women! O our frail, frail sex!
No wonder tragedies are made from us.
Always the same: nothing but loves and cradles.
O friend! O Lampito! If you and I
Are of one mind, we yet may pull things through;
Won't *you* vote with me, dear?

LAMPITO: Haith, by the Twa',
'Tis sair to bide your lane, withouten men.
Still it maun be: we maun hae peace, at a' risks.

LYSISTRATA: O dearest friend; my one true friend of all.

CALONICE: Well, but suppose we do the things you say,
Pray heaven avert it, but put case we do,
Shall we be nearer peace?

LYSISTRATA: Much, much, much nearer.
For if we women will but sit at home,
Powdered and trimmed, clad in our daintiest lawn,
Employing all our charms, and all our arts
To win men's love, and when we've won it, then
Repel them, firmly, till they end the war,
We'll soon get peace again, be sure of that.

LAMPITO: Sae Menelaus, when he glowered, I ween,
At Helen's breastie, coost his glaive awa'.

CALONICE: Eh, but suppose they leave us altogether?
LYSISTRATA: O, faddle! Then we'll find some substitute.
CALONICE: If they try force?
LYSISTRATA: They'll soon get tired of that
    If we keep firm. Scant joy a husband gets
    Who finds himself at discord with his wife.
CALONICE: Well, then, if so you wish it, so we'll have it.
LAMPITO: An' our gude folk we'se easily persuade
    To keep the peace wi' never a thocht o' guile:
    But your Athanian hairumscairum callants
    Wha sall persuade *them* no play the fule?
LYSISTRATA: O, we'll persuade our people, never fear.
LAMPITO: Not while ye've gat thae gallies rigged sae trim,
    An' a' that rowth o' siller nigh the goddess.
LYSISTRATA: O, but, my dear, we've taken thought for that:
    This very morn we seized the Acropolis.
    Now, whilst we're planning and conspiring here,
    The elder women have the task assigned them,
    Under pretense of sacrifice, to seize it.
LAMPITO: A' will gae finely, an' ye talk like that.
LYSISTRATA: Then why not, Lampito, at once combine
    All in one oath, and clench the plot securely?
LAMPITO: Weel, you propound the aith, an' we'se a' tak' it.
LYSISTRATA: Good; now then, Scythianess, don't stand there gaping.
    Quick, set a great black shield here, hollow upwards,
    And bring the sacrificial bits.
CALONICE: And how
    Are we to swear, Lysistrata?
LYSISTRATA: We'll slay
    (Like those Seven Chiefs in Aeschylus) a lamp
    Over a shield.
CALONICE: Nay, when our object's peace,
    Don't use a shield, Lysistrata, my dear.
LYSISTRATA: Then what shall be the oath?
CALONICE: Could we not somehow
    Get a gray mare, and cut her up to bits?
LYSISTRATA: Gray mare, indeed!
CALONICE: Well, what's the oath will suit
    Us women best?
MYRRHINA: I'll tell you what I think.
    Let's set a great black cup here, hollow upwards:
    Then for a lamb we'll slay a Thasian wine jar,
    And firmly swear to—pour no water in.

LAMPITO: Hech, the braw aith! My certie, hoo I like it.

LYSISTRATA: O yes, bring out the wine jar and the cup.

(*A maiden brings out a jar of wine and an immense cup.*)

CALONICE: La! Here's a splendid piece of ware, my dears.
Now, that's a cup 'twill cheer one's heart to take.

LYSISTRATA: (*to the servant*): Set down the cup, and take the victim boar.
O Queen Persuasion, and O Loving Cup,
Accept our offerings, and maintain our cause!
(*The servant pours the wine into the cup, the women all
pressing round to see.*)

CALONICE: 'Tis jolly colored blood, and spurts out bravely.

LAMPITO: Ay, an' by Castor, verra fragrant too!

MYRRHINA: Let *me* swear first, my sisters?

CALONICE: Yes, if *you*
Draw the first lot; not else, by Aphrodite.

LYSISTRATA: All place your hands upon the wine cup: so.
One, speak the words, repeating after me.
Then all the rest confirm it. Now begin.
I will abstain from love and love's delights.

CALONICE: *I will abstain from love and love's delights.*

LYSISTRATA: And take no pleasure though my lord invites.

CALONICE: *And take no pleasure though my lord invites.*

LYSISTRATA: And sleep a vestal all alone at nights.

CALONICE: *And sleep a vestal all alone at nights.*

LYSISTRATA: And live a stranger to all nuptial rites.

CALONICE: *And live a stranger to all nuptial rites.*
I don't half like it though, Lysistrata.

LYSISTRATA: I will abjure the very name of love.

CALONICE: *I will abjure the very name of love.*

LYSISTRATA: So help me Zeus, and all the powers above.

CALONICE: *So help me Zeus, and all the powers above.*

LYSISTRATA: If I do this, my cup be filled with wine.

CALONICE: *If I do this, my cup be filled with wine.*

LYSISTRATA: But if I fail, a water draught be mine.

CALONICE: *But if I fail, a water draught be mine.*

LYSISTRATA: You all swear this?

MYRRHINA: O yes, my dear, we do.

Motse

shows that the gentlemen of the world are confused about the difference between righteousness and unrighteousness

MOTSE [Mo Ti, c. 470-391 B.C.] *was born in the Chinese feudal state of Lu, the home of Confucius, and was disciplined in Confucian philosophy. For a short time he was minister of the state of Sung. He advocated universal love, and his opposition to war was so great that when he heard of neighboring states planning to engage in battle, Motse would travel to see the rulers and try to convince them to avoid warfare.*

Suppose a man enters the orchard of another and steals the other's peaches and plums. Hearing of it, the public will condemn it; laying hold of him, the authorities will punish him. Why? Because he injures others to profit himself. As to seizing dogs, pigs, chickens and young pigs from another, it is even more unrighteous than to steal peaches and plums from his orchard. Why? Because it causes others to suffer more, and it is more inhumane and criminal. When it comes to entering another's stable and appropriating the other's horses and oxen, it is more inhumane than to seize the dogs, pigs, chickens and young pigs of another. Why? Because others are caused to suffer more; when others are caused to suffer more, then the act is more inhumane and criminal. Finally, as to murdering the innocent, stripping him of his clothing, dispossessing him of his spear and sword, it is even more unrighteous than to enter another's stable and appropriate his horses and oxen. Why? Because it causes others to suffer more; when others are caused to suffer more, then the act is more inhumane and criminal.

All the gentlemen of the world know that they should condemn these things, calling them unrighteous. But when it comes to the great attack of states, they do not know that they should condemn it. On the contrary, they applaud it, calling it righteous. Can this be said to be knowing the difference between righteousness and unrighteousness?

The murder of one person is called unrighteous and incurs one death penalty. Following this argument, the murder of ten persons will be ten times as unrighteous and there should be ten death penalties; the murder of a hundred persons will be a hundred times as unrighteous and there should be a hundred death penalties. All the gentlemen of the world know that they should condemn these things, calling them unrighteous. But when it comes to the great unrighteousness of attacking states, they do not know that they should condemn it. On the contrary, they applaud it, calling it righteous. And they are really ignorant of its being unrighteous. Hence they have recorded their judgment to bequeath to their posterity. If they did know that it is unrighteous, then why would they record their false judgment to bequeath to posterity?

Now, if there were a man who, upon seeing a little blackness, should say it is black, but, upon seeing much, should say it is white, then we should think he could not tell the difference between black and white. If, upon tasting a little bitterness one should say it is bitter, but, upon tasting much, should say it is sweet, then we should think he could not tell the difference between bitter and sweet. Now, when a little wrong is committed people know that they should condemn it, but when such a great wrong as attacking a state is committed people do not know that they should condemn it. On the contrary, it is applauded, called righteous. Can this be said to be knowing the difference between the righteous and the unrighteous? Hence we know the gentlemen of the world are confused about the difference between righteousness and unrighteousness.

Buddha
pities a man who abuses him

BUDDHA [c. 560-483 B.C.] *was the son of a wealthy king of the Sakyas in India. When he was twenty-nine Buddha renounced his easy life and left home to wander and study, and after six years of this he attained "enlightenment" while meditating under a tree. His ethical ideals of love and respect, forgiveness and peace, nonviolence and humility, form the basis of the Buddhist religion he founded. He spent the rest of his life as a wanderer preaching his gospels to the populace.*

If a man by causing pain to others, wishes to obtain pleasure for himself, he, entangled in the bonds of sefishness, will never be free from hatred.

Let a man overcome anger by love, let him overcome evil by good; let him overcome the greedy by liberality, the liar by truth!

For hatred does not cease by hatred at any time; hatred ceases by love; this is an old rule.

Speak the truth; do not yield to anger; give, if thou art asked; by these three steps thou wilt become divine.

Let a wise man blow off the impurities of his self, as a smith blows off the impurities of silver, one by one, little by little, and from time to time.

Lead others, not by violence, but by law and equity.

He who possesses virtue and intelligence, who is just, speaks the truth, and does what is his own business, him the world will hold dear.

And the Blessed One observed the ways of society and noticed how much misery came from malignity and foolish offences done only to gratify vanity and self-seeking pride.

And Buddha said: "If a man foolishly does me wrong, I will return to him the protection of my ungrudging love; the more evil comes from him, the more good shall go from me; the fragrance of goodness always comes to me, and the harmful air of evil goes to him."

A foolish man learning that Buddha observed the principle of great love which commends to return good for evil, came and abused him. Buddha was silent, pitying his folly.

The man having finished his abuse, Buddha asked him, saying: "Son, if a man declined to accept a present made to him, to whom would it belong?" And he answered: "In that case it would belong to the man who offered it."

"My son," said Buddha, "you have railed at me, but I decline to accept your abuse, and request you to keep it yourself. Will it not be a source of misery to you? As the echo belongs to the sound, and the shadow to the substance, so misery will overtake the evildoer without fail."

The abuser made no reply, and Buddha continued:

"A wicked man who reproaches a virtuous one is like one who looks up and spits at heaven; the spittle soils not the heaven, but comes back and defiles his own person.

"The slanderer is like one who flings dust at another when the wind is contrary; the dust does but return on him who threw it. The virtuous man cannot be hurt, and the misery that the other would inflict comes back on himself."

The abuser went away ashamed, but he came again and took refuge in the Buddha, the Dharma and the Sangha.

Lao-Tse

*says that he who rejoices at the destruction of
human life is not fit to be trusted with power*

L A O - T S E [c. 604-531 B.C.], *born Li Err of K'u Province, Ch'u State,
was a Chinese philosopher; the classic book,* Tao Tê Ching, *which has
been attributed to him, inspired the cult of Taoism. He was an original
thinker, always searching for disciples to carry on his ideas. According
to legend, when Lao-Tse was an old man he began a journey to the
west, passed through the gates of his city, and was never heard of again.*

He who in the use of Tao renders assistance to a human ruler does not
use weapons to force the people. His actions are such as he may well
accept the results of [or, such as he would wish rendered to himself
again].

Where legions are quartered, briars and thorns grow. In the track
of great armies, there must follow bad years.

The good soldier is brave in need only [to effect some good pur-
pose]. He ventures nothing for the sake of power. He is brave in need,
but not a bully. He is brave in need, but not a boaster. He is brave in
need, but is not overbearing. He is brave in need, but he cannot be less.
He is brave in need, but not violent.

When things reach their highest pitch of vigor, they become old.
This is called not Tao. What is not Tao is soon at an end.

Ornamental weapons are not instruments of joy, but objects of
hatred to every creature. Therefore he who has Tao will not stay where
they are.

The superior man in his home makes the left hand [the weak side]
the place of honor. But he who goes forth to use weapons of war honors
the right [the strong] hand. They are instruments of evil omen. They
are not the tools of a superior man. He uses them only when he cannot
help it. Peace is his highest aim. When he conquers he is not elated. To
be elated is to rejoice at the destruction of human life. And he who rejoices
at the destruction of human life is not fit to be entrusted with power in
the world.

In a prosperous state of affairs, the left side is preferred; and in an
adverse state of affairs, the right side is preferred. The adjutant general
takes his place on the left, and the general-in-chief takes his place on the
right. Now, I say, this is just the order of a funeral. He who has been

instrumental in killing many people should mourn over them with bitter tears. Therefore, those who have been victorious in battle are disposed after the order of a funeral.

A certain person of military experience has said, "I dare not be the host [to lead on the fight]; I would rather be the guest. I dare not advance an inch [to make the first attack]; I would rather retire a foot." Now, this [principle, if carried out] would, I say, result in there being no following of ranks, no baring of the arm, no charging of the enemy, no grasping of weapons.

There is no calamity greater than making light of the enemy. By making light of the enemy, we are almost sure to lose our treasure. Therefore, when opposing warriors join in battle, the pitiful is always the conqueror.

SELECTED BIBLIOGRAPHY

Addams, Jane, *Peace and Bread in Time of War*, The Macmillan Company, New York, 1911.

——, *The Long Road of Woman's Memory*, The Macmillan Company, New York, 1916.

Allen, Devere, *The Fight For Peace*, The Macmillan Company, New York, 1930.

——, *Pacifism in the Modern World*, Doubleday, Doran & Co., Inc., Garden City, New York, 1929.

Angell, Norman, *After All*—The Autobiography of Norman Angell, Farrar, Straus & Young, New York, 1957.

——, *Peace with the Dictators?*, Hamish Hamilton, London, 1938.

Archer, William, *To Neutral Peace-Lovers—A Plea for Patience*, Sir Joseph Causton & Son, Ltd., London, 1916.

Arnoldson, K. P., *Pax Mundi*, Swan Sonnenschein & Co., London, 1892.

Baha, Abdul, *The Promulgation of Universal Peace*, Bahai Publishing Committee, Wilmette, Illinois, 1943.

——, *Talks*, The Unity Press, Surrey, 1912.

Bainton, Roland H., *Christian Attitudes Toward War and Peace*, Abingdon Press, New York, Nashville, 1960.

Ballou, Adin, *Autobiography, 1803-1890*, The Vox Populi Press, Thompson & Hill, Lowell, Massachusetts, 1896.

Barth, Karl, *The Church and the War*, The Macmillan Company, New York, 1944.

Beales, Arthur C. F., *The History of Peace*, Lincoln MacVeagh, The Dial Press, New York, 1931.

Beckwith, George C., *The Peace Manual*, American Peace Society, Boston, 1847.

Bender, Harold S., *Conrad Grebel, c. 1498-1526*, The Mennonite Historical Society, Goshen College, Goshen, Ind., 1950.

Benet, S. T. et al., *Zero Hour, A Summons to the Free*, Farrar & Rinehart, Inc., New York, Toronto, 1940.

Berkman, Alexander, *What Is Communist Anarchism?*, The Vanguard Press, New York, 1929.

Bondurant, John Valerie, *Conquest of Violence*, Princeton University Press, 1958.

The Book of Peace, A Collection of Essays on War and Peace, George C. Beckwith, Boston, 1845.

Boudin, Louise B., *Socialism and War*, New Review Publ. Assoc., New York, 1916.

Bourne, Randolph S., *Towards Enduring Peace*, American Association for International Conciliation, New York, 1916.

Bowman, Paul H., *The Adventurous Future*, The Brethren Press, Elgin, Illinois, 1959.

Brandis, Georg, *The World at War;* translated by Catherine D. Groth; The Macmillan Company, New York, 1917.

Brewer, William C., *Permanent Peace*, Dorrance and Company, Philadelphia, 1940.

Brittain, Vera, *Testament of Youth*, The Macmillan Company, New York, 1933.

——, *Testament of Experience*, The Macmillan Company, New York, 1958.

Brock, Peter, *The Political and Social Doctrines of the Unity of Czech Brethren in the 15th and Early 16th Centuries*, Moulton & Co., 's Gravenhage (The Hague), Netherlands, 1957.

Brumbaugh, Martin G., *A History of the German Baptist Brethren in Europe and America*, Brethren Publishing House, Mt. Morris, Ill., 1899.

Bryan, William J., *The Forces That Make For Peace*, World Peace Foundation, Pamphlet Series 1-2, 1911-12.

Buber, Martin, *Between Man and Man*, The Macmillan Company, New York, 1948.

——, *Pointing the Way;* translated from the German and edited by Maurice Friedman; Harper & Brothers, New York, 1957.

Burritt, Elihu, *A Memorial Volume;* edited by Chas. Northend; D. Appleton & Co., New York, 1879.

——, *Lectures and Speeches*, Sampson Low, Son & Marston, London, 1869.

Butler, Nicholas Murray, *Why War?*, Charles Scribner's Sons, New York, London, 1941.

Cadoux, C. John, *The Early Christian Attitude to War*, Headley Bros. Ltd., London, 1919.

——, *Christian Pacifism Re-examined*, Oxford, Blackwell, 1940.

Carey, Cynthia Sally, *A Comparative Study of Civil Disobedience and Parliamentarianism in the Indian National Congress 1930-1940;* dissertation submitted to University of Chicago faculty of Division of Social Sciences for M.A., International Relations, June, 1951.

Carlyle, R. W. and A. J., *A History of Mediaeval Political Theory in the West*, 6 vols., William Blackwood & Sons, Ltd., Edinburgh, London, 1903-36.

Case, C. M., *Non-Violent Coercion*, The Century Co., New York, London, 1923.

Channing, William Ellery, *Lecture on War*, Dutton and Wentworth, Boston, 1839.

Chander, Jag Parvesh, *Tagore and Gandhi Argue*, Indian Printing Works, Lahore, 1945.

Clark, G. N., *The Cycle of War and Peace in Modern History*, University Press, Cambridge, 1949.

Clarke, John, *Physical Science in the Time of Nero*, with notes on the treatise by Sir Archibald Geikie; Macmillan and Co., Ltd., London, 1910.

Coleman, McAlister, *Eugene V. Debs*, Greenberg, Publisher, Inc., New York, 1930.

Collin, Christen, *The War Against War*, Macmillan and Co., Ltd., London, 1917.

Conklin, Robert J., *Thomas Cooper—The Chartist, 1805-1892*, University of the Philippines Press, Manila, 1935.

Conway, Moncure Daniel, *The Sacred Anthology*, Henry Holt & Co., New York, 1877.

Corkey, Robert, *War, Pacifism and Peace*, Society for Promoting Christian Knowledge, London, 1940.

Cornell, William M., *Charles Sumner—Memoir and Eulogies*, James H. Earle, Boston, 1874.

Coudenhove-Kalergi, Richard, *From War to Peace;* translated from the German by Constantine Fitzgibbon; Jonathan Cape, London, 1959.

Coulton, G. G., *Five Centuries of Religion*, University Press, Cambridge, 1936.
——, *The Main Illusions of Pacifism*, Bowes and Bowes, Cambridge, 1916.
Cronbach, Abraham, *The Jewish Peace Book*, Dept. of Synagogue and School Extension of the Union of American Hebrew Congregations, Cincinnati, 1932.
Cousins, Norman, *Who Speaks For Man?*, The Macmillan Company, New York, 1953.
Crosby, Ernest, *Garrison the Non-Resistant*, The Public Publishing Company, Chicago, 1905.
Curti, Merle, *The American Peace Crusade*, Duke University Press, Durham, N.C., 1929.
——, *Peace or War—the American Struggle, 1636-1936*, W. W. Norton & Co., New York, 1936.
——, *The Learned Blacksmith*, Wilson-Erickson, Inc., New York, 1937.
D'Alviella, Goblet, *The True and the False Pacifism*, T. Fisher Unwin, Ltd., London, 1917.
Darton, F. J. Harvey, *From Surtees to Sassoon*, Morley & Mitchell Kennerley, Jr., London, 1931.
Davis, Jerome, *Peace, War and You*, Henry Schuman, New York, 1952.
Debs, Eugene V., *Writings and Speeches of . . .* , Hermitage Press, Inc., New York, 1948.
De Ligt, Bart, *The Conquest of Violence*, George Routledge & Sons, Ltd., London, 1937.
Dingwall, E. and Heard, E. A., *Pennsylvania, 1681-1756, the State Without an Army*, The C. W. Daniel Company, Ltd., London, 1937.
Diwakar, Ranganath Ramachandra, *Satyagraha—The Power of Truth*, H. Regnery Co., Hinsdale, Illinois, 1948.
Dolci, Danilo, *Outlaws*, The Orion Press, New York, 1961.
Eddy, Sherwood, *Eighty Adventurous Years—An Autobiography*, Harper & Brothers, New York, 1955.
Ellis, Havelock, *The Philosophy of Conflict and Other Essays in War-Time*, Houghton-Mifflin Co., Boston, New York, 1919.
——, *The Task of Social Hygiene*, Constable & Company, Ltd., London, 1912.
Field, G. C., *Pacifism and Conscientious Objection*, University Press, Cambridge, England, 1945.
Finch, Roy, "The New Peace Movement," *Dissent*, winter, 1963, pp. 86-95; spring, 1963, pp. 138-148.
Fischer, Louis, *Gandhi—His Life and Mission for the World*, New American Library, New York, 1954.
Fischer, Louis, ed., *The Essential Gandhi*, Vintage Books, New York, 1963.
Fogelklou, Emilio, *James Nayler—The Rebel Saint, 1618-1660*, Ernest Benn Ltd., London, 1931.
Fox, George, *Journal of George Fox*, Cash, London, 1852; vol. I, 7th ed., Beacon Press, Boston.
Frank, Jerome, *Fate and Freedom—A Philosophy for Americans*, Simon and Schuster, New York, 1945.
Fried, Alfred H., *The German Emperor and the Peace of the World*, Hodder and Stoughton, London, New York, Toronto, 1912.
Friedman, Maurice, *The Covenant of Peace*, Pendle Hill, Wallingford, Pennsylvania, 1960.
Friedrich, Carl Joachim, *Inevitable Peace*, Harvard University Press, Cambridge, 1948.
Fry, Anna Ruth, *Victories Without Violence*, Peace Book Club, 1939.

Galpin, W. Freeman, *Pioneering for Peace,* The Bardeen Press, Syracuse, New York, 1933.

Gandhi, M. K., *Non-Violence in Peace and War,* Navajivan Publishing House, Ahmedabad, 1942, 1944.

——, *Non-Violent Resistance,* Schocken Books, New York, 1961.

Gairdner, James, *Lollardy and the Reformation of England,* 4 vols., Macmillan & Co., Ltd., London, 1908.

Garrison, William Lloyd—The Story of His Life, told by his children, 4 vols., T. Fisher Unwin, London; The Century Co., New York, 1885.

Gelber, Lionel, *Reprieve From War,* The Macmillan Company, New York, 1950.

Genung, Dan B., Jr., *A Survey of Pacifist Techniques in the Modern Period;* dissertation submitted to faculty of Divinity School, University of Chicago, for M.A., Chicago, 1940.

Giddings, Franklin Henry, *Democracy and Empire,* The Macmillan Company, New York, 1900.

——, *Democracy and Empire,* The Macmillan Company, New York, 1900.

Gierke, Otto, *Political Theories of the Middle Age,* University Press, Cambridge, 1900.

The Gist—A Peace Digest (Sponsors: Fellowship of Reconciliation, National Council for Prevention of War, 1944.)

Glover, Edward, *War, Sadism and Pacifism,* George Allen & Unwin Ltd., London, 1933.

Goldman, Emma, *Living My Life,* Garden City Publishing Co., Garden City, New York, copyright Alfred A. Knopf, Inc., 1931.

Gummere, Amelia Mott, *The Quaker in the Forum,* The John C. Winston Co., Philadelphia, Pennsylvania, 1902.

Hancock, William Keith, *War and Peace in This Century,* University Press, Cambridge, 1961.

Hearnshaw, F. J. C., *The Social and Political Ideas of Some Great Mediaeval Thinkers,* George G. Harrap & Company, Ltd., London, Calcutta, Sydney, 1923.

Hemleben, Sylvester John, *Plans For World Peace Through Six Centuries,* The University of Chicago Press, Chicago, 1943.

The Herald of Peace and International Arbitration Peace Society for the years 1844-45.

Hershberger, Guy Franklin, *War, Peace and Nonresistance,* The Herald Press, Scottdale, Pa., 1944.

Hirst, Margaret E., *The Quakers in Peace and War,* The Swarthmore Press, Ltd., London; George H. Doran Company, New York, 1923.

Hook, Sidney, "The Philosophy of Non-Resistance," *The Open Court,* vol. 36, no. 1, January, 1922.

Holmes, John Haynes, *New Wars For Old,* Dodd, Mead & Co., New York, 1916.

——, *I Speak For Myself,* Harper & Brothers, New York, 1959.

Horowitz, Irving Louis, *The Idea of War and Peace in Contemporary Philosophy,* Paine-Whitman Publishers, New York, 1957.

Horsch, John, *Mennonites in Europe,* Mennonite Publishing House, Scottdale, Pa., 1942.

Hunter, Allan A., *White Corpuscles in Europe,* Willitt, Clark & Co., Chicago, New York, 1939.

de Huszar, G. B., *New Perspectives on Peace,* University of Chicago Press, 1944.

Huxley, Aldous, *An Encyclopedia of Pacifism, 1937,* Harper & Brothers, New York, London, 1937.

——, *Ends and Means,* Chatto & Windus, London, 1937.

Huxley, Aldous, *Science, Liberty and Peace,* Harper & Brothers, New York, London, 1946.

——, *What Are You Going To Do About It?—The Case For Constructive Peace,* Chatto & Windus, London, 1936.

Jackson, Elmore, *Meeting of Minds,* McGraw-Hill Book Company, Inc., New York, Toronto, London, 1952.

Jacob, Philip E., and Sibley, Mulford Q., *Conscription of Conscience,* Cornell University Press, Ithaca, New York, 1952.

Jászi, Oscar, and Lewis, John D., *Against the Tyrant,* The Free Press, Glencoe, Illinois, 1957.

Jones, Rufus M., *The Church, the Gospel, and War,* Harper & Brothers, New York, London, 1948.

——, *Spiritual Reformers in the 16th and 17th Centuries,* Macmillan and Co., Ltd., London, 1914.

——, *Studies in Mystical Religion,* Macmillan and Co., Ltd., London, 1909.

——, *The Nature and Authority of Conscience,* The Swarthmore Press Ltd., London, 1920.

Juvenal, *The Satires of . . .* ; translated and illustrated by Francis Hodgson, Payne and MacKinlay, London, 1807.

Kant, Immanuel, *Perpetual Peace,* George Allen & Unwin, Ltd., London, 1915.

King, Martin Luther, Jr., *Stride Toward Freedom,* Harper & Bros., New York, 1958.

Kirkland, Edward Chase, *The Peacemakers of 1864,* The Macmillan Company, New York, 1927.

Knight, W. S. M., *A Mediaeval Pacifist, Pierre du Bois,* Sweet & Maxwell, Ltd., London, 1924.

Knight, Rachel, *The Founder of Quakerism,* George H. Doran Company, New York, 1923.

Kuhlman, Charles, *Pacifism as the Unifying Thesis of All Social Reform,* Richard G. Badger, The Gorham Press, Boston, 1922.

Kuper, Leo, *Passive Resistance in South Africa,* Cape, London, 1956; Yale University Press, New Haven, 1957.

Laidler, Harry W., *A History of Socialist Thought,* Thomas Y. Crowell Company, New York, 1927.

La Motte, Ellen N., *The Backwash of War, The Human Wreckage of the Battlefield,* G. P. Putnam's Son, New York, London, 1916.

Lawrence, William L., *Men and Atoms,* Simon and Schuster, New York, 1946.

Lee, Umphrey, *The Historic Church and Modern Pacifism,* Abingdon-Cokesbury Press, New York, Nashville, 1953.

Legge, James, *The Life and Works of Mencius,* J. B. Lippincott and Co., Philadelphia, 1875.

Luthuli, Albert, *Let My People Go,* McGraw-Hill, New York, 1962.

MacGregor, George Hogarth C., *The New Testament Basis of Pacifism,* Fellowship Publications, Nyack, New York, 1960.

Macphail, James M., *The Heritage of India—Asoka,* Oxford University Press, London, 1926.

Magnes, Judah L., *War-Time Addresses, 1917-1921,* Thomas Seltzer, New York, 1923.

——, *In the Perplexity of the Times,* The Hebrew University, Jerusalem, 1946.

——, *Let Jews and Arabs Meet,* Union Pamphlet No. 2, Ihud (Union) Association, Jerusalem, 1945.

Masland, John W., "Pressure Groups and American Foreign Policy," *Public Opinion Quarterly,* vol. 6, Spring 1942.

Maude, Aylmer, *The Life of Tolstoy, Later Years*, vol. 2, Constable & Company, Limited, London, 1910.

Mayer, Milton, *Conscience and the Commonwealth*, n.d.

Mead, Edwin D., *The Literature of the Peace Movement;* published quarterly, World Peace Foundation, Boston, October, 1912, Nov. 7, Part IV.

———, *Organize the World!*, American Peace Society, Boston, 1898.

Mei, Yi-Pao, *Motse, the Neglected Rival of Confucius*, Arthur Probsthain, London, 1934.

Melia, Pius, *The Origin, Persecutions and Doctrines of the Waldenses*, James Toovey, London, 1870.

Melman, Seymour, *The Peace Race*, George Braziller, New York, 1962.

Menninger, Karl, *Love Against Hate*, Harcourt, Brace & Co., New York, 1942.

The Mennonite Encyclopedia, Mennonite Publishing House, Scottdale, Pa., 1955; Mennonite Publication Office, Newton, Kansas; Mennonite Brethren Publishing House, Hillsboro, Kansas, 1955-59.

Milck, Joseph, *Hermann Hesse and His Critics*, The University of North Carolina Press, Chapel Hill, 1958.

Millis, Walter, *Road to War, America 1914-1917*, Houghton Mifflin Company, Boston, New York, 1935.

Mills, C. Wright, *The Causes of World War Three*, Simon and Schuster, New York, 1958.

Milne, A. A., *Autobiography*, E. P. Dutton & Co., Inc., New York, 1939.

———, *Peace With Honour*, Methuen & Company, London, 1935.

———, *War With Honour*, Macmillan & Co., Ltd., London, 1940.

Mockail, J. W., *Erasmus Against War*, The Merrymount Press, Boston, 1907.

Morrison, Charles Clayton, *The Outlawry of War*, Willett, Clark & Colby, Chicago, 1927.

Morrison, Sybil, *I Renounce War*, Sheppard Press, London, 1962.

Mo-Tse, *The Ethical and Political Works of Motse;* translated by Yi-Pao Mei; A. Probsthain, London, 1929.

Mumford, Lewis, *In the Name of Sanity*, Harcourt Brace & Co., New York, 1954.

Muste, A. J., *Non-Violence in an Aggressive World*, Harper & Brothers, New York, London, 1940.

Nef, John U., *War and Human Progress*, Harvard University Press, Cambridge, Mass., 1950.

Nehru, Jawaharlal, *Toward Freedom*, John Day, New York, 1941.

Newton, J. T., "The State and the Individual Conscience," *London Quarterly Review*, 166, April, 1941.

Niebuhr, Reinhold, *Faith and History*, Charles Scribner's Sons, New York, 1949.

———, *Moral Man and Immoral Society*, Charles Scribner's Sons, New York, London, 1941.

———, *Reflections on the End of an Era*, Charles Scribner's Sons, New York, London, 1936.

Ogburn, Mary Cornelia Aldis, *Pacifist Attitudes Toward American Foreign Policy From Dunkirk to Pearl Harbor;* dissertation submitted to faculty of Division of Social Sciences, Department of Political Science, University of Chicago, for M.A., December, 1950.

Owen, Harold, *Disloyalty: The Blight of Pacifism*, Hurst and Blackett, Ltd., London, 1918.

Page, Kirby, *National Defense*, Farrar & Rinehart, Inc., New York, 1931.

———, *A Study of the Origins, Results and Prevention of War*, Farrar & Rinehart, Inc., New York, 1931.

Paine, Albert Bigelow, *Mark Twain—A Biography*, Harper & Brothers, Publishers, New York, London, 1912.

Paullin, Theo., *Introduction to Non-Violence*, The Pacifist Research Bureau, Philadelphia, 1944.

Payne, Ernest A., *The Anabaptist of the 16th Century*, The Caray Kingsgate Press, Ltd., London, 1949.

Peace Calendar, 1962, 1963, War Resisters League, New York.

Peace Society, London, Tracts #1-12, 1831-33.

Perry, Ralph Barton, *The Free Man and the Soldier*, Charles Scribner's Sons, New York, 1916.

——, *Puritanism and Democracy*, The Vanguard Press, New York, 1944.

Peterson, H. C., and Fite, Gilbert C., *Opponents of War 1917-18*, The University of Wisconsin Press, Madison, 1957.

Phelps, Christina, *The Anglo-American Peace Movement in the Mid-Nineteenth Century*, Columbia University Press, New York, 1930.

Philanthropos, *The Essays of Philanthropos on Peace and War*, John T. Burnham, Exeter, New Hampshire, 1827.

Potter, Charles Francis, *The Great Religious Leaders*, Washington Square Press, 1962.

Pringle, Cyrus, *Record of a Quaker Conscience;* introduction by Rufus M. Jones; The Macmillan Company, New York, 1918.

Randall, John Herman, Jr., *The Making of the Modern Mind*, Houghton Mifflin Co., Boston, 1940.

Reed, Louis S., *The Labor Philosophy of Samuel Gompers*, Columbia University Press, New York, 1930.

Reynolds, Earle L., *The Forbidden Voyage*, David McKay Company, New York, 1961.

Richards, Leyton, *Christian Pacifism After Two World Wars*, Independent Press Ltd., London, 1948.

Rougemont, Denis De, *Love in the Western World*, Pantheon Books, Inc., 1956.

Roy, Dilip Kumar, *Among the Great*, Nalanda Publications, Bombay, 1945, 1947.

Runciman, Steven, *The Medieval Manichee—A Study of the Christian Dualist Heresy*, University Press, Cambridge, 1947.

Russell, E., *The History of Quakerism*, The Macmillan Company, New York, 1942.

Schilpp, Paul Arthur, *The Quest For Religious Realism*, Harper & Brothers, New York, London, 1938.

Schweitzer, Albert, *Peace or Atomic War?*, Henry Holt and Company, New York, 1958.

Schrugham, Mary, *The Peaceable Americans of 1860-61, A Study in Public Opinion*, Columbia University, New York, 1921.

Scott-Craig, T. S. K., *Christian Attitudes to War and Peace*, Charles Scribner's Sons, New York, 1938.

Scott, Job, *The Works of That Eminent Minister of the Gospel, Job Scott*, J. Comly, Philadelphia, Pennsylvania, 1831.

Scott, Michael, *A Time To Speak*, Doubleday, New York, 1958.

Sen, Amulyachandra, *Asoka's Edicts;* with preface by Suniti Kumar Chatterji; publ. for The Institute for Indology, by The Indian Publicity Society, Calcutta, July 1956.

Sharp, Gene, *Tyranny Could Not Quell Them*, Publications Committee of Peace News, London, 1954.

Sheppard, H. R. L., *We Say "No,"* John Murray, London, 1935.

Shridharani, Krishnalal, *War Without Violence*, Harcourt, Brace & Company, New York, 1939.

Sibley, Mulford Q., and Jacob, Philip E., *Conscription of Conscience*, Cornell University Press, Ithaca, New York, 1952.

Silver, Abba Hillel, *The World Crisis and Jewish Survival*, Richard R. Smith, New York, 1941.

Simonds, Frank H., "The Collapse of the Peace Movement," *The Annals of the American Academy of Political and Social Science*, 174, July, 1934.

Simons, Menno, *The Complete Writings of Menno Simons, c. 1496-1561;* translated from the Dutch by Leonard Verdwin and edited by John Christian Wenger, with a biography by Harold S. Bender; Herald Press, Scottdale, Pa., 1956.

Smith, C. Henry, *The Mennonites of America*, published by the author, Goshen, Indiana, 1909.

Sneath, E. Hershey, *The Evolution of Ethics*, Yale University Press, New Haven, 1927.

Speak Truth to Power, A Quaker Search for an Alternative to Violence, American Friends Service Committee, Philadelphia, Pennsylvania, 1961.

Sumner, Charles, *The Duel Between France and Germany With Its Lesson to Civilization*, Wright and Potter, printers, Boston, 1870.

Suttner, Bertha von, *Memoirs of . . .* ; Published for the International School of Peace, Ginn and Company, Boston, London, 1910.

Tagore, Rabindranath, *Letter to a Friend*, George Allen & Unwin Ltd., London, 1928, 1929, 1931.

——, *My Reminiscences,* The Macmillan Company, New York, 1917.

——, *Nationalism*, The Macmillan Company, New York, 1917.

——, *Sādhanā, The Realization of Life*, The Macmillan Company, New York, 1929.

Thomas, Evan W., *The Positive Faith of Pacifism*, pamphlet, Plowshare Press, New York, n.d.

——, *The Way to Freedom*, War Resisters League, New York, April, 1943.

St. Thomas Aquinas, *The Summa Theologica*, Volume 2, Benziger Brothers, New York, 1947-48.

Thompson, James Westfall, *An Economic and Social History of the Middle Ages, 300-1300*, The Century Co., New York, London, 1928.

Tilden, W. P., *All War Forbidden by Christianity*, M. D. L. Stevens, printer, Dover, New Hampshire, 1847.

Tolstoi, Lyof N., *Essays, Letters, Miscellanies*, Thomas Y. Crowell & Co., New York, 1899.

Tolstoy, Leo, *The Law of Love and the Law of Violence*, R. Field, New York, 1948.

Tomlin, E. W. F., *Simone Weil*, Yale University Press, New Haven, 1954.

Toynbee, Arnold J., *War and Civilization*, Oxford University Press, New York, 1950.

Troeltsch, Ernst, *The Social Teaching of the Christian Churches*, George Allen & Unwin, Ltd. London, 1931; The Macmillan Company, New York, 1931.

Trueblood, Benjamin F., *The Development of the Peace Idea and Other Essays*, Boston, 1932.

Van Kirk, Walter W., *Religion Renounces War*, Willett, Clark and Co., Chicago, New York, 1934.

——, Walter W., "The Churches and World Peace," *International Conciliation*, Nov., 1934, no. 304, published by Carnegie Endowment for International Peace.

Walker, Amasa, *The Suicidal Folly of the War-System*, American Peace Society, Boston, 1863.

Walling, William English, *The Socialists and the War*, Henry Holt and Co., New York, 1915.

Warren, Josiah, *True Civilization*, Part I, Benj. R. Tucker, Princeton, Mass., 1875.

Weigall, Arthur E. P., *The Life and Times of Akhnaton, Pharaoh of Egypt*, G. P. Putnam's Son, New York, 1923.

Wells, H. G., *The Common Sense of World Peace*, Leonard & Virginia Woolf at the Hogarth Press, London, 1929.

——, *The Outline of History*, Garden City Publishing Co., Garden City, New York, 1920-1929.

White, Anna, and Taylor, Leila S., *Shakerism, Its Meaning and Message*, Press of Fred J. Heer, Columbus, Ohio, 1904.

Wilkins, Ernest Hatch, *Students Against War, Two Addresses*, Press of the Oberlin Printing Co., Oberlin, Ohio, 1935.

Willibrand, William Arthur, *Ernst Toller and His Ideology*, University of Iowa Studies, VII, August, 1940, published by the university, Iowa City, Iowa.

Winger, Otho, *History and Doctrines of the Church of the Brethren*, Brethren Publishing House, Elgin, Illinois, 1920.

Wright, Edward Needles, *Conscientious Objectors in the Civil War*, University of Pennsylvania Press, Philadelphia, 1931.

Young, Rose, *Why Wars Must Cease*, The Macmillan Company, New York, 1935.

Young, Wilmer, *A Testimony For Radical Peace Action*, Pendle Hill, Wallingford, Pennsylvania, 1961.

SOURCES

Angell, Norman, "If A German Attacked Your Wife," *New Republic*, January 6, 1917.

Aristophanes, *The Comedies of Aristophanes, The Lysistrata*, vol. IV, 1902-1916.

Ballou, Adin, *Non-Resistance in Relation to Human Governments*, Non-Resistance Society, Boston, 1839.

Barclay, Robert, *An Apology For the True Christian Divinity*, 4th ed., T. Sowle, London, 1701.

Benezet, Anthony, *Several Considerations on Several Important Subjects*, Joseph Crukshank, Philadelphia, 1778.

Blanchard, J. P., *Address to 13th Anniversary of Massachusetts Peace Society*, Wait, Greene & Co., Boston, 1829.

de Bloch, Jean, *The Future of War*, Ginn & Company, Boston, 1903; Doubleday & McClure Co., 1899.

Bourne, Randolph, "The War and the Intellectuals," *Seven Arts*, June 1917.

Burritt, Elihu, *The World's Workingmen's Strike For Peace*, from Swarthmore College Peace Collection, Swarthmore, Pa.

Carlyle, Thomas, *Sartor Resartus, Collected Works*, London, 1897.

Carus, Paul, *The Gospel of Buddha*, The Open Court Publishing Company, 1895.

Chalmers, John, *"The Old Philosopher" Lau-Tsze*, Trübner & Co., London, 1868.

Channing, William Ellery, *The Works of . . .*, James Monroe & Co., Boston, 1848; C. S. Francis & Co., New York, 1848.

Clarkson, Thomas, *An Essay on the Doctrines and Practice of the Early Christians as They Relate to War*, from Tract No. III of the Society for the Promotion of Permanent and Universal Peace, R. Clay, London, 1832.

Cooper, Thomas, *Two Orations Against Taking Away Human Life*, Chapman Brothers, London, 1846.

Darrow, Clarence, *Resist Not Evil*, C. H. Kerr and Co., Chicago, 1903.

Dell, Floyd, "Non-Resistance, Utopian and Scientific," *The Masses*, December 1916.

Dymond, Jonathan, *An Inquiry Into the Accordancy of War*, Mahlon Day & Co., 1844; W. Brown, printer, Philadelphia.

Eastman, Max, "Conscription for What?", *The Masses*, July 1917.

Emerson, Ralph Waldo, *Miscellanies*, Houghton, Mifflin and Company, Boston, 1885.

Erasmus Against War, The Humanists' Library, edited by Lewis Einstein, introduction by J. W. Mackail, The Merrymount Press, Boston, 1907.

Fried, Alfred H., *The Restoration of Europe,* tr. by Lewis Stiles Gannett, The Macmillan Company, New York, 1916.

Garrison, William Lloyd, *Selections From the Writings and Speeches of . . . ,* R. F. Wallcut, Boston, 1852.

Goldman, Emma, "Preparedness: the Road to Universal Slaughter," *Mother Earth,* December 1915.

Grimke, Thomas S., *The Principles of Peace,* G. F. Olmsted, Hartford, Conn., 1832.

Grotius, Hugo, *Rights of War and Peace,* Old South Pamphlet No. 101, Directors of the Old South Work, Boston, 1902.

Hancock, Thomas, *The Principles of Peace,* H. H. Brown, Providence, 1832.

Hugo, Victor, *The United States of Europe,* World Peace Foundation, Boston, Oct. 1914.

Jay, William, *War and Peace,* Oxford University Press, New York, 1919 (reprinted from original of 1842).

Jefferson, Charles E., *Militarism and the Christian Church,* sermon preached in Broadway Tabernacle Church, 1908.

John, Pope XXIII, *Pacem in Terris,* issued in Rome, April 10, 1963.

Josephus, Flavius, *Josephus's Works,* R. Penny, London, 1733.

Ladd, William, *Peace and War,* John T. Burnham, New Hampshire, 1827.

Liebknecht, Karl, *The Future Belongs to the People,* ed. by S. Zimand, The Macmillan Company, New York, 1918.

London, Meyer, *Congressional Record,* 65th Congress, House of Representatives, April 5, 1917.

Love, Alfred H., *Vindicating the Principles of Peace, and Non-Resistance by Force of Arms,* August 22, 1861, from the Swarthmore College Peace Collection, Swarthmore, Pa.

Luthuli, Albert, 1960 Nobel Peace Prize acceptance speech—at a dinner in Oslo, Norway, December 11, 1961; *New York Times,* December 12, 1961; and *Pax et Libertas,* April-June 1962.

St. Martin, *A Select Library of Nicene and Post-Nicene Fathers of the Christian Church,* vol. XI; The Christian Company Literature, Oxford and London; Parker and Company, n.d.

Mei, Yi-Pao, translator, *The Ethical and Political Works of Motse,* Arthur Probsthain, London, 1929.

Nearing, Scott, *The Trial of Scott Nearing and the American Socialist Society,* The Rand School of Social Science, New York, 1919.

Origen, *Ante-Nicene Christian Library,* T. & T. Clark, Edinburgh, 1867-1872.

Parker, Theodore, *The Works of . . . ,* vol. II, Amerian Unitarian Association, Boston, 1907-1913.

Passy, Frédéric, "The Future of Arbitration," *The Independent,* March 13, 1902.

Penn, William, *Plan For the Peace of Europe,* Old South Leaflet No. 75, The Directors of the Old South Work, Boston, 1906.

Reed, John, "Whose War?", *The Masses,* April 1917.

Schwimmer, Rosika, *In re Petition for Naturalization,* District Court of the United States, 1927.

Scott, Job, "War Inconsistent with the Doctrine and Example of Jesus Christ," *The Herald of Peace* for 1844-45, vol. IV.

Sumner, Charles, *The Works of . . . ,* vol. I, Lee & Shepard, Boston, 1870.

Suttner, Bertha von, "How I Came to Write 'Lay Down Your Arms'," *The Independent,* February 1906.

Tertullianus, *The Writings of . . . ,* vol. I, T. & T. Clark, London, 1869.

Thoreau, Henry David, *Friendship and Other Essays,* Little Leather Library Corporation, New York, n.d.

Toller, Ernst, "Fight for Peace," *Golden Book magazine,* October 1934.

Tolstoy, Leo, *The Complete Works of Count Tolstoy,* vol. 23, J. M. Dent & Co., London, 1905.

Worcester, Noah, *A Solemn Review of the Custom of War,* Stevens, Schenectady, New York, 1817.

36-401